• Human Sexuality •
in
Cultural
Context

Callista Lee

Kendall Hunt
publishing company

Cover image © Shutterstock.com

www.kendallhunt.com
Send all inquiries to:
4050 Westmark Drive
Dubuque, IA 52004-1840

Contents in Brief

Contents

Chapter 3

Chapter 4

Chapter 5

Chapter 6

Chapter 9

Chapter 10

Chapter 11

Chapter 12

Chapter 13

Chapter 14

Chapter 15

Chapter 16

Sexual Dysfunction, Sex Therapy, and *Sexual Enhancement*   425

Preface

As an introductory text in human sexuality, *Healthy Sexuality* is based on the fundamental information and concepts that have evolved from the body of research in this field. We firmly believe in a biopsychosocial model of human sexuality. In this view, humans become sexual beings and evolve as a result of a continual interaction between biological and psychosocial forces.

We also believe that human sexuality is intimately tied to overall health and wellness. Our overall level of health and wellness plays a big part in our sexuality. *Healthy Sexuality* examines how the components of wellness—physical, intellectual, emotional, social, spiritual, and environmental/occupational—influence our sexual health. Additionally, our sexuality is a key component of our health. The book points out how the healthy expression of our sexuality can improve our overall level of health and wellness.

Essential to being healthy, people have to come to grips with themselves as human beings, to make sound sexual decisions and self-actualize their sexual selves. Although we do cover sexual health concerns and risks (unintended pregnancy, sexually transmitted diseases, date rape, and so on), *Healthy Sexuality* takes a pro-sex rather than a problem-oriented approach to sexual issues. We make no apologies for focusing on the positive, life-enhancing aspects of healthy sexuality instead of presenting sexual topics as a series of problems to overcome.

In the spirit of diversity, we have included information relative to differences between races and ethnic groups, as cited in the most current data generated by the Centers for Disease Control. We use the federally sanctioned language in referring to these groups. We have carefully integrated issues of sexual orientation throughout the book wherever appropriate rather than presenting this as a stand-alone topic in a single chapter. We have incorporated sexual orientation issues into the body of the text, through case studies and in illustrations and photographs. In this way, we hope to project the view of sexual orientation as a healthy part of human sexuality, not a "problem" to be discussed in a separate chapter.

Features of the Text

- The opening page of each chapter begins with a set of **Student Learning Objectives** designed to put the chapter's content into a meaningful framework, to introduce readers to the content of each chapter and personally connect them to the material.
- **Case Studies** throughout each chapter are drawn from the authors' work with students and clients over the years in a number of settings. The case studies cover a diverse cross section of people and are designed to illustrate how the material in the chapter connects to real individuals in everyday situations. You'll meet people like Jorge, a college student who learned the meaning of no the hard way. Although the names have been changed, the cases are authentic.

- **Critical Thinking** questions are inserted next to each case study and bring up questions for readers to answer for themselves. In Chapter 15, for instance, you'll be asked to ponder the issue of discussing one's sexual/medical history with a potential sex partner. You'll be asked to assess the pros and cons of this approach and how a person actually goes about such a task. These questions have no right or wrong answers; they are exercises in critical thinking and represent possible topics for the instructor to consider for group discussion.
- **Personal Exploration Activities** in each chapter allow students to participate in a fun and revealing activity, in which they can explore their feelings and opinions on issues of sexuality. In Chapter 4, for example, students can discover all the things they would never do if of the opposite sex.
- **Healthy Sex Hints** within each chapter are practical, step-by-step suggestions for achieving optimal sexual health and well-being related to the accompanying discussion. Healthy Sex Hints cover a broad range of topics from aphrodisiacs in Chapter 7 to how to perform breast or testicular self-exams in Chapters 2 and 3 respectively.
- **Sex in Society** boxes throughout the text present unusual, interesting, and sometimes controversial material related to the discussion. They add interest and expand upon the basic topic. Sex in Society boxes explore a range of topics such as "Body Image as a Lifelong Concern" in Chapter 4 to the "The HIV Highway" in Chapter 17.
- Each chapter integrates **Wellness Syntheses** into key content areas throughout the chapter. These are designed to tie the chapter content to the six dimensions of health and wellness—physical, intellectual, emotional, social, spiritual, and environmental/occupational in a meaningful way. A key facet of our text, this feature demonstrates the linkages between sexuality to health and wellness throughout the text.
- Throughout the text, **Marginal Definitions** identify and highlight key terms that are defined in the margins. These marginal definitions are used to clarify the chapter's content and give the student easy access to the meanings of vocabulary essential to their understanding.
- To further personalize learning, we have added **Personal Assessment** for each chapter can be found on the accompanying companion website. These assessment activities are tools for readers to use to apply what they have learned to their own lives—and thereby improve their health and well-being. These assessments range from "Things that Turn Me On" in Chapter 7 to a "Sexual Communication Satisfaction Questionnaire" in Chapter 11.
- The **Test Yourself** quiz for each chapter can be found on the accompanying companion website. offer readers an opportunity to assess their mastery of the course material.
- Each chapter contains a list of **References** that includes all of the works cited in the chapter. We have tried to blend the classic works in the field with new material from reputable sources. Besides these features we incorporate data to support the textual presentation through **illustrative tables** and **figures** from the most current sources available, complemented by the classic studies by Kinsey, Masters and Johnson, Laumann and colleagues, and other respected researchers in this field. Finally, the judicious use of **diverse photographs** and **drawings** illustrates important information under the principle that a picture is worth a thousand words. Additional References for Ms. Lee's articles will be found at the accompanying companion website.

Acknowledgments

First, I acknowledge two people who were early influences in my development as a human sexuality professional. Drs. Richard Cross and Sandra Leiblum of the University of Medicine and Dentistry of New Jersey first opened my eyes to the field and my own sexuality many years ago in one of their intensive sexuality seminars for medical students and invited professionals. Their ease and professionalism in dealing with sexual matters left a lasting impression on me. They provided my first exposure to the scientific, professional study of sexuality and validated sexuality as a scientific discipline worthy of serious study.

I'd also like to thank my mentor and role model, Dr. Marvin Levy of Temple University, for standing out as the epitome of what I consider a "healthy sexuality professional." With his rugged, athletic masculinity, scholarly wisdom, and health background, Marv created an image in my mind of someone able to place sexuality squarely in the framework of health rather than a series of problems to be addressed and feared. I was lucky to come under his influence at a crucial time in my life as a young husband and developing professional. I'm thankful for his guidance in both areas of my life.

I'd like to thank Clifford G. Freund, my mentor with the New Jersey State Department of Health (NJSDH). Cliff nurtured my early career as an STD professional and supported my initial interests in sexuality and education. He had the faith in my work and the wisdom to give me the freedom to explore issues and develop as a sexuality professional.

Lastly, I'd like to thank my co-authors for their contributions to the text. The fact that *Healthy Sexuality* is a balanced, diverse, health-oriented sexuality book is due in great part to the hard work of Jean Levitan and Lillian Cook Carter. Both of these wonderful women have dedicated their professional careers to teaching human sexuality in an honest, open, and supportive way and it shows in their writing and attention to detail. Thanks, Jean and Lillian.

—R.B.

It is not possible to express the thanks I owe to Murray Vincent, an incredible teacher who inspired me to become a health educator. His sexuality class was creative, thought provoking and an amazing growth producing experience. It was because of him that I got my first job teaching sexuality in a college and it was a perfect gift. I also want to thank my students who have taught me probably more than I have taught them. It is because of them that I continue to love working in the area of sexuality. And finally, thanks to Bal, my urologist husband, who is a great resource for confusing issues in the medical aspects of sexuality, and to Rich and Jean who have been wonderful partners in this book.

—L.C.C

We'd like to thank the following people at Kendall/Hunt Publishing: We thank Sue Saad for the original opportunity to write this book. Without Sue's belief in the book there would be no second edition of *Healthy Sexuality*. She saw a great book that was about to die and resurrected it. Thanks Sue for your persistence in bringing this book back.

We'd like to thank our Project Coordinator Jordan Hoftender and Author Account Manager Samantha Smith for framing out the project and keeping us on task. Thanks for helping us with the resources we needed to get the book to press in a record-breaking window of opportunity. We'd also like to thank Caroline Kieler for her help with securing the necessary permissions to key material.

Thanks to Will Blonna for a beautiful new cover. The colors are dazzling. Many thanks to Susan Willis for her time and expertise in photographing the various contraceptives methods for Chapter 14.

To our reviewers and class testers—Scott Acrement, Canyon College; Consuelo Bonilla, Kean University; Carol Chenault, Calhoun State; F. Scott Christopher, Arizona State University; Paul Finnicum, Arkansas State; Kay Foland, South Dakota State; Lois Goldblatt, Arizona State University; Elyse Gruttadauria, State University of New York College at Brockport; Lynne Hamelton, West Chester Community College; Edward Hart, Bridgewater State College; Dianna Hurlbut, Irvine Valley College; Eileen Johnston, Glendale Community College; Andrew Kanu, Virginia State University; Richard Larkin, Harper College; Katrina Lubbers, University of Nebraska; Don Matlosz, California State University–Fresno; Susan Molstad, Northwestern State University of Louisiana; Lin Myers, California State University–Stanislaus; Marilyn Myerson, University of South Florida; Bobby Ogletree, Southern University of Illinois at Carbondale; Christine Osgood, Mesa Community College; Dianna Peck, Western Illinois University; Miguel Perez, California State University–Fresno; Valerie Pinhas, Nassau Community College; Catherine Sherwood-Puzzello, Indiana University; Stanley Snegroff, Adelphi University; Sherm Sowboy, California State University–Fresno; Richard Stacy, University of Nebraska; Sonja Swanson, Palm Beach Community College; Tom Tatchell, University of Toledo; Maria Theresa Wessel, James Madison University; William Yurkiewicz, Millersville University—we extend thanks for their time, dedication to thoroughly reviewing the text, and their thoughtful comments that enabled us to improve the manuscript.

Finally, we thank our colleagues in the Department of Public Health at William Paterson University and the Department of Health Sciences at Towson University for providing a supportive work environment.

Richard Blonna   Lillian Cook Carter

My deep gratitude to all of the folks at Kendall-Hunt for encouraging me to take on this project and seeing me through the editing and writing process for both the print book and the website. To Richard Blonna and Lillian Cook Carter, thank you for providing an excellent foundation upon which I could build my own custom text.

I also wish to thank my colleagues at Fullerton College, Dr. Julie Felender and Dr. Robert Byde, who have inspired and encouraged me to continue my growth as an educator. And of course I am grateful to my students who keep me on my toes with their desire for practical and up-to-date materials.

Callista Lee

About the Authors

RICHARD BLONNA, ED.D, CHES, NCC, Professor Emeritus, has been teaching human sexuality for more than 30 years. His initial work in the field was in education and control of sexually transmitted diseases. He served as an STD investigator, counselor, supervisor, and trainer for the New Jersey State Department of Health (NJSDH) STD Control Program. He also worked for the NJSDH as a health education consultant for the AIDS and family planning programs. He has taught human sexuality at Temple University and, most recently, William Paterson University, where he also taught health counseling, epidemiology, and stress management. He currently works as a Health and Wellness Coach, Trainer, and Writer.

LILLIAN COOK CARTER, PH.D, CHES has been teaching human sexuality at the university level for more than 30 years. She is a health educator at Towson University teaching human sexuality, mental health and stress reduction, and wellness.

CALLISTA LEE, M.S., Professor of Psychology, has been teaching human sexuality for over 30 years. She made her way into teaching psychology at the Community College level after earning a Master of Science degree at California State University, Long Beach in Community-Clinical Psychology and working as Director of Education at the Coalition Concerned with Adolescent Pregnancy (CCAP) in Orange County, California. In addition to Human Sexuality, Ms. Lee also teaches Cross-Cultural Psychology and Psychology of Adjustment at Fullerton Community College. She is active in the College's Study Abroad Program, having taught our local students in Athens, Rome, and Paris.

Chapter

one

Exploring Healthy Sexuality

Student Learning Objectives

After reading this chapter, students will be able to:

- Define *human sexuality.*
- Describe the key components of healthy sexuality.
- Explain how the six dimensions of health and wellness impact one's sexuality.
- Compare and contrast behaviors that enhance or inhibit healthy sexuality.
- Describe the key sources of sexual information.
- Evaluate sources of sexuality information.
- Explain the importance of the work by sex research pioneers Kinsey, and Masters & Johnson.
- Describe the components of informed decision making.
- Compare how matrilineal and patrilineal cultures view sexuality and gender roles.

Self-esteem A way of looking at oneself; may be high or low

Sexuality remains a critical force shaping our lives. It is part of how we see ourselves and impacts our **self-esteem**. It is ever-present as we relate to others on both romantic and platonic levels. Students, as well as the population at large, are constantly confronted with media messages on enhancing sexuality through the use of various products. Sexual themes remain prominent in all forms of entertainment, including books, film, television, and music. As we continue living in the 21st century, students may be struggling to sort out the conflicting messages about "healthy sexuality." Compared to students growing up in the previous century, so much more information is open and accessible. There are choices that are better understood, with the power of the Internet to answer questions that in previous generations may not even have been asked. More and more, individuals are demanding their rights to be who they are in terms of their sexuality.

Our Sexual Climate

To try to figure out how best to make healthy personal decisions in a climate of contrasts is confusing and problematic. Americans talk about sex and sexuality all the time. It is a favorite subject of the media. Some conservative media pundits criticize our culture for its overemphasis on sex. They claim that sexual themes dominate our culture and the media and that the government has gone too far in allowing the free expression of sexuality. Some liberal commentators say exactly the opposite. They claim that our culture is sexually restrictive and downright puritanical. As examples of a restrictive culture, they cite abstinence-until married sexuality education in the schools, restrictions on reproductive rights, and lack of acceptance of the LGBT community. Still others claim that our culture sends mixed messages about sexuality. It is used to market and sell almost everything, yet many schools are not allowed to teach about sexuality in a comprehensive, forthright way.

The reality is that government and society influence our sexuality in many ways, some positive, some negative, and some ambiguous. We are sexual beings from conception to death, and our sexuality evolves and grows regardless of official sanctions or restrictions. We learn about sex whether we do or do not have sexuality education in our schools. It is not a question of *whether* we learn. It's more a matter of the *quality* of what we learn. A key to understanding sexual learning is to realize that we learn about sexuality and what it means to be a man or woman even if no one ever sits us down and has a heart-to-heart talk about the "birds and the bees." And that classic explanation of where we came from is only a small part of understanding ourselves.

Quality sexuality programs result from well-thought-out curricula, with goals and objectives for student learning. Curricula are based on accurate information, in which the pursuit of knowledge is encouraged rather than restricted. Students have a chance to examine their values and the factors that contribute to healthy and appropriate personal decisions. All states do not require sexuality education and in some states certain topics may be prohibited. In our information-rich culture, such censorship further highlights the conflicts students face when attempting to move toward sexual health.

In many ways the sexual learning that takes place outside any classroom is far more influential, as it is constant, both verbal and nonverbal, and often insidious. Students can easily relate the types of misinformation they acquired from friends throughout their childhood and simultaneously often report that their parents didn't talk with them about sexuality issues. In reality, though, parents convey information, impart values, and serve as **role models** whether a formal, face-to-face, serious conversation ever takes place between parent and child. A frown or a raised eyebrow can convey disapproval just as a nod, smile, or laugh indicates support. To be silent on an issue, to omit sexuality from the daily discourse in our lives, to never bring up sexuality as part of the conversation around the dinner table sends a strong message about its being a taboo subject.

Role model A person whose behaviors are imitated by others

Some of what we see and learn, unfortunately, does not present the healthiest picture of sexuality. Sometimes our parents, caregivers, friends, teachers, and media figures do not provide us with the best role models or information for healthy sexuality. The sexual scripts we receive may not promote healthy relationships and in some cases may actually jeopardize our lives. For example, if women are taught that they must be thin to be sexually attractive, what connection might that "lesson" have to eating disorders such as anorexia and bulimia? If men are taught that they are entitled to sex and that women want to be dominated, what connection does that "lesson" have to dating violence and rape? Sometimes the very people and institutions charged with teaching us and nurturing us fail or, worse yet, sexually abuse us.

So what is human sexuality? **Sexuality** is a broad term that refers to all aspects of being sexual. Many people think human sexuality refers to sexual behavior—what people do, how often they do it, and so on. Although sexual behavior is an important part of being sexual, human sexuality encompasses much more than that. Sexuality involves our genetic inheritance, our anatomy and physiology, and the reality of being a sexual creature in a biological sense. It also encompasses our thoughts and feelings about our body and what it means to be a man or a woman. It involves our ethics, values, and the cultural mores we've assimilated through our family, ethnic group, and religious affiliation.

Sexuality A broad term referring to all aspects of being sexual

Our sexuality extends beyond the self to encompass our friendships, intimate relationships, and sexual relationships. Lastly, our sexuality does not exist in a vacuum. It is influenced by and influences our environment. Our institutions (schools, governments, and so on), neighborhoods, communities, campuses, states, and countries, and their policies, help shape the person we are and our options as a sexual being.

Factors That Contribute to Our Sexuality

Without being able to clearly determine which factor is most influential, we do know that we all receive strong and perhaps conflicting messages

Sexologists Specialized researchers of sexual subjects from a variety of disciplines including psychology, biology, medicine, nursing, and health

about sexuality from family, friends, school, media, religion, and the culture. **Sexologists**, those who study sexuality through various rigorous research methodologies, provide input into our knowledge base. Developing a healthy sexuality involves processing that information and, as individuals, internalizing that which is useful.

Family

Are we the persons we are because of how we were reared? In a social sense, the term *family* has taken on broader connotations as people's living arrangements take on a variety of forms. Divorce, remarriage, stepfamilies, blended families, and single families introduce new models.

Nuclear family A family made up of the mother, father, and their children

The traditional **nuclear family**, consisting of a married man and woman and their biological children, represents less than half of all households in the United States today. The primary caregiver thus may assume a greater role in a child's development than previously. The challenge comes in trying to evaluate the impact of various family arrangements on a family's members.

The impact of parental influence on sexuality is still open to debate. For example, the societal concern with homosexuality has led courts—almost exclusively, until more recent times—to award children to the heterosexual parent in custody cases resulting from divorce. The concern is that gay or lesbian parents will influence their children to be gay or lesbian. That the heterosexual parents of the gay and lesbian adults were unable to influence their children's orientation is not given the same credibility.

As we will discuss later, good parenting skills, rather than the parents' sexual orientation, are key to raising healthy children. The family influences the development of healthy sexuality in numerous ways. Through family,

© Andresr, 2010. Shutterstock, Inc.

Children learn about sex from their families without it ever being mentioned.

we learn gender roles and expectations, are taught about love and affection, learn patterns of touch, develop a sense of our physical selves, and assume patterns of social interaction. In each of these areas, our experiences can lead to healthy or unhealthy development.

In some areas of parenting, a number of approaches can lead to healthy sexual development. It is generally accepted that parents should be loving and supportive toward their children. Children who receive physical affection will, in turn, be more likely to be able to give affection to others. Embedded in such general advice, however, are individual patterns that may be criticized. For example, research has shown that boy children stop receiving physical affection earlier than girls, who may continue to be hugged and kissed throughout their lives. Does the change in the type of touch boys receive impact their adult patterns?

In terms of **gender role** expectations, most parents reinforce gender-stereotyped behaviors very early on. Boys are expected to play aggressively and to enjoy trucks, Legos, action figures, and the like. Girls get socialized to plan for motherhood, beauty, and domestic tasks. The women's movement of the late 1960s and early 1970s questioned the impact of gender stereotyping on the healthy development of boys and girls. Years later, television commercials for children's toys reveal little departure from the traditional gender role expectations. Toy manufacturers, in their defense, claim they are marketing to the children who will buy their products. When they have attempted to market toys in a more gender-neutral manner, their efforts have not been successful. Families have different views on what is socially acceptable and what toys they want to purchase, yet children seem to develop their own preferences regardless of their parent's efforts.

Gender role The different behaviors and attitudes that society expects of females and males

Friends

One's peer group has always maintained a powerful role in shaping our attitudes and values about sexuality. Depending on the friends with whom we socialize, we have various experiences at different ages. Teens may refer to others as "loose or fast"—which may mean that more sexual activity and drinking take place. Kids may refer to others as "nerds"—meaning that, though smart, they seem to lack social skills and have interests that are "not cool." Regardless, peer pressure, social judgments, and opportunities all interact to influence healthy development. At the same time, those very influences can leave a negative mark dominated by low self-esteem, depression, and feelings of inadequacy.

Most students report that the bulk of their sexuality education comes from talks with friends. They say that some friends passed along accurate information, and others spoke with authority while dispensing inaccurate information. Students have reported that, as children and teens, they saw sexually explicit pictures, magazines, and videos at a friend's home—all supposedly belonging to "my friend's dad." The sneaking around and the searching through hidden material convey a message about sexuality.

Society is the people who live in a country or region, their organizations, and their way of life. It usually involves a shared government.

Culture The sum of the learned set of rules governing the behavior of people, often focused on the influences of race, class, religion, and ethnicity

Patriarchy is a cultural pattern in which males hold the primary positions of social, economic and political power. It is supported by Patriliny, a family system in which family is defined by the male line (wives and children are given the husband/father's last name). As on Earth, the Heavens are ruled by a deity who is perceived as male (God the Father).

Society and Culture

Source: Callista Lee

The USA is a **society** that is democratic, youth-oriented, and capitalistic. The dominant **culture** is western-style **patriarchy**, heavily influenced by Christianity, specifically the Puritanism of early British colonists. All of these factors affect our sexuality. Laws regulate who can legally marry (changed in 2015 to include same-sex couples), age of consent, responsibilities of parents and/or the state to children, which sexual behaviors are legal, availability of reproductive health services, and public nudity. Government policies promote equal rights for men and women in education and in the workplace. Our economic system has favored males, especially anyone who can amass vast sums of money. With money, you can hire lobbyists to promote your social or business interests to legislators. And of course, money also allows for access to the best education, healthcare, safest neighborhoods, and powerful social and business networks. The ability of the wealthy to influence business and financial policy for their own benefit is today in conflict with a core cultural belief that every hard-working American has an equal opportunity to be successful. Americans tend to be uncomfortable discussing the very real barriers of poverty, racism, and sexism, preferring to believe that success or failure is totally in the control of the individual. We tend to be fascinated by the lives of the wealthy (*Keeping up with the Kardashians, Housewives of Beverly Hills, Lifestyles of the Rich and Famous*, etc.). We enjoy showing off our material wealth by wearing branded clothing, driving upscale cars, and filling our homes with as many goods as will fit. And when our materialism overflows our home, we rent a storage unit. While people in less wealthy societies value *time* spent with family or friends over a long meal, we tend to rush about, often preferring a quick text over a long, in-person conversation. We invented "fast food." We even rush our online dating: swipe left and move on. Our orientation toward youth is part of the reason we are in such a hurry. We like innovation, change, new ideas, and new products, and we are eager to get on to the next adventure. We also have big dreams. We are taught "you can grow up to be anything you want." We expect a lot out of life, and our romantic partners. We focus a lot on the highs of infatuation, but have a tough time figuring out how to keep a long-term marriage interesting and fulfilling (Rapaille, 2007).

Men have traditionally been the primary bread-winners for families, and even today with most women working, men still tend to earn more, and old social expectations remain for men to spend more of their earnings than women when seeking romance (paying for dates, vacations, engagement rings, etc.). In a society in which wages have stagnated while costs for housing, food, education, transportation, and healthcare have steadily risen, most males have had to adapt to the fact that it is now necessary for them to view their wives as co-breadwinners. Most young people today expect to be equal partners in their romantic relationships.

In Patrilineal societies, the easiest way for a man to be sure that a child is indeed his biological offspring is to ensure that his bride is a virgin when she marries him and that she remains monogamous throughout the marriage. Our religions encourage both men and women to save sex for marriage, but there is a double standard; men are more likely to be called a "player" if they have sex with various partners, whereas women are still called "sluts." Young women today who feel it is their right to engage in "hookups" for fun are still aware that their "number" (of partners) mustn't get *too high* or they will be socially ostracized. Without being aware of its older meaning, most of these young women still want their fathers to "give them away" at their weddings. What that practice originally symbolized was that her father was the guardian of her virginity as well as the man responsible for her overall support. In the wedding, he "gives her" over to her husband, who now takes on those responsibilities and claims her sexuality as "his." It wasn't until the 1970s that US states began to recognize that a wife could be raped by her husband; prior to that, he apparently still "owned" her sexuality. Today, spousal rape is recognized as a crime in all fifty states. The earliest laws of western culture described rape of an unmarried girl as a property crime against the victim's father, for which a financial penalty had to be paid by the rapist. It wasn't until the eleventh and twelfth centuries of the Common Era (CE) that rape began to be considered more as a violent crime against the victim (Bishop, 2018). Unfortunately for male victims, it was only in 2012 that the US Department of Justice finally changed its definition of rape to include them. States did have laws against sexual assault on men, but many did not consider the crimes to be as serious as when perpetrated against women. The **#MeToo** movement has increased awareness about sexual assault. The movement has mainly focused on female victims, but recognizes male and trans victims as well, encouraging all to get help, heal, and advocate for the end of sexual violence in our society.

In a Patrilineal society, there is no need for male virginity. If he fathers a child out of wedlock, he can claim it isn't his child … though that has changed with DNA paternity testing! The double standard goes even further, though. Men are given more social permission to enjoy their sexuality by themselves (masturbation) and to ask for what they want from a partner. Many women have never masturbated because they've been taught that sexual pleasure is only "right" when it is enjoyed within the context of a loving relationship; being sexual all by yourself is still a foreign concept to many women. When they finally get together with a partner, they don't really know what kind of touch they would like, because like Sleeping Beauty, they are waiting for their sexuality to be "awakened" by some dreamy "Prince Charming." And many males, conscious of their expected role as leaders, are not comfortable accepting sexual direction from females. Somehow, the male partner is just supposed to know what the female partner will enjoy, based on what feels good to him (Eisler, 1995). Perhaps it should not be surprising that several researchers have found that lesbians have more satisfying sexual encounters than heterosexual women (Bagshaw, 2016). They are not starting from the false assumption that what feels great for a man will also feel great for a woman. In Chapter 2, you will find out why this assumption fails us.

Our western culture carries with it quite a bit of sex guilt. Many young people feel uncomfortable walking into a drugstore to purchase condoms, worrying what others will think of them. And although we've been taught that we *should* have conversations with our sexual partners about safe sex, most young people say that is just too embarrassing. Unfortunately, many also find it embarrassing to get tested for STIs or to talk with a doctor about which methods of birth control are most effective. Yet most of us agree that sex is an important part of a romantic relationship, not just for the physical pleasure but also for the emotional closeness it affords. But the old belief—that sex is only for reproduction—is still

with us in sex education courses that only focus on reproduction, or in arguments about abortion in which people will say "well, if you didn't want to deal with a baby you shouldn't have had sex." We are stuck with a lot of mixed messages. Music, movies, TV, and advertising are encouraging the pleasures of sex every day. And yet many of us feel uncomfortable about letting go of our worries to fully enjoy it.

Although the US is filled with diverse peoples, adhering to a wide variety of religious faiths, Christianity is still the one that most influences American culture. Going back into the history of Christianity, we can see some very clear messages that sex is sinful. Many theologians have suggested that the "Original Sin" was more than simple disobedience. To St. Augustine (354–430 CE), that first sin was actually sexual desire. It was hot bodily desire that led to the eating of the apple, rather than cool logic (Wijngaards Institute). He believed that in Paradise, humans would have been able to reproduce without "foul sexual passion." There would have been no need for passion or pleasure. The man's seed could pass to the woman's womb without destroying her virginity. This idea that both desire and pleasure are "foul" took root and flourished in early Christianity. Hundreds of years later, it was confirmed by philosopher/theologian Thomas Aquinas (1224–1275 CE) that sexual pleasure was sinful. He argued that the only sex that was *not* sinful was sex that he decreed to be *natural*: between a man and a woman with the man on top, for the purpose of procreation, and without the hunger of desire or excessive pleasure. He even went so far as to argue for a hierarchy of which sexual sins were worse than the others (Kainz, 2012). In his time, the Catholic Church considered itself to be the only official voice of Christianity. Priests were held to a vow of chastity, not just to keep them from sexual sin but also to assure that they would not have offspring who might demand a portion of their wealth upon their deaths. During the Protestant Reformation (during the 1500s in Western Europe), many complaints were made against the Catholic Church, including an argument that sex was not quite so sinful as had been taught. And so Protestant Christians have taught a slightly more "sex-positive" message than have Catholics. The Eastern Orthodox Christian Church was and is also more "sex-positive" than the Roman Catholic Church. They didn't agree with Augustine or Aquinas, and saw no reason for priests to be celibate.

The Catholic Church still teaches that sex should be only for reproduction and, for that reason, unnatural methods of contraception are forbidden . . . at least officially. In the US, most Catholic couples DO use birth control. Interestingly, it wasn't until the 1869 that the Church determined that abortion before "quickening" (approximately thirteen to sixteen weeks, when the mother feels the fetus moving) was a sin (Brind'Amour, 2011). Prior to that, whatever a pregnant woman did was her business because God had not yet ensouled the fetus. Today there is a wide range of opinions about when a fetus gains personhood, and therefore legal rights.

As you consider the many ways in which your culture and society shape your sexuality, it is hoped that you will begin to wonder how people in other cultures view their sexuality differently. Likely you are aware that LGBT persons are more accepted here than in some other countries. Basic understandings about what it means to be male or female differ too. In fact, within the US there are Native cultures that consider humans to have anywhere from four to five different genders (Davis-Young, 2019). Acceptance of LGBT persons fits easily into their worldview.

Although most cultures today are patriarchal, there are matriarchal groups in some remote areas, such as the **Mosuo** people of Tibet. There is no shame in sex and no value in virginity for women. It is not necessary to know who is the father of a child. Children are raised by the men and women of the mother's family. Men visit their lovers but do not live with them. People live with their maternal family members. Both men and women have a say in how the villages are run, with the grandmother having the final say (Booth, 2017).

Understanding that expectations about gender and sex are socially constructed by each culture allows us to look into the past to better understand how we got to where we are today. Instead of assuming that the way things are today in the US "is just the way things are and always have been," we can see that there are other ways—maybe better ways—that humans have viewed their sexuality. Are there things about your own cultural view of sexuality that you might want to rethink?

personal exploration activity
All That Glitters Is Not Gold

The goal of this activity is to stimulate you to take a critical view of ideas and actions related to sexuality that are presented in the media as normal and healthy. Your task is to determine whether they are healthy or unhealthy for relationships and whether they fit your values. Gather a few of your friends together to watch one of your favorite television shows that deals with romantic relationships. *How I Met Your Mother* and *Modern Family* are the kinds of shows that fit well with this activity. Your task while watching the show is to individually list the relationship behaviors as either healthy/realistic or unhealthy/unrealistic. Examples to watch for are couples talking at the same time and never listening to what the other says, one partner treating the other with respect, and similar behaviors. When the show ends, compare your list with the lists of your friends. Do you all see the behaviors in the same way, or do your friends see something as healthy when you think it is unhealthy? If you find differences, explore with your friends the reasons for your views. Ask your friends what healthy/realistic behaviors they would like to have in a loving relationship. Do they think the behaviors we watch in the media hurt the way we relate to one another?

When Sex Was Sacred

Source: Callista Lee

Long before ancient peoples worshiped an all-spiritual, father-God, most cultures of the world imagined their creator as a Great Mother Goddess: the mother of everything in nature. Evidence of widespread worship of a Mother Goddess goes back as far as 30,000 BCE (Christ, 1997; Downing, 1981; Eisler, 1995; Lerner, 1986).

In these cultures, sex was without sin. The Goddess was most often portrayed in art as naked, because her power came from her body. She birthed and nourished all of creation from her exaggerated hips and breasts. Although human women were not viewed as goddesses themselves, they did hold the mystery of life within their wombs.

Venus of Willendorf. Dan Shachar/Shutterstock.com

Even after humans figured out the male role in reproduction, the Goddess was worshiped as the primary deity for thousands of years. Eventually, a male God joined the Goddess, and in some cultures the rite of "Sacred Marriage" was celebrated in which the Goddess and God would make love to create new life. The sexual act could be sacred. It took many thousands of years before the male Gods began to be viewed as superior to the Mother Goddess. At the same time, cultures were changing from matriarchies to patriarchies. As above, so below.

There remain arguments among anthropologists about whether it is accurate to refer to these early societies as Matriarchies (rule of the Mothers), but they do agree that the usual family system was **Matrilineal** (family line determined by the mother). Evidence suggests that these ancient cultures tended to be egalitarian in that men and women shared social, economic, and political power. An excellent example is the Minoans of the ancient Aegean Sea (now part of Greece).

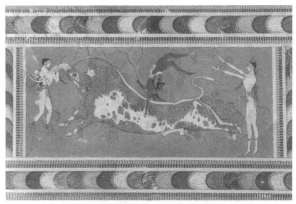

Bull Leaping, Fresco from Knossos, Crete, Greece.
Pecold/Shutterstock.com

Minoan Goddess. Anna Pakutina/Shutterstock.com

These island people worshiped a Great Mother, but were led in their society by both a King and a Queen who appear to have held equal power. The

Matrilineal a family system in which family membership is determined by motherhood. Children belong to their mother's family, rather than the father's as in patriliny. In matrilineal societies, it is unnecessary to know who a child's father is.

breasts of the Goddess were not hidden because there was no shame in them. She is shown with animals because she was the Goddess of all life. And she was magical, able to tame even dangerous snakes. Equality between the sexes appears to have been the norm, as was a relatively high standard of living among all social classes. Both men and women competed in the physically challenging sport of bull jumping. The Minoans were sailors and traders, preferring to do business with their neighbors rather than war with them. Peace held until mainlanders were able to take advantage of their defenselessness following a series of catastrophic earthquakes, a devastating volcano eruption, and resulting tsunamis (Christ, 1997; Ensler,1995; Goodrich, 1989)

Fertility figure from the Ancient Mediterranean. The Met. Bequest of Walter C. Baker, 1971.

Before the thirteenth century CE, the people of India were far more liberal with regard to sexuality than they are today. The Kama Sutra, a detailed text on sexuality, eroticism, and emotional fulfillment in life was written in the third century CE and later

illustrated in graphic detail. Several Hindu temples built between the eighth and twelfth centuries CE feature intricately carved figures of men, women, and animals in erotic poses. Celebration of lovemaking was considered totally appropriate for a place of worship and learning. Lovemaking was considered an important art to be learned for general well-being of both sexes. Thankfully, the rather puritanical Indians of today have not banned access to these temples (as most pornography is banned), and a few still attract worshipers (Chakraborty and Thakurata, 2013).

Erotic Sculptures at the Kajuraho Temples at Madhya Pradesh, India. mdsharma/Shutterstock.com

CE The term used by anthropologists for our current time period, measured in years since the birth of Christ. In recognition that not every culture is Christian, the term "Common Era" (CE) has been put to use in place of the Catholic term, AD (Latin for Anno Domini, meaning "in the year of our lord").

BCE The time period prior to that when we count backward from the year zero, instead of using BC (Before Christ), anthropologists now use the term BCE (Before the Common Era).

K–12 Schools

Schools are charged as the institutions primarily responsible for transmitting knowledge and helping children learn about the world. As a logical extension, schools are to play a key role in sexuality education. Even so, the debate has raged for decades regarding the role schools should play, the depth of information they should convey, at what ages children should learn information about sexuality, and how, if at all, schools can teach in a "value-free" way. Programs that have been successful have been conducted by working closely with parents, clergy, and community leaders to develop curricula that are acceptable. The efforts in this regard far exceed those in other subject areas such as English or history. Research shows that most parents support sexuality education in the public schools.

The National Guidelines Task Force, under the auspices of SIECUS (1997), identified six key concepts that should be part of comprehensive sexuality education programs: human development, relationships, personal skills, sexual behavior, sexual health, and society and culture. A broad spectrum of professionals, including the American Medical Association, National Education Association, U.S. Centers for Disease Control, and Planned Parenthood Federation of America published *Guidelines for Comprehensive Sexuality Education,* which expands on the teaching of 36 sexuality-related topics presented from an age-appropriate perspective (SIECUS, 1996).

Since the *Guidelines'* publication in the early 1990s; however, opponents to comprehensive sexuality education have seen their position supported with federal funding for programs that teach abstinence until marriage. There is little doubt that concerns about sexually transmitted disease (STD) and HIV infections among young people have fueled the abstinence education movement. In 1997, the federal government earmarked multimillion-dollar grants to the states for the development of abstinence-based curricula. Such funding was both continued and increased in 2002, with presidential and legislative support. However, President Obama, in his proposed 2017 federal budget, removed all federal funding for abstinence only sex education (New York Times, 2016). This decision reflects the views of the general population who in two large studies supported comprehensive sexuality education instead of abstinence only education. Both the NPR, Kaiser Family Foundation and Harvard University (2004) national study and the Kaiser Family Foundation (2000) conducted a national study found that the overwhelming majority of parents, teachers, principals, and students want sexuality education taught in secondary school. The majority of parents wanted students to learn about how to deal with the pressure to have sex, the emotional issues and consequences of being sexually active, how to make choices based on personal values, how to use and get birth control methods and abortion, STD's and HIV/AIDS, masturbation, and issues related to sexual orientation.

College

Our college years are a time of great personal growth. Many of us develop intimate, loving, sexual relationships in our college years that remain with us for a lifetime.

College life also is a time for making choices. The decisions we make also can remain with us for a lifetime. Our decision-making ability is put to the test on a regular basis. Sexual choices are among the most important decisions we have to make. Decisions about who we are and what it means to be men and women, who we are attracted to, how we want to live and express our sexuality, what our sexual needs and wants are and how we will fulfill them are but a few of the decisions we will make during our college years.

Evaluating Sexuality Research

Research Methods and Sources of Information

Sexology is the discipline that scientifically studies sexuality

As we strive toward a personally healthy sexuality, a critical task for all of us is to evaluate the information we receive. **Sexology**, the discipline that scientifically studies sexuality, is often conducted by researchers, some of whom refer to themselves as *sexologists*. Because the field of sexuality is truly interdisciplinary, researchers may primarily identify themselves as biologists, psychologists, sociologists, anthropologists, health educators, nurses, historians, physicians, and so on. Wiederman (2001) identifies 19 professional journals whose primary focus is publishing research on human sexuality. In addition, professional organizations in the field also publish newsletters and reports, which add to the knowledge base.

It has often been difficult for researchers to secure adequate funding for sexuality research. Government funding has been most available if the research agenda can be closely demonstrated to impact public health. To some, however, the very study of human sexuality is suspect; others can appreciate the need to know and how much there is to learn. The studies were conducted in different ways—some through questionnaires, some through interviews, some by observation, and so forth—although it would be fair to argue that better funding may have yielded broader samples and more comprehensive information.

As mentioned, a growing number of professional journals are focused on sexuality research. At the same time, there are limitations on the types of research conducted. Although a wide variety of questionnaires have been designed and administered, most sexuality research involves surveying selected populations. Often, university academics rely on the input of students, groups who are at the very least better educated and literate. In contrast, it would be far more difficult to assess information from populations who may not speak English, trust researchers, or even communicate about sexuality issues.

Ethical and practical considerations also impact what kinds of research are conducted. Observing and surveying children may be problematic, as parental permission must be secured; determining when an issue may be most related to the developmental stage of the child can become political and contentious. Some research is best conducted as a longitudinal study, where a population can be examined over time; the costs associated with such a design, however, can be prohibitive. In other cases, topics such as understanding sexual functioning related to a particular disease may pose challenges in securing an adequate sample size.

Because disciplines have their own established perspectives, the research presented may have other limitations or biases. Key criteria separate good research from poor research. Issues such as bias, sampling issues, honesty, and access, all contribute to the quality of sexuality research findings.

When applying research findings to one's personal life, practical questions to consider include the following: Are you like most people? If not, how aren't you? If you are part of a sexual minority—identifying, for

sex in society 1.1

Criteria Associated with Good Research

We are bombarded with sexual information every day. Countless studies and reports are released and presented by the media. "Experts" report new findings that challenge our notions about sexual issues. Here are some guidelines for evaluating sources of sexual information and research:

1. **Evaluate the researchers.** Reputable researchers are well known in their fields, have some kind of university or agency affiliation, and are members in good standing in professional organizations, and their research is not connected to or funded by for-profit businesses.
   - Who did the research?
   - Was the study done by reputable researchers?
2. **Evaluate the researchers' track record.**
   - Have they conducted scientific studies before?
   - Is their previous research respected and accepted in the field?
3. **Evaluate the sample.** Two issues related to the population studied will tell you the most about the quality of the study: sample size and randomness.
   - How large is the sample? (In general, the larger the sample, the better the study.)
   - Were the samples chosen randomly (subjects chosen at random from a larger pool of eligible), or were the subjects taken from a convenience sample (an intact group; students in a certain

class—prison population, army recruits, subscribers to a certain magazine, and so on)?
4. **Evaluate the methods.** In general, first-person observable reports (person-to-person interview or direct observation) are better than other ways of gathering data (such as mailed questionnaires and telephone interviews). Sexuality research is unique, though. Anonymity protections in many situations will help guarantee better results. Unfortunately, when facing a questioner, respondents may be sensitive to reactions to their answers and consequently give desired answers rather than honest ones.
   - How was information about the subjects obtained?
5. **Evaluate replication.** Studies that are replicated with different samples and come up with similar findings are more likely to stand the test of time. Research linking smoking to lung cancer, for example, has been replicated with samples from different countries over the past decade and yielded similar results.
   - Has the study been replicated with a different population resulting in the same findings?
6. **Examine the impact.** Read reviews and reports of the study in reputable journals.
   - Have other researchers in the field received the study well?

example, as bisexual—how does this affect your lifestyle? If some expert claims that a sexual behavior is problematic and you engage in it, will your behavior change? Should it? Who *is* this expert when it comes to helping you make decisions about your sexuality?

Sexuality Researchers

Because of the interdisciplinary nature of the field of sexology, individuals and teams of researchers have conducted research exploring various aspects of sexuality. Some of the prominent names in the field have examined human sexual response and subsequently developed strategies to help people respond more fully and positively. Others have focused their

American Pioneers

Source: Callista Lee

Throughout this textbook, you will read about the work of many researchers, both historic and contemporary. Among the important historical figures are sex research pioneers **Alfred Kinsey and Associates**, who interviewed thousands of Americans to learn about their sexual behaviors in the 1940s and 1950s. The diversity of sexual behavior they found shocked many. The now famous "Kinsey Scale" is still used in discussions of heterosexuality, homosexuality, and bisexuality today.

William Masters and **Virginia Johnson** developed physiological measuring devices to determine the effects on the body of sexual arousal and orgasm in the 1960s and 1970s. They determined that both men and women go through four distinct phases of arousal that affect not only the genitals but also major systems including respiration and blood flow. Their findings of both similarities and differences between men and women will be described in detail in Chapter 2.

work on patterns of behavior, differentiating for gender, race, culture, and ethnicity, where possible. Theorists have worked on questions of gender, orientation, and identity. Others have looked at relationship patterns. Almost all traditional styles of research have been utilized over the years to help provide a fuller understanding of human sexuality. Descriptive research formats have been widely used to survey a myriad of attitudes, values, and experiences. Experimental designs have yielded better understanding of sexual functioning and dysfunction. Qualitative research, in which individuals have been interviewed in depth, has provided the richness and contexts that statistical reports omit.

A Wellness Approach to Understanding Sexuality

One way to explain and understand our sexuality is to look at it from a more holistic approach. Think of how Maria from Case Study 1.1 described how the dimensions of health affected her sexuality. A person cannot study something such as body image, for example, without looking at issues related to individual personality, family and peer influences, and societal expectations. The focus of this textbook is on healthy sexuality and strategies for maximizing our sexual potential.

Healthy sexuality enables a person to develop to the fullest potential. It requires being knowledgeable. It involves personalizing information and using it to make informed decisions about your life and the world around you. Making good decisions about yourself and others is an essential part of healthy sexuality.

It involves our personal level of well-being, the health of our relationships with others, and the nature of the environment in which everything occurs. The best way to conceptualize this approach to understanding human sexuality is to use a health and wellness model to describe it.

Healthy sexuality is the safe and open exploration and development of our potential as human beings

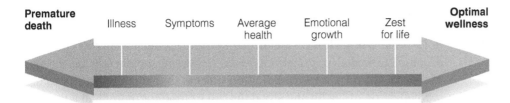

| Premature death | Illness | Symptoms | Average health | Emotional growth | Zest for life | Optimal wellness |

Figure 1.1 *Health and Wellness Continuum* Health can be viewed as a continuum. Where we are on the continuum at any given time is strongly influenced by our lifestyle.

© Kendall Hunt Publishing Company.

Wellness The state of optimal health and wellbeing

sex in society 1.2

Diversity in Sex Research

One of the long-standing criticisms of many human sexuality studies is the lack of diversity in their subjects. Most of the classic studies in the field have focused on white, heterosexual, middle-class subjects. The two best-known sexuality works—Kinsey's studies of male and female sexual behavior and Masters and Johnson's work on sexual response—are both based on such a sample. Both were conducted decades ago, when diversity received much less attention. The lack of diversity seems to affect three distinct minority subgroups: lower socioeconomic status populations, racial minorities (blacks, Asians, and Hispanics/Latinos), and gays, lesbians, and bisexuals.

To complicate matters, although these three categories of populations are underrepresented in major studies of sexual response and behavior, they are overrepresented in other types of sex research, such as those focusing on STDs and teen pregnancy.

The problem may represent a lack of aggressive recruitment of nonwhite, non-middle-class, nonheterosexual subjects in major sexuality research (particularly studies that are privately funded) and an overreliance on sampling from public clinic populations (people with STDs, family planning), which tend to have higher minority representation.

Studies of gay, lesbian, and bisexual populations also have been clouded by methodological problems associated with sampling. Studies of gay men draw heavily from men who frequent gay bars, subscribe to gay publications, are incarcerated, or attend gay public events. Less is known about lesbian women.

A true cross-sectional sample of gay men and lesbians representing various socioeconomic and racial/ethnic lines is needed.

Methodological issues related to sampling and sample size have been cited as the primary problems related to obtaining more diverse samples. It is harder to target recruitment efforts for lower socioeconomic status, minority, and gay/lesbian populations. Targeting narrow segments of these populations (for example, gay men attending gay bars) is easier and has a higher-yield recruitment than mainstream sources such as newspapers, random-digit telephoning, and the like. Narrowing the scope of recruitment, however, means that sampling may miss a true cross-section of the population targeted for study.

Can these studies accurately reflect human sexual behavior and response if they omit large segments of the population? Are there differences between and among various racial and ethnic groups, socioeconomic segments, and different sexual orientations, that might lend greater insight into the true nature of human sexuality?

Finally, newer research has attempted to draw conclusions and examine differences in attitudes, values, and behaviors of groups drawn from a broader range of backgrounds. Students must remember, however, that the United States has increasingly drawn immigrants into our midst who do not answer surveys, may not speak English, or may even feel that sexuality is not a topic to be discussed with anyone outside the immediate family circle.

Health and Wellness Defined

Health Total mental, physical, and social wellbeing, not merely the absence of disease

In 1947 the World Health Organization (WHO) defined **health** as "the state of complete mental, physical, and social well-being, not merely the absence of disease" (p. 35). WHO's definition was the first globally accepted conceptualization of health and stood the test of time for more than a decade.

Although multifaceted, this definition of health was flawed, according to members of a new movement called **holistic health**. The holistic health movement came into being in the 1960s as an attempt to expand the view of health that WHO had promulgated.

Holistic health The process of moving toward optimal functioning across the physical, social, spiritual, emotional, and intellectual dimensions

The Six Dimensions of Wellness

Physical well-being A component of wellness reflected in how well the body performs its intended functions

Body composition The fat and nonfat components of the human body; important in assessing recommended body weight

Intellectual well-being A component of wellness referring to the ability to process information effectively and rationally

Emotional well-being A component of wellness that refers to being in touch with one's feelings, having the ability to express them, and being able to control them when necessary.

Social well-being A component of wellness that involves connection to others through various types of relationships

Environmental well-being A component of wellness that reflects our ability to function in our immediate environment, such as home, school, and work, as well as being able to deal with the world at large

Micro-environment The part of one's environment that is immediate and includes living situation, campus, neighborhood, home, and work site and family, friends, and associates who populate these places

The first dimension, **physical well-being**, is reflected in how well the body performs its intended functions. Absence of disease—although an important influence—is not the sole criterion for health. The physical domain is influenced by one's genetic inheritance, nutritional status, fitness level, **body composition**, and immune status, to name just a few.

Intellectual well-being is the ability to process information effectively. It involves the capability to use information in a rational way to solve problems and grow. It includes issues such as creativity, spontaneity, and openness to new ways of viewing situations. To maintain a high level of intellectual well-being, one must seek knowledge and learn from one's experiences.

Emotional well-being means being in touch with one's feelings, having the ability to express them, and being able to control them when necessary. Optimal functioning involves the understanding that emotions are the mirror to the soul. Emotions help us get in touch with what is important in our lives. Our emotions make us feel alive and provide us with a richness of experience that is uniquely human.

Social well-being involves being connected to others through various types of relationships. Individuals who function optimally in this domain are able to form friendships, have intimate relationships, give and receive love and affection, and accept others unconditionally. They are able to give of themselves and share in the joys and sorrows of being part of a community. This community includes both formal and informal networks. Formal networks include organizations such as churches, professional organizations, fraternities, sororities, and campus groups requiring official membership, dues, and standards. Informal networks such as an intramural sports team do not have rigid rules for membership. In a sense, your social networks are a big part of your environment.

Environmental well-being involves high-level functioning on two levels. The most immediate environment, the **micro-environment**, consists of school, home, neighborhood, and work site. The people with whom we interact in those places link the environment to the social aspects of our health. This environment greatly affects our health and personal safety by influencing whether we are at risk for and fear issues such as theft, crime, and violence. The quality of our air and water, noise pollution, crowding, and other issues that impact our stress levels are also affected. Our social support system is also part of this environment.

The components of wellness

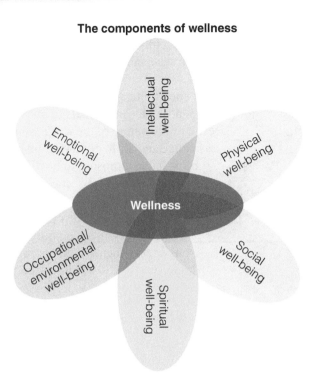

Figure 1.2 *Six-Dimensional Wellness Model* Wellness is a multifaceted phenomenon. Source: Adapted from Bill Hettler, M.D., 1979; http://hettler.com, 2003.

The **macro-environment**, the level of well-being at a larger level—state, country, and the world at large—also affects our wellness. The impact of things discussed earlier in the chapter—the wars in Iraq and Afghanistan, the terrorist attacks of 9/11, and other things such as violence, international disputes, racism, sexism, heterosexism, ageism, and so on—all influence us daily to some extent. Decisions that our political leaders make, such as engaging in wars or determining where we store radioactive wastes, affect the way we think and live our lives. Our ability to stay focused and whole is constantly challenged by the media, which bring the entire world and its problems into our living rooms each night. We need to learn to think globally, act locally, and be happy despite the myriad of problems in the world.

Macro-environment
The environment that extends beyond the micro and includes one's city, state, country, and the world at large

Spiritual well-being involves feeling connected to something beyond oneself. One way to express spirituality is by participating in organized religious activities. This usually means believing in a supreme being or higher supernatural force and subscribing to a formalized code of conduct to live by. In a secular sense, spirituality could manifest itself through connection to something greater than oneself. Whether it is being part of a community, working to save the environment, helping feed the needy, or being committed to world peace, the underlying feeling is a perception of life as having meaning beyond the self.

Spiritual well-being A component of wellness that involves feeling connected to something beyond oneself

Finally, **occupational/vocational well-being** involves issues related to job wellness. Occupational/vocational well-being encompasses everything from the safety of our particular work site to the nature of your career. Work site wellbeing includes physical (air, water, physical plant, machinery, and so on) and social (relationships with coworkers, management, health and wellness facilities and activities) factors. Our personal wellness is affected by the health of our work site. Employers and work sites vary tremendously

Occupational/vocational well-being A component of wellness that reflects our ability to use our unique skills/talents to work that is meaningful and rewarding in relation to health. Some strive for optimal levels, encouraging employees to take advantage of a myriad of health-enhancing programs and services, whereas others meet the minimum acceptable standards for health and safety set by the government.

Besides the specific health of the workplace, different jobs/careers pose varying threats to our well-being as a result of the nature of the work. Some jobs such as police and military service are risky because of possible exposure to hostile combatants. Other occupations such as firefighters, emergency medical service workers, coal miners, and oil rig operators are risky because they place employees in dangerous environments. Other occupations entail high stress due to deadlines, competition, or other factors.

© Monkey Business Images, 2010. Shutterstock, Inc.

Friends are an important part of social well-being.

Wellness and Human Sexuality

Our sexuality both contributes to overall health and well-being and is affected by it. High-level sexual health can be a positive force in our lives. It contributes to the full functioning of our body, mind, spirit, and social relationships. When we are engaged in healthy sexual activity and have a healthy outlook concerning our sexuality, we can maximize our potential as men and women. Conversely, our sexuality is affected by our overall level of health and well-being. Sexual response (from desire to arousal and orgasm) is greatly influenced by our overall level of well-being. We simply are less interested in sex and perform poorly when we have low-level health and wellness.

The important thing is to be moving toward optimal health, even if you never achieve it. If your current level of health is lower than you would like, the main thing is to take steps to improve it. The experience and process of improving, the journey, is as important as the current level of functioning.

Many of us have limitations that keep us from achieving the high levels of health that others enjoy. A wellness perspective of health and sexuality helps us accept our limitations and maximize the potential within us. You may never have the body of the man or woman of your dreams, but you can enjoy healthy sexuality if you strive to be the best you can be.

Applying the Wellness Model to Sexuality

Source: Callista Lee

Now that you have read about the six dimensions of wellness, how would you apply each of them to human sexuality and romantic relationships? With a couple of friends or classmates, take a few minutes to come up with examples for each dimension:
Physical well-being:

Intellectual well-being:
Emotional well-being:
Social well-being:
Occupational/environmental well-being:
Spiritual well-being:

Donna's Journey to Sexual Health

I'm 40 years old, and I like myself. I accept myself. I can be who I am. But it wasn't always like that. As I look back, I realize that my sexuality has played a very significant role in my life.

Sexuality is a significant part of everyone's life, yet if you stray from the center, the average, the expected, then the journey at the very least has more bumps in it than for most.

We can get into a whole list of identities—woman, daughter, lover, student. I see labels as political designations. You try them on to see which ones fit. Can you find "one" that encompasses a total human being? I don't think so. In the last 5 years I've taken "transgender" as one of my primary identities, yet I am also a mother of two boys. I am committed to a woman as a partner. I am a recent college graduate with a full-time job that isn't what I've always hoped to be doing with my degree, but it pays the bills. And when I clear out some of my debts, I hope to pursue graduate school at some point.

I've always been "inappropriate." My mother was always into dressing me to be the pretty little girl, and in 6 seconds I would destroy her efforts. I wanted to climb trees, play in the dirt, and have fun—all sorts of things you couldn't do in a dress. My hair was always very long to please my mother. My way to manage that was to always keep it in pigtails. Once on my own, I started dressing in drag, with short hair and men's clothing. I came out to my family when I was 16, but to my painful surprise found the reception in the lesbian community most unwelcome. Being butch and dressing like a man back in the 1970s was not "politically correct." I remedied my sense of not fitting in and trying to sort everything out by marrying a man and trying to live as a heterosexual woman. I was very successful at that game for close to 20 years, being the dutiful wife and mother.

Today it's a 50–50 shot as to whether people think I'm a man or a woman. It used to bother me a lot when people were confused. Now, I find it amusing and really don't care. I have a job where I can be free to be who I am, sharing the ups and downs of my life with people who are friends. I don't fit neatly into the transgender community, nor do I have "gender dysphoria." My body is my body, and I accept it. I wear men's clothing primarily because they fit better, both body and psyche. I build muscle in "male-patterned" ways, my voice has gotten deeper over time, and my neck is thick. The blood tests I've had in the past all indicate "normal hormone parameters" for a woman.

I feel that I've experimented a lot to find out what is most comfortable and to learn who I am as a sexual person. Not that my journey has ended, but I better understand the road to healthy sexuality. And self-acceptance is a great place to start.

Critical Thinking

How does Donna illustrate some of the problems associated with trying to attach a label to someone's sexuality?

healthy sex hints 1.1

Making Informed Decisions

The following is a simple decision-making model that may help you make better decisions about your sexuality.

1. *Establish your goal.* Try to put in a broader context the decision you are making about an issue. ("How will this decision affect my goal?")

2. *List the pros and cons.* In two columns on a sheet of paper, list the consequences of saying either yes or no to the question you are trying to make a decision about. Don't scrimp. Put down all of them, no matter how trivial they might seem.

3. *Prioritize the pros and cons.* Rank the pros and cons from most important to least important.

4. *Weigh the pros and cons.* Although one column might be greater than the other (many more pros than cons, for instance), the top one or two items on the shorter list might carry much more weight.

5. *Ponder the results.* Examine the lists, and discuss them with one or two people whose opinions you value.

6. *Listen to your instincts.* Sometimes something may seem to be right for the average person but may not feel like the best thing for you. Your rational/intellectual evaluation of your lists, and your significant other's advice, provide you with two pieces of information; your gut-level intuition provides you with another.

7. *Decide.* Action is important. You must make a decision and move on with your life.

8. *Give it time.* Once you make a decision, give yourself time to experience the effects of that decision. At first it may seem that you made the wrong decision. Only time will tell.

9. *Reevaluate.* Go through this model again to reevaluate your decision once a sufficient amount of time has passed.

10. *Don't beat yourself up!* You are human! Sometimes you will make the wrong decisions. Learn from your mistakes, and try not to make the same ones twice. Persecuting yourself and putting yourself down are not productive and will not help you make better decisions.

References

Ardell, D. (1985). *The history and future of wellness.* Dubuque, IA: Kendall/Hunt.

Boulard, G. (2001, December 24). After September 11th students find themselves under a magnifying glass. *Community College Week, 14*(10), 2–4.

Davey, J. (2002, September 30). One day in September. *Community College Week, 15*(4), 4.

Dettmer, J. (2001, October 29). New York shows strength in adversity. *Insight on the News, 17*(40), 13.

Dunn, H. (1962). High-level wellness in the world of today. *Journal of the American Osteopathic Association, 61,* 9.

Garmon, J. (2001, December 24). Making sense, not war. *Community College Week, 14*(10), 4–6.

Henry J. Kaiser Family Foundation. (2000). *Sex education in America: A view from inside the nation's classrooms.* Chart pack. Menlo Park, CA: Author.

Mindlin, A. C., Wallace, E. E., & Kapell, M. (2002). Cultural and religious determinants of sexual behaviors: A crosscultural analysis of the available literature. *Michigan Academician, 34*(1), 6–8.

National Abortion and Reproductive Rights Action League Foundation. (2001). *Who decides? A state-by-state review of abortion and reproductive rights.* Washington, DC: NARAL and the NARAL Foundation.

National Public Radio, the Henry J. Kaiser Family Foundation, Harvard University Kennedy School of Government (2004, January). Sex education in America: General public/ parents survey. Retrieved from http:// kaiserfamilyfoundation. org.

National Wellness Institute. (2002). Definition of wellness Retrieved from http://www .nationalwellnessinstitute.home.

New York Times (2016, February 18) *President Obama cuts funding for all abstinence-only sex education.* Retrieved from http://www.nytlive .nyt.com

Office of the Surgeon General. (2001). *The surgeon general's call to action to promote sexual health and responsible sexual behavior.* Washington, DC: U.S. Government Printing Office.

Sexuality Information and Education Council of the U.S. (1996). *Guidelines for comprehensive sexuality education* (2nd ed.). New York.

Sexuality Information and Education Council of the U.S. (1997). Guidelines for comprehensive sexuality education fact sheet. Retrieved from http://www.siecus.org/pubs/fact/fact0003.html.

Sexuality Information and Education Council of the U.S. (2001, August–September). Issues and answers: Fact sheet on sexuality education. *SIECUS Report, 29*(6). Retrieved from http:// www.siecus.org/pubs/fact/fact0007.html.

Straw, D. (2001, December 24). A separate peace in a wartime classroom. *Community College Week, 14*(10), 4–6.

Tsigos, C., & Chrousos, G. P. (1996). Stress, endocrine manifestations and disease. In C. L. Cooper (Ed.), *Handbook of stress, medicine, and health.* New York: CRC.

Weis, D. (2002, May). Another stab at sexual theory [a review of *The Role of Theory in Sex Research,* edited by J Bancroft]. *Journal of Sex Research, 39*(2), 158–160.

Wiederman, M. (2001). Why understanding research? In *Understanding sexuality research.* Belmont, CA: Wadsworth.

World Health Organization. (1947). Constitution of the World Health Organization. *Chronicles of the World Health Organization, 1,* 29–43.

Chapter
two

Female Sexual Anatomy and Physiology

Student Learning Objectives

After reading this chapter, students will be able to:

- Identify and locate the key structures of the female sexual anatomy;
- Describe the main functions of the key female sexual structures;
- Identify and describe the functions of the key female sex hormones;
- Explain the erogenous potential of the female sexual structures;
- Identify the signs, symptoms, and treatment for common female sexual disorders;
- Describe a variety of screening tests used to diagnose common female sexual disorders.

case study 2.1

Critical Thinking

It is important for women to love and accept their genitals. We take better care of that which we love. We may then choose to share our genitals only with those who deserve us.

Is it comfortable for you to examine your genitalia?

Why is it important for women to look and understand how they are built?

"The Vagina Workshop" from *The Vagina Monologues* by Eve Ensler

The subject of this piece is an anonymous woman in her late 30s to 40s.

Ensler prefaces this piece as belonging to one of the women she interviewed from a group in their late 30s and early 40s. The woman had learned about her body and orgasm at one of the body workshops taught by Betty Dodson.

. . . I found it quite unsettling at first, my vagina. Like the first time you see a fish cut open and you discover this other complex world inside, right under the skin. It was so raw, so red, so fresh. And the thing that surprised me most was all the layers. Layers inside layers, opening into more layers. My vagina, like some mystical event that keeps unfolding another aspect of itself, which is really an event in itself, but you only know it after the event.
*   . . . It was better than the Grand Canyon, ancient and full of grace. It had the innocence and freshness of a proper English garden. It was funny, very funny. It made me laugh. It could hide and seek, open and close. It was a mouth. It was a morning. And then it momentarily occurred to me that it was me, my vagina: it was who I was. It was not an entity. It was inside of me.*

Many of the structures and functions of sexual anatomy are really quite similar when comparing females and males. Indeed, an underlying theme in this book is the emphasis on how women and men are more similar than different. That being said, however, women's unique role in reproduction and the experiences associated with monthly menstruation across much of a woman's life require women to be aware of their bodies in a way different from men. Those experiences also make it challenging to separate the sexual from the reproductive function of the anatomy.

External Female Sexual Structures

Vulva The external female genitalia

The formal term used to describe all of the external female genital structures collectively is the vulva. The **vulva** includes the mons pubis (also known as mons veneris), labia majora and minora, clitoris, hymen, introitus, and vestibule. There is wide variety in how vulva look: the shapes, sizes, colors are all different, just as our faces have a unique look. In pornography, labias are often photo shopped to look a certain way convincing some women to get labiaplasty to achieve this look (Newman, 2016). However, simply understanding that we are all different and celebrating this difference can help us accept and be proud of our genitalia and the way we look. These are shown in Figure 2.1.

■ Mons Veneris

The mons veneris is named after the Greek goddess of love. In Latin, mons veneris means "the mound of Venus." The mons veneris, commonly called the pubic area, is the softly protruding cushion of fat, skin, and pubic hair that covers the pubis symphysis, the juncture of the pubic bones of the

personal exploration activity
What Do You Know?

After drawing and labeling the female sexual anatomy, you will be able to identify what is accurate and inaccurate about your knowledge of the female anatomy.

Before reading this chapter on female anatomy, take a few minutes to see how much you know or don't know about the female sexual anatomy. Take a sheet of paper and draw from memory the internal and external female sexual anatomy. If possible, get one of your friends of the opposite sex to team up with you to do this drawing. This will be more fun and will show which sex has the most knowledge of the female anatomy. Once you have drawn the anatomy, label the following parts: clitoris, ovaries, uterus, vagina, cervix, labia majora, labia minora, mons pubis, urethra, ureter, fimbria, and bladder.

When you have finished, compare your drawing to the one in this chapter. Are you surprised by how little or how much you know? How comfortable were you drawing this sexual anatomy? Ask one of your friends to do this activity. Does your friend's drawing indicate that they have good knowledge of the female anatomy? How comfortable were they drawing the sexual anatomy?

pelvis. Although it serves no reproductive function, the mons is sensitive to stimulation during sexual arousal. Its pad of fatty tissue provides a soft cushion to maximize pleasure during sexual activities, particularly those involving grinding circular movements.

Labia Majora

The two **labia majora** form the outermost vaginal lips. The labia are folds of skin covering fatty tissue and are covered with hair on the outside. The inner portion of the labia majora is covered with numerous sweat and oil glands.

Labia majora The larger, outer vaginal lips

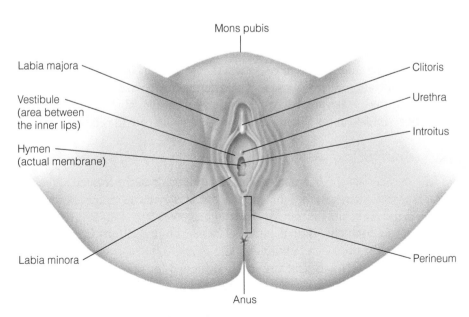

Figure 2.1 *The External Genitalia*

In the unaroused state, the labia majora remain closed, providing protection for the vaginal opening and clitoris. The skin of the labia, like that of the male scrotum, is normally darker in color than the rest of a woman's body. During sexual arousal, underlying erectile tissue engorges with blood, causing the labia to swell, deepen in color, and open like "the petals of a flower" (see "Betty Dodson's Art"- Sex in society 2.1), exposing the vaginal opening and clitoris.

The sweat and oil secretions of the labia majora are capable of producing a cheesy substance called *smegma, which can collect under the clitoral hood causing irritation.* Routine washing with soap and water around the labia and after pulling back the clitoral hood helps ensure cleanliness and prevents the accumulation of smegma under the clitoral hood.

Labia Minora

Labia minora The smaller, inner vaginal lips

The **labia minora** are a second set of vaginal lips located within the larger labia majora. Thinner than the labia majora, the labia minora have spongy tissue containing oil and sweat glands and are richly endowed with blood vessels and nerve endings. The top portion of the labia majora fuse to form the clitoral hood, or *prepuce.* Unlike the labia majora, the minora are hairless. In the unaroused state they, too, remain closed, providing a second line of protection for the vaginal opening and clitoris.

The labia minora are highly sensitive to sexual stimulation and engorge with blood during sexual stimulation, opening up and exposing the vaginal opening and clitoris. Within the labia minora are **Bartholin's glands**, which secrete a small amount of lubricating fluid during sexual arousal. Once thought to provide the major portion of lubrication during arousal, it is now understood that vaginal lubrication comes from the walls of the vagina, rather than any significant amount of secretion from these glands. Bartholin's glands are homologous in structure and function to the bulbourethral (Cowper's) glands in males.

Bartholin's glands Small glands adjacent to the vaginal opening that secrete a small amount of lubricant during arousal

The media has convinced some women that their labia minora hang down too far or are the wrong shape and so they need labia plasty- surgery to reduce size and reshape the labia. The procedure is often described as minor but it is important to remember that no surgery is risk free. The American College of Obstetrics and Gynecology (2014) has stated that these surgeries are not medically indicated and that the safety and effectiveness has not been shown. In addition, they believe women should be warned of the complications such as infection, altered sensation, pain during intercourse and adhesions and scarring from these procedures. As discussed earlier, labia come in various shapes, size and color making us all very individual, not in need of surgery.

Clitoris

Clitoris A small, highly sensitive, organ located at the top of the labia minora

The **clitoris** is a small structure made up of erectile tissue located at the top of the vestibule where the labia majora join. It is made up of three parts—the glans, the shaft, and the root, or *crura,* and evolves from the same tissue that develops into the penis on the male. The glans of the clitoris is exposed by retracting the prepuce or clitoral hood.

The clitoris is a structure solely designed for sexual pleasure; it has no urinary or reproductive function. It is not involved in the passing of any body fluid, in contrast to the penis, which has a role in sexual response,

sex in society 2.1

Betty Dodson's Art

The vulva has long been the subject of artistic expression. The vulva has often been portrayed as a flower, with the labia representing its petals, moist with the dew of sexual arousal, unfolding to reveal the secrets of love and lust contained within.

For more than 30 years, author, artist, and lecturer Betty Dodson has been celebrating female form and function. She has had over 100 exhibitions, and her artwork has adorned countless galleries throughout the world. Her sketches of the vulva capture the variety and uniqueness of female external genitalia. She combines artistic expression with sexual health activism.

Her book *Sex for One: The Joy of Self Loving* is a celebration of female sexuality. In the book, Dodson chronicles her own personal journey from a woman who questioned her own sexual response and ability to enjoy orgasm to a champion of women's sexual health. For decades, Dodson has run workshops devoted to helping women become orgasmic by using masturbation to liberate their sexual energy. Her artwork adorns her book, illustrating the sensual nature of female sexuality.

Source: From *Sex for One: The Joy of Self Loving* by Betty Dodson, copyright © 1974, 1983, 1987 by Betty Dodson.

---

reproduction, and urination. Because of this, many females don't discover their clitoris until preadolescence or older. Figure 2.2 depicts the clitoris.

The clitoris is richly endowed with nerve endings. Although it appears externally as much smaller than the male penis, the clitoral glans has 8000 sensory nerve endings, more than any other body part (Cornforth, 2009). Because of its dense concentration of nerve endings, the clitoris is sensitive to over stimulation, and the prepuce will move forward to cover and protect it from excessive stimulation. The glans is exposed during sexual arousal but the underlying structures of the clitoris are not. New research suggests that these underlying structures may play a larger role in sexual arousal than previously believed. Johnson (2004) uses an iceberg analogy to explain how the glans of the clitoris is similar to the tip of an iceberg. Most of the mass of the clitoris continues under pelvic bone, turns down and surrounds the vagina from above and both sides.

In the unaroused state, the clitoris is hidden by the prepuce. During sexual arousal, the spongy tissue of the clitoris engorges with blood, causing the clitoris to grow, become erect, and protrude from the prepuce, which retracts as the labia minora unfold. The clitoris is highly sensitive to sexual stimulation. Because of this high sensitivity, females often find it more arousing and comfortable when the clitoris is stimulated gently on either side instead of being directly stimulated. Adequate clitoral stimulation plays a key role in female sexual response and orgasm.

Methods effective for arousal include manual, oral, and mechanical stimulation of the clitoris. During intercourse, if there is no pressure on the clitoris, manual stimulation can be used to enhance arousal. Discussion of the clitoris has often been missing from the education of young women. The clitoris is the

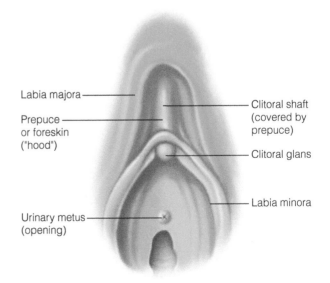

Labia majora

Prepuce or foreskin ("hood")

Clitoral shaft (covered by prepuce)

Clitoral glans

Labia minora

Urinary metus (opening)

Figure 2.2 *The Clitoris*

center of sexual arousal, and U.S. culture has historically been reticent to discuss sexual pleasure with young girls. See chapter 3, sex in society 3.1, Rethinking the Role of the Clitoris in Sexual Arousal, for a more detailed description of the role of the clitoris during sexual arousal.

Vestibule

Vestibule The area within the labia minora that includes the hymen, introitus, and urethral opening

The **vestibule** is the area between the labia minora that is covered with the hymen and contains the openings to the vagina and urethra. In a sense, the vestibule represents the entrance to the vagina. During sexual arousal, the vestibule is sensitive to stimulation of all kinds. Like the labia and clitoris, it is richly endowed with nerve endings.

Urethral Opening

Urethral opening The opening to the urethra, lying behind the clitoris and in front of the vaginal opening

The **urethral opening** in the female lies behind the clitoris and in front of the vaginal opening. Because it is difficult for a female to see and locate, some people have mistakenly thought that a female urinates out the vagina. The urethra itself is an internal structure.

Hymen and Introitus

Hymen The membrane that lines the introitus

Introitus The vaginal opening

The **hymen**, named for the Greek god of marriage, is a thin mucous membrane that partially covers the opening to the vagina, the **introitus**. There is no biological function for the hymen. The hymen is intact at birth but typically becomes perforated by the time a young woman reaches puberty, allowing the passage of menstrual flow. Various activities ranging from sports and exercise to inserting fingers or other objects into the vagina during masturbation are capable of perforating the hymen.

Although the hymen is durable, its opening is capable of being stretched or enlarged through intercourse, masturbation, or insertion of a tampon. Many people believe that the presence of a hymen is proof of a woman's virginity. This belief also is not true.

Figure 2.3 illustrates the three main types of hymens. The most common is the *annular*, in which the tissue surrounds the entire opening of the vagina and is open in the middle. The *cribiform* hymen has a web of tissue over the introitus and several small openings. The *septate* has a single band of tissue that divides

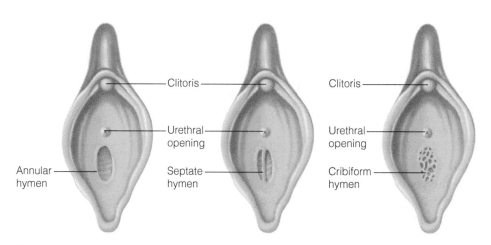

Figure 2.3 *Types of Hymens*

the introitus into two parts. In rare occurrences, girls are born with the hymen completely covering the opening of the vagina, which is not discovered until she starts menstruating. This causes the fluid to build up in the vagina. When this happens, a physician must make a small opening to allow the menstrual flow.

If the hymen is still present at the time of first intercourse, penetration by the penis can produce some discomfort or even bleeding if the hymen is torn. Prior to first intercourse, a female can stretch her hymen by inserting 1 to 2 finger(s) into the vagina and pushing toward the front , sides and back of the vagina. If necessary, a physician may also cut the hymen or stretch the hymen with dilators. However, there is usually little trouble inserting the penis through the hymen if the male is gentle and has taken enough time in foreplay to allow the female to become adequately lubricated.

Perineum

The female **perineum** is the area between the thighs bounded in the front by the pelvis joint (the *symphysis pubis*) and in the rear by the coccyx (tailbone). The muscular tissue is covered by a layer of skin. Although it is not normally considered part of the female sexual anatomy, the perineum plays a part in sexual response because the entire area is endowed with nerve endings and is highly responsive to sexual stimulation. As with men, the nature and intensity of stimulation desired in this area varies from woman to woman and encounter to encounter.

Perineum The area of muscle and skin between vagina and anus

The major difference between the perineum in women and men is its role in childbearing. The perineum of pregnant women is subject to tearing of the skin and muscle tissue during childbirth. This is usually the time when they first become aware of this region. During delivery, pressure from the emerging fetus can exert a tremendous force on the perineum, first stretching, then tearing, the muscle and skin. The muscles and skin will heal, although some women report less sensitivity, as nerve endings can be injured and require additional time to recover. Women are encouraged to massage the perineum with vitamin e oil during pregnancy to minimize the risk of tearing.

Anus

The anus in women is exactly the same as in men and, as such, is capable of similar responsiveness during sexual activity. Sexual stimulation can be enjoyed manually, orally (**anilingus**), and through anal intercourse. Some women use anal intercourse as an alternative to vaginal coitus because they think that by doing this, they can "preserve their virginity" and still enjoy sex. (See Healthy Sex tips 8.5)

Anilingus Oral stimulation of the anus

Underlying Structures

Although only the vulva is visible, there are underlying structures that are important to sexual arousal (see Figure 2.4). The area is rich in erectile tissue, with a network of nerves and blood vessels that become engorged, comparable to the spongy tissue of the penis. The vestibular bulbs run along the

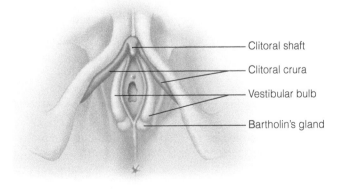

Clitoral shaft

Clitoral crura

Vestibular bulb

Bartholin's gland

Figure 2.4 *Underlying Structures*

sex in society 2.2

Female Genital Mutilation

The practice of female genital mutilation (FGM) is a centuries old tradition in some cultures, primarily in western, eastern and north-eastern Africa, and in some countries in Asia and the Middle East (World Health Organization, 2016).

It is estimated that 200 million girls and women worldwide are living with the consequences of female genital mutilation. (World Health Organization, 2013). The procedure ranges from removal of the clitoris, removal of the clitoris and labia minora, or removal of the clitoris and entire labia with the area stitched closed. Other harmful procedures include piercing, scraping and cauterizing the genital area. Although the procedure is most commonly performed between the ages of 2 and 15, some girls have had it done within the first week of life (Rising Daughters Aware, 1999; WHO, 2013). This cultural and religious custom has been done to reduce females' ability to experience sexual pleasure and ensure marital fidelity. The cultures that practice FGM do not believe a woman should derive pleasure from sex. The physical health risks of the procedure are many with immediate consequences including shock, bleeding, sepsis, urinary retention, open sores in the genital area, and damage to nearby genital tissues. Long term consequences include infertility, recurrent bladder infections, the need for more surgery, childbirth complications and the deaths of newborns (WHO, 2013).

Female genital mutilation is recognized internationally as a violation of human rights of girls and women. According to the World Health Organization (2016), "It reflects deep routed inequality between the sexes and constitutes an extreme form of discrimination against women." In 2012 the United Nations General Assembly accepted a resolution on the elimination of female genital mutilation. In recent years many organized groups, most prominently the World Health Organization and the United Nations Children's Fund, have condemned this treatment of females and are continuing to pressure the countries and cultures that still practice genital mutilation to end it. U.S. representatives to the World Bank and other financial institutions oppose loans to countries that widely practice genital cutting and have no anti-FGM educational programs. In 26 African countries there are laws prohibiting FGM. In most countries, there is a decline in female genital mutilations and most women and men in these practicing countries support the elimination of the practice (WHO, 2016).

In the United States, the Federal Prohibition of Female Genital Mutilation Act of 1995 passed in September 1996, provides for prison sentences for anyone who performs this procedure on a female under 18 years of age. That law does permit the surgery if it is "necessary to the health of the person on whom it is performed." Other countries that outlaw the procedure include England, Canada, France, Sweden, and Switzerland.

---

vagina, with the crura of the clitoris extending up toward the pelvic bone. The structures engorge with blood during sexual arousal, causing the labia, clitoris, and vagina to enlarge, swell, and deepen in color.

The muscles in the area also play a significant role in arousal. As discussed in Healthy Sex Hints 2.1, strengthening the pelvic floor muscles through Kegel exercises has clear health and sexual benefits.

Breasts

Lactation The process of producing and secreting milk from the breasts

Although the main function of the female breast is **lactation**, it has taken on erotic and sexual significance in American and other cultures. Breasts. like the labia, are varied and come in all sizes and shapes. The breasts are composed of mammary glands, fatty tissue, the nipple and areola, and underlying muscle and ligaments.

For many, breast have become markers for attractiveness, and sexiness, leading women—even teen girls—to surgically alter their breasts. Large-breasted females may choose reduction surgery for appearance and comfort while small breasted women may want to increase the size of their breast.

Mammary Glands

The **mammary glands** are divided into 15 to 20 lobes or compartments separated by fatty tissue. Each lobe is made up of several smaller components called lobules.

Imbedded in the lobules are milk-secreting cells called alveoli. Following childbirth, special hormones trigger the production and secretion of milk from the alveoli. Milk secreted from the alveoli is stored in chambers called mammary ducts and are drained through nursing.

Swelling of glandular tissue and storage of milk typically cause the breasts of nursing women to enlarge significantly. Breast size returns to normal after nursing ceases. (We will discuss lactation and nursing more fully in Chapter 13.)

Breast swelling, and in some cases painful tenderness, often precedes menstruation, as the breasts (like the uterus) prepare for potential pregnancy.

Mammary glands Glands within the breasts that produce milk for lactation

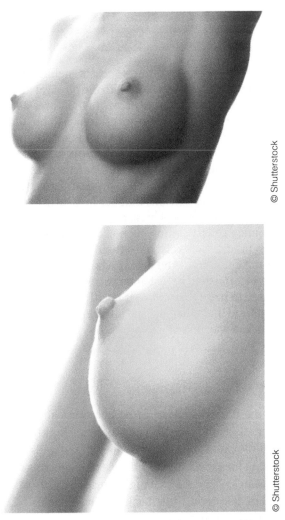

© Shutterstock

© Shutterstock

The female breast comes in a variety of shapes and sizes.

Fatty Tissue

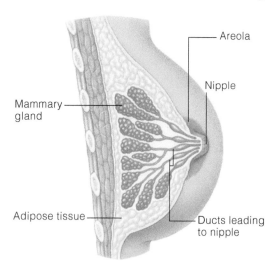

Areola

Nipple

Mammary gland

Adipose tissue

Ducts leading to nipple

Figure 2.5 *Structures of the Female Breast*

Breast size and shape in a woman who is not nursing are determined primarily by heredity and the amount of adipose or fatty tissue present in the breast. Figure 2.5 highlights the different structures of the breast.

Because of the cultural emphasis on breast size, surgical breast augmentation (enlargement) and reduction procedures have become much more common. In 2015, breast augumentation was the number one plastic surgery performed with approximately 280,000 women having breast augmentation surgery. In addition, 99,143 women had breast lifts and 650 had breast reduction surgery (American Society of Plastic Surgeons, 2015). The number of augmentation procedures had been as low as 32,000 in 1992. A 2008 study of women who had had breast augmentation, lift, or reduction found the women reported improved self esteem and quality of life. Of these women, 99 percent were so satisfied that they would have the surgery again (Swanson, 2013). As with any surgery, breast augmentation and reduction procedures are not without risks. Anyone considering this surgery should research the specific procedure to make an informed decision

❧ *Physical and Emotional Wellness* ❧

Concern for the appearance of one's breasts highlights how the emotional dimension of health interfaces with the physical dimension. Many females spend money to increase the size of their breasts with implants or to decrease the size. Plastic surgeons are available to make breasts smaller, larger, more even, or higher and/or to replace one or both that may have been removed due to disease. Because breasts in American culture are sexualized and significant to women's sense of being attractive, focusing on breast health from the physical perspective may become secondary to a woman's concern that her breasts are "acceptable."

The physical dimensions of breast health can change with menstruation, pregnancy, breastfeeding, menopause, and aging. Some females are prone to breast cysts related to their menstrual cycles. Some are amazed at the changes in the breast when they breastfeed, whereas for others concerns over breast changes can stand as an impediment to their desire to breastfeed. Breast health requires paying attention to the breasts and their changes and ensuring that emotional concerns do not get in the way of proper care.

Areola and Nipple

Areola The brownish or pink ring of tissue surrounding the nipple of the breast

At the end of the breast is a ring of darker skin called the **areola**. In the center of the areola is the nipple. The areola is slightly rougher in texture than the rest of the breast because it contains oil glands that help lubricate the nipples during breastfeeding. The areola also contains small muscles and many nerve endings. This makes it highly responsive to sexual stimulation. Nursing mothers also report that suckling their babies can cause sensual feelings that can be a source of confusion.

Pubic Hair

When I was younger, I could not wait for my body to change and become a 'grown up' body. My first pubic hair was greeted with great excitement and pride. I grew the most wonderful bushy pubic hair and looked forward to showing it off to the future love of my life. The time finally came when I thought I had found the perfect guy with whom to share my body. I was so proud when I first undressed only to find that he thought my pubic hair was ugly and disgusting. He pressured me until I agreed to remove it to please him. What a disaster! I shaved, only to find that it grew back in a few days and itched like crazy. So then I went to a salon to have a bikini wax. That took longer to grow back but was it was pretty uncomfortable when they pulled the wax and hair off and it really seemed expensive on my budget. For my grand finale, I tried tweezing since that would be cheap but it almost killed me. After all that, I decided my pubic hair was just fine as it was. I liked it and if he did not, then maybe he wasn't truly the right one for me. This experience really made me look at what I am willing to do to my body to please someone. I am now with this amazing guy who loves all parts of my body, just as they are. His attitude makes our physical intimacy so relaxing and this relaxation makes the physical pleasure incredibly intense.

case study 2.2

Critical Thinking

Do sexual partners have the right to persuade a partner to make physical changes? How far are you willing to go to change for your partner?

The nipple is located within the areola and contains smooth muscle fibers, milk ducts, and many nerve endings. The nipples and areola are highly sensitive, and their smooth muscle fibers can contract upon stimulation, causing them to stiffen and become erect. Nipples also can stiffen and become erect in response to cold and nonsexual tactile stimulation.

© Shutterstock

Breastfeeding is strongly encouraged as a healthy and economical way to nourish a baby.

Breast health was once thought to include monthly breast self exams by all women. The philosophy and thinking about this action has changed however. The US Preventative Services Task Force (2009) and the Canadian Preventative Services Task Force both recommend against women doing monthly breast self exam (BSE). There is no data to support that breast self exams decrease breast cancer deaths. However, these exams are likely to increase the chances of her going for a clinical assessment and biopsy. Therefore both groups recommend against doing breast self exam. Mammograms are recommended every two years for women age 50–74 for early detection of breast cancer to help protect breast health. Deciding to screen women under 50 should be on an individual basis (USPSTF, 2016).

Internal Female Sexual Structures

The internal structures of the female anatomy include the vagina, uterus, cervix, fallopian tubes, and ovaries (Figure 2.6). The urethra in the female lies outside the reproductive system, yet, along with the bladder, it is affected by pregnancy, menstruation, and sexual behavior.

■ Urethra and Bladder

The urethra in the female runs from the bladder to the vestibule, and it is much shorter than that of the male (1 inch compared to 9 inches in the male) making her more vulnerable to infections. It is relatively easy for bacteria from outside the body to enter the urethra and lead to bladder infections known as **urinary tract infections (UTIs)**. *Escherichia coli* bacteria from the rectum and irritation from sexual intercourse can lead to bacterial bladder infections, necessitating antibiotic treatment. Using the diaphragm as birth

Urinary Tract Infections (UTI)
Bacterial infection of the bladder

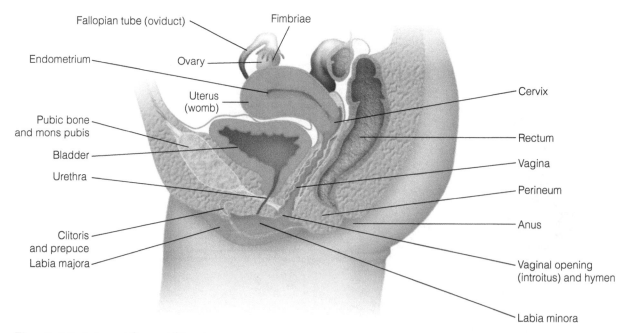

Figure 2.6 *Internal Sexual Structures*

control can also increase a woman's risk of bacterial UTI's. An inflammation of the bladder, called **cystitis**, can occur due to irritants such as feminine hygiene sprays or spermicidal jellies(Mayo Clinic, 2012). Drinking plenty of fluids, urinating frequently, washing gently around vagina or anus with mild (not harsh) soaps, urinating after intercourse and wiping from the front to back when you use the bathroom can enhance urinary health. The bladder in the female lies next to the anterior wall of the vagina and in close proximity to the uterus. The role of the bladder is to hold urine and when this stretchy pouch is full, the female feels the need to urinate. Listening to your body by urinating when you feel the urge will decrease the risk for urinary tract infections.

Cystitis Bladder inflammation

Vagina

The **vagina** is a thin-walled muscular tube, about 3 to 4 inches long, lying between the bladder and the rectum, which connects to the cervix at one end and opens up to the outside of the body at the other. The vagina is tilted upward at a 45-degree angle extending toward the small of the back.

Vagina A tubular organ connecting to the uterus, which serves both reproductive and erotic functions

The walls of the vagina contain an outer layer of muscular tissue and an inner layer of mucous membrane. The mucous membrane tissue produces a thin, clear, moderately acidic (pH 3.5–4) discharge that provides an efficient self-cleaning mechanism. During sexual arousal, these same tissues engorge with blood, producing a thin, slippery lubrication that reduces friction and facilitates intercourse.

The outer third of the vagina contains the most muscle tissue and nerve endings. The interior and rear part, which connects with the cervix,

healthy sex hints 2.1

Pelvic Floor (Kegel) Exercises

You can practice contracting your pelvic floor muscles to prevent or reduce sagging of the organs and urinary incontinence (losing urine when you cough, sneeze, or laugh), to strengthen your orgasms, and to prepare for childbirth. Before you begin your exercises make sure your bladder is empty. A good way to locate these muscles is to spread your legs apart while urinating and to then start and stop the flow of urine. Your ability to do this is one indication of how strong your muscles are. If you are not sure if you have found the correct muscle, insert your finger into the vagina and tighten the muscles as if you are stopping the flow of urine, then release, You should feel the muscle tighten on your finger.

When you have correctly identified the muscles, begin exercising these muscles by squeezing, and holding for 6–8 seconds, then relax for 10 seconds. It is essential to isolate the pelvic floor muscles. If you contract your buttocks or abdomen while doing the exercises, you are doing them incorrectly. Repeat these contractions 10 times in a row. to make up one set of exercises. Repeat the set of 10 contractions 3 times every day. The exercises are only effective when done regularly and the more you do them, the more they will help. You can do them at any time—sitting in a car or bus, talking on the telephone, or even as a "wake-up" exercise. After just 6 weeks, many report better muscle tone, increased sexual pleasure during intercourse, and stronger orgasms. Kegel exercises have also been shown to decrease premature ejaculation for males, underscoring the importance of Kegels for sexual health of both sexes.

Source: *Mannheim, J. (2012). Kegel exercises-self care. Online:http: //www.nlm/nih.gov*

is relatively devoid of nerve endings. In the unaroused state, the vagina resembles a collapsed space similar to a balloon without air in it. Because the vagina is a muscle, it can expand to accommodate objects of varying sizes ranging from a tampon, penis, or sex toy to a newborn's head. Myths and stories exist, nonetheless, alluding to male or female partners being incompatible: "He's too big for me," "She's too loose for him," and so on. Being sexually active or having a baby will not make the woman's vagina "too big" since the vagina is a muscle. However, all females need to perform Kegel exercises three times a day to maintain and strengthen the muscle tone of the vagina and pelvic floor. (Mannheim, 2012). The technique guidelines are explained in healthy sex hints 2.1.

G-spot An area on the front wall of the vagina

On the front wall of the vagina, midway between the introitus and cervix, is an area known as the **G-spot**, or Grafenberg spot, named for the physician who first identified that portion of the vagina as having erotic potential. Research conducted in the 1980s focused on whether all women had such a spot, if all women found stimulation to the area arousing, and what exactly was the chemical makeup of the fluid propelled from the urethra in some women at the time of orgasm. Deep manual stimulation or penile stimulation can cause the area to swell, leading to an orgasm that has a strong, vaginal component. Overall, research on the G-spot has been related to discussions of female ejaculation, tissue referred to as a female prostate gland, and a redefining of the components of female orgasm (Zaviacic & Whipple, 1993).

The vagina is also known as the birth canal because of its function as the exit point for the newborn during childbirth. The vagina has both reproductive and sexual pleasuring functions. Unlike the penis, the vagina is not involved during urination. Urine is excreted through the urethra, whose opening is located above the vaginal opening in the introitus.

The vagina is actually a self-cleansing structure. To ensure vaginal health, the average, healthy woman needs to do nothing more than shower or bathe daily (making sure to wash the vulva with mild soap or water). She has no need to douche, wear minipads (if not menstruating), or use feminine hygiene sprays to perfume the vaginal area. Douching and/or using feminine hygiene sprays can change the pH of the vagina and cause a vaginal infection.

The walls of a normal, healthy vagina produce a thin, clear to yellow colored, slippery discharge that cleanses the vaginal lining and does not indicate any problem. The discharge and the vagina in general have a characteristic musky odor that sex partners often consider erotic.

Changes in the amount, consistency, color, and odor can be used to assess whether you have a vaginal infection. If the amount of discharge increases, changes in color (from clear to bright yellow, green, or white), consistency (from thin and slippery to thick and clumpy), or odor (becomes foul smelling), it could indicate a vaginal infection.

Vaginal health can be enhanced by taking steps to increase overall health and vaginal health. Using condoms when sexually active and being in a monogamous relationship will help protect the vagina from STDs. All females should be vaccinated for human papillomavirus that can cause warts and vaginal cancer. In addition, they should also be vaccinated for hepatitis A and B, which are spread through sexual contact, The vaginal tissues are very sensitive so avoid douching, perfumed soaps, feminine sprays and scented tampons. If sex toys are used, be sure to clean them after each use. Antibiotics can cause vaginal yeast infection and should be taken only when really needed. Some antihistamines used for allergies can cause vaginal dryness which can be irritating during and changing to a medication that does not have this side effect can alleviate this issue. Spermicides and the NuvaRing can cause vaginal irritation so finding a different and effective contraceptive will protect vaginal health. Anxiety and stress can decrease sexual arousal and vaginal lubrication so relaxing before intercourse will decrease vaginal dryness and irritation (Mayo Clinic, 2012). Marijuana use before and during intercourse may contribute to vaginal dryness so avoid using before intercourse. She may also want to use a water based lubricant to protect against irritation during intercourse. The couple could make using the lubricant an erotic, fun part of foreplay. Cosmetic vaginal surgeries, such as "G-spot amplification" and "vaginal rejuvenation" have no medical indication and have never been shown to be safe or provide long term satisfaction. Potential complications include altered sensation, infection, painful intercourse and scarring. These procedures are not supported by the American College of Obstetricians and Gynecologists (ACOG, 2014).

Uterus

The **uterus** is an organ that is sized and shaped like a pear. It is connected to the vagina at its narrow end. The end, or cervix, of the uterus is attached to the vagina and protrudes into the end of the vaginal canal. The wider end (the fundus) extends backward and is held in place by a broad uterine ligament. The uterus is tipped slightly forward.

Uterus Also called the womb, a fist-sized muscular structure that houses the developing fetus during gestation

The uterus is composed of three layers of tissue. The innermost layer, called the **endometrium**, undergoes a cycle of transformation each menstrual period as it prepares for implantation of a fertilized egg. The endometrium is where a fertilized egg implants and grows during pregnancy. If fertilization does not occur, the endometrium breaks down and is shed during menstruation.

Endometrium The inner blood lining of the uterus

The next layer of tissue, the **myometrium**, makes up the bulk of the uterus. This is thick muscular tissue capable of providing the powerful contractions necessary to dislodge endometrial tissue during menstruation or deliver a developed fetus during childbirth. This layer is capable of expanding the size of the uterus from that of a pear, pre-pregnancy, to a small watermelon during pregnancy, and then returning to near its original size within 2 months after birth.

Myometrium The muscular, middle layer of the uterus

The myometrial contractions associated with menstruation can cause severe cramping and pain which is called dysmenorrhea. At the end of this chapter, we will discuss self-help strategies to reduce these and other symptoms associated with menstrual discomfort. The third and outermost layer of uterine tissue is called the **perimetrium**.

Perimetrium The outer lining of the uterus

Cervix

The **cervix**, located at the lower end of the uterus, is described as the neck of the uterus and is about one inch long. It resembles a small ring

Cervix The neck of the uterus, which extends into the inner end of the vagina

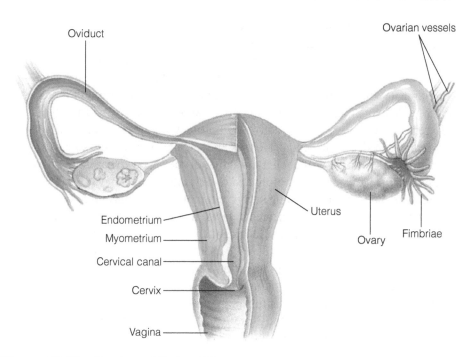

Oviduct

Ovarian vessels

Endometrium
Myometrium
Cervical canal
Cervix
Vagina

Uterus

Ovary   Fimbriae

Figure 2.7 *The Cervix and Related Structures*

or button, the center portion tightly contracted and blocked with a plug of mucus. The cervix feels similar to the way the tip of your nose feels. Running through the cervix is the cervical canal, a small passageway connecting the vagina to the uterus. It is filled with irregularly shaped spaces called *crypts.* The cervical opening, or *cervical os,* remains closed and blocked with mucus during most of a woman's menstrual cycle. As a woman's fertile time approaches, the mucous plug thins, allowing a passageway through the cervix into the uterus. Figure 2.7 shows the cervix and related structures. The cervix is a common site for the development of cancer in women with Human Papillomavirus (HPV) being the main cause.

To protect the health of the cervix, the Human papillomavirus vaccine is recommended for routine use in females and males ages 11–26. If the vaccine is given prior to age 15, two shots are required. The vaccine is also recommended for those 15-26 and for these ages the three shot series is recommended. Shots should be given before the first sexual contact, to ensure the greatest protection from the virus. Human papillomavirus is spread by skin to skin contact during any type of sexual activity with another person (Center for Disease Control, 2013). Starting at age 21, cervical cancer screening (a pap smear), is recommended every three years. It is recommended that women not be screened before age 21 (US Preventive Services Task Force, 2012). In addition to the HPV vaccine and cervical cancer screening starting at age 21, consistently using condoms, reducing the number of sexual partners, and not smoking is a great combination of actions to best protect the cervix (Centers for Disease Control, 2017).

Fallopian Tubes

The two **fallopian tubes**, also known as *oviducts* and *uterine tubes,* approximately 4 inches long, stretch from either side of the fundus of the uterus to the ovaries. Unlike the male vas deferens, which connects to the epididymis, the fallopian tubes do not actually connect with the ovary. Each fallopian tube stops just short of the ovary and is held in place with ligaments that attach it to the peritoneal cavity. The open end of the fallopian tube is funnel shaped, with fingerlike projections called *fimbriae,* which shadow but do not connect with the ovaries. The fallopian tubes are made up of smooth muscle tissue and are lined with hair like projections called *cilia.*

During ovulation, an egg released from the ovary is drawn into the fallopian tube by the fimbriae. No one knows for sure how this happens, but once inside the tube, the egg is moved along by a combination of smooth-muscle contractions and the wavelike action of the cilia. For the egg to be fertilized and implanted within the uterus, a viable sperm must be waiting in the fallopian tube or reach the egg within 24 hours. Figure 2.8 shows how the female egg develops and moves.

Fallopian tube cilia are highly susceptible to destruction from infection. Destruction of these cilia is a common byproduct of infection with gonorrhea or chlamydia. Once the cilia are destroyed, they do not grow back. In addition, infections can cause scarring of the fallopian tubes. Either of these can result in infertility or **ectopic pregnancy**. The term ectopic refers to the process in which the fertilized egg implants in a part of the body other than the uterus, most often in the fallopian tubes. Fertilized eggs can also implant in the abdominal area or cervical canal. Ectopic pregnancies cannot go to term and, if not treated promptly, can be life-threatening. The most common early symptoms of an ectopic pregnancy include abdominal or pelvic pain and light bleeding (Mayo Clinic, 2015).

It is estimated that 1 in 15 sexually active adolescents has Chlamydia. Therefore, to protect the health of the fallopian tubes sexually active women must make sure they do not have Chlamydia. The CDC and the American College of Obstetricians and Gynecologists (2016) recommend yearly Chlamydia screening for all sexually active women age 25 and under. A urine test is all that is needed and allows non invasive screening. Chlamydia is a silent infection and if left

Follicle development

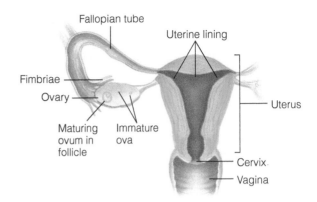

Ovulation

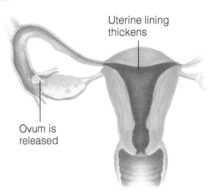

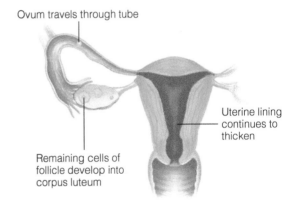

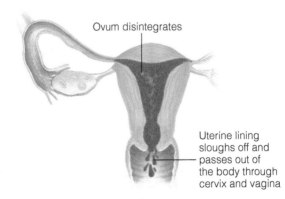

Figure 2.8 *Movement of the Egg*

Fallopian tubes Also called oviducts, extending from the fundus of the uterus to the ovaries; serve as the passageway for the ova

Ectopic pregnancy Implantation of an egg outside the womb

Ovaries Two almond shaped structures that contain and release ova and secrete the hormones estrogen and progesterone

untreated it may cause pelvic inflammatory disease (PID) and if this is not treated it may cause infertility, ectopic pregnancy or chronic pelvic pain. Annual screening of sexually active women is also recommended for gonorrhea since it has the same destructive effects on the fallopian tubes.

Ovaries

The **ovaries** are the size and shape of almonds. Each is located adjacent to a fallopian tube and is held in place in the peritoneum by connective tissue that anchors them to the broad uterine ligament. Like the male testes, the ovaries have two primary functions: fertility and hormone production. The ovaries produce ova (eggs) and the two important female sex hormones, estrogen and progesterone.

Reproductive Physiology

Two distinct cycles—the menstrual (also known as *uterine*) and ovarian—work in concert to control reproduction. Each cycle is regulated by hormones secreted by various endocrine glands. These cycles and their respective hormones are introduced here and described in greater detail in Chapter 13, "Human Reproduction."

Menarche The onset of the menstrual cycle in girls

Menarche is the term to define the onset of the menstrual cycle in girls. The age of menarche is typically between 11-14 but can be as early as 8 and as late as 15. The age of menstruation is similar to what it was in 1973 with only ten percent of girls experiencing menarhe before 11 and ninety percent of girls reaching menarche by age 14 (Chumlea, Schubert, Rohe, Kulin, Lee, Himes & Sun, 2003).

Menopause The absence of a period for 12 consecutive months, without surgery or medical treatment

Menopause has become a term somewhat harder to define, yet the traditional definition is 12 consecutive months of amenorrhea, meaning the absence of a period, without a woman having had surgery or any medical treatment that stops menstruation. The average age for menopause is 51 (Mayo Clinic, 2015). Overall, females menstruate approximately 13 times a calendar year, over a 40-year time frame, minus pregnancy. Consequently, menstruating is a fundamental part of being female, occupying a significant part of a woman's life.

Ovarian Cycle

Unlike male sperm, which are freshly produced in unlimited numbers, women are born with approximately 400,000 immature ova. The health and viability of the ova are affected by age and various environmental factors. Exposure to radiation, toxic chemicals, and other hazards can impair the health of the ova. In general, the viability of ova declines with age.

Ovarian cycle A three phased period of time covering maturation of a follicle, release of ovum, and secreting role of corpus luteum

In a normal cycle, one immature egg matures, is released, and either is fertilized or dies and is discarded with the menstrual flow. This three-phased process is called the **ovarian cycle** (see Figure 2.9). Each cycle has a follicular, ovulatory, and luteal phase. For purposes of illustration, a typical 28-day cycle is used here.

Women's cycles can vary significantly; hormonal changes, stress, weight loss, exercise, and other factors can all impact cycle length. A woman who is monitoring her body to determine ovulation needs to understand that ovulation occurs 14 days from the end of the cycle. While the follicular phase can vary in length, the luteal phase tends to be consistently 2 weeks in length.

1. The *follicular phase* consists of the first 10 days. During this time, a **follicle** grows, preparing to release a mature egg.

   Follicle An egg sac in the ovary

2. The *ovulatory phase,* days 11 to 14, consists of final preparation for and release of a mature egg.

3. The *luteal phase,* days 14 to 28, revolves around the activity of the **corpus luteum.** The corpus luteum's role of secreting progesterone to sustain the rich endometrial lining necessary for implantation varies depending on whether fertilization occurs.

   Corpus luteum The follicle after it has released its ovum and begins to produce progesterone

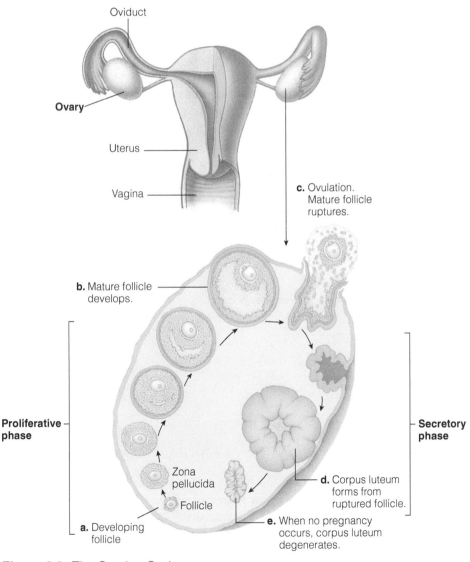

Figure 2.9 *The Ovarian Cycle*

healthy sex hints 2.2

Taking Care of Your Reproductive Health

For many women, going to the gynecologist or other reproductive health care provider is a visit they don't look forward to. In particular, the pelvic exam tends to arouse the most anxiety and discomfort. Draped from the waist down, lying on their back on the exam table with their feet in stirrups, legs spread wide apart, vulva completely exposed, they wait, feeling vulnerable.

Even when performed by the most sensitive of clinicians, the pelvic examination can be stressful. The examination is designed to allow the clinician to examine visually and manually a woman's internal and external sexual anatomy. To facilitate this examination, a speculum is used to spread the walls of the vagina, and a light is used to illuminate the vaginal walls and cervix.

The examination consists of looking at the vulva and internal structures for any abnormalities—unusual growths, erosions, lumps, rashes, or discharges. After visually examining the area, the clinician manually probes the various structures, feeling for any changes in size or shape. A *bimanual examination* means using two hands to palpate structures such as the cervix, uterus, fallopian tubes, and ovaries. During this procedure, the clinician places one hand on the patient's abdomen and inserts two fingers from the other hand into the vagina. The clinician then feels for any abnormalities. Often these palpations will cause pain if disease is present.

Patient-centered clinicians take extra time and care to prepare patients for what is about to happen. They explain each procedure before it is done, helping the patient adjust to the probes and prods that are part of the examination. They also offer patients the option to see what is happening through the use of floor and handheld mirrors. Little things such as warming a speculum before inserting it and helping patients relax with breathing exercises can go a long way toward making the examination less offensive.

Women are encouraged to understand their bodies, prepare for the exam by thinking through the questions that they have, and make sure their concerns are dealt with in a sensitive manner. Three excellent reference books to have in your home library include these:

> *Our Bodies, Ourselves,* Boston Women's Health Book Collective (New York: Simon & Schuster, 2011)

> *The New Harvard Guide for Women's Health,* Karen J. Carlson, Stephanie A. Eisenstat, and Terra Ziporyn (Boston: Harvard University Press, 2004)

> *The V Book: The Doctor's Guide to Complete Vulvovaginal Health,* Elizabeth Stewart and Paula Spencer (New York: Bantam, 2002)

Menstrual or Uterine Cycle

Although the main function of the uterus is to house the implanted and developing embryo, the cyclic nature of reproduction allows this for only a few short days each month. The menstrual cycle coincides perfectly with the ovarian cycle to ensure the union of sperm and egg at the best possible time to enhance successful implantation in the endometrium. The phases of the menstrual cycle are depicted in Figure 2.10.

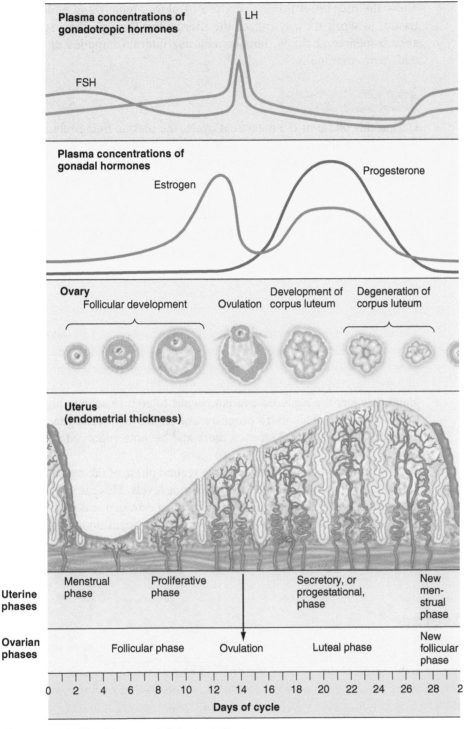

Figure 2.10 *The Menstrual (Uterine) Cycle*

Menstrual Phase

During the menstrual phase, which lasts approximately 3 to 5 days, the uterus sheds its endometrial lining. The strong muscles of the uterus contract and slough off the rich network of tissue and blood vessels built up to support fetal implantation and development. The cervix dilates to allow the menstrual fluid, a mixture of blood. mucus and endometrial tissue, to work its way out of the uterus and through the vagina. To absorb menstrual fluids, females can use internal tampons or sanitary pads worn externally.

Proliferative Phase

During this phase of the menstrual cycle, the uterine lining rebuilds. The endometrium literally proliferates with a rich network of tissue and blood vessels, preparing the uterus for pregnancy. To support a pregnancy, the lining must be thick enough and endowed with the complex network of blood vessels necessary to sustain successful implantation and development of an embryo for the 9 months of prenatal development. During the buildup, the endometrium relies on a constant source of the hormone estrogen. This phase takes about 9 days and ends with ovulation which occurs 14 days before menstruation starts.

Secretory Phase

The secretory phase begins with ovulation and lasts about 14 days or until the onset of the menstrual phase. The secretory phase is divided into two parts. During the first half of the phase, the uterus prepares for implantation of a fertilized ovum. Luteinizing hormone (LH), secreted by the pituitary gland, triggers the ruptured ovarian corpus luteum to secrete high levels of progesterone. This extra progesterone mixes with estrogen, causing the endometrium to thicken even more and become engorged with blood vessels.

If fertilization does not occur, the second phase of the secretory cycle begins with a decline in LH, and progesterone levels. This causes the corpus luteum to degenerate and causes a decrease in estrogen and progesterone. This loss of hormones causes the endometrium to begin sloughing, starting the menstrual phase again.

Your Body Isn't Average

Source: Callista Lee

All of the textbooks on human sexuality present the "average" menstrual cycle, but what if you are not average? You likely already know that not every woman's cycle is twenty-eight days long, so you would be correct in guessing that ovulation does not always occur on day fourteen. If you read about the menstrual cycle carefully, you noted that the proliferative phase ends with ovulation, and that ovulation occurs about fourteen days before the next period starts. That's right, ovulation occurs, and then it takes about fourteen days until the uterus figures out that there has been no pregnancy and so it is time

for another period (menstruation) to start the cycle over again. If you wanted to know when ovulation occurred you would count about fourteen days *backwards* from the first day of your period. Actually, fourteen days is an average, so make it twelve to sixteen days that you count back.

You can know in hindsight when you last ovulated, but it is a little trickier to know in advance when you will ovulate *next*. This is important for two groups of people: (a) those hoping to get pregnant—they want to be sure that sperm are present in the uterus and fallopian tubes at ovulation, and (b) those desperately wanting to *avoid* pregnancy—they want to make sure there are *no sperm* present at the time of ovulation. But if you assume that your next cycle will be twenty-eight days long and just count fourteen days from the first day of your period, you could be very wrong! What if your cycle is twenty-four days that next month? Counting backward from day twenty-five (the first day of your next period after a twenty-four day cycle), by twelve to sixteen days means that you would have ovulated anytime from day nine to day thirteen. And if your cycle is longer than twenty-eight days? If it is thirty-three days, long, you would count backward from day thirty-four by twelve to sixteen days and find that you probably ovulated sometime between days eighteen to twenty two. See how far off you could be if you don't have twenty-eight-day cycles every month?

There is yet another factor to consider, and that is how long sperm survive in the woman's reproductive system. Some researchers have found that at least some sperm can survive and be able to fertilize an ovum for up to a week! If you are using a calendar to calculate your "safe time" to have sex without risking pregnancy, you need to avoid the days of when ovulation is likely *plus* a week prior to that for long-lasting sperm.

But wait! It gets even more complex. Although most women ovulate just once per cycle, it is not all that unusual for a woman to ovulate twice in a cycle. Scientists are still trying to understand why this happens (Vince, 2003). The bottom line is that there is no 100 percent "safe" time to engage in heterosexual intercourse without use of contraceptives if you hope to avoid pregnancy.

Menopause

The cessation of the menstrual period, called menopause, generally occurs between ages 40 and 55 and on average begins at 51. Women typically experience 5 to 10 years of what is termed **perimenopause**, a period of gradually declining estrogen levels produced by the ovaries, culminating in no more menstrual periods. Physical changes from declining hormones include hotflashes, thinning of the genital area that may lead to discomfort during intercourse, sleep disturbances and increased risk for osteoporosis. Declining estrogen levels have been related to higher rates of osteoporosis and heart disease in postmenopausal women. Some women may be prescribed either estrogen replacement therapy (ERT) or hormone replacement therapy (HRT), which is a combination of estrogen and progesterone to decrease menopausal symptoms. In addition, some hormone protocols include testosterone replacement therapy, which can help improve sex drive. There is some controversy surrounding the use of hormones for menopause so women should educate themselves and discuss it with their health care provider.

Perimenopause A period of gradually declining estrogen levels produced by the ovaries

Vaginal dryness can affect sexual enjoyment but can be improved with estrogen applied directly on the vaginal tissues with a tablet, ring or cream. Low dose antidepressants or the drug Gabapentin can help reduce hot flashes. There are several drug choices that will help women avoid osteoporosis (Mayo Clinic, 2013).

Many women want to avoid using drugs or may want to do more in addition to the above ideas. Taking control of one's health during menopause is an important step in this life transition. Some women gain weight during this period due to the slowing of metabolism. Regular daily exercise will increase metabolism and help her regulate her weight. Weight bearing exercises, running/weight lifting, are also effective in preventing osteoporosis. Exercise reduces anxiety; an issue brought on by changing hormones. Do not smoke since it increases risk of osteoporosis, heart disease and hot flashes. Menopause is a perfect time in life to focus on eating in a healthy way and decreasing the empty calorie foods that increase body weight. Getting plenty of sleep by avoiding too much caffeine and alcohol are effective in improving health and managing menopause. Yoga, tai chi and qi gong are also helpful in reducing hot flashes. If she is experiencing vaginal dryness, water based vaginal moisturizers and lubricants will help. Staying sexually active will increase blood flow to the vagina resulting in improved vaginal health (Mayo Clinic, 2013.) All of the healthy changes listed can be practiced early in life to help females achieve a healthy body and mind long before the change of menopause.

❧ *Emotional and Social Wellness* ❧

Because the menstrual cycle is such a fundamental part of being female, it is important that women learn to manage this part of their health. For some, menstruation means little more than remembering to carry the necessary hygiene products. To others, however, each cycle can be fraught with intense pain, mood swings, irritability, and an overall desire to be left alone.

The cessation of menstruation can bring relief and joy to some women. No more cramps. No more hassles. No fear of pregnancy. Others, however, feel a loss when they no longer experience the menstrual cycles that have been a part of their lives for so long.

Health Issues

Although most women can expect to stay healthy, various health issues/disorders can affect female sexual anatomy and physiology. For many of these health issues, making healthy behavior choices can decrease the likelihood of experiencing the disorder.

■ Endometriosis

Endometriosis A condition in which pieces of the endometrium migrate to the fallopian tubes, ovaries, or abdominal cavity

Endometriosis, one of the most common gynecological diseases, is a disorder of the endometrium resulting from migration of the byproducts of menstruation into the fallopian tubes, ovaries, and abdominal cavity. The shed endometrial tissue, called *implants,* adheres to these structures and continues to respond to the effects of hormones during the menstrual cycle. The most common symptoms of endometriosis are sharp pain, cramps, and heavy bleeding during menstruation. The first choice of treatment for endometriosis is oral contraceptives.

■ Breast Cancer

Breast cancer develops when cancerous cells proliferate, causing one or more tumors.

These tumors may metastasize, with malignant cells spreading throughout the body in lymph fluid and the bloodstream. Excluding skin cancer, breast cancer is the most common cancer of American women and is the second leading cause of deaths from cancer in women, surpassed only by lung cancer. The often quoted, "1 in 8 chances of getting breast cancer", is scary for most women. It is also a misleading quote since it is more accurate to examine the chances of getting breast cancer by age group as shown below.

A mammogram can detect lumps too small to feel during breast self-exam.

A 40 year old has a 1 in 14 chance of getting breast cancer by age 70

A 60 year old has a 1 in 28 chance of getting breast cancer by age 70

A 70 year old has a 1 in 14 chance of ever developing breast cancer (Sohal, Baustian, Rao, Choy, Sweet, & Jones, 2010)

There is increasing concern that women are being scared into early mammograms and that we are over treating breast cancer. Because mammography has both benefits and harms, the recommendation is to have a mammogram every other year if you are between the ages of 50–74. If you are outside of that age group it should be a personal decision after being fully informed of the risks (USPSTF, 2016). All breast cancers are not alike; there are at least four genetically distinct breast cancers. The most likely treatment for early stage breast cancer will be surgery with either chemotherapy, hormonal therapy or radiation (Mayo Clinic, 2016).

Age and a having a parent, sibling or child with breast cancer are the strongest predicting factors for having breast cancer. These factors cannot be controlled but there are ways a woman can reduce her risk for developing breast cancer. Moderate risk factors include smoking, alcohol consumption and obesity. A woman can take control and avoid smoking, drink only in moderation and either maintain a healthy weight or lose weight if needed.

Exercise has been shown to protect against breast cancer so women should incorporate daily exercise into their lives. Additional risks under a woman's control include late childbearing (after 35), never having children, and never breast feeding a baby. If a woman is planning to have children she may wish to consider doing so before age 35 and breast feeding her baby (National Cancer Institute, 2016).

Vaginitis

In **vaginitis**, the vagina becomes inflamed, resulting in one or more of the following symptoms: discharge, dryness, burning upon urination (if the inflammation spreads into the urethral opening), and pain during intercourse. The discharge associated with vaginitis is often overlooked or mistaken for a woman's normal vaginal fluid. Three characteristics of vaginal discharge—quantity, color, and odor—can vary in response to vaginitis. The discharge associated with vaginitis is usually profuse (quantity), ranging from frothy white to greenish yellow (color), and changes from a woman's normal scent to a foul, even fishy-smelling odor. Sometimes vaginitis causes vaginal dryness instead of discharge. This unusual dryness results in pain.

Vaginitis Inflammation and irritation of the vagina

The urethra can become inflamed as a result of either the discharge or unusual dryness. When the urethra is inflamed, urination is painful. Painful intercourse is another common symptom of vaginitis.

healthy sex hints 2.3

Promoting Optimal Vulvovaginal Health

1. Do not make your private parts private to you. Examine yourself.
2. Get involved in your health care. Go on the Internet. Get information. Ask questions.
3. Wash the vulva daily with warm, soapy water.
4. Avoid douching. The vagina is a self-cleansing organ. Douching does not prevent pregnancy or infection and can destroy healthy bacteria present in the vagina.
5. Avoid scented products such as vaginal hygiene sprays and perfumed soaps. Do not use talcum powder on the vulva.
6. Be careful about what you insert into your vagina (make sure all sex toys and other objects are safe and clean before inserting them).
7. Do not progress from anal intercourse to vaginal intercourse (a common way to transfer germs from the rectum to the vagina) without first washing your partner's penis.
8. Never force vaginal penetration (make sure your vagina is well lubricated before inserting anything into it).
9. Become familiar with the amount, consistency, color, and odor of your normal daily discharge.
10. If the discharge changes, see a health care provider.

Source: Elizabeth G. Stewart and Paula Spencer, *The V Book: A Doctor's Guide to Complete Vulvovaginal Health* (New York: Bantam, 2002).

Vaginitis is diagnosed through a combination of clinical examination and laboratory tests. Various forms of vaginitis have different combinations of symptoms. An experienced clinician often can make the diagnosis based on the symptoms and will most likely treat with prescription or over the counter drug therapy. Self-treatment of vaginitis (especially involving douching) is not recommended without an accurate diagnosis of the condition.

Premenstrual Syndrome (PMS)

Premenstrual syndrome (PMS)
A condition preceding menstruation, characterized by a myriad of physical and psychological symptoms

Premenstrual syndrome (PMS) is characterized by a myriad of physical and psychological symptoms that appear anywhere within 2 weeks of the onset of menstruation and end after menstruation begins. Up to 85% of women report having one or more of a variety of physical and psychological symptoms. Some common symptoms include bloating, weight gain, breast swelling and tenderness, fatigue, difficulty in sleeping, headache, appetite change or food cravings- especially sugary foods, chocolate and carbohydrates, joint or muscle pain, tension, irritability, mood swings, anxiety, depression and difficulty concentrating. The cause is not yet determined but may be linked to sensitivity to changing hormone levels during the menstrual cycle and fluctuations in serotonin in the brain. Stress is not thought to be a cause but can make it worse. The symptoms of PMS are so varied that women often attribute to the menstrual cycle symptoms that are not related. Women may find it helpful to note on a calendar the dates they experience certain symptoms and the dates they have their menstrual

healthy sex hints 2.4

Self-Help for PMS

Various treatments are available to help women who have PMS. For years, stress management and dietary changes have been advocated as part of a comprehensive PMS treatment program. Recently, prostaglandin inhibitors have been recommended. The following are some strategies that might work for you:

1. Have a daily exercise program.
2. Eat a well-balanced diet high in healthy foods such as fruits, vegetables, and whole grains. Eat at least three meals a day (it may be preferable to eat 5 smaller meals). This will provide the best fuel and an even release of energy throughout the day.
3. Avoid excess sugar and snacks high in sugar and fat. This step, coupled with tip 2, will help avoid the extreme high and low blood sugar levels associated with mood swings.
4. Avoid excess sodium intake (table salt and salt in food), which will help reduce bloating related to fluid retention.
5. Have an orgasm. This activity can help release pent-up vaginal and uterine muscle tension.
6. Try relaxation activities such as diaphragmatic breathing, imagery, meditation, and systematic muscle relaxation.These activities can help reduce stress and induce relaxation.
7. Have your partner (or a professional) give you a lower-back massage. It will help relieve muscle tension and induce relaxation.
8. Soak in a warm bath, Jacuzzi, or hot tub, or apply heat to the abdominal area with a heating pad or water bottle.The warmth will help you relieve muscle tension and induce relaxation.
9. Try antiprostaglandin medications. Prostaglandin inhibitors reduce the intensity and duration of cramps. Prostaglandin inhibitors include ibuprofen (Motrin), naproxen (Aleve), and ketoprofin (Orudis KT).

cycle. After a few months it will be easy to identify the symptoms that are consistently related to the menstrual cycle and those that are simply "life symptoms." This information can be helpful in planning around problem days if there are any (womenshealth.gov).

Dysmenorrhea

Often, the myometrial contractions associated with menstruation cause dysmenorrhea, resulting in cramping and pain that can be severe. As you might recall from our discussion earlier in this chapter, the myometrium is a thick layer of muscular tissue capable of providing the powerful contractions necessary to dislodge endometrial tissue during menstruation or expel a developed fetus during childbirth. Myometrial contractions are triggered by the release of powerful hormones called **prostaglandins**. Dysmenorrhea is often caused by excessively high levels of prostaglandins. This can cause more intense contractions that last longer than usual (Ferri, Baustian, Murray, Danakas, Jain, & DeMarco (2011). Pain usually occurs right before menstruation begins and decreases as menstruation continues. Hormonal contraceptives can be effective in treating dysmenorrhea (American College of Obstetricians and Gynecologists, 2015).

Dysmenorrhea Painful menstruation

Prostaglandins Hormones that can cause muscle contractions and have been associated with menstrual pain

References

American Cancer Society. (2008). American Cancer Society Recommendations for Human Papillomavirus (HPV) Vaccine Use To Prevent Cervical Cancer and Pre-Cancers. Retrieved from http://www.cancer.org.

American College of Obstetricians and Gynecologists. (2014). *Vaginal rejuvenation and Cosmetic VaginalProcedures*. Retrieved from http:// www.acog.org

American College of Obstetricians and Gynecologists. (2015,December). *Dysmenorrhea*. Retrieved from http:// www. acog.orgAmerican

American Society of Plastic Surgery (2015). *Plastic Surgery Statistics*. Retrieved from: http://www.plasticsurgery.org

Barot, S. (2015, Winter). Sexual and reproductive health and rights are key to global development: The case for ramping up investment. *Guttmacher Policy Review*, 18(1).

Boston Women's Book Collective. (1998). *The new our bodies, ourselves*. New York: Simon & Schuster.

Burnstein, G., Jacobs, A., Kissin, D., & Workowski, K. (2013). Changes in 2010 STD Treatment Guidelines. Available: www.acog.org

Centers for Disease Control and Prevention (2016, October). *CDC recommends only two HPV shots for younger adolescents*. Retrieved from http:// www.cdc.org.

Centers for Disease Control and Prevention (2017, January). *Cervical cancer*. Retrieved from http:// www.cdc.gov

Chulea, W., Schuber,C., Roche, A., Kulin, H., Lee, P., Himes, J. & Sum, S. (2003). Age and menstruation and racial comparisons in girls. *Pediatrics*. 111(1), 110–113.

College of Obstetricians and Gynecologists. (2016, December). *Chlamydia, gonorrhea, & syphilis*. Retrieved from http:// www. acog.org

Comforth, T., (2009, July 17). The Clitoral Truth. Womens Health About .com. Available: http://womenshealth.about.com/cs/sexuality/a/clitoraltruthin_31

Dodson, B. (1996). Sex for One. New York: Three Rivers Press.

Ensler, E. (1998). The vagina workshop. In The vagina monologues. New York: Villard.

Ferri, F., Baustian, G., Murray, J., Danakas, G., Jain, T., & DeMarco, B. (2011). *Dysmenorrhea. First Consult*. Retrieved from http://www.mdconsult.com

Johnson, J (2004). Exposed at last; the truth about your clitoris. pp 387–389. In Worcester N,

Mannheim, J. (2012). Kegel exercises-self care. MedlinePlus. Available: http://www.nlm.nih.gov

Mayo Clinic (2012, February). Ectopic Pregnancy. Retrieved from: http://www.mayoclinic.com

Mayo Clinic (2012, February). *Vagina: What's normal and what's not*. Retrieved from: http://www.mayoclinic.com

Mayo Clinic (2015, January). *Menopause*. Retrieved from http://www.mayoclinic.com

Mayo Clinic (2016, August). *Breast Cancer*. Retrieved from www.mayoclinic.org

Mayo Clinic (2016, November). *Urinary Tract Infections*. Retrieved from http://www.mayoclinic.org

National Cancer Institute (2016, October). *Breast cancer prevention*. www.cancer.gov/breast

National Cancer Institute (2012, September 24). *Breast Cancer Risk in Women*. Retrieved from http://www.cancer.gov

National Cancer Institute (2016, October 13). *Breast Cancer Prevention*. Retrieved from www.cancer.gov

Newman, N (2016, September 16). Vaginal Dispatches: What you don't know about your vulva. *Our Bodies Ourselves*. Retrieved from http://ourbodiesourselves.org.

Sister Song (2017) *Sister Song: Women of Color Reproductive Justice Collective*. Retrieved from http://www.sistersong.net.

Swanson, E. (2013, May). Prospective outcome study of 225 cases of breast augmentation, *Journal of Plastic Surgery*,131(5), 1158–1166.

Sohal, D., Baustian, G., Rao, D., Choy, C., Sweet, E., & Jones, R.(2010). *Breast Cancer*. First Consult. Retrieved from http://www.mdconsult.com

Stewart, E. G., & Spencer, P. (2002). The V book: A doctor's guide to complete vulvovaginal health. New York: Bantam.

US Preventative Services Task Force (2012). *Cervical Cancer Screening*. Available: uspreventativeservicestaskforce.org

US Preventative Services Task Force (2013). Screening for breast cancer appendix F. Retrieved from http://uspreventativeservicestaskforce.org

WebMd (2007, April 3). Normal menstrual cycle: Menarch and the teenage menstrual cycle. Available: www.Webmd.com

WebMd (2009, August 12) Kegel exercises: an overview. Available: www.webmd.com

WebMd (2012) What to know about ectopic pregnancy. Available: www.webmd.com

Whipple, B., Gerdes, C., & Komisaruk, B. (1996). Sexual response to self-stimulation in women with complete spinal cord injury. *Journal of Sex Research*, 33(3), 231–240.

World Health Organization (2013, February). Female Genital Mutilation Available: www.who int/en/

Writing Group for the Women's Health Initiative Investigators. (2002, July 17). Risks and benefits of estrogen plus progestin in healthy postmenopausal women. *Journal of the American Medical Association*, 288(3).

Zaviacic, M., & Whipple, B. (1993). Update on the female prostate and the phenomenon of female ejaculation. *Journal of Sex Research*, 30, 148–151.

Chapter three

Male Sexual Anatomy and Physiology

Student Learning Objectives

After reading this chapter, students will be able to:

- Identify and locate key structures of the male sexual anatomy;
- Describe the main functions of the male sexual structures;
- Identify and describe the functions of the key male sex glands;
- Explain the erogenous potential of the key male sexual structures;
- Perform a testicular self-exam;
- Identify the signs and symptoms of, and treatment for, eight common male sexual disorders;
- Describe a variety of screening tests used to diagnose common male sexual disorders;
- Describe a variety of disabilities and their effects on male sexuality.

case study 3.1

Critical Thinking

How far would you go to change a feature of your body that you currently are dissatisfied with?

Penis Size and Self-Esteem

Jordan, a sophomore, attends a large urban northeastern university.

For the longest time I can remember being hung up on the size of my penis. I remember, as a kid, getting my mom's tape measure and measuring the length and circumference of my penis. I never talked to my friends about size because I was convinced mine was smaller than theirs. My dad used to kid me about how small mine was when he'd see me in the shower. I'd get intimidated by his because it seemed so big. I probably should have talked to him about it, but I couldn't. He wasn't so approachable, and, like I said, he always seemed to be making fun of mine. Maybe this was his way of trying to break the ice and get a conversation going. I don't know. I doubt it.

Anyway, I guess I just kind of felt that mine was small, and if I tried to bring it up with my friends, they'd laugh at me or, worse yet, I'd find out that theirs were really bigger than mine. I sent away for this stuff from the back of a magazine that was "guaranteed" to make your penis grow. The only thing it did was make my penis burn. It must have been some kind of liniment or something. I decided from that point on that I'd have to be satisfied with what I have. My current lover thinks my penis is big enough to satisfy him and that has really put me at ease.

One of the more interesting things about healthy sexuality is the great diversity we are capable of bringing to our sexual response. Whether we are straight or gay, male or female, our bodies are capable of responding in a myriad of pleasurable ways if we take the time to understand them and explore their potential. After our discussion of female anatomy in Chapter 2, we will now focus on male anatomy and physiology as an additional step in understanding our bodies.

Much of male sexual anatomy is external. Most men touch their genitals frequently during urination, and because of this, men tend to be familiar with the external parts. Even though men tend to be comfortable with their external sexual anatomy and physiology, sexual health extends to understanding the proper functioning of the internal structures also. Many of the internal and external sexual structures of both men and women are capable of responding sexually. Proper stimulation can provide intense sexual pleasure. We vary tremendously in how we like to stimulate (and have our partners stimulate) these structures. We will discuss this further at various points in this and other chapters.

External Male Sexual Structures

The external structures of the male sexual anatomy (see Figure 3.1) include the penis and scrotum, as well as the perineum, anus, and breasts. The last three, although not traditionally considered parts of sexual anatomy, are included here because of their potential as **erogenous** structures.

Erogenous Capable of producing sexual excitement

Penis

Like many structures in the human body, the penis has more than one function. Both sperm and urine pass through the penis on their way out of a man's body. The same organ used to pass liquid waste is capable of providing exquisite sexual pleasure. This duality of function is often cited as a reason for feeling squeamish about engaging in **fellatio.**

Structure of the Penis

The penis (Figure 3.2) consists of two main parts: the shaft and the glans. The shaft of the penis consists of two cylinders of spongy tissue—the larger cavernous body (*corpora cavernosa*) and one smaller spongy body (*corpus spongiosum*)—wrapped in thick membrane sheaths. Similar to a common household sponge, this cylindrical tissue has many pockets of open space or cavities that are richly endowed with blood vessels, allowing them to fill with blood during sexual arousal. This is how a penis becomes erect during sexual arousal.

   A key to understanding this is to visualize how a sponge expands as its cavities fill with water. Contrary to popular belief, the penis has no bone or cartilage and very little muscle tissue. Slang terms such as *boner* and *hard-on* derive their origin from the firm, protruding nature of the spongiosum during erection. The spongy cylinders are held together by **connective tissue** attached to a loose wrapping of skin. The penis is capable of great expansion and changes in size because of its spongy tissue and loose covering of skin.

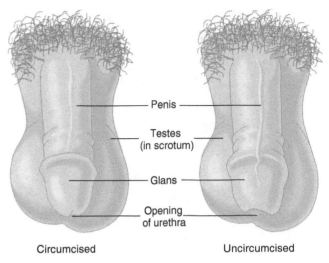

Figure 3.1 *Male External Genitalia* The male external genitalia includes the penis, scrotum, and perineum.

Fellatio Oral stimulation of the penis

Connective tissue Tissue that supports or binds other tissue

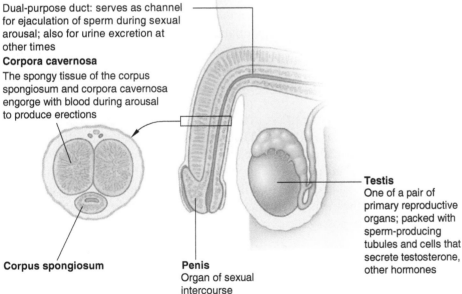

Urethra
Dual-purpose duct: serves as channel for ejaculation of sperm during sexual arousal; also for urine excretion at other times

Corpora cavernosa
The spongy tissue of the corpus spongiosum and corpora cavernosa engorge with blood during arousal to produce erections

Corpus spongiosum

Penis
Organ of sexual intercourse

Testis
One of a pair of primary reproductive organs; packed with sperm-producing tubules and cells that secrete testosterone, other hormones

Figure 3.2 *The Structure of the Penis* The penis consists of three cylinders of spongy tissue wrapped in a muscular sheath.

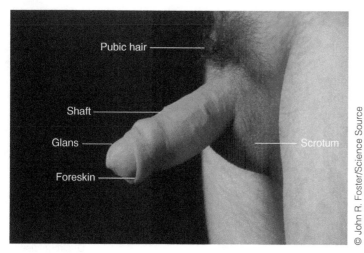

Figure 3.3

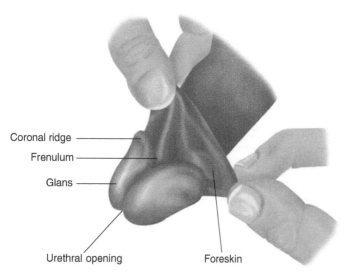

Figure 3.4 *Glans and Foreskin* The frenulum, located on the underside of the glans, is the most sensitive part of the penis.

Glans penis The end of corpus spongiosum, which is composed of the head of the penis and the urethral opening

Urethra Dual-purpose duct: serves as channel for ejaculation of sperm during sexual arousal; also for urine excretion at other times

The corpora cavernosa run side by side along the entire length of the penis, attaching to the abdominal cavity by their roots, the crura. The cavernous body lies above the corpus spongiosum and wraps around it, appearing to create two cylinder-like structures on either side. The corpus spongiosum also runs the entire length of the shaft, forming the head or **glans penis.** When the penis is erect, the corpus spongiosum is what gets hard and protrudes, forming a pronounced ridge along the underside of the penis. The **urethra** runs through the corpus spongiosum.

The entire penis is responsive to touch. The amount and type of touch that men like vary from man to man and sexual encounter to encounter. Even though the entire penis is responsive to touch, the greatest concentration of nerves is on the glans penis, illustrated in Figure 3.4. Two regions of the glans in particular—the coronal ridge and the frenulum—are the most richly endowed with nerve endings and capable of providing the greatest pleasure.

The *coronal ridge* forms the mushroom-like cap of the penis, separating it from the shaft. The *frenulum* is the triangular patch of tissue on the underside of the penis where the ridge pinches in to give the glans its distinctive shape. Both the corona and the frenulum are involved during arousal but are stimulated more precisely through oral sex and manual stimulation. The latter two forms of stimulation allow more individual control over the type and amount of pressure and stimulation than through intercourse.

The loose layer of skin that covers the shaft of the penis attaches at one end to the base of the penis near the abdomen and at the other end just behind the coronal ridge of the glans. The skin continues forward, extending beyond the glans penis, forming the prepuce or *foreskin.* In the unaroused state, the foreskin extends over the glans, covering and protecting it. During arousal, as the penis grows and expands, the foreskin retracts and stretches backward, exposing the glans for sexual activity.

Penis Size

The average penis is approximately 3 to 4 inches when flaccid (soft). In a recent study of penis size, when erect, the average length among subjects was found to be 6.02 inches, with a variation from 3.4 to 9.44 inches.

Circumcision

Source: Callista Lee

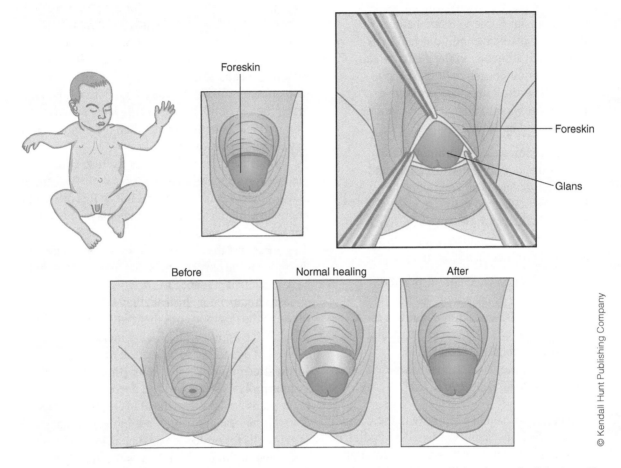

Foreskin

Foreskin

Glans

Before

Normal healing

After

© Kendall Hunt Publishing Company

Male Circumcision. Before surgery, an anesthetic (topical cream or injectable) is applied to the penis. Prior to cutting the foreskin, it must be carefully torn from the surface of the glans. A guide/clamp is then placed over the glans to decrease risk of accidental cutting. The foreskin is then cut off, with suturing if necessary to stop the bleeding. The clamp will be left on the penis after surgery and will normally fall off during healing. Note that the glans is redder in color than the skin of the shaft and foreskin. Over time the glans will grow extra layers of skin to protect itself, and its coloring will become closer to the color of the skin of the shaft, and it will eventually lose its shiny moist appearance.

Male Circumcision

Source: Callista Lee

Around the world, less than 1/3 of males undergo surgical **circumcision**, mostly either shortly after birth or as a rite of puberty. It is most common in countries that are primarily Muslim or Jewish as it is an important religious rite in those faiths. Elsewhere, it has been a cultural or aesthetic choice, with moderate-to-high rates of circumcision seen in North America, Australia, and parts of Africa. The practice is rare in non-Muslim Asia and Africa, Eastern and Western Europe, South America, and Central America (UNAIDS, 2010). As a multicultural nation of immigrants, people of the United States hold divergent views.

In the US, the popularity of circumcision dates back 140 years to Dr. Lewis

Circumcision Surgical removal of foreskin of penis

Sayre, one of the founders of the American Medical Association, says David Gollaher author of <u>Circumcision: A History of the World's Most Controversial Surgery.</u> Sayre believed that many medical conditions had their root in a dysfunction in the genital area, and that circumcision could be used to **treat a startling array of problems**, from depression to mental health issues, syphilis and epilepsy.

Circumcision was also promoted as a way of discouraging masturbation, and was regarded as clean and hygienic. It was particularly popular among the higher classes, and was seen as a sign of being well-off enough to afford a birth at hospital rather than at home.

Sayre's theories were later debunked, but not before being widely picked up in other English-speaking countries, in particular in the UK, Canada, Australia and New Zealand, Gollaher says (Hebblethwaite, 2012, https://www.bbc.com/news/magazine-19072761).

Circumcision increased in popularity in the US until 1971 when the American Academy of Pediatrics (AAP) announced that there was no medical support for the routine circumcision of baby boys. Meanwhile in Britain, rates had dropped back in 1948 with the advent of the National Health Service, which determined that routine circumcision was not medically necessary and therefore not covered by the national health plan. Today, only about 9 percent of men in the UK are circumcised. Rates have been dropping in the US and are now at around 55 percent nationwide, with rates much lower in the Western States, perhaps even as low as 20 percent in California according to some estimates (Elliot, 2013; Hebblethwaite, 2012). In 2012, the AAP reversed itself slightly by stating that the benefits outweigh the risks of infant male circumcision. But one of their most commonly cited reasons for this statement rests on a problematic study that found a small but significant decrease in HIV infection in circumcised vs. uncircumcised men in **South Africa**. The study is problematic in that there was no consideration of personal hygiene practices in the South African males as compared to males in other nations. It may well be that there would be no difference in HIV risk if uncircumcised boys and men at risk for HIV would simply wash beneath their foreskin on a daily basis. Using this study to promote circumcision in South Africa for the purpose of HIV prevention has remained controversial for this reason. Why choose surgery when simple soap and water washing provides the same health benefit? The most effective means of protection against HIV transmission continues to be the use of condoms. It is feared that if men in South Africa get the idea that circumcision will make them "clean," then they may use that as another reason to *not* use condoms.

Because circumcision has been so common in the US for so many years (along with the attitude that an intact penis is dirty and ugly), it is difficult to know how big a role cultural bias plays, even in the thinking of the medical establishment. So although they argue that the benefits of circumcision outweigh the risks of the surgery, they accept that they do not have sufficient evidence to *strongly advise* parents to choose circumcision. Instead, they *encourage* parents to weigh the pros and cons themselves (Brady, 2016). Those in the *Intactivist* (anti-circumcision) movement claim that it is unfair to cause risk to a baby for pain, surgical errors, and infections (though they admit serious problems are rare) and decrease in sensitivity to the glans penis. When the glans loses its protective cover, it makes up for it by adding additional layers of skin cells for protection against irritation by diaper and other clothing, which leaves the glans penis less sensitive to sexual stimulation as the boy grows up. Research into the functions of the foreskin itself show that it is a highly specialized bit of skin that not only protects and lubricates the glans but is also **highly enervated**, especially at the site of the **frenulum**. The damage done by cutting these nerve fibers may result in the pain (from continued movement after orgasm) that some men feel just after orgasm (Bloodstainedmen.com, 2018).

Parents must now grapple with the ethical question of whether it is right for them to make this decision for their infants or if it is better to wait and let their sons decide later in life. A small number Jews and Muslims are even questioning this practice within their religions and argue for a replacement ritual that causes no lasting damage to the penis (Hebblethwaite, 2012; Kesvani, 2018).

Highly enervated having a large number of sensory nerves

Anti-Circumcision Protest.

different from what they are used to. Certainly, you wouldn't want your son to get the idea from you—even unintentionally—that there is something wrong with the way his penis looks.

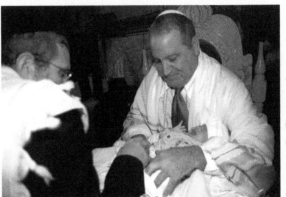

Jewish Circumcision Ritual.

Even those who argue in favor of circumcision admit that simple washing with soap and water provides the same protection against infections as the surgery. A little education goes a long way in helping parents to properly care for their son's penis and to teach him how to bathe himself properly as he gets older. No special care is needed for at least the first year or two of life. As the boy grows, the foreskin becomes loose from the glans and freely retracts (usually by age three), at which point the boy needs to be taught to gently pull back the foreskin to wash beneath it, something most boys don't mind doing at all. Some parents have remarked that it is much easier than teaching them to brush their teeth! Parents are warned to avoid forcing the foreskin to retract before it becomes loose on its own as this can cause pain and scarring that may create problems with the foreskin in the future. Any parent with questions specific to their son's health should consult their pediatrician. Only in cases of **phimosis** or **paraphimosis** is surgical circumcision necessary (Mayo Clinic, 2019).

Around the world, male circumcision is becoming less and less common, with some European nations even considering a ban on the practice of infant male circumcision, which has caused an uproar in Jewish and Islamic communities who feel their religions are under attack (Hebblethwaite, 2012). One common attitude among parents choosing to leave their son's penises intact (uncircumcised) is "If it's not broken don't fix it." But others worry about what will happen if the son's penis differs from his father's, or how many of his peers will be like him. If they have been brought up to believe that the intact penis is dirty or ugly, they may worry about his ability to find a sexual/romantic partner in adulthood. And some parents are just not comfortable with an intact penis because it is

Whether you choose circumcision or not, your son will have plenty of company among his peers. If you choose circumcision, be sure to talk with your doctor about the type of anesthesia that will be used to decrease the pain of the procedure and what you can do afterward during healing to keep your baby as comfortable as possible. And for those of you wondering if you should worry about your son looking like his father, it may help to know that the question most boys have is why their penis is so much *smaller* than their father's. There will be a topic of comparison up for discussion regardless of your decision about circumcision. It is easy enough to explain that his penis will grow bigger after puberty, and that different decisions were made regarding the foreskin given the information that parents had at the time. Understanding that an intact penis is natural and normal is comforting to most children, even if they notice that dad was circumcised. Although the surgery is a bit more complex later in life, it is always an option if you son decides that he does prefer to be circumcised. But once this surgery is done, there is no getting that specialized skin back again.

Phimosis a relatively rare condition in which the foreskin is too tight to retract properly when a man gets an erection.

Paraphimosis a condition in which the foreskin retracts from the glans penis only to become tightly wound up and unable to slide back over the glans afterward. Less common than phimosis.

healthy sex hints 3.1

Weighing the Pros and Cons of Circumcision

- **Easier hygiene.** Circumcision makes it simpler to wash the penis. **However, boys with uncircumcised penises can be taught to wash regularly beneath the foreskin.**
- **Decreased risk of urinary tract infections.** *The risk of urinary tract infections in males is low*, but these infections are more common in uncircumcised males. **Simple hygiene also decreases this risk.**
- **Decreased risk of sexually transmitted infections.** Circumcised men *might* have a lower risk of certain sexually transmitted infections, including HIV. **Simple hygiene also decreases this risk.** Still, safe sexual practices remain essential whether the man is intact or circumcised.
- **Prevention of penile phimosis.** Occasionally, the foreskin on an uncircumcised penis can be difficult or impossible to retract. This can lead to inflammation of the foreskin or head of the penis. **This problem is rare, so surgery to prevent it is viewed as extreme.**
- **Decreased risk of penile cancer.** Although cancer of the penis is *rare*, it is less common in circumcised men. In addition, cervical cancer is also *slightly* less common in the female sexual partners of circumcised men. **Simple hygiene also decreases this risk.**
- **The risks of accidents during surgery or serious infection afterward are low. Of course, the risk is zero if there is no surgery.**
- **Despite concerns from *Intactivists*, men who are circumcised manage to function sexually without knowing that they are missing anything.** With the benefits of circumcision being small, and the alternative of simple hygiene being sufficient for most men, **why choose a surgery with permanent effects?**

Source: Callista Lee

Erection Filling of the penile spongy tissue with blood during vasocongestion, resulting in a hard, erect, penis

Average penis girth (circumference) at erection was found to be 4.96 inches with a variation from 2.24 to 7.4 inches (Harding & Golombok, 2002). Most of the variation in penis size occurs during erection. **Erection** has been called "the great equalizer" because smaller penises seem to grow more during erection than larger ones, so the extremes tend to equalize when erect.

Obsession with penis size has a long history. Most young boys are curious about their penis size, and use rulers and tape measures to actually measure their penises. They are concerned that their penises are smaller than their peers'. By late adolescence, most boys grow out of their fears and obsessions about the size of their penises.

Much of the adult male concern about penis size stems from the perception promoted through inaccurate media coverage suggesting that size equates to virility and sexual performance. Penis size is a central theme in both straight and gay erotica and pornography. Male pornographic actors are recruited as much for the size of their penises as their ability to act.

Researchers Masters, Johnson, and Kolodny (1996) found that penis size had little physiological effect on women's sexual response. The vagina, they point out, is capable of adjusting to penises of varying sizes from small to large. The inner depth of the vagina can be reached by a man with an average-size penis by using intercourse positions (such as rear entry)

Penis Size throughout History

People have been preoccupied with penises and penis size throughout time. Penis artifacts, ranging from pottery to temple decorations to statues with grinning characters possessing huge penises, have been recovered across the globe. Nearly 2,000 years ago, the Romans worshiped Priapus, the god of fertility. Priapus symbolized both passion and fertility. Although small in stature, Priapus had a huge penis. Every bride of the Roman aristocracy was supposed to lose her virginity by sacrificing it on the altar of Priapus.

In Greece, giant penises adorned the classic columns used to support its massive structures. In India, the temple of Kama Sutra is decorated with characters having oversized penises. The erotic pen-and-ink art of Japan has, as its focal point, couples lost in their passion, their elaborate silk robes parted, capturing their

Courtesy of the authors

Priapus was always portrayed with an unusually large penis.

genitalia. The men all possess oversized penises that they are thrusting into their enraptured lovers.

No wonder that men are convinced that the size of their penises determines their masculinity.

that facilitate deeper penetration. An unusually long penis can extend beyond the depth of the vagina. A slightly shortened vagina also can be the byproduct of a hysterectomy. Partners can accommodate for any discomfort by adjusting intercourse positions and avoiding those that facilitate deeper penetration.

The inner depths of the vagina, the area stimulated by the probing of a larger penis, is relatively devoid of nerve endings. Most of the nerve endings in the vagina are located in the outer third, thereby accessible to all sizes of penises. The most sensitive area for sexual stimulation is actually the clitoris, not the vagina. Female arousal is related to adequate clitoral stimulation; clitoral stimulation is not contingent on penis size (or even the presence of a penis) at all.

The relationship of penis size to anal sexual intercourse is similar to that of vaginal sex. The length of the rectum and bowel is longer than the vagina, allowing for either deeper penetration or a longer penis. Unlike the vagina, the rectum does not produce lubrication. Men and women who engage in anal intercourse should use water-based lubricant to facilitate ease of penetration and thrusting. In Chapter 7 (sexual behavior), we offer a full range of health hints associated with anal sexual activity.

Although penis size has little physiological relationship to sexual response, it can play a big part in one's psychological functioning. Men, whether straight, gay, or bisexual, who are overly concerned with or anxious about the size of their penis seem to be more likely to develop sexual disorders than men who don't share this concern (Masters et al., 1996). Men who are overly concerned about their penis size can become anxious about sexual relations and develop sexual arousal disorders and even inhibited sexual desire.

Scrotum

Scrotum A double-chambered pouch of tissue that hangs loosely from the base of the penis, containing the testicles

The **scrotum** is a sac or pouch with two chambers that house the testes. Each testicle is cradled in its own scrotal pouch, suspended by a *spermatic cord* and *cremaster muscle*. A midline, or *raphe,* divides the scrotum into left and right halves. The scrotum has a sparse covering of hair and is usually darker in pigmentation than skin elsewhere on the body.

The scrotum normally hangs loosely, away from the body. This provides an optimal temperature of about 93 degrees Fahrenheit for the testicles. In a sense, the scrotum acts like a thermostat, regulating temperature by pulling the testicles closer to the abdominal cavity in colder temperatures and letting them hang loosely and away from the body under warmer circumstances.

The scrotum is composed of a thin layer of muscle tissue called the *tunica dartos* covered by skin. The skin attaches to the body at the base of the penis. During sexual arousal, exposure to cold, or threat of physical harm, the tunica dartos contracts and works together with the cremaster muscle to pull the testicles closer to the abdominal cavity for warmth and protection. In doing this, the scrotal sac shrinks and becomes taut.

Like the penis, the scrotum is responsive sexually to various forms of stimulation and pressure. When stimulating the scrotum, care must be taken, since each man varies in sensitivity to stimulation.

Perineum

Perineum The erogenous area of skin extending from the base of testicles to the anal opening

The **perineum** is an area between the thighs, bounded in the front by the pelvis joint (symphysis pubis) and in the rear by the coccyx (tail bone). The perineum can be divided into two triangles of muscle tissue, the first containing the base of the penis and the scrotum and the second containing the anal opening. The muscular tissue is covered by a layer of skin. Although not normally considered part of male sexual anatomy, the perineum plays a part in the male sexual response because the entire area is endowed with nerve endings and is responsive to stimulation.

Again, the nature and intensity of stimulation to this area vary from man to man, and encounter to encounter.

Anus

Anus The opening of the bowel, through which fecal matter is eliminated from the body

The **anus,** or opening of the bowel, is another body part with multiple functions. Although the primary function of the anus is to eliminate solid waste from the body, it also serves as a part of male sexual anatomy.

The anal canal is about 11.5 inches long and is composed of two sets of sphincter muscles. The internal anal sphincter muscle is made up of smooth muscle tissue, and the external anal sphincter is composed of skeletal muscle. The anal sphincters act like the strings of a purse to open and close the anus. The anus is normally closed, except during defecation and sexual stimulation. Anal tissue is slightly elastic. The bowel or anus produces no natural lubrication.

The anus is richly endowed with nerve endings, can be stimulated manually or orally, and is enjoyed sexually by gay and straight men alike.

As a result of the AIDS epidemic, this behavior is being talked about more openly. Gay and straight couples have discovered that sex toys can be inserted into the anus to provide sexual pleasure that entails less risk than anal intercourse. We will discuss this in greater detail in Chapters 7 and 15.

Breasts

The breast is not usually discussed as a part of the male sexual anatomy. Although men's breasts are not typically thought of as erogenous, heterosexual women and gay men find the sight and feel of men's breasts to be sexually appealing. In addition, many men enjoy having their breasts stimulated manually or orally during sexual contact.

Structurally, men's breasts have the same components as women's: nipple, areola, fat, and glandular tissue. Men's breasts, however, have much less underlying fatty and glandular tissue than women's do, and men do not lactate. Men's breasts normally do not enlarge during puberty. A small percentage of men develop a condition known as *gynecomastia,* which will be discussed in greater detail later in the chapter.

Breast size and concerns about other external sexual anatomy and body shape in general are a source of stress for many men. A "manly" torso, with well-developed pectoral (chest) muscles, broad shoulders, and a tapered waist, is the ideal that the media and society present to us. Many men become obsessed with trying to achieve the perfect body and, toward that end, try everything from binging and purging to taking steroids. Separating good health from physical perfection is something we have to learn (see Case Study 3.3 Charlie: All Bulked Up and Nowhere to Go).

The standards for male perfection promoted by media images are often unattainable for the vast majority of men.

Internal Male Sexual Structures

The internal male sexual structures are illustrated in Figure 3.5.

Testes

The **testes** are oval-shaped male **gonads** housed in the scrotum. During the third trimester of fetal development, the testes form inside the abdominal cavity, and descend into the scrotum. The testes are held in place within the scrotal sac by the spermatic cord, which passes through the inguinal canal attaching to the wall of the abdomen and the cremaster muscle, which connects with the lower part of the internal oblique abdominal muscle (see Figure 3.6).

When one or both testicles have not descended by birth, the infant is diagnosed with **cryptorchidism.** In most cases the testicles will descend by the end of 5 years. If they do not descend by this time, surgical or hormonal treatment may be necessary to get them to fall into place. Undescended testicles are a risk factor for infertility, inguinal hernia, and testicular cancer.

Testes Two almond-shaped male gonads responsible for sperm and hormone production

Gonads The primary endocrine glands in men (testes) and women (ovaries) that influence sexuality

Cryptorchidism Undescended testicle(s)

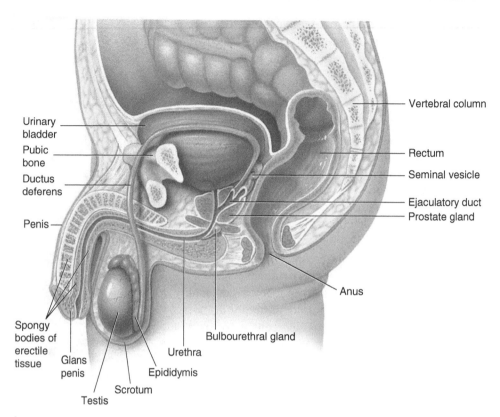

Urinary bladder
Pubic bone
Ductus deferens
Penis
Spongy bodies of erectile tissue
Glans penis
Testis
Scrotum
Epididymis
Urethra
Bulbourethral gland
Anus
Prostate gland
Ejaculatory duct
Seminal vesicle
Rectum
Vertebral column

Figure 3.5 *Male Internal Sexual Structures* The male internal sexual structures have reproductive and sexual arousal functions that are similar to female internal structures.

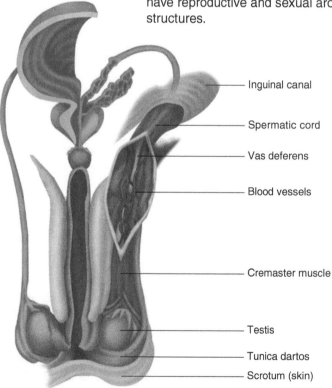

Inguinal canal
Spermatic cord
Vas deferens
Blood vessels
Cremaster muscle
Testis
Tunica dartos
Scrotum (skin)

Figure 3.6 *Testes and Spermatic Cord* The testes are anchored to the abdominal wall by muscles in the spermatic cord.

The testes have two primary functions: sperm production and hormone production. Each oval-shaped (1.5 inches long by 1 inch in diameter) testis is divided into 300 to 400 cone-shaped lobules. Each lobule contains two to three tightly coiled *seminiferous tubules* and endocrine cells called *interstitial* or *Leydig cells*. **Spermatogenesis** occurs within the seminiferous tubules. The Leydig cells produce the male sex hormone testosterone. If laid end to end, the seminiferous tubules (each between 1 and 3 feet long) from both testicles combined would stretch almost 0.5 miles.

Sperm production begins at puberty and can continue until death, although the rate of production does diminish with aging. Some men fear "running out" of sperm. In fact, sperm are produced on an ongoing basis. Many things can interfere with sperm production, resulting in a low sperm count. Examples of the range of conditions that can lower sperm production as a result of damage to the testicles are injuries incurred during participation in sports and other circumstances, tight clothing, and exposure to toxic chemicals. **Testosterone**, the main hormone associated with sexual desire, also is produced first during puberty, and its production ends with death.

No evidence shows that sperm have anything to do with energy production and loss. Many men (including athletic coaches, trainers, and associated personnel) erroneously believe that depletion of sperm (through sexual activity) will weaken athletes and hamper their performance.

Because of this, coaches sometimes sequester their teams before games or matches to prevent these athletes from having sex. We will discuss the influence of testosterone and other hormones on sexual response in greater detail in Chapter 7. Sex in Society 3.2, provides an interesting view of how castration, eunuchs and sexual desire among other things.

Spermatogenesis Sperm production

Testosterone the main hormone associated with sexual desire

Epididymis

The **epididymis** is a *C*- or comma-shaped, coiled duct that sits on top of and extends along the back of each testis. Each of its heads merges the sperm-producing seminiferous tubules, and each tail connects with the vas deferens (*ductus deferens*). Within the coiled, 20-foot-long epididymis, immature sperm produced in the seminiferous tubules become motile and fertile. The journey of the sperm from head to tail takes about 20 days. During this time, the sperm receive nutrients and mature fully, and the inactive sperm undergo a quality-control procedure. Defective and immature sperm are "weeded out" before they are able to be ejaculated. This process helps ensure that only healthy, viable sperm are available for potential fertilization of a ripe female ovum (egg).

Epididymis A C- or comma-shaped structure that sits along top of each testicle and serves as storage chamber for immature sperm

Vas Deferens

The **vas deferens** are two long, thin ducts that originate in the base of the testis and extend up and around the bladder and into the prostate gland. There, they merge with the urethra. Each vas deferens is responsible for transporting mature sperm from the epididymis to the urethra. Each vas deferens joins the ejaculatory duct of the seminal vesicles just prior to entering the prostate gland.

The smooth muscle tissue of the vas deferens contracts during ejaculation, moving sperm as it does so. The sperm mix with secretions of the seminal vesicles, prostate gland, and Cowper's glands to form the milky-white fluid released through ejaculation. Each ejaculate contains about 1 teaspoon of fluid.

During a **vasectomy**, the vas deferens are located, a piece is cut out of each, and the end is tied or burned off. This prevents sperm from mixing in the ejaculate. We will discuss this method of male sterilization more fully in Chapter 14.

Vas deferens A tube extending from testicles to prostate gland, where it converts into urethra; responsible for transporting sperm and other ejaculatory fluid

Vasectomy A male contraceptive method resulting in sterilization by cutting the vas deferens Inguinal canal

Seminal Vesicles

The **seminal vesicles** are two saclike glandular structures located behind the urinary bladder. Each gland is about 2 inches long, and tapers into a short duct that joins with the vas deferens to form the ejaculatory duct. The seminal vesicles produce an alkaline fluid that is high in the sugar fructose. The alkalinity helps neutralize the acidity of the urethra, protecting sperm as they pass through it. The fructose provides energy the sperm need to reach

Seminal vesicles Small structures connected to the vas deferens which release fluids that nourish and buffer sperm as they are ejaculated

personal exploration activity
What Do You Know?

After drawing and labeling the male sexual anatomy, you will be able to identify what is accurate and inaccurate about your knowledge of the male anatomy.

Before completing this chapter on male anatomy, take a few minutes to see how much you know or don't know about the male sexual anatomy. Take a sheet of paper and draw from memory the internal and external male sexual anatomy. If possible, get a friend of the opposite sex to team up with you to do the drawing. This will be more fun and will show which sex has the most knowledge of the male anatomy. Once you have drawn the anatomy, label the following parts: penis, bladder, testicles, Cowper's glands, ureter, scrotum, urethra, vas deferens, seminal vesicles, epididymis, ampulla, corona, glans penis, and prostate gland.

When you have finished, compare your drawing with the one in this chapter. Are you surprised by how little or how much you know? How comfortable were you drawing this sexual anatomy? Ask one of your friends to do this activity. Does your friend's drawing indicate that he or she has good knowledge of the male anatomy? How comfortable was your friend drawing the sexual anatomy?

their ultimate destination, a mature female egg, or ova. Seminal vesicle fluid contributes 60 to 70 percent of the total amount of fluid ejaculated.

Prostate Gland

Prostate gland A chestnut-sized gland connected to the neck of the bladder and vas deferens, which secretes alkaline fluid and enzymes that are part of ejaculatory fluid

The **prostate gland** is about the size and shape of a chestnut. The prostate produces several enzymes that play a role in activating sperm. These enzymes are released in a milky-white alkaline fluid that mixes with seminal vesicle fluid and sperm to make up about 30 percent of the total fluid ejaculated.

The prostate is located immediately in front of the rectum, enabling digital (by finger) examination to detect any changes in shape and size. A routine prostate examination is recommended for all men over 40 years of age as part of their preventive health checkups. Some men find stimulation of the prostate (through digital penetration or receptive anal intercourse) sexually arousing. Others find any contact with the prostate uncomfortable.

Cowper's Glands

Cowper's glands Bulbouretheral glands, located below seminal vesicles, which produce pre-ejaculatory fluid that lubricates the vas deferens and urethra and protect sperm that are being ejaculated

The **Cowper's glands,** also known as the *bulbourethral glands,* are ducts that secrete a thick, clear mucus during the plateau stage of sexual arousal, prior to ejaculation. This alkaline, preejaculatory fluid provides an additional buffer for sperm against the acidic environment of the urethra as the sperm make their way out of the body.

Advocates of birth control have long speculated that enough live sperm can be present in preejaculatory fluid to cause an unintended pregnancy. This has not been proven, however, in scientific studies of preejaculatory fluid. Two studies intended to determine the ability of preejaculatory fluid to transmit HIV found that the preejaculate was free of spermatozoa (Ilaria et al., 1992; Pudney, Oneta, Mayer, Seage, & Anderson, 1992). Some sperm may remain in the urethra following ejaculation.

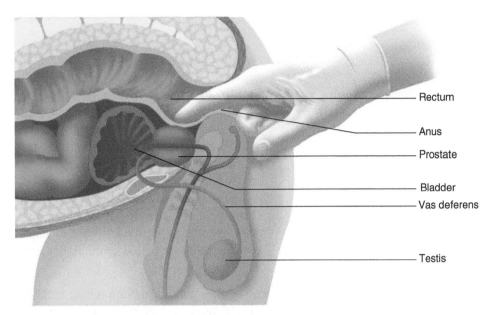

Figure 3.7 *Digital Rectal Examination* A digital rectal examination is a routine examination performed in a clinician's office.

The two variables that contribute to the presence or absence of live sperm within the urethra are *time* (sperm live 3 to 5 days) and *urination* (urination flushes the urethra and the acidity kills sperm). If live sperm are present in the urethra before a man urinates, they possibly could get mixed into the preejaculatory fluid secreted by the Cowper's glands and thus increase the risk of pregnancy.

Diseases and Disorders Related to Male Sexual Anatomy

Prostatitis

Prostatitis is an inflammation of the prostate gland. The symptoms of prostatitis are lower back and pelvic pain, a sensation of heat and tenderness in the area, a thin discharge from the penis, and swelling in the genital area. The two types of prostatitis are infectious and congestive.

Prostatitis Inflammation and irritation of the prostrate gland

- *Infectious prostatitis* is caused by bacterial or viral infection. Treatment usually involves taking antibiotics.
- *Congestive prostatitis* is associated with failure to ejaculate prostatic fluid.

Prostate secretions are produced in response to a man's sexual behavior patterns. Reducing the frequency of sexual activity disrupts the pattern of production and removal of prostatic fluid. If prostatic fluid is not ejaculated, it begins to decompose and build up, causing congestion. Congestive prostatitis usually responds to warm baths and prostate massage (ACS, 2003d).

Prostate Cancer

Source: Callista Lee

Prostate cancer is one of the most common types of cancer in older men. It usually grows slowly and is initially confined to the prostate gland, where it may not cause serious harm. However, some types are aggressive and can spread quickly to other organs. It is rare in men under age forty. The average age of diagnosis is sixty-six. Discuss prostate cancer screening with your doctor.

Factors that can increase your risk of prostate cancer include the following:

- **Age.** Your risk of prostate cancer increases as you age.
- **Race.** For reasons not yet determined, black men carry a greater risk of prostate cancer than do men of other races. In black men, prostate cancer is also more likely to be aggressive or advanced.
- **Family history.** If men in your family have had prostate cancer, your risk may be increased. Also, if you have a family history of genes that increase the risk of breast cancer (BRCA1 or BRCA2) or a very strong family history of breast cancer, your risk of prostate cancer may be higher.
- **Obesity.** Obese men diagnosed with prostate cancer may be more likely to have advanced disease that is more difficult to treat.

Complications may include incontinence, erectile dysfunction, and damage to other organs if the cancer metastasizes beyond the prostate.

Information provided from The Mayo Clinic and The American Cancer Society.

 # healthy sex hints 3.2

Preventing Urethral Trauma

Many cases of urethral trauma can be prevented by using risk-reducing protective devices. Protective plastic cups that fit securely in athletic supporters provide excellent protection against most sports-related trauma. Newer bicycle seats are designed with a protective groove or gap along the middle of the surface that comes in contact with the urethra.

Other ways to avoid trauma are to always read user manuals and understand safe ways to operate equipment and machinery that can cause blunt force to the lower body.

Do you routinely use these strategies?

໑ *Emotional Wellness* ໑

Issues related to men's sexual health can provoke strong emotions. A diagnosis of testicular cancer, for example, can conjure images ranging from deformity to death. High-level emotional well-being can make the difference between facing the challenge of cancer and working with health care providers to ensure that everything possible is done, or turning your back to the problem and hoping it will go away by itself. High-level emotional wellness involves recognizing, accepting, and working with our emotions. It involves asking for help when needed, and taking responsibility for your feelings.

Testicular Cancer

Testicular cancer is a relatively rare form of cancer (representing less than 2 percent of all cancers). Although fairly uncommon, it is the leading cancer killer of men under 35 years of age. Most cases of testicular cancer affect men between the ages of 15 and 40 years (ACS, 2003c; Bernard & Sweeny, 2015).

Risk Factors

The major risk factor for testicular cancer is cryptorchidism (undescended testicle). About 14 percent of the cases of testicular cancer are attributed to cryptorchidism (ACS, 2003d). Most of these cases occur in the undescended testicle, but 25 percent occur in the normally descended testicle. Some experts believe that performing surgery to lower the testicle prior to the onset of puberty can reduce the risk of developing some tumors in the testicle (ACS, 2003d).

Family history can also increase risk. Research indicates that a history of testicular cancer in one brother can increase risk in other male siblings. Cancer in one testicle slightly increases the risk for cancer in the other testicle. Certain occupations (mining, oil and gas workers, food- and beverage-processing workers, janitors, and utility workers) have an increased risk for testicular cancer.

The rate of testicular cancer has increased for both white and black men although the rate of increase is greater for white men. The incidence among white American men is five times that of African American men and double that of Asian American men. The reason for this difference is unknown. Worldwide, the risk of developing this disease is highest among men living in the United States and Europe, and lowest among men living in Africa or Asia (ACS, 2005).

Symptoms

Ninety percent of all men with testicular cancer have a painless or uncomfortable lump in the testicle or testicular enlargement or swelling. The remaining 10 percent notice no specific problem in their testicles but often report a sensation of heaviness or aching in the lower abdomen or scrotum. In rare cases, men with certain testicular tumors notice breast tenderness or swelling caused by an overproduction and release of the hormone human chorionic gonadotropin (HCG).

Many conditions can mimic the signs and symptoms of testicular cancer. The most common are injury and orchitis, both of which often cause pain and swelling that can be mistaken for testicular cancer symptoms. These can easily be ruled out by a physician, through examination and testing.

Testicular Cancer Stages

There are three stages of testicular cancer:

Stage 0: Preinvasive cancer of the testicular germ cells is present.

Stage 1: No cancer has spread to the lymph nodes or distant organs.

Stage 2: The cancer has spread to regional lymph nodes.

Stage 3: The cancer has spread to nonregional lymph nodes.

Diagnosis and Treatment

Most cases of testicular cancer are diagnosed through a combination of medical history (to rule out injury, preexistent medical conditions, and so forth), blood tests (to look for proteins and enzymes associated with the disease), ultrasound (to rule out fluid buildup and other conditions), and biopsy (to detect the presence of cancer growth) (Schmidt, Mettlin, Natarajan, Mench, McGinnis, & Piver, 1986; ACS, 2003d).

Treatment of early-stage testicular cancer typically consists of removing the cancerous tumor and administering chemotherapy. The chemotherapy is usually a prophylactic treatment to reduce the likelihood that the cancer has spread beyond the local lymph nodes. More rigorous combinations of surgery, chemotherapy, and radiation treatment might be indicated for later-stage testicular cancer. The long-term survival rates for early-stage testicular cancer treatment are excellent. Most men treated for testicular cancer have no loss of fertility, sexual desire, or sexual response (ACS, 2003e).

healthy sex hints 3.3

Testicular Self-Exam

Why It's Done

Testicular self-exams help you learn the normal feel and appearance of your testicles. That may make it more likely that you'll notice subtle changes, should they occur. Changes in your testicles could be a sign of a common benign condition, such as an infection or a cyst, or a less common condition, such as testicular cancer.

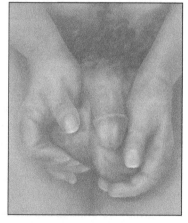

Testicular self-exam should be performed monthly while in the shower.

Testicular Cancer

Source: Callista Lee

Unlike most cancers, testicular cancer is a younger man's problem, with most cases occurring between the ages of fifteen and forty-nine. The good news is that it is relatively rare. Although it has not been proven that monthly testicular self-exams (TSE) reduce the risk of *death* from this cancer, both the Mayo Clinic and the American Cancer Society recommend TSE. Most cases are diagnosed after a man visits his doctor to report a lump or swelling on his testes. In about 10 percent of cases, the man will not experience a lump or swelling but will complain of a sense of heaviness or pain in the lower abdomen or scrotum. The doctor will work to rule out other causes, test the blood for substances linked to testicular cancer, and do an ultrasound and a biopsy of the lump. Treatment begins with surgical removal of the cancerous tumor, followed by chemotherapy. In later stages of testicular cancer, radiation treatment may also be needed. Survival rates are excellent when the cancer is detected and treated early, generally without loss of sexual or reproductive functioning.

Testicular Self-Exam: How Its Done: https://www.hopkinsmedicine.org/health/conditions-and-diseases/testicular-cancer/how-to-perform-a-testicular-selfexam-advice-from-urologist-philip-pierorazio

References

Abdulwahab-Ahmed, Abdullahi; Mungadi, Ismaila A. *Journal of Surgical Technique & Case Report*. Jan-Jun2013, Vol. 5 Issue 1, p1–7. 7p. DOI: 10.4103/2006-8808.11858

AIDS Weekly Staff. (2002, September 30). *AIDS Weekly,* pp. 4–6.

American Academy of Pediatrics (2012). Circumcision Policy Statement. *Pediatrics Vol. 130 No. 3 September 1,* 2012. pp. 585–586

American Cancer Society (2005a). Cancer Reference Information. Detailed Guide to Testicular Cancer. Revised: 07/01/2005 http://www.cancer.org/docroot/CRI/content/CRI_2_4_3X_Can_Testicular_Cancer_Be_Found_Early_41.asp

American Medical Association. (2003). *Neonatal circumcision* [Online]. Council on Scientific Affairs Report #10. Available: www.ama-assn.org/ama/pub/article/2036-2382.html.

Bernard, B, Sweeny, C (2015). Diagnosis and Treatment of Testicular Cancer: A Cliniaian's Perspective. *Genitourinary Pathology; Surgical Pathpology Clinics*. December 2015 8(4), 717–723.

Blank, Susan; Brady, Michael; Buerk, Ellen; Carlo, Waldemar; Diekema, Douglas; Freedman, Andrew; Maxwell, Lynne; Wegner, Steven. Circumcision Policy Statement, Task Force on Circumcision Source: Pediatrics. Vol. 130 (3). SEP 2012. 585–586.

Brady, M,T. Newborn Male Circumcision with Parental Consent, as Stated in the AAP Circumcision Policy Statement, Is Both Legal and Ethical. *Journal of Law, Medicine & Ethics*. Summer2016, Vol. 44 Issue 2, p256–262. 7p. DOI: 10.1177/1073110516654119.

Freedman, Andrew L. *Pediatrics*. May2016, Vol. 137 Issue 5, p1–2. 2p. DOI: 10.1542/peds.2016-0594.

Harding, R., & Golombok, S. E. (2002, August). Test–retest reliability of penile dimensions in a sample of men. *Archives of Sexual Behavior, 31* (4), 351–358.

How, A. C. S. W., Ong, C. C. P., Jacobsen, A., & Joseph, V. T. (2003). Carbon dioxide laser circumcisions for children [Online]. Available: http://link.springer-nv.com/ link/service/journals/00383/contents/02/00894/s00894/s00383-002-089.

Ilaria, G., Jacobs, J. L., Plosky, B., Koll, B., MacLow, C., Armstrong, D., & Schlegal, P. N. (1992). Detection of HIV-1DNA sequences in pre-ejaculatory fluid. *Lancet, 340* (8833), 1469.

Landis, S. H., Murray, T., Boldon, S., & Wingo, P. A. (1999). Cancer statistics, 1999. *CA: A Cancer Journal for Clinicians, 49,* 8–31.

Lawson, W (2003). Mammograms for Men? Breast Cancer is not just a Woman's Disease. Psychology Today. 36 (5) September/October, 2003, p 28.

Mayo (2013). *Testicular Self-Examination. Mayo Foundation for Medical Education and Research.* Available online at: http://www.mayoclinic.com/health/testicular-exam/MY00776/DSECTION=why-its-done.

Masters, M. H., Johnson, V. E., & Kolodny, R. (1996). *Human sexuality* (6th ed.). New York: HarperCollins.

Otto, Richard; Evans, Grant; Boniquit, Christopher; Peppas, Dennis; Leslie, Jeffrey. **Pediatric** Urology: Why Desired Newborn **Circumcisions** Are Not Performed: A Survey In *Urology*. November 2016 97: 188–193 Language: English. DOI: 10.1016/j.urology.2016.06.054, Database: ScienceDirect

Pudney, J., Oneta, M., Mayer, K., Seage, G., & Anderson, D. (1992). Pre-ejaculatory fluid as a potential vector for the transmission of HIV-1. *Lancet, 340* (8833), 1470.

Wasserburg, R (2004). Eunuch Power in Old Byzantium. Gay & Lesbian Review, (11) # 3, pp18–20. May/June, 2004.

Chapter *four*

Sexual Identity

Student Learning Objectives

After reading this chapter, students will be able to

- ☞ Identify the components of sexual identity and appreciate its complexity.
- ☞ Describe the components of gender development.
- ☞ Evaluate the impact of biological, psychological, sociological, and cultural factors on gender development.
- ☞ Evaluate the impact of biological, psychological, sociological, and cultural factors on sexual orientation.
- ☞ Analyze the similarities and differences in the development of a variety of sexual orientations.
- ☞ Understand the challenges of "coming out."
- ☞ Discuss the more common forms of gender incongruities.

From *Healthy Sexuality*, 4th edition, by Richard Blonna and Lillian Cook Carter. © 2017 by Richard Blonna and Lillian Cook Carter. Reprinted by permission of Kendall Hunt Publishing Company.

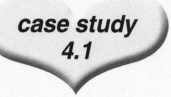

case study 4.1

Critical Thinking

How do you feel about the use of the word queer? In what ways does our sexual identity become a political issue?

Emily

Emily, 23

In these past 6 years, I haven't hooked up with a man, but I still feel uneasy about identifying as either lesbian or bisexual. "Lesbian" speaks to the fact that I date women, but naming myself as a lesbian does not mean that I am closed off to the potential of being with a man. "Bisexual," although allowing for fluidity, isn't really me. I pursue sexual and romantic relationships with women, not men. Queer—that's the word that says me best. "Queer" is like the antilabel label for me, a way to say "I'm here and I'm different" but at the same time not demand that I make any promises about what choices I might make in the future. "Queer" connects me to a political community that is inclusive of many different expressions of gender and sexuality. I identify as a queer femme, and what attracts me the most are alternative forms of masculinity, butch women, and female-to-male transgender people.

Of course, many LGBT (lesbian, gay, bisexual, transgender) people find the term queer offensive because the term has been derogatory. For this reason, I am deliberate about which label I use depending on whom I'm talking to. When I talk to someone who does not have much experience or knowledge of the LGBT community, I usually identify as a lesbian because that label is easier for them to understand. Because I am a queer femme, most people assume that I am straight. I identify as queer or femme with other queers and with straights who are both supportive of and sophisticated in their understanding of queer identity. Being queer celebrates my gender and sexuality in all its fabulousness and lets me feel comfortable being myself.

We are using the term *sexual identity* in a comprehensive way, to include the various factors that affect how we see ourselves. Individual sexual health requires that we appreciate the impact biology has on our being. The experiences one has in life, occurring in varied social and cultural contexts, help frame how we see ourselves. Sexual identity becomes a part of who we are as whole people: we have physical bodies, we show them to the world in a variety of ways, and we form romantic attachments with others. Ideally, our healthy sexual identities leave us comfortable with our bodies, expressing ourselves in ways that are true to who we "are." Our sexual identities develop from the interaction of several variables:

Biological/anatomical sex
Categorizing individuals based primarily on their reproductive organs, chromosome makeup, and hormone levels; traditionally, one sex is labeled male and the other female

1. **Biological/anatomical sex** focuses on the anatomical parts associated most closely with reproductive capabilities and sexual arousal, specifically internal and external reproductive organs. The term *natal sex* has been used to describe that part of identity connected to what is visible at birth (Kliegman, Stanton, Geme, & Schor, 2016). Included as

well are the influences of the endocrine system hormones, as reflected in **secondary sex characteristics** and the process of sexual differentiation in the brain.

2. **Gender identity**, an individual's sense of being a boy/man/, girl/woman, or other/transgender, and **gender role**, behaviors and characteristics expected in one's culture for the assigned biological sex, bring sexual identity beyond the physical domain. In the scheme of things, how we see and express ourselves is expected to correlate with our anatomy.

3. **Sexual orientation** defines the sexual and emotional attractions in choice of partners. One can be drawn to male partners, or to female partners, or be receptive to both men and women.

The question of why we are the sexual beings we are has no simple answer. Sexuality is complex, and our understanding of it continually grows. A number of questions have been, and are continuing to be, researched:

- What factors contribute to the individuals we are? Can those factors be controlled? Altered?
- At what point, if any, is our sexual identity fixed? Is this locked in our genes?
- Are parents and other caregivers the principal forces in shaping our sexuality?
- How powerful are the actual experiences we have in determining how we see ourselves, and how we make decisions?

To be sexually healthy, we have to become introspective, examine our past, look for explanations and answers, and work through aspects of our sexual identity that are uncomfortable for us. To promote greater sexual health, society, too, has to become better educated and respectful of people with diverse sexual identities.

Secondary sex characteristics Physical traits that develop during puberty and signal sexual maturity; examples are developed breasts, armpit and pubic hair, and coarse facial hair

Gender identity One's personal perception and sense of being male, female, or other

Gender role Behaviors expected of males and females in their society or culture

Sexual orientation Refers to attractions, behaviors, fantasies and emotional attachments to men, women, or both. *Heterosexuality* refers to attraction to a partner with different anatomy; *homosexuality* refers to a same-sex partner; *bisexuality* refers to attraction to both men and women.

© Andresr, 2010. Shutterstock, Inc.

Being better educated and respectful of people with diverse sexual identities promotes greater sexual health.

Continua of Sexuality

Sandra Bem (1995), Charlene Muehlenhard (2000), and others have challenged the approach to sexuality that limits the individual to dichotomous choices about his or her sexuality. You are either "male" or "female." You are either "masculine" or "feminine." You are either "heterosexual" or "homosexual." Needless to say, the culture at large seems to have mandated the dichotomy while simultaneously confusing issues of physical sexuality, gender identity, and sexual orientation. Greater sexual health and freedom may come from viewing identity along the continua described in this chapter.

Self-acceptance, as well as a more sophisticated and accurate assessment of others' sexuality, benefits from the recognition that three continua influence our sexual identity (see Figure 4.1). For each variable, the individual can place him or herself at any point along the continuum. Permutations of the intersections are many. As a result, the tremendous diversity within sexuality becomes apparent.

For example, in the traditional model of female sexuality, the female has female reproductive organs—clitoris, vagina, uterus, and so on—and female secondary sex characteristics such as developed breasts, broader hips, and narrow waist. To be viewed as an attractive female, the culture further prescribes an acceptable presentation of those characteristics. The female identifies herself as female, adopts the prescribed female role, enjoys feminine things, and behaves in feminine ways. She sees herself as heterosexual, making herself attractive to males in the culture. This person assumes positions at the extremes of the three continua.

Above and beyond fundamental questions regarding "feminine things and feminine ways" is the basic reality that this description defines only certain females in the culture. Relying on a broader model of sexual identity, someone who is female can possess female reproductive structures but

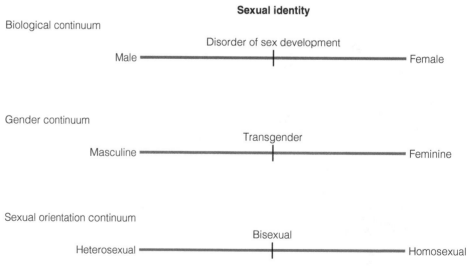

Figure 4.1 *Conceptualization of Sexual Identity* Identities can be fluid and form at various intersections.

appear more "masculine" to others. A female could enjoy male clothing and be attracted to women. She could have both male and female reproductive structures and enjoy relating to both men and women sexually. The possibilities and realities are numerous.

The *biological continuum* of identity is often thought to be separated clearly into "male and female," yet some individuals have reproductive structures from both and are categorized as having ovotesticular disorder of sex development (previously called hermaphrodite).

The *gender identity* continuum offers numerous points for placement. It is predicated on the cultural ability to distinguish female traits from male traits. Individuals who consider themselves **androgynous** make choices about how they look and act without adhering to sexual stereotypes. Earlier literature defined androgyny in positive terms, in which the individual adopted the healthier traits of both male and female. For example, a woman would not be afraid to voice her opinions, and a man would not hesitate to express his emotions. Clothing, and more significantly one's occupation, would be chosen without gender restrictions. In essence, each would freely choose characteristics and behaviors that best suit his or her personality, not the cultural stereotypes.

Androgynous Psychological and Social expression of a combination of stereotypically masculine and stereotypically feminine traits.

Woodhill and Samuels (2003) propose that individuals may be "positively androgynous" or "negatively androgynous" by incorporating desirable or undesirable characteristics. Gender-based characteristics can be positive or negative. The positively androgynous person may demonstrate high levels of compassion, a positive female quality, along with high levels of independence, a positive male quality. In contrast, the negatively androgynous person would demonstrate high levels of submissiveness, a negative female quality, and selfishness, a negative male quality. Their research findings identify positive androgyny as the developmental ideal, associated with higher scores on indicators of mental health and well-being; such individuals have the potential to live a more fulfilled life.

As discussed later in this chapter, those identifying as **transgender** also place themselves at varying points on the gender identity continuum. For some, their physical appearance is of primary concern. For others the core gender identity is under question, and at some point hormonal and surgical interventions may be sought to become more authentic.

Transgender An umbrella term used to describe a range of people whose gender identity and/or gender role do not match what we associate with their sex assigned at birth

Placement along the *sexual orientation* continuum allows for erotic connections to males, females, or both. Exclusive **heterosexuality** involves erotic relationships with members of the other sex; males would connect with females and females with males. Exclusive **homosexuality** involves erotic relationships between members of the same sex—that is, males with males and females with females. **Bisexuality** is reflected by erotic connections in which the individual relates to both males and females.

Heterosexuality Forming sexual relationships with members of the other sex

Homosexuality Forming sexual relationships with members of the same sex

Figure 4.1 is intended to provide a visual model for understanding sexual identity. Individuals may place themselves at different points along each continuum, and those points may vary at different times in their lives. The continua can also intersect at various points, resulting in a great diversity of sexual identities.

Bisexuality Forming sexual relationships with both men and women

What if I Am Queer, Pansexual, or Asexual?

Source: Callista Lee

Today, many young people are expressing a desire to be perceived as beyond the traditional labels that have been used to categorize our sexuality. The term **Queer** has been used to describe people who don't fit the definition of heterosexual yet don't feel comfortable with the labels of homosexual or bisexual. It has also been used to describe people who don't feel that the labels of male or female adequately match their sense of gender identity, as in "gender queer." Often people who prefer this term see their sexuality as **fluid** (changing according to the situation). Often, what a person who labels themselves as "queer" is saying is, "don't put me in a box; don't expect me to meet some old expectation of typical behavior." The term "queer" comes with a lot of baggage, as it has been used in the past as an insult against LGBT persons. The term means "strange" or "odd." Some older people in the LGBT community are uncomfortable with it because that term has been hurled against them in anger. Today, it is being reclaimed as a positive term.

Another term you may be hearing lately is **Pansexual**, usually as a sexual orientation. Its use indicates that their sexual orientation doesn't fit within the expectations for a **bisexual**. In addition to being open to romance with both men and women, they may be open to partners who are transgender (at varying stages of transition). Less often, the term also includes those who are open to a wide variety of sexual and romantic practices, including **polyamory** (a romantic relationship including more than two partners) or **BDSM** (bondage, domination, submission, sadism, masochism). If you want to know what someone means when they use this term to describe themselves, *ask* them!

Asexuals are a more diverse group than most people imagine. It may mean that they have no (or very little) interest in sex or romance at all. But more often, it means that they desire romance, but without sex. Or they may be open to sex to satisfy their partner but just don't feel a sexual interest emerging from themselves. It may *also* mean that although they have an interest in masturbation, they do not desire partnered sex. They may or may not be interested in nonsexual expressions of physical affection such as kissing and snuggling. Again, you have to ask what they mean if you really want to understand what they mean by this term.

Sexual Anatomy—Its not Just Between Your Legs!

Source: Callista Lee

Back in High School you probably learned a little about genetics; specifically that if you have an XX pair of chromosomes you will be a girl and if you have an XY pair you will be a boy (refer to Figure 4.2). But anatomical development is actually more complex than that. In the womb, the development of biological sex is dependent upon chromosomes, plus **gonads**, plus hormonal levels. All 3 factors play critical roles in our development in utero as well as later in life.

Typically, an egg (ovum) contains a single X chromosome along with its other genetic material from the mother, and sperm may contain either an X or a Y chromosome in addition to the other genetic material from the father. The genes provide guidance for development. At approximately 6 weeks into pregnancy, the genes direct gonadal development. In XY individuals, testes are supposed to develop, and in XX individuals, we expect ovaries, and that is what happens in most cases. If the gonads have developed normally, the testes will produce androgens (we focus most on testosterone) and ovaries produce estrogens. These hormones direct the development of the rest of the internal reproductive structures as well as the external genitals. Meanwhile, the fetal **adrenal glands** begin to produce small amounts of both androgens and estrogens in both males and females.

The sex hormones not only assist the fetus in in continuing to develop the sexual and reproductive structures but also certain areas of the brain. The developmental effects of these hormones create lifelong effects on our **gender identity** and sexual behavior.

Gonads Ovaries or Testes.

Adrenal glands Adrenal Glands: Above each kidney, the adrenal glands produce a variety of hormones in addition to the sex hormones, including adrenaline and cortisol.

Gender identity one's psychological sense of self as male or female.

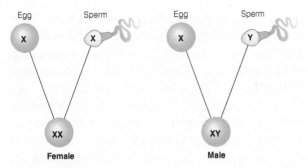

Figure 4.2 *Genetic Sex*

In early studies researchers found that an initial "bath" of hormones was needed between weeks 6-12 for the normal development of the genitals and internal reproductive structures, but that some time during the second half of pregnancy the sex hormones also play an important role in the development of the an areas of the brain that determines gender identity and sexual orientation (Hofman & Swaab, 1989; Allen & Gorski, 1990). In studies in both rats and humans, a part of the **hypothalamus** called the *pre-optic area* (POA) has been found to be larger in males than in females, and also larger in transgender men (but not transgender women). Another area of the hypothalamus that differs between men and women is the "bed nucleus of the stria terminals (BNST), also larger in men and transmen than in women or transwomen (Allen & Gorski, 1990; Kruijver, 2000). More recently, researchers have begun to question whether gender identity itself is determined by these structures or whether it is just sexual behavior and gendered *behavior* (childhood toy preferences, adult career choices) and other differences we observe between male and female brains such as spatial abilities (Berenbaum & Beltz, 2016). Research is ongoing to better understand the role that sex hormones play in the brain both before birth and afterward.

The tragic case of **a boy whose penis was accidentally destroyed** during circumcision provides additional support for the brain being the source of gender identity. Canadians Janet and Ron Reimer welcomed twin boys into the world on August 22, 1965; Bruce and Brian. At 7 months old both boys were having troubles urinating due to overly tight foreskins. The Reimers dropped their sons off at the hospital and enjoyed an evening to themselves. Although this was a simple procedure the hospital wanted to keep the boys overnight. The Reimers were shocked when they received a telephone call the next morning explaining that Bruce had been involved in an accident and that Brian's surgery had been can-

celled. For reasons unknown, the doctor chose to use a *cautery* tool rather than a scalpel, and the cautery tool was not calibrated correctly. As soon as the surgeon touched it to Bruce's penis, the surge of electricity caused the entire penis to burn up. All that was left was a blackened stump. Broken-hearted, the Reimers took their children home to cope with this devastating loss. How does one raise a boy with no penis?

Several months had passed when the Reimers happened to see a television program featuring **Dr. John Money** of Johns Hopkins Medical Center in Boston discussing his research on intersex children. He cited examples of intersex children who had undergone surgeries to normalize their genitals and stated that he had found that these children were well adjusted in whichever sex they had been assigned regardless of their genetic sex. He concluded that it was nurture, not nature that created the sense of gender identity. At that time the primacy of social learning was a popular view in psychology. Parents were being advised to be careful in raising their children because of the huge impact they could have on their child's personalities and mental health. Mrs. Reimer wasted no time in reaching out to Dr. Money to see if he could help her son. Money, who had never researched what would happen if you raised a normal boy as a girl or a normal girl as a boy was thrilled to have an opportunity to put his theory to the test, confident that he was right.

He advised the Reimers to raise Bruce as a girl and to have him castrated (removal of the testicles) as soon as possible. Needless to say, the Reimers were hesitant. No one had ever heard of such a thing. But Dr. Money was insistent; not only must they follow his instructions, but they mustn't delay. He never explained to the Reimers that their child would be the first genetic and hormonal male to be raised as a girl. Precious time was ticking away. He knew that gender identity appears early in childhood. At age 22 months, the Reimers finally agreed to the surgery; **Bruce became Brenda**. Dr. Money kept in touch with the mother through letters and met with the children in person once a year to check on their progress. As they grew older they also saw a psychologist at home in Canada. Mrs. Reimer did her best to encourage Brenda to be feminine, but it was a struggle. At the time it wasn't common for people to question author-

Hypothalamus A small but critical area of the brain that regulates such basic functions as sexual desire, sexual behavior, body temperature, appetite, thirst, and the sleep-wake cycle.

ity, and doctors tended to blame mothers when their children failed to behave properly. So she hesitated to report the problems, focusing instead on anything that Brenda did that was feminine to please her mother. According to Money's reports on the case published in the leading sexuality journals, Brenda's transition was a wonderful success and his theory of gender neutrality was supported. However, those published reports did not match the facts of Brenda's life. She was a miserable little girl, with no friends, a lack of interest in girls' toys or girls' clothing, teased at school and called "cavewoman" because of her clumsiness in trying to be girly. Eventually she was removed from school to be homeschooled. She was depressed and confused, eventually becoming suicidal. When she started taking hormones to stimulate female puberty (mother told her they were vitamins) she hid her body in oversized clothing, uncomfortable with its new curviness. At her annual visits with Dr. Money he became angry with her for refusing to undergo surgery to create a vagina. The twins also report (in adulthood) that Dr. Money would ask them embarrassing questions about sexuality and even insisted that they look at each other's genitals to note the differences. At age 14 Brenda rebelled and her parents finally told her what had happened to her as a baby. Brian was angry. Brenda was relieved. Shortly thereafter, Brenda changed her name to David and adopted a male gender identity. None of the teaching by his parents or the doctor, the castration, or the female hormones could convince Brenda that she was a girl. His brain knew that something was terribly wrong. Many years passed before the medical and psychological community learned of Money's failure. He was finally outed by Dr. Milton Diamond, a biologist at the University of Hawaii who had been fascinated by the case but frustrated by the secrecy that Money maintained. With all that he knew about biology he was skeptical that a normal human male could be raised successfully as a female. He finally tracked down the twins and learned that they had abandoned Dr. Money, and Brenda was now living fairly happily as David. David was more than a little angry that Money was continuing to declare his case a success. At that point Money published reasons for the failure of the trial, primarily blaming the mother. He never accepted responsibility for making a terrible mistake and refusing to see the unhappiness that Brenda exhibited. David went on to have surgery to construct a penis and testicles. He found a woman who was happy to marry him despite his lacking full penile function and occasional bouts of depression. The stress on the family was involved in the breakup of the parents' marriage and on brother Brian's mental Health. He was diagnosed with schizophrenia and killed himself in 2002. Following a breakup with his wife, David also committed suicide, in 2004. He was just 36 and a half years old. Dr. Money continued in his career and died as an old man in 2006. Many of his colleagues, still not knowing the full extent of his failure in "the twins case" gave him a standing ovation at the Society for the Scientific Study of Sexuality (SSSS) that year. Seated in the audience were Milton Diamond and several sexologists (including myself) who never forgave Money for his treatment of the twins or his failure to accept responsibility for their pain. Dr. Diamond founded the Pacific Center for Sex and Society where he has continued to work past his retirement from the University of Hawaii. He continues to receive awards for his work in sexual health.

During the years of Money's "success stories" surgeons had grown comfortable doing sex surgeries on intersexed infants because they could be confident that the children would be happy psychologically with whichever sex they were assigned. It has taken many years following the news that Money's "experiment" was not a success that they became cautious again. Today, they wait until the child is old enough to express their own gender identity before doing any "corrective" surgery, on advice from Dr. Diamond and others who study the biological factors involved in gender identity (Kruijver et.al.,2000; Diamond & Sigmundson, 1997; Lehmiller, J.J. (2012).

It is interesting to note the similarities between male and female fetuses in the first weeks of pregnancy, before **sexual differentiation**. We all start out as "bipotential" meaning that we have the basic structures to create either a male or a female. It is only the action of the genes, and later the hormones that allow us to develop an anatomical sex (see Figure 4.3).

When all goes well, a simple **sex assignment** is made at birth. It's a boy! Or, it's a girl! But as com-

Sexual differentiation The process by which the embryo develops into a male or a female.

Sex assignment the sex proclaimed at the birth of a baby, based on visual inspection of the genitals. This "assignment" may or may not match the development of the internal reproductive structures or the development of the brain.

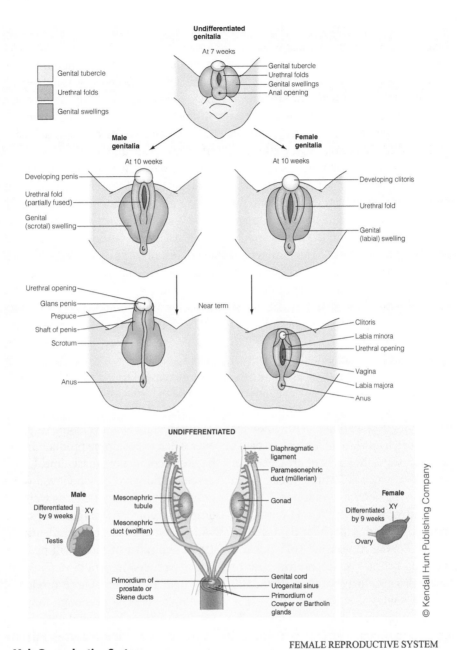

Figure 4.3 *Differentiation of Internal and External Reproductive Structures*

plex as our development is, things can go awry. There may be hormonal or genetic abnormalities which we will discuss here.

Sometimes we don't get a perfect set of XX of XY chromosomes which leads to one of several genetic conditions. **Klinefelter Syndrome** is one of the most common sex variations, occurring once in every 1,000 male births (Blackless et.al., 2000). It occurs when the egg has not one but two X chromosomes, resulting in a combination of XXY. Because of the Y chromosome, development will be along the male pathway and the baby will be male in appearance when it is born. Many Klinefelter males are not diagnosed until puberty or even later. The testicles are smaller than normal and sperm production is generally low. There is an increased risk of autoimmune diseases such as diabetes and lupus. Common physical signs include a rounded (feminine) body type, lack of facial and chest hair, breast enlargement in puberty (often temporary), and they tend to be taller and heavier than average. There is also increased risk of osteoporosis. Most will experience a delay in language development and need extra help with reading and writing. Many will be slow in crawling and walking. With guidance they will eventually catch up with their peers. Because of the extra X chromosome their risk of breast cancer is equal that of women, which is 50 times greater than in normal XY males ("Klinefelter Syndrome," 2019).

Turner's Syndrome girls have one normal X chromosome but the second X is either damaged or completely missing. For this reason, 99% of cases end in miscarriage during the first or second trimester of pregnancy. This syndrome affects only 1 in 2000-2500 female births (Wolf, vanDyke & Powell, 2010). The external genital development is normal but internally their ovaries are underdeveloped which leads to infertility in most cases (Morgan, 2007). There is a range of symptomology from mild to severe that includes slow or no sexual development at puberty, puffy hands and feet, extra folds of skin on the neck, soft upturned finger nails and kidney, heart and hearing difficulties. They tend to be shorter than average and have a greater risk of bone thinning (osteoporosis) and diabetes. Cognitively, they are of normal intelligence but have learning disabilities especially related to math and spatial relationships. For both Klinefelter's boys and Turner's girls medical treatment and assistance with learning disabilities can allow them to lead normal lives without any obvious clues as to their genetic conditions.

As you may have guessed by now, things can go wrong at the hormonal level as well. **Androgen**

Insensitivity Syndrome (AIS) is a condition in which a male fetus is insensitive to his own androgens. The male hormones are present but his body appears to be blind to them. Because he is not responding to the presence of androgens during his time in development, he will be born with feminine appearing genitals and will likely be sex assigned female at birth. The diagnosis is often not made until puberty when a visit to the doctor because of a lack of menstruation reveals undescended testicles (or just one) in the lower abdomen. Most are raised as girls, accept a female gender identity and show a sexual interest in males. AIS is one of the conditions that causes **Intersex**, which affects between 1-2% of babies. In some cases the genitals look like a combination of both male and female structures and in others it is unclear which sex was *trying* to develop. Related to AIS is 5-alpha-reductase deficiency (also known as **DHT deficiency**). This occurs when a male fetus is unable to convert testosterone into dihydrotestosterone (DHT) because of the deficiency of the 5-alphareductase enzyme. DHT is necessary for the development of male external genitalia. In most cases the children are raised as girls and accept a female gender identity. They are in for an unwelcome surprise at puberty however when testosterone production increases and their bodies become more masculine. Usually the testes will descend and what they believed was a clitoris begins growing into a small penis as well as facial hair and a deepening voice. At this point most of these individuals will switch to a male gender identity (Mendonca et.al., 1996) and most of these will be interested in female sexual partners (Imperato-McGinley et.al, 1979). They may or may not be able to produce viable sperm or develop a penis large enough for penetrative sex.

One other hormonal abnormality is worth discussing here – **Congenital adrenal hyperplasia (CAH).** This can happen in male or female fetuses and occurs when their adrenal glands produce excessive amounts of androgens during pregnancy and throughout their lifetime. No significant problems in genital development have been found in males with CAH but females will be born with partially or completely male genitals which may lead to a gender assignment of intersex or even male. In the past, both doctors and parents were eager to "correct" the genitals of CAH girls surgically but today parents are

Intersex formerly diagnosed as "disorders of sex development," is when sex assignment at birth is difficult because the genitals are neither clearly female nor clearly male.

discouraged from rushing into this surgery which is quite delicate and not without risk of creating problems later in life. Internally, the ovaries and other female reproductive structures are present, but function is hampered by the high levels of androgens. It is important for the overproduction of androgens to be treated medically or the girl can experience early puberty with excessive body and facial hair, irregular periods and fertility problems later in life. CAH boys also require hormonal treatment to prevent problems such as tumors on the testes and low sperm count. In both boys and girls there may be problems with overweight and stunted growth. (Boyse, Sands, & Sandberg, 2011). Most CAH females will adopt a female gender identity but will be more masculine both physically and psychologically and express interests in things that males usually prefer such as working with things (or technology) rather than working with people. Although most CAH females report a sexual interest in men, some studies have found there to be a larger than expected number of same-sex or bisexual attractions among CAH girls compared to the general population of females (Meyer-Bahlburg et.al.,2008). **Sexual Orientation** also has its links to brain structure and hormones.

Now you understand that our sexual anatomy extends way beyond our genitals, into our reproductive organs throughout the endocrine system (hormones) and even into the brain. Of course, all of your sexual beliefs, attitudes, emotions, motivations, and memories are in your brain too! But the physical brain you were born with is not the only determinant of your sexuality identity. Who we are as individuals is a complex combination of biological, environmental and sociocultural factors. In the next section we will discuss some of the sociocultural factors.

Sexual Orientation The sex of the individuals to whom a person is romantically, emotionally and sexually attracted.

Table 4.1 Atypical Chromosomal and Hormonal Patterns in Prenatal Development

Syndrome	Chromosomal Sex	Gonad	Internal Reproductive	External Reproductive	Secondary Sex Characteristics	Gender Identity
Klinefelter syndrome	Male, XXY	Testes	Normal male	Small penis and testes	Female secondary sex characteristics develop at puberty	Male
Turner syndrome	Female, XO	Nonfunctioning or absent ovaries	Normal female except for ovaries	Underdeveloped genitals	No breast development or menstruation at puberty	Female
Androgen insensitivity syndrome	Male, XY	Testes, but body unable to utilize testosterone	Shallow vagina, lacking normal male structures	Labia	Female secondary sex characteristics develop at puberty; no menstruation	Female
Congenital adrenal hyperplasia	Female, XX	Ovaries	Normal female	Ambiguous, tending toward male appearance; enlarged clitoris may be mistaken for penis	Female secondary sex characteristics develop at puberty	Usually male
DHT deficiency	Male, XY	Undescended testes	Partially formed, but no prostate	Ambiguous until puberty when penis enlarges and testes descend	Male secondary sex characteristics develop at puberty	Female until puberty when male identity taken

Gender Role Socialization

Source: Callista Lee

Even before a baby is born parents, family and friends often want to know the sex so they can start thinking about who this little person is going to grow up to be. They select "gender-appropriate" toys and clothing for newborns and decorate the nursery accordingly. If there is no "gender reveal" prior to birth, the first question asked is usually, "What did you have? A boy or a girl?" When we meet a stranger with an infant, we look for clues about the sex. Is there a bow in the hair? What colors is it dressed in? Does it have a girl's name or a boy's name? We don't even think about these things consciously, but clearly gender is important to us. Numerous studies have found that both parents and strangers respond to babies differently based on their assumptions of its sex. In one type of study (replicated dozens of times), adult men and women were given the opportunity to interact with an infant that was presented as either male or female (by means of wrapping it in either a blue or a pink blanket). In reality, they were all interacting with the same infant. When they believed the child was a girl, they tended to be more verbal and nurturing, and they tended to select stereotypically feminine toys to amuse the baby. When playing with boys, they tended to select masculine toys such as trucks and tools. For a review of these studies see Stern and Karraker (1989). Even the adults' perceptions of the baby differed according to the assumed sex. Newborn girls are described as soft, fine-featured, petite, delicate, and beautiful by their parents, whereas newborn boys are described as strong, big, and determined regardless of how physically similar they are (Fausto-Sterling, Coll, & Lamarre, 2013). Mothers tend to interact with greater emotional warmth and responsiveness with girls but encourage greater independence with boys.

Children are not only given "gender-appropriate" toys, but they are also reinforced for playing with them, which can create a self-fulfilling prophecy that the child will like this toy because they are a girl (or a boy). Behaviors we reinforce are repeated (ask someone who has taken an Introductory Psychology class about Operant Conditioning). Children who may not have an innate attraction to certain kinds of play may be willing to engage in it because it makes their caretakers happy and more willing to spend time with them. Some children though, will reject what they don't want regardless of how much encouragement they get from adults. Children as young as two have already picked up information about what it means to be male or female, by age three most have a pretty clear sense of their own gender identity, and by age five they understand that boys grow up to be fathers and girls grow up to be mothers. By age seven, they have developed the more complex cognitive concept of *gender constancy*, which is the understanding that regardless of what they wear (dress/pants or long hair/short hair) or what they do (play baseball or princess), their sex/gender will never change (Cunic, 2019).

Besides parents and family, children learn from their peers, teachers at school, the media, and religious training about what is expected of them. A trip to the toy store makes it very clear which toys they are expected to play with, as the toys tend to be segregated by gender. The girls' aisle will be full of bright packages, often in pink or light purple, with sparkles and words in curvy fonts. Many girls' toys focus on the importance of being pretty or caring for others. Boys' aisles are darker, featuring blues, greens, black, and some red with words promising ACTION and POWER! They get to practice skills like building, eye-hand coordination in throwing and catching, and of course fighting the bad guys.

As toddlers become social, they tend to show preference for same-sex friends, which further reinforces the gender role messaging. This preference continues through childhood and into adolescence. While playing together with their peers, boys learn to use commands, threats, and physical strength to gain compliance from other children. But girls learn "obliging strategies," involving quieter and more refined methods for obtaining what they want, including polite requests and other verbal persuasion (Riley & Jones, 2007). At school, teachers spend more time attending to boys than to girls. Often this is because boys display a higher level of activity, which if not controlled is disruptive to the classroom. They have also been observed to allow boys to break the rules more frequently and more blatantly than girls before administering punishment (Leaper & Friedman, 2007). When students have difficulties problem solving, teachers tend to guide girls quickly to the answer, whereas they encourage boys to keep working until they can reach a solution on their own (Huang et al., 1998).

It has long been assumed that boys are naturally more aggressive than girls, but child psychologists point out that if you include *social alienation* in the definition of aggression then girls are *least* as aggressive as boys (Crick & Gropeter, 1995; Marsee et al., 2014 Wilbert, 2008).

Social Wellness

Source: Callista Lee

Social alienation as discussed in "How Girls Bully" (2014) includes:

- Playing jokes or tricks designed to embarrass or humiliate
- Deliberate exclusion of other kids for no real reason
- Whispering in front of other kids with the intent of making them feel left out
- Name calling, rumor spreading, and other malicious verbal interactions
- Being friends one week and then turning against a peer the next week with no incident or reason for the alienation
- Encouraging other kids to ignore or pick on a specific child
- Inciting others to act out violently or aggressively against another child

The media is also a major player in spreading stereotyped gender roles, showing males to be the leaders, heroes, problem-solvers, decision-makers, and dominant over females. When men are shown taking care of children, they are often portrayed as clumsy and inept. Studies have found that children who grew up without a television were be less stereotyped about gender. And children who regularly watch programs that violate traditional gender roles (women as brilliant doctors or men as patient and caring elementary school teachers) tend to exhibit less traditional gender roles in their own behaviors (Witt, 2000).

Your sense of how well you match (or don't match) the gender role that society expects of you is another important part of your sexual identity. Some people are quite comfortable not fitting the cultural norms, whereas others worry themselves sick over their failure to live up to expectations. They may be taunted by both kids and immature adults for being different. Parents and teachers play an important role in teaching young people to be accepting of gender role diversity. Traditional gender roles are stereotypes, and as stereotypes we know that not everyone will fit them. In recent years, there has been greater social permission for kids to stray from these expectations, but there is a double standard. Girls are generally accepted if they are "tomboys" and even to grow up to enter traditionally male sports or careers. It is harder for boys. His GI Joe is an "action figure" not a doll. He is warned to "man up" if he gets scared or hurt, even if he is just four years old. There is almost nothing worse than being called a "sissy." An adult male who chooses a career in nursing is likely to be asked if he just couldn't get through medical school even though nursing school is plenty difficult, and a very different type of work than being a doctor. Men who choose careers working with children may be suspected of being pedophiles. The women's movement of the 1970s opened the doors for women to move out of their narrow roles of wife, mother, or secretary, but it didn't free up men to break out of their roles of leader, provider, and hero. There are some men's groups today that support such freedom. They want to learn how to be men in the modern era where it is no longer necessary to be the physically strongest to be the best worker, and how they can use their strength to help others rather than just hurting the bad guys. They gather to discuss feelings that society has not allowed them the freedom to express: depression, fear, doubt, and the exhaustion of having to be the one with all the answers. Take a look at Figure 4.4 to review the many factors that work together to develop one's sexual identity.

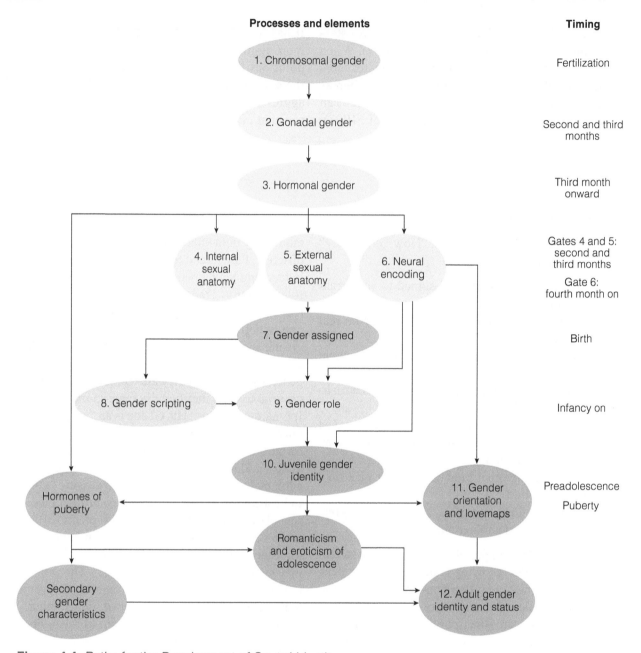

Figure 4.4 *Paths for the Development of Sexual Identity*

Francoeur, Robert T., *Becoming a Sexual Person,* 2nd Ed., © 1991. Reprinted by permission of Pearson Education, Inc., New York, New York.

ဗ   *Physical Wellness*   ဗ

As we age, particularly at puberty, our physical selves become a statement of gender. Heredity and hormones play a significant role in size, structure, and, to some extent, shape. Once we've matured, we make decisions about appearance—what clothes to wear, how to cut our hair, what we accentuate, what we hide.

The Flower Boy

The flower boy was 4 at the time.

When my sister was planning her wedding, she asked us if our 4-year-old son could be the flower boy. He would walk down the aisle just before the bride and throw rose petals along the path as he went. Though neither of us had ever seen or heard of a flower "boy," we thought that it was a wonderful idea. When we asked our son, he was excited about his important job. It never occurred to us that there would be a problem until we started mentioning, in casual discussions, that our son was going to be the flower boy at the upcoming wedding. Reactions we got from family members and friends (not all, luckily) ranged from astonishment to disgust: "Boys don't throw flowers." "That is a girl's job." "How can you do that to your son? You will humiliate him." "You'll confuse him," and so on. Frankly, we could not believe the reactions people had. After all, we argued, we weren't planning to put him in a dress, and since when were flowers the sole purview of girls? Remember, we are talking about a 4-year-old—a boy who happens to love picking flowers for his mommy and daddy.

In the face of scandal, we became even more committed to seeing this through. The day came, and our son, along with everyone else in the wedding party, was very excited and very nervous.

As he came down the aisle, dressed in his tuxedo, a basket of rose petals in his hand, spontaneous "oohs" and "aahs" could be heard from those assembled. People saw not a radical, genderbending experiment but an adorable 4-year-old spreading beauty and love. We were so proud of him!

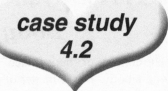

case study 4.2

Critical Thinking

If and when you have children, how far will you be willing to go to encourage their role flexibility? What will you do that your parents' did or did not do? How will you respond to those who have strong, negative reactions to you encouraging role flexibility in your children?

In the past several years, males and females alike have been using steroids as a way to increase muscle mass. The evidence is clear that steroids used in this way can be dangerous. Women bodybuilders, for example, may have the desired large muscles but will notice diminished breast size, changes in the menstrual cycle, and more masculine contours to the face, not to mention increased facial hair. Males who use steroids may be excited by the size and strength of their muscles but unprepared for what is commonly called "roid rage," a pronounced and intense level of anger, and decrease in testicle size.

Changes to our health, such as depression or having a serious accident can influence the physical aspects of our identitiy. Having or developing a disability may affect movement, which in turn may affect how we see ourselves and how others react to us. Our view of our body is very closely tied to how we feel about our sexuality.

Our physical body is the machine through which we express our sexuality, therefore taking care of it, in whatever condition it is, and learning to love and accept it is essential for healthy sexuality.

sex in society 4.1

Body Image as a Lifelong Concern

The concept of "body image" refers to how one views one's body. It is a matter of self-perception, formed over years of looking in the mirror, receiving comments both critical and complimentary from others, comparing oneself to friends and models in magazines, and experimenting with looks. Who hasn't looked back at old photographs and wondered " How could I have thought I looked so good?" What is fashionable one year can be passé in the next. Changes in what is seen as desirable can certainly have an impact on a person's health, in all its dimensions.

Eating disorders, a powerful result of body image pressure, more often develop in the teen years or young adulthood but can even begin in elementary age students. The rates among women are two and a half times greater than men but men also suffer from distorted body image. The social pressure for men to have highly developed muscles can lead to muscle dysmorphia, an extreme concern for being more muscular (National Institute of Mental Health, 2016). Anyone can have a "bad hair day," want to hide his or her head under a hat, and generally feel self-conscious. However, individuals with body dysmorphic disorder (BDD), have a clinical diagnosis, and they see themselves as ugly, often becoming obsessive about one particular part of their body. Their disordered thinking about appearance can disrupt all aspects of their everyday lives, with some becoming housebound.

Concern for appearance and positive body image is very entrenched in the American culture. Some choose to enhance their bodies in a positive way by continuing to exercise daily and eating nutritiously to maximize their appearance. To find the right balance between attending to appearance and taking care of oneself versus getting caught up in the momentum of ever-increasing pressure to choose healthy options for improving appearance remains a challenge.

personal exploration activity

All the Things I Would Never Do If I Were the Opposite Sex

The goal of this activity is to inspire you not only to look at behaviors of the opposite sex that annoy you but to identify your own behaviors that hinder your relationships with the opposite sex.

Imagine that you have the ability to change what really irritates you about the opposite sex. All you have to do is make your wish list, and everything you wanted would be granted.

Take a minute and make a list of all the things that the opposite sex does that you really wish they would never do again. After you have finished making your list, show your list to your best same-sex friend and see whether he or she has the same wishes or can add to your list. Then be very brave and show it to your best opposite-sex friend. How does he or she react to your list? Ask this best opposite-sex friend if he or she could make any changes in the behavior of your sex, what would they be? Notice all the behaviors on your friend's list that you presently do. Are you willing to make those changes?

For example: If I were a female I would never
- lead a guy on sexually.
- wear so much makeup.
- always expect the guy to pay for everything.

If I were a male, I would never
- scratch my genitals in public.
- expect sex because I pay for dinner.
- talk with the guys about my sexual experiences.

Source: Callista Lee

Biological research has already been discussed in the section on Sexual Anatomy, earlier in this chapter. The preponderance of evidence supports the theory that a predisposition for one's sexual orientation is built into the brain's structure before birth. After birth additional individual experiences and socio-cultural factors further influence this primary predisposition. In some the predisposition may be strong enough to exert itself despite social pressure to be otherwise, while in others the predisposition may be weaker, leaving the individual more vulnerable to social pressure or life experiences. Of one thing we are certain; sexual orientation is not a choice made by the individual (Kleigman, 2011).

Sexual Orientation

Sexual orientation is a blending of sexual identity as a homosexual or heterosexual, sexual behavior, and sexual attraction to males or females or both (Bailey, Vasey, Diamond, Breedlove, Vilaine, Epprecht, 2016). In attempting to explain sexual orientation, theorists have often focused their efforts on explaining why some people identify as homosexual or bisexual. There is thought to be no need to explain heterosexuality, as that is the norm. That is what is expected. The strongest arguments for heterosexuality lie in the reproductive aspects of heterosexual behavior. Without heterosexuals, the argument goes, no children would be born. The species would die.

Some individuals look to their religious doctrines, citing passages that condemn behavior between same-sex individuals. And history is replete with violence, gay bashing, arrests, and even death for those thought to be homosexual. LGBT people are more likely to be targets of hate crimes than any other minority group. In 2014, twenty percent of all hate crimes were because of a person's sexual orientation. This level of violence and hate is thought to be a reaction by some to the trend of a more accepting attitude toward the LGBT community in the United States (Park & Mykhyalyshya, 2016).

Although we appreciate the strength of various convictions, we take the position that sexual health requires accepting our sexual orientation and that individuals who are comfortable with themselves are less likely to feel threatened by people who have orientations that are different from their own. The gay and lesbian rights movement has often pointed out, "We are everywhere. We are your children, your brothers and sisters, your parents, your friends." The issue is whether an individual can be open about his or her sexuality, and whether you are willing to know that aspect of those with whom you are close.

Theories of Sexual Orientation

Theories on sexual orientation abound, but no one theory of sexual orientation has gained wide spread support. Theories involving genetic and environmental influences are the most generally accepted. Biological theorists have looked toward genetic, hormonal, and structural differences in the brain to explain homosexuality. Social theorists emphasize learning as a key factor in determining orientation. Wiederman (2001), in his critique of research on orientation, elaborates on the difficulties inherent in studying orientation. While the question of causality may be the primary focus, the experimental research that would be needed to systematically identify key factors cannot be conducted.

It is unethical, for example, to manipulate genetic material in an attempt to identify difference. It would be just as unethical and impossible to manipulate the behavior of parents, or experiment with childhood experiences, in order to assess the impact on later interpersonal attachments. Consequently, much of the research on orientation ends up being speculative and correlational; for example, researchers will survey and interview adults about their past to identify related variables (Wiederman, 2001).

Environment Theories

In looking to environment theories, particularly psychoanalytic and learning theories, explanations of sexual orientation again have limited uses or reliability. In his *Three Essays on the Theory of Sexuality,* published in the early part of the 20th century, Freud spoke of the child as having an undifferentiated sexuality and having to learn appropriate responses as he or she ages. Part of that learning would be to identify with the parent of the same sex, and to seek out a partner of the opposite sex. To be homosexual then could be construed as inappropriate identification. The female child, for example, would identify with her father and seek out women as partners.

For years, the field of mental health, led by psychiatrists, psychoanalysts, and psychologists, considered homosexuality a form of mental illness. Not until 1973 did the American Psychiatric Association remove homosexuality from its *Diagnostic and Statistical Manual of Mental Disorders* (DSM). It is now understood that homosexuality does not cause mental illness. However, society's reaction to homosexuality and treatment of homosexuals can certainly contribute to depression and other mental health issues for some gays.

Very popular for years was the notion that homosexuality in males resulted from a weak or absent father and a strong, domineering, overly intimate mother. Research has not supported this theory of parents being responsible for their child's sexual orientation thus parents do not need to wonder what they did to influence their child's sexual orientation.

One study extensively interviewed and compared responses from close to 1,000 gay and lesbian adults with those from a sample group of approximately 500 heterosexual males and females (Bell, Weinberg, & Hammersmith, 1981). The interviewees were asked about their child and adolescent years. The results showed no patterns of family dysfunction, no prevalence of positive or negative sexual experiences to explain orientation.

Another false notion has been that homosexuals were seduced into their lifestyle by an older adult. This myth is particularly destructive, for it sets up gay and lesbian adults as seducers, likely to seek out children and adolescents for their personal pleasure. As a result, professions where adults have contact with children (teacher, coach, and so on) become particularly risky places to "come out."

Although the genesis of sexual orientation is different for individuals, orientation is thought to be stable and not under our conscious control. "What we have learned over the last 30 years is that you apparently cannot change a person's sexual orientation, though you can change others views about sexual orientation" (Dreger, 2009). Homosexual, bisexual, and heterosexual children can and do have the same biological parents, grow up in the same households, and end up differently along the continuum of sexual orientation.

Biological Theories

Simon LeVay (1991) reported that the *third interstitial nucleus of the anterior hypothalamus* (INAH3) in heterosexual men was more than twice the size as it was in homosexual men. For gay men, the INAH3 was more similar in size to heterosexual women. This research was done by observing brains post-mortem which left researchers wondering if this was caused by fetal development or life experience. More recently brain imaging technology used on living persons found that self-reported sexual orientation was linked to some other brain structures. Gay men's brains looked more like those of heterosexual women in that they tended to be more symmetrical than heterosexual males' brains (right and left hemispheres were of similar size) and possessed a greater number of neural connections to the left side of amygdala (a region of the brain that plays a key role in processing emotions). In addition to brain symmetry, facial symmetry is also related to sexual orientation. Heterosexuals tend to have more symmetrical faces than gay men or lesbians (Hughes & Bremme, 2011).

Lalumiere, Blanchard, & Zucker (2000) found that homosexuals are more likely to be left-handed than heterosexuals. And others have found an atypical finger-length ratio in gay men and lesbians. Among heterosexual women, the length of the index finger (the one next to the thumb) tends to be the same length as the ring finger, but in heterosexual men the index finger is usually a little shorter than the ring finger. This tends to be more often true of the right hand than the left. Lesbians tend to exhibit the pattern found in heterosexual males, while gay men tend to exhibit an even greater difference in length than found in heterosexual men. For reasons unknown, the exaggerated difference in gay men only shows up in studies of predominantly white gay men. However multiple studies have found the lesbian vs. heterosexual woman difference across races (Grimbos et.al.,2010; LeVay, 2011).

Another interesting factor is the *fraternal birth order effect*. Blanchard & Bogaert (1996) found that for each extra older brother a man has, his odds of being gay increase by 33%. It has been suggested that each time a woman bears a male child there is a change in her body that somehow affect sons who come later. The exaggerated finger length was also more likely to be found among gay men who had a larger number of older brothers. All of the biological differences in sexual orientation discussed thus far appear to be related to hormones. But there is also important genetic support for a biological cause of sexual orientation.

Twin studies have found higher concordance (how often both twins share a given trait; in this case the same sexual orientation) among identical twins (they share 100% of their DNA) than among fraternal twins (who share about 50% of their DNA). No "gay gene" has been identified but it is supposed that having the same DNA will mean that genetically identical twins will also share identical internal hormonal environments as they develop in the womb which predispose them to the same sexual orientation (Hershberger, 2001).

Biology—Environment Interaction

Source: Callista Lee

While the old environmental theories have been debunked, we do know that the social environment and life experience play a role in human development. Sex researcher Daryl Bem (1996, 2000, 2008) has proposed a theory of sexual orientation development that explains both heterosexual and homosexual development by taking a closer look at the interaction of biological and environmental factors. He calls it the **exotic becomes erotic (EBE)** theory of sexual orientation. Bem suggests that instead of being born with a predisposition toward a certain sexual ori-

entation, we are born with predispositions to childhood temperaments (aggression, shyness, high or low activity level, and others) that affect our behaviors. These behaviors may be either **gender-conforming or gender-nonconforming**. Most children exhibit gender-conforming behaviors, which allow them to be welcomed into same-sex play groups where they will fit in relatively comfortably. Gender-nonconforming children will be more likely to fit in with playmates of the other sex.

The effect of spending so much time with one sex or the other is that the playgroup becomes the in-group and the other sex becomes the out-group. Bem suggests (and other researchers agree) that negative emotional arousal develops about the out-group and is expressed in comments such as "I hate girls" or "Boys are mean." This mocking of the outgroup is reinforced by other children (and sometimes parents) and often leads to pressuring members of one's own sex to "act right." For boys, it is "don't be a sissy" and for girls, "you play too rough." Years pass, these friendships deepen, and these feelings continue.

But at puberty, there is a sexual awakening. Members of the out-group become interesting for all of their strangeness...exotic even. The accompanying emotional arousal changes from the former negative association of "I hate girls" to a desire "I want a girlfriend." Thus, the exotic becomes erotic. Whichever sex made up your childhood in-group will continue to be your source of close friends, but the sex of your childhood out-group will become the source of your romantic interests. This theory is not just an interesting idea that Bem came up with. After more than fifteen years of research, there is ample evidence that the sex we find sexu-

Biological variables
Genetics, exposure to prenatal hormones

Childhood temperaments
Differences in activity level, aggression, and other factors

Gender conforming or nonconforming behavior
Engagement in activities that are typical or atypical for one's sex; selection of playmates

Feelings of difference from same-sex or other-sex peers
Feeling different from peers who are "exotic" and have other interests

Physiological arousal to same-sex or other-sex peers
Generalized, nonsexual arousal in the presence of "exotic" peers

Erotic attraction to same-sex or other-sex peers
Around puberty, general arousal transforms into sexual arousal

© Kendall Hunt Publishing Company

Exotic Becomes Erotic theory

Gender-conforming behaviors Behavior that is consistent with traditional cultural expectations for a child's sex. Example: girls playing quietly and cooperatively vs. boys playing at more rough and tumble activities.

Gender-nonconforming behaviors Behavior that is inconsistent with traditional cultural expectations for the child's sex and considered more appropriate for children of the other sex. Example: boys playing house and girls playing army.

ally attractive in adolescence and adulthood is the one that was our out-group in childhood, whether we are gay or straight. Bem doesn't really have an answer for what allows for some people to become bisexual. Perhaps he will find that bisexuals did not have a strong attachment to one sex or the other in childhood. Or perhaps this will remain a mystery. It should be noted that not all gender-nonconforming children grow up to be homosexual or bisexual. But the vast majority of homosexuals studied were gender-nonconforming as children. There is still much to learn.

Labels and Categories

Alfred Kinsey's work on male and female sexuality continues to provide a reference point for work on sexual orientation (Kinsey, Pomeroy, & Martin, 1948; Kinsey, Pomeroy, Martin, & Gebhard, 1953). Along with his colleagues, he developed a 7-point scale that categorized sexual experience, shown in Figure 4.5.

After interviewing more than 10,000 people, Kinsey found it useful to categorize behaviors on a continuum based on sexual experience with same-sex and other-sex partners. If one's behavior was exclusively with a member of the other sex, that person was referred to as a "Kinsey 0." A person whose behavior was exclusively with members of his or her own sex was labeled a "Kinsey 6." All other positions between 1 and 5 represented interest in both men and women. Those in this part of the continuum are the ones most likely to fluctuate in their attraction and commitment to one particular sex (Savin-Williams & Cohen, 2004). This fluctuation, called sexual fluidity, is more common among women than men and is dependent upon the situation. One could be attracted to a female based on the person and the situation yet in the next relationship be attracted to a male (Diamond, 2008).

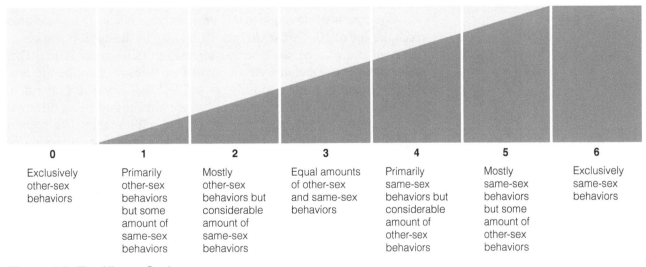

0	1	2	3	4	5	6
Exclusively other-sex behaviors	Primarily other-sex behaviors but some amount of same-sex behaviors	Mostly other-sex behaviors but considerable amount of same-sex behaviors	Equal amounts of other-sex and same-sex behaviors	Primarily same-sex behaviors but considerable amount of other-sex behaviors	Mostly same-sex behaviors but some amount of other-sex behaviors	Exclusively same-sex behaviors

Figure 4.5 *The Kinsey Scale*

Because the culture often seems to want to classify or label people regarding orientation, only Kinsey 0's would fit the definition of heterosexual. Individuals categorized as Kinsey 6's would be homosexual, and those falling within categories 1 through 5 would be bisexual or ambisexual. The mean age for self labeling as a non heterosexual is middle adolescence. However, many choose not to share this with others causing the mean age for coming out to be after high school, or young adulthood (Savin-Williams & Cohen, 2004).

Later researchers and theorists have objected to classifying individuals based only on their behavior, as well as questioning the need to classify and label at all. Fred Klein pointed out the limitations of using behavior as the sole variable for labeling. Common sense dictates that *what we do* is only a part of *who we are* and what identity we have. Klein proposed that orientation be assessed on seven factors (Klein, 1978; Klein, Sepekoff, & Wolf, 1985):

1. *Sexual attraction:* To whom do we find ourselves attracted? Who turns us on? Do we respond only to women? Only to men? To both?
2. *Sexual behavior:* When you've engaged in sexual behavior, who have been your partners?
3. *Sexual fantasies:* When you fantasize or masturbate, what sex/gender is your partner?
4. *Emotional or affectional preference:* To whom do you connect on an emotional level? With whom do you "fall in love"?
5. *Social preference:* With whom do you prefer to socialize? With whom do you "go out"?
6. *Lifestyle:* In your community, with whom do you spend most of your time? Are your friends primarily lesbian or gay? Bisexual? Heterosexual?
7. *Self-identification:* How do *you* label yourself? Where do you place yourself on the Kinsey grid?

Awareness of attraction to the same sex often occurs before children reach the age of 10. This sexual attraction may be the earliest and strongest predictor of a person's sexual orientation (Kliegman, 2011). This reality lead The American Academy of Pediatrics to describe the four stages of identity formation for gays and lesbians (Ryan & Futterman, 2001). First, there is "Sensitization," where a feeling of being different is experienced by prepubertal children and adolescents. The second stage, "Sexual Identity Confusion," is marked by a self-awareness of same-gender attraction yet confusion reconciling oneself with what are negative societal stereotypes. The third stage, "Sexual Identity Assumption," is the process of acknowledgment and social and sexual exploration of one's identity. Delving into the gay and lesbian community is more common in late adolescence. Finally, the fourth stage, "Integration and Commitment," represents the individual's ability to incorporate being gay or lesbian into positive self-acceptance, and sharing that part of oneself with others. This stage, if and when reached, typically occurs in adulthood. However, in the face of society's lack of acceptance of gays, some gay people marry and have children before finally admitting to themselves that they are gay. This can take a tremendous toll not

sex in society 4.2

Dealing with the Categories

Audre Lorde, a feminist writer, highlighted our culture's need to categorize and stigmatize individuals around issues of race, sex, class, and sexual orientation. "As a fortynine-year-old Black lesbian feminist socialist mother of two, including one boy, and a member of an interracial couple, I usually find myself a part of some group defined as other, deviant, inferior, or just plain wrong" (Lorde, 2001, p. 588). She speaks to the constant drain of energy it takes to respond to a world that oppresses individuals for a variety of qualities—sex, race, social class, ethnicity, and sexual orientation—and challenges the culture to redefine the way it deals with difference.

For sexual health, it is necessary to realize that issues of race and ethnicity cannot be separated from the ways the individual functions in his or her community. The Families of Color Network is a coalition of Asian–Pacific Islanders, Latinos, African Americans, Arab Americans, Native Americans, Caucasians, and biracial individuals who come together as an activist and advocacy group around LGBT issues.

Nila Marrone (2001), in an article for *The SIECUS Report,* identifies issues in the Latino culture, for example, that make dealing with LGBT concerns more difficult:

- Very strong family ties are more common and all family problems must be solved internally by its members.
- The family name and image must be protected.
- Traditions are highly valued, and change is generally not welcome.
- Respect for elders is highly prized.
- There is no tradition for forming or joining support groups.
- Privacy is highly prized.
- Limited economic resources are a serious obstacle to joining civic or support groups.
- Most Latinos are Catholic.

Other racial and cultural groups may share some of these values and characteristics, adding others that are unique to them. Overall, the LGBT community must address its diversity on race, class, ethnicity, religion, politics, and other issues as it works to build the connections stemming from sexuality.

Source: Adapted from N. Marron (April/May 2001), "Advice to Latino Parents of GLBT Children," *SIECUS Report,* 29 (4).

healthy sex hints 4.1

Advice on Coming Out

The decision to be open about one's homosexuality is a personal one, one that heterosexuals don't have to confront. It is almost as if lesbian and gay individuals have to explain to the world that they are not heterosexual, rather than "the world" having considered that possibility.

The risks a person takes for being open about sexual orientation depend on a variety of factors including age, geography, employment, and financial solvency, among others. Although civil rights protections are gradually being extended to people at the local and state levels, no constitutional amendment guarantees civil rights protection regardless of sexual orientation.

The following guidelines are adapted from the brochure *Be Yourself* * (Sauerman, 1998):

1. *Are you sure about your sexual orientation?* Don't raise the issue unless you're able to respond with confidence to the question "Are you sure?" Confusion on your part will increase your parents' confusion and decrease their confidence in your judgment.

(Continued)

2. *Are you comfortable with your gay sexuality?* If you're wrestling with guilt and periods of depression, you'll be better off waiting to tell your parents. Coming out to them may require tremendous energy on your part; it will require a reserve of positive self-image.

3. *Do you have support?* In the event your parents' reaction devastates you, there should be someone or a group that you can confidently turn to for emotional support and strength. Maintaining your sense of selfworth is critical.

4. *Are you knowledgeable about homosexuality?* Your parents will probably respond based on a lifetime of information from a homophobic society. If you've done some serious reading on the subject, you'll be able to assist them by sharing reliable information and research.

5. *What's the emotional climate at home?* If you have the choice of when to tell, consider the timing. Choose a time when they're not dealing with such matters as the death of a close friend, pending surgery, or the loss of a job.

6. *Can you be patient?* Your parents will require time to deal with this information if they haven't considered it prior to your sharing. The process may last from six months to two years.

7. *What's your motive for coming out now?* Hopefully, it is because you love them and are uncomfortable with the distance you feel. Never come out in anger or during an argument, using your sexuality as a weapon.

8. *Do you have available resources?* Homosexuality is a subject most non-gay people know little about. Have available at least one of the following: a book addressed to parents, a contact for the local or national Parents and Friends of Lesbians and Gays, the name of a non-gay counselor who can deal fairly with the issue.

9. *Are you financially dependent on your parents?* If you suspect they are capable of withdrawing college finances or forcing you out of the house, you may choose to wait until they do not have this weapon to hold over you.

10. *What is your general relationship with your parents?* If you've gotten along well and have always known their love—and shared your love for them in return—chances are they'll be able to deal with the issue in a positive way.

11. *What is their moral societal view?* If they tend to see social issues in clear terms of good/bad or holy/sinful, you may anticipate that they will have serious problems dealing with your sexuality. If, however, they've evidenced a degree of flexibility when dealing with other changing societal matters, you may be able to anticipate a willingness to work this through with you.

12. *Is this your decision?* Not everyone should come out to their parents. Don't be pressured into it if you're not sure you'll be better off by doing so—no matter what their response.

Be Yourself highlights the process that most parents go through when told that their child is gay. The stages include shock, denial, guilt, expression of feelings, personal decision-making, and true acceptance. It highlights that each family is unique, and offers suggestions of resources and support.

Source: *Read This Before Coming Out to Your Parents* by T. H. Sauerman, PFLAG Philadelphia, 1998. For ordering information: PFLAG Philadelphia, P.O. Box 176, Titusville, NJ 08560-0176; vrb@pupgg.princeton.edu.

only on the gay person, but on the spouse and especially the children. With greater societal acceptance of all orientations, each person would be free to explore and accept his or her orientation early in life. Since this orientation is established early in life, it seems a great loss for so many to struggle even into late adulthood to accept this essential aspect of personhood.

The subject of sexual orientation has often led to a need to document "how many." How many people are heterosexual? How many are lesbian

healthy sex hints 4.2

Support in Faith Communities

Spiritual health needs get met in many ways, and having a sense of community is one of them. One of the challenges of considering yourself "religious" and part of the LGBT community is to be able to reconcile religious teachings with your lifestyle. The Internet has enabled groups within various religious communities to provide support and resources. Here is a sample of sites organized by Lambda Families (E. Schroeder, personal communication, September 3, 2002):

Source: Activism to Stop Spiritual Violence: **www.soulforce.org**

Baptist: Association of Welcoming and Affirming Baptists: **www.wabaptists.org**

Catholic: Dignity: **www.dignityusa.org**

Episcopalian: Integrity: **www.integrityusa.org**

Evangelical: Evangelicals Concerned: **www.ecinc.org**

Jewish: The World Congress of GLBT Jews: **www.glbtjews.org**

Lutheran: Lutherans Concerned: **www.lcna.org**

Methodist: Reconciling Ministries Network: **www.rmnetwork.org**

Metropolitan Community Churches: **www.ufmcc.com**

Mormon: Affirmation: **www.affirmation.org**

Presbyterian: More Light: **www.mlp.org**

Quaker: Friends for Lesbian, Gay, Bisexual, Transgender, and Queer Concerns: **www.quaker.org/flgbtqc**

Seventh-Day Adventists: Kinship International: **www.sdakinship.org**

Unitarian Universalist: Interweave: **www.interweave.uua.org**

United Church of Christ: Coalition for LGBT Concerns: **www.ucccoalition.org**

and gay? How many are bisexual? As researchers attempt to count, a number of problems arise. What criterion will be used? How easily assessed is a sample, and can it be determined to be generalizable to the population at large?

Kinsey reported that 37 percent of males and 13 percent of females had engaged in adult same-sex behavior to the point of orgasm. He estimated that 2 percent of males and 1 percent of females could be categorized as Kinsey 6's (Kinsey et al., 1948, 1953). A limitation of Kinsey's work, particularly as it pertains to the Heterosexual-Homosexual Rating Scale, is that behavior is emphasized without attending to the other factors that Klein identified. As researchers continue to investigate the prevalence of homosexuality, a compilation of studies finds that fewer than five percent of respondents in Western surveys identify as gay or lesbian. The rate has been stable over time with no evidence that increased tolerance and acceptance of gays and lesbians has led to an increase in behavioral expression of same sex activities (Bailey et al., 2016). A recent Gallup

Gender variant gender identity or role that varies from what is typical for the person's biological sex

Gender role a behaviors expected of males and females in their society or culture

Poll found that only 3.8 percent of Americans actually identify as lesbian or gay (Newport, 2015).

Gender variance and **gender role** non conformity in children can make some adults uncomfortable. Gender variance in childhood describes behaviors that do not conform to the expected behaviors for that child's sex in the culture in which he or she lives. A young boy who wears skirts because his beloved sister wears them and a little girl who will only play with guns and trucks are examples of gender variance or gender non conformity. Gender variance reflecting the exploration of gender identity and gender role is part of normal development. These behaviors may or may not continue after childhood and into adolescence. However, extensive gender variance in adolescence often persist into adulthood. (Kleigman et al, 2016).

Children with transgender or gender variant identity differ not just in behaviors but in their core gender identity. The transgender group includes a diverse population that does not fit into the culturally defined description of gender. There are two major sources of stress for the transgender person. One stressor is the confusion and discomfort with the difference in the sex assigned at birth and gender identity. This discomfort is often referred to as gender dysphoria. The other source of distress is the feeling of not fitting in, of being different from what is expected by society and not being accepted by friends and family (Kleigman, 2011).

Children with transgender or gender variant identity exhibit some characteristic behaviors. Boys may identify as a girl at an early age and expect to grow up to be a girl. They prefer typical girl toys such as dolls and enjoy playing house. They avoid rough play and prefer to dress like girls. These boys may wish they were a girl or wish to grow up to be a woman. Girls with gender variant identity may identify as a boy and wish to grow up to be a man. They avoid the traditional girl activities and seek tomboy play and boys as friends. They may dress as a boy, may refuse to urinate sitting down, and believe they will grow a penis. Only a minority of gender variant children develop an adult transgender identity. Most will develop a gay or lesbian identity and some a heterosexual identity (Kleigman et al, 2016).

Increasingly, college students are "coming out," as transgender, with campus organizations addressing LGBT issues. More openness and recognition of LGBT issues has inspired some colleges and universities to recognize gender-non conforming students by allowing transgender students to room with their preferred gender; going a step further, the University of Iowa has added a transgender box to the college application (Schulman, 2013).

Gender dysphoria discontent with ones biological sex or gender role

As previously discussed, the transgender group includes transsexual individuals, those who feel their biological sex does not match who they really are as a person. Transsexual people often have **gender dysphoria** and want to change their bodies so that the body more closely matches their gender. The first step is to be thoroughly evaluated to ensure that gender dysphoria is the correct diagnosis. Cross-dressing is encouraged, followed by hormonal interventions to feminize male-to-female gender affirmation or masculinize female-to-male transsexuals. Changes in body hair, changes in the face, and fat deposits all move these individuals in their desired direction. These interventions are reversible if necessary and, for some, represent the extent of treatment that is both comfortable and affordable.

Gender Dysphoria in Children

Source: Callista Lee

As the numbers of children diagnosed with gender dysphoria grow and make it into the news, so do concerns that this condition may be overdiagnosed. As stated earlier, only a minority of gender variant children will identify as transgender in adulthood. Most will grow up to identify as gay or lesbian. For those who do continue to experience gender dysphoria, being able to publicly identify as the gender they believe themselves to be is a welcome relief from trying to fake it as their assigned sex. A change of name, wardrobe, hairstyle, social expectations, and **puberty blockers** (drugs similar to a natural hormone, gonadotropin-releasing hormone/GnRH) allow them to skip going through puberty as "the wrong sex" and to be accepted as the gender they know they know themselves to be. Puberty blocking medications are *mostly* safe, but they do increase the risk of losing bone density and a condition known as osteoporosis (brittle bones). Facing a lifetime of having to worry about breaking a bone every time you fall or even bump into something is not something that anyone would look forward to. That risk must be weighed against the psychological pain that transgender patients experience as well as the physical changes of puberty that will have to be surgically and hormonally remedied in adulthood. One transwoman described her experience of male puberty as "testosterone poisoning." Despite hormonal treatments and surgeries, she still looks quite masculine due to that "poisoning." Because puberty blockers have only been prescribed to treat gender dysphoria since 2004, we don't yet have information about their long-term effects on this population. It should be noted however, that these drugs have been used for over thirty years to treat children who were experiencing *precocious puberty* (puberty that is too early) or CAH. Transgender patients do not have the hormonal conditions that children experiencing precocious puberty or CAH have, so will the long-term results differ? We don't yet know. Before these drugs are prescribed by a medical doctor, there is a requirement that a psychologist report on the severity of the gender dysphoria, which is the best predictor of the persistence of these feelings into adulthood. The primary argument for allowing children to take them is that it buys them more time to sort out their feelings about their gender and reduces their anxieties about going through puberty the "wrong way." At age sixteen, the youth may go off of the puberty blockers and on to the hormones of their identified gender. And at age sixteen, they are allowed to seek genital surgery to affirm their identified gender. The medical treatment of children and teens for gender dysphoria remains controversial, which makes many doctors hesitant to prescribe puberty blockers. Parents should seek out well-respected endocrinologists to discuss the medical pros and cons, and at least one psychologist to discuss the severity of their child's gender dysphoria. It may also be helpful to consult with parents of children who have had these treatments as well as those who did not.

The surgical interventions, if desired, are more complicated. Transsexual men will have the testicles and penis removed, and the skin of the penis is used to construct a vagina that can respond to sexual stimulation. **Transsexual** females will have a complete hysterectomy and a double mastectomy and will have a penis constructed. Because the clitoris is small and behind the penis, it can be left to improve sexual response.

Transgender communities share a variety of concerns with their gay, lesbian and bisexual peers. Issues such as coming out, violence, self-esteem, discrimination and access to health care are similar in these groups. (Wolraich, 2007; American Psychological Association, 2014). At the same time, there are unique concerns, such as what physician to use to get comprehensive health care, perhaps hormone treatments and even sex reassignment surgery. The World Association for Transgender Health works to bring together professionals to promote health, research, education, respect, dignity and equality for transgender, transsexuals and gender

Transsexual people whose gender identity is different from their assigned sex and who often wish to alter their bodies to match their gender identity

non-conforming people (World Association for Transgender Health, 2017). This group provides a free, online data base to help patients find health care providers that promote and meet these criteria (WPATH, 2013).

Transgender activists and those who work with transgender clients claim that the emotional, social, and occupational stress that interferes with daily functioning is not due to the person's gender identification but is caused by society's reaction to it (Klein, 2002). Perhaps if our society did not have such rigid expectations of how each sex must act and feel, we would have little need for the classifications we have been discussing. In an ideal world, we would accept and support all people, no matter how they dress or who they have as a sexual partner, without needing to label each person or their actions.

✎ *Emotional Wellness* ✎

The cornerstone of emotional well-being is positive sexual self-esteem. Feeling good about ourselves and accepting who we are is vital to health. What is unique about emotional health is that it derives from the other dimensions of health. Feeling good about yourself may result from others liking you, or feeling good about yourself may depend on your liking your body, or a combination of these.

All of us need to have realistic expectations about who we are. As the lyrics from "I Am Who I Am" highlight, though, "Life is not worth a damn until you can shout 'I am who I am.'" In essence, we all need to accept ourselves.

The road to positive self-acceptance is longer for some than others. If you cannot be open about who you are, secrecy and oppression take their toll. Support groups and mental health professionals trained in the area of sexuality can be extremely helpful to those who are struggling with identity issues, seeking acceptance of their orientation, and figuring out how to negotiate environments that prove to be hostile. The use of resources available in books, journals, and online can greatly add to positive sexual self esteem.

Because our emotional health is also connected to others' behavior, we must focus attention on the need to reduce the hostility and discrimination faced by those who are perceived as "different." Improving the mental health of others and their ability to accept differences are critical factors in reducing oppression and permitting variations in lifestyle to coexist.

References

American Psychological Association (2014). *Answers to your questions about transgender people, gender identity, and gender expression.* Retrieved from www.apa.org

Bailey, J. & Benishay, D. (1993). Familial aggregation of female sexual orientation. American Journal of Psychiatry, 150, 272–277.

Bem, S. (1993). *The lenses of gender: Transforming the debate on sexual inequality.* New Haven, CT: Yale University Press.

Bem, S. (1995, April). *Dismantling gender polarization: Shall we turn the volume down or shall we turn the volume up?* Keynote address, 1995 Eastern Region Annual Conference,

Society for the Scientific Study of Sexuality, West Atlantic City, NJ.

Diamond, L (2008). Female sexuality from adolescence to adulthood: Results from a 10 year longitudinal study. *Development Psychology*, 44, 5–14.

Jenkins, W., (2010) Can anyone tell me why I'm gay? What research suggest regarding the orgins of sexual orientation. *North American Journal of Psychology*, vol. 12, No 2, 279–296.

Kinsey, A., Pomeroy, W., & Martin, C. (1948). *Sexual behavior in the human female.* Philadelphia: Saunders.

Kinsey, A., Pomeroy, W., Martin, C., & Gebhard, P. (1953). *Sexual behavior in the human female. Philadelphia: Saunders.*

Klein, F. (1978). *The bisexual option.* New York: Arbor House.

Klein, F., Sepekoff, B., & Wolf, T. J. (1985). Sexual orientations: A multivariable dynamic process. In F. Klein & T. J.

Lorde, A. (2001). Age, race, class, and sex: Women redefining difference. In P. S. Rothenberg (Ed.), *Race, class, and gender in the United States: An integrated study* (5th ed., pp. 588–594). New York: Freeman.

Marrone, N. (2001, April/May). Advice to Latino parents of GLBT children. *SIECUS Report, 29* (4).

Maurer, L. (1999, October/November). Transgressing sex and gender: Deconstruction zone ahead? *SIECUS Report, 28* (1).

Muehlenhard, C. (2000, May). Categories and sexuality. *Journal of Sex Research, 37* (2), 101–107.

National Institute of Mental Health (2016). *Eating disorders*. Retrieved from http:// www.nimh .nih.gov.

Newport, F. (2015). *American greatly overestimate percentage of gays and lesbians in the United States.* Retrieved from http:// www.gallup.com

Park, H., & Mykhyalyshyn, I. (2016, June). L.G.B.T. people are more likely to be targets of hate crimes than any other minority group. *The New York Times*. Retrieved from http:// www:nyt.com

Pillard, R. & Weinrich, J. (1986). Evidence of familial nature of male homosexuality. *Journal of Psychiatry,* 43, 272–277.

Ryan, C., & Futterman, D. (2001, April/May). Social and developmental challenges for lesbian, gay, and bisexual youth. *SIECUS Report,* 29(4).

Sauerman, T. H. (1998). *Read this before coming out to your parents.* Philadelphia: PFLAG Philadelphia.

Sexuality Information and Education Council of the U.S. (2001, April/May). Lesbian, gay, bisexual, and transgender sexuality and related issues: Annotated bibliography and website directory. *SIECUS Report Supplement, 29* (4).

Schulman, M., (2013) Generation LGBTQIA, *The New York Times*. Retrieved from http:// www. nyt.com.

Vance, C. (1988). Anthropology rediscovers sexuality: A theoretical comment. *Social Science Medicine, 33* (8), 875–884.

Wiederman, M. W. (2001). Orientation: What determines sexual attraction to men or women? In *Understanding sexual research* (pp. 74–81). Belmont, CA: Wadsworth/ Thomson Learning.

Woodhill, B. M., & Samuels, C. A., (2003, June). Positive and negative androgyny and their relationship with psychological health and well-being." *Sex Roles: A Journal of Research.*

Wolraich, M., (2007). Developmental-Behavioral Pediatrics, 1st edition. Mosby Publisher.

World Association of Transgender Health (2017). *Mission and Values.* Retrieved from http:// www.wpath.org

Zieman, G., (2005). Gender Identity Disorder-Patient Handout Retrieved from http://www. mdconsult.com.

Chapter *five*

Human Sexual Response

Student Learning Objectives

After reading this chapter, students will be able to

- ☞ Identify the key brain structures involved in the human sexual response.
- ☞ Describe how the nervous and endocrine systems interact during sexual response.
- ☞ Explain how psychological and physiological factors interact during sexual response.
- ☞ Describe the effects of major disabilities on sexual response.
- ☞ Compare and contrast a variety of sexual response theories.
- ☞ Diagram and describe the four phases of the Masters and Johnson sexual response cycle.
- ☞ Define aphrodisiac and evaluate the effects of aphrodisiacs on sexual response.
- ☞ Describe factors that enhance vasocongestion and sexual response.
- ☞ Describe a variety of theories of sexual response.

From *Healthy Sexuality,* 4th edition, by Richard Blonna and Lillian Cook Carter. © 2017 by Richard Blonna and Lillian Cook Carter. Reprinted by permission of Kendall Hunt Publishing Company.

If you were to ask the average person which part of the body is the most important for controlling sexual response, the answer most likely would be "the penis" or "the vagina." Most people equate sexual response to genital functioning. In reality, sexual response begins and ends in the brain. The brain, not the genitals, is the seat of human sexual response. Human sexual response originates with the brain's perception of desire. What makes you want to respond? What allows you to become comfortable and to relax so the response will happen? In this chapter, we'll examine sexual response and try to answer these and many other questions.

∽ *Social Wellness* ∽

The quality of our social relationships plays a big part in our sexual response. Being able to relax, feel secure, and trust our partner is crucial for good sex. Another key to good sex is open communication. Getting to know your partner requires time. Intimacy builds over time as a result of shared experiences and open communication about our innermost thoughts, feelings, needs, and wants. As you can see in Case Study 5.1 with John and Michelle, an intimacy, trust, and a sense of playfulness spring from this social bond between them. Their sensuality and sexuality are easy, not forced, and are a hallmark of high-level social wellness.

Physiology of Sexual Response

Sexual response is the result of a complex interaction between psychological and physiological factors originating in the brain and spreading through various body parts and systems. We'll trace the sexual response, describing the key components and mechanisms of action that control it.

The Nervous System and Sexual Response

Central nervous system Brain and spinal cord

Peripheral nervous system All other nerves connecting to spinal cord

Somatic nervous system The part of the peripheral nervous system under voluntary control

Autonomic nervous system The part of the peripheral nervous system that is automatic and involuntary

The human nervous system is composed of two parts: the **central nervous system** and the **peripheral nervous system**. The central nervous system is made up of the brain and spinal cord. The peripheral nervous system consists of all other nerves, and connects the spinal cord to various target organs, glands, and tissue. Figure 5.1 shows the nervous system. The peripheral nervous system is made up of two divisions: the **somatic nervous system** and the **autonomic nervous system**. We'll start with a discussion of how the central nervous system works during sexual response.

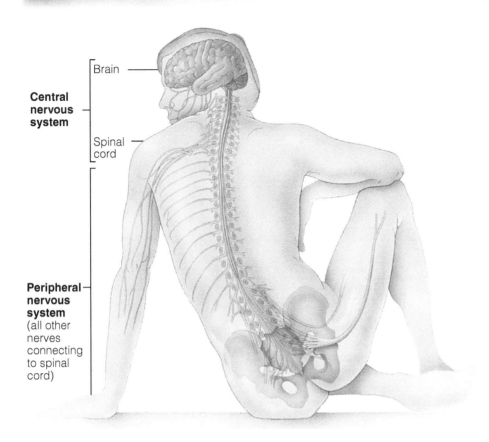

Figure 5.1 *The Nervous System* The nervous system receives and sends sexual messages electrically throughout our body.

The Central Nervous System (Brain and Spinal Cord)

The brain and spinal cord together comprise the central nervous system. Both the brain and the spinal cord play key roles in sexual response. Sexual arousal usually is the end result of a complex interplay among our sensations, thoughts, memories, and feelings that come together in our brains and are interpreted as being sexual. We'll begin our exploration of human sexual response with a discussion of how the brain is involved in this process.

The Brain

The brain has four major divisions (see figure 5.2):

1. Cerebrum (containing the cerebral cortex and limbic system)
2. Diencephalon (comprised of the thalamus, hypothalamus, & pineal body)
3. Brain Stem (comprised of the medulla oblongata, pons, and midbrain)
4. Cerebellum (Martini, 2005)

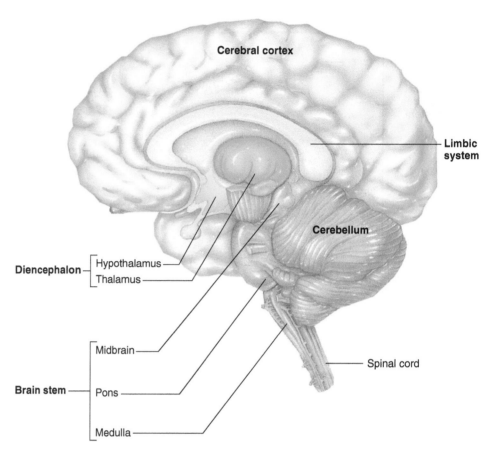

Figure 5.2 *Parts of the Brain* The brain can be divided into four main parts when studying sexuality: the cerebrum, the diencephalon, the brain stem, and the cerebellum.

Hemispheres The two halves of the cerebrum, each controlling the functions of the opposite side of the body

Motor Relating to nerve impulses going out to muscles

Sensory Relating to nerve messages coming into the brain

Associational Connecting together individual sensory inputs

Cerebrum The cerebrum is the largest and uppermost part of the brain. The cerebrum is irregularly shaped, with ridges and shallow and deep grooves, and is divided into two halves called **hemispheres.** The cerebral hemispheres form the outermost part of the brain and are divided into sections called lobes. Four of the lobes are named after the bones in the skull that they lie over. These four are; the frontal lobe, the parietal lobe, the temporal lobe, the occipital lobe. The fifth lobe, the insula, is hidden from view. The frontal, parietal, occipital, and temporal lobes of each hemisphere are responsible for controlling a variety of **motor, sensory,** and **associational** brain functions that are directly involved in sexual response. Each of the lobes controls many functions besides those related to sexual response (Martini, 2005; Fisher, 2004).

Cerebral Cortex The surface of the cerebrum is called the Cerebral Cortex. The conscious awareness of sensations (sight, sound, smell, taste, and touch) is controlled by the parietal, occipital, and temporal lobes of the cerebral cortex, the thinking part of the brain. These sensations, in some combination, enter one's consciousness through the sensory areas of the cerebral cortex and are interpreted as sexual. The cortex picks up the messages, and the associational areas interpret them.

Although each sensory stimulus is entered as a distinct, separate entity, it is quickly assimilated, sorted out, deciphered, and combined with others to form a potentially "sexy" signal. This interplay relies on stored memories (whether real or imagined) of past experiences that influence one's assessment of the present incoming stimuli as sexual and one's expectations of what is to follow (Martini, 2005, Fisher, 2004).

Limbic System The limbic system is a complex arrangement of nerve tissue that links the emotional brain with the thinking, rational brain (cerebral cortex). In this way, the limbic system establishes a relationship between our thoughts and our feelings. Sometimes this relationship is clear-cut and appropriate; other times it is not. Sometimes our emotions get the best of us so we don't think clearly. We might interpret someone's verbal communication, body language, or behavior as conveying interest in having sex when they really are not. The cerebral cortex does have the ability to shut down sexual response through conscious control of behavior at any point (Fisher, 2004).

ҩ *Intellectual Wellness* ҩ

Knowing how our perceptions can influence our sexual response opens the door to relearning things about our sexuality that until now might have been barriers to our sexual fulfillment. If we believe in the cognitive basis of sexual response, we can unlearn negative sexual information and learn new, healthy ways of viewing ourselves and our sexuality. Knowing about the sexual response patterns in men and women and the areas that are most responsive to stimulation can make us better lovers, regardless of whether we are straight, gay, lesbian, or bisexual. Knowing our limitations and capabilities, and how to work around certain disabilities and health conditions, can help us improve our sexual response and maintain our self-respect and self-esteem. Knowing what to expect concerning sexual response can make the difference between allowing ourselves to relax and let things happen or becoming overly concerned with the process and worrying that it won't happen. Knowing that our sexual desires and responses vary from day to day will help us understand the differences, and enable us to relax and go with the changes. Understanding that our needs and responses won't always perfectly mirror our partner's can help us devise ways to work around these and other differences. Understanding the effects of drugs, fatigue, stress, and other substances on our sexual response empowers us and helps us moderate their effects. Knowledge also can prepare us for the future, by enabling us to anticipate the changes in sexual response associated with aging.

Diencephalon The diencephalon forms the central core of the brain and contains the **thalamus** and **hypothalamus**. This area plays a crucial role in the continuation of sexual response that begins with the interpretation of an incoming stimulus as sexual. The thalamus, a hidden region of the brain, might best be described as the relay center for all inputs to the cerebral cortex. The hypothalamus is located directly beneath the thalamus at

Thalamus The part of the brain that relays all inputs to the cerebral cortex

Hypothalamus The part of the brain that correlates activities between the nervous centers and the pituitary gland

Flirting is often perceived as a sign of sexual interest.

the end of the brain stem. Despite its small size, the hypothalamus exerts a tremendous amount of control over body functioning.

The hypothalamus works in concert with the nervous and endocrine systems to initiate sexual arousal. The hypothalamus sends both electrical (nerve impulses) and chemical (releases hormones) messages throughout the body during sexual response. These messages orchestrate a host of physiological reactions that we will describe in detail later in the chapter.

Brain Stem The structures of the brain stem produce the autonomic functions necessary for our survival, in addition to serving as the pathway for connections between the higher and lower brain functions. One of the key functions of the midbrain is the release of the **neurotransmitters serotonin** and **dopamine**, which are antidepressants that elevate mood and increase energy. These neurotransmitters, combined with the hormones epinephrine and nor-epinephrine play a major role in fueling sexual desire and arousal. We will discuss the interplay of neurotransmitters and hormones later in the chapter. A key part of the brain stem, the *reticular activating system* (RAS), is a collection of neurons running through the three regions of the brain stem. It is responsible for both arousing the brain and filtering out unnecessary information. During arousal, the RAS is responsible for magnifying and increasing our awareness of specific stimuli. It allows us to hone in or focus on details of the stimulus. During sexual arousal this helps us focus our attention on important stimuli (Martini, 2005).

Cerebellum The cerebellum works with the cerebral cortex to produce skilled movement of muscles and muscle groups. It helps skeletal muscles control posture and produce smooth, coordinated, muscle movements. An example of such control would be the coordinated thrusting, grinding, and other motions associated with sexual intercourse (Martini, 2005).

The Peripheral Nervous System

During sexual response, nerve impulses travel from the hypothalamus, through the spinal cord to the peripheral nervous system, and ultimately to the specific glands, organs, and tissues involved in sexual response.

Neurotransmitters chemicals that transmit nerve impulses from one nerve to another

Serotonin a neurotransmitter that is an anti-depressant, energy and mood elevatorv

Dopamine a neurotransmitter that is an anti-depressant, energy and mood elevator

case study
5.1

Jorge: Mistaken Perceptions

Jorge is a college sophomore. He shared a story about mistaking a date's expressions of affection as an invitation to have sexual intercourse.

I'm a little embarrassed about talking about this, but I think it's exactly what we were just talking about in class. I dated a girl last semester who was really fine. I was instantly attracted to her when I saw her at the student center. I went up to her, and we hit it off, so I asked her out. We went to one of the jazz concerts on campus and hung out afterward. We walked around campus, and after a while, she kind of snuggled up against me on one of the benches by the auditorium. She smelled real good, and it felt great having my arm around her. We started to kiss and make out. Everything seemed to be going great. We were laughing and snuggling, having a great time.

It started to get late, so I suggested I walk her back to her room. Her roommates had gone home, so she invited me in, and we started making out again. I really thought she wanted to have sex. I mean, she was hot and rubbing up against me. By now I had an erection, and I started to unbutton her blouse. When I got about halfway she stopped me and said, "No." I said, "No what?" She said, "Listen, I like you a lot, but I really don't want to have sex." I must admit, I was shocked and upset. In the past I had never gotten this far without having sex.

I wasn't sure what to do. My penis was throbbing, and I really was horny. I said, "Can you take care of me?" She said "I'm really sorry. I just don't want to do this anymore. Could you please leave?" I really didn't know if she was serious or not, so I asked her, "Are you serious?" She said she was, and I got myself straightened up and left. I was surprised, but by the time I got out of her dorm and started to walk back to my place, I had lost both my erection and my desire. I found out the next week that she had just broken up with her boyfriend that day, and I guess I came along at the wrong time. I never could bring myself to call her again.

Critical Thinking

Has something like this ever happened to you? Have you ever either unintentionally sent sexual signals that you did not want to or misinterpreted signals sent from someone else? If given the chance, how would you handle those situations now?

For many years it was generally assumed that sexual arousal in men and women was a simple spinal reflex located in the genital area. Figure 5.3 illustrates the simple spinal reflex arc responsible for penile erection in men. During a simple spinal reflex erection, stimulation of the penis (manual, oral, etc.) sends nerve messages along the parasympathetic nerves connecting the penis to the **erection center** in the spinal cord. The erection center sends back new nerve transmissions to the smooth muscle tissue of the arteries in the penis causing it to relax. This allows the tissue to fill with blood, causing erection. Clitoral engorgement and erection in women work similarly. When the clitoris is stimulated manually or orally, nerve transmissions travel along the **pudendal nerve** to the sacral region of the spinal cord, where it also connects to a reflex center in the spinal cord. The reflex center sends back new nerve transmissions

Erection center An area of the lowest part of the spinal cord, the sacral region, where the parasympathetic nerves of the penis connect

Pudendal nerve One of the nerves of the pudendal region of the spinal cord that encompasses the second, third, and fourth sacral regions of the spinal cord

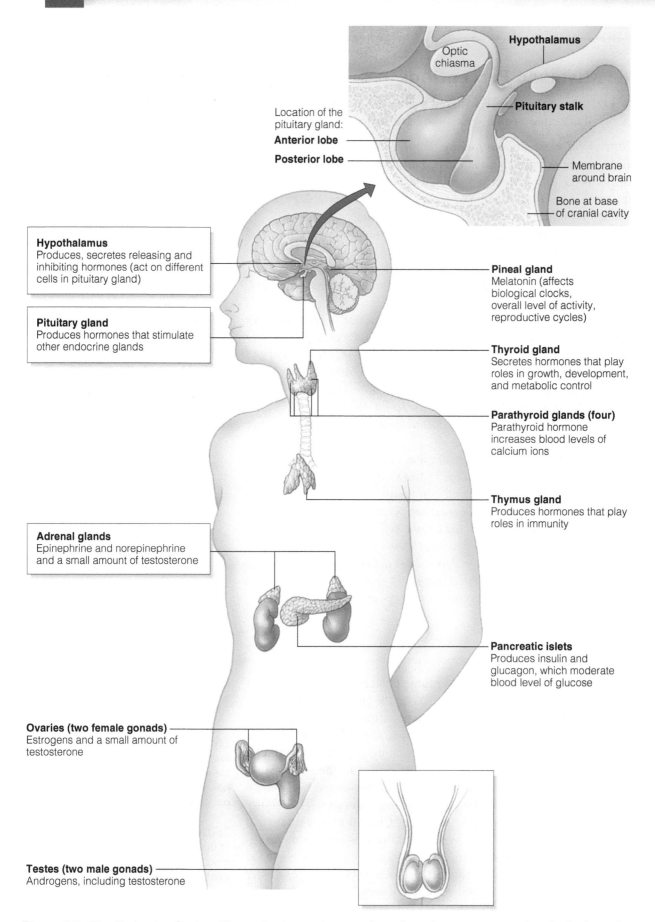

Location of the pituitary gland:
Anterior lobe
Posterior lobe

Optic chiasma

Hypothalamus

Pituitary stalk

Membrane around brain

Bone at base of cranial cavity

Hypothalamus
Produces, secretes releasing and inhibiting hormones (act on different cells in pituitary gland)

Pituitary gland
Produces hormones that stimulate other endocrine glands

Pineal gland
Melatonin (affects biological clocks, overall level of activity, reproductive cycles)

Thyroid gland
Secretes hormones that play roles in growth, development, and metabolic control

Parathyroid glands (four)
Parathyroid hormone increases blood levels of calcium ions

Thymus gland
Produces hormones that play roles in immunity

Adrenal glands
Epinephrine and norepinephrine and a small amount of testosterone

Pancreatic islets
Produces insulin and glucagon, which moderate blood level of glucose

Ovaries (two female gonads)
Estrogens and a small amount of testosterone

Testes (two male gonads)
Androgens, including testosterone

Figure 5.3 *The Endocrine System* The endocrine system sends and receives messages chemically throughout our body.

to the smooth muscle tissue of the blood vessels in the clitoris, causing them to relax, engorge with blood, and enlarge, resulting in clitoral erection (Berman, 2000).

We now know that although initial sexual response can be the result of a simple spinal reflex, in most cases initiation or continuation of arousal involves the complex interplay between the brain and the body discussed earlier.

Endocrine System

The endocrine system is responsible for the production and secretion of potent hormones that initiate and perpetuate the sexual response, in addition to a variety of other functions, ranging from the stress response to growth. The endocrine system is made up of the pituitary, thyroid, parathyroid, adrenal, pancreas, thymus, and pineal glands, as well as the ovaries and the testes.

The endocrine system works on the principle of feedback, with the hypothalamus acting as a thermostat that senses the level of a hormone circulating in the bloodstream. Just as the thermostat in your home senses the level of heat and turns on the heating or cooling system to regulate the temperature, the hypothalamus senses the level of circulating hormones in your bloodstream. If the level of a hormone is too low, the hypothalamus secretes specific releasing factors that travel through the bloodstream to the target endocrine gland, prompting it to begin producing hormones.

Sex Hormones

The role of sex hormones in human sexual response is tremendously confusing. Part of the problem stems from categorizing "male hormones" as androgens and "female hormones" as estrogens. In fact, the primary "male hormone," testosterone, is produced in both males and females. In addition, the primary "female hormone," estrogen, is similarly produced in males and females. What vary are the level of each hormone and their sites of production (Lemonick, 2004; Fisher, 2004).

Androgens

Testosterone is the main androgen that seems to exert the most dramatic effect on sexual response. It is the main hormone associated with sexual desire in both men and women. The average man produces between 6 and 8 mg of testosterone daily. Most of the male testosterone (about 95%) is manufactured in the testes, and the remainder is produced in the adrenal glands. The average woman produces about 0.5 milligrams of testosterone daily, manufactured in the ovaries and adrenal glands. Prior to puberty, testosterone is produced in similar quantities in boys and girls, in the adrenal glands (Lemonick, 2004; Fisher, 2004).

Although men produce much more testosterone than women daily, women seem to have a lower threshold for testosterone sensitivity; they need less in circulation to derive the effects of this potent hormone. Regardless of the overall level of testosterone in men or women, deficiencies of this hormone result in a drop-off in sexual desire (Fisher, 2004; Bancroft, 2002). Studies have shown that a drop-off in androgen levels associated with surgery, anti-androgenic drugs,

Overwork can diminish one's interest in sex.

© Monika Wisniewska, 2010. Shutterstock, Inc.

and other causes can result in diminished sexual desire (Reagan, 1999, Traish, Kim, Munarriz & Goldstein, 2002). Conversely, increasing androgen levels in men and women with diminished blood levels results in heightened sexual desire (Cama, Colleluori, Emig et al., 2003).

Men are especially dependent on testosterone levels for sexual performance. When testosterone levels drop, they have difficulty obtaining and maintaining erections. Women's sexual performance does not seem to be affected as much by testosterone levels. When their levels of testosterone drop, they still are able to experience lubrication, orgasm, and other changes associated with sexual performance (Traish et al., 2002).

Estrogens

Although commonly referred to as "female hormones," estrogens are also produced by men. Women manufacture estrogens in their ovaries, whereas men produce estrogen in their testes. Estrogen levels also are related to sexual response. Estrogens play a role in maintaining vaginal lubrication, thus facilitating intercourse (Traish et al., 2002).

Women who have had their ovaries removed through hysterectomy and other procedures do not experience a reduction in sexual drive, although they may experience vaginal dryness and subsequent pain, which can diminish their interest and desire in sex. Women with high levels of estrogen do not experience heightened (or reduced) levels of sexual desire. Men also do not seem to be affected by too little estrogen. Excessive estrogen in men can have a "feminizing" effect that includes breast enlargement and erectile difficulties.

Progesterone

Progesterone is another major female sex hormone produced in the ovaries. It seems to play a primary role in reproduction by ensuring the viability of the endometrium. Its role in sexual desire and functioning is not understood very well. It may actually suppress the sexual interest of men and women alike (Reagan, 1999).

The Interaction between the Nervous and Endocrine Systems

Becoming aroused may seem to be a relatively simple phenomenon, but in actuality it involves a complex interplay between the nervous and endocrine systems. The two systems work in consort with the other major systems (circulatory, respiratory, muscular, etc.) of the body to get the body ready for sexual activity. The hypothalamus sends electrical (direct nerve transmissions) and chemical (hormones) messages to switch on the body parts responsible for initiating the sexual response. The heart, responding to electrical and chemical stimulation, increases the volume of blood pumped throughout the body by raising its rate and pressure. This increased pumping of blood is necessary for supplying the extra oxygen and energy used during sexual activity. Blood vessels supplying the genitals, brain, and skeletal muscles dilate, allowing greater blood flow to the areas involved in sexual response. The lungs respond instantly by increasing the rate and depth of breathing. The airways expand, allowing maximum intake of air so its vital oxygen is mixed with the blood. The skeletal muscles began to contract and build tension (Martini, 2005, Fisher, 2004).

The Chemicals of Sex

Chemicals, neurotransmitters, and hormones interact is a variety of ways to trigger sexual arousal and keep the fires of desire ablaze. Once our brain interprets any stimuli (sensations, thoughts, feelings, etc.) as sexy, it sends nerve transmissions along our parasympathetic nervous system to the cells in our genital tissue that synthesize a complex molecule called **nitric oxide synthase (NOS)**. NOS interacts with another chemical, a **nucleotide, Guanosine Triphosphate (GTP)**, converting it to **Guanosine Monophosphate (GMP).** This starts a chain reaction resulting in the relaxation of smooth muscle tissue in the genitals allowing it to engorge with blood (de Tajada, 2002).

Nitric oxide synthase (NOS)
A complex chemical produced in genital tissue that starts a chain reaction initiating sexual arousal in men and women

In men, NOS is released in the spongy erectile tissue of the penis. In women, it occurs in the erectile tissue of the vestibular bulbs, the body and crura of the clitoris and in the tissue of the walls of the vagina. O'Connell, Sanjeevan & Hutson (2005), report that NOS causes the smooth muscle tissue of the corpora cavernosa in the penis and clitoral structures to engorge with blood, causing erection and increased sensitivity to stimulation. NOS also causes increased blood flow to the vaginal walls, resulting in lubrication.

Nucleotide A chemical compound that is the basic structural unit of nucleic acids (RNA, DNA etc.) that are found in all living cells

While NOS is working its magic, the same sexual stimuli trigger the brain to release the neurotransmitters dopamine and serotonin. As we've already discussed, serotonin and dopamine are powerful antidepressants that elevate mood and increase energy. Both of these neurotransmitters have been linked to sexual arousal in men and women. When released in response to sexual stimuli, they act to increase desire and facilitate sexual arousal (Lemonick, 2004, Fisher, 2004).

Guanosine Triphosphate (GTP)
An energy-rich nucleotide necessary for protein synthesis

Guanosine Monophosphate (GMP) The converted form of GTP that is associated with the relaxation of genital smooth muscle tissue

While all of this is going on, a powerful hormonal response is also initiated in the brain. The hypothalamus secretes chemicals called **hormonal releasing factors** that travel through the bloodstream to the adrenal glands. These chemical messengers trigger the adrenal glands to release epinephrine and norepinephrine, powerful stimulants that speed up a host of metabolic processes including breathing, heart rate, and blood pressure just to name a few. These hormones combine with the neurotransmitters dopamine and serotonin to provide the energy that fuels sexual desire and arousal.

Hormonal releasing factors
Chemicals secreted into the bloodstream by the hypothalamus. They travel through the bloodstream to specific endocrine glands and trigger them to release their hormones into circulation

Circulating levels of testosterone, also play a part in sexual desire and arousal. As we mentioned previously in this chapter, testosterone is produced in the adrenal glands in women and the testes in men. New data on the effects of testosterone on vaginal and clitoral tissue shows that androgens enhance nitric oxide synthase activity (Traish et al., 2002a; Munarriz, Kim, Goldstein & Traish, 2002). While testosterone has long been recognized as the hormone of desire (Kaplan, 1974), this newer research may shed light on the specific actions of testosterone during the desire and arousal phases of sexual response.

While these findings clearly identify the chemicals of desire, the exact timing and interplay of these individual components is murky. For example, while we know that these chemicals, neurotransmitters, and hormones work together during sexual arousal we are not sure if their release must occur in a specific sequence to work properly. We also do not know if neurotransmitters can stimulate desire or if an elevated mood and more energy just set the stage for feeling sexy. Can the presence of hormones, chemicals, and neurotransmitters overcome the effects of thoughts, feelings and old memories?

Aphrodisiacs

Source: Callista Lee

People have believed that certain foods, scents, herbs, drugs, or other substances can act as aphrodisiacs for thousands of years. They have tended to either resemble the genitals, sperm, ova, or they are delicious, sensual treats. Some cause a tingling in the genitals, while others affect mood. But do any of them actually make people horny? NO. None of them do; not oysters, passion fruit, caviar, chocolate, powdered rhinoceros horn, Spanish fly, or even horny goatweed. What does make people horny? **the mind**. If you *believe* that consuming a certain item will increase your sexual desire, your belief can stimulate the placebo effect. The **placebo effect** is when the body reacts according to the mind's expectations.

Some supposed aphrodisiacs can actually be harmful. **Spanish fly** is ground up, dried blister beetles, which causes warmth throughout the body, not because of sexual desire or arousal but because of inflammation due to irritation, which can be severe. Yohimbe is an herb found in Africa and India. It works by stimulating nerve centers in the spine, thereby improving the capacity for erection *without* increasing sexual excitement. Unfortunately, there are side effects to taking this herb, which include anxiety, weakness, overstimulation, paralysis, and hallucinations. **Horny goatweed** has been shown to help men suffering from erectile dysfunction (ED) to maintain a stronger erection, but it doesn't make anyone horny. It comes from a plant known as "yin yang huo" in Chinese medicine. If you buy some in a sex store, you can't be sure that is actually what you are getting or at what dosage, as it is not regulated. Taking large doses or long-term use can cause serious side effects.

While some of the foods touted as aphrodisiacs may be good for your overall health (**oysters** are high in zinc), they will not cause an increase in sexual desire or performance. However, you may have heard that drinking **pineapple juice** will sweeten semen, and this does appear to be the case! You may also find that drinking other fruit juices will sweeten your bodily fluids. The effect is not long lasting, so you'll want to weight this advantage against the cost in calories, especially if the bottled juice has added sugar to make it sweeter. **Chocolate** is another one that comes with calories from fat and sugar that need to be weighed against its healthy effects. To experience any positive effects from chocolate, it must be at least 70 percent cocoa. The flavonoids in chocolate have a wide range of beneficial health effects, as do flavonoids in many fruits, vegetables, teas, and red wine. And dark chocolate can improve feelings of calmness and contentment, but … not horniness.

While there is no "magical" aphrodisiac out there, you can use your own mind to build positive attitudes about sex, and to create sensual delights for yourself and your partner. Check the website for more information about aphrodisiacs.

Aphrodisiac a substance that increases sexual desire and performance when consumed.

Placebo effect a beneficial effect produced by a placebo drug or treatment, which cannot be attributed to the properties of the placebo itself, and must therefore be due to the patient's belief in that treatment.

healthy sex hints 5.1

Effects of Aphrodisiacs

People are always searching for a magic potion that will enhance their sexual response and enable them to respond quicker, last longer, and become re-aroused quicker. This has enabled a multi-million-dollar aphrodisiac market to flourish. Certain foods, nutrients, and other aphrodisiacs are promoted as aids to sexual response. But do they work? The answer is yes and no.

Although no true aphrodisiac (a potion that increases desire and performance) exists, if you think it's helping, it probably is, as is the case with any placebo. Because the mind and the body work together in initiating and perpetuating sexual response, it makes sense that if a person perceives that a substance will help promote sexual response, it just might (Bergeson, 2005, Scelfo, 2002).

Physiologically, however, the effects of aphrodisiacs are mixed. In general, they can be categorized by the way they work: provide energy, increase blood flow to the genitals, decrease the sensitivity of genital tissue, and increase desire in the brain.

Various "pep pills" are promoted as increasing energy levels. These are featured in fitness and "muscle" magazines, and claim to enhance sexual desire by increasing overall energy levels. Although we believe that sexual desire is enhanced through high-level well-being, we think this should emanate from a healthy lifestyle, not a "pep pill." Other aphrodisiacs, in the form of salves and creams, claim to work by enhancing vasocongestion (firmer erections, more responsiveness)—sending more blood to the genital area. In reality, vasocongestion is a result of dilation and constriction of blood vessels and changes in blood pressure, not extra surface blood in the smaller capillaries.

Still other aphrodisiacs claim to work by decreasing sensitivity, which hypothetically allows men to "last longer." These topical creams and ointments often inflame sensitive genital tissue, creating painful irritation. Using a condom to cover the head of the penis is a better way to decrease sensitivity.

Psychoactive drugs and alcohol work by altering perception. Alcohol deadens the parts of the brain that control conscious thought. This can reduce negative thoughts and feelings that might inhibit sexual response. Other drugs, such as marijuana, heighten sensations such as touch and smell. Enhancing the ability to perceive sensations can heighten enjoyment of sexual activity and promote sexual response.

Viagra, a treatment recommended for men (and under study in women) with erectile disorders associated with impaired genital blood flow, has also been touted as an aphrodisiac. Although Viagra is very effective in enhancing blood flow in people with this problem, its utility in enhancing sexual response in men and women with adequate blood flow is questionable.

The best "aphrodisiacs," in our opinion, are summarized as the following:

Become physically fit.
Develop healthy eating habits.
Reduce stress through relaxation techniques and behavior management.

Your Brain on Orgasm

Source: Callista Lee

Researchers using fMRI and PET scans have learned that multiple parts of the brain are involved in having an orgasm. The thalamus helps integrate information about touch, movement, and any sexual memories or fantasies that someone might call upon to help them reach orgasm. Meanwhile, the hypothalamus is busy producing oxytocin and may help coordinate arousal (Mitrokostas, 2019). During orgasm, the brain releases a surge of dopamine, often referred to as the neurotransmitter of pleasure. But it is more than that; it teaches the brain that whatever is happening is so pleasurable that the brain should seek out this behavior again in the future. Oxytocin (created in the pituitary gland) is also secreted from the brain, specifically, from the hypothalamus. Oxytocin has a reputation as a *bonding hormone* since it is released during breast-feeding and is known to facilitate love and attachment. Prolactin, also associated with breast-feeding, is also released at orgasm to produce a feeling of satisfaction. In men, there is just the single surge of oxytocin and prolactin, but in women oxytocin continues to be released after orgasm, which may explain the desire that most women have for postsex cuddling.

"Surprisingly, the brain doesn't differentiate much between sex and other pleasurable experiences. The parts of your brain that make you feel good after indulging in dessert or winning at poker are the same areas that light up during orgasm" (Mitrokostas, 2019). In this way, to the brain, pleasure is pleasure regardless of the source. The same reward pathways are activated by recreational drug and alcohol use.

In addition to this feel-good neurochemistry, endorphins are released, which makes us less sensitive to pain when we are sexually aroused, which allows us to enjoy things during sex that we would ordinarily find uncomfortable (hair-pulling, a smack on the behind, or a lover's scratch on your back). Interestingly, sexual stimulation and pain stimulation activate the same areas of the brain's cortex, which may help explain how some people can experience sexual pleasure from pain. Or perhaps those sexual facial expressions so similar to those of a person experiencing pain. After orgasm, serotonin is released, which promotes good feelings and relaxation and, in some cases, drowsiness.

In addition to encouraging us to engage in sex due to pleasure, the brain activity during sexual arousal and orgasm appears to be healthy for the brain because of the great increase in blood flow to diverse areas of the brain. The old saying that horny guys act stupid because all of the blood from their brain goes to their penis is not supported. Our bodies are designed to keep sufficient blood flow to the brain at all times. Blood flow into the genitals comes from the body's core, not the brain. However, both men and women are likely thinking less rationally while under the spell of sexual arousal. "The lateral orbitofrontal cortex becomes less active during sex. This is the part of the brain that is responsible for reason, decision making, and value judgments. The deactivation of this part of the brain is also associated with decreases in fear and anxiety," clinical psychologist Daniel Sher told INSIDER (Mitrokostas, 2019). So it appears that it is wisest to make ones important sexual decisions before actually becoming sexually aroused!

As we'll see in the next section of this chapter, Models of Sexual Response, there is much controversy regarding viewing sexual desire and arousal in a purely biomedical way. While drugs like Viagra can help NOS relax genital muscle tissue and facilitate erections, many question whether this really equates to sexual desire. We'll explore this and other issues in the rest of this chapter and in Chapter 12 in the section on sexual dysfunction.

Models of Sexual Response

Four models of sexual response are discussed here. By far the best known is the one by William Masters and Virginia Johnson, pioneers in the study of sexual response.

Masters and Johnson Four Phase Model

In 1966, Masters and Johnson published their ground-breaking work, *Human Sexual Response*. The book was ground-breaking for several reasons. Although previous researchers (Alfred Kinsey being the most notable) had published reports concerning self-reported sexual behavior, Masters and Johnson's was the first large-scale study of sexual response. Masters (a gynecologist) and Johnson (a psychologist) were the first researchers to study sexual response in a laboratory setting. They were the first mainstream scientists to apply the scientific rigor necessary to quantify and qualify a very private act. Their work provided a graphic depiction of the actual sexual processes in action.

Masters and Johnson invented the technology and instruments necessary for studying our most intimate body parts. They devised clear, plastic, penis-shaped cameras to photograph things such as changes in vaginal lubrication. They invented electromyographic devices to measure the most intimate of all muscular contractions, those of the penis, vagina, and anus. Many of these instruments and methods also were used to treat sexual dysfunction. The Masters and Johnson Institute in St.Louis became world-renowned for the study and treatment of sexual dysfunctions.

Besides creating the technology, they operationally defined **orgasm**. An operational definition was a prerequisite for experimental research of the phenomenon. They created a language of sexuality that included words such as *orgasm, vasocongestion, myotonia,* and others, which allowed professionals in the field to communicate with each other and disseminate their research findings.

Orgasm The stage of sexual response characterized by ejaculation in males and involuntary muscular contractions followed by relaxation in both males and females

Masters and Johnson were the first researchers to divide sexual response into phases that blend into one another as sexual response continues. They identified four phases:

1. Excitement
2. Plateau
3. Orgasm
4. Resolution

This sequence was the same regardless of the nature of sexual stimulation (masturbation, intercourse, and so forth) or sexual orientation (heterosexual, homosexual, bisexual) studied. The four stages are depicted in Figure 5.4 for women and Figure 5.5 for men.

Finally, Masters and Johnson discovered that the seat of women's sexual response is the clitoris, not the vagina. This broke new ground for understanding and conducting future research concerning women's sexual response. It opened the door for future research concerning issues such as the **G-spot**, differences in response patterns in women before and after a hysterectomy, and a host of other areas. Heterosexual and lesbian women (as well as their partners) have had the opportunity to apply Masters and

G-spot An area in the upper, rear section of the vagina named after Ernest Grafenberg, who claimed it to be an erogenous zone

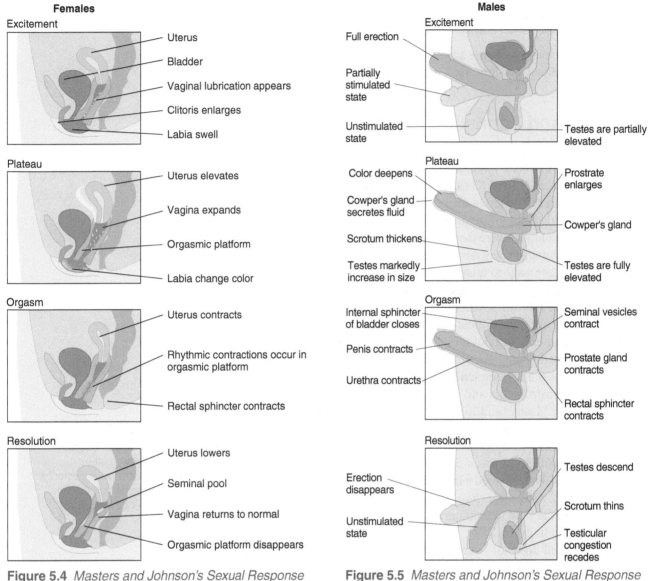

Females

Excitement
- Uterus
- Bladder
- Vaginal lubrication appears
- Clitoris enlarges
- Labia swell

Plateau
- Uterus elevates
- Vagina expands
- Orgasmic platform
- Labia change color

Orgasm
- Uterus contracts
- Rhythmic contractions occur in orgasmic platform
- Rectal sphincter contracts

Resolution
- Uterus lowers
- Seminal pool
- Vagina returns to normal
- Orgasmic platform disappears

Males

Excitement
- Full erection
- Partially stimulated state
- Unstimulated state
- Testes are partially elevated

Plateau
- Color deepens
- Cowper's gland secretes fluid
- Scrotum thickens
- Testes markedly increase in size
- Prostrate enlarges
- Cowper's gland
- Testes are fully elevated

Orgasm
- Internal sphincter of bladder closes
- Penis contracts
- Urethra contracts
- Seminal vesicles contract
- Prostate gland contracts
- Rectal sphincter contracts

Resolution
- Erection disappears
- Unstimulated state
- Testes descend
- Scrotum thins
- Testicular congestion recedes

Figure 5.4 *Masters and Johnson's Sexual Response Cycle in Women* This cycle has four phases.

Figure 5.5 *Masters and Johnson's Sexual Response Cycle in Men* The cycle for men has four phases.

Johnson's discoveries to enhance their sexual pleasure by better understanding their sexual functioning.

Excitement

During the first stage of Masters and Johnson's human sexual response—excitement—sexual arousal is initiated. Excitement can be triggered by a limitless array of cognitive and sensory stimuli ranging from viewing erotic films to listening to romantic music or getting a whiff of a familiar cologne or perfume.

The excitement stage is characterized by engorgement of erectile tissue in the genitals and a buildup of muscle tension throughout the body. The brain processes sensory and motor stimuli as being sexual in nature and passes a message to the hypothalamus, which initiates the nerve and hormonal sexual response.

Many cardiovascular changes are set into motion during excitement. The heart rate increases, and blood vessels throughout the body constrict, raising blood pressure. Blood vessels in the genitals dilate, resulting in increased blood flow to the genitalia. The increased blood flow fills up the spongy tissue that makes up this region. Blood flow into the genitals is greater than outflow. As this tissue fills with blood, it becomes engorged, enlarging in size, deepening in color, and increasing in sensitivity. Masters and Johnson called this engorgement process **vascongestion.** In men, the major changes associated with vasocongestion are erection of the penis and deepening of the color of the genitalia. In women, vasocongestion is responsible for labial swelling, deepening of the color of the vulva, vaginal lubrication, and increased size and sensitivity of the breasts.

Vasocongestion The movement of blood flow into the genitals resulting in a variety of responses, including erection in men and lubrication in women

Prior to Masters' and Johnson's research, sex researchers believed that vaginal lubrication was caused by sweat and oil glands within the vagina. Masters and Johnson discovered, and documented through special intravaginal photography, that lubrication is a by-product of vasocongestion. Vaginal mucosal tissue becomes engorged with blood and produces a clear, slippery fluid that empties from the cells directly into the vagina. They called this process **transudation** and discovered that it was directly linked to the level of sexual excitement. Masters and Johnson found that insufficient lubrication is often the result of too little foreplay and low levels of excitement or high levels of anxiety.

Transudation The production of vaginal lubrication because of sweating of vaginal tissue engorged with blood during vasocongestion

The second characteristic associated with excitement is **myotonia,** the gradual heightened tension in the skeletal muscles throughout the body. Unlike the muscle tension associated with stress, myotonia is a gradual buildup that is progressive and pleasurable. Employing specially developed instruments and methods, Masters and Johnson were able to quantify the level of muscle tension in various parts of the body during sexual arousal. This was done by placing electrodes on strategic parts of the body to measure **electromyographic** activity during sexual arousal.

Myotonia Involuntary skeletal muscle contractions

During excitement in men, the testes elevate, moving closer to the body. In women, the inner two-thirds of the vagina expand, and the uterus is pulled backward.

Electromyographic Refers to measurement of muscle tension through electrical sensors at skin surface

✍ *Physical Wellness* ✍

Physical wellness contributes directly to healthy sexual response. When we are physically fit, our bodies respond and perform better sexually. High-level cardiorespiratory endurance can facilitate maximum blood flow and staying power. Vasocongestion hinges on efficient blood flow through the blood vessels to the genitals. Atherosclerosis, the narrowing and hardening of blood vessels, can inhibit maximum blood flow. Smoking also can speed up atherosclerosis and lead to constriction of blood flow. This affects overall health and also sexual response. Increasing the overall level of fitness (particularly, cardiorespiratory fitness and flexibility), improving the diet (minimizing fats and cholesterol), limiting use of alcohol and other illicit drugs, and maximizing body composition can increase overall physical well-being and improve sexual response.

Although being fit doesn't *ensure* good sex, it can enhance the physiological (body strength and endurance, increased blood flow, and the like) and psychological (higher self-esteem, positive outlook, enhanced body image) components of good sex. Conversely, having a disability or illness, or being unfit, doesn't necessarily preclude sexual satisfaction. People with disabilities and chronic illnesses that impact their sexual response can learn to maximize their sexual potentials and abilities, whatever they are. People who do not have the highest levels of fitness still can have good sex as they work their way toward becoming fit.

Plateau

In the second phase of Masters' and Johnson's sexual response cycle, called the *plateau*, processes set into motion during the excitement phase reach their maximum levels. Vasocongestion creates peak levels of engorgement, color changes, and lubrication; muscular tension also reaches its maximum level.

In men, the testes become fully elevated, and the prostate gland enlarges. The Cowper's gland releases clear, slippery, preejaculatory fluid (we will discuss the sperm-carrying capability of this fluid in Chapter 14). In women, the labia reach their maximum size, the vagina forms the "orgasmic platform," and the clitoris retracts under its protective hood. Both men and women experience a "sex flush," a rashlike reddish tinge to the skin of the chest and back associated with dilation of the blood vessels and increased blood flow in these areas.

Masters and Johnson found that the plateau was the most variable stage in terms of time. More experienced couples, for instance, were able to prolong the plateau if they desired, whereas younger, less sexually experienced subjects had much shorter plateau periods.

© Galina Barskaya, 2010. Shutterstock, Inc.

High-level cardiorespiratory fitness can enhance vasocongestion.

Orgasm

The third phase of Masters and Johnson's response cycle, orgasm, is characterized by the dramatic release of tension and other physiological processes (heart rate, blood pressure, increased breathing, and so on) associated with the excitement and plateau stages. During orgasm, most of the male and female sexual structures undergo rhythmic, muscular contractions. These are responsible for the release of pent-up muscular tension in men and women, and ejaculation in men.

Masters and Johnson found that women have a one-step orgasm, whereas it is a two-step process in men. The first step in men is called **ejaculatory inevitability.** During this step, men sense the release of tension and feel the inevitability of ejaculation. During the next step, **emission** contractions of the vas deferens and other structures move sperm and other ejaculatory fluids through the vas deferens and out of the urethra. Masters and Johnson found that women did not ejaculate during orgasm.

Prior to Masters and Johnson, researchers studying sexual response used much more subjective criteria for determining whether an orgasm had or had not occurred. Masters and Johnson quantified the muscular contractions, fluid expulsions (in men only), and physiological reversals associated with the release of tension as a result of orgasm.

Ejaculatory inevitability The first step in male ejaculation; beginning of smooth-muscle contractions that trigger release of ejaculate

Emission The release of secretions from various organs and glands that produce male ejaculate

Resolution

The last phase of the sexual response cycle is resolution, return of the body to the unaroused state. Masters and Johnson found that after orgasm, the two key physiological processes—vasocongestion and myotonia—reverse. Orgasm triggers the brain to normalize the dilation of blood vessels, heart rate, and blood pressure, allowing blood flow to return to normal and vasocongestion to reverse. With this reversal, the erection begins to shrink, lubrication ceases, and color changes disappear. In addition, the buildup of muscular tension followed by contractions stops, and muscle tissue returns to normal.

Masters and Johnson (1966) coined the term **refractory period** to describe the time required after an orgasm before a person could enter the excitement stage again. They found tremendous variability in this time between men and women, and among individual men. They found that women did not have a refractory period. Women did not need recovery time to get excited again and reach orgasm.

Refractory period The time from last orgasm to the next beginning of excitement

Vasocongestion and lubrication could remain at optimal levels if the source and intensity of stimulation and interest in maintaining activity with the partner were to continue. The significance of this finding was that it proved that women could have multiple orgasms without a refractory period. This is both a difference between men's and women's sexual response patterns and a significant finding in terms of women's ability to extend and enjoy sexual relations if they desire.

For most women in Masters and Johnson's study, however, sexual stimulation ceased after their partner's orgasm. Often, this is because of preset agendas that couples have about trying to achieve orgasm simultaneously or a "me first, then you" pattern in achieving orgasm. In follow-up studies, Masters and Johnson (1976) found that most male partners did not realize that they could continue to stimulate their partners (if desired, through pubic contact or manual/oral stimulation), even if they were to lose their erection.

Unlike women, men need a certain amount of downtime before they can achieve another erection. The amount of time varies significantly. Among the variables related to the amount of time needed to obtain another erection, the most significant were age and time since last orgasm. In general, the younger the man, the shorter the refractory period. The longer the duration since the last orgasm, the shorter the refractory period. Thus, a younger man who hadn't had an orgasm in some time would become re-aroused much more quickly than an older man who recently had an orgasm. Other variables, such as overall level of health, stress, and obesity, were also found to be related to the length of refractory period.

Figures 5.6 and 5.7 show the patterns in sexual response that Masters and Johnson discovered for the men and women in their study. Figure 5.7, their classic cycle for men, shows a steady buildup in excitement followed

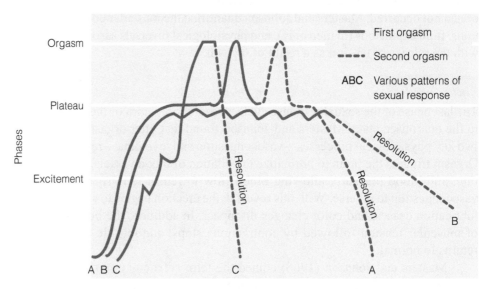

Figure 5.6 *Masters and Johnson's Sexual Response Patterns in Women* Masters and Johnson found three major sexual response patterns in women.
Source: *Human Sexual Response* by W. Masters and V. Johnson (1966).

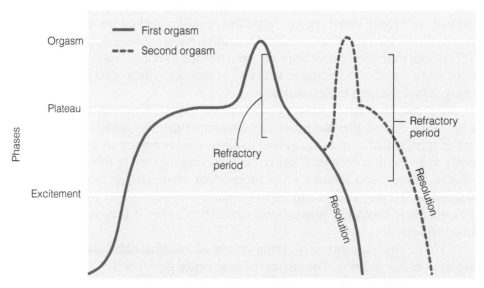

Figure 5.7 *Masters and Johnson's Sexual Response Patterns in Men*
Masters and Johnson found one primary sexual response pattern in men.
Source: *Human Sexual Response* by W. Masters and V. Johnson (1966).

sex in society 5.1

Tantric Sex

For most Americans, orgasm is the whole point of sexual activities. As a culture, we're obsessed with orgasm. We keep track of orgasms like box scores for baseball: number of at-bats (sexual encounters), number of hits (orgasms), and whether they are singles (OK), doubles (slightly better orgasms), triples (really good orgasms), and home runs (really, really, great orgasms). We are not only obsessed with our own orgasms, but we also want to know about our partner's orgasms. "Was it good for you?" we ask. Our ultimate criterion is to achieve simultaneous orgasm with our partner—the ultimate: two home runs at the same time! None of these scoring measures correlates perfectly with sexual satisfaction or healthy sexuality. Frequency, intensity, and mutuality of orgasms vary in their relationship to sexual satisfaction for people.

One can even enjoy sex without orgasm. The idea of having intercourse but intentionally not having an orgasm may seem strange, but that's exactly the point of Tantric sex: an Indian sexual/spiritual practice based on *conserving orgasm*. The origins of Tantra can be traced back over 20,000 years to markings on cave walls that resemble those still in use today in Tantric training. Tantra, originally associated with fertility worship and paganism, is based on the belief that life itself is the result of sex and love.

Sacred temples decorated with the sexual positions of the Kama Sutra were built to provide places of worship for the Tantric religion in India starting in 800 C.E. Indian spiritual leaders taught their disciples about the spiritual power of sexual energy. They believed the energy that emanates from sexual arousal could be shared with one's partner and used to transcend the couple's sexual union to bring them closer to spiritual oneness with a higher power. Tantric sex is part of the spiritual form of yoga. The spiritual form of yoga is practiced to achieve a transcendent state of being (see www.tantric.com).

In the West, the practice of Tantra borrows liberally from Hinduism, Taoism, Buddhism, Native American spirituality, and Wiccan. Disciples view Tantric sex as a spiritual activity that unites partners in transcendence and also as a technique to enhance sexual intensity. Couples focus on sexual pleasuring, not the outcome of orgasm. This de-emphasis on orgasm allows couples to relax and enjoy the sensations without being so goal directed. Some organizations run Tantric sex training programs and retreats.

by a moderate level of plateau. The level of stimulation in the plateau stage reaches its zenith with orgasm. This is followed by the cessation of stimulation and a rapid drop-off into resolution.

Figure 5.6 diagrams multiple orgasms in women. The pattern is similar to that in men, except that following orgasm, stimulation continues and the woman is able to achieve multiple orgasms before entering the resolution phase.

Pattern B in Figure 5.6 shows what happens when the level or type of stimulation is insufficient to trigger orgasm. Excitement builds with the stimulation, and plateau is achieved. The level or type of stimulation, however, lacks the intensity (or stops before it can build to high enough levels) to trigger orgasm, which is responsible for reversing the effects of vasocongestion. This results in a protracted resolution stage until the pelvic area and genitals return to their unaroused levels.

This phenomenon in men has been called "blue balls." Although no equivalent slang term applies to women, females experience similar effects: pelvic congestion, swollen genitalia, throbbing pelvic area, and so on. Although Masters' and Johnson's findings added valuable information about the objective experience of sexual response, the analysis is physiological and is open to a more subjective interpretation.

sex in society 5.2

Rethinking the Role of the Clitoris in Sexual Arousal

Since Master's & Johnson's pioneering research on human sexual response in the 1960s the presence of penile erection and vaginal lubrication have been considered the gold standard as far as proof of sexual arousal in men and women respectively. Clitoral engorgement and erection, though noted in the literature, has not been considered to be as significant an indicator of sexual arousal in women as vaginal lubrication. Recent research findings in sexual anatomy and the physiology of sexual response are shedding new light on the nature of clitoral erection in female sexual arousal.

O'Connell et al (2005) believe that while it is appealing to use a single, simple term, the clitoris, to refer to a "cluster of erectile tissue," it can be misleading, and it de-emphasizes the complexity of female sexual response. Their research, based on autopsies of cadavers and MRI studies shows that the vascular structures of the pelvic area in women (the distal vagina, distal urethra and clitoris including the vestibular bulbs, crura, body and glans) actually form a unified cluster of structures that can be identified using MRI technology and surgical removal.

As we mentioned in Chapter 2, most of the clitoris is not visible before or during sexual arousal. The glans is exposed during sexual arousal but the underlying structures of the clitoris are not. New research suggests that these underlying structures may play a larger role in sexual arousal than previously believed. Johnson (2004) uses an iceberg analogy to explain how the glans of the clitoris is similar to the tip of an iceberg. Most of the mass of the clitoris continues under pelvic bone, turns down and surrounds the vagina from above and both sides. Starting from the exposed glans and working back are the clitoral shaft, two crura, and two vestibular bulbs. The clitoral shaft is about 2.5 centimeters long and, like the penis, contains two corpora cavernosa. The two crura (also referred to as the legs) extend back from the top, and are five to nine centimeters long, anchoring to the hip girdle. Inside of the two crura are the two vestibular bulbs.

Johnson (2004) and O'Connel et al (2005) found that the underlying structures are richly endowed with nerve endings and all, with the exception of the glans, are comprised of erectile tissue that engorge with blood during sexual arousal. Johnson (2004) and O'Connell et al (2005) have found that these underlying structures also surround the female urethra and their contractions during sexual arousal squeeze the urethra shut. Johnson (2004) believes that so-called "vaginal" or "G Spot" orgasms and female ejaculation are a byproduct of these underlying structures working in consort with the urethra and its paraurethral glands. In their findings on cadavers and on MRI analysis, O'Connell et al (2005) "did not reveal any additional structure separate from the bulbs, glans, or corpora of the clitoris, urethra and vagina that could be regarded as the G spot." Furthermore, O'Connell et al's (2005) findings clearly indicate that the erectile tissue of these interrelated vascular structures wrap around the urethra and vagina forming a midline core to the clitoris.

O'Connell et al (2005) believe that referring to this cluster of vascular structures as a unified entity with a different name would provide a new, inclusive way to describe female sexual anatomy. Such an inclusive description, O'Connell et al (2005) and Johnson (2004) believe, would end artificial discussions of female sexual response that separate clitoral from vaginal orgasms and highlight individual areas within this region such as the "G Spot" that are actually interrelated.

For instance, even though an orgasm, according to Masters' and Johnson, is characterized by a certain number of muscular contractions at a certain intensity and other physiological parameters, a person could have an enjoyable sexual experience without having an official Masters and Johnson orgasm.

What operationalizing a concept such as orgasm does is to allow us to study it more rigorously. For instance, if researchers want to study the effects of alcohol on orgasm, their research will be easier and more accurate if they are able to operationally define orgasm. The same kind of rigor need not enter into our human relations.

Kaplan's Triphasic Model of Sexual Response

Helen Singer Kaplan (1974) disagreed with Masters' and Johnson's four-phase sexual response cycle. She argued that the model neglects the importance of sexual desire in human sexual response. Furthermore, she agreed with others in the field who claimed that the plateau stage is really indistinguishable from excitement and that the two stages would more appropriately be merged together.

Kaplan's original model had two stages: excitement and orgasm. She modified it, however, after her work with dysfunctional individuals and couples revealed that many of them had problems with low levels of interest in sex. She then proposed a triphasic model of sexual response that included the phases of desire, excitement, and orgasm (Kaplan, 1985). She placed most of the emphasis on desire and the role of the brain in initiating sexual response.

Desire

During the desire phase, some activating thought, emotion, fantasy, or sensation arises in the cortex or limbic system and triggers the activation of neural and hormonal sexual stimulation. The emphasis here is on the key role the cerebral cortex plays in initiating sexual response, and the subjective, emotional nature of arousal. As we mentioned at the beginning of this chapter, the brain is the sexiest organ in the body and plays the key role in determining whether the sexual response continues.

Excitement

Kaplan accepted Masters' and Johnson's findings concerning the physiology of sexual arousal. She agreed that vasocongestion is the key physiological process involved in excitement. She disagreed, however, with the idea of separating the plateau from excitement. She argued that the plateau is really nothing more than end-stage excitement or culmination of the excitement phase. When excitement peaks, the person reaches the plateau, or level of maximum arousal. As such, however, to clinically distinguish plateau from excitement is next to impossible, and, therefore, the two phases should be merged.

Orgasm

Once again, Kaplan accepted Masters' and Johnson's findings concerning the physiology of orgasm. She also described orgasm as the one phase that is clearly distinguishable for most people. Unlike the transition from desire to excitement, which is hard to pinpoint, the onset of orgasm is an event most people readily identify.

Criticisms of Kaplan's and Masters' and Johnson's Models

Although Kaplan's model of sexual response is important because it expands Masters' and Johnson's conceptualization by adding the dimension of desire to the cycle, it still left gaps in fully understanding the nature of sexual response in men and women.

Lieblum (2000), a renowned sex therapist and educator, notes how Kaplan's model doesn't always match up to women's experiences of sexual response. Lieblum describes how many women do not have spontaneous feelings of sexual desire, and for those who do, it doesn't always lead to arousal. She found that most women rely on their male partners to initiate sexual activity, and they may or may not participate, depending on a host of sexual and nonsexual factors, such as intimacy.

Lieblum adds that for many women *and* men, arousal comes *before* desire. A man's morning erection may trigger feelings of desire and interest in initiating intercourse with a partner. The feeling of pleasurable genital sensations or touch may ignite feelings of desire in women. In other words, the order of the response is reversed from what Kaplan found.

Lastly, Lieblum (2000) found that Kaplan's and Masters' and Johnson's models do not take subjective feelings of sexual satisfaction into account. A purely physiological explanation of sexual response is inadequate, according to Lieblum, because it doesn't attend to the subjective feelings of satisfaction or dissatisfaction, which contribute greatly to future desire and arousal. For many women, satisfaction with sexual activity with their partner did not necessarily revolve around whether or not they had an orgasm (as it usually does with men).

❧ Emotional Wellness ❧

Good sexual response hinges on our emotional well-being. As Lieblum, Basson, and the other sexual response theorists in this chapter point out, our sexual response involves both physiological and psychological variables. We have to be in the right frame of mind for vasocongestion to happen. When we are nervous, angry, sad, worried, or in a number of other negative emotional states, we have trouble relaxing enough to allow our brain to trigger efficient vasocongestion. Even if we allow ourselves to become sexually excited, we may not be able to have an orgasm. The best sex is usually when we are able to let down our guard, free our mind, and relax. High-level emotional wellness allows us to do this. We are in control of our emotions; they don't control us. We feel good about ourselves and about our partners, and we trust ourselves and our partners enough to relax and let the sexual responses happen.

sex in society 5.3

Expanding Your Perception of Lovemaking and Orgasm

Sex is a goal-oriented activity for many people. It seems they view sex as a race, with both partners competing to see who crosses first with an orgasm. Even better, both partners cross at the same time and have the ultimate prize—mutual orgasms. The prize is the perfect orgasm, achieved together. The ultimate victory is the quest for perfect sex. Is this really the best sex? Is sex best viewed as a competition, a race? We like to think of sex as more of a multicourse gourmet meal. With each course the couple anticipates something special, a unique taste delight.

A before-dinner aperitif sets the mood for the evening and whets the appetite for the next course, appetizers. Appetizers delight the palate. They come in an infinite variety, each with its own special ability to please.

Next comes a soup, followed by a special salad. Each tickles the taste buds and is savored for its uniqueness. Between these courses we pause and have a refreshing sorbet to cleanse the palate. We stop and sit back, savoring the exquisite gastronomical delights we've already sampled, and we eagerly anticipate the rest of the meal to follow. We enjoy good conversation and admiring looks.

The entree comes next—not too much food, just enough to satisfy our cravings and delight our palate.

We pause again to savor our meal before dessert is served. Dessert provides just a taste of sweetness to round off our meal.

Finally, we sit back, sipping our after-dinner brandy. This brings our meal to a close.

When we eat a meal such as this, who can argue that the entree is the only or most important part of the meal? Sometimes the entree isn't as special as the other parts of the meal, and we only sample it. We can view lovemaking as a feast, a multicourse meal that first involves the buildup of desire through kissing, hugging, massage, and noncoital foreplay.

The lovemaking continues with a variety of techniques including oral sex, vaginal intercourse, and so on, extending the plateau as long as we desire. We pause frequently to talk, laugh, touch, have a drink, and the like. We continue into and through orgasm, and we finish by staying coupled and basking in each other's pleasure until we go limp.

If we envision sex as a feast for the senses rather than as a race, perhaps we will enjoy our orgasms more when they occur, and not feel as though we've missed something if we don't have them once in a while.

Stayton's Spiritual/Theological Model

William Stayton (2002), a Baptist minister, has an interesting spiritual/theological perspective on sexual response and pleasure. In 1965, in his early years as a minister, Stayton was asked by his church's youth group to develop an education program on sexuality. He admits to have been both excited and scared by the prospect. He was excited because he felt such information was needed and who better than the church to provide it to the congregation. He was afraid, however, because sex was very controversial, and he was not sure how his congregation would view his program.

⤷ *Spiritual Wellness* ⤶

By definition, spirituality revolves around transcending ourselves and connecting with something greater than ourselves. Whether we believe our spirituality connects us with God, some higher power, or all other living things, transcendence of the self is the key to spirituality. We've often heard people describe orgasm in terms of feeling "uplifted," "out of this world," or "at one with the universe." We believe the transcendence that orgasm offers is inherent in our sexual response and not totally reliant on our emotional connections to another. We also believe, however, that sex and orgasm with someone we love and are committed to gives a heightened level of spirituality. Sharing an intense orgasm with another person can, at times, make you feel instantly at one with the universe. If one positive human experience is capable of linking all of us together, it just might be orgasm. Humans and other animals seem to share the ability to respond sexually to one another. Sexual activity with a partner, by its nature, connects us to someone else in a unique way. A high level of spiritual wellness can help us form sexual relationships based on caring and mutual respect, instead of exploitation and disrespect.

His fears were assuaged when 60 young people, parental permission slips in hand, showed up for his first session. His program was such a success that the local school district asked him to develop a curriculum for the Glouchester, Massachusetts, Board of Education.

Stayton's basic premise is that it is not by coincidence that sexual response is undeniably pleasurable. The theological significance of sexual pleasure and response is that God created humans in such a way to respond to sexual pleasure. He cites Masters' and Johnson's discovery of the clitoris as the center of sexual response in women as evidence that God intended humans to be sexual creatures and enjoy this blessing. Why else would he make such an organ that has no other function except to provide sexual pleasure?

Stayton uses sexual research about sexual response as proof that God created humans with the ability to derive extreme pleasure from loving each other. In fact, Jesus' core teachings were about love. Stayton explains that Jesus, God's son, never, even in his teachings of self-denial, condemns sexual pleasure. Jesus' primary teachings revolved around love, not condemnation of pleasure. Stayton's "theology of sexual pleasure" is that love, spirituality, and sexuality are inextricably bound together and that God created people who are sexual in the fullest sense of the word. To be fully sexual in God's world is to be both physical and spiritual.

Love, Stayton believes, has both sexual and spiritual dimensions. Why would God create in us the ability to feel such intense sexual pleasure if it were not his intention to connect it to the pursuit of love? Doesn't "making love" have a strong spiritual component that transcends the act of sexual intercourse with the loved one? Aren't we truly at one with the universe when making love to another person?

Steve and Tracy: What Good Sex Means to Us

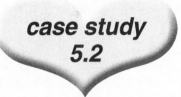

case study 5.2

Steve is a senior majoring in small business administration. He took some time off after high school and worked in construction before starting college. Tracy is an education major and a fifth-year senior, having worked her way full-time through college.

STEVE: Good sex to me is being able to relax with my partner. With Tracy, I don't have to worry about anything. I trust her.

TRACY: Yeah, that's it—trust. Before I met Steve, I went through a lot of one-night stands or real short relationships where I think the guys just wanted to get laid. I never felt I could trust any of them.

PROFESSOR: What do you mean by "trust them"?

TRACY: I guess I mean trust them about *anything*. Would they respect me and my wishes? Would they have my interests at heart or just their own? I also was worried about pregnancy and disease. Could I trust them to be disease-free, wear a condom, those sort of things? Oh, yeah, I also wanted to be able to trust that they'd respect my privacy. I didn't want them to go bragging to their friends about me or tell other people the most intimate aspects of my sex life.

STEVE: I feel the same way. I like to be able to let down my guard in order to enjoy sex. I guess you could say that, for me, it's sexy to be vulnerable with a woman. With Tracy, I can tell her about my desires, concerns, and fears, and trust her to act in my best interests. I remember telling one woman I had sex with that I liked it when she played with my anus during sex but that I always worried that this might mean I was gay. I later found out she had told this to a sorority sister, and before long everyone in the house knew, as well as some members of the fraternity they were little sisters to.

PROFESSOR: How does trust affect your sexual response?

TRACY: For me, it allows me to let down my guard and relax. I trust Steve completely, and that allows my mind and body to relax. I've never been as responsive with anyone else as I am with Steve. I can get sexually aroused and have an orgasm with very little effort.

STEVE: I feel the same way. With Tracy, I feel so relaxed that things just naturally happen. I remember with other women worrying that I might not perform up to their standards, and that made it real difficult to get excited and erect. I know I can please Tracy, and even if I have an off-night, she'll understand and not use it against me.

TRACY: I hope I don't make it seem that because I'm so relaxed, there's no spark or sexual tension between Steve and me. Nothing can be farther from the truth. Even though I'm completely relaxed in bed with him, I can get aroused just thinking about sex with him. I hope this never changes.

Critical Thinking

How has trust, or lack of trust, in a sexual partner influenced your enjoyment of sex with that person? What role would trust play in your future sexual relationships?

Stayton believes that God intended sex researchers to continue his mission by guiding them to understand more about this gift he bestowed on us. Like theologians who interpret God's word through studying the Bible, sex researchers interpret God's gift of sexual pleasure by studying sexual response.

Lastly, Stayton believes that when people combine love, sex, and spirituality, God's intentions are born anew in the world. Sexual pleasure is not a hindrance to God's mission; it is part of it. He cites "creation" as something God did for humans but also as something God intended to create us to be able to derive sexual pleasure through our love for each other and to create new life.

Basson's Model

The newest sexual response model was developed by Rosemary Basson, a sex therapist, in 1999. Basson's (2000) model is both similar to and different from those that preceded it, and grew out of her work as a sex therapist. As we will see in Chapter 12, traditional diagnostic criteria for sexual dysfunction are based on the widely accepted sexual response phases of Masters and Johnson (arousal, and orgasm) and Kaplan's (desire) models. Basson does not believe that these models hold the key to treating women with sexual dysfunction. A new model of sexual response in women was needed, one that would serve as the basis for treating women's sexual dysfunction.

Basson does not take issue with the physiology of sexual response. She doesn't dispute the physiological processes involved in arousal, orgasm, and resolution. Her dispute is with the interplay of psychosocial and physiological factors during sexual arousal, and the lumping of men's and women's sexual response patterns together.

Basson also believes, like Walen and Roth (1987), that cognitive factors continually mediate the physiology of sexual response. Positive thoughts and feelings (trust, caring, happiness) about one's partner are necessary for intimacy to exist and for sexual response to occur. Negative thoughts and feelings (anger, fear, unhappiness) can sabotage intimacy and make desire and arousal difficult, if not impossible.

Basson's model also revolves around the premise of gender-based differences in sexual response between men and women. Basson believes that emotional factors and intimacy issues are central to understanding sexual response in women. She feels that female sexual response doesn't begin with desire or arousal as it does in men; it begins with intimacy. Basson believes that for many women, the starting point for the sexual response cycle is not the desire for sex (physical sexual release) but the desire for intimacy (being close emotionally and physically with one's partner).

The desire to initiate intimate contact could occur either for positive reasons or to avoid negative consequences. For instance, a woman could initiate an intimacy because she wants to hug and talk, to get close to her partner (positive reason). She might also initiate intimacy because she feels she has neglected her husband (or vice versa), and she doesn't want this to create any anger, resentment, or displeasure in her relationship with him.

Alyssa: A Case of Fear and Mistrust

Alyssa is a college junior. She recently broke up with Carla, her girlfriend of 2 years. She and Carla had been having sex for about 1.5 years. Alyssa has had little sexual desire and some problems having an orgasm ever since she broke up with Carla about 3 months ago.

COUNSELOR: Tell me about what's been troubling you.

ALYSSA: I've been having a hard time having an orgasm lately when I have sex. I seem to be able to get excited, but something seems to keep me from being able to come.

COUNSELOR: Have you ever had this kind of problem before?

ALYSSA: No, I never had problems coming when I was going out with Carla.

COUNSELOR: When did you break up with Carla?

ALYSSA: About 3 months ago.

COUNSELOR: How many times have you had sex since then?

ALYSSA: I still masturbate about twice a week, but I've had sex only four or five times—once with a woman I met at a party and the other times with a gal from one of my classes. In each case, I didn't have sex on the first date, only after we went out a couple of times.

COUNSELOR: Do you achieve orgasm when you masturbate?

ALYSSA: Yes. Always.

COUNSELOR: Tell me about your feelings toward these two women.

ALYSSA: The first woman, Jill, is fun to be around. She's a real party gal, likes to dance, go to karaoke bars. . . . We have a good time together, but I worry about her past. I try to talk to her about her past sex life, but she kind of blows it off. It's hard to talk about this stuff. One of my girlfriends told me that she heard that Jill was bisexual and has had a lot of different sexual partners in her life. This worries me. I don't want to get AIDS.

COUNSELOR: What are you doing about this?

ALYSSA: I insisted that we practice safe sex until we got to know each other better. It basically worked. We didn't go down on each other and got off other ways, but I got the sense that she really wasn't into it. She's never said as much, but I could pick it up from her attitude. It didn't make for great sex. I kind of anticipated that it was going to be a problem, so it put a damper on things for me. I never really relaxed. I didn't come.

COUNSELOR: Tell me about the other woman.

ALYSSA: The other woman, Luz, is very nice. I know her from class last year, and she's in my psychology class this semester. She asked me out when she

case study 5.3

Critical Thinking

How is the issue of trust in lesbian and gay relationships similar to and different from that in heterosexual relationships? What special trust issues might gay and lesbian people face that heterosexuals don't?

found out I broke up with Carla. She was very tender and understanding. She encouraged me to talk about Carla and get a lot of things out. We've had sex a few times, but I still haven't been able to come.

Luz has a real temper. I've seen her almost lose it a couple of times over silly things like getting cut off by another driver on the highway. She seems to respect me, but I worry about her going ballistic on me if I ever get on her bad side. I can't fully relax around her when we're in bed. I've heard of date rape, and I'm afraid if I ever refuse her because I'm not in the mood for sex, she might force me. Not a real good way to start a relationship, huh?

In either case, the primary motivation isn't a feeling of sexual tension and the desire for sexual release. It was a desire for intimacy.

The woman herself may have no conscious feeling of need of sexual release (desire) to initiate an intimate connection with her partner. Once the intimate connection is made, however, classic stimuli (internal and external) for sexual arousal are introduced.

The woman's partner may tell her he finds her attractive, desirable, and the like (internal stimuli). They may hug, listen to music, or share a bath (external stimuli). Desire and arousal emerge from these elements of intimacy between them. In many cases, the woman makes a conscious decision to become aroused.

Basson (2004) points out a problem with using the same models and evidence of sexual arousal in men and women. Studies in men traditionally have pointed to erection and other physiological changes as evidence of sexual arousal and desire. While this is adequate in most cases for studying men because most men equate physical arousal with desire, it may not be suitable for use as the model and evidence for studying sexual response in all women. Basson (2004) feels that while women might show *evidence* of sexual arousal (vaginal lubrication and clitoral engorgement) this may not be an accurate indicator of their true arousal. Using the latest magnetic resonance imaging (MRI) technology, Basson (2004) found that women's *subjective* experience and description of arousal does not always correlate with her *objective* physiological (vaginal lubrication, clitoral structures engorged with blood, etc.) *evidence* of arousal. What this research suggests is that even though women show genital physiological evidence of sexual arousal, this doesn't always correlate with their thinking about and feeling desire and arousal in their brain.

Another difference in Basson's theory is her belief that desire *follows* arousal and results in greater levels of arousal. Because the two are so closely related, it is often difficult to distinguish when one starts and the other ends. Basson believes that sexual response in this sense is more circular than linear. A woman doesn't move from intimacy to arousal and then to desire, and then to orgasm, and so forth. Intimacy leads to arousal, which sparks desire, which leads to greater feelings of intimacy, which leads to higher levels of arousal and therefore more desire. The cycle could end in orgasm, but it doesn't have to in order for the woman to feel satisfied and desire more intimacy. At every point in the cycle, cognitive factors (positive or negative) affect what is going on. Levels of desire, arousal, and satisfaction are always mediated by the subjective perception of cognitive factors such as trust, mistrust, fear, anger, and so on (Basson, 2002).

Another key difference is the reference to an end point of sexual response other than orgasm or resolution. Basson believes that a subjective end point relating to satisfaction is critical to understanding women's sexual response. Many women, she found, report enjoying a sexual encounter, even if it didn't end in orgasm. Men typically equate satisfaction with orgasm, but Basson found that for many women, that wasn't the case. Rather than equate "good" sexual response with achieving orgasm, Basson feels that sexual response should be evaluated on whether the person enjoyed the experience. In fact, attaining orgasm may not always be related to an enjoyable sexual encounter. Lieblum (2000) found that men and women can go through an entire sexual response cycle (including orgasm) while reporting that the encounter wasn't enjoyable. Consequently, Basson feels there should be some end point such as feelings of satisfaction, disappointment, frustration, and so on, that characterizes the cycle rather than just the presence of orgasm.

Reed's Erotic Stimulus Pathway Model

Source: Callista Lee

Psychiatrist David Reed reinterpreted the work of Masters & Johnson and Kaplan to focus on a more psychological and interpersonal approach to sexual response. He labeled his four stages in order as Seduction, Sensations, Surrender, and Reflection. The first stage, seduction, correlates with Kaplan's stage of desire. But Reed adds that during seduction, people engage in behaviors that they believe will make them more sexually attractive to a potential partner. These include they way they dress, making eye contact, flirting, nonsexual touching, sending love notes, engaging in self-disclosure (to increase emotional intimacy), offering small gifts, and signaling desire for sex. Reed's sensations stage includes what Masters and Johnson include in their stages of excitement and early plateau. He suggests that heightened sensations, fantasy, and imagination feed sexual arousal. Reed views orgasm as surrender; giving over oneself both mentally and physically to the sensations of the sexual peak. He views the period after orgasm not just as a time to return to normal but as an important psychological phase of reflection; the opportunity to interpret the emotional and physical feelings of the sexual encounter and to consider whether this is something they would want to do again with this partner under similar circumstances.

Feeling secure and being safe are essential to healthy sexuality. Our sexual response depends on a safe and comfortable environment. If we can't relax and feel safe and secure, we won't be able to relax enough to let the sexual response flow.

Have you ever been in a strange house as a guest and felt uncomfortable having sex? Think about being in a strange environment (your boyfriend's/girlfriend's fraternity/sorority house, a tent in a campground, a bed and breakfast with thin walls, your partner's parent's house) and how it feels to try to relax fully and let your sexual response flow. Even meeting potential sex partners requires a safe environment.

Think about going out to a bar, club, or other public place and feeling that people there don't like you or want you around, or having to suppress your natural urges to hold hands, dance, or make out. This is what many gay and lesbian people face every day in trying to meet potential friends and lovers. This environment may also include the work site.

personal exploration activity

How Do You See Yourself?

How we feel about our bodies can either enhance or inhibit sexual response and pleasure. Our society places an incredible emphasis on looks, thus often leading us to have very unrealistic expectations about how we should look. The goal of this activity is to encourage you to take a realistic look at your body and accept who you are.

Take a full sheet of paper, and cover the entire page with a drawing of your body. You do not need to be an artist, but be as realistic as possible. Make your drawing a nude one of yourself. Once you have drawn your body, put an X over the parts of your body that you think need work and a star over the parts of your body that you like or that inspire pride. Once you have finished, your entire body should be clothed in X's or stars. Take a minute and write a short analysis of what has influenced your view of your body and how this view affects the way you respond in a romantic relationship, both physically and psychologically. Conclude by making a contract with yourself to work on the parts that you are really willing to change, or accept yourself as you are and like who you are. Lack of body acceptance has a very negative impact on our sexuality, so eliminate this by loving and accepting who you are.

References

Bancroft, J. (2002, February). Biological factors in human sexuality. *Journal of Sex Research, 39*(1), 15–21.

Basson, R. (2000). The female sexual response: A different model. *Journal of Marital Therapy, 26,* 51–65.

Basson, R. (2002). Are our definitions of women's desire, arousal and sexual pain disorders too broad and our definition of orgasmic disorder too narrow? *J Sex Marital Ther.* 2002 Jul–Sep; 28(4): 289–300.

Basson, R. (2004). Recent advances in women's sexual function and dysfunction. *Menopause.* 2004 Nov–Dec; 11(6 Pt 2): 714–25.

Bergeson, L. (2005). The Big Organic O. Utne Reader no. 129 (May/June 2005) pp. 20–1.

Cama, E., Colleluori, D. M., Emig, F. A., Shin, H, Kim, S. W., Kim, N. N., Traish, A. M., Ash, D. E., Christianson DW. (2003). Human arginase II: crystal structure and physiological role in male and female sexual arousal. *Biochemistry.* 2003 Jul 22; 42(28): 8445–51.

deTejada, I. S. (2002). Molecular mechanisms for the regulation of penile smooth muscle contractility. *International Journal of Impotence Research* 2002 (14) Supplement 1, pp. 6–10.

Fisher, H. (2004). Why we love; the nature and chemistry of romantic love. New York: Henry Holt and Company.

Johnson, J. (2004). Exposed at last; the truth about your clitoris. pp. 387–389. In Worcester N., Whatley, M. H. (2004). *Women's Health: readings on Social, Economic, and Political Issues.* Dubuque IA: Kendall/Hunt Publishing.

Kaplan, H. S. (1974). *The new sex therapy.* New York: Times Books.

Kaplan, H. S. (1985). *Comprehensive evaluation of disorders of sexual desire.* Washington, DC: American Psychiatric Press.

Ladas, A., Whipple, R., & Perry, T. (1982). *The G-spot.* New York: Holt, Rinehart, & Winston.

Lemonick, M. (2004). The Chemistry of Desire. Time, Jan 19th, 2004, pp. 62–68.

Lieblum, S. R. (2000, November). Redefining female sexual response. *Contemporary Obstetrics and Gynecology, 45*(11), 120–131.

Martini, F. (2005). *Fundamentals of Anatomy and Physiology*, 5th Edition. San Francisco: Benjamin Cummings Publishing.

Masters, W., & Johnson, V. (1966). *Human sexual response.* Boston: Little, Brown.

Masters, W., & Johnson, V. (1976). *The pleasure bond.* New York: Bantam.

Munarriz, R., Kim N. N., Goldstein, I., Traish, A. M. (2002). Biology of female sexual function. *Urol Clin North Am.* 2002 Aug 29(3):685–93.

O'Connell, H. E., Sanjeevan, K. V., Hutson J. M. (2005). Anatomy of the clitoris. *J Urol.* 2005 Oct;174 (4 Pt 1):1189–95.

Reagan, P. C. (1999, Spring). Hormonal correlates and causes of sexual desire: A review. *Canadian Journal of Human Sexuality, 8*(1), 1–29.

Scelfo, J. (2002). Bored with sleeping? Sleep and Sex. Newsweek v. 140 no. 3 (July 15 2002) p. 45

Stayton, W. R. (2002, April–May). A theology of sexual pleasure. *SIECUS Report, 30*(4), 27–30.

Traish, A. M., Kim, N. N., Munarriz, R., & Goldstein, I. (2002, October). Biochemical and physiological mechanisms of female genital sexual arousal. *Archives of Sexual Behavior, 31*(5), 393–400.

Traish, A. M., Kim, N., Min, K., Munarriz, R., Goldstein, I. (2002a). Role of androgens in female genital sexual arousal: receptor expression, structure, and function. Fertil Steril. 2002 Apr; 77 Suppl 4: S11–8.

Chapter six

Sensuality and Sexual Behavior

Student Learning Objectives

After reading this chapter, students will be able to

- ☞ Compare and contrast sensuality and sexuality.
- ☞ Compare and contrast celibacy and abstinence.
- ☞ Describe a variety of non-penetrative sexual behaviors.
- ☞ Evaluate the myths associated with masturbation.
- ☞ Compare and contrast a variety of positions for vaginal intercourse.
- ☞ Identify the factors associated with healthy anal sexual behavior.
- ☞ Describe a variety of oral sex behaviors.
- ☞ Explain the effects of spinal cord injury on sexual behavior.

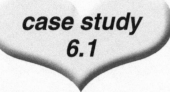

case study 6.1

Delores: Sex in Pregnancy

Delores is a 26-year-old nontraditional sophomore. She is married and the mother of a 6-month-old son, Greg. Delores describes her sexual experiences during her pregnancy.

Before I got pregnant, I was very concerned about the effects it would have on my sex life with my husband, Joe. We were married for 3 years and had a very satisfying sex life. I was worried about that changing. I've always liked sex, and I've kept in shape through running and lifting weights. I was concerned about gaining weight and my body changing shape. But I decided that I wouldn't limit my weight gain and make the baby suffer.

During the first trimester, my sex drive dropped a lot. I wasn't as horny as I normally was, and I had terrible morning sickness. Actually, I had morning, afternoon, and evening sickness and could hardly keep any food down. Other than that, though, nothing much changed. The frequency of sex dropped in half, but the kinds of things we did—positions—didn't change.

During the second trimester, my morning sickness disappeared, and I felt much better. I had put on some weight, but it really didn't affect our intercourse. I was concerned about bouncing around too much and things like rolling off the bed, but for the most part we didn't change our behaviors. The good news was that my sex drive returned to normal.

During the third trimester, things changed again. I had put on over 20 pounds and had a big belly. I was really concerned about deep penetration. I worried that it might hurt the baby, but my doctor reassured me that everything would be OK. I didn't have much energy, so we made love less often. We couldn't use any man- or woman-on-top positions. I've always liked the woman-on-top position with me sitting on my husband's lap, and I had to give that up, too.

I found that the only position we could use was the spoon [side-by-side] position. That allowed us to have full-body contact without putting pressure on my belly. It also allowed my husband to massage my breasts and belly. I had no desire for him to perform oral sex on me, but sometimes I liked to satisfy him that way, particularly on those days when I didn't have much energy. Overall, I think our sex life survived my pregnancy very well.

Critical Thinking

Pregnancy is a time of physical, emotional, social, and other changes. Pregnant women and their partners react to these changes in a myriad of ways in regards to sexual response and desire. If you have never been pregnant, how do you think being pregnant will influence your sexual desire and response? If you have been pregnant before, how did it influence your sexual response and desire? How can pregnant women and their partners maintain or enhance their sexual desire and response during this period?

As Delores has shown us, one's sensuality and sexual behavior manifest themselves in many ways. In this chapter, we'll start by examining sensuality and how it is related to sexual behavior. Then we'll consider the full range of sexual behaviors, starting with celibacy.

Sensuality

As we discussed in Chapter 5, sexual response originates in our brain and senses. But what *is* sensuality? What makes a person sensual? Is it the richness and texture of her features (thick, long hair; distinct, angular nose; high cheekbones; long, exotic nails; tantalizing perfume/cologne; self-assured body language)? Is it his attitude (a deep thinker, caring/loving personality, down-to-earth simplicity)? Could it be her appreciation of life (enjoys great food, appreciates music, likes nature, enjoys physical activities)? We will answer these questions and provide hints on how to enhance and develop one's sensuality since it is the basis for all sexual response and behavior.

Although they are intimately related, sexuality and sensuality are different. **Sensuality** is the quality of being sensual, of experiencing life fully through all of the senses. **Sexuality,** you will remember, is a broad term that refers to all aspects of being sexual, encompassing a variety of biological, psychological, and cultural variables.

Sensuality Experiencing things through all five senses

Sexuality Broad term that refers to all aspects of being sexual

Sensuality is a part of our sexuality. People who are very sensual have a heightened awareness of sight, sound, taste, touch, and smell. They use this increased awareness to experience life through all of these senses whenever possible. They approach each experience, every day, through this context or frame of reference. A walk in the woods or down a bustling city street is a symphony of sounds, colors, scents, tastes, and textures (Spayde, 2001).

This increased sensitivity to and appreciation of all sensory stimuli carries over into their sexuality and lovemaking. The heightened awareness of all the senses enhances lovemaking. Sensual lovers delight in all aspects of their partners and their surroundings, making sex a feast for the senses. Sex isn't just a genital-driven quest for orgasm. It is a five-course gourmet meal that may include climax as the entree.

Developing Sensuality

William Burnham, a pioneering educational psychologist, believed that all humans are born as sensual creatures (Burnham, 1932). As newborns, we experience life through all of our senses. Burnham referred to this as being "fully integrated." Little separates our intellect and our senses. A good example of this integration is how children play in the grass.

Think about how toddlers play in the grass. They roll around in it, close their eyes, lie back in it, and listen to the sounds the wind makes as it blows through the high blades. They pull out handfuls of grass, throw them up in the air, and watch the blades fall to earth. They take a blade of grass and examine it carefully, rolling it around in their fingers, maybe even against their cheeks with their eyes closed. As they squeeze the grass between their fingers, they notice that oils are secreted. They smell this oil and taste it. Satiated with the grass, they move on to the next activity.

How many of us as adults take the time to get into the "grassiness" of life anymore? Have we lost our ability to revel in the "grassiness," or do we still have it but don't utilize it? We authors believe that we still have the ability to be fully integrated with the Here and Now of our lives but do not take advantage of it as often as we could. Along the course of our lives, most of us, for many reasons, stop experiencing life with all of our senses. We pay less and less attention to anything other than sight and sound (the primary senses we need to get through our work day). Of course we still occasionally remark about "how good something tastes" or how "nice something smells," but these observations are more often than not isolated and not part of our overall orientation to life.

Types of Sexual Behavior

One way to present the many forms of sexual behavior is to place them on a continuum from celibacy to oral/anal sex. This presentation is useful in understanding safer sex options, as well as choices in fertility control.

■ Celibacy and Abstinence

Celibacy Abstaining from sexual intercourse

Celibacy is defined as abstaining from sexual intercourse. Although the formal definition of celibacy refers specifically to abstaining from sexual intercourse and never marrying, many people assume that celibacy and abstinence mean total avoidance of all forms of sexual release and the absence of sexual desire. Celibacy may or may not include masturbation and fantasy as forms of sexual release.

Celibate people also have varying degrees of sexual desire. Not all celibate people lack sexual interest and desire; they merely choose to channel that energy and desire into different avenues of expression.

Celibacy is usually associated with a spiritual or religious sacrifice and is considered to be a lifelong commitment. Priests and nuns, for instance, declare a vow of celibacy so they may devote themselves fully to serving God and never marry. It is a conscious, willful diversion of sexual energy into nonsexual activity. Kathleen Norris (1996) uses the phrase "celibate passion" to describe how celibate monks are able to transform sexual energy into a sense of deep caring and love that she found to be unique among celibate people.

Not all people who choose celibacy, however, do so as part of a religious commitment. Actually, all of us choose to wait before we engage in intercourse. Many people choose celibacy because they are not ready to begin having intercourse, and they satisfy their sexual needs through other behaviors. We all develop at our own pace, and some of us are simply not ready as soon as others are.

We sometimes choose celibacy because we need time to recover or grieve from relationships that have ended. We need time to heal emotionally and are not interested in forming sexual relationships at the time. Others choose celibacy because they do not have the time or energy to sustain a commitment (sexual or otherwise) with another person. They think they need all of their energy for school or work, especially if they are beginning a new career or starting school. They don't want to divert time and energy from these areas. Some students find being celibate helps them focus more attention on their schoolwork and improve their academic performance (Rajen, 2004). Netting & Burnett (2004) found that about 30 percent of the students they studied in a 30-year prospective study in British Columbia, Canada were celibate.

Abstinence Self-restraint or self-denial, as in not engaging in sexual activity

The generic definition of **abstinence** is self-restraint or self-denial. Sexual abstinence, therefore, refers to self-restraint or self-denial of sexual activities (Foston, 2004). Many people assume that abstinence means denial of all forms of sexual behavior. Actually, one can choose to abstain from unprotected intercourse but not other forms of sexual behavior. Abstinence usually is not discussed as a lifelong spiritual or religious commitment. It is more situational; a person can abstain for a day, a week, a month, a semester, and so on. It doesn't have to be an all-or-nothing proposition. Most of us have voluntarily chosen to abstain from sexual intercourse at various times during our lives. Once abstinence is viewed as a situational choice and not a lifetime commitment, it becomes easier to accept and understand as a viable sexual option. We also believe that although abstinence is a valid option for people, it is not the only option.

Fantasy

Source: Callista Lee

Sexual fantasies serve many positive purposes:

- Provides a sexual outlet free of risk of pregnancy, STIs, or relationship stress
- Enhances sexual arousal prior to or while being sexual with a partner as well as during masturbation
- Relieves boredom, not just in everyday life but also in your sex life. Fantasizing can spice things up.
- Relieves sexual anxieties by allowing an opportunity to consider one's sexual values, replay sexual scenes, or explore one's sexual identity.
- A sex therapy tool can be used as an opportunity to get to know oneself and/or one's partner better, practice techniques, and/or relieve sexual tension autoerotically while working on relationship issues (Hock, 2016).

Most people report using sexual fantasy during masturbation, and many people fantasize while engaging in sex with a partner (Stockwell & Moran, 2013). Fantasizing while with a partner is not only *NOT* a sign of a problem with the relationship, but research has found that people who fantasize more tend to be better sexually adjusted, have fewer sexual problems, and report the greatest overall satisfaction in their sexual relationships (Gagnon & Simon, 2011). Males and females fantasize about a lot of the same things, but there are some topics that are more common among one sex versus the other. Women are more likely than men to fantasize about: getting married, being rescued by a partner, and having same-sex fantasies if they are straight or heterosexual fantasies if they are lesbian. Males are more likely than women to fantasize about: sex with a virgin, being with two or more lovers at the same time, or sex with a mysterious stranger.

It is important to note that sometimes we fantasize about our favorite things to do in real life, but other times we enjoy fantasizing about things we would never do in real life. Compare this to the types of movies you like to watch. You probably enjoy watching some movies about things you would never want to be a part of, like those horror films so popular around Halloween. But you probably also like watching films about characters that remind you of yourself or perhaps a life you would like to be living. Your fantasy is your own private trip to the movies. It is especially important to keep this in mind when sharing fantasies with your partner. It may be necessary to ask if this is something they just enjoy fantasizing about or if it is something they actually hope to do one day? The fantasies that are probably the most disturbing are when forced sex is part of the plot line. In a rape fantasy, nobody is getting hurt, while in real life the psychological trauma can be life changing, even to the point of becoming suicidal. But the enjoyment of a *fantasy* of being raped has none of the fear of violence of an actual rape, nor the feelings of betrayal (most victims are raped by someone they know at least casually), or self-doubt (am I to blame for what is happening?). In a rape fantasy, the fantasizer is writing the script and playing all of the roles. Researchers have found that many women who report enjoyment of rape fantasies see themselves as the powerful one in the fantasy script, being so irresistible that the rapist can't hold back, or she allows the *illusion* of his dominance to give *her* pleasure (Strassberg & Lockerd, 1998).

If a partner wants to discuss making a fantasy come true in real life, such as having sex with multiple partners at the same time, the couple must have some serious conversations about how a real-life orgy would be different from the fantasy. As stated earlier, in fantasy, the fantasizer is the writer, director, and all of the actors. But in real life, you are dealing with people who have their own ideas about how things ought to go. And there are real-life issues of insecurity, jealousy, emotional disconnects, how to meet people you can trust, how to avoid becoming emotionally involved with them, maintaining positive consent throughout the entire event, and STIs. If all that is just a little too real, a couple may choose to act out or talk through a fantasy without other people being actually involved. The same is true for fantasies that may be illegal, such as sex in a public place. The reality of being arrested for public lewdness is nobody's idea of a good time.

Non-Penetrative Sexual Activity

Non-penetrative sexual activities offer a wide variety of pleasurable behaviors that can be carried out to the point of orgasm and involve little risk of pregnancy or disease. This activity has been called "outercourse" and includes options ranging from kissing and hugging to using sex toys. To us, non-penetrative sexual activity includes any sexual behaviors that do not involve genital-to-genital, mouth-to-genital, or insertive anal sexual contact.

Kissing

Kissing can provide intense sensual and sexual delight. The sucking, licking, rubbing, and tongue probing associated with kissing is pleasurable and carries no risk for pregnancy. Volumes have been written about kissing.

As we age, we seem to become more genitally focused and lose some of our interest in kissing. Kissing becomes an ancillary activity associated with the real objective—orgasm—rather than a satisfying activity in and of itself (Gulledge, Stahmann, Wilson, 2004: Gulledge, Gulledge, Stahtmann, 2003).

Hugging/Rubbing

Kissing is usually associated with hugging and rubbing. These activities, once commonly called *petting,* can take on new meaning if we can visualize them as viable forms of sexual expression. Hugging and rubbing, even with one's clothes on, can be intensely pleasurable and can be carried to the point of orgasm with no risk of pregnancy or disease. These activities also can serve as a prelude to other non-insertive forms of sexual activity such as masturbation and use of sex toys.

A delightful way to use rubbing as a safe sexual release is to rub against your partner to the point of orgasm. Typically this is done with both partners fully clothed. You rub your penis or vulva against your partner's groin, leg, arm (or another convenient body part) to the point of orgasm.

You control the pressure, rhythm, and intensity. Although students sometimes call this "dry humping," it doesn't have to be either. You can enhance your enjoyment by doing it with your clothes off and adding oil or lotion to the equation. Try spreading lotion on your partner's breasts or chest. Take your clothes off, lie on your back, and let your partner rub your penis or vulva back and forth and up and down between her breasts or his chest until you come. Try spreading some lotion or oil on your partner's buttocks and the small of his or her back. Straddle the backside and ride back and forth to the point of orgasm. If this seems too messy, try rubbing your

Kissing is an almost universal form of sexual expression.

healthy sex hints 6.2

10 Good Reasons for Choosing Abstinence

Abstinence has gotten a bad rap over the years. It's almost politically incorrect to talk about abstaining from sexual intercourse (and penetrative sex, if you're gay or a lesbian). Here are 10 good reasons to choose abstinence:

1. To retain your virginity for someone special
2. To get to know your partner better (you want to become more comfortable with your partner and come to trust him or her)
3. To ascertain your partner's STD/HIV status (you'd rather wait to have intercourse but might consider safer-sex options)
4. To wait to be in the mood (you'd rather be doing something else)
5. If you're heterosexual, to avoid pregnancy if neither of you has contraception (you might consider a low-risk sexual outlet other than intercourse)
6. To find a suitable partner (sure, you've had offers, but no one turns you on)
7. To recuperate from an illness or surgery (you're not feeling very sexy or are feeling downright lousy)
8. To get a medical opinion on unusual genital symptoms (these might represent an STD)
9. To get some sleep (you're tired and need sleep, not sex)
10. To adhere to your personal moral code (regarding premarital, extramarital, and other sexual taboos that make up your personal code of ethics)

What other good reasons for abstaining from intercourse can you come up with?

penis or vulva through your partner's hair and against his or her head and neck. You can use hugging and rubbing in many ways to enjoy a highly erotic sexual episode without fear of disease or pregnancy.

Massage

Non-genital massage is one of the greatest sensual delights you can share with your partner. Massage can be a stand-alone sensual activity or can be part of activities culminating with orgasm. Sex therapists often prescribe non-genital massage for clients as a way to help them reestablish touching each other's bodies again. Massage allows us to explore every nook and cranny of our partner's bodies in a relaxed, sensual way.

Separating our sensuality from our sexuality is sometimes difficult when it comes to massage. The only time many of us touch others in such an intimate way is when we are being sexual. Massage is not an inherently sexual activity. It *is* sensual, though. Kneading, stroking, and manipulating another person's flesh require us to be in tune with the sensation of touch. We must be acutely aware of pressure and motion when we give a massage. Also, many of the massage oils available are scented and bring into play our sense of smell. Visually, the sight of exposed flesh has the potential for arousal.

sex in society 6.1

Variations on Kissing

We asked our students to talk about kissing—their likes, dislikes, the role it plays in their relationships. Here's what they had to say:

Marcia 19, single, freshman, identifies as Latina.

I love kissing. I especially like long, deep, French kissing with my boyfriend. I really enjoy deep tongue thrusting—you know, like when he tries to run his tongue all the way down my throat. What a turn-on.

Mary 18, single, freshman, identifies as Italian American.

I like gentle kissing. I like lighter pressure—soft pecks, nuzzles, gentle tongue probing. I hate it when a guy tries to ram his tongue down my throat. It's disgusting. Oh, and I hate hickeys. Why do some guys feel compelled to leave their mark on my neck? I never go out with a guy again if he tries to lay a hickey on me. How gross.

John, 20, single, junior, identifies as Asian American.

I like kissing. It's kind of like a game, tongues darting back and forth, in and out. There's almost a rhythm or method to kissing. I like to work my tongue around my girlfriend's whole mouth.

Sonja, 20, single, junior, identifies as African American.

I personally think French kissing is overrated. I prefer lip action. I like to nip and suck, just using my lips. I like it when my boyfriend nibbles on my lips and when we just use the tips of our tongues around our lips and the outer parts of our mouths. I find this kind of darting tongue action preferable to all of that deep tongue thrusting. That makes me gag.

Glen, 41, married, nontraditional senior, identifies as African American.

At this point in my life, I find that my wife and I are more gentle in our kissing. We still get into all the deep French kissing every once in a while, but most of our kissing is more affectionate than passionate. Don't get me wrong—our sex is great, and intercourse is usually pretty passionate. We just seem to kiss more as an expression of love and affection. Kissing during sex is less frequent than when we were in our 20s.

The ability to enjoy giving and getting a massage and viewing these as sensual delights that don't have to lead to sexual activity may take time. Of course, giving a massage with the intent to arouse your partner sexually is a natural way to initiate erotic activities if that is the intention. Being able to give and receive sensual pleasure without sexual release is excellent training in becoming a compassionate lover.

Giving a massage is a natural behavior. Instinctively, we believe that if it feels good to us, it will feel good to the person we are massaging. Usually, giving a massage is easier if you use some form of lubricating oil. Some people prefer powder to reduce friction, and they like the sensation of powder. Most people, however, prefer oil. Oil should be warm or at room temperature. Cold oil on the skin can get the massage off to a bad start. The oil should sit at room temperature or be warmed in the container

personal exploration activity

Boosts and Blocks to Arousal

There are so many differences in what each person finds sexually arousing and what blocks each person's arousal. Too often we don't even recognize what are our own boosts or turn-ons and our blocks or turn-offs to being aroused. Remember that arousal does not just happen as a prelude to sexual intercourse. Arousal can happen while we are walking across campus and notice a great body. The goal of this activity is to help you recognize what is sexually significant and important to you.

To identify your own personal boost and blocks to sexual arousal, keep a diary for 1 week where you list all the little things that sexually arouse you. Include not just physical but social and psychological factors that arouse you. (You can keep this in code if you don't want anyone to know what you are doing.) Notice all the little contributors such as reading an erotic passage in a novel, having someone you find attractive brush your hand, how you respond when you are being kissed, and so forth. When the week is finished, examine your list and star the ones that are the most effective in arousing you. These are the things you want to enhance in your sensual activities to increase your arousal. Next put an X by those that most effectively block your arousal, and try to eliminate these factors when possible. If you have a partner, you may want to share what you discovered about yourself and suggest he or she keep a diary for a week. Your partner can then share the findings with you. The two of you can use your list to enhance what is really important to both of you in your sensual life together.

under hot water in the sink before starting. The oil should be poured into the hands and rubbed onto the body rather than squirted directly onto the person's skin (Good Arts, 2003).

Massage should be done with sufficient room to get completely around the person without having to lean on or jump over him or her. When straddling a person, you should not sit directly on him or her. You should be able to position yourself over the person so you can apply firm pressure during some strokes. A massage table or high bed is ideal because it allows you to stand while giving a massage. You also could kneel next to the person receiving the massage. It allows the person to lie comfortably with the face down, facilitating easy access to the neck, shoulders, and head. A professional table isn't necessary. You could place a pillow under the person's head for support and have him or her rest the head gently to the side.

Most important in giving a massage is to take your time. The other person will sense if you feel obligated to do this and are rushing through it. Giving a massage is an act of kindness and must be done slowly, lovingly, with no expectations for getting anything in return.

healthy sex hints 6.3

Giving a Massage

You can give full-body or partial massages. Sometimes just a back massage or a foot massage will do the trick. At other times, a full-body massage, complete with scented candles, is preferred. When giving a full body massage, try these pointers:

- Start anywhere. Wherever you start, move in the direction toward the heart to facilitate venous blood flow.
- If you start with the feet, work up to the head, and finish at the hands. Or work in the reverse order.
- Or start at the abdomen, as it is the center of the body and, when stressed, is the place where blood pools.
- Cover the entire body in a systematic way. Finish a part thoroughly, then move on to the next. Don't jump around from feet to head to toes. Massage both hands/arms or feet/legs before moving to the next body part.

After a massage, allow the person some quiet time to savor the results—and maybe even to reciprocate. Massage can be a prelude to other forms of sexual activity. In sensual massage, the focus shifts to providing more direct contact with the genitals and other erogenous zones.

case study 6.2

Critical Thinking

How does your own background and upbringing affect your ability to give and receive sensual massages with your partner? How does this influence your use of professional massage services? Does the gender of the massage therapist matter when seeking professional massage services?

Chrissy and Ken: Sensual Massage

Chrissy and Ken are single and in their senior year of college. They have been dating and having sex for 2 years and are planning to get engaged sometime before graduation in June. They have worked massage into their sexual lifestyle.

KEN: We got into massage as a way to relax and enjoy the sensual part of it. I didn't want Chrissy to think the only time she'd get a massage was when I wanted to have sex.

CHRISSY: We talk about what our needs are. If we want just a massage, we know this going into it, and that's what we do. If we're feeling sexy, we sometimes use massage to feel more sensual and get excited. We spend a lot of time massaging each other's erogenous zones.

KEN: I really get excited when Chrissy uses oil to massage my toes. I also love it when she uses long, slow strokes up my inner thighs and gently kneads the skin there.

Chrissy: I really go wild when Ken uses small, circular strokes around my temples or kneads the base of my skull. I start to get wet when he spends a few minutes doing that.

Masturbation

One of the first activities linking our sensuality to sexual behavior is **masturbation**. Masturbation usually evolves out of sensual exploration of our own body. We notice that it feels good when we unintentionally or intentionally rub (or rub up against) our genitals. In her book *Liberating Masturbation,* feminist writer, artist, and sex educator Betty Dodson (1996, p. 11) describes masturbation as "our primary sex life, our sexual base." According to Dodson, all other forms of sexual expression are a result of socialization. The expression of healthy sexual relationships between individuals begins with self-exploration of sensual and sexual pleasure from the time of birth.

Masturbation Individual or mutual stimulation of genitalia by hand or using other objects

Most of us learn the joy and security of cuddling, hugging, and warm, caring touch early in our lives, from contact with our parents and other caregivers. Although our earliest bonding experiences with our mother and father are not sexual in nature, they provide a sensual connection that leads to healthy sexuality.

Besides laying the foundation for developing trust and self-esteem, physical bonding with, and nurturing by, parents sets the stage for recognition and acceptance of our own body as a potential source of pleasure. Solitary sexual behavior, or masturbation, provides our first, and usually lifelong, source of sexual pleasure. Too many of us, however, associate masturbation with sinful, inappropriate behavior.

Masturbation can be a solitary sexual behavior or can be enjoyed with a partner. As a solitary behavior, masturbation may or may not be accompanied by sexual fantasy and other autoerotic activity. Many people combine masturbation with viewing erotic material or engaging in simulated sexual activities with someone online (Daneback, Cooper, Mansson, 2005). Couples can masturbate each other simultaneously, take turns pleasing each other, or masturbate themselves simultaneously.

Separating Sex and Love: In Praise of Masturbation

Source: Callista Lee

This is the title of Part 2 in Nancy Friday's third book of women's sexual fantasies (Women on Top, 1991) in which she discusses women's attitudes about masturbation. Women have been traditionally taught that they are to be sexual only in relationships. We aren't even taught about the clitoris or female orgasm in high school sex ed. Its like we are all just like Sleeping Beauty, waiting for a handsome prince to awaken us with a kiss. Friday suggests that sex outside of a romantic relationship is the greatest taboo for women. Even though her book came out in 1991, after the "sexual revolution" of the 1970s, she found that women were still having a difficult time owning their own sexuality. It was something that they were waiting for "Mr. Right" to awaken in them. Friday describes masturbation this way, "a simple, private act ... the most natural thing in the world, our own hand on our own genitals ... not a difficult skill like playing the violin. Our hand naturally

moves there in infancy ... and yet we feel guilty as thieves when we should feel mastery and self-love. Something or someone gets between us and our genitals so early that we cannot even remember" (p. 22). She continues by pointing out the benefits of masturbation (pp. 33–34):

- It teaches us that we are sexual all by ourselves
- It teaches to separate (the feelings of) love and sex
- It helps us to become more orgasmic and better partners
- It helps us to be better candidates for contraceptive responsibility
- It is one of life's greatest sources of sexual pleasure—thrilling in itself—a sweet sedative before sleep, and an effective tension reliever.

Female Techniques

Masters and Johnson noted that women exhibit much greater variation in masturbatory behavior. Even when women had a similar style of stimulation, the tempo, timing, and approach to masturbation varied. The most common form of female masturbation is to stimulate the clitoris, labia, and mons by hand through stroking, pulling, or rubbing (Hite, 1976).

Most women prefer to masturbate while lying on the back. A smaller percentage chooses to sit or stand while stimulating the genitalia. Between 5 and 10 percent of women prefer to masturbate while lying on their stomach, either placing a hand between their legs to stimulate the clitoris or rubbing the vulva against a pillow or some other object (Hite, 1976). Figure 6.1 illustrates female masturbation.

Masters and Johnson reported the following patterns of masturbatory behavior in order of preference: (1) manually stimulating the vulva, (2) using a vibrator to stimulate the clitoris/vulva, (3) inserting something into the vagina, (4) rubbing up against an object, (5) pressing the thighs together, (6) using water massage, and (7) all other methods. About half of the younger women reported using sex toys (vibrators, dildos, or other devices) to masturbate, choosing either to insert these or to use them to apply external vibration. A smaller percentage of women report using these devices in a similar fashion to stimulate the anus during masturbation. The variety and complexity have increased markedly as more women (and their partners) express interest in these products.

Male Techniques

In her study of male sexuality, Shere Hite (1981) reports the following male masturbatory techniques in order of preference: (1) stimulating the penis by hand, (2) lying down on the stomach rubbing against a bed, and (3) with water in the shower.

Few men choose to masturbate using sex toys such as vibrators, dildos, plastic sleeves, penile pumps, and inflatable dolls, although these devices are readily available. Though still relatively uncommon, proponents of these sex toys claim that they can enhance

Figure 6.1 *Female Masturbation* Lying on the back and massaging the genitals with one hand is a common position for masturbation.

sexual pleasure, provide a change of pace from routine masturbatory practices, and add variety to safe-sex options.

Masters and Johnson found that many men masturbate by rubbing, stroking, or pumping the shaft of the penis with one hand (Masters, Johnson, & Kolodny, 1996). The tempo of movement usually builds gradually in response to the increase in arousal. Slow, deliberate touch gradually gives way to more forceful, rapid movements, often accompanied by increases in pressure and tension. A small percentage of men studied spend time stimulating the frenulum on the underside of the glans of the penis. Uncircumcised men seem to spend more time stimulating the glans and frenulum through pulling the foreskin back and forth. Ejaculation varies more, some men preferring to slow down and relax their grip and others desiring to increase pressure, squeezing out the last drops of semen. Figure 6.2 illustrates male masturbation.

Because the male penis is not lubricated, and masturbation usually involves a buildup of heat and friction, most men use some form of lubrication while masturbating. Body lotion and baby oil are two commonly used lubricants.

Health Aspects of Masturbation

Early critics of masturbation posed pseudoscientific charges that masturbation was neither "healthy" nor "normal." There is no evidence to support the claim that masturbation has adverse health consequences. In fact, recent studies indicate just the opposite. Several recent studies have shown that masturbating on a regular basis may decrease one's risk for prostate cancer. It does not cause any physical problems. It carries no risk for any physical or psychological illness. Most safe sex educators encourage their students to masturbate to relieve sexual tension or to enjoy an orgasm whenever they want one. It is also an excellent way to learn what feels good and how their bodies respond.

From a physiological perspective, a person cannot masturbate to excess. It is a self-limiting behavior; we ultimately lose our interest in it. As long as people follow basic hygienic precautions (clean hands, toys, and so on) and have adequate lubrication, they can masturbate as often as they want to. Rather than being a source of problems, masturbation is a healthy outlet for sexual desire, can reduce risk for sexually transmitted diseases in people who don't have safe sexual partners, and is an alternative to having sex with prostitutes or anonymous partners.

Figure 6.2 *Male masturbation*

An Orgasm a Day Keeps the Doctor Away

Source: Callista Lee

Health Benefit	Research Findings
General health	An orgasm at least once or twice a week strengthens the immune system's ability to resist flu and other viruses.
Pain relief	Some women find that orgasm reduces the pain of menstrual cramps.
Lower cancer rate	Men who have five or more ejaculations per week during their twenties have a significantly lower risk of prostate cancer later in life.
Mood enhancement	Orgasms increase estrogen and endorphins, which tend to improve mood and ward off depression in women.
Longer life	Men who have two or more orgasms per week live significantly longer than men who have fewer.
Increased intimacy	Oxytocin release increases five-fold at orgasm; it is linked to feelings of love and emotional intimacy.
Less heart disease	Men who have at least three orgasms per week are 50 percent less likely to die of heart disease.
Better sleep	Dopamine (released at orgasm) triggers a stress-reducing, sleep inducing response that may last up to two hours.

Sources: Giles et al. (2003); Komisaruk & Whipple (1995); Resnick, (2002); Komisaruk, Beyer-Flores, & Whipple (2006); Levin (2007); Smith, Frankel, & Yarnell, (1997); Weeks & James, (1999); Whipple (2000).

ℰ Intellectual and Emotional Wellness ℰ

Intellectual wellness provides the objective basis for understanding sexual behavior. It allows you to separate fact from fiction, truth from myth, science from theology. It empowers you to gain access to information and make informed choices that are free from dogma and outside pressures. Emotional wellness allows you to understand your emotions about the information without being overwhelmed by them. Perhaps nothing illustrates this interplay more than the topic of masturbation.

Centuries upon centuries of misinformation based on religious dogma, pseudoscience, and Puritanism have clouded the truth about masturbation and shrouded the topic in a veil of shame, guilt, and punishment. While the scientific "truth" about the behavior (it is a harmless outlet for sexual tension and a viable sexual behavior in itself) is well documented, the emotions it arouses often makes it difficult for people to deal with masturbation honestly and openly. People with high-level intellectual and emotional well-being about masturbation realize that it is a normal, healthy sexual behavior, and they try to work with their emotions regarding it rather than to suppress them or feel worse because of them. They talk about these issues with their partner(s) and seek help if they need it.

Sexual Intercourse

Many people think that being a good lover means being particularly adept at sexual intercourse. Actually, being a good lover means having certain skills (knowing how to arouse your partner, using various sexual behaviors, and so on), as well as having good psychosocial skills (knowing how to communicate, when to initiate, and the like). In this section, we will focus on a variety of intercourse positions.

Vaginal Intercourse

Vaginal intercourse, also known as **coitus**, is one of the most common forms of heterosexual sexual activity, although sexual paraphernalia (strap-on or hand-held dildos and the like) allow lesbian women to penetrate their partner's vaginas if they desire. The three starting points for vaginal intercourse are face-to-face, side-by-side, and rear entry. We call these starting points rather than positions because each starting point offers a limitless array of positions, depending on how you place the rest of your body (arms, legs, torso, and so on).

Coitus Vaginal intercourse

✎ *Spiritual Wellness* ✎

A key component of spirituality is the sense of being connected with something beyond the self. In one sense, a person can't become more "interconnected" with another human being than through sexual intercourse. When our sexual relationships are based on respect, mutuality, and caring, our union with another person creates something that we cannot experience as individuals. In contrast, when our sexual relationships are based on exploitation, power, mistrust, fear, or other destructive intentions, we become disconnected from others, mere sexual mercenaries, out for ourselves only. Regardless of whether we are religious, we each have a moral code, a sense of right and wrong that can enhance our connectedness to others or destroy it. Those with high-level spirituality view their sexual relations with others with integrity and morality.

Face-to-Face

Face-to-face positions have two variations: man on top and woman on top.

Woman on Top. The woman-on-top position, shown in Figures 6.3 (heterosexual couple) and 8.4 (lesbian couple), allows women greater control in the depth, pace, and motion of her partner's thrusting. It allows the woman on the top the greatest control in clitoral stimulation and is the easiest intercourse position for manual clitoral stimulation. Orgasm rates for heterosexual women are better for this position than any other. This position is also good for helping heterosexual male partners control premature ejaculation. The woman can get to this position in two ways: She can start with her partner on top and roll over into this position or start with her partner on his or her back and move on top. In the latter case, the partners

Figure 6.3 *Woman on Top Sitting; Heterosexual Couple* This position allows for the partner on the bottom to use his hands to massage his partner's breasts and upper body.

Figure 6.4 *Woman on Top Lying; Lesbian Couple* Lying on top of one's partner while facing her allows both partners to kiss as they make love.

must have enough room on the bed so they won't find themselves rolling off the bed and onto the floor.

When starting with the man on his back, the woman kneels over him with one knee on either side of his legs. Either partner can part the vaginal lips as the woman lowers herself onto the erect penis, guiding it in with a free hand.

With the penis inside, the woman can rock or thrust her hips or move them in a circular fashion. The rocking and thrusting motions allow maximum penile penetration, whereas the circular grinding motion stimulates the clitoris more directly. Each of these three creates entirely different sensations.

Lesbians can use this position in a similar fashion with the aid of a strap-on dildo. The motions, activities, and benefits are the same as those for heterosexual couples. The partner on the bottom can be passive and allow the woman on top to control all movements or move with her, synchronizing motion with hers. The bottom partner can also initiate thrusting and grinding if the woman on top becomes tired or desires it.

In this position the woman also has more freedom to use her hands in ways similar to those of the man-on-top position. From this position she can caress and manipulate either her partner or herself. One option that the woman-on-top position offers is the ability to rotate her torso, while still being penetrated by her partner, so that her back is to her partner. In this position she can lean forward or sit back and achieve different depths of penetration and sensations. Her partner can fondle her buttocks and back while maintaining penetration.

An interesting variation of the woman-on-top position is to move from kneeling or lying on to actually sitting on her partner. By sitting on her partner, the woman-on-top position affords maximum penetration and intimacy as the couple can embrace, kiss, and talk.

Man on Top (Missionary). The man-on-top position, illustrated in Figure 8.5, is also known as the "missionary position." It is the most commonly used intercourse position in the United States. In this position, the partners stimulate each other until they are sufficiently aroused. The man then moves on top of the woman. Either partner spreads the female's vaginal lips and inserts the penis into the vagina. The man supports his weight on his elbows, hands, knees, or across his partner's entire body as his penis moves in the vagina.

The most typical penile movements involve thrusting in and out as the female either remains still or moves her hips in concert with her partner's thrusting. These motions provide direct sexual stimulation of the male's penile nerve endings (on the shaft, glans, and corona). The woman's clitoris usually is stimulated as the clitoral hood (top of the labia minora) pulls back and forth over it or the man's pubic area rubs against it. The vagina is stimulated as the penis slides in and out. The deeper recesses of the vagina (cervical area) may or may not be stimulated depending on the depth of the strokes and the positions. An option to thrusting in and out is a circular motion, known as *grinding,* which involves more pubis-to-pubis contact and stimulates the female's clitoris differently. This provides more direct and intense stimulation of the clitoris and the base of the man's penis and can be done even if the man has ejaculated. If he hasn't withdrawn the penis before it has become limp, he can continue stimulating his partner with the circular motion. Sometimes this can go on through his refractory period, and

Figure 6.5 *Man on Top, Heterosexual Couple* The man-on-top position is commonly referred to as the "missionary position" and is the most common heterosexual intercourse behavior.

he can achieve another erection without removing his penis. This allows his partner to be stimulated and have additional orgasms even though he has climaxed. Many men find this type of stimulation enjoyable even though they have a limp penis and already have had an orgasm.

Variations of this starting point involve changing the position of the legs and arms. The woman on the bottom can experience a variety of different sensations and depths of penetration by wrapping her legs around the partner's ankles, legs, or waist. Or she can throw her legs over her partner's shoulders as he thrusts in and out, which affords the deepest penetration.

One of the advantages of this position is that it allows the partners to look into each other's eyes and communicate. It also allows the partners to rub and caress each other's chest and shoulders. Furthermore, it allows use of the hands to enhance stimulation by touching or rubbing the partner's genitals during intercourse.

The woman may enjoy stretching her arms over her head, arching her back. This allows her partner better access to caress the breasts and nipples. She may enjoy having the partner pin her arms back over her head. This mild form of domination/submission allows her to "lose control" in a safe way. Individuals should participate in domination/submission only with someone they trust and must understand that "no means no" if either partner wants the activity to stop.

The missionary position can also be used by lesbian women if the partner on top is using a strap-on dildo to penetrate her partner's vagina. The positioning, motions, and benefits are similar to those experienced by heterosexual couples.

Rear Entry

The rear entry starting point (Figure 6.6) is also known as "doggie style" because it is the way in which dogs and most other animals have intercourse. In rear entry positions, the partner enters the woman's vagina from behind. This usually is accomplished with the woman kneeling on her hands and knees and the man kneeling behind her, either between or straddling her legs. Either partner parts the vaginal lips and guides the penis in. This position

Figure 6.6 *Rear Entry, Heterosexual Couple* The rear-entry intercourse position is commonly referred to as "doggie style."

creates deep vaginal penetration but little direct clitoral stimulation. For this reason, either the man or the woman stimulates the clitoris manually.

This position also offers stimulation of the anus and perineum through pressure and friction from the man's pubis rubbing or grinding against it. Once engaged, the woman can lower her head and raise her hips higher to achieve maximum penetration. The rear-entry position can also be used by lesbian women with the aid of a strap-on dildo for vaginal penetration. The positioning, motions, and benefits are similar.

Two other rear-entry position variations are (1) the couple can lie down with the man on top of the woman, or (2) they can lie on their sides. The latter is commonly known as the "spoon" position. One disadvantage of this position is that the partners do not face each other, which makes communication and kissing more difficult.

Side-to-Side

The side-to-side vaginal intercourse can involve face-to-face positioning (Figures 6.7 and 6.8) or rear-entry positioning. Because neither partner is bearing the full weight of the other, the side-to-side position is ideal for leisurely lovemaking or the rest period between more vigorous sessions. The easiest way to get into the side-to-side position is by rolling into it from the man-on-top or woman-on-top or the rear-entry position.

Besides being a comfortable position for leisurely lovemaking, the side-to-side variation has many advantages. It also is good for obese people, as it minimizes weight-bearing. The rear-entry variation (Figure 6.8) is good for pregnant women whose developing fetus and protruding abdomen make the man-on-top position impossible. The side-to-side position also

Figure 6.7 *Side-by-Side, Heterosexual Couple* The side-by-side facing and rear-entry intercourse positions are very comfortable and are often used to relieve pressure on the partner.

Figure 6.8 *Side-by-Side, Pregnant Heterosexual Couple*

facilitates good communication and kissing while leaving the hands free for hugging and forms of manual stimulation.

Anal Intercourse

In anal intercourse, a man inserts his penis into his partner's rectum. Heterosexual and homosexual couples both practice anal intercourse. Like vaginal intercourse, anal intercourse can take place from the three starting points: side-to-side, rear-entry, or face-to-face. The advantages and disadvantages associated with these starting points for vaginal intercourse are similar to those for anal intercourse. Rear-entry is the most commonly used starting point for anal intercourse, although anal penetration can be accomplished through all of the positions previously described (Figure 6.9).

Oral Sex

Oral sex, also known as oral-genital sex, mouth-genital sex, giving head, and going down, is the stimulation of the partner's genitals with the lips, mouth, tongue, and face. The three main types of oral sex are fellatio (mouth-to-penis contact), cunnilingus (mouth-to-vulva contact), and anilingus (mouth-to-anus contact). All three are common forms of sexual expression for straight, gay, lesbian, and bisexual people.

Fellatio Oral stimulation of the penis

Figure 6.9 *Rear Entry Anal Intercourse, Gay Couple* The rear entry position is commonly used by gay couples.

Fellatio Also known as a "blow job," **fellatio** involves licking and sucking a man's penis. The term is derived from the Latin word *fellare,* which means "to suck." During fellatio, the partner begins by licking and sucking the flaccid penis while holding it. As the penis begins to grow, a man usually enjoys having his penis move in and out of his partner's mouth. The

healthy sex hints 6.4

Reducing Health Risks Associated with Anal Intercourse

Although the anus is richly endowed with nerve endings and has erogenous potential, it differs from other body parts and requires a few special considerations. One major difference between the tissue of the anus and rectum and that of the vagina concerns the blood vessels that supply the area. The blood vessels of the anus and rectum are very close to the surface. Any minor tearing or scraping of this tissue will result in bleeding and exposing these blood vessels to germs that could enter the bloodstream in this way.

Another major difference involves lubrication. Unlike the vagina, anal and rectal tissue does not produce natural lubrication as a product of vasocongestion. Therefore, care must be taken to adequately lubricate the anal opening and rectum with some other product. Saliva or a commercial water-based sterile lubricant is advisable. Saliva is not as slippery as most commercial products, such as K-Y Jelly, but it is free and can be used at any time. Because petroleum-based products can erode the latex in condoms, these products, such as Vaseline, should not be used in conjunction with a condom.

Lubricants should be spread liberally on the penis and the anus. Gently inserting a lubricated finger into the rectum will lubricate this area and relax the sphincter that keep the anus closed. (Make sure your fingernails are trimmed!)

The lubricated penis is inserted gently and begins controlled thrusting to work the penis deeper into the rectum. Once the penis is inserted comfortably into the rectum, the couple can decide on the nature and intensity of pelvic thrusting. From this rear-entry starting point, couples can try most of the positions described in the section on vaginal intercourse.

Sex involving the anus and rectum also carries an increased risk for transmitting a range of infections ranging from hepatitis B to HIV. Organisms that are transmitted through contact with fecal matter or blood are easily transmitted through insertive or receptive anal intercourse or anilingus.

To reduce the likelihood of disease transmission and increase sexual response associated with anal stimulation:

1. Do not engage in anilingus or anal intercourse with an anonymous (don't know at all) or a casual (don't know that well) partner.
2. Before engaging in anal activities, be sure your sex partner is HIV-negative and free of other STDs. This means getting to know your potential partner better and, sometimes, being tested.
3. With disease-free partners, shower normally with soap and water before having sex to provide adequate hygiene.
4. Always use a water-based lubricant when anal penetration is involved.
5. Do not insert foreign objects (other than specially designed dildos, vibrators, and the like) into the rectum. Be careful not to let things you insert slip past the anal sphincter muscle. The object can get "lost" in the rectum and may require surgical removal.
6. If your partner's STD/HIV status is unknown, use a condom for anal intercourse.

man can accomplish this by gently thrusting his hips, driving the penis in and out of his partner's mouth. The partner can do this by moving his or her head up and down, moving the penis deeper into the mouth and then letting it slide back again.

The sliding motion is accompanied by sucking, which can vary in intensity depending on the man's preference. The tongue is used to lick, flick, or swirl around the penis as it moves in the mouth. Using these tongue motions to stimulate the glans and the coronal ridge (particularly the underside where the shaft meets the glans) provides maximum stimulation for the man.

These movements, if continued, usually provide enough stimulation to trigger orgasm. Many men find that a combination of oral and manual stimulation is necessary to provide enough stimulation for orgasm. The partner can grasp the penis at its base or along the shaft and pump it while simultaneously stimulating it with the mouth and tongue. Grasping the penis in one hand while licking and sucking it can also give the partner a sense of control over the depth and intensity of the man's thrusting.

When the penis is thrust into the throat, it typically initiates a gag reflex, which can be minimized by using your hand to control the depth of the partner's thrusting. To minimize this, the partner can relax the throat muscles and control the depth of thrusting by holding the penis.

Couples need to discuss their feelings about ejaculation. As discussed in Chapter 3, the male ejaculate is typically about 1 teaspoon of fluid when he comes. The ejaculate is milky-white in color, has a slippery texture resembling egg whites, and leaves a salty aftertaste. Most men enjoy the sensation of ejaculating into the partner's mouth. This also can be enjoyable to the partner. If the partner finds swallowing ejaculate distasteful, an alternative is fellatio to the point of orgasm, then to withdraw the penis and ejaculate outside the partner's mouth, or to switch to some other form of sexual behavior prior to the point of orgasm.

✎ *Environmental Wellness* ✎

In this chapter, we openly discuss sexual behaviors from a scientific/health perspective. We discuss the pros and cons of such things as oral and anal intercourse, heterosexual, homosexual, and bisexual variations on these behaviors, and how to engage in them with minimal health risks. We realize, however, that people don't engage in these behaviors in a vacuum. There are still places in the United States where century-old statutes regarding *sodomy* (a term that can be broadly interpreted to include such things as oral sex between consenting marital partners) laws are still enforced. You need to know what laws are still on the books regarding sexual behavior in your city, town, county, and state. This is vital information that can help you make informed choices about your sexual behavior and lifestyle.

Cunnilingus

Cunnilingus Oral stimulation of the vulva

The oral stimulation of a woman's vulva through licking, sucking, and nibbling or rubbing with the face is called **cunnilingus**. It is a common sexual practice of straight, lesbian, and bisexual men and women. Although cunnilingus (from the Latin words *cunnus* [vulva] and *lingere* [to lick]) by definition refers to oral stimulation of the vulva, often the perineum and outer parts of the vagina are also stimulated during this act.

Cunnilingus typically begins as the partner kisses and licks the partner's inner thighs, abdomen, and mons area. The partner then gently parts the labia majora and uses the tongue to lick, flick, or swirl around the vaginal lips, clitoris, and introitus.

Pressure can be applied by pressing the tongue against the vulva with greater force. Circular motions are often used to stimulate the vulva in a somewhat different fashion. Care must be taken not to apply too much pressure directly to the clitoris, as it is the part of the female sexual anatomy that is most richly endowed with nerve endings.

The mouth can be used to gently suck on the vaginal lips and clitoris. Gently sucking one or more lips into one's mouth can provide intense pleasure. The clitoris also can be sucked on gently. Some women find it arousing to have their partner gently nibble the vaginal lips and clitoris. The tongue also can be used to penetrate the vagina with thrusting motions.

The face (chin, cheeks, and forehead) can become involved in cunnilingus while the mouth and lips are busy providing stimulation. A partner can intentionally use the face to provide additional stimulation through direct pressure or circular motion. For instance, the bridge of the nose can provide clitoral stimulation while licking or sucking on the labia.

As with fellatio, cunnilingus can be performed with or without manual stimulation. Many women derive pleasure from having their partner insert a well lubricated finger into their vagina or anus while performing cunnilingus. Saliva or vaginal lubrication can be used to make the fingers slippery. The partner also can stimulate the woman's clitoris with manual stimulation while licking or sucking on another part of the vulva.

Anilingus

Anilingus Oral stimulation of the anus

Although it isn't as common as fellatio or cunnilingus, **anilingus,** also known as *rimming,* is another form of oral sex practiced by people of all forms of sexual orientation. During anilingus, a person kisses, licks, or sucks the partner's anus. The motions and activities of anilingus are similar to both cunnilingus and fellatio.

Performing anilingus affords a good opportunity to stimulate the perineum, an area richly endowed with nerve endings. Some men and women enjoy having their partners insert their tongues into their anus during anilingus. Others prefer that their partner insert a well-lubricated finger into the rectum. When performing anilingus on a woman, care must be taken to avoid spreading *Escherichia coli* bacteria into the vagina. The tongue or fingers never should be inserted directly from the anus to the vagina without first being washed.

Another concern is the spread of hepatitis and other STD organisms through anilingus. We do not recommend performing anilingus with a casual sex partner or someone whose STD status is unknown, as this could result in ingesting disease-causing organisms. (This topic is discussed in greater detail in Chapter 15.)

Mutual Oral Sex

Heterosexual **Mutual oral sex** is often referred to as *sixty-nine* because of the shape couples form when engaged in it. This usually is accomplished in the side-to-side starting point, with each partner's head at the other's genitals (see Figures 6.10 and 6.11). From this position, both partners have easy access to their partner's genitals. From the side-to-side starting point, it is easy to roll into the man or woman on either the top or bottom positions. By being on the top or the bottom, a person can control for deeper penetration of the tongue when performing cunnilingus, or the penis during

Mutual Oral Sex The term used to describe simultaneous cunnilingus and fellatio is sixty-nine.

Figure 6.10 *Mutual Oral Sex Heterosexual Couple* Mutual oral sex is often referred to as sixty-nine because of the shape couples form when engaged in it.

Figure 6.11 *Mutual Oral Sex, Lesbian Couple*

fellatio. Mutual oral sex is enjoyed by heterosexual, gay, and lesbian couples.

This procedure does not normally affect sexual response, and it doesn't impede engaging in a variety of sexual behaviors ranging from oral sex to different forms of intercourse. However, learning to manage these and other sexual activities while wearing a colostomy bag (or temporarily removing it) depends on the willingness of the person with the disability to accept the colostomy and work around it (Chance, 2002).

References

Bender, M. (1999). The secret to living a sensuous life. Cosmopolitan, 227, pp. 236–242.

Brand, H. (2001). Sexual chemistry (the use of pheromones) Soap, Perfumery & Cosmetics, *74*(9), p. 19.

Burnham, W. H. (1932). *The wholesome personality.* New York: Appleton Century.

Daneback, K., Cooper, A. L., Mansson, S. A. (2005). An Internet Study of Cybersex Participants. Archives of Sexual Behavior v. 34 no. 3 (June 2005) pp. 321–8.

Dodson, B. (1996). *Sex for one: The joy of selfloving.* New York: Crown.

Eiseman, L. (1999). *Colors for your every mood.* New York: Capitol.

Foston, N. A. (2004). Is Celibacy The New Virginity? Living The Single Life Without Sex. Ebony v. 59 no. 3 (January 2004) p. 118, 120, 122.

Giles, G. G., Severi, D. R., English, M. C., Credie, M. R., Borland, R., Boyle, P., Hopper, J. L. (2003). Sexual Factors and Prostate Cancer. BJU International 92, pp. 211–216.

Goins, L. (2001). 5 secrets for making sex supersensual. Cosmopolitan, *230*(4), pp. 156–160.

Good Arts. (2003). *Sensual massage* [Online]. Available: www.goodarts.com.

Gulledge, A. K., Gulledge, M. H., Stahmann, R. F. (2003). Romantic Physical Affection Types and Relationship Satisfaction. The American Journal of Family Therapy v. 31 no. 4 (July/ September 2003) pp. 233–42.

Gulledge, A. K., Stahmann, R. F., Wilson, C. M. (2004). Seven Types of Nonsexual Romantic Physical Affection among Brigham Young University Students. Psychological Reports v. 95 no. 2 (October 2004) pp. 609–14.

Hite, S. (1976). *The Hite report: A nationwide study of female sexuality.* New York: Dell.

Hite, S. (1981). *The Hite report on male sexuality.* New York: Knopf.

Inkeles, G., & Austin, K. K. (1992). *The new sensual massage.* Bayside, CA: Arcata Arts.

Kemp, K. (2000). How to touch a naked man. Cosmopolitan, 228 (4), pp. 194–206.

Kraus, D. K. (2000, October 27). Realm of the senses. San Francisco Business Times, pp. 29–33.

Marrone, S. (2002). Indulge your sensual side: Eat a mango, sniff some cinnamon, and other fun, fast ideas for putting more pleasure into your life. Redbook, *198*(5), pp. 84–86.

Masters, W. H., Johnson, V., & Kolodny, R. (1996). *Human sexuality.* New York: HarperCollins.

Netting, N. S., Burnett, M. L. (2004). Twenty Years of Student Sexual Behavior: Subcultural Adaptations to a Changing Health Environment. Adolescence v. 39 (Spring 2004) pp. 19–38.

Norris, K. (1996, September–October). Celibate passion. *Utne Reader,* 51–53.

Rajen. P. (2004). T*he Times Educational Supplement* (October 29 2004 Friday supp) p. 20.

Spayde, J. (2001). Hear sensuality, think sex? Utne *Reader* no. 108 (November/December 2001) pp. 57–58.

Chapter
Seven

Child *and* Adolescent Sexuality

Student Learning Objectives

After reading this chapter, students will be able to

- ☞ Discuss how political forces shape sex education.
- ☞ Describe signs of unhealthy childhood sex play.
- ☞ Discuss the effects of parenting practices such as bonding, and nudity on healthy sexual development.
- ☞ Compare the biological consequences of puberty with the psychosocial aspects of adolescence.
- ☞ Describe the findings of a variety of studies concerning adolescent sexual behavior.
- ☞ Compare the adolescent sexual behavior of people in the United States with those from other cultures.
- ☞ Evaluate the positive and negative aspects of sexual activity during adolescence.

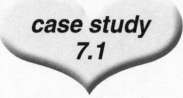

case study 7.1

Rebecca and Jake

Rebecca, 24, and Jake, 25.

Rebecca and Jake became parents for the first time in their mid-20s. They both were so excited at the birth of Adam yet nervous at the same time about how to be good parents.

REBECCA: I grew up in a very puritanical household. My parents rarely touched or showed any kind of physical affection toward each other or my brother and me. I know they loved each other and us, but it just wasn't their way to express it physically, in public. Nudity also was not tolerated, and sex was never discussed. Being with Jake has taught me that the physical expression of affection and love is a natural and positive thing.

JAKE: I come from a very physical, touchy family. Our whole family loves to hug and kiss, and visitors rarely get in or out of the house without a big hug hello and good-bye. When Rebecca and I got together, differences in our attitudes about touch had to be worked out between us. I love being naked, and for me touch does not always mean "I want some sex." I felt it was really important that Rebecca commit to breastfeeding Adam . . . she knew the health benefits, but the reality of it all seemed to scare her a bit.

We often just sit and look at Adam, our precious little baby. We want him to grow up healthy and comfortable with his sexuality. We've been taking turns getting up to change and feed Adam. When it's Rebecca's turn, she gets up, goes into Adam's room, and nurses him while rocking in the chair in his room. When it's my turn, I bring Adam into our bed and then put him back in his crib after nursing. We both love the skin–skin contact we share with the baby and each other.

REBECCA: Despite how tired we both are, we know that this phase of being parents is only the beginning. There will be so many more challenges down the line. What we know for sure is that we will work together to help Adam navigate through the sexual challenges of childhood and the teen years.

Critical Thinking

Those who want to be really good at a sport or playing a musical instrument often take lessons, get coaching and read to develop and improve their skills. Why do so many people think they "just know" a skill as complex as parenting a child? What will you and your partner do to learn how to effectively parent? Are you willing to take classes together, work with your pediatrician, read books together? How do parents develop parenting strategies that bridge the gaps among how they each were raised, what they have learned to be healthy for their child, and what they are each comfortable with as parents?

As you sit here reading, you may want to ask yourself, "How did I get to be the sexual person that I am?" You look a particular way and have your own unique thoughts, feelings, attractions, and needs. Despite what is often a cultural desire to protect children from things sexual, the reality is that profound aspects of sexual development occur in childhood and adolescence. How you are as an adult stems from the varied influences and experiences you have had "growing up." And as we explore adult issues in Chapter 6, you may want to question when, if ever, development *stops*.

Psychosexual development is the process of becoming a sexual person. The term traditionally refers to the psychological aspects of sexual development. As we've mentioned throughout this text, though, to completely separate the psychological from the physical, intellectual, emotional, social, spiritual, and environmental facets of our sexuality is not possible.

Psychosexual development
The blending of sexual aspects of one's development with other psychological factors

Early Development

There are some common themes related to early sexuality that influence sexual development: bonding, other expressions of physical intimacy, self-exploration and masturbation, and nudity. These critical sexual development issues surface during infancy and childhood and remain throughout life. How our caregivers initially handle these issues strongly influences the direction our development takes.

The major task of infancy, according to Erikson, is to develop a sense of trust. For trust to win out over mistrust is essential to continuing healthy psychological development in all of us.

Bonding

One of the earliest behaviors that helps foster trust and satisfies our most primal physiological needs is bonding. **Bonding** is a process of developing a close physical and psychological relationship with one's primary caregiver. Bonding between mother and child begins almost immediately as the newborn and mother are brought together to share the first moments of life. Bonding continues as mother and child are brought together during feeding, diaper changing, and simple things such as smiling, talking to the child, and acknowledging the child when approaching him or her.

Fathers also fulfill a bonding role. They are often present at the birth of the baby and develop strong, close physical bonds with their children, sharing in their care and feeding. The increased use of the word parenting rather than mothering and fathering reflects social changes around the raising of children. Raising children as a team has advantages for both parents and their children. Parents increasingly divide child-rearing responsibilities to fit with their work schedules and time at home.

During the bonding process, infants learn to associate the mother and father with fulfilling the most basic needs for sustaining life. Trust in

Bonding The close physical emotional attachment between infants and their primary caregiver(s)

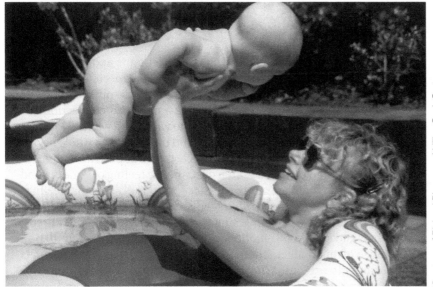

Bonding can take many forms. Here a mom plays in the pool with her child.

Courtesy of Richard Blonna and Lillian Cook Carter.

© S. Tucker, 2010. Shutterstock, Inc.

Grandparents can lavish love and attention on their grandchildren, bringing extra sources of affection.

Thriving Pattern of normal weight gain, neuromuscular development, and other developmental attributes of infants

the world as a whole begins by trusting in mothers and fathers. Infants respond positively to touch. **Thriving**— a term pediatricians use to describe physical and psychological growth—is enhanced by touch and bonding. Failure to thrive has been noted in infants who, among other things, have been deprived of sufficient physical nurturing during infancy. As children, these infants often lack the cognitive and motor abilities of their peers.

Other Forms of Physical Intimacy

In addition to bonding as a contributor to the development of sensuality and sexuality, other forms of touch play an important part. Beyond the basic need of touch for infants to thrive, touch is related to the development of sensuality. Our entire skin surface is capable of acting as an erogenous zone. It is sensitive to touch in all of its manifestations. Babies love to be held, stroked, and rocked. In his classic book on the importance of touch, Ashley Montague describes how our ability or inability to respond positively to physical intimacy is believed to be rooted in the time our parents spent touching and stroking us as infants (Montague, 1986).

How we touch babies varies from generalized hugging and stroking to infant massage and baby exercise. Infant massage strokes are similar to those used with adults, but much gentler. Observe how your baby responds and continue if he/she seems happy. However, when the baby turns his/her head away or seems unhappy, it is a good time to end the massage. Beyond the closeness and benefits from touch that massage affords, research has identified additional health benefits that result from the effect massage has on the body. Infant massage has been found to help babies reduce crying, positively influence hormones that control stress, adjust their circadian rhythms and move toward better sleeping habits, as well as promote better health and development (Mayo Clinic, 2015; Ferber, Laudon, Kuint, Weller, & Zisapel, 2002; Globus, 2002).

❧ *Spiritual and Emotional Wellness* ❧

Although we are not always cognizant of it as infants and children, we begin to develop a sense of connectedness or disconnectedness during this stage. Probably the earliest manifestation of spirituality is the bonding with primary caregivers. This is a powerful connection not only to other human beings but also to the world as a whole. Developing a sense of trust in ourselves, others, and the world as a whole begins with the skin-to-skin nurturing we receive from our parents in times of need. Parents and caregivers often describe the feeling of bonding and nurturing of an infant as one of the most profoundly spiritual feelings they have ever experienced. Many rediscover a sense of awe and faith in the power of love by connecting with and nurturing our children.

Infant and childhood emotional development forms the foundation for much of our adult emotional makeup. Basic personality constructs such as self-esteem, trust, happiness, and optimism begin to take shape during infancy and childhood. As Maslow and other developmental theorists point out, the ability to fully self-actualize as adults requires people to meet basic emotional needs early in life. It's harder to love others as adults if a person was not loved as an infant and if pieces of one's emotional development were left scattered on the floor of childhood and adolescence. Those who were not loved as children can learn to love themselves and others, it is just more difficult. Nurturing infants, children, and adolescents, attending to their needs, and providing a safe haven and outlet for their desires are all essential for their continuing emotional development and healthy sexuality.

Adolescence Time period representing the psychosocial transition from childhood to young adulthood

Self-Exploration and Masturbation

All infants discover the joys of genital pleasure inadvertently. They discover what it feels like to have their genitals rub against things in their immediate environment (crib, blanket, toys, diaper, clothing, their mother and father). If allowed to do so, infants between 6 and 12 months of age will touch their genitals. They will learn that they are capable of initiating the same pleasurable feelings they felt when rubbing against objects.

This behavior is not considered sexual behavior. Although it is definitely sensual and erotic, it lacks the associated sexual connotations that older children and adults have concerning genital pleasuring. These associations are learned later. This genital play should be evaluated exactly for what it is—play (Leung, 1993; Kaplan, 1974). It feels good, and children become frustrated if their hands are kept away from their genitals.

Infant self-exploration and masturbation also lay the foundation for developing a broad continuum of sexual feelings and behaviors. **Masturbation** is a normal developmental act, one of the earliest forms of sexual activity. Most children discover masturbation quite innocently as a physical, not sexual, act.

Masturbation Individual or mutual stimulation of genitalia by hand or using other objects

Boys' penile erections often occur as sexual reflexes in response to a variety of stimuli ranging from self-touching to breastfeeding. Girls experience clitoral erection and lubrication and orgasm under similar circumstances.

These earliest attempts at self-exploration teach us about our body and the potential it has for providing pleasure. This healthy exploration can be the foundation for an exploration that continues in adolescence and adulthood. Conversely, self-exploration has the potential for negatively influencing sexual development if parents overreact to their children's attempts at self-stimulation. Adults who punish children for masturbating may be denying them valuable opportunities for learning about self-pleasuring and may set the stage for negative attitudes (shame, guilt, fear) about sex. Parents who say nothing about masturbation send negative messages through their omission. Children learn that these omissions represent areas that are off-limits for discussion.

Nudity

Infants and children are nudists at heart. Most infants and young children are perfectly comfortable lying and running around the house naked. They do not associate nudity with morality. To be naked to them is simply to be

Babies are sensual creatures. They like to be nude and feel softness and textures of things such as sheepskin throws.

© y. van eekelen, 2010. Shutterstock, Inc.

without clothes. Parents and other caregivers (and, later, society at large) teach infants and children that nudity has sexual overtones.

In contrast, Scandinavian cultures have nude beaches that cater to families. Being naked with one's family is considered normal and healthy.

Unlike some other cultures that accept nudity as part of life and don't make a big deal about it one way or another, U.S. culture frowns upon most public displays of nakedness. We owe this to our Puritan heritage. When they came to America, the Puritans enacted many laws that attempted to curtail public displays of nakedness and sexual behavior. To this day, laws dating back to the early 1800s still are on the books concerning things such as proper swimming attire. The rigid views concerning sex and nudity grew out of Victorian England in the 19th century. In that formal, rigid culture, visions of naked flesh were linked to uncontrolled sexual desire and giving into the will of the devil. In an almost comical adherence to covering their exposed limbs, the Victorians went to extremes such as putting "skirts" onto the legs of pianos and chairs lest they offend and tempt their owners to engage in lewd behavior.

 healthy sex hints 7.1

Becoming an Askable Parent

Becoming an askable parent is a lifelong process. A neon sign doesn't suddenly appear during adolescence signaling approachability. Being an askable parent is a reward earned after years of sending subtle messages about the desire to listen and willingness to help. The following are guidelines on how to be an askable parent:

1. *Start early.* Body language and nonverbal behaviors concerning bonding, nudity, and toilet training send messages about approachability.
2. *Don't worry about giving too much information.* Scientific evidence doesn't indicate that too much information too soon will overstimulate children. If a child is getting too much information, he or she will simply get bored, tune you out, and change the subject.
3. *Communicate even if you're not entirely comfortable about the topic.* If you are uncomfortable with a specific sexual issue, you can still address it openly and honestly with your children. The child might respond positively to your admission that you have difficulty talking about an issue.
4. *Admit your ignorance.* You don't know it all. Even the best teachers don't know everything about their subject. If your child asks a question you can't answer, admit it and offer to look it up. Better yet, look it up together.
5. *Realize that less is better.* Concise, simple answers that address the question at hand are better than longwinded answers.
6. *Don't worry about offering information that children can't understand.* If you make a mistake by being too technical, children will extract what they need or understand, and the rest will go over their head.

7. *Don't be afraid to make mistakes.* Everyone makes honest mistakes. Handle these as you would any other mistakes: Admit you were wrong, and try to correct the mistake, if possible.

8. *Relate your values.* Children want to know how you feel about sexual matters. Take every opportunity to share relevant values with them.

9. *Have a sense of humor.* Lighten up. Sexuality education gives rise to opportunities to laugh and learn at the same time. Children feel less inhibited about an adult's talking about sexual matters if sex isn't always portrayed as a deadly serious topic.

Development in Early Childhood

Self-exploration continues during early childhood (ages 3 to 5) and often extends to playmates. The more mobile child now begins to interact with other children more frequently. Games such as "doctor" and "nurse" typically provide opportunities for sex play and exploration. The availability of playmates often influences the nature of play. Same-gender versus opposite-gender exploration is a function of who is available to play with rather than representing any adult sexual orientation (such as heterosexual or homosexual).

As we pointed out in Chapter 4, gender identity is established by age 3 so it is already strongly established by this stage. Little boys and girls know what being masculine and feminine means, and they continue to explore and

When Is **Childhood** Sex Play NOT Normal?

Source: Callista Lee

What generally differentiates normal childhood sex play from problematic behaviors is the pervasiveness and intensity of the behavior. It is normal to develop a fascination with something that is pleasurable and new, but normally a child will not become *preoccupied* with masturbation or sex play with others to the exclusion of other activities. Repeatedly touching another child sexually even when doing so causes the other child to become upset is certainly not normal. Young children do not generally have an opportunity to learn about such adult behaviors as oral or anal sex, so if your child is engaging in these acts with another child, animal or a toy, it is time to calmly ask where they learned about that. It is also unusual for children to attempt to engage in sex play with an adult, unless some adult has taught them to do so. If there is concern about molestation, professionals suggest looking for behavioral signs that may include:

- Sexual behavior that is inappropriate for the child's age
- Bedwetting or soiling the bed, if the child has already outgrown these behaviors

- Not wanting to be left alone with certain people or being afraid to be away from primary caregivers, especially if this is a new behavior
- Tries to avoid removing clothing to change or bathe

Emotional signs may include:
- Excessive talk about or knowledge of sexual topics
- Resuming behaviors that they had grown out of, such as thumb sucking
- Nightmares or fear of being alone at night
- Excessive worry or fearfulness

Do not hesitate to bring your concerns to the attention of the child's teacher, doctor, school nurse, or counselor. An excellent source of information about child sexual abuse as well as sexual abuse of adults is the Rape, Abuse & Incest National Network (RAINN). They can put you in touch with your local sexual assault victims center.

Remember, you are not alone. If you suspect sexual abuse, you can talk to someone who is trained to help. Call the National Sexual Assault Hotline at 800.656.HOPE (4673) or chat online at online.rainn.org.

refine these roles. The more freedom they are given to explore behaviors and roles, the greater opportunity they will have in moving toward a more flexible gender identity. For instance, little girls who are allowed to play with boys and engage in active, physical play and sports might find that they enjoy this type of activity. Little boys who are allowed to play house and with dolls might find this an enjoyable addition to or replacement of more traditional roughhouse activities.

Development in Childhood

Children continue to explore and mimic gender role behaviors and scripts they learn from their parents and the culture. "Playing house" is a common script for 5- to 7-year-olds. The boys play the "daddies," and the girls play the "mommies." Often these games include kissing, hugging, and cuddling. Children at this age talk about people they love and will marry someday. Children often have a "special friend" to whom they are attracted and for whom they have loving feelings. Elementary school children exchange valentines and other symbols of endearment.

By 8 or 9 years of age, children begin to become more segregated in their play. Boys tend to play with other boys, and girls with their girl-friends. Although they still have the same interest in the opposite gender, the socialization process begins to segregate them more and more. Formal activities such as team sports and school-based extracurricular activities are often segregated, sometimes formally but usually informally. Little

healthy sex hints 7.2

Education for Children and Teens

Source: *Callista Lee*

Sexuality educators agree that parents are the primary sexuality educators of their children whether they realize it or not. What you say as well as what you *don't* say make important impressions on your kids. There is a lot of help available for parents. One can check any bookseller for titles. Planned Parenthood has an easy-to-navigate website with resources for parents, teens, and young adults. Check out their resources for parents, which include websites, books you can read with your children, and books for children https://www.plannedparenthood.org/learn/parents/resources-parents

Their information for teens is quite extensive, including topics to read as well as an opportunity to submit questions to the experts. Topics extend beyond what you might expect at Planned Parenthood (pregnancy and STIs) to include relationships, bullying, and LGBTQ issues. https://www.plannedparenthood.org/learn/teens

A couple of titles suggested by the Sexuality Information and Education Council of the United States (SIECUS) include: Deborah Roffman's "Talk to me first: Everything you need to become your kids' Go To Person on sex" (2013), and Debra Hafner's "Beyond the Big Talk", Revised Edition. Every Parent's Guide to Raising Sexually Healthy teens from middle school to college (2008.)

girls who might have played touch football with the guys last season may try out for cheerleading this year. Boys who played sandlot baseball with the neighborhood boys and girls may sign up for Little League, while their female counterparts sign up for softball. Leagues in some towns encourage mixed-gender participation.

In addition to cultural influences that help shape boys and girls and influence which direction they might take regarding sports, economic and political factors play a big part. Often, funding for girls' sports and recreational activities does not equal that earmarked for boys. Consequently, girls haven't always been offered the same opportunities as boys to compete in youth sports. To attempt to rectify that, Title IX of the Civil Rights Act was passed to ensure parity in funding. The law refers to all benefits and activities available in schools. Most of the controversy regarding Title IX revolves around sports and athletic programs. Title IX has been instrumental in getting more girls and women involved in sports and athletic activities.

Development in Preadolescence

Many of the books available for children and teenagers reinforce the idea that children develop at their own pace.

Studies show that although segregation of the sexes is more pronounced during this time, feelings of desire and affection are strong. Most boys and girls of this age view relationships with other preadolescents as important and something they desire. Children in this age range are learning how to interact with members of the same and opposite sexes they find desirable. They are learning the scripts and rehearsing the behaviors necessary to make the transition from childhood to young adulthood. Adults may find some of the behavior amusing, yet the fact that we use the term social skill literally means that skill development is crucial.

Hedgepeth and Helmich (1996), as they developed materials for sexuality educators, have noted that young adolescents between the ages of 12 and 14 are dealing with the following developmental issues:

1. They're worried about their bodies.
2. They're engaged in a search for identity, including sexual orientation identity.
3. They are very centered on the self yet influenced by peer attitudes.
4. They intellectually understand that behavior has consequences but don't necessarily think the consequences will happen to them.
5. They're fearful of asking questions of adults that may make them appear uninformed.

∽ *Intellectual Wellness* ∽

Individuals begin to learn about sexuality from the day of birth. Infants and children learn symbolically. They learn about what feels good through direct physical exploration. They learn about what is taboo by the reactions of significant others.

Children continue to grow as they become more verbal and are able to communicate by asking questions and seeking clarification. Development takes shape according to the answers received and the nonverbal messages attached to the information. If children grow up in a household where sexual questions are allowed and teachable moments are encouraged, the natural curiosity about sex is satisfied.

This learning continues through childhood and adolescence. What differs is the sheer quantity of information to which people are exposed and the sources from which it is derived. Infants and young children receive sexual information mostly from parents and other caregivers. By the time of adolescence, sexual information flows in torrents from sources ranging from parents to friends to mass media to the Internet.

Today, more than ever before, many excellent sources of information about sexuality are available—books, recordings, educational television shows, Web sites, and more. Unfortunately, many poor sources of information and negative gender roles also bombard us daily. The ability to process all of this information and make sense of it is aided by our ever-growing intellectual development and rests on a foundation of "askable parents" and a school environment and curriculum that encourage questions and make information readily available.

Development in Adolescence

Adolescence denotes a period of years (roughly between 12 and 18). The major task associated with adolescence is to develop a self-identity (Erikson, 1978). Adolescence can be a time of great excitement and joy as individuals literally move from childhood to adulthood. During adolescence, both the body and the mind change and grow. They outgrow not only their old clothes but often their old ideas as well, and sometimes their old friends, as they struggle to come to grips with who they are and where they are going.

Experts have come to understand that the promotion of good health behaviors at this stage has a critical impact on adult lifestyles (Hatcher & Scarpa, 2002). Consequently, health programs directed at teens often focus on adolescent risk-taking behaviors with particular attention to tobacco and alcohol use, exercise and nutrition, sleep, accident reduction, and sexuality.

Puberty is the time of myriad physiological events that characterize adolescence. It is a time of profound physiological change as the body matures and becomes "reproductively ready" with fully adult genitalia, a reproductive system, and hormones coursing through the bloodstream, sending messages to the brain of arriving sexually.

Reproductive readiness Pubertal development resulting in full growth of genitalia and onset of fertility

Psychosocial readiness for sexual activity with another person takes a while to catch up to **reproductive readiness.** Adolescents become caught in a state of confusion as the body sends the mind messages about sex that the adolescent may not be ready to handle psychosocially.

Michael Carrera, a respected adolescent sexuality expert, has been working for some time to help teenagers emerge from adolescence as young adults who are strong, competent, and whole. Along with the Children's Aid Society, Carrera (2003) has developed a model for working with youth that has had demonstrable positive results on adolescent health. His program includes getting participants involved with work and money management, educational support that includes tutoring and test preparation designed to move students toward college, a family life/sex education program, involvement in the arts, and participation and development of lifetime individual sports. Simultaneously, students have access to comprehensive medical care including reproductive health care and mental health counseling. Students in his program have shown lower pregnancy rates, delayed onset of intercourse, better sexual health behaviors, and higher graduation rates. The program is currently serving 4000 students per year (Childrens Aid Society, 2017).

Today's teenagers, even those not participating in such a program, seem to be more successful at working toward healthy behaviors and healthy sexuality than those of their parents and grandparents generation. Today's teens smoke less marijuana, use fewer illegal drugs and drink less than their parent's generation. They are also much less likely to get pregnant or have sexual intercourse than their parent's generation (Parker-Pope, 2012).

✎ *Physical, Psychological, and Social Wellness* ✎

Child and adolescent health is positively impacted by participation in exercise and organized sports. Historically, organized sports were seen as important for boys' development, yet of little interest to most girls. Title IX of the 1972 Education Amendments Act outlawed discrimination in secondary and postsecondary educational institutions receiving federal funding. Its impact on reducing gender discrimination in sports has been significant.

In 1971, 1 in 27 girls participated in high school sports compared to 1 in 2 boys. By 2001, the ratio for girls was almost the same as for boys, with 1 in 2.5 girls participating compared to the 1 in 2 ratio for boys (childtrends.org, 2015; Lopiano, 2001). Participation in sports helps teens learn about teamwork, goal setting, and the pursuit of excellence. Physical activity can enhance self-esteem and improve body image. Research has also shown that teenage female athletes are less likely to get pregnant, delay their first sexual intercourse, and report that they had not had sexual intercourse compared to nonathletes (Lopiano, 2001).

Figure 5–1 highlights the physiological changes associated with puberty. In general, these can be grouped into changes associated with primary and secondary sex characteristics.

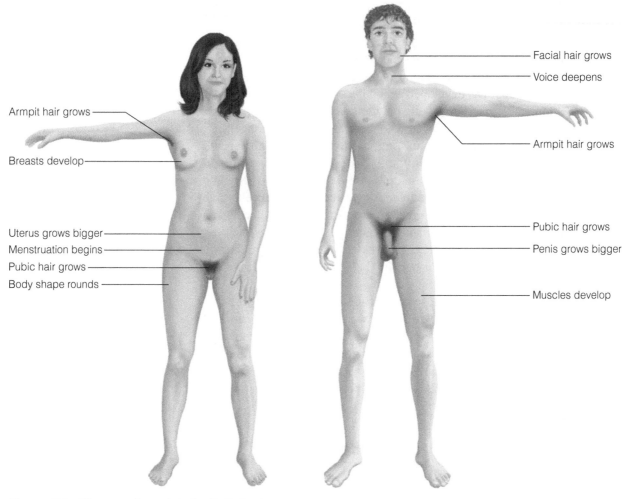

Armpit hair grows ———

Breasts develop ———

Uterus grows bigger ———
Menstruation begins ———
Pubic hair grows ———
Body shape rounds ———

——— Facial hair grows
——— Voice deepens

——— Armpit hair grows

——— Pubic hair grows
——— Penis grows bigger

——— Muscles develop

Figure 7.1 *Changes Associated with Puberty*

Primary Sex Characteristics

Primary sex characteristics Growth of the sex organs

Primary sex characteristics are associated with the full growth and development of the sex organs. A boy's penis and testicles grow and reach full adult size by the end of puberty. The testes begin to produce sperm and androgens, and first ejaculation signals the onset of reproductive readiness.

In girls, the major internal (vagina, ovaries, uterus, and fallopian tubes) and external (labia, mons, clitoris) sexual structures reach maturity. First menstruation is the sign that puberty has arrived.

Secondary Sex Characteristics

Secondary sex characteristics Nongenital changes associated with puberty; include growth of pubic, facial, and underarm hair, breast development, increases in height and weight

Secondary sex characteristics are nongenital changes associated with puberty. Boys and girls both experience a growth spurt and begin to attain their subsequent adult height. They both grow pubic, underarm, and body hair. Although boys characteristically grow significantly more facial hair than girls do, this generally represents a continuum with a range of possibilities for boys and girls, from relatively hairless to very hairy.

Body contours begin to develop. Girls naturally deposit more fat on their hips, thighs and breasts than boys do, but, as with facial and body hair, there is a wide continuum of growth possibilities for both boys and girls. The voice box in boys enlarges, creating a deeper, more resonating sound. The transition period involved in this change causes a squeaky quality to boys' voices.

By the end of puberty, the body has reached a stage of reproductive readiness with two major components: mature reproductive anatomy and hormonally influenced sexual desire. The sex organs are fully developed and capable of procreating as well as recreating. Not only are parts such as the penis and vagina fully mature and capable of responding to sexual desire, but ovaries and testes are also fully able to produce viable ova and sperm, respectively. This is often the time when a young girl discovers that her clitoris is capable of providing sexual pleasure.

In nature's eyes, humans are able and ready to propagate the species. Nature gives a boost in that our **gonads** (testes and ovaries), which have long been silent, now begin to produce hormones that stimulate sexual desire. **Androgens,** primarily **testosterone,** stimulate sexual receptor centers in the brain, which trigger feelings of sexual desire. All of the cold showers in the world will not quell this sexual desire because, to a certain extent, it is fueled by hormones circulating in the bloodstream.

Adolescence has a profound impact on sexuality for the rest of our lives. Often our body image and initial impressions about our masculinity and femininity that were formed at this time color how we view ourselves for the rest of our lives. Old labels and images such as "I'm not a good dancer" or "I'm shy" or "I'm not very good-looking" influence our self-concept and can stay with us for years to come.

Gonads The primary endocrine glands in men (testes) and women (ovaries) that influence sexuality

Androgens A group of naturally occurring steroid hormones produced by both men and women

Testosterone The most notable androgen, recognized for fueling sexual desire and aggressiveness in males

Body Image Issues

Both males and females at some point during the preteen and adolescent years may become obsessed with physical appearance. So many changes are happening to the body, and comparisons to peers and "the rich and famous" can be all consuming. The media standard for female attractiveness is thin, large breasted, tall and beautiful. Males are increasingly also portrayed in an unrealistic

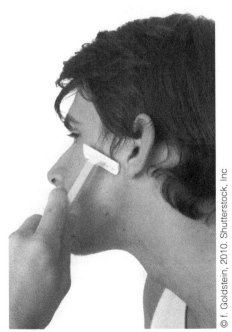

© f. Goldstein, 2010. Shutterstock, Inc

Shaving is an exciting rite of passage for teens.

© Carla Dapino, 2010. Shutterstock, Inc.

manner as they are expected to be tall, broad shouldered, muscular and to have no body hair or odor.

There is a major disconnect between the media's ideal and reality. Adolescents are becoming increasingly overweight, partly due to lack of exercise as well as increased consumption of high-calorie foods. In 2016 the CDC reported that 46% of high school students were trying to lose weight and that 16% were overweight and 14% obese. Not surprisingly the same CDC survey found that 51% did not meet the recommended levels for physical activity (CDC, 2016). Although states mandate that students have regular physical education classes, other programs often interfere with regular, daily exercise. There are barriers to participation in organized sports such as costs, lack of transportation, competing time commitments, competitive pressures, and lack of facilities (American Psychological Association, 2002). In fact, when asked, 14% of adolescents said they had not participated in vigorous physical activity in the past 7 days (CDC, 2016). Former first Lady Michelle Obama made a mission of improving the health of children and adolescents by promoting healthier school lunches and promoting movement and exercise. These much needed changes can go far in helping children and adolescents achieve a healthy weight and positive body image.

Learning to love, accept, and respect one's body is essential for becoming sexually healthy. The impacts of body image on sexual behavior and choices are numerous. Positive body image helps in expressing sexual needs and desires and facilitates sexual health. However the effects of poor body image are significant for both females and males. Females with poor body image are less likely to be assertive and ask for what they want sexually and are less likely to practice safer sex (Zamboni et al, 2006). Males with poor body image are also less likely to practice safer sex and are more likely to withdraw emotionally from their partners. However, men who are comfortable with both their bodies and women's real, not ideal, bodies have a higher level of intimacy with women and participate in more kissing, an intimate sexual activity (Schooler & Ward, 2006).

Adolescent Sexuality

"Becoming a sexually healthy adult is a key development task of adolescence…. Sexual health encompasses sexual development and reproductive health, as well as such characteristics as the ability to develop and maintain meaningful interpersonal relationships; appreciate one's own body; interact with genders in respectful and appropriate ways; and express affection, love and intimacy in ways consistent with one's own values." (Haffner, 1995, p.4). Thus begins the consensus statement of the National Commission on Adolescent Health, endorsed by well respected groups such as the American Medical Association and the American College of Obstetricians and Gynecologist. They believe adolescence is in stages, early-ages 9-13 for women, 11-15 for men; middle- ages 13-16 for girls and 14-17 for males; and late- ages 16 and older for females and 17 and older for males. During early adolescence, youth work to develop a sense of identity, connection, power and joy. If they are not supported in the development of their identity in healthy ways, sexual experimentation may be the easy way for them gain these feelings. The Commission believes that young adolescents do not have the emotional or cognitive maturity to be involved in intimate relations, especially intercourse, so parents, schools and society need to provide positive outlets. During middle adolescence, adolescents seek more independence and begin to value their peers more highly. Sexual expression and experimentation are important in their lives. In late adolescence, they begin to develop more empathetic relationships and begin to transition to adult roles. The Commission believes both families and communities have responsibility in promoting adolescent sexual health. Parents can promote sexual health in ways such as valuing their adolescents and being knowledgeable and openly discussing sexuality. The community can promote comprehensive sexuality education, community programs and accessible health care. (Haffner,1995) What the Commission advocates would bring us closer to the Dutch, German and French model where adolescents are viewed as assets, are valued and respected, and expected to act responsibly. Families in these countries have open, honest discussions with teens about sexuality and support educators and health care providers in making services available to teens. The sexual health outcomes for these teens compared to the U.S. are much more positive. The teen pregnancy rate in the U.S. is more than 4 times higher than the Netherlands and over 3 times higher than Germany. In addition, European teens are much more likely to use contraception than American teens. (Advocates for Youth, 2017). Though we in the United States have much to learn from our European counterparts, some recent trends in adolescent sexual behavior do indicate a move toward healthier behavior.

Masturbation

Conscious, erotic self-stimulation is thought to be among the most common expressions of adolescent sexual behavior, particularly for males. Kinsey and his associates discovered that the rate of masturbation was different for boys and girls (Kinsey, Pomeroy, & Martin, 1948). Among boys in that early study, the level of masturbation increased from 21 percent of 12-year-old boys to 82 percent of 15-year-old boys. Among girls, the level of masturbation increased from 12 percent of 12-year-old girls to 20 percent of 15-year-old girls. By the end of adolescence, more than 90 percent of the boys and about 35 percent of the girls had masturbated.

Compared to Kinsey's study, a 2011 study shows an increased rate of female masturbation with 58% masturbating by the end of adolescence. As in Kinsey's study, males report higher rates (74%) of masturbation than females. Masturbation is more common among 14-17 year olds than any partnered sexual behavior. (Robbins, Schick, Reese, Herbenick, Sanders, Dodge, & Fortenberry, 2011). Unfortunately, there is much silence and discomfort surrounding the topic of masturbation. This lack of openness is a lost opportunity for helping adolescents learn body awareness and healthy expression of sexual desire and experimentation. Masturbation is a way for adolescents to explore their bodies and identify what they find pleasurable. If parents encourage their children to masturbate, it may lessen the guilt children sometimes feel. As a result adolescents may be more comfortable choosing masturbation as an alternative until they are emotionally ready for sexual expression with a partner.

Oral Sex

Source: Callista Lee

The Centers for Disease Control (CDC) reports that about half of males and females aged fifteen to nineteen have engaged in oral sex (Copen, Chandra, & Martinez, 2013). Especially concerning is that many teens don't consider oral sex as "counting" as having sex. For some, oral sex occurs prior to first intercourse, but for nearly 75 percent oral sex is co-occurring with intercourse (Lindberg, Jones, & Santelli, 2008). Most are not aware that sexually transmitted infections (STIs) can be spread that way, and so they consider it to be "safe sex." Neither are they aware that many common STIs can be present (and transmissible) without obvious symptoms. Unfortunately, these facts are often not taught in health classes in middle school or high school, leaving many young people at risk for an unpleasant surprise. This has become a concern for public health agencies.

Sexual Intercourse

The number of teens choosing to have sexual intercourse has greatly declined over the past 20 years. In 1991, over half (54%) of all 9-12th grade students had experienced sexual intercourse and by 2015 the number had fallen to 41%. Males are no more likely to have had sex than females (Kaiser Family Foundation, 2014). The decline in sexual activity among males has been especially steep. Males are now expressing the desire to not be sexually active for the same reasons we hear expressed by females. They wait because they have not met the right person or they are in a relationship and are waiting for the right time. Contrary to popular belief, males are as emotionally invested as females in relationships (Schalet, 2012). Of these sexually active teens, the majority do not have multiple partners in a given time period but instead practice serial monogamy (Kirby, 2007).

Very few teens (3.9%) choose to have sexual intercourse before age 13 (CDC, 2016). This low number is encouraging since those who initiate early intercourse are not likely to be emotionally ready for that level of intimacy (Siecus, 1995). Eighty-five percent of female and 89% of males used some form of birth control the first time they had intercourse (CDC, 2011). The US has witnessed a large (64%) decline in the teen pregnancy rate, dropping from 117 pregnancies per 1000 females age 15–19 in 1990 to 22 per 1000 in 2015 (National Campaign to Prevent Teen Pregnancy, 2015). The abortion rate has also continued to decline from 24 per 1000 women ages 15–17 in 1994 to 9 per 1000 women in 2009 (Pazol, Creanga, & Jamieson, 2015). The overall decline in teen pregnancy can likely be attributed to the decrease in sexual activity and the improved use of reliable contraceptives.

First Sex Among Lesbian/Gay Youth

Sexual behavior patterns in gay and lesbian youth are more complex because of the added dimension of coming to terms with a sexual identity that is different from their heterosexual peers. Sexual behavior seems to be the fourth step in a five-step coming-out process that involves these stages:

1. Fear and suspicion that one's sexual desires and attraction are different (although still not clearly defined)
2. Labeling of those feelings as homoerotic (sexual feelings for someone of the same sex)

personal exploration activity
What Is Right for You?

It is easy to avoid openly examining our beliefs and values concerning sexual activity. Often our sexual behavior is dictated by the moment, not by our values and rational decisions. The goal of this activity is to help you clarify the sexual behavior that is comfortable and acceptable for you, and to identify a plan for making sure you can stick to your sexual values.

Take a few minutes to really examine what you believe and respond to the following questions honestly and openly. You do not need to share this with anyone; however, you might enjoy discussing it with a close friend.

What would be some good reasons or advantages for you to choose to have premarital sex? (If you are married, substitute *extramarital* for *premarital* in each question.) *Example:* "It's fun."

What would be some good reasons or disadvantages for you to choose not to have premarital sex? *Example:* "I could get hurt."

What are some guidelines you need to follow if you choose to have premarital sex? *Example:* "Be honest with my partner about my motives for having sex."

What are some guidelines you need to follow if you choose not to have premarital sex? *Example:* "Don't drink too much."

List the reasons you might choose to have premarital sex in two columns, reasons that would make you feel guilty *Example:* "using a partner for sex" versus guilt-free reasons *Example:* "love".

How can you tell when a premarital sexual relationship becomes unhealthy *Example:* "sex is the only good part of the relationship" or harmful *Example:* "you are doing things you are not comfortable with"?

3. Defining oneself as gay or lesbian
4. Having one's first gay love affair
5. Becoming involved in the gay or lesbian subculture (Troiden, 1988)

Having sexual feelings for someone of the same sex (homoerotic feelings) almost always precedes sexual activity by several years among gay and lesbian people. Gay and lesbian youth today recognize feelings for same-sex partners and act on them earlier than their peers of 20 years ago (Savin-Williams & Rodriguez, 1993).

Cultural Attitudes about Adolescent Sexuality

How does U.S. society view adolescent sexuality? It seems to view adolescent sexual behavior in general, and intercourse in particular, as a "problem" that will lead to negative outcomes (such as unintended pregnancy, sexually transmitted diseases including HIV, and sexual abuse, among others). Many other cultures view this matter entirely differently and celebrate this time in a young person's sexual life as a natural part of maturity. Indeed, in some Pacific Island cultures, adolescent sexual behavior is encouraged, not merely tolerated. This is not to say that these cultures advocate promiscuity. Most have rules pertaining to adolescent sex.

The United States has a conservative sexual history. American culture evolved from devoutly religious, puritanical ancestors who escaped persecution for their views in Europe by coming to this country. The American

sex in society 7.1

Other Cultures, Other Ways

Over the years, researchers have studied societies that recognize and celebrate the onset of puberty in adolescent boys and girls. Ford and Beach (1951) found that more than 70 societies celebrated the onset of puberty in girls and more than 65 that in boys. In a sample of 192 societies, Schlegel and Barry (1979, 1980) found that 80 had no rites of passage, 17 had ceremonies for boys only, 39 had rites for girls only, and 46 had ceremonies for both sexes. Larger societies, with intensive agricultural and manufacturing bases, and those with more complex forms of social organizations, tended not to have initiation rites.

Of the societies celebrating puberty in girls, these celebrations usually coincide with the onset of first menses and are directly related to the sexual significance of menstruation. Schlegel and Barry found that first menses signified fertility and the tribe's continued existence.

These ceremonies often included seclusion of the young women, prohibiting any contact with men. In many instances, the ceremonies included instruction from older women in matters pertaining to sex and marriage. In some cultures, the young women were "deflowered" or subjected to piercing, tattooing, or genital adornment or mutilation. Frequently, the occasion was also marked by a feast or celebration.

Schlegel and Barry found that segregation from males at this time is usually based on avoiding contact with menstrual flow, which is feared because of its supposed ability to weaken a hunter's abilities or contaminate the tribe's meat sources.

For boys, unlike with girls' first menses, no clear demarcation indicates that puberty has begun. Generally, boys are given the rites when evidence is sufficient (usually secondary sex characteristics) that they have reached puberty. Boys' ceremonies are similar to girls' in that they usually include some form of seclusion, instruction, and ritualistic physical sacrifice (often circumcision).

The Sexual Culture of Mangaia

In the 1950s, anthropologist Donald Marshall studied the sexual attitudes and activities of the people of Mangaia, the southernmost island in the Polynesian Cook chain. There, he found, the people were exposed to sexuality from early childhood. They listened to folk stories that included detailed accounts of sex acts and sexual anatomy, and they watched sensual ritual dances.

As adolescents, males underwent *superincision,* a surgical procedure in which the tissue at the end of the penis was cut and folded back, which exposed the glans. They were taught how to stimulate a woman's genitals and breasts with the mouth, how to bring female partners to orgasm, and how to control the timing of ejaculation. Mangaian girls were taught to be responsive and to participate actively during sexual activity.

In a practice called "night-crawling," a young male would sneak into the home of a young woman with the intent to have sexual intercourse. Because most homes had a single sleeping area, this act tended to be more public than private, though the other family members feigned sleep. The parents approved of night-crawling and listened for their daughter's laughter—a sign that she was happy with her partner. The parents encouraged their children to have more than one sexual partner before marriage, to find the most sexually compatible mate.

After marriage, couples in Mangaia continued to engage in sex more often than most Western countries. The emphasis, though, shifted from the number of orgasms during a single session to a goal of copulation every night. Throughout life, the emphasis for males and females alike was on pleasing the partner (Marshall, 1971).

patriarchal culture emphasized the family and historically has viewed sex as something that occurs within the context of a marriage, with the primary function being procreation.

Besides having a moral tradition that prohibits adolescent sexual education and experimentation, U.S. culture, like that of many industrialized societies, prolongs adolescent and young adult dependency. To succeed, adolescents, in most cases, need to further their education. For most of them, this means remaining indebted to their parents and pursuing additional training and education while either living at home or remaining financially obligated to their parents. In a sense, what this does is delay the transition from childhood to adulthood, and delaying with it adult privileges such as sexual experimentation. In many other cultures, adolescents are encouraged to begin to separate from their parents earlier, and this separation is often institutionalized in a formal rite of passage.

Perhaps, a shift in American attitudes toward adolescent sexuality are long overdue. Viewing sexuality as a natural part of adolescent development is essential. Following the European model, American parents can encourage adolescents to be fully informed and to give them the rights, respect and responsibility they need and deserve. Talking openly about sexual behavior, sexual values and decisions can help guide young people in making more responsible decisions (Berne and Huberman, 1999). We can learn lessons from those teens who do choose to practice healthy behaviors. Teens who have more parental supervision, who come from two parent households and who do well in school are more likely to delay sexual intercourse until late teens or beyond (Parker-Pope, 2009).

Education and Sexual Development

Ideally, sexuality education would be infused in all parts of the developing child and adolescents life. It would begin early, with open honest discussions and questions among parents and children. The education would then continue in the pediatricians office. According to the American Academy of Pediatrics, (2001) " Children and adolescents need accurate and comprehensive education about sexuality to practice healthy sexual behaviors as adults." They believe the pediatrician has a responsibility to provide good sexuality education to his/her patients. In the churches, synagogues, mosque, and in the community, discussions on sexual values and behaviors add to the sexual education of children and adolescents. In addition, sexuality education should begin early in the school career. If education is to be effective in delaying onset of intercourse it needs to be implemented by 5th grade (Frost & Forrest, 1995). However, abstinance only education has not been shown to delay onset of intercourse or increase safer sex practices (Frost and Forrest, 1995). Early comprehensive sexuality education that includes practical skills such as decision making and refusal skills should be an integral component of the early educational experience.

Fortunately, the support for sex education in the schools is at an amazingly high rate of 93% of Americans saying sex education should be taught in the schools, according to the NPR/Kaiser/KennedySchool poll (2003). As of January, 2017, twenty four states and the District of Columbia mandated sex education in the schools (Guttmacher, 2017). However, this leaves far too many students without access to reliable information about sexuality provided by well-trained educators.

Federal Support of Sex Education

Source: Callista Lee

Although each state is free to teach sexuality education as they wish, the availability of federal funding does influence their decision-making. The teen pregnancy rate was considered a national crisis in the 1980s and 90s. During the Clinton administration (1993-2000), federal dollars for abstinence-only sex ed rose to US$80 million annually, while dollars for more comprehensive sex ed remained at zero. During the George W. Bush administration (2001-2008), spending on abstinence-only sex ed more than doubled, peaking at US$177 million annually. If a state accepted the money, it had to assure that *only* abstinence-only sex was allowed in its public schools. California was one of only four states that refused the funding so that its school districts could continue to make local decisions about what to teach. With the election of Barack Obama, funding for abstinence-only sex ed dropped to Clinton-era levels, and funding finally appeared for more comprehensive sex ed. More than twice the money for comprehensive sex ed was available than for abstinence-only programs. Today, sexuality educators fear that we may be headed back to the days when the federal government only supports abstinence-only sex ed programs due to a more conservative Senate and Presidency (Donovan, 2017).

Being aware of how changes in politics can affect sexuality education is part of supporting one's social well-being. Clinton's Surgeon General, Dr. Joycelyn Elders, kept her post for just a little over a year due to her belief that Americans should be talking more about sex during high school rather than less. She supported schools providing condoms and even suggested teaching young people to consider masturbation as an alternative to sexual intercourse as a way of preventing pregnancy and the spread of STIs. Her comments about masturbation brought about such outrage from the religious right that Clinton felt that he needed to fire her. An interview with her is included in a 2016 documentary, "Sticky: A (Self) Love Story" (Schonfeld, 2016). Throughout this time, researchers have known that abstinence-only sex education is not effective in its stated goal of getting teens to abstain from sex until marriage. It does not raise the age of first sexual intercourse or decrease pregnancy rates. And because condoms are condemned in these curricula, it does not help to prevent the spread of sexually transmitted infections But still, the federal government has funded it despite there being zero benefit (Donovan, 2017). As a taxpayer, you might care about this waste of tax dollars.

Sexuality researchers and educators have been promoting a more comprehensive approach to sexuality education since the 1970s because it has been shown to help teens to make healthier decisions. Public fears that it encourages young people to experiment with sex have not been supported (Guttmacher Institute, 2007). While many Americans feel that the teen pregnancy crisis is over now that we have seen a large decrease, the rate is still too high. The US' teen pregnancy rate is six times that of the Netherlands, four times that of Germany and almost three times that of France despite there being a similar number of teens having sex. As for STIs, the US rate for Gonorrhea is thirty-three times that of the Netherlands, and the US rate for Chlamydia is nineteen times higher. The differences lie in culture and policy. Rather than viewing adolescents as problems, in Germany, France, and the Netherlands they are viewed as assets to the community. Respect is shown to teens along with an expectation that they will act responsibly. *Research rather than politics or religious pressure* is the basis for their national health and education policies. Educators provide accurate and complete information to youth, and sexuality is included at all grade levels in age-appropriate discussions. Families have open and honest discussions with teens and support educators and health providers in making information and services available to teens. Youth have convenient access to free or low-cost contraception through national health insurance (Advocates for Youth, 2009). As you consider what your sex education experience has been, you might want to think about the legacy you would like your generation to leave the youth of America.

Communication about Adolescent Sexuality

An open, honest and positive approach may be the best way to address adolescent sexuality. Teaching adolescents to value and respect their bodies may improve sexual decision making. If parents think their adolescent children would be better off to delay sexual intercourse or other forms of sexual activities with a partner, it is best for them to tell their children this and explain why. The healthy way to do this is to admit honestly to young people that sex is a natural, healthy but powerful force in their lives and that, as parents, you would prefer them to redirect that sexual energy from sexual intercourse into other, less risky sexual outlets, such as hugging, kissing, and masturbation. To deny the power of adolescent sexual urges or, worse, not mention it and hope the subject will never come up is unhealthy and dishonest.

Included in this open discussion should be an examination of the sexual attitudes and behaviors portrayed in the media, including film, television, music, and the internet. The media may be one of the most powerful influences on an adolescent's views of sexuality. By the time an adolescent graduates from high school, he/she will have watched more hours of television, 15,000, than hours spent in the classroom, 12,000 (Strasburger, 1993). According to a 2005 study by the Kaiser Family Foundation, the number of sexual scenes on television has nearly doubled since 1998. While the inclusion of safer sex discussions has increased since 1998 it has recently leveled off. The study found that sexual content was a part of 70% of all shows and that they average 5 sexual scenes per hour (Kaiser Family Foundation, 2005). Sexual references are common in prime time TV, music videos, and music. Educating teens to critically view the media and accept it as fantasy and entertainment is an important step in minimizing this negative influence.

© G. barskaya, 2010. Shutterstock, Inc.

Parents can be a great source of support and information.

Gay adolescents can face even more issues. Not only do they have to deal with the mixed messages and pressures associated with this part of their lives, but they also face a wall of silence concerning their own emerging preferences. Gay adolescents may learn early on that discussing their attraction to same-gender partners is taboo. Often there are too few social supports and people are available to turn to for these adolescents. Local chapters of Parents and Friends of Lesbians and Gays (PFLAG) and other gay and lesbian organizations are excellent places to find help and information about resources.

Helping teens and adolescents learn to accept themselves and develop tolerance and respect for the sexuality of others remains an ongoing challenge to parents, schools and agencies working with youth.

References

Advocates for Youth (2017, January). *Adolescent sexual health in Europe and the United States.* Retrieved from http://www.advocatesforyouth.org

American Academy of Pediatrics(2001). Sexuality Education for Children and Adolescents, Pediatrics, 108, 498–502.

Berne, L &Huberman, B (1999). European Approaches to Adolesecent Sexual Behavior and Responsibility. Advocates for Youth. Washington, D.C.

Carrera, M. (2003, October). The Children's Aid Society—Carrera Adolescent Sexuality and Pregnancy Prevention Program. Paper presented at the Network for Family Life Education's 20th Anniversary Conference, "20 Years of Great Sex(Ed): Lessons from the Past, Plans for the Future."

Child Trends (2015, October). *Participation in school athletics.* Retrieved from http://www.childtrends.org.

Children's Aid Society (2017). Carrera adolescent pregnancy prevention program to stop teen pregnancy. Retrieved from http://www.childrensaidsociety.org

Elliott, V. (2002). Health risks make some fashion trends " don'ts.' American Medical News. Retrieved from http://www.amednews.com.

Ferber, S. G., Laudon, M., Kuint, J., Weller, A., & Zisapel, N. (2002, December). Massage therapy by mothers enhances the adjustment of circadian rhythms to the nocturnal period in full-term infants. *Journal of Developmental & Behavioral Pediatrics, 23*(6), 410.

Ford, C. S., & Beach, F. A. (1951). *Patterns of sexual behavior.* New York: Harper.

Globus, S. K. (2002, Spring). Touch me, I'm yours: The benefits of infant massage. *Special Delivery, 25*(1), 8.

Gordon, S., & Gordon, J. (1983). *Raising a child conservatively in a sexually permissive world.* New York: Simon & Schuster.

Gunter, T & Mcdowell, B. (2004). Body piercing: issues in adolescent health. Journal for Specialists in Pediatric Nursing, 9, 67–69.

Haffner, D. (Editor) (1995). Facing facts: Sexual health for America's adolescents. Sexuality Information Council of the United States.

Hall, C. S. (1954). *A primer of Freudian psychotherapy.* New York: Mentor.

Hatcher, J. L., & Scarpa, J. (2002, July). *Encouraging teens to adopt a safe, healthy lifestyle: A foundation for improving adult behaviors.* Child Trends Research Brief. Washington, DC: Child Trends.

Hedgepeth, E., & Lemich, J. (1996). *Teaching about sexuality and HIV.* New York: New York University Press.

Kaiser Family Foundation (2004). *NPR/ Kaiser/ Kenndy School Poll-Sex education in America.* Retrieved from http://www.kkf.org.

Kaiser Family Foundation (2005, November). *Number of sex scenes on TV nearly doubles since 1998.* Retrieved from http://www.kff.org.

Kaiser Family Foundation. (2008, September). *Sexual Health of Adolescents and Young Adults in the United States.* Retrieved from http://www.kff.org./womenshealth/upload/3040

Kaiser Family Foundation (2014 January). Sexual Health of Adolescents and Young Adults in the United States. Retrieved from http://www.kff.org/womenshealth/3040.cfm

Kaplan, H. S. (1974). *The new sex therapy.* New York: Brunner/Mazel.

Kinsey, A. C., Pomeroy, W. B., & Martin, C.E. (1948). *Sexual behavior in the human male.* Philadelphia: Saunders.

Kirby, D. (2007) Emerging Answers 2007: Research Findings on Programs to Reduce Teen Pregnancy and Sexually Transmitted Disease. *National Campaign to Prevent Teen and Unplanned Pregnancy.* Washington D. C.

Leung, A. (1993). Childhood Masturbation. *Clinical Pediatrics.*

Lopiano, C. (2001). *Equity in women's sports: A health and fairness perspective.* Retrieved from http:// www.womenssportsfoundation.org.

Marshall, D. (1971). Sexual behavior on Mangaia. In D. Marshall & R. Suggs (Eds.), *Human sexual behavior: Variations in the ethnographic spectrum.* Englewood Cliffs, NJ: Prentice Hall.

Mayo Clinic (2015, April 17). Infant massage; Understanding this soothing therapy. Available: mayoclinic.org

Montague A. (1986). *Touching* (3rd ed.). New York: Columbia University Press.

Parker-Pope, T. (2009, January 27). The Myth of Rampant Teenage Promiscuity. New York Times.

Parker-Pope, T. (2012, February 5). The Kids are more than all right. The New York Times.

Pazol, K., Creanga, A., Zane, S. Burley, K., Jamieson, D. (2012). Abortion surveillance- United States, 2009. Available :www.cdc.gov

Robbins, C. Schick, V. Reece, M. Herbenick, D. Sanders, S. Dodge, B. Fortenberry, D. (2011). Prevalence, frequency & association of masturbation with partnered sexual behaviors among U.S. adolescents. Archives of Pediatrics. Available online: http://archpedi.jamanetwork.com.exproxy.

Savin-Williams, R., & Rodriguez, R.G. (1993). A developmental, clinical perspective on lesbian, gay male, and bisexual youth. In T. P. Gullets et al. (Eds.), *Adolescent sexuality.* Newbury Park, CA: Sage.

Schalet, A. (2012, April 6). Caring, romantic American boys. The New York Times.

Schlegel, A., & Barry, H. (1979). Adolescent initiation ceremonies: Cross-cultural codes. *Ethnology,* 18, 199–210.

Schlegel, A., & Barry, H. (1980). The evolutionary significance of adolescent initiation ceremonies. *American Ethnologist,* 7, 696–715.

Schooler, D. & Ward, M. (2006). Average Joes: Men's relationships with media, real bodies, and sexuality. Psychology of Men and Masculinity. Vol. 7, no. 1, 27–41.

Sonenstein, F. L., Pleck, J. H., & Hu, L. C. (1989). Sexual activity, condom use, and AIDS awareness among adolescent males. *Family Planning Perspectives,* 2(14), 152–158.

Strasburger, V.C. (1992) Adolescents and the media: five crucial issues. Adolescent Medicine, 4, 479–493.

Troiden, R. (1988). *Gay and lesbian identity: A sociological analysis.* New York: General Hall.

Watson, J. *Behaviorism* (1970). New York: Norton.

Zamboni, B. Robinson, B. & Brockting, W. (2006). Body image and sexual functioning among bisexual women. Hawthorn Press.

Chapter
eight

Adult Sexuality

Student Learning Objectives

After reading this chapter, students will be able to

- Describe the typical developmental tasks associated with young adulthood through older adulthood.
- Relate the findings of a variety of studies concerning the sexual behavior of college students and young adults.
- Assess a variety of living arrangements of the college years and young adulthood.
- Examine the major developmental tasks associated with adulthood.
- Assess a variety of sexual lifestyles in adulthood.
- Explain the impact of aging on sexual response and behavior.
- Describe the developmental course of long-term straight, gay, and bisexual relationships.
- Identify the major areas of discord and stress in marital and long-term intimate relationships.
- Discuss the effects of divorce and widowhood on adult sexuality.

case study 8.1

Maria, aka Supermom

Maria, 35, has been married for 15 years and has three children, ages 12, 10, and 7. Married as soon as she finished at the local community college with an associate's degree, she worked full-time for a year at an accounting office. As soon as she started having children, however, the idea of continuing to work and pay for day care made no financial sense. She and her husband decided she should stay home with the kids, and she could bring in some money doing child care in her home.

Once the kids were in school all day, Maria realized that she wanted to finish her own education and earn her bachelor's degree in accounting. All along she'd taken primary responsibility for the child rearing, cooking, cleaning, and chauffeuring the kids to appointments, activities, and play dates. She was an officer with the PTA, den mother for the Cub Scouts, Sunday school teacher, and all-around busy stay-at-home mom. The change of going back to school has markedly increased her stress but, in an odd way, also energized her.

Maria is finding that her relationships with her kids and husband are changing. She seems to have less time to give each the attention they want. Maria heads off for her own classes as soon as the kids are on their way. She carries a cell phone for emergencies and has been lucky that the kids have stayed well and she hasn't been beeped in the middle of her classes. Dinners aren't quite as nutritious as they had been, with more drive-through pickup meals than she'd like. She likes to get up at 5:30 A.M to enjoy the quiet of the morning before all the chaos sets in. That has been a good time for her to study while running the wash.

She and her husband find that they have to schedule "dates" now in order to be together as a couple. At the end of the week, it takes purposeful planning to keep the romance alive. It hasn't been easy, juggling the demands of motherhood, housework, and school, but everyone is adjusting. Maria feels she's making a successful passage into another phase of her life.

Critical Thinking

Can you identify some strategies Maria and her family could develop to reduce her workload and stress levels?

Intimacy A gradual process of sharing one's innermost feelings with another

The primary task we face as young adults, according to Erik Erikson (1978), is the development of **intimacy**—forming committed, intimate, loving relationships. We begin to move away from the adolescent focus on ourselves toward exploring mutually satisfying relationships. This stage emphasizes commitment, both in intimate relationships and in work.

This is an exciting time of life. We meet new friends, explore intimate, loving relationships, and test the waters for work and career possibilities. This is the first time many college students are living apart from their parents. It is a time of unparalleled freedom. It is a perfect time to become the person we really want to be and a time to explore new ways of being us. Students who have mastered the developmental tasks of adolescence and childhood enter this period in their lives ready and eager to sample all that life has to offer. Maria's life, as described in Case Study 8.1, highlights the many demands of adulthood, some of which compete for time and attention.

Dating and Intimate Relationships

Friendships fill a special place in our lives

© y. arcurs, 2010. Shutterstock, Inc.

Every society has some rituals or norms for pairing and courtship. Although the "rules" for dating and courtship vary from culture (and subculture) to culture, every society has traditions that it passes along from one generation to the next. Adults who came of age in the late 1960s and early 1970s in the United States vividly remember the differences between the rigid rules of the 1950s and the more liberated late 1960s and early 1970s. Prior to the cultural revolution of the 1960s, a young woman would not even consider asking a man out for a date. Men were expected to ask women out, pay for the evening's activities, and be responsible for picking up and dropping off their dates. Women were expected to wait for men to call them, even if a woman was interested and wanted to initiate contact. The popular media played out these and other traditional dating scenarios, and mothers and fathers passed them on to their daughters and sons. Everyone was assumed to be heterosexual, and sex was not a part of the evening's activities. Although we have moved toward equality for both sexes, there is still comfort in and acceptance of these traditional dating behaviors (Paynter & Campbell, 2016). However, these traditional gender rituals often do not encourage power sharing in romantic relationships. Research suggest that the equality and cooperation shown in friendship can be a better foundation for a healthy romantic relationship (Paynter & Campbell, 2016 Eaton & Rose, 2011).

For many, the face of dating today looks dramatically different. As will be discussed in this chapter, it may be more comfortable for students to use the terms talking, *hooking up and seeing someone* rather than *date* (Crawford & Popp, 2003). Regardless of the term used, the behavior involved can reflect greater role flexibility. A woman can initiate a date, pick up her date, and pay for the date. Straight, gay, and bisexual men and women have their own clubs, organizations, and dating services that make finding a partner easier and safer.

Although the rituals and rules of dating change over time, the purpose of dating hasn't changed much. Dating serves the important function of helping us decide with whom we want to spend more time and the characteristics we desire in a potential partner. Dating is an effective mechanism for developing intimate relationships.

❧ *Emotional and Social Wellness* ❧

The emotional dimension of wellness requires that we acknowledge the full range of emotions associated with our changing roles and responsibilities. Most of the major developmental tasks associated with the adult stages of our lives are part of social wellness: forming intimate relationships, committing ourselves to others and to our work, being productive—in relationships, work, and so on. Understanding our emotional responses and developing interpersonal social skills become critical as we navigate the challenges associated with adulthood.

The social legacy we develop and leave behind can be one of a caring child, loving partner, and/or devoted parent. We can move through the stages of our relationships eagerly anticipating the changes and tasks that await us. We can also move through life and relationships with a self-centeredness that obscures all propensities for caring, sharing, and nurturing. Adulthood and older age may be viewed as opportunities for continued growth, reflection, and self-acceptance; for some, this stage of life may be marked by bitterness and regret. Overall health is enhanced by positive attitudes and a willingness to be a loving, caring individual who is fully engaged in living.

College Sexual Standards and Relationships

A review of the research confirms that sexual attitudes may have become more egalitarian in recent years, yet there are still differences for males and females. Females may be judged for having had sex at an early age, having had many partners in the past, and for having sex outside a committed relationship. Males may also judge behaviors differently when seeking dating partners as opposed to long-term partners (Crawford & Popp, 2003).

Because of sampling issues, it is more difficult to assess lesbian, bisexual, and gay student mores. The process of "coming out," finding a partner, and being free to date openly is of paramount concern to the gay, lesbian, and bisexual community of students. Like their heterosexual peers, however, gay, lesbian, and bisexual individuals may judge a potential partner's past sexual history.

All students, irrespective of sexual orientation, however, need to assess their personal levels of interest, sexual involvement, and commitment as they form pairs with others. Engaging in behavior that is consistent with one's personal values and feeling comfortable in sexual situations is essential. When our behaviors do not match our personal values, we often experience the effects of guilt. Guillt is a signal to us that we need to reevaluate our behavior and or values and make changes so that our behavior consistently reflects our values.

Sexual Behavior among College Students

Hooking up A sexual encounter between two people who may or may not know each other well and are not seriously dating

Although a common perception is that **hooking up** is the universal behavior at colleges and universities, the data do not support this belief. A valuable source of information on sexual behavior of college students is the American College Health Association's yearly assessment of college behaviors. Data for the 2016 survey were gathered from 95,761 surveys taken at 137 colleges and universities. The researcher assessed how many sexual partners students had in the last year for the activities often associated with hooking up: oral sex, vaginal sex or anal sex. One out of 3 (33%) students reported having 0 sexual contacts in the past year while almost 1 out of 2 (44%) reported only 1 contact. Less than 1 in 10 (9%) reported having 4 or more contacts refuting the idea that all students are active with multiple partners. The number was similar in the 2003 American College Health Association survey when 75%

of students reported having 0-1 sexual contacts during the past year. However, only 14% of students thought the typical student had only 0-1 sexual contacts in the past year (American College Health Association, 2012).

The perception that all college students have had sexual intercourse is also not accurate. One in three (30%) college students report never having had vaginal sex while less than 1 in 2 (48%) reported having done so within the last 30 days. Similarly less than one in three (30%) of students have never tried oral sex while less than half (44%) have experienced oral sex within the last 30 days. The number of students who had never had anal sex was even higher at three out of four (75%) (American College Health Association, 2016). These data reinforce the variety of sexual choices students are making and underscore the fact that many are choosing not to hook up. It is common for us to believe that everyone has more sexual partner, more friends, more money and other things than we have. Examining actual data about sexual behavior of college students can help in understanding where the truth really lies and understanding that there are other students making the same sexual choices we are making.

Cohabitating

Cohabitating is the most common type of relationship among women and men in their twenties and will precede more than half of all marriages (Jay 2012; Scott, Schelar, Manlove, & Cui, 2009). The rates of cohabitation among college age people have dramatically increased in recent years. In a study by Child Trends, a nonprofit research group, 1 in 5 young adults was unmarried and living with a romantic partner (Scott et al, 2011). Of those who cohabit, half will marry within three years and if they are college graduates, the marriage will last at least 10 years (Wang, 2014; Roberts,

Cohabitation Living together without being married

---

personal exploration activity

Relationship Contract: How Much Am I Willing to Compromise?

The goal of this activity is to help you decide what you really need to have a healthy, happy, and supportive long-term relationship.

The following questions could be made into a relationship contract by which you and your future long-term partner agree to abide. Answer the questions as if you could have your ideal in the relationship. If you are in a relationship now, ask your partner to do the same and then compare your answers. This should cause a lively debate.

Freedom

Will we still maintain our outside friendships? Do we have the freedom to make new friends? Are we free to spend time with our same and opposite-sex friends without our partner? In what types of activities can we participate? Will we participate in sexual relationships outside this one?

Money

How will we make sure money is not a problem for our relationship? Will we have a budget, and, if so, what do we do if one does not follow the budget? Will we keep our own money or have a joint bank account? What will be our financial priorities? Will we make financial decisions as a team?

Chores

How will we divide our responsibilities so that neither of us feels overwhelmed or taken advantage of?

Who will do the laundry, pay the bills, clean the house, take care of the yard, shop for groceries, cook, buy gifts for our families, run the errands?

Free Time

Will we spend all of our free time together? What types of activities will we do to keep the relationship from becoming boring? Will we spend most of our free time with friends, family, or alone?

Children

Will we have children? How many? What lengths are we willing to go to if one of us is infertile? Will one of us stay home to raise the children? Will we raise them as a team?

2010). Motivations for cohabitating include testing compatibility, spending more time together and sharing the financial burden. Data from one study showed very positive views toward cohabitation among those 20-24. Fifty seven percent agreed with the following statement: "It is all right for an unmarried couple to live together even if they are not interested in considering marriage" and only 25% disagreed. (Scott et al, 2009).

Does Cohabitation Prepare Couples for Marriage?

Source: Callista Lee

Most people assume that if living together goes well for a couple, then their marriage is likely to go well too. Yet most researchers have found that couples who cohabit prior to marriage report *lower* marital satisfaction (Jose, O'Leary, & Moyer, 2010) and a higher rate of divorce than those who waited to live together until after the wedding. Students sometimes suggest that maybe it is because they used up all of their excitement while living together and don't have any left for marriage. But if that were the problem, any married couple would eventually run out of the excitement of a new relationship and divorce, which is not the case. As it turns out, those responsible for the higher divorce rate among premarital cohabita-

tors are individuals who were not great candidates for long-lasting marriage in the first place (Thornton, Axinn, & Xie, 2010). They may have moved in and out of relationships in the past, setting a pattern of giving up on relationships when things get tough. Or they may not be very committed to the institution of marriage, viewing it as an antiquated social norm. Or they may have poor relationship skills. After all, bad experiences in the past don't automatically teach us how to do better in the future. To do better, we have to acknowledge our own mis-steps as well as those of our exes. Next comes learning how to actually behave differently, which is easier said than done. Some couples may develop poor habits while cohabitating prior to marriage but enter marriage with high hopes that things will be better ... by the "magical power" of their wedding day. Learning to be better partners is something they should be doing *before* getting married.

Adults who grew up in homes in which the parents exhibited poor communication and problem solving, or verbal, physical, or emotional abuse have missed out on the opportunity to grow up with role models who could show them how to have a successful and happy marriage. As kids, they may have vowed to not have an unhappy marriage like their parents, but just having good intentions is not enough.

Relationships require behavioral skills as well love and good intentions. More on that topic in Chapter 10. For people wanting to be different from their role models, it may help to seek out other role models such as relatives or friends in a happy long-term relationship. Pay attention to how they treat each other, how they handle disagreements, and how they talk about each other. Books and courses on marriage may be helpful, but for people who came from truly *broken* homes, spending time in therapy may be needed. You will find additional advice in the section on cohabitation in the section on Adult relationships later in this chapter.

Married

Today, most undergraduates who plan on marriage wait until they graduate to marry. Recent data from the Child Trends study finds only 1 in 5 college age respondents were married. These low rates of marriage reflect the trend toward waiting to marry. In 1960 the median age for marriage for men was 23 and by 2016 rose to 29. A similar trend can be seen for women whose median age for marriage in 1960 was 20 compared to 27 in 2016 (Census Bureau, 2016; Scott et al, 2011: Cohen, 2011).

Adult Sexual Behavior

Both masturbation and sexual intercourse are common behaviors throughout the life span. The largest nationally representative and comprehensive study on sexual behavior ever conducted in the United States, the National Survey of Sexual Health, found masturbation common in the 30-39 age range for both men (80%) and women (63%). These rates were only slightly lower than the rates for college age men (83%) and women (64%). Sexual intercourse patterns in the 30-39 age group revealed intercourse to be a norm for both men (85%) and women (74%) (NSSHB, 2017).

Physical and Intellectual Wellness

As we move through adulthood, we continue to be responsible for maintaining and enhancing our physical well-being. The experiences we've had earlier on may "catch up," making physical health no longer something to be taken for granted. The choices we made, behaviors we adopted, and lifestyles we lived will either enhance or undermine our sexuality. Abusing our bodies and letting our physical well being decline will have a negative impact on our sexuality. Everything from body image to sexual response to overall energy level may decline. This will impact negatively on our social relationships with lovers, spouses, employers, and others. Better body image, sexual response, and energy level will help us meet the demands of our ever-changing sexuality. This state of wellness will not only enhance our personal functioning but also positively influence our relationships.

The ability to gather information, critically analyze it, and make good decisions is a hallmark of high-level mental functioning. Rational thinking and logical reasoning can help us understand the nature of our ever-changing sexuality as we pass through young adulthood into adulthood and older age. Having reasonable expectations about our sexuality, based on solid information, can guide us in decision making. It also can help us avoid unrealistic expectations about relationships and sexuality that are likely to lead to personal unhappiness and dissatisfaction with partners. It is important to determine the personal value of the information to which we're exposed —what relates to us, what can constructively impact our sexual health.

Laumann et al. (1994) have examined masturbation in light of its relational context. They believe that masturbation, like all forms of sexual expression, is driven by a variety of social and biological factors throughout the life cycle and can have complementary, supplementary, or independent status with reference to partnered sex. This means that masturbation can enhance partnered sexual activity. It also can be an additional source of sexual expression within the context of the relationship, and last, it can serve as a solitary source of sexual pleasure independent of partnered sex. The level of masturbation is not related to relationship status.

Rather than reinforce the stereotype that masturbation is a substitute for partnered sex, this finding shows that this isn't necessarily so. Masturbation can actually improve partnered sex by helping each identify what feels the most pleasurable so this can be shared with a partner. The frequency of individual masturbation is as likely to be a function of social factors and a variety of reasons as it is the availability of alternative outlets.

Addendum to Adult Sexuality

Source: Callista Lee

Sexuality in middle adulthood may need to be redefined, especially in long-term cohabitating or marital relationships. Habit, competing family and work obligations, fatigue, and unresolved conflicts may erode the passion of a couple's earlier sex life. This is a time when couples need to make their sexual relationship a priority, finding new ways to keep that spark alive. Accepting one's changing body is another adaptation in middle adulthood. Variations in sexual frequency among long-term couples differ widely, although all couples do report a decrease in frequency over time. That said, married couples do report having more sex than single people, who are often without partners. Most couples don't report that the declining frequency of sex is a major problem if their overall relationship is satisfying (Sprecher & McKinney, 1993). And their level of sexual satisfaction, despite the decreased frequency, is higher than when they were single. More than 50 percent of married men report that they are extremely satisfied physically and emotionally with their partner, while forty to forty-five percent of married women report extreme satisfaction (Lindau & Gavrilova, 2010). Adult relationships tend to have complex expectations: emotional support, shared time and values, personal enrichment, security, companionship, love, and commitment. Long-term couples have been able to learn each other's likes and dislikes and feel more comfortable communicating than newer couples. Their general comfort level with one another is also greater as they have built trust in each other and commitment to staying together. Sexual satisfaction is very important to overall marital satisfaction (Brezsnyak & Whisman, 2004).

Adult Relationships

One of the major developmental tasks of adulthood is the continuation and deepening of the commitment to relationships that began in young adulthood. For many Americans, this means a commitment to marriage and a family. For others, the commitment to someone else does not involve marriage but, instead, cohabitation. This is also a period frequently marked by divorce or the death of a spouse. In the remaining part of this chapter, we'll examine the changing nature of adult relationships.

Singlehood

A significant percentage of Americans are choosing to remain single for life. Reasons for remaining single include changes in sexual standards, greater financial independence for women, changing economic times, and shifting conceptions of marriage. Even being a single parent has lost much of it stigma and presently, one third of all births are to single women (Bumpass, 2004). Sometimes, postponing marriage results in an inadvertent slide into permanent singlehood (Cavanaugh, 1993). According to Pew Research projections based on census data, when today's young adults reach their mid 40's to mid 50's, a record high (25%) will have never been married. However, slightly more than half of those not married would like to eventually marry (Wang & Parker, 2014). Others realize that they can live satisfying lives being single. In today's society, there is less urgency to marry, especially if they feel no desire to have children.

Regardless of the reasons, most people who chose to remain single for life reported that they were quite happy. Contrary to popular beliefs, most singles are not lonely, and they develop alternative social patterns based on friendships and non- marital love relationships. The satisfaction that singles derive from these relationships and their careers is more than adequate for their happiness (Phillis & Stein, 1983).

Cohabitation

Cohabitation in the United States has increased an amazing 1,500 percent in the last fifty years (Jay, 2012). Over half of those under age 45 have lived with someone of the opposite sex and when they marry, fifty percent of all couples have lived together. One often reads about the higher divorce rate of those who live together before marriage. Bumpass (2004) points out that during the period when cohabitation became more popular, the divorce rate remained constant. He proposes that "many of the relationships that at an earlier time would have resulted in marriage and then divorce now dissolve prior to marrying." This testing of relationships may have, in actuality, helped the divorce rate stop rising and level off (Bumpass, 2004). Others argue that cohabitating is not risk free. An important risk of cohabitating is "sliding, not deciding." Couples may go from dating and sleeping over to sleeping over more often and then to cohabitating, thus sliding into the arrangement. There is no discussion about why they want to live together and what it really means. Often the standards for a live in partner are lower than they would be for a spouse. However, after living together for some time it becomes difficult to disengage from the arrangement. Couples can spend months and years in a relationship that is unfulfilling and unhappy. To avoid this trap, couples can discuss their intentions before moving in and view living together as a step toward marriage. This change may help some couples avoid making the mistake of living with someone who does not really meet their needs. In a poll by the Pew Research Center, two thirds of Americans believed that living together is a step toward marriage. This is indeed good news since couples will be more selective in choosing the live in partner making the marriage more likely to succeed (Jay, 2012).

Unmarried adult couples who live together face similar relationship challenges of those who marry. They must learn to effectively communicate, share, compromise, argue, and make decisions about money, sex, and household labor. Parenting is also a challenge since two fifths of births to unmarried women are to those in cohabiting, two parent families (Bumpass, 2004). Though many view living together as a step toward marriage, fewer cohabitations are now transitioning into marriage (Guzzo, 2014). The reasons for adults living together but not marrying are many and varied. It may be that the bar for marriage has been set so high that many just continue to live together or end the relationship rather than marry. Generally speaking, three forms of cohabitation are casual or temporary involvement, preparation or testing for marriage, and a substitute for or alternative to marriage.

Marriage

Marriage is a life goal for the majority of those who have never been married. As discussed earlier, about half of never married adults would like to eventually marry (Wang & Parker, 2014) However, the Pew Research Centers' analysis of the latest census data finds a record low number of adults are married, barely half. In 1960, 3 in 4 (72%) of those age 18 and older were married compared to only 1 in 2 (50%) today. The data analysis also found a steep five percent drop in new marriages between 2009 and 2010, perhaps due to the poor economy. This trend began to reverse when the economy improved. Interestingly, the majority of the new marriages (87%) were among the college educated (Fry, 2014). Even with this increase in marriages, a record number (one in five) of American adults 25 and older has never married compared to 1960 when only one in ten were classified as never married. (Wang & Parker, 2014).

There are so many options for living arrangements that may be more appealing than marriage to some. As we discussed earlier, more Americans are living together and also more are also living alone or living as single parents.

The expectations for marriage are much different today than for previous generations. Historically, marriages were intended to provide a stable economic unit in which to rear children. Today, people expect marriage to fulfill their social, emotional, financial, and sexual needs. When people marry, they find that many of these expectations are unrealistic and cannot be fully realized. This discovery can lead to frustration, disillusionment, separation, and divorce. They also find that marriage is hard work. Even under the best of circumstances and with a good match in a partner,

© iofoto, 2010. Shutterstock, Inc.

Weddings allow couples to openly show their love and commitment to family and friends and society.

successful marriage requires continual nurturing, assessment, communication, commitment, and willingness to change. Perhaps we should consider marriage as similar to driving a car. The relationship needs continual attention and small adjustments to make it healthy and strong, If neglected the small issues may become large enough to derail a good relationship just as one may drive off the road if not making small steering corrections.

Ingredients for a Healthy, Happy Relationship

There are many ingredients that make up a happy, long term relationship and none is more important than the choice of a partner. The romantic partner must have some of the characteristics needed to make the relationship a happy, healthy one. Once the excellent ingredients- the partner—are chosen there are some essential characteristics that help the relationship succeed. Equality between the partners will encourage them to work as a team and to treat each other with respect. Respect for one another helps couples treat each other as best friends and keeps the relationship positive. Best friends often play together, laugh and have fun, which are other key ingredients to the success of a relationship.

John and Julie Gottman have done years of research with couples and can predict with 90% accuracy which couples will have successful relationships after just three hours of listening to their interactions. They suggest seven principles to keep the relationship strong. First principle is for couples to be intimately familiar with each other's life. Each should know what their partner loves and what bothers them. Second principle is that it is essential to nurture fondness and admiration for one another. This is helpful during arguments and during the difficult times. Third, couples should turn toward one another when looking for support or humor rather than toward others. Fourth, the happiest and most stable marriages have equal sharing in power and decision making. The traditional husband role of making all the decisions may contribute to the deterioration of the relationship.

Fifth, all couples have problems that need to be solved and the Gottmans suggest good manners and the following four steps will help couples solve these issues with grace. Step one is to soften the start up- state feelings without blame. Second step is to make and accept repair attempts. This involves de-escalating the fight and expressing appreciation. Fights can bring on a flooding of emotion so step three is to take a break to sooth and distract yourself and your spouse. Finally, compromise is essential.

For the last two principles of a healthy relationship, couples need to overcome gridlock of repeated conflicts by honoring each other's dreams and goals. And finally, create customs and rituals that make you a family or a team (Gottman & Gottman, 2012). When asking married couples what was most important for their happiness, a surprising finding was that sharing household chores ranked number three in importance and was ranked even more important than having children and an adequate income. The two top ranking contributors were having shared interest and a satisfying sex life (Geiger, 2016). These couples appear to value the equality and fun that have been found to be so important in relationship satisfaction.

Sexual satisfaction and happiness in marital and other partnered relationships have two dimensions: physical satisfaction and emotional happiness (Laumann et al., 1994). The relationship between the two is complex with sexual satisfaction being one of the most important components of marital happiness. (Litzinger & Gordon, 2005). Highly satisfying physical relationships usually bring with them high emotional happiness. High levels of emotional satisfaction, however, don't necessarily indicate high levels of physical satisfaction. It has been shown that when couples are good at communicating, sexual satisfaction fails to contribute significantly to marital happiness (Litzinger & Gordon, 2005). Overall, a fairly high proportion of men (47 percent) and women (41 percent) described their partnership as extremely physically pleasurable with satisfaction varying with age. Among men, the level of physical satisfaction was high to begin with and increased with age. Among women however, high levels of physical satisfaction dropped significantly after age 55. Findings are similar regarding emotional satisfaction. Laumann et al. account for this by explaining that men in their 50s and older are more likely than similar-aged women to acquire new sex partners after divorce. Equitable sharing of housework appears to improve marital happiness and the couples sex life. When husbands share housework, their wives feel more affection for them and have a higher interest in sex (Coleman, 2008).

healthy sex hints 8.1

Lessons from Happy Marriages

In a happy marriage:

1. The partners find their prime source of joy in each other but maintain separate identities.
2. They are generous and giving out of love, not because they expect repayment or are keeping score.
3. The partners enjoy a healthy and vigorous sexual relationship.
4. The partners "fight" in a constructive way, airing feelings and frustrations without attacking or blaming the other.
5. The partners communicate with each other openly and honestly.
6. The partners trust each other.
7. The partners treat each other with respect.
8. Both talk about their future together. They have mutual goals.
9. The best marriages tend to be ones in which the partners are similar in these ways:
   - ethnicity
   - locality (geography; urban or rural)
   - maturity (emotional and social)
   - goals and ideals
   - intelligence levels
   - amount of education
   - economic level and financial resources
   - social strata
   - value system
   - religious beliefs
   - common interests

sex in society 8.1

Midlife Crisis or Middle-Age Myth?

You have heard the story before. A happy, successful 45-year-old businessman quits his job, leaves his wife and kids, and runs off to Tahiti with his 25-year-old personal trainer. Or, perhaps it is the 40-year-old mother of two facing the "empty nest" who jumps into her convertible BMW with her 25-year-old co-worker and heads west into the sunset in a torrid blaze of passionate sex.

These and other "midlife crises" that have been popularized by the print and film media make interesting stories and pose a romantic solution to many of the difficult issues that appear during middle age. In real life, however, relatively few people experience such catastrophic, radical changes. New information fueled by long-term research on aging is showing that middle age is the very best time of life. It is a developmental stage unlike most others, because it is not tied particularly to changes in the body, such as early childhood, adolescence, and old age. Midlife is characterized more by psychological adaptations and is reality based.

By midlife, many of the stressful questions that faced us as young adults are answered, such as, Will anyone ever love me? Will this marriage work out? Will I ever find a job? What kind of lifestyle can I afford to lead? By midlife, most people have found love. If they are married, they are more likely to stay married (the overwhelming majority of divorces occur within the first 6 to 8 years of marriage). They have settled into a job and have a pretty good idea of where they are headed (most professionals who are going to "make it" have made it by this time). They have a good sense of their earning capacity and therefore can gauge the kind of lifestyle they can expect.

Although the myth of midlife is that this period is characterized by unrest, discomfort, dissatisfaction, and upheaval, the reality is that it is a comfortable, satisfying time. It is a time to enjoy the rewards of 10 to 20 years of scuffling. It is a time to push a little easier at work, to get off a little early to watch your kid's Little League game. It is a time to focus on vacations and social gatherings, to take a class to learn how to paint or improve your backhand. It is a time to lighten up a little.

Midlife is a period of gradual adjustment, not tumultuous change. It gradually unfolds and is based on several adjustments to reality. For most people it is based in reality, not fantasy. Those most likely to experience a true crisis (about 5 percent) are people who generally have experienced similar crises in all developmental stages of their lives. Their lives are based on unrealistic (therefore unrealized) notions and expectations. One of the major criticisms of earlier studies of midlife is that they were based on small numbers of case studies of atypical populations (mostly affluent, professional, and white). In the recent cross-sectional studies of more representative samples of Americans, researchers found that the average person's midlife adjustment is based on reality. People gradually adjust their expectations to fit the reality of their lives. By the time they settle into midlife, they have learned to make the best of what they have and are not constantly longing for things that are beyond their reach.

Source: R. Blonna, *Coping with Stress in a Changing World* (3rd ed.) (Dubuque, IA: McGraw-Hill,), p. 537.

Parenting and Relational Satisfaction

Children can be a major source of stress and change for couple's established patterns of interaction. Adding children to a marriage can be extremely pleasurable but also stressful. Unfortunately, for 40-70 percent of couples, marital happiness declines (Gottman & Notarius, 2000). This decline has been shown to be especially prevalent during the first three years of a baby's life when 67% of parents experience a precipitous drop in relationship satisfaction (Shapiro and Gottman, 2005). As we've seen from the Berry and Williams analysis of marital happiness and adult developmental phases, satisfaction within a marriage reaches its lowest point about the time the children reach adolescence. Even though this seems to indicate that adolescents are responsible for their parents' stress, the demands of parenting pose formidable stressors at all stages of child development. However, there is some evidence that when both partners equally want to have children the relationship satisfaction does not seem to drop (Parker-Pope, 2010). This powerfully argues for couples to discuss if and when they want to have children.

Children can also be a source of great personal pleasure for parents. The Pew Research center found that parents find time spent with their children more meaningful than time spent at work. The level of enjoyment they find with their children is only slightly less than enjoyment from leisure activities. Parents also report feeling less stressed spending time with their children than the stress they experience at work (Wang, 2013).

Parenting requires a tremendous amount of time and effort and as a result, children decrease up to half the amount of time parents have to share activities with each other (Cavanaugh, 1993). With all the demands of parenting, remaining a "couple centered" and not "child centered" marriage is a challenge. Couples need to take time to nurture their relationship in order to maintain a healthy marriage because the marriage is the foundation of the family. If the marriage fails the family will also fail. It is essential for parents to spend time as a couple, going out alone, having date nights, talking and working on their relationship. This commitment to their marriage necessitates a balancing of all needs and time demands. Perhaps it is not as important for parents to attend all sporting and school events of every child but instead spend time improving the relationship that is the key to the family stability.

Divorce

The commonly held belief that "half of all marriages end in divorce" is not accurate and can be very discouraging for those considering marriage. In reality, the age at which one marries and the education level are strong factors in determining if the marriage ends in divorce. According to the Bureau of Labor Statistics, for those with a bachelor's degree or higher, seventy percent of marriages succeed and only thirty percent end in divorce. Those with a college degree tend to marry later and have a higher income, both of which are contributors to the success of a marriage. For those who did not graduate from high school, the divorce rate is a much higher fifty percent. At the fifteen year anniversary, seventy-five percent of those with a college degree are still married. (Auginbaugh, Robles, & Hugette, 2013) These statistics should give all of those considering marriage hope that they too can have a successful marriage.

When examining data about divorce, raw numbers are misleading. The divorce rate, which examines numbers of divorces in relation to numbers of marriages, rose steadily for 20 years, reaching a high of 5.3 divorces per 1,000 Americans in 1981, then began declining. The divorce rate is now at its lowest level since 1970. In 2016, there were a reported 3.2 divorces for every 1,000 people, an encouraging decrease in the rate of divorce. (National Center for Health Statistics, 2016).

Most people marry with the hope that the relationship will last forever. Divorce, therefore, often represents a loss of this hope. This often is accompanied by the loss of economic status (particularly for low- and middle-income women), lifestyle, security, friends, and sometimes children. The psychological effects of divorce can be compared with those of the grieving process associated with death of a loved one. First, shock sets in ("Is this really happening to me?"), followed by disorganization ("Everything feels so confused."). Volatile emotions, then guilt ("It's my fault.") usually follow. Loneliness, too, often accompanies divorce. Finally, after several months to a year, these feelings are replaced by a sense of relief and acceptance. Adjusting takes time but one year after divorce both men and women are happier (Cowen, 2007).

The grieving process leads to healing, a cleansing of wounds, that allows divorced people to move on with their lives. If, after a year or so, the divorced person hasn't gotten over the divorce and begun to accept what has happened, counseling and psychotherapy may be helpful. Approximately three in four divorced persons remarry, most within 3 years after their divorce. Although most remarried people report that their second marriage is better than their first, the likelihood that this marriage also will end in divorce is greater than that among first marriages. No one knows why this is so for sure, but some of the reasons given are less willingness to stay in the second marriage when they are embittered, closer scrutiny of the second marriage, financial problems (such as alimony and child support), and the trauma of divorce being less threatening after having experienced it once.

Long-Term Gay, Lesbian, and Bisexual Relationships

Most research regarding relationships has related to married heterosexuals, with far less written regarding long-term gay, lesbian, and bisexual relationships. Now that gay marriage is legal in the United States, there will be many more opportunities to study these long term relationships.

Domestic partnerships
Registered relationships between gay and lesbian couples

In addition to being legal in the United States, gay marriage also has legal status in twenty-two countries worldwide. The Netherlands in 2000 became the first nation to make same-sex marriage legal, and was followed by Belgium, Spain, and Canada. South Africa, Norway, Sweden, Argentina, Iceland, Portugal, New Zealand, Uruguay, France, England, Luxembourg, Scotland, Greenland, Ireland, Columbia, and some jurisdictions in Mexico followed these early countries in legalizing same sex marriage (Masci, Sciupac, & Lipka, 2015).

Support for the issue of marriage equality in the US has steadily increased in many arenas. In March of 2013, after extensive review of the scientific literature, The American Academy of Pediatrics issued a policy statement in support of same sex marriage. This esteemed organization concluded that same sex marriage is in the best interest of children since it helps guarantee rights, benefits, and long term security for children (Saint Louise, 2013).

One of the benefits of being in a same sex relationship is the absence of social norms for thus allowing the relationships to be more egalitarian as opposed to gender stereotypical. The lack of hard-and-fast gender role stereotypes forces homosexual men and women to communicate more effectively and to be more flexible and creative in meeting relationship needs. Gay men and women are more willing to communicate, experiment, and be more attentive to detail in their sexual behavior (Kurdek, 1993).

Some interesting research by John Gottman and Robert Levison (2017) found that overall relationship satisfaction and quality are about the same whether a couple is heterosexual or homosexual. However, some strengths unique to homosexual relationships include the ability of homosexual couples to be more positive in the face of conflict. Gay and lesbian couples use more humor during disagreements and are more likely to be positive after the disagreement. The use of controlling emotional tactics is less common suggesting more equality in power sharing.

Because of better planning throughout their relationship, homosexual men and women may be more prepared to deal with losses such as the death of their partner and retirement. Many homosexuals have planned for their own financial support and have consciously developed supportive social networks. They also may be better prepared to cope with hardship, having lived a life of adversity as a member of a stigmatized group. This combination of attitude, social and financial resources, and self-reliance may help gay men and women cope with the demands of aging.

Sexuality in Older Adults

In Erik Erikson's (1978) final stage, older age, our major developmental task is to maintain integrity in the face of death. This last stage begins in older adulthood with the growing awareness of the nearness of death. This is a time for facing our mortality and accepting the worth and uniqueness of our lives.

Maintaining integrity entails evaluating our lives and accomplishments. In a sense, we are verifying our existence and seeking its meaning. We do this by looking back at where we've been, what we've accomplished, whom we have touched (Erikson, 1978). This process often involves reminiscing with family, friends, and others.

Sexual Response and Aging

Sex doesn't necessarily get better or worse as we age; it just gets different. Many myths have arisen in regard to sexual response and aging. The following three are common ones that usually surface during classroom discussions in our classes:

Once you start to get older (over age 60), you lose interest in sex.

Older people aren't sexually attracted to each other.

Older people can't perform sexually or have orgasms.

Physiologically, most men and women change very little during their 30s and early 40s. The most noticeable changes in sexual response in women are associated with menopause.

The changes in sexual physiology among most men in their 40s and 50s are less noticeable. Although sperm production slows down after age 40, it continues into the 80s and 90s. Similarly, male sexual hormone levels decline gradually after age 55, and men may notice a decline in sexual desire and sexual activity as they age. These physiological changes, in men and women, which basically revolve around the sexual response slowing and the intensity of response lessening slightly, are more than offset by greater comfort about sexuality, no fear of pregnancy, familiarity with one's partner, and extending the sex act.

Social Factors Affecting Aging

Source: Callista Lee

Our culture has associated romance and sexual passion with youthfulness. There is an assumption that people just lose their interest in this part of life as they age. We may see an elderly couple holding hands or sharing a kiss and remark, "Oh that is so cute!" Although well intentioned, that is actually a bit insulting. It sounds like something you might say about a couple of fourteen-year-olds. As people get into their sixties, seventies, and eighties, we have a tendency to treat them as if they aren't capable of making their own decisions. While this may be true of individuals suffering from dementia, most seniors are cognitively and emotionally fit. And while they may not be up on the latest technology, they do have a lifetime of experience and wisdom to draw upon. Elderly persons are often as interested and actively seeking romance and sexual expression as people decades younger. Some dating sites popular with "mature adults" include: Zoosk, Our Time, Elite Singles, Silver Singles, eHarmony, and Match.

While older adults do have to adapt to their changing bodies, the bigger problem is sociocultural. The main roadblock they face is society's discomfort with romance and sexuality among the elderly. Couples in nursing homes often find the staff is not receptive to their requests for privacy, which is a terrible blow to them as individuals and as a couple. Just because a person needs the services of a nursing home does not automatically mean that they are at risk medically if they have sex. Each couple needs to discuss their physical activities with their doctor. As discussed earlier, sex is so much more than intercourse. The full range of sexual behaviors is available to people as they age. Not every old man needs Viagra, and not every older lady needs hormone replacement therapy, though many will benefit from some store-bought lubricant. Couples who have enjoyed a satisfying sex life throughout earlier periods of adulthood are likely to continue their enjoyment physically and emotionally into their golden years. The principle of "use it or lose it" does apply somewhat, as it is easier to continue something you have been doing regularly than to start up after years of inactivity. The number one reason that older individuals stop having sex has nothing to do with their wrinkly skin or decreased mobility. Buying into the cultural expectation that elderly people are not supposed to "act that way" is what leads them to stop enjoying their sexuality (Laumann et al., 2009).

Give some thought to how good it feels to you *now* to experience emotional closeness and physical affection. Why would you ever stop enjoying that? The fact is, that you don't have to.

Marital Satisfaction

As married couples reach mid adulthood, happiness that was at an all-time low in their early 40s begins to rebound when the adult children leave home (Berry & Williams, 1987). The children are leaving home resulting in multiple changes for the relationship. The couple finds they have the time, money, and privacy to reestablish the things in their relationship that provide pleasure, as well as investigate new things together. They can travel, dine in new restaurants, and learn a new hobby and other things they have been unable to fit into their lives.

healthy sex hints 8.2

Changes in Sexual Response Associated with Aging

Women

The following changes are associated with sexual response in women who have gone through menopause:

1. The vagina is less elastic and not able to expand as much.
2. Physiological responses to sexual stimuli take more time.
3. Vaginal lubrication takes longer and may be less effective in reducing vaginal irritation.
4. The clitoris is smaller but not less responsive.
5. The intensity of orgasmic contractions diminishes slightly.
6. The ability to have multiple orgasms does not change.

Men

The following physiological changes have been observed in men older than age 55:

1. Arousal takes longer and may require manual stimulation of the penis.
2. Erections tend to be less firm.
3. Less semen is ejaculated.
4. There is less need to ejaculate to enjoy sexual activity.
5. The intensity of orgasmic contractions is slightly diminished.
6. More time is necessary to get another erection.

Marital happiness continues to rise in the later adult years and carries over into retirement. Depending on a number of factors ranging from health to retirement income, the couple continue to enjoy their freedom and, in some cases, relationships with their children's families and grandchildren (Cavanaugh, 1993). Many who age remain healthy and active and can enjoy these retirement years enjoying the new interests and hobbies they have developed.

Along-term study of 17 happily married couples found that the most significant factor related to marital satisfaction was their ability to adapt to change and "roll with the punches" (Weishaus & Field, 1988). These couples had the ability to adapt to changing circumstances that normally might be interpreted as stressful and potentially damaging to the relationship. In a later study supporting these findings, the psychological well-being of each person in the relationship was found to be the major influence on the quality of the couple's relationship (Walker, Isherwood, Burton, Kirtue-Magambi, & Luszo, 2013). They might view a serious illness, for instance, as an opportunity for caring and closeness rather than anger and alienation.

Divorce

In many cases, marital dissatisfaction in older adulthood is not related to any age specific cause but, rather, resurfaces after years of being. With the children grown and out of the house, old tensions and discontent surface

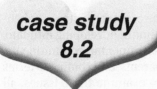

case study 8.2

Critical Thinking

The ratio of men to women in many adult residences is such that "partner sharing" may become necessary for heterosexual individuals.

How do you think you would react to such an arrangement? Would sharing a partner be acceptable if the alternative meant being unattached?

Happy Harry

Harry, 78, is living in an apartment at a newly developed senior residence. The residence is private and costs approximately $6,000 a month. Harry doesn't mind the cost because his meals are free, the staff takes care of most of his needs, and his pension, fortunately, provided nicely for his retirement. Harry's children no longer need his financial support, so he's enjoying life without worrying about taking care of anyone else.

Harry had been happily married to June, but when she passed away 5 years earlier, he decided he could no longer live in their house by himself. Little did he know how much in demand he would be once he arrived at the residence! The ratio of ladies to gentlemen is 4:1, and Harry is very popular. He knows he's not the best-looking guy, but he is agile and loves to dance, go out to movies, and generally have a good time. He's decided not to commit to any one woman, although he's had plenty of offers. At this point, being a free man with a lot of attention is just fine.

As for sex . . . well, he does have one or two special ladies with whom he spends the night. He feels a bit like a teenager again, sneaking around the residence hoping that one doesn't see him enter the room of the other.

and become a source of stress. Dependency is a key issue in the level of marital satisfaction in older couples. When dependence is mutual and the level is relatively equal for both partners, relationships are strong and close. When dependence is not equal and one partner's needs are much greater than the other's, marital conflict is much more likely (Cavanaugh, 1993). When dependence is not equal or mutual, one partner may perceive normal developmental issues such as retirement and relocation as threatening, and, therefore, they become a source of resentment, discontent, and stress. While divorce rates in the younger age groups have decreased, divorce rates in those over 50 have increased. Knowing that we live longer may make those whose children have left the house, less inclined to live in a marriage that is devitalized and more willing to take on the challenges of making a new, more fulfilling life (Ellin, 2015).

Widowhood

Although a person can become widowed at any time during a marriage, it is much more likely later in life. The grieving process when someone loses a spouse can be similar to that of divorce discussed earlier. Widowhood can be stressful in a number of ways besides ending a partnership. U.S. society does not have well-defined social roles for widowed people. Therefore, they often are left alone by family and friends who don't know how to respond to them. Widowed individuals also may feel awkward as single people trying to fit into their previously coupled world. Remaining an independent person, no matter the marital status, and making sure we are well balanced in all dimensions of health can be instrumental in successfully weathering the loss of a spouse.

Widowhood The period of time between loss of spouse and remarriage

❧ Spiritual Wellness ❧

Adulthood and old age are potentially a time of great spiritual awakening and renewal. For most people this is a time of developing intimate, loving relationships, making permanent (sacramental) commitments, having children, caring for sick and dying parents, and coming to terms with our own mortality. We are forced to examine these issues, all of which have a spiritual dimension. Understanding the meaning of these events, coping with them and their universality, help us develop a sense of connectedness with something other than ourselves. If we allow ourselves to look beyond the self and gain strength through connecting with others, we can enhance our spirituality, which can help us lead more satisfying and productive lives.

References

Health Association (2016). *National college health assessment (ACHA-NCHA), Spring 2016 reference group report.* Retrieved from http://www.acha-ncha.org

Auginbaugh, A., Robles, O., & Hugette, S. (2013, October). Marriage and divorce: patterns by gender, race, and educational attainment. *Department of Labor Statistics Monthly Review.* Retrieved from http://www.bls.gov

Bumpass, L. (2004). Social Changes and the American Family. Annals of the New York Academy of Science. 1038, 213–219.

Bogle, K. (2008) Hooking Up: Sex, dating and relationships on campus. New York University Press, New York, NY.

Cavanaugh, J.C. (1993). *Adult development and aging.* Belmont, CA: Wadsworth.

Census Bureau (2017). *Median age at first marriage.* Retrieved from http://www.census.gov

Clark, A.E., & Oswald, A.J. (2002). A simple statistical method for measuring how life events affect happiness. International Epidemiological Association, 31, 1139–1144.

Cohen, D. (2013, February 13). *Love and marriage.* Retrieved from http://www.pewsocialtrends.org

Cohen, D (2010, June 4). At long last divorce. Pew Research Center Publications. Retrieved from http:// www.pewsocialtrends.org

Cohen, Passel, J., Wang,W., & Livingston, G. (2011, December14). Barely half of U.S. adults are married-a record low. Pew Research Social & Demographic Trends. Retrieved from http://pewresearch.org

Coleman, J.(2008). Parents need to get out of the house sometimes! Contemporary Families. Retrieved from http://www.contemporary families.org

Cowen, T. (2007, April 19). Martimony has its benefits, and divorce has a lot to do with that. The New York Times.

Crawford, M., & Popp, D. (2001, February). Sexual double standards: A review and methodological critique of two decades of research. *Journal of Sex Research*, 40 (1).

Easterlin, R.A. (2003). Explaining happiness. PNAS (National Academy of Sciences of the USA, 100(19), 11176–11183.

Ellin, A. (2015, October 15). After full lives together, more older couples are divorcing. Retrieved from http://nytimes.com.

Erikson, E. (1978). *Childhood and society* (2nd ed.). New York: Norton.

Fields, J. (2001, June 29). [Report.] *U.S. Department of Commerce News.* U.S. Census Public Information Office. Washington, DC: U.S. Government Printing Office.

Flannery, D., Ellingson, L., Votaw, K., Schaefer, E. (2003). Anal intercourse and sexual risk factors among college women, 1993-2000. American Journal of Health Behavior, 27(3), 228–234.

Fry, R. (2014, February. New census data show more Americans are tying the knot, but mostly it's the college-educated. Retrieved from http://www.pewresearch.org.

Geiger, A. (2016, November). Sharing chores a key to good marriage, say majority of married adults. Retrieved from http://www.pewresearch.org.

Gottman, J. & Gottman, J. (2013). How to keep love going strong. Retrieved from http://www.gottman.com

Gottman, J. & Gottman, J. (2017). *Same sex couples.* Retrieved from http://www.gottman.com

Gottman, J. & Notarius, C.(2000) Decade Review; Observing Marital Interaction. 62. 927–947.

Guzzo, K. (2014, August). Trends in cohabitation outcomes: Compositional changes and engagement among never married young adults. *Journal of Marriage and the Family*, 76, 826–824.

Hughes, R. (2003). The demographics of divorce: United States and Missouri Retrieved from http://www.missourifamilies.org.

Jay, M. (2012, April 14). The downside of cohabiting before marriage. The New York Times.

Kurdek, L. (1993). The allocation of household labor in gay, lesbian, and heterosexual married couples. *Journal of Social Issues,* 49(3), 127–139.

Lambert, T. A., Kahn, A. S., & Apple, K. J. (2003). Pluralistic ignorance and hooking up. *Journal of Sex Research,* 40(2), 129–133.

Laumann, E., Gagnon, J. H., Michael, R. T., & Michaels, S.

(1994). *The social organization of sexuality: Sexual practices in the United States.* Chicago: University of Chicago Press.

Laumann, E. O., & Michael, R. T. (2001). *Sex, love, and health in America: Private choices and public policies.* Chicago: University of Chicago Press.

Litzinger, S. & Gordon, K.C. (2005) Exploring relationships among communication, sexual satisfaction, and marital satisfaction. Journal of Sex And Marital Therapy, 31, 409–424.

Michael, R. T., Gagnon, J. H., Laumann, E. O., & Kolata, G. (1994). *Sex in America: A definitive survey.* Boston: Little, Brown.

Mixon, B. (2008, April 28). Chore wars: *Women & house work.* Retrieved from http//:www.msf. gov/discoveries/disc_summ.jsp?cnta_id=1114!

National Survey of Sexual Health and Behavior (2017). *Percentage of Americans performing certain sexual behaviors in the past year.* Retrieved from http://www.nationalsexstudy. indiana.edu

Parker-Pope, T, (2010), For Better: how the surprising science of happy couples can help your marriage succeed. New York, NY: Plume,

Paul, E. L., McManus, B., & Hayes, A. (2000). Hookups: Characteristics and correlates of college students' spontaneous and anonymous sexual experiences. *Journal of Sex Research,* 37(1), 76–88.

Paynter, A. & Leaper, C. (2016, October). Heterosexual dating double standards in undergraduate women and men. *Sex Roles.* 75(7) 393–406.

Phillis, D. E., & Stein, P. J. (1983). Sink or swing? The lifestyles of single adults. In E.R. Allegeir & N. B. McCormick (Eds.), *Changing boundaries: Gender roles and sexual behavior.* Palo Alto, CA: Mayfield.

Roberts, S. (2010, March 2). Study finds cohabiting doesn't make a union last. The New York Times.

Saint-Louise, C. (2013, March 21). Pediatric group back gay marriage saying it helps children. *The New York Times.*

Scott, M., Schelar, E., Manlove, J., & Cui, C. (2009). Young adult attitudes about relationship and marriage: times may have changed, but expectations remain high. Child Trends Research Brief. Available: www.childtrends.org

Scott, M., Steward-Streng, M., Manlove, J., Schelar, E., & Cui, C. (2011, January). Characteristics of young adult sexual relationships: Diverse, sometimes violent, often loving. *Child Trends Research Brief.* Retrieved from http:// childtrends.org.

Shapiro, A. & Gottman, J. (2005). Effects on marriage of a psycho-communicative educational intervention with couples undergoing the transition to parenthood, evaluation at 1 year post intervention. *Journal of Family Communication,* 5(1) 1–24.

Thomas, J. A. (2000, October 10). Childcare and laboratory schools on campus: The national picture.

National Coalition for Campus Children's Centers. Retrieved from http://www.campuschildren.org.

Wang, W. (2015, December 4). *The link between a college education and a lasting marriage.* Retrieved from http://www.pewresearch .org.

Wang, W. (2014, September 24). *Record share of Americans have never been married.* Retrieved from http://www.pewresearch.org.

Weishaus, S., & Field, D. (1988). A half century of marriage: Continuity or change? *Journal of Marriage and the Family,* 50, 763–774.

Chapter
nine

Sexual Assault

Student Learning Objectives

After reading this chapter, students will be able to

- ☞ Define *rape,* and differentiate it from other forms of sexual assault.
- ☞ Describe the typical pattern of rape by a stranger, and develop a personal plan to reduce the risk for this form of rape.
- ☞ Define *acquaintance rape* and identify the risks.
- ☞ Develop a personal plan for reducing the risk for date rape.
- ☞ Describe the risks associated with the major "date rape" drugs.
- ☞ Assess the impact of alcohol abuse in sexual assault.
- ☞ Describe the characteristics of rapists.
- ☞ Evaluate common myths associated with rape and rapists.
- ☞ Define *sexual assault* and *sexual victimization* and the three forms highlighted in this chapter: harassment, rape, and child sexual abuse.
- ☞ Explain and give examples of the three conditions that constitute sexual harassment.
- ☞ Describe the dynamic of power over subordinates in determining sexual harassment.
- ☞ Describe the preconditions of child sexual abuse.
- ☞ Evaluate ways to reduce the risks for child sexual abuse.

case study 9.1

Critical Thinking

Assuming that both Marc and the third woman were really interested in *some form* of sexual encounter, how could this scene have ended differently?

Marc: Learning That No Means No

Marc, a senior, was a student in one of Dr. Blonna's human sexuality classes. He submitted a written assignment about how he learned the difference between yes and no.

I'm embarrassed to write this, but I think the story needs to be told. I grew up learning that when a woman said no, she really meant yes. My brother and his friends explained it to me by saying that women do this so they can remain ladies but still get laid. It made sense to me then, even though I now realize this kind of thinking is crazy.

I didn't encounter this with the first two women I had sex with. They both willingly went along. I went out with my second girlfriend for almost 2 years. When we broke up, I had to start dating again and didn't get anywhere with the first two girls I went out with. They didn't even let me get to first base.

The third woman was very sexy. I met her at a frat party, and she was hot. We danced a little and had a couple of beers, and then she wanted to leave. I walked her back to her room, and she invited me up. Her roommates had gone home for the weekend, and we started making out on the couch. She was so sexy, and I thought she really wanted to have sex. She let me feel her breasts and put my hand in her pants, but every time I tried to unzip her jeans, she pulled away and said no. I figured she was just teasing and really wanted me to continue, so I kept pushing the limit.

After about 20 minutes of this, she suddenly pushed me off of her and literally dumped me on the floor. She screamed at me, "Look, I told you no five times! I don't want to fuck you. Now get out before I call the campus cops!" I was shocked and very upset. I really didn't want to rape her, just push her until she gave in. I felt embarrassed and wanted to explain how I felt, but she told me if I didn't leave immediately, she'd call the police. I ran out of there zipping up as I left. I've seen her on campus, but she won't even look at me. I learned that no really means no!

Sexual Assault

Sexual assault is defined as any unwanted sexual contact

Sexual coercion Any nonconsensual sexual behavior that occurs as the result of arguing, pleading, and cajoling, and includes, but is not limited to, force

Sexual victimization Depriving a person of free choice and forcing him or her to endure, observe, or comply with sexual acts

Sexual assault is defined as any unwanted sexual contact. The legal definition varies state-to-state but sexual assault advocates consider any unwanted sexual conduct or activity, including rape, and attempted rape, to be sexual assault. Sexual assault may or may not involve force and includes grabbing or fondling in addition to penetration. (Women'sLaw.Org, 2016). **Sexual coercion, a form of sexual assault is** any nonconsensual sexual behavior that occurs as the result of arguing, pleading, and cajoling, and includes, but is not limited to, force.

Rape is the unlawful penetration of a person against the will of the victim, with use or threatened use of force, or attempting such an act. Rape includes psychological coercion and physical force, and forced sexual intercourse means vaginal, anal, or oral penetration by the offender. Rape also includes incidents where penetration is from a foreign object (e.g., a bottle), victimizations against male and female victims, and both heterosexual and homosexual rape. **Attempted rape** includes verbal threats of rape. (Truman & Morgan, 2015).

Sexual harassment is defined as unwelcome sexual advances, requests for sexual favors, and other verbal or physical conduct of a sexual nature in the workplace or educational setting when: (1) submission of such conduct is made explicitly, or implicitly a term or condition of an individual's employment or academic advancement, (2) submission or rejection of such conduct by an individual is used as the basis for academic or employment decisions affecting the individual, or (3) such conduct has the purpose or effect of unreasonably interfering with an individual's work or academic performance or creating an intimidating, hostile, or offensive working or educational environment. (EEOC, 2003).

> **Sexual harassment** is defined as unwelcome sexual advances, requests for sexual favors, and other verbal or physical conduct of a sexual nature in the workplace or educational setting

Child sexual abuse is any sexual contact between an adult and a child under 18 years of age. Child sexual abuse runs the gamut from inappropriate fondling and touching, to masturbation, to oral sex, to penetration of the anus or vagina with fingers or a penis. These and other forms of sexual behavior are considered evidence of child sexual abuse despite the child's consent or sexual precociousness (Schetky & Green, 2014).

> **Child sexual abuse** Any sexual contact between an adult and a child under 18 years of age

California Law—Sex with Minors

Source: Callista Lee

California Penal code differentiates between child sexual abuse and sex with a minor. The age of differentiation is fourteen. Child Abuse codes relate to anyone having sexual contact with a child under the age of fourteen. Codes against sex with minors relate to adolescents ages fourteen to seventeen. **No person under the age of eight is able to provide legal consent for sex**, so technically, if two sixteen-year-olds agree to have sex they are breaking the law. This is known as **statutory rape**. However, It would be a rare case for such teens to be arrested. A more typical response would be to bring the minors to the police station and call their parents to come get them. This doesn't happen very often because most teens choosing to have sex find a place to do it that is not likely to bring their behavior to the attention of adults who might contact police. But if there is evidence that one teen coerced or forced the other to have sex, then the laws of sexual assault would be applied.

Statutory rape cases rarely proceed to trial because the District Attorney (DA) must balance the potential harm done to teens in involving them in the Justice System versus potential harm of their sexual relationship. An exception is made when one of the teens is three years (or more) older than the other. In these situations, there is concern that the older teen is taking unfair advantage of the cognitive and emotional immaturity of the younger person. The three-year policy also applies to young adults having sex with minors. No charges are likely to brought against a nineteen-year-old having consensual sex with a seventeen-year-old, but if the adult is twenty and the partner is seventeen, it could be a very different situation. Many adults charged with statutory rape plead innocence based on their lack of knowledge that their partner was underage; the teen may have even lied about their age. But the law puts the responsibility on the adult to be certain that their sex partners are not only providing consent for sex but also have the legal ability to do so. Each case is considered individually by the DA regarding harm done to the victim, intentions of the perpetrator, as well as strength of the evidence. Cases without strong evidence are rarely brought to trial. Prosecutors want to bring forward cases they believe they can win, otherwise it is a questionable use of public resources as well as trauma to both the alleged perpetrator and

> **Statutory rape** consensual or nonconsensual sex with a minor or other person deemed incapable of providing legal consent due to mental disability.

victim. In California, whenever a report of sexual assault is brought to police, the police are obligated to notify their local **Rape Crisis Center** to provide a victim's advocate who will accompany the victim during police questioning, the **"rape kit"** forensic exam, meetings with the DA's office, and, if the case goes to trial, the advocate accompanies the victim to the trial. There is a special team trained specifically to work with children. If you would like to discuss or report child abuse, you may call 714-940-1000 or 800-207-4464, twenty-four hours a day, seven days a week.

Source: WaymakersOC.org

Rape Crisis Center Local service provider for victims of sexual assault. Most provide 24/7 hotline service as well as in-person counseling for victims whether their assault was recent or years ago. Clients are not required to make a police report to receive services, but they will be encouraged to consider the pros and cons of making a police report. Client advocates accompany them throughout the entire legal process if they do make a police report. Counseling generally includes both 1:1 sessions as well as group therapy sessions. Self-defense classes are often offered as well. Victims are also referred to services available for all victims of crime, which may include a safe place to stay, transportation, payment of medical services related to the crime, assistance in obtaining a restraining order, and more. All services are provided free of charge. Orange County's Rape Crisis Center is WaymakersOC.org Hotlines: **Call (714) 957-2737 or (949) 831-9110**

Rape kit a nice name for an unpleasant medical examination. A specially trained forensic nurse follows state-protocol for examining the primary crime scene, in this case the victim's body and clothing. The process may take from two to four hours and consists of carefully taking biological samples and photographs to substantiate the rape accusation. Any place on the victim's body touched by the perpetrator is examined.

Rape

Rape is the unlawful penetration of a person against the will of the victim, with use or threatened use of force, or attempting such an act

Sexual aggression Any form of forced sexual contact, including but not limited to intercourse, without the person's consent

Rape is the unlawful penetration of a person against the will of the victim, with use or threatened use of force, or attempting such an act (Truman & Morgan, 2015). The word *rape* comes from the Latin term *rapere,* which means to steal, seize, or carry away. Rape has been a common theme in literature, art, and popular culture throughout history.

Chilling examples of rape occur regularly in cartoons, comic strips, and other "children's entertainment." The caveman, replete with club and knuckles dragging the earth, is out and about to find a mate. When he spies the female he desires, he hits her with the club, knocks her out, and drags her away by her long hair (presumably to make her his wife).

More than 95 percent of rapes are committed by men against women or other men (Rand, 2008). Although 9 of 10 rapists are men, this does not mean that all men rape, nor are all men potential rapists. If you were to take a sample of 100 rapists, more than 90 would be men. If you were to take a random sample of 100 men, fewer than 10 would be rapists or potential rapists. The statistic does mean, however, that most of the rapes are committed by a small percentage of men who achieve power over women and other men by forced sexual aggression.

Rape is a form **sexual aggression**, a broader term that encompasses all forms of nonconsensual physical sexual activity against men, women, children, and gay people as victims (Truman & Morgan, 2014). It includes fondling, oral sex, and anal sex, as well as vaginal intercourse.

Sexual coercion, the broadest term, covers all nonconsensual sexual behavior that results from arguing, pleading, and cajoling, in addition to force.

The term *victim* is gradually being replaced by words such as *target* and *survivor,* in some contexts. This language avoids further degradation of the person who was raped. The new terminology connotes the encouragement for survivors to reclaim control over their lives.

The Bureau of Justice Statistics however uses victimization as the basic unit of analysis in their ongoing National Crime Victimization Survey (NCVS) and for their reports. A victimization is a crime as it affects one person or household. For personal crimes, the number of victimizations is equal to the number of victims present during a criminal incident. The number of victimizations may be greater than the number of incidents because more than one person may be victimized during an incident (Bureau of Justice Statistics, 2015).

In most states, to be considered rape, the target's body (usually the vagina) has to be penetrated. Forced oral sex and the insertion of fingers and other objects into the vagina, anus, or mouth don't automatically qualify as rape. Although these sexually aggressive acts are still illegal and can result in prosecution, they are tried as less serious offenses than is rape. Rape includes acquaintance rape (also known as date rape), stranger rape, marital rape, gang rape, and statutory rape. A last category of rape, male rape, usually is committed by men against other men but does occur, rarely, with women as the perpetrators.

Here are some common myths associated with rape:

Myth: Rape is a sexual act, not a violent one.

Fact: Although the rapist achieves sexual gratification through his actions, the rape is first and foremost an act of violence. If sexual release were all that a rapist desires, he could achieve that by finding a willing partner, masturbating, or paying a prostitute for sex. The rapist seeks to dominate his victim, to exert power, and to humiliate by using threat and violence. In contrast, sex is a consensual act of pleasure, not a violent act of power.

Myth: Women secretly want to be raped.

Fact: Even though many men and women have rape fantasies, there is a world of difference between using fantasy to become sexually aroused and actually desiring to be assaulted, forced to submit to another's sexual onslaught, and humiliated or beaten in the process. In a fantasy, you control the situation, orchestrate the script, and create the happy ending. In a rape, someone assaults you and controls you. Women do *not* want to be raped.

Myth: A woman can't be raped if she really doesn't want to be.

Fact: The logic of this myth revolves around the difficulty surrounding inserting a penis into a vagina that is thrashing to and fro. Men who rape use force to hurt women, to injure them to the point of submission. They have been known to break a woman's hip to stop it from moving. Rape is not about two lovers playfully teasing each other into submission. Rape is about force, domination, and pain.

Myth: Women "ask for it" by the way they act and dress.

Fact: Women don't dress provocatively to invite rapists. The idea of a woman wanting to attract a man and initiate a sexual liaison by acting in a sexy way is much different from the notion of a woman dressing in revealing clothing because she wants to be raped. If a woman intentionally acts and dresses provocatively to attract a man, that style doesn't give any man the right to rape her.

Myth: *No* really means *yes.*

Fact: Where does the notion that *no* means *yes* come from? Is it a rationalization, made up by men, to justify their domination and overpower women into submission? Or is it a leftover piece of baggage from the Victorian era, reminding women that ladies are not supposed to enjoy sex? In that line of thinking, because a lady can't ask for sex, she has to say no even though she means yes. That way she can have it both ways: maintain her status as a lady and still have sex ("He did it to me"). Wherever this belief came from, it's time to stop it and realize that *no* means *no.* When in doubt, don't continue.

Myth: Rape is justifiable under certain circumstances.

Fact: Rape is never justifiable. No one—husband, lover, boyfriend, father, or any man—ever has the right to force sex on anyone.

Myth: Most rapists are crazy.

Fact: Most rapists are not crazy. They are similar to the average man except for three distinguishing characteristics: (a) They are

California Law—Consent

Under California law, an individual is only consenting if he or she engages in the activity freely and willingly, and if he or she understands the nature of the act. A relationship of any kind does not automatically qualify as consent.

In California in late 2015, Gov. Jerry Brown approved a requirement (SB 695) for sex education to include a "yes means yes" as the standard for consent. Today, schools must use this affirmative consent standard when investigating the validity of sexual crimes claims (SB 967). High schools must teach the standard as part of a health graduation requirement. College campuses are also required to teach affirmative consent.

What "Yes Means Yes" or Affirmative Consent Means for You

The affirmative consent standard is designed to change the way people approach sexual encounters. Instead of assuming the other partner is ready for and okay with engaging in any sexual activities, the standard asks that you receive verbal confirmation at some point in the process. Furthermore, the standard highlights the need for individuals to consider a partner's ability to give consent. After several drinks or doing drugs, many individuals are too impaired to understand the nature of the act.

Source: The Law Office of George Gedulin https://www.gedulinlaw.com/blog/2017/march/overview-of-california-consent-laws/

hostile toward women and have a harder time handling it; (b) they have more traditional beliefs about gender roles; and (c) they are more willing to use force to achieve their ends.

Myth: Women are responsible for preventing rape.

Fact: *Everyone* is responsible for preventing rape.

Characteristics of Rapists

Most of what we know about men who rape comes from research conducted on convicted rapists. It is estimated that less than 10 percent of all rapists are convicted of this crime. FBI statistics in 1992 on convicted rapists, similar to those for perpetrators of other serious crimes, indicate that most are under 25 years of age, are from single-parent or foster parent homes, are marginally employed, have a low income, and have little formal education.

Because less than 10 percent of all rapists are ever convicted of their crimes, several researchers have studied populations of men who rape who have not been convicted or incarcerated. In one of the most comprehensive reviews of the literature, Cate and Lloyd (1992) identify seven characteristics of men who rape:

1. They are much more likely than their nonrapist peers to hold traditional beliefs about women and women's roles and female stereotypes. These beliefs range from nonsexual views concerning a woman's place (in the home) to sexual beliefs that men are the initiators during sex and that women want men to initiate.
2. They believe in rape-supportive myths—women secretly want to be overpowered during sex; they like it rough; *no* really means *yes*—and other stereotypical beliefs about women.
3. They use exploitative techniques such as coercing women into sex using alcohol and other drugs.
4. They accept the use of violence as a way to solve problems and dominate others.
5. They are more likely to vent their anger and express their need to dominate sexually rather than find other outlets for these feelings.
6. They devalue all that is feminine. They are hostile toward "feminine" personality attributes such as nurturance and collaboration, and devalue traditional female pursuits such as child care and homemaking.
7. They are generally more sexually active than their peers who do not rape.

What to Do if You Are Sexually Assaulted

Source: Callista Lee

1. Get yourself to a safe place, and call someone you can trust to stay with you. You might not want to talk right now, but you do need to be able to feel safe so you can get some rest.
2. If there is a chance that you might want to report the assault to police, put off taking a shower, and save the clothing you were wearing during the assault. If you can avoid eating or drinking that is also helpful. Your body was a crime scene, so you want it to be as close to how it was during the assault as possible when examined by the forensic nurse.

3. If you are unsure about whether or not you want to report the crime to police, at least call the Rape Crisis Hotline to talk with a counselor. For Orange Country, that is (714) 957-2737. They can explain what the process will be like and help you weigh the pros and cons. It is their job to help you recover, not to report crimes to police. All calls are confidential, and services are free whether you report your crime to the police or not. If you want to get in-person counseling or just have a longer telephone discussion with a sexual assault victim's counselor, the hotline staffer can help you to arrange that. Feel free to call them day or night, any day of the year.

4. If you have decided to make a police report, call the police department in the city in which the crime occurred. They will come to wherever you are to take your report, and if it is decided that it makes sense for you to be examined by a forensic nurse for the "rape kit" exam, they will transport you to the hospital where those examinations are done. In OC, we have a special ward for victims of sexual assault, near the emergency room at Anaheim Regional Medical Center. Do not take yourself there yourself. The rape kit exam will not be done unless the police bring you there. They are also responsible for calling out the Forensic Nurse and the Victim's Advocate to come to the hospital to meet you. In California, every sexual assault victim must have a trained victim's advocate present at the hospital during the exam, and at any further meetings with representatives of the justice system. The advocate is there to make sure the victim's rights are respected at all times, to provide emotional support, and to provide referrals for other services the victim may need. They are sometimes able to arrange for emergency housing, transportation, clothing, and food aid if the victim cannot safely go home.

5. It is totally okay to make a police report days or even weeks after the assault occurred, but for the sake of information gathering, sooner is better. Your case against the perpetrator will be stronger if the forensic nurse is able to get their DNA from your body. Anywhere they touched you is part of the crime scene.

6. If you decide that you do not want to make a police report but do want medical attention, you have a couple of options. You can call the Hotline to find out where you can go to get a rape kit done without a police report (there is at least one clinic in LA County that will do that). That will allow for the evidence to be held for you in case you change your mind. And while you are there, you can ask for any medical attention that you need, including tests for STIs and Emergency Contraception if you are concerned about pregnancy. Your other option is to either go to an emergency room or your regular doctor's office to be checked out. You can tell them that you are concerned because of "rough sex" that you had. If you tell them that you were raped, they are mandated reporters and must call the police. So if you don't want to talk to police, don't say anything to indicate that you were the victim of a crime. Just get your medical concerns taken care of.

7. Remember that even if the sexual assault was not particularly violent, you have suffered a serious psychological trauma that isn't going to just go away on its own. You can't drink or drug or sleep it away either. Spend time talking with a counselor trained in helping victims of sexual assault. Be gentle with yourself and expect for healing to take time. Share what happened with people you trust, so they can be supportive while you are learning how to move from victim to survivor. Let them know that part of your healing includes being able to make your own decisions about how you want to proceed. The rapist took your choices away; now is the time for you to regain control of your life.

8. Even if the assault(s) happened to you many years ago, you have the right to reach out for services. Call your local Rape Crisis Center. They are happy to help whether your assault happened last week or thirty years ago. It is never too late for counseling to be helpful. Adults molested as children often find that issues come up many years later.

Source: https://waymakersoc.org/, 2019.

Incidence and Effects of Sexual Assault

Source: Callista Lee

Throughout history and across cultures, sexual assault occurs more frequently when women are devalued and negative outcome of the assault is perceived to be low by the perpetrator (Yarber & Sayad, 2018). According to the US Centers for Disease Control (CDC), "Sexual violence affects millions of people each year in the United States. Researchers know that the numbers underestimate this significant problem as many cases go unreported. Victims may be ashamed, embarrassed, or afraid to tell the police, friends, or family about the violence. Victims may also keep quiet because they have been threatened with further harm if they tell anyone or do not think that anyone will help them" (CDC, 2019). Although anyone can become a victim, this type of violence often occurs when the victim is young, and ethnic and minority persons are more affected (Simon et al., 2017). The CDC has data to show that:

Sexual violence is common. One in three women and one in four men experienced sexual violence involving physical contact during their lifetimes. Nearly one in five women and one in thirty-eight men have experienced completed or attempted rape, and one in fourteen men was made to penetrate someone (completed or attempted) during his lifetime.

Sexual violence starts early. One in three female rape victims experienced it for the first time between eleven and seventeen years old, and one in eight reported that it occurred before age ten. Nearly one in four male rape victims experienced it for the first time between eleven and seventeen years old, and about one in four reported that it occurred before age ten.

Sexual violence is costly. Recent estimates put the cost of rape at US$122,461 per victim, including medical costs, lost productivity, criminal justice activities, and other costs.

Health and social consequences. The consequences of sexual violence are physical, like bruising and genital injuries, and psychological, such as depression, anxiety, and suicidal thoughts. The consequences may also be chronic. Victims may suffer from post-traumatic stress disorder and experience reoccurring gynecological, gastrointestinal, cardiovascular, and sexual health problems. Sexual violence is also linked to negative health behaviors. For example, victims are more likely to smoke, abuse alcohol, use drugs, and engage in risky sexual activity. The trauma resulting from sexual violence can have an impact on a survivor's employment in terms of time off from work, diminished performance, job loss, or being unable to work (CDC, 2019). In addition to anxiety, depression, substance abuse, PTSD, and suicidality, researchers have found a greater risk of bipolar disorder and obsessive-compulsive disorder among victims of sexual assault (Yates, 2017).

Like female victims, most **male victims** were assaulted by males. Rape of males is not limited to prisons. Both in and out of prison, men who sexually assault other men do it to demonstrate their power over the victim, and to extract the ultimate humiliation—treating him as if he were no better than a woman. In addition to suffering the same psychological traumas that female victims do, male victims often find themselves questioning their manhood for not being able to keep themselves safe from attack. They may wonder if they put off a "gay vibe" that drew the assailant(s) to them. Another very concerning factor is that they are likely confused if their body responded to the sexual assault by developing an erection. However, this is a normal, involuntary, physiological reaction of the parasympathetic nervous system's fear response and *not* an indication that he secretly enjoyed the assault (Rosin, 2014).

The majority of sexual assaults are not reported to police. Only 230 out of every 1,000 (23 percent) sexual assaults are reported to police. That means about three out of four go unreported (National Crime Victimization Survey, 2017). Males are even less likely than females to report, for reasons stated earlier. Male victims are also less likely to reach out for counseling to help them heal psychologically. Our local Rape Crisis Center's most common initial contact with a male victim occurs after he has been admitted to the hospital for attempted suicide (WayfindersOC, 2017).

■ Sexual Assault among College Students

Acquaintance rape, also known as **date rape**, is a form of rape defined as forced sexual intercourse by a dating partner. Many experts consider acquaintance rape to be the most common and least reported of all forms of rape (Cate & Lloyd, 1992). Previous research has shown that college campuses, contrary to public opinion, are not safe havens from sexual coercion. College women are at a greater risk for rape and other forms of sexual assault than women in the general population or in a comparable age group (Fisher, Koss, Gidycz, & Wisnewski, 1987). This is due in part to the nature of the college environment where large concentrations of young women come into contact with young men in a variety of public and private settings at various times on and off their college campuses.

In the late 1990's the National Institute of Justice, the research arm of the United States Bureau of Justice Statistics chartered a study by Fischer et al's (2000) called "The National College Women Sexual Victimization Study (NCWSV)," The NCWSV was designed to overcome the shortcomings of previous studies that attempted to estimate the incidence of sexual victimization of college women. Previous studies were flawed by multiple methodological issues.

The study was designed as a telephone survey of 4,446 female college students. Schools were randomly chosen from a probability proportional to total female enrollment. Subjects were then randomly chosen from the institutions picked for the study Each subject was interviewed over the phone by a trained female interviewer (Fisher et al., 2000).

Screening questions were very graphic in their depiction of the potential sexual victimization events. No previous sexual victimization surveys used such specific screening questions that, in a sense, operationally defined the event under study.

Incident report questions covered all aspects of the event, ranging from the relationship of the perpetrator to the subject, the environment in which the event occurred, whether the victim used force to repel the perpetrator, and additional details.

Rape Trauma Syndrome (RTS)

Source: Callista Lee

RTS is no longer a formal clinical diagnosis but it provides a framework for understanding some of the psychological and physiological phases victims commonly experience in the aftermath of rape. RTS parallels the progression of PTSD (posttraumatic stress disorder); in fact, rape is the most commonly reported cause of PTSD in women (Cloitre, 2004; Zinzow et al., 2010). The symptoms can be divided into several phases (Butcher, Hooley, & Mineka, 2013):

Anticipatory—the horrible realization that one is about to be raped. Attempts are made to stop the rape from happening.

Impact—experiencing the terror of the event itself. Some victims continue to try to stop the attack but others fear that they must comply to avoid being severely beaten or killed. It is very common for victims to report that they were afraid for their lives. In both of these first two phases, the victim may *freeze* physically and emotionally, feeling helpless to do anything to stop it. The event may even have a sense of unreality about it—"This cannot possibly be happening." Fear, anxiety, and anger are the most commonly reported emotions of these first two phases.

Recoil—surviving the trauma in the days and weeks following the assault. Shock and numbness typically set in, which mask other emotions. Friends may mistakenly think that the victim is handling things eerily well. There are often physical symptoms unrelated to the physical attack like appetite and digestion upsets, or difficulty sleeping. As the shock wears away, deeper feelings of humiliation, fear, anger, degradation, shame, and guilt are common.

Reconstitution—the months or even years during which healing occurs with the help of counseling, the support of friends and family, taking legal steps, and reorganizing one's life. Many survivors move their residence, change phone numbers and social media profiles, hide out with friends or family members, get a dog, install an alarm—anything that helps them to feel safer. Frightening nightmares about the assault may keep them from wanting to go to sleep at night. It is an important time to be able to talk through uncomfortable emotions and nightmares. Talking through them often reduces their power, rendering them less frightening. They may find it difficult to concentrate at work or school, so it is important for them to understand that it's okay to not always be performing at your highest level. Like many people suffering from PTSD, they may experience hypervigilance—an enhanced state of sensory sensitivity accompanied by an exaggerated intensity of behaviors whose purpose is to detect danger. Where most people might say "Ooh! You scared me by coming up behind me," a person with PTSD may scream loudly and/or go into a defensive pose to fight the intruder. Many survivors will develop phobias of being alone, or being with strangers, being in the dark, or being in a place similar to the one in which they were attacked, or experience fear so great of starting a new romantic relationship that they develop a social phobia. If symptoms fail to improve, additional professional therapy is strongly advised. Although some fears may never completely go away, survivors can learn to cope with them in ways that allow them to get back to a mostly normal lifestyle. It is not unusual for the person to be well for a time and then experience symptoms again months or years later. Having people around they can rely upon during these times is very important.

Key Findings of the NCWSV

The most startling finding of the study was the overall high incidence of sexual victimization and attempted sexual victimization among college women. Overall, 2.8 percent of the sample had experienced either a completed rape (1.7%) or an attempted rape (1.1%). This accounts for a rape victimization rate of 27.7 rapes per 1,000 female students (Fisher et al., 2000).

Another disturbing finding of the study was the small percentage of women who actually defined their victimization as rape (even though they said yes when asked whether someone had "by force or threat put their penis into your vagina"). Fisher et al (2000) explain that this reluctance may be due to reasons such as feeling embarrassed, not clearly understanding the legal definition of rape, or being reluctant to label someone they are intimate with and who victimized them as a rapist (Fisher et al., 2000).

A third finding of the study was the overall incidence of other forms of sexual victimization. The types of sexual victimization ranged from threats of rape and sexual contact to completed sexual coercion. The study found that overall percentage of women who were sexually victimized in the study exceeded 15 percent (Fisher et al., 2000).

A fourth finding of the study was the relationship of the perpetrator to the victim. For both completed and attempted rape, 9 out of 10 women knew the perpetrator. The relationships most often cited were a boyfriend, ex-boyfriend, classmate, friend, acquaintance, or coworker (Fisher et al., 2000).

Reducing Risks of Acquaintance Rape

Source: Callista Lee

Communication—Whether you are male, female, gay, or straight, communicating your expectations clearly is a must. If a partner moves past your comfort zone, speak up immediately; your silence may be taken for agreement. If your expression of discomfort is ignored, become more forceful with a loud "No!" or "Back Off!" If you feel like you want to leave, then leave. A socially awkward moment is much less painful than being raped.

Remember the "Yes Means Yes" Law: make sure you get a verbal "yes" from your partner before moving ahead. Some people think it's a turn off to ask because they haven't seen it in the movies. But getting an enthusiastic, freely offered "yes!" should be the goal if you want to enjoy sex with someone. Asking "May I?" with a smile is usually appreciated.

Flirting is a form of nonverbal communication that isn't always interpreted the same way by both parties. Men often perceive it as an expression of sexual desire. So you may have to use your words to thank them for the fun flirtation but let them know that you are not interested in going further. Going up to someone's bedroom is another commonly misinterpreted behavior. Be clear about your intentions.

Watch for red flags—Have they been trying to get you drunk? Does your date/friend use power stares or body language to intimidate others? Are they dismissive of the feelings of others? Are they cruel to animals? Do they have trouble controlling their anger? Do they espouse traditional views in which the male is expected to be dominant and the female passive and obedient? Do they ignore your "no" when they make nonsexual requests? Do they behave like entitled brats who always get what they want? Remember that good looking people who can get sexual partners willingly may also like exercising their dominance over others once in awhile. They may not be prepared to accept a "no" from you.

Consider their point of view—Your partner may not be as interested in being as sexual as you are. Instead of trying to read their mind or nonverbal signals, ASK!

Be aware that if you are bigger and stronger than they are your size may be intimidating. Try to help your partner feel safe and comfortable with you even when it means accepting their "no."

Remember that if your partner doesn't want sex, that doesn't necessarily mean that they don't want YOU. Find out what they DO want from you.

Have a basic safety plan—Your phone should be charged and your wallet full of enough money to get you home safely. Got out in groups while you are getting to know one another. Know your limits when it comes to alcohol. Use the buddy system. Your designated sober driver friend should also be charged with looking out for drunken friends who might wander off with someone that they wouldn't if sober. If you are going to lay down for a nap at a party, lock the door behind you or lay down where others will be able to keep an eye on you. And don't accept open drinks from people you don't trust with your life.

Trust your gut—Rape victims often tell us that they had a "creepy feeling" before the assault occurred but didn't get out of the situation because it would have been awkward. If your body is signaling you that there is danger, take care of yourself whether that feeling makes sense to you or not.

Start changing the culture—Be the one who speaks up to say "that's not cool" when someone makes a joke about rape, objectifies women, or supports a victim-blaming myth. Get into the habit of looking out for one another. If you see something sketchy, report it, don't just video it on your phone. Be the bystander who steps up. Talk to younger people about what is cool and what's not—they look up to you!

❧ Environmental Wellness ❧

High-level environmental wellness implies safety, security, and respect. A safe home environment includes appropriate parenting, setting boundaries for behavior, and getting help with emotional problems.

A neighborhood that offers high-level environmental wellness is well lit and policed, and it has neighbors looking out for one another. The schools are safe and do not tolerate sexual harassment and discrimination. The community has safe playgrounds and parks that are well patrolled and not inviting for sex offenders. A college that offers high-level environmental wellness is a microcosm of any community. It has policies and procedures in place for dealing with harassment and discrimination and offers safety and protection. Its students don't fear walking to their cars after class or attending social functions. In addition, enforcement is swift, fair, and equal for all on campus.

Drinking and Sexual Assault

Many college students use alcohol and other drugs to "fit in," cope with college stressors, and reduce inhibitions related to dating and sex. Unfortunately, alcohol consumption is often linked to sexual coercion and other forms of violence. The National Advisory Council on Alcohol Abuse and Alcoholism's Report on College Drinking estimates that more than 70,000 students are the victims of alcohol-related sexual victimization (sexual assault and rape) (Task Force, 2002).

Often, this alcohol is consumed in large quantities for the express purpose of getting drunk. Weschler, Davenport, Dowdell, Moeykens, and Castillo (1994) coined the term **binge drinking** to describe such a pattern of alcohol consumption. Binge drinking is operationally defined as "having five or more drinks in a row, at least once during the previous 2 week period" (Weschler et al., 1994, p. 1673). The greatest predictors of binge drinking were living in a fraternity or sorority house, engaging in drinking games, and living a "party-centered" lifestyle (Weschler et al., 1994).

Binge drinking Having five or more drinks in a row, at least once during the previous 2 week period

Bingeing on alcohol often becomes part of the social fabric of the college experience. Weschler et al (1994) studied the binge drinking behavior of more than 17,000 students on 140 four-year college campuses across the United States. About one in six (16%) of all the respondents were nondrinkers (15% of the men, 16% of the women). About two in five (41%) were drinkers but did not binge. Almost half (44%) of all the students were binge drinkers. About one in five (19%) were frequent binge drinkers (17% of the women and 23% of the men). These students had three or more binge drinking episodes within the past 2 weeks.

Weschler and colleagues found binge drinking to be associated with unplanned and unsafe sexual activity, physical and sexual assault, other criminal violations, physical injury, interpersonal problems, and poor academic performance. Binge drinkers were more likely than non-binge drinkers and abstainers to engage in unplanned sexual activity, not use protection when having sex, get hurt or injured, damage property, argue with friends, miss classes, get behind in schoolwork, and do something they later regretted. Frequent binge drinkers were 10 times more likely than bingers to have unplanned and unprotected sex, get into trouble with campus police, and get injured or damage property. When asked to evaluate the seriousness of their bingeing and its repercussions, less than 1 percent of the binge drinkers designated themselves as problem drinkers (Weschler et al., 1994).

Current research confirms Weschler's earlier findings. Recent studies show that the consequences of college drinking include missed classes and lower grades, injuries, sexual assaults, overdoses, memory blackouts, changes in brain function, lingering cognitive deficits, and death (White & Hingston, 2014).

College students who have high rates of heavy drinking are more likely than their non-drinking peers to be both perpetrators and victims of sexual victimization. In addition for both females and males, sexual victimization was positively associated with child sexual abuse, hooking up more often, and heavier drinking (Kimberly et al., 2015,White & Hingston, 2014).

The odds of committing a sexual assault increased for men with higher bar and party attendance and in semesters in which party or bar attendance was higher than their own average. Evidence suggests that party and bar drinking was connected to hookup behavior. The likelihood of committing a sexual assault was more likely in semesters in which the number of hookups exceeded one's own average. In other words, drinking in bar and party settings was related to increased hooking up in certain semesters among those who engaged in such behavior. This type of pattern was found to be related to being a sexual assault perpetrator(Testa & Cleveland, 2017).

Rohypnol A depressant drug also known as the "date rape drug," because it causes loss of memory and makes women vulnerable to uninvited sexual intercourse

These and other findings findings illustrate the importance of drinking contexts (bar & party drinking and hooking up) rather than drinking per se, as predictors of college men's sexual assault perpetration.

Other Date Rape Drugs

Many other drugs, used alone or in consort with alcohol have been implicated in sexual victimization. Marijuana, cocaine, gamma hydroxybutyrate (GHB), benzodiazepines, ketamine, barbiturates, chloral hydrate, methaqualone, heroin, morphine, LSD, and other hallucinogens have all been used to facilitate rape (Higher Education Center, 2003). When combined with alcohol (which they often are), many of these drugs cause reduction of inhibitions, weakness, memory loss, and blackout. These incapacitating effects are used by sexual victimization perpetrators to take advantage of their targets (Higher Education Center, 2003).

Two drugs in particular, **Rohypnol** and GHB, have been dubbed "date rape drugs" because of their increased use and association with sexual assault and rape. Rohypnol was the key target in the Drug-Induced Rape Prevention and Punishment Act of 1996. This legislation was developed in response to the threat posed by Rohypnol. The act established harsher penalties for the use of even the smallest quantities of flunitrazepam (the chemical name of Rohypnol) for the purpose of facilitating a violent crime (U.S. Congress, 1996).

© Mark Stout Photography, 2010. Shutterstock, Inc.

Rohypnol and GHB, available in liquid or pill form, are often mixed into the drinks of unsuspecting victims.

Rohypnol—also known as roofies, rophies, Mexican valium, ropies, and the "forget me" drug (to name a few)—is the trade name for flunitrazepam, a benzodiazepine. Benzodiazepines are depressant drugs. Rohypnol is similar to Valium in its effects on the body, only 10 times more powerful. The United Nations Commission on Narcotic Drugs has transferred Rohypnol from a Schedule IV to a Schedule III drug. Several states in the United States have already moved Rohypnol to Schedule I [Office of National Drug Control Policy (ONDCP), 2002b].

Rohypnol is a tasteless, odorless, clear drug available in powder form. It mixes easily in liquids and is virtually undetectable when mixed in alcoholic beverages (its preferred delivery by date rape perpetrators). When swallowed, it takes effect in 15 to 20 minutes, and its effects last for more than 12 hours. Users experience a slowing of psychomotor performance, muscle relaxation, sleepiness, and/or amnesia. Rohypnol leaves the body after 72 hours and is undetectable after that time (ONDCP, 2002b).

GHB—also known as cherry meth, liquid X, organic Quaalude, and fantasy, to name a few—is similar in its nature and effects to Rohypnol. It is also a tasteless, odorless, clear, depressant drug. It is available in either powder or liquid form, and easily mixes in alcoholic beverages, where it is undetectable. GHB is not produced legally in the United States. It is produced in clandestine laboratories. Users claim it can produce euphoric, hallucinogenic states, and act as a growth hormone that stimulates muscle growth. Because of this latter claim, GHB is often marketed through the same channels (gyms, health clubs, rave clubs, and so forth) where anabolic steroids are sold (ONDCP, 2002a).

Both drugs have been implicated in date rape in the United States. Both drugs, besides having classic depressant drug characteristics (slowing central nervous system functioning), can cause memory loss and loss of consciousness. Because of this, women who have been assaulted and raped while under the influence of these drugs are unable to resist the perpetrator or recall any of the details concerning the incident. The assailant mixes the drug into the drink of the unsuspecting woman, allows it to take effect, takes advantage of her, and denies any knowledge of the event if the woman realizes or suspects what has happened. Because both drugs pass through the victim's system within 72 hours, she typically does not have the opportunity to get tested for the drugs (ONDCP 2002a, 2002b).

Stranger Rape

Stranger rape is rape by a person whom the target does not know. The overwhelming majority of rapes reported to the police and resulting in prosecution are stranger rapes. Although stranger rape can involve a premeditated assault with an anonymous assailant descending upon the victim totally without warning, statistics prove otherwise. Most cases of stranger rape seem to spring out of chance meetings that create the potential for assault. The assailant targets the victim in a park, a shopping mall parking lot, while driving in a car, and so on. The perpetrator initiates contact, appears friendly and "safe," and lulls the victim into relaxing her (usually the victim is female) guard, allowing the perpetrator to strike. The assailant maneuvers the target to one or the other of their cars or lures the victim into an alley, stairwell, or other remote location, then commits the rape.

Stranger rape Forced intercourse by a person who is unknown to the target person

Stranger rapes are more likely to involve guns, knives, and other weapons than other forms of rape (Rand 2008). Older persons are more likely to be raped in their homes than in public places, and the assailant often gains access by overpowering. A relatively recent type of stranger rape involves targeting women who are driving by themselves. The perpetrators intentionally rear-end the cars of their potential victims, forcing them to pull off the road, where they are assaulted when they leave their car to investigate the accident. Often the rape is combined with stealing the woman's car.

Reducing risks for assault by strangers

Source: Callista Lee

Whether you are hoping to a sexual assault or robbery, you should have a basic safety plan:

- Be aware of your surroundings
  - Use only one earplug to listen to music while walking or jogging so you can hear others approaching
  - Look up from your phone to check your surroundings frequently
- Lock windows and doors
- Don't open your door to anyone you did not invite to your home
- Get to know your neighbors so you can call on them for help if needed
- If you are in an accident, stay in your car until the police arrive
- Avoid being alone in strange surroundings, especially at night
- Use the campus police escort service to walk you to your car at night
- Avoid getting drunk outside of the presence of a buddy who is looking out for you
- Remember all of your stranger-danger training from childhood—it's still relevant!
- Take a self-defense course and practice, practice, practice

- Avoid carrying weapons that can be taken and used against you; if you carry one, you need to be able to get to it and deploy it quickly and without thinking. Practice so that the movements come automatically when you are fearful.
- If you are assaulted by a robber, give them what they want and get yourself to safety
- If you are assaulted by someone wanting to beat or rape you, trust your gut. Does it tell you to fight? Then fight long enough to create an opening for you to get to safety. Research tells us that survivors feel better about themselves if they tried to fight their attacker, but you have to trust yourself in that moment. If your gut tells you that you should comply so they won't kill you, then comply. Survive.
- One thing that many victims do that has been shown to NOT be effective is to beg for mercy. For rapists who enjoy the fear they create in their victims, this only reinforces their behavior. What DOES work, however, is making a lot of noise. If you can make enough noise to get other people to come out to see what is going on, the chances are good that the assailant will leave.

■ Marital Rape

For many years, police were reluctant to investigate and prosecute marital rape. In a landmark case from 1978, Greta Rideout of Oregon filed charges against her husband for nonconsensual sex, bringing marital rape to national attention. Approximately 13 percent of married women have been raped by their husbands (Russel, 1990). In most cases, the husband used force (84%) or the threat of force (9%). The rape was an isolated incident for 31 percent of the victims. Another 31 percent reported being raped more than 20 times, and the rest fell somewhere in the middle (Russel, 1990).

Perpetrators of marital rape share some of the same personality traits as other rapists—namely, anger, power, and sadism. Husbands who rape are also more likely to abuse their wives verbally, psychologically, and physically. More than 30 percent of wives who were raped also reported having been targets of physical abuse during their marriage (Frieze, 1983).

Verbal and psychological abuse often prove more damaging than physical abuse. The verbal and psychological abusers create an environment of endless criticism, suspicion, and torment. Abusers often undermine their mates' confidence and self-esteem through constant criticism of everything from the way they look to their level of competence in performing simple household tasks. Abusers are extremely jealous and turn even the most casual remark or involvement with another person into suspicions of flirting or having an affair. This constant flow of criticism, insults, and accusations is tormenting and can result in a host of psychological problems (Marano, 1996).

Survivors of marital rape suffer after-effects that are similar to those of women who have been sexually assaulted by someone they know (date rape). Because they know their assailants intimately and have an established history of trust, they feel especially betrayed, humiliated, and angry.

❧ *Environmental/Occupational Wellness* ❧

A work environment with high-level environmental wellness is a place where workers coexist without fear of abuse, discrimination, or harassment. Policies to guard against harassment and discrimination are in place and are enforced swiftly, fairly, and equally for all levels of workers. Healthy workplaces are environments where people pursue their occupations in a safe and supportive atmosphere. Sexual harassment exists in exactly the opposite environment—one that is hostile, where those in power use their positions to take advantage of others. Each person has the responsibility to report coworkers and bosses who abuse the work site and thus turn it into a hostile environment for everyone.

Conditions of Sexual Harassment

Sexual harassment has three attributes that transcend individual perception and set the context for any interaction between individuals:

- A power differential in the relationship
- Inappropriate approach
- Pressure after expression of disinterest

A hallmark of sexual harassment is the use and abuse of power to secure sexual favors. Power differentials exist in the workplace and the classroom based on roles and responsibilities. The boss, supervisor, and professor have power over workers and students by the nature of their roles and authority. A boss or supervisor is responsible for evaluating work performance, giving assignments, and the like. A professor evaluates papers, tests, and exams, and ultimately assigns a grade to students in the class.

When someone holds power over another by virtue of a "superior" role, the subordinate person has a harder time refusing the advances. The subordinates fear reprisal—in a poor performance review, no raise, undesirable work assignments, even termination. In a school environment, the students fear a less objective review of their work and lower grades. Also, being approached in a respectful, inquiring way is vastly different from being approached in a harassing way.

Finally, if the pursuing person stops the pursuit once the subordinate has expressed noninterest or displeasure, it's not harassment. Persistence and an attempt to pressure the other person into responding, however, are more likely to be considered harassment, especially if the first two criteria are also present.

Sexual Harassment

Source: Callista Lee

Title VII of the Civil Rights Act of 1964 first made various kinds of discrimination, including sexual harassment, illegal in the workplace. Title VII applies to employers with fifteen or more employees. In 1980, the US Office of Equal Employment Opportunity Commission (EEOC) issued guidelines regarding both verbal and physical harassment in the work and education environments. The EEOC defined sexual harassment as *unwelcome* sexual advances, requests for sexual favors, and other verbal or physical conduct of a sexual nature when this conduct: (1) explicitly or implicitly affects an individual's employment, (2) unreasonably interferes with an individual's work performance, or (3) creates an intimidating, hostile, or offensive work environment. A major component of the guidelines is that the behavior is unwanted and might affect workplace conditions negatively. It is also unlawful for an employer to retaliate against an individual for filing a discrimination charge or opposing employment practices that discriminate based on sex (US EEOC, 2009).

Except for very small businesses, every employer must have a sexual harassment policy that adheres to the EEOC guidelines. Violation of these policies is not quite the same as breaking a law. If someone breaks the law, we call the police to report it. If someone violates sexual harassment *policy*, it is reported to the employer. If the employer does not comply with their responsibility to adequately follow-up and protect workers, a claim against them may be made directly to the EEOC. Most workers will find that a report of sexual harassment made to the Human Resources department of the company will be investigated, and appropriate action taken.

The process is only slightly different in educational settings because schools are governed by US Education Code. Title IX of the Education Code protects people from discrimination based on sex in education programs or other school-based activities that receive Federal financial assistance. Title IX states that:

> No person in the United States shall, on the basis of sex, be excluded from participation in, be denied the benefits of, or be subjected to

discrimination under any education program or activity receiving Federal financial assistance.

Source: https://www2.ed.gov/about/offices/list/ocr/docs/tix_dis.html

At school, a report of sexual harassment may be made to any instructor, dean, administrative supervisor, the Health Center, or Campus Safety. From there the report moves to the Title IX Coordinator who is charged with investigating the complaint. While the complaint is being investigated, the school will take actions to protect the reporter, which may include shielding a student from ongoing contact with the individual being investigated, removing the individual from class, issuing a no-contact order, or assigning the individual to another work/study setting. It is against policy for students to harass other students, for students to harass employees of the school, for employees of the school to harass students, or for employees to harass other employees. Most private schools who do *not* receive federal education funding also have sexual harassment policies and procedures for handling complaints. And being an employer, they are required to have a policy for protecting their employees as well. See the Resources section at the end of this chapter for more information about where to seek help at Fullerton College.

Persons found guilty of breaking sexual harassment policy may suffer penalties at work (or school) or be fired (dismissed from school) and/or sued in civil court. But they do not go to jail unless they crossed over the line from sexual harassment to sexual assault, a police report was made, and the person found was guilty in a court of law.

In Sex in Society 9.2 we take a look at a case that was pivotal in awakening Americans to the widespread problem of sexual harassment in the workplace: Anita Hill vs. Clarence Thomas. Although Judge Thomas suffered no ill employment effects from Dr. Hill's charges, the nationally televised hearings brought discussions about sexual harassment into every home, school, and workplace. Sadly, despite all of the mandatory trainings on how to avoid sexual harassment by employers and repeated clarifications from the EEOC about what constitutes sexual harassment, it has remained all too common in the United States. Recently, the **#MeToo** movement has sparked renewed conversation about both sexual harassment and sexual assault, particularly in the workplace. The movement hit Hollywood hard in 2017, beginning with "The New York Times and The New Yorker publishing stories that cracked open the decades-long predation of movie mogul Harvey Weinstein. Since then, the producer has been banished from the glitterati's ranks, and more victims began speaking up about the horrors behind Hollywood's doors" (Mandell, 2018). Decades after the Hill–Thomas hearings, another high-profile hearing on Capitol Hill occurred in September of 2018 during the Supreme Court confirmation hearings of Judge Brett Kavanaugh. This time, the reluctant accuser was making allegations of sexual assault rather than sexual harassment, but the outcome was similar in that the victim had not made an official report at the time the event occurred, in part because she didn't think she would be believed because the perpetrator was a prominent young man in the community. As with Thomas, Kavanaugh was confirmed onto the US Supreme Court, and the female accuser (Dr. Christine Blasey Ford) had to cope with hate mail and death threats. Indeed, many victims of sexual harassment hesitate to make a complaint for fear of social fallout, retaliation, and increased stress in the workplace. Sometimes the situation cannot be resolved quickly or satisfactorily enough for the victim to feel safe, and so they wind up being the one to leave the workplace or school, rather than the harasser. This outcome is certainly not what the creators of sexual harassment policies had in mind.

sex in society 9.1

A Historical Look at Rape

In *Against Our Will,* one of the most definitive works on the subject, author Susan Brownmiller (1975) described the evolution of our current attitudes toward rape and the laws against it. According to Brownmiller, rape has a long, sordid history. In antiquity, women were considered one of the spoils of war, objects to be taken and used in whatever way one wished. After a battle, the conquering army routinely rounded up all female survivors and had free rein to do what they wanted with them. Women who resisted were routinely slaughtered. Women who were spared were often sold off as slaves once their captors became bored with them.

Although rape seems to have been a part of all cultures, it has not always been considered a crime against a person. The earliest statutes against rape were laws related to property. Women were not considered persons. Instead, they were valued as property. They could provide labor and bear children—two important commodities in an agrarian economy dependent on the availability of workers.

Under Hammurabi's Code (a Babylonian law approximately 4,000 years old), a woman was not considered to be a free, independent human being. She was considered to be some man's (father's, husband's) property. Therefore, if someone violated the woman, he committed a crime against that man's property and was prosecuted accordingly.

Women also were categorized according to their marital status and virginity. Virgins were considered purer than nonvirgins in relation to sex-related crimes. The purest of all virgins were those engaged to be married. A man convicted of raping a betrothed virgin was put to death and his victim set free. A man convicted of raping a married woman also was put to death. His victim, however, also was put to death because she was considered a willing victim or accomplice in the crime. Presumably, the feeling was that she somehow led the rapist on, or consented to the act. The two early beliefs briefly described here about women and rape—that a woman is a man's property and that rape cannot occur unless a woman somehow consents—still exist and form the foundation of much of the legislation and belief systems that people share about rape.

sex in society 9.2

The Clarence Thomas–Anita Hill Hearings

The Thomas–Hill Congressional hearings in 1992 had effects far beyond the matter of deciding whether Clarence Thomas should sit on the U.S. Supreme Court. As a result of these hearings, the issue of sexual harassment came to the fore and led to a whole new zeitgeist of how people are to conduct themselves in the workplace. The hearings were also noteworthy in that this event involved two prominent blacks—Thomas, a judge, and Hill, a law professor at the time of the hearings—with opposing political ideologies.

In her testimony, Hill described her position as an employee of Thomas at the Equal Employment Opportunity Commission (EEOC). She claimed that, beginning in 1982, Thomas had pressured her to go out on dates, and that he had made lewd comments to her, including references to a pubic hair on a Coke can and the size of his penis. She stated that, because Thomas was well connected and could help advance her career, she was reluctant to speak out at the time. She produced three witnesses who testified to Hill's having told them that she was being harassed, though they did not recall Hill's having accused Thomas by name.

Hill's critics charged that she waited too long (10 years) to speak of the harassment, and that she had agreed to testify to members of committee only under condition of anonymity. Her detractors took this as an indication that she made the charges only to try to derail Thomas's chances to gain a Supreme Court

berth. They produced a number of witnesses who had worked for Thomas at the same time as Hill did, and these witnesses testified that they had observed no evidence of harassment and were not harassed themselves. Finally, Hill's critics questioned why she had followed Thomas to another job subsequent to the alleged harassment.

Thomas denounced the charges as completely untrue and a "high-tech lynching." In a close vote, he was confirmed to the Supreme Court. Irrespective of the outcome, the legacy of the hearings was far-reaching and has an enduring symbolic value. Major changes include the recognition of sexual harassment in the workplace, its definition, and enactment of legislation making sexual harassment easier to prove. Monetary awards and settlements also increased dramatically. In 1990, sexual harassment awards handled through the EEOC totaled $7.7 million; by 1996, settlements had reached $27 million.

Awakened by the prospects of costly lawsuits, the public and private sectors alike have gone on the defensive. Sexual harassment training is becoming common. Formal policies now are the rule rather than the exception in the workplace. More women (and men) are filing suit and supporting the victims of harassment. As a result of the Thomas–Hill hearings, public attitudes and actions regarding sexual harassment were irrevocably changed.

Helping a Friend Who Has been Sexually Assaulted...

Source: Callista Lee

1. Listen and believe. You probably don't want to believe that something so awful could happen (especially if the perpetrator is a mutual acquaintance), but believing your friend is part of truly "being there" for them.
2. Avoid asking a lot of questions; especially any that may suggest that your friend might have avoided the assault if they had done things differently. Most "why" questions can sound that way to the victim.
3. Express empathy. "I'm sorry this happened to you." "I'm glad you got out of there alive!"

"You did the right thing in telling me; I want to support you."

4. Encourage them to call the local Rape Crisis Hotline to talk with a counselor trained to help sexual assault survivors. Look up the phone number for them.
5. You may want to tell them that they "must" call the police to report the crime, but *don't*. ASK them if they want to report it to police. Look up the phone number for them. But remember that the rapist took away their choice by forcing sex on them. Don't be

another person taking away their choices. Be the person who *respects* their right to make their own decisions. Offer to go through the process with them if they want to make a report but are afraid.

6. Ask them what you can do to help them feel safe. Offer to check the house for them. Offer to run errands for them. Keep checking in with them over the weeks that follow. They may start to feel like they are asking too much of you, so you may have to keep offering your assistance rather than waiting for them to ask.

7. Learn more about what your friend might be going through by reading about Rape Trauma Syndrome. Know that your patience will be needed and appreciated. Consider talking to a rape counselor yourself, to both learn more about how to be helpful as well as to de-stress yourself. Helping someone go through trauma can be traumatizing in itself. Engage in self-care.

Sexual Harassment in College

In covering President Obama's declaration making sexual assault on campuses a core priority for his administration, the Huffington Post reported that while the commitment made by the administration to sexual assault on campus were applaudable, it wasn't enough. The Post reported that to truly ensure safe, secure campus environments would require a response not only to sexual assault, but to the entire spectrum of sexual violence taking place on college campuses today including sexual harassment, an issue that is often minimized (May et al, 2014).

Hill & Silva (2005) reported that about two-thirds of college students (male and female) experience some type of sexual harassment, yet less than 10 percent report it to a college or university employee or officially report them to a Title IX officer.

In their report, Drawing the Line on Sexual Harassment on Campus, Hill and Silva (2005) reported that sexual harassment is common on college campuses with a majority of students experiencing it. Further, they found that more than one-third encounter some form of sexual harassment during their first year. In many cases this is so traumatic that it forces students to drop out before finishing the year.

Physical intimidation often plays a big part in creating a hostile environment.

Most of this harassment is noncontact in nature. It comes in the form of sexual remarks or electronic messages. About one third of students surveyed experienced some form of physical harassment, such as being touched, grabbed, or forced to do something sexual (Hill & Silva, 2005).

These data support findings from The National College Women Sexual Victimization (NCWSV) study. The NCWSV, although not designed to measure sexual harassment per se, found that approximately 11 percent of the 4,446 women studied had been sexually victimized (other than rape). These incidents included sexual coercion, sexual contact with or without force, threats of rape, sexual contact, and penetration. About 10 percent of the women had also been victimized in the past. Even more startling is the percentage of women who reported being stalked in the previous academic year. The NCWSV defined stalked as "repeatedly followed, watched, phoned, e-mailed, or communicated with in some way that seemed obsessive to you and made you afraid or concerned for your safety." Fully 13.1 percent of the women, using these criteria, reported being stalked in the previous academic year. Although none of these NCWSV data meet the classic criteria for sexual harassment, many would argue that this scenario could represent a hostile environment for some campus women (Fisher et al., 2000).

healthy sex hints 9.1

Sexual Harassment: How to Fight Back

The following guidelines may be helpful in fighting back if you think you have been the victim of sexual harassment on campus or at work.

1. If the harassment includes rape or attempted rape, file criminal charges against the perpetrator.
2. If the act does not include rape or attempted rape, confront the person who is harassing you. Write a letter to the offender, and follow up with a meeting. Be as clear and specific about the offender's actions as possible.
   - Be specific about the incidents, times, and dates. A history and pattern of events are important. Most harassers are repeat offenders.
   - Describe exactly what happened, your feelings about the incidents, and how you reacted. Include a short statement indicating your desire for the harasser to stop.
   - Sign and date the letter, and make duplicate copies.
   - Send a copy to the perpetrator, and indicate that if the behavior doesn't stop immediately, you will press charges using the letter as evidence.
3. Seek support. Don't hide what happened.
   - Talk to coworkers, fellow students, and people identified with the issue. This may help put pressure on the offender to stop.
   - Contact a local support group, and talk to others who have experienced the same problem.
   - Relate your incidents to your significant other.
4. If the behavior doesn't stop, meet with the offender's supervisor. Discuss the incidents and give a copy of your letter to the supervisor
   - In a work setting, this is the offender's immediate supervisor.
   - In a college setting, this person may be the department chairperson, the student center director, a member of the sexual harassment panel, or the dean of students.
5. Know your rights. Sexual harassment is against the law. You do not have to put up with it.
   - Obtain the company's/school's sexual harassment policy. Read it thoroughly, and make sure you follow its guidelines for handling your case.
   - Identify the administrative office and person responsible for handling sexual harassment violations in your workplace or school.

Although it may seem frightening, it's better to act quickly than to wait and see what happens. Harassers rarely stop their activities if they are not challenged. ॐ

Hill & Silva (2005) found that both men and women were equally likely to be harassed, but in different ways. Female students were more likely to be the target of sexual jokes, comments, gestures, or looks while their male counterparts were more likely to be called gay or a homophobic name.

While both men and women are equally likely to be harassed, *men are more likely* than women to *harass*. In addition, both men and women on campus were more likely to be harassed by a man than by a woman. Almost half of the male students interviewed and about one third of the females admitted to sexually harassing someone in college (Hill & Silva, 2005).

An interesting finding was that more than half of harassers think their actions were funny. About one-third thought the personbeing harassed

personal exploration activity
Coercive Sex in the Media

We all know that it is immoral to push, coax, or force someone to have a sexual interaction when they do not want to be sexual. However, this type of behavior is fairly common in today's music. The music we listen to may influence the way we think and act, so it is important to recognize the messages we are receiving. This activity will help you start to critically analyze the impact of the music in your life.

For the next week, list all the songs you hear on a sheet of paper in two columns: sexually coercive lyrics and nonsexual or healthy sexual lyrics. To really analyze the songs, you will have to listen closely to the lyrics. If you cannot understand the words, try looking on the group's Web site for the lyrics. You may be quite surprised at the song's message when you see the actual words. At the end of the week, evaluate your choices of music. Is your favorite music reflecting a healthy, positive view of sexuality or a negative, destructive one? Are you willing to reduce or eliminate the songs that reinforce the idea that sex is to be gotten at all cost and replace these with songs that reflect a healthy, positive approach to sexuality?

Bethany: A Proposition from Her Professor

case study 9.2

Bethany, a college senior, was having trouble with one of her classes and went to see her professor, a 35-year-old married man.

When I went to see him, I was a little surprised that he shut the door. It was after our late-afternoon class, and there wasn't anybody around in his department. He had this weird little smile on his face when he asked me to sit down. I sensed something was wrong and should have left then, but I didn't. When I sat down, his first remark was about how good I smelled. I smiled and thanked him but thought to myself that the comment was totally inappropriate.

I explained to him that I was there because I was worried about my grade for the semester. I had gotten a D on the last test and didn't want to lower my grade below a B–. He told me not to worry; he didn't like to see me so sad. Again I smiled but thought that this remark was also inappropriate. He said he'd take care of me, that I was one of his favorite students. With that, he slid his hand over the table and began rubbing my hand with his.

I was getting very uncomfortable by now and moved my hand away. He said, "Don't be so tense; let me rub your shoulders." He started to get up, but I stood up and said, "I don't think that's necessary. I must be going." He said, "Sit down. I thought you wanted to talk about your grade." I sat back down, and he proceeded to explain to me that he'd had his eye on me all semester and was hoping I'd come to visit him. He explained that other female students in the past had worked out "special arrangements" to boost their grades. I asked him, "What kind of special arrangements?"

Critical Thinking

Have you ever been in a situation where a grade was so important you said, "I'd do anything to get a better grade in this class?" What makes class grades this important?

He said, "Come on now, Beth, don't be so naive. You're a very sexy girl. We could have lots of fun together." At this point, I was so flustered that I got up quickly and excused myself. I had to beat him to the door because he got up as if to block my exit, but I already had opened the door. He smiled and told me not to do anything foolish. I didn't tell anyone because I was afraid he'd flunk me. He kind of ignored me the rest of the semester but did wind up giving me a higher grade than I thought I earned.

actually *wanted* the sexual attention, and another third believed that it was just a part of school and everybody did it. In general, the students who did the harassing did not see themselves as harassers, but instead as misunderstood jokesters (Hill & Silva, 2005).

As with previous studies, most victims don't even report their sexual harassment. More than one-third of all college students didn't tell anyone about their with sexual harassment. They are reluctant to talk openly and honestly about their sexual harassment and are more apt to joke about or ignore the matter (Hill & Silva, 2005).

Lastly, the effects of sexual harassment on campus can be serious. It can harm the emotional and academic well-being of students, promote conflict among students, and contribute to a hostile learning environment. The financial costs to universities can be staggering and the harmful press that follows can severly damage their reputations (Hill & Silva, 2005).

Reports such as *Drawing the Line on Sexual Harassment on Campus* have increased awareness of the problem and have resulted in many reforms ranging from the adoption of stricter policies to enhanced enforcement through Title lX and other legal actions.

Child Sexual Abuse

Child sexual abuse Any sexual contact between an adult and a child who is under 18 years of age

Child sexual abuse is any sexual contact between an adult and a child under 18 years of age. Child sexual abuse runs the gamut from inappropriate fondling and touching, to masturbation, to oral sex, to penetration of the anus or vagina with fingers or a penis. These and other forms of sexual behavior are considered evidence of child sexual abuse despite the child's consent or sexual precociousness.

Often sexual abuse starts off as normal hugging, kissing, and playful behavior. It then progresses to more intimate touching, manual and oral stimulation, and finally intercourse. The perpetrator often tells the child that he or she is not doing anything wrong but "Don't tell anyone because they might not understand." The perpetrator often uses bribes and rewards to get the child to conceal the illicit behavior. Or, physical threats or threats of desertion scare the child into silence. Children also may not report abuse because of fear and guilt. They sense that something is wrong but can't bear the shame of others finding out. Often, fear of reprisals from the perpetrator or other family member stands in the way of the victim's reporting abuse. In many cases, even when children report the behavior to a parent, they are not believed.

Child sexual abuse involving nonfamily members is generally referred to as **child molestation**. Child sexual abuse involving genetically related family members is called **incest**. Often, the perpetrators are adults who fall between the two forms, such as steprelatives, the mother's boyfriend, or a caregiver brought into the house to watch the children. As we discussed in Chapter 9, a **pedophile** is an adult who is sexually aroused by children and initiates contact with them out of sexual desire. A non-pedophilic **child molester** is not motivated by sexual desire but, rather, by power, the desire to control, or out of affection.

Child molestation Abuse of a child by nonfamily members

Incest Child sexual abuse involving genetically related family members

Pedophile An adult who is sexually aroused by children and initiates contact with them out of sexual desire

Child molester One who makes indecent sexual advances to children

∾ Intellectual and Emotional Wellness ∾

As adults, we have the intellectual and emotional maturity to make informed choices regarding when and with whom we want to be sexual. Although "age of consent" is a gray area chronologically, theoretically it is the age where intellect and emotion work together in the mature person to make informed choices regarding their behavior. Society has long believed that children must be "protected" sexually from sexual predators until they are mature enough to make informed decisions regarding their behavior. Sexual predators are often very smart and develop elaborate plans for deceiving, luring, and trapping their victims. They observe and note their victim's behavior, patterns, and weaknesses. Their cognitive abilities, although they may be high-level, are without the self-regulating moral/ethical controls that most of us have.

∾ Social Wellness ∾

As we have just described, sexual predators do not have strong social relationships. Starting with their dysfunctional relationships with their own parents, sexual predators have not developed mature, egalitarian relationships based on caring, respect, and tolerance. From those who harass, to those who rape, to those who abuse children, a common thread is immature, dysfunctional, unsatisfying social relationships. Those who engage in coercive sex often have limited experience with relationships based on love and caring, trust, respect, mutuality, sharing, and commitment. Their relationships are exploitive, self-centered, and destructive. They use power differentials in relationships to take advantage and inflict pain and suffering. Their relationships are really not relationships at all. They are artificial arrangements set up to trap and abuse.

Incidence of Child Sexual Abuse

The actual number of cases of child sexual abuse is unknown. Like rape, child sexual abuse is often unreported for many reasons. However, following a sustained 15-year increase from 1977 to 1992, reported cases of child sexual abuse have been decreasing since then (Jones & Finkelhor, 2001). Numbers of cases of reported child sexual abuse reached an estimated peak of 149,800 in 1992. Since that time, cases declined 2 to 11 percent each year through 1998 (Jones & Finkelhor, 2001). In 1998, estimated cases of child sexual abuse reached a low of approximately 103,600, which represents a total decline of 31 percent over that 6-year period (Jones & Finkelhor, 2001). This sustained decline in the number of cases contrasts significantly with the 1980s, when the United States experienced 10 percent annual increases in the number of cases of child sexual abuse (Jones & Finkelhor, 2001).

Explanations for the Decline

Wilson (2001), reporting in the Office of Juvenile Justice bulletin, identifies several reasons for the decline in child sexual abuse cases. The past two decades have seen a dramatic increase in public information and information about child sexual abuse. There has been an increase in child abuse prevention programs. The increase in awareness and prevention has led to the arrest and incarceration of more sex offenders. With the onset of Megan's Law (which we will discuss in detail later), new laws have been passed in many states to increase and improve the monitoring of sex offenders (Jones & Finkelhor, 2001).

The decline in child sexual abuse parallels declines in other criminal offenses that may be related to victimizing children. As we mentioned previously, the number of cases of all violent crime, rape, sexual assault, and other types of female victimization are down nationally. Factors that may be related to the declines in these crimes could also be related to the declines in child sexual abuse (Jones & Finkelhor, 2001).

Effects of Child Sexual Abuse

Several factors have an impact on the future well-being of the victim. Four factors are related to the need for long-term treatment and the prognosis for the child (Krugman, Bays, Chadwick, Levitt, McMugh, & Whitworth, 1991). The closer the victim's relationship to the perpetrator, the longer the abuse, the more violent the contact, and the more intrusive the relationship, the greater is the need for treatment and the poorer the hope for an effective outcome.

As adults, child sexual abuse victims report extremely sad, pain-filled childhoods. They recollect feelings of betrayal, fear, and loss of innocence, painting a picture of a lost childhood (Felitti, 1991). Victims of child sexual abuse often have difficulty forming intimate relationships as adults. They have feelings of shame and guilt, depression, a lack of trust, and revulsion at being touched, and they often are alcohol and other drug abusers (Frazier & Cohen, 1992). When victims are able to form relationships, they are often characterized by a lack of emotion and sexual interest and gratification (Jackson, Calhoun, Amick, Maddeve, & Habif, 1990).

Megan's Law

Megan's Law Legislation requiring notification that a sex offender has been released and is residing in a community

On October 31, 1994, the New Jersey State Legislature enacted the Registration and Community Notification Laws (RCNL), also known as **Megan's Law**. The law is named after Megan Kanka, who was lured into the house of a neighbor, whose son, a convicted sex offender, raped and murdered her. Only one family, neighbors of the perpetrator, had any knowledge of him living on the block.

Lucy: A Victim of Child Abuse

A 16-year-old girl was referred to the STD clinic by her high school nurse. The report showed a classic macular/papular rash on her hands and feet and a blood test confirming secondary syphilis. This girl, Lucy, probably used drugs, had a few boyfriends, and was a dropout candidate. Dr. Blonna saw these kids all the time. Here he relates Lucy's case.

When I first interviewed Lucy, I knew from the start that this was not a cut-and-dried case. She was young, fresh-faced, and preppy-looking in her Catholic schoolgirl's pleated skirt and white socks.

Lucy was quiet, almost sunken in her posture. She averted eye contact, obviously embarrassed. After my usual introduction, explaining why I needed to talk to her, I began to explain the nitty-gritty of sexually transmitted diseases and how they are spread. By the time I got around to asking her about her sexual contacts, she was on the verge of tears.

Lucy's initial response to my asking for the names of her sexual contacts was "There's only one—my boyfriend, Hector." When pressed for Hector's address and telephone number, Lucy hemmed and hawed, said she didn't know where he lived or went to school, and tried to move the interview along.

Finally, I had enough and said, "Look, I know you're lying to me. What's going on here?" It took but a second for Lucy to break down and the floodgates to open up, her tears pouring forth in a torrent followed by shakes, sobs, and near hyperventilation. She couldn't contain herself any longer. Between gasps of air and body-wracking sobs, she told her story. There was no boyfriend Hector. Rather, there was a 45-year-old man, Luis. Luis was the boyfriend of her mother, Maria. He mostly lived with them and had free rein to come and go. It seemed that he liked to come around when Maria was still at work and Lucy and her younger sister were home from school. Luis had started sexually abusing Lucy about 5 years ago. It started out with her sitting on his lap and his fondling her. It progressed to his exposing himself to her, demanding fellatio, and, for the past couple of years, vaginal intercourse. When it began, Lucy was confused, but Luis told her not to say anything to her mother. Lucy thought her mother knew what was going on because there were times when Lucy didn't want to be left home with Luis, but her mom made excuses for him and didn't let Lucy leave.

When Luis began to force fellatio and intercourse on Lucy, he warned her not to tell her mother or he'd leave them or, worse, hurt her mother and little sister. Lucy was beginning to worry about her little sister. She'd seen the way Luis was eyeing her sister lately, and Lucy didn't want her to have to go through the same thing that she did.

I'm not sure how the story ended. I brought Lucy downtown to the child welfare agency that afternoon. I had to fill out forms and was still there when they returned with her little sister, afraid but unmolested. The social worker told me that they were removing Lucy and her sister from the home, arresting Luis and probably Maria, and would find a safe home for the girls. The last image I have of Lucy is her sitting on the wooden bench in the child welfare office, her arm around her little sister, smoothing the pleats on her school uniform, looking much older and more tired than her 16 years.

Critical Thinking

Social workers and other mental health professionals are trained to pick up on cues like the ones Lucy presented. Should these people be held liable for missing the same cues? Why?

Megan's Law requires that certain convicted sexual offenders must register with law enforcement authorities and provide for community notification depending on the degree of risk that they represent to the community. The law applies to those who have been convicted of specified sexual offenses and has a grandfather's clause that includes offenders who were convicted of similar offenses prior to the passage of the law.

Over 40 states rushed to enact Megan's Laws of their own, and in May 1996, President Bill Clinton signed into law a federal version of the legislation. The federal version of Megan's Law was a revision of the Federal Violent Crimes and Law Enforcement Act of 1994. The revised law, entitled Megan's Law, required all states wishing to continue to receive federal funding for law enforcement to comply with its identification and notification of sex offenders criteria (*Economist,* 1997). The law came under intense scrutiny from civil libertarian groups, who claimed it denies convicted sex offenders their constitutional rights to privacy and protection (Brooks, 1996).

The various versions of Megan's Law all contain provisions for identifying convicted sex offenders and ranking them on the aforementioned three-tiered scale according to their likelihood to offend again. The level of community notification varies according to the offender's level. Tier 1 offenders must register with local authorities, but their status is not released to the community (Webby, 2003). High-risk residents (all day care center operators; supervisors of Boy Scouts, Big Brothers, Big Sisters; and the like) are notified of Tier 2 offenders. All immediate neighbors and others likely to come in contact with Tier 3 offenders are sent registered letters notifying them of the presence of the offender in their neighborhood (*Economist,* 2002). In addition to registered letters, other means of community notification include posting of pictures and descriptions of sex offenders; mailings to families, community groups, and organizations deemed at risk by local authorities; and postings on Internet bulletin boards.

Critics of Megan's Law legislation claim that, in addition to being unconstitutional, it does not work. Just knowing that a sex offender lives on your street is not sufficient to protect your children (Webby, 2003; Bai, 1997). Neighbors of Megan Kanka, for instance, knew that at least one sex offender (the roommate of Megan's killer) already lived on their street (Knight Ridder/Tribune Services, 2003).

Strategies to Prevent Child Sexual Abuse

Parents, teachers, and other helpful adults might use the following strategies to help prevent child sexual abuse:

1. *Provide sex education.* One of the cornerstones of any good school-based sexuality education program is a child sexual abuse prevention component. The unit should be comprehensive and cover issues including self-esteem, communication skills, inappropriate adult physical contact, refusal skills, and escape skills. This unit should be presented early in the child's curriculum, as most sexual abuse begins before 8 years of age.

2. *Become an approachable parent.* Open lines of communication early with your children. Continually underscore the fact that your children can come to you with any question involving sex. Do not punish your children for asking questions.

3. *Discuss inappropriate sexual behavior with your children.* Let your children know that you do not approve of any adult-child sexual contact (explain kissing, hugging, and so forth). Tell them that you would never punish them for telling on another adult (no matter how close their relationship-stepfather, baby-sitter, coach). Differentiate "good touch" and "bad touch" while letting your children know that they have the right to want "no touch."

4. *Let your children know they can decide how, when, and by whom they want to be touched.* Do not force them to hug, kiss, or be affectionate with adults with whom they do not want to behave this way. This reinforces their trust in their intuition about other people's sexual behavior.

5. *Discuss refusal skills.* Have your children practice how to say no in an assertive way. Teach them how to refuse an offer to engage in any behavior in which they do not want to be involved.

6. *Discuss escape skills.* Teach your children how to escape from potentially dangerous or abusive situations. Tell them it is OK to yell, scream, hit, and run away from any adult who does not stop touching them when asked to. Help children identify trusted friends, neighbors, and family members with whom they can seek shelter.

7. *Discuss telling.* Your children have to understand that they absolutely must tell you if they have been approached or touched inappropriately by any adult, no matter how close that person's relationship is with you. Children need to understand that this isn't tattle-telling and is the best way to deal with the situation.

Adults Molested as Children (AMAC)

Source: Callista Lee

Not all, but many adults who were sexually abused as children will experience long-term effects that are wide ranging and may include:

- Depression—the most frequently reported symptom of AMAC clients
- Self-destructive tendencies including suicidal ideation and attempts
- Somatic disturbances and dissociation including anxiety and nervousness, insomnia, chronic pain, eating disorders, irritable bowel syndrome, feelings of "spaciness" or being out-of-body, and feeling that things are "unreal"
- Health risk behaviors including tobacco use, alcoholism, obesity, and unsafe sexual behaviors
- Negative self-concept, including feelings of low self-esteem, isolation, and alienation
- Interpersonal relationship difficulties like problems relating to people, trusting others, and even trouble relating to their own children
- Revictimization, in which women abused as children are more vulnerable to marital violence
- Sexual function difficulties in which victims find it difficult to relax enough to enjoy sex, avoid sex, lack desire, or experience trouble experiencing full arousal and orgasm. It should be noted that some AMACs go the opposite direction, becoming promiscuous as a way of taking back their sexuality or proving to themselves that they are desirable and powerful. A small number of AMACs become molesters themselves.
- Counseling during childhood and the adolescent years can help to prevent many of these difficulties, but many AMACs need to come back for additional therapy during their adult years.

Sources: Darkness to Light (2015), and RAINN.org

References

Bai, M. (1997). A report from the front in the war on predators: Years after Megan's murder, her law is still on trial. *Newsweek, 129*(20), 67.

Brownmiller, S. (1975). *Against our will.* New York: Simon & Schuster.

Burgess, A. W., & Holmstrom, L. L. (1974). Rape trauma syndrome. *American Journal of Psychiatry, 131,* 981–985.

Cate, R. M., & Lloyd, S. A. (1992). *Courtship.* Newbury Park, Calif.: Sage.

Deming, M. E., Krassen-Covan, E. Swan, S C, Billings, D. L. (2013) Exploring Rape Myths, Gendered Norms, Group Processing, and the Social Context of Rape Among College Women: A Qualitative Analysis. Violence Against Women. Volume: 19 issue: 4, page(s): 465–485.

Chmielewski, C. M. (1997). Sexual harassment meets Title IX: New federal rules to combat sexual harassment and place schools at the battlefront. *NEA Today, 16*(2), 25.

The Economist. (1997). Pointing the finger at Megan's Law. *342*(8004), 27–29.

The Economist. (2002, November 16). A scarlet letter: Megan's Law, changing the law for sex offenders. *365*(8299).

Equal Employment Opportunity Commission. (2003). Sexual harassment charges: EEOC and fair employment practices agencies (FEPA) combined, FY 1002-FY 2001 [Online]. Available: www.eeoc.gov/stats/harass.html.

Felitti, V. (1991). Long-term medical consequences of incest, rape, and molestation. *Southern Medical Journal, 84,* 328–331.

Frazier, P., & Cohen, B. (1992). Research on the sexual victimization of women. *Counseling Psychologist, 20,* 141–158.

Frieze, I. H. (1983). Causes and consequences of marital rape. *Signs, 8,* 532–553.

Higher Education Center. (2003). Sexual assault: Alcohol and other drugs [Online]. Available: www.edc.org/hec/pubs/factsheets/fact_sheet1.html.

Hill, C., Silva, E (2005). Drawing the Line on Sexual Harassment on Campus. Washington, DC: American Association of University Women Educational Foundation.

Jackson, I., Calhoun, K., Amick, A., Maddever, H., & Habif, V. (1990). Young adult women who report childhood intrafamilial sexual abuse: Subsequent adjustment. *Archives of Sexual Behavior, 19,* 211–221.

Jones, L. M., & Finkelhor, D. (2001, January). The decline in child sexual abuse cases. *Juvenile Justice Bulletin.* Washington, DC: Bureau of Justice Statistics, Office of Juvenile Justice and Delinquency Prevention.

Kaufman, L. (1997). A report from the front: Why it's gotten easier to sue for sexual harassment. *Newsweek, 129*(2), 32.

Knight-Ridder/Tribune Services. (2003, January 13). Public must be involved to make Megan's law work. *San Jose Mercury News,* p. 7485.

Krugman, R., Bays, J., Chadwick, D., Levitt, C., McMugh, M., & Whitworth, J. (1991). Guidelines for evaluation of sexual abuse of children. *Pediatrics, 87,* 254–260.

Malamuth, N. M., Sockloski, R. J., Koss, M. P., & Tanaka, J. S. (1991). Characteristics of aggressors against women: Testing a model using a national sample of college students. *Journal of Consulting and Clinical Psychology, 59,* 670–781.

Marano, H. E. (1996). Why they stay: A saga of spouse abuse. *Psychology Today, 29*(3), 56–66.

May, E, Roy, D, Cameron, J (2014). What About Sexual Harassment on Campus? The Huffington Post. 01/27/2014 04:28 pm ET | Updated Mar 29, 2014.

Montgomery, R. L., Benedicto, J. A., & Hammerke, F. M. (1993, December). Personal U.S. social motivation of undergraduates in using alcohol. *Psychological Reports,* 960–962.

Muram, D., Miller, K., & Cutler, A. (1992). Sexual assault of the elderly victim. *Journal of Interpersonal Violence, 791,* 70–76.

New Jersey Law Network. (2003, February 18). New Jersey law [Online]. Available: www.njlawnet.com/megan.html.

Office of National Drug Control Policy. (2002a). Gamma hydrobutyrate (GHB) [Online]. Available: www.whitehousedrugpolicy.gov/publications/factsh/tgamma/index.html

Office of National Drug Control Policy. (2002b). Rohypnol [Online]. Available: www.whitehousedrugpolicy.gov/publications/factsht/rohypnol/index.html

Rantala, R. R., & Edwards, T. J. (2000, July). *Effects of the NIBRS on crime statistics.* Bureau of Justice Statistics Special Report (NJC 178890). Washington, DC: U.S. Department of Justice, Office of Justice Programs.

Ruskin, L. (2002, November 12). Sex registry goes to court; John Doe: Alaskans say law amounts to retroactive punishment. *Anchorage Daily News* p. 1.

Russel, D. E. H. (1990). *Rape in marriage.* Bloomington: Indiana University Press.

Sanday, P. (1987). The socio-cultural context of rape: A crosscultural study. *Journal of Social Issues, 37*(4), 5–27.

Schetky, D. H., Green, A. H. (2014). *Child Sexual Abuse: A Handbook For Health Care And Legal Professions.* New York: Brunner/Mazel Publishers.

Task Force of the National Advisory Council on Alcohol Abuse and Alcoholism. (2002). *A call to action: Changing the culture of drinking at US colleges.* NIH Publication 02-5010.

Testa, M, Cleveland, M. J. (2017). Does Alcohol Contribute to College Men's Sexual Assault Perpetration? Between-and Within-Person Effects Over Five Semesters. *Journal of Studies on Alcohol and Drugs*, 78(1), 5–13 (2017).

Tyler, K. A., Schmitz, R. M., Adams, S. (2015). Alcohol Expectancy, Drinking Behavior, and Sexual Victimization Among Female and Male College Students. *Journal of Interpersonal Violence*, June-30-2015 pp 1-25HYPERLINK "http://dx.doi.

org/10.1177%2F0886260515591280" 10.1177/0886260515591280 Washington, DC: National Institute on Alcohol Abuse and Alcoholism.

United States Congress. (1996).The Drug-Induced Rape Prevention and Punishment Act of 1996. 21 USC 841(b)(7).

United States Department of Justice, Federal Bureau of Investigation (FBI). (2015). *2015 Crime in the United States.* 2015 U.S. Department of Justice—Federal Bureau of Investigation Released Fall 2016 https://ucr.fbi.gov/crime-in-the-u.s/2015/crime-in-the-u.s.-2015/tables/table-1

Webby, S. (2003, January 13). Lack of funding, personnel hinder enforcement of Megan's Law. *San Jose Mercury News,* p. 1058.

Wechsler, H., Davenport, A., Dowdell, G., Moeykens, B., & Castillo, S. (1994). Health and behavioral consequences of binge drinking in college. *Journal of American Medical Association, 272*(21), 1672–1677.

White, A., Hingson, R. (2014). The Burden of Alcohol Use: Excessive Consumption and Related Consequences Among College Students. Alcohol Res. 2014; 35(2): 201–218.

Wilson, J. J. (2001, January). Explanation for the decline in child sexual abuse cases. *Juvenile Justice Bulletin.* Washington, DC: Bureau of Justice Statistics, Office of Juvenile Justice and Delinquency Prevention.

Women'sLaw.Org (2016). What is sexual assault? March 10th, 2016. http://www.womenslaw.org/laws_state_type.php?id=13048&state_code=PG

Chapter

ten

Love & Communication in Intimate Relationships

Student Learning Objectives

After reading this chapter, students will be able to

- ☞ Describe the key elements of healthy relationships.
- ☞ Identify issues related to meeting potential partners.
- ☞ Compare a variety of theories regarding love.
- ☞ Evaluate a variety of barriers to intimacy.
- ☞ Describe various techniques used to overcome barriers to intimacy.
- ☞ Identify characteristics of unhealthy relationships.
- ☞ Become aware of markers for abusive relationships.
- ☞ Examine a variety of ways to end unhappy relationships.
- ☞ Describe some of the key elements that make sexual communication different and difficult.
- ☞ Assess the importance of communication in sexual relationships.
- ☞ Describe a variety of verbal sexual communication techniques.
- ☞ Describe a variety of nonverbal sexual communication techniques.
- ☞ Describe some barriers to effective sexual communication.

College provides opportunities to meet a wide variety of people.

Intimacy Connectedness to another person characterized by respect, equality, mutual caring, openness, self-disclosure, honesty, attentiveness, sharing, commitment, trust, empathy, and tenderness

Our quality of life depends to a large extent on the types of relationships we develop. Relationships define our connectedness to others and provide opportunities for **intimacy**. Intimate relationships are characterized by respect, equality, identity, honesty, caring, sharing, trust, commitment, empathy, and tenderness. Intimacy requires us to self disclose and be vulnerable and open in order to have this richer level of affection. (Lewis, 2010) This can be somewhat scary since we must trust the other person enough allow ourselves to be vulnerable.

Intimacy is often linked with being sexual with another but in reality there others forms of intimacy. Cognitive intimacy happens when we exchange opinions and ideas freely. Experiential intimacy is the sharing of activities. Having a variety of these activities is essential for preventing boredom in relationship thus blocking intimacy. Excitement in a relationship promotes closeness (University of Michigan, 2009). In emotional intimacy we try to understand how the other feels. And finally is sexual intimacy which is the physical part of intimacy. This physical form of affection includes not only intercourse but activities such as hugging and holding hands. (University of Florida, 2013).

Forming healthy relationships with others is a skill a person develops and practices. For relationships to be intimate, we have to be ourselves and let others be who they are. Good relationships derive from good role models and require giving thought to the outcome of our actions.

As we age, we form social relationships with others on many levels including family, friends, working colleagues, neighbors, and partners. Although this chapter focuses primarily on partner relationships, we have to realize that becoming sexually intimate with someone does not necessarily mean that we automatically have an emotionally intimate relationship.

We learn patterns of relating to others from our families, friends, and past experiences. Some people are extroverted and outgoing, and they enjoy having many different types of relationships. Developing relationships is easy for them. Other people are introverted and enjoy doing many things alone. They develop fewer relationships in their lives and may have difficulty forming new relationships. Regardless, human contact is essential for health and wellness.

Establishing Relationships

Friends share activities, thoughts, and feelings. They help each other out. When a life experience tests a friendship, we often hear the comment "That really let me know who my true friends are!" A healthy romantic relationship, one that is founded on intimacy, requires the same expectations as a friendship, yet we may find ourselves not being authentic with our thoughts and feelings, second-guessing the other person, and sometimes tolerating behaviors we would never accept from our friends. The erotic piece of the puzzle is what changes the interaction. We often become self-conscious in ways we hadn't anticipated, and we might lose our identity in pursuit of the relationship. Healthy relationships are based on being able to clearly identify who we are, what we want, how we want to be treated, how we want to live, and recognizing that we deserve to have a relationship that meets our needs and one that encourages us to be our true selves.

Meeting People

Before overcoming the issues of where and how to meet a prospective partner, people have to be ready for a relationship. Are they open to a relationship? Are they comfortable with themselves? If they were hurt in a previous relationship, they may not have let go of the pain and hurt. Too often people approach a new relationship with defensiveness, negative past associations that become expectations with a new partner, and patterns of relating that prevent new relationships from developing. A healthier response is to look at past relationships as a learning experience. We are better able to decide what we need and what is important to us in a partner and a relationship when we experience ones that are not ideal for us.

Meeting people and forming relationships are social skills and are behaviors that are modeled, taught, and practiced. People have to feel comfortable enough with themselves to believe they are worth getting to know, a fundamental aspect of self-esteem. People who consider themselves "shy" may find social settings very intimidating. They may not be able to identify the behaviors and words needed to make social contact with others.

Shyness

Shyness has been found to be a risk factor that can decrease relationship quality. A lack of social skills, communication skills and self-doubt of shy partners may contribute to a decrease in satisfaction for both partners (Tackett, Nelson, Busbee, 2013). Zimbardo's (1977) classic work on shyness provides a framework for understanding what is a nearly universal experience of being shy at some point in one's life. More than 80 percent reported feeling shy at some time, 25 percent described themselves as chronically shy, and 4 percent described themselves as being shy all the time, in all situations, with virtually all people. Since that classic work, the percentage of people who describe themselves as chronically shy has risen to 48% (Marano, 2005). Some believe the changes in our society such as the focus on electronic communication, telecommuting, the internet, e-mail, cell phones, and the fast, loud pace of life, have all contributed to this increase (Carducci, 2000). The ability to overcome shyness is essential to forming relationships.

Shyness is revealed in a number of ways. People who are shy may experience or demonstrate one or more of the following characteristics:

Overly concerned with themselves: how they look, how others perceive them

Speaking softly

Not making eye contact

Have difficulty introducing self

Blushing

Experiencing "butterflies" in the stomach

Feeling embarrassed

Feeling self-conscious and unfairly comparing themselves to others

Although everyone has those experiences and feelings at times, shyness becomes a problem when the level and frequency of those experiences impede the development of relationships. Shy individuals may see themselves as unacceptable and unworthy, and they typically lack the social skills of knowing how to initiate conversation and make connections. Zimbardo found that overcoming shyness is possible if individuals are willing to work on making changes in the way they think about themselves and others and in how they behave.

Shyness can become painful enough that professional intervention may be warranted. Individuals may choose to avoid social situations, cancel out at the last minute, avoid pleasurable activities, and/or choose to spend the majority of time at the computer rather than in face-to-face interactions. Additionally, chronic low moods, use of alcohol and drugs to manage social situations, or excessive time spent on academic work and professional activity to the exclusion of socializing can be symptoms of painful shyness (Henderson, Zimbardo, & Rodino, 2001).

Approximately 12% of those who are shy use alcohol to help themselves feel comfortable in social situations. Since drinking interferes with cognitive functioning, they are less likely to improve their social skills through good practice. In addition, they are likely to over consume alcohol, making it not a surprise that a significant number of problem drinkers are shy (Young, DiBello, Traylor, Zvolensky, Neighbors, 2015; Carducci, 2000).

Another impediment to forming intimate relationships is the fear of being rejected. Some people enter social situations with an expectation that they will be rejected. They become anxious about being rejected, expect to be rejected, and overreact to what may be ambiguous behavior in others (Downey & Feldman, 1996). Again, having a frame of mind that allows one to approach others in a positive way, without worrying about rejection, is more likely to lead to better interactions and a possible friendship or relationship. When interacting, think positively, control your emotional reactions and add a little humor to make it all easier and more successful (Carducci, 2000).

Choosing a Partner

What is it that attracts us to someone? Some generalizations have been formed based on the research on partner choice and attraction. Most people are drawn to partners from similar backgrounds and form relationships with people who are close in age, race, ethnicity, and social status. The National Health and Social Life Survey (NHSLS) conducted by the National Opinion Research Center (NORC), found that race, education, age, and religious background were similar in a significant number of couples (Michael, Gagnon, Laumann, & Kolata, 1994).

The authors reported that about 90 percent of couples were of the same race. Having similar educational backgrounds was also the predominant pattern as individuals chose sexual partners. Men who had less than a high school education seldom had a partner who had gone to college, and men with a college degree almost never reported having sex with women who had much less or much more education than they did (Michael et al., 1994). Religion and age comparisons also yielded choices based on similarity. The authors of the NHSLS study concluded that couples with more marked differences in background tend to be the exception rather than the rule. Most people choose partners and marry someone who is the same race, same educational background, same religion, and within 5 years of their age. Our society tends to be structured in segregated ways. Consequently, where you live, work, and with whom you socialize have an influence on your choice of partner (Michael, et al., 1994).

Attraction is based on a variety of physical and personality attributes.

Attraction

Researchers have long concluded that people prefer romantic partners who are physically attractive and that there is some cultural consistency in what is deemed attractive (Berscheid & Walster, 1974; Dion & Dion, 1987; Hatfield & Sprecher, 1986). An image of the ideal female and male physique emerges from the media and advertising, and though it may be hard to attain in reality, the standard is set in many people's minds. How we each think we measure up to cultural ideals also may influence our sexual self-esteem. Are we acceptable? Are we attractive? We have found in our classes that just as students can identify what they find attractive in others, they can identify aspects of themselves they deem attractive, as well as characteristics they do not like. Individuals will become sexually healthier when they can accept themselves or make constructive changes that allow them to interact in a healthier way. It is helpful to assess what you like about your body and what you think needs work. Following this assessment, make a decision about what you are willing to do to improve your body and do the work needed to improve. If you find that you are really not willing to make changes, then accept and love your body just the way it is. It is essential to stop being critical if you are not willing to work to improve your body. It is also important to accept the body of your partner and celebrate and enjoy each as they are.

Research on attraction has found that physical attraction is important for both sexes (McClintock, 2011). However, looks alone do not define attractiveness, nor can looks sustain a relationship. Most of us have admired someone for their looks only to discover that this person had a personality that detracted from their appearance and values that we found objectionable, making that person unappealing after all. Over time, looks diminish in importance, as we develop loving feelings toward our partners and fully accept them for who they are.

Social psychologist Donn Byrne (1971) developed a theory of attraction focusing on rewards and punishments. He postulated that we tend to like people who reward us by making us feel good about ourselves and tend to dislike people who punish us and are nasty. Researchers have also documented that people tend to be attracted to those who share similar

Guidelines for Safer Online Dating

Source: Callista Lee

Nearly everyone does it at some point, but youthful naïvete (lack of wisdom, experience, or judgment) must be guarded against by following a few sensible rules. The following sources offer some great advice about increasing your safety online, as well as ranking some online dating sites. All of the authors agree on these five basic rules:

1. **Meet in a public place.** Even if your goal is a quick hook-up, your first meeting should take place at a coffee shop, museum, café, park, or some other public venue. This gives you time to get to know a person at least a little bit, so you can identify obvious red flags before agreeing to meet in a more private setting.
2. **Tell someone what you're doing.** Make sure at least one friend or family member knows who you are meeting, where, and when. Arrange to check in with that person at least once during your date.
3. **Pay your own way.** If the other person wants money or gifts from you, or wants to shower you with money or gifts, walk away. This is not normal behavior early in a relationship!

4. **Dress appropriately.** If you're seeking long-term romance, leave the super-sexy outfit in your closet. If you are looking for a hook-up, show your assets.
5. **Trust your instincts.** This is the most important safety tip of all. If a situation doesn't feel right to you for any reason at all, ***get out***.

For additional safety suggestions and details about dating apps, check out these articles:

https://www.asecurelife.com/online-dating-safety/ —the main focus is on the safety measures built into the dating sites/apps themselves

https://www.cosmopolitan.com/uk/love-sex/relationships/a19603997/online-dating-safety-tips/—women discuss what they do to guard their safety

https://www.psychologytoday.com/us/blog/love-and-sex-in-the-digital-age/201802/five-tips-safe-online-dating—the basic five safety tips

https://www.getsafeonline.org/social-networking/online-dating/—from the Online Dating Association; lots of advice from passwords, to payments, to scammers, to setting up a safe first meeting, and how to file a report

healthy sex hints 10.1

Tips for Assessing the Health of a Relationship

- Are you comfortable with yourself—know who you are, what you want, what you believe in? This is a critical first step toward being able to relate to others.
- Are you able to communicate freely and openly without being criticized for your thoughts and feelings?
- When you're with this person, do you feel good about yourself? Do you feel appreciated and important? Do you feel you receive a lot of support?
- Are you treated as an equal? Do you respect and show respect for one another?
- Is your relationship based on shared interests? Are your personal values close enough in perspective to allow for becoming close?
- Can you tolerate differences? If you two are different, are those differences critical? For example, can your relationship surpass differences in age, race, philosophy about money, and political outlook?
- Can you maintain a sense of individuality within the relationship?
- Do you laugh and have fun when you are together?

attitudes on issues (Smith, Becker, Byrne, & Przybyla, 1993). Relationships can develop and function well when we get along with our partners. Although this point sounds like common sense, too many people invest time and energy in relationships that are not working, with people who do not treat them well, and where they do not feel good about themselves.

Women were found to be more conservative in their views toward love and relationships, incorporating concerns over finding a mate who would be a good provider and partner. Males, on the other hand, tended to respond early on to beauty and the playful aspects of relationships, and they were less concerned with commitment.

❧ Environmental/Occupational Wellness ❧

People today seem to spend more and more hours at work. Many students juggle classes and jobs. Consequently, the people one meets and spends a lot of time with can be classmates, coworkers, teachers, and employers. What continues to be a thorny question is whether people should become romantically involved with those at work. Prohibitions about workers becoming involved romantically may be included in sexual harassment policies. Colleges and universities also have such policies, dictating the acceptable parameters of romantic relationships. At work, romantic involvements may be permitted as long as the two involved are not in the same division or unit. At the university level, professors are not to get involved with those they grade and mentor. In reality, the prohibitions do not always prevail.

For LGBT (lesbian, gay, bisexual, transgender) individuals, romantic relationships become more complicated. If one is "out" at work and school, secrecy and fear of reprisals can be minimal. Job discrimination based on gender and sexuality is outlawed in many states, yet harassment still occurs both overtly and subtly.

Our overall health is enhanced when we can share and be open about the positive love relationships we have.

Sexual Chemistry

Many times friends and family offer to "fix up" a person with someone they're "sure you'll like." A man may be told, "She's attractive, very nice, interested in a lot of different things." Or a woman may be told, "I have just the man for you! He's smart, handsome, talented, and has a great sense of humor." So, with such glowing testaments, they agree to a blind date. They go out. They have an OK time but can't see anything romantic developing. They don't disagree about their date's attributes; he or she is objectively attractive, has a nice personality, and so on, but just doesn't excite the other person. The explanation to the matchmaker is "Well, there was just no chemistry—no spark." Despite a host of attractive traits, chemistry may be lacking.

People respond to the smell of others. Bad breath may turn us off while certain colognes, perfumes, and aftershaves are designed to turn us on. On an unconscious level, we may be responding to **pheromones**, which are sex-attractant chemicals, more familiar in lower animal forms. For example, a female dog "in heat" puts out an odor that male dogs can pick up from some distance. Even though human attraction is not grounded so heavily in reproductive issues, odors may have a larger role than we recognize (Kohl & Francouer, 1995).

Pheromones Body chemicals that attract potential sexual partners

Studies have begun to look at the impact of chemicals in male sweat and female vaginal secretions, examining their role in increasing attraction between a male and a female; their role in same-sex couples has yet to be assessed. The intense feelings associated with the early phases of a relationship, when we feel excited and caught up with the newness of the relationship, may have a chemical connection to higher levels of phenylethylamine (PEA) and possibly dopamine and norepinephrine, stimulants the body produces. As a consequence, we literally can be on a "romantic high" that can be explained through chemistry (Botting & Botting, 1996).

An online matchmaking service has taken a new, creative approach to finding the right chemistry between two people. Chemistry.com uses neuroscience to find just the right person for each subscriber. Subscribers answer a lengthy questionnaire to uncover their individual brain's "love map." This profile is then run through a computer algorithm to find the ideal match for each person (Arnst, 2005).

More Factors that Affect Attraction

Source: Callista Lee

The Halo effect—When we first meet someone, we don't know much about them except for their appearance and their current observable behavior. That is really not very much information, but we make snap judgments about them anyway. The "halo effect" is our tendency to infer other positive qualities based upon good looks; if they look good, they *are* good. We take that one positive trait we know and we extend it to the point of assuming positive things about them regarding their values, their interests, their coolness, and their behavior in other settings. Scent researchers have found the same inferences are made based upon how a person smells to us. In the case of smell, it is a more profound effect however; if they smell good they *are* good; if they smell bad they *are* bad!

Scent—You may have noticed that you experience a very pleasant feeling when you smell your partner's clothing, but that same smell doesn't do anything for a friend of yours. You probably assumed that their scent had become associated with all of your positive feelings about them. But research with both humans and mice have found that we are primed to be sexually attracted to others whose immune systems are genetically different from ours and to reject suitors who are too much like us. That benefits our offspring by providing them with broader immunity than if their parents' immune systems were much more alike. However, even if a suitor's genes were a good match, the person could be turned off if their scent is too *strong*. This is our nose's way of warning

us that they may suffer from disease (Furlow, 1996). Scent is different from pheromones, which our noses do not detect. When human pheromone was presented to the Vomeronasal Organ/VNO (a portion of the brain atop the nose), response was simply a pleasant feeling, not sexual attraction. If you purchase an expensive bottle of pheromone-based perfume or cologne, you are probably wasting your money.

A lot of work has gone into creating scents that will boost sexual attraction, and Dr. Alan Hirsch of the Smell and Taste Treatment Research Foundation in Chicago found that sexual attraction is more closely related to the scents of certain foods than those nose-blind pheromones. He found that the scent of a mixture of lavender and pumpkin pie increased penile blood flow by 40 percent. Next was the black licorice–doughnuts mixture at 32 percent; and the pumpkin pie–doughnuts combination at 20 percent. The smell of buttered popcorn increased male arousal an average of 9 percent; cheese pizza, an average of 5 percent; baked cinnamon buns, an average of 4 percent; and women's perfume an average of 3 percent. He did not find any scent that was a turn off to men. So where is that Lavender–Pumpkin Pie perfume for people who want to attract men? He followed by researching increase in blood flow to the vagina and learned that women had very different interests: Certain odors did *diminish* female arousal. The scent of cherry decreased women's arousal an average of 18 percent and charcoal barbecue smoke decreased women's arousal an average of 14 percent. Men's colognes also *decreased* women's arousal an average of 1 percent.

His Good & Plenty candy–cucumber combination increased female arousal an average of 13 percent, as did the scent of baby powder. The Good & Plenty-banana nut bread mixture increased female arousal an average of 12 percent. The pumpkin pie–lavender combination increased female arousal an average of 11 percent. The baby powder–chocolate combination increased female arousal an average of 4 percent. Women's perfumes increased female arousal an average of 1 percent (Hirsch, 2014). So, it appears that if you are looking to attract a woman, you can just splash on some baby powder under your clothes! For bisexuals, the pumpkin pie–lavender combination ought to work quite well!

Proximity effects—Just being physically close to someone on repeated occasions can increase the likelihood of a relationship beginning; the more we are exposed to the person, the more we come to like them … unless our initial response was negative. If it was neutral, we are likely to see an increase in attraction over time (Festinger, Schachter, & Back, 1950). Think about where you should sit in class to get liked by someone!

Physiological arousal—There is a large body of research demonstrating that meeting a person when one is already physiologically aroused (heartbeat and respiration are both up, etc.) increased the likelihood of developing an attraction toward the person. While you cannot (and should not!) control how another person's physiology will be when you meet them, you may consider doing something exciting on your first date, or even a nondate when you are with a group of friends that includes possible partners. Your professor experienced this first-hand when she went on a double date at Magic Mountain. In the now classic 1974 experiment by Dutton and Aron, they sent out their attractive female research assistant to meet men on one of two bridges: one was a high and shaky suspension bridge and the other was a lower and more stable bridge. The female assistant asked the men to fill out a survey (including a narrative about a picture they were given) while standing at the middle of the bridge, after which she provided them with her name and phone number with an invitation to call her if they wanted to learn more about the study. The men on the shaky bridge wrote much more romantic and sexual narratives about the picture and were much more likely to actually call the research assistant than the men on the not-scary bridge. A decade later, another group of researchers created the same effect by having men exercise for a few minutes prior to rating the attractiveness of a female assistant (Lehmiller, 2018).

Is all this all the same for gay men and lesbians? The answer is "mostly." **Similarity *does not*** appear to be as important for same-sex couples as it is for heterosexual couples. Proximity also appears to have less of an effect for same-sex couples. Both of these differences may be related to the fact that lesbians and gay men are working with a smaller *field of eligibles* (Lehmiller, 2018).

Compatibility

In the long run, what makes a relationship work is how compatible the two individuals are. A healthy relationship allows two people to be who they truly are, with no attempt to change their partners. The values and lifestyles of the two, therefore, must mesh closely.

Popular books abound, offering advice on finding the right partner and making the relationship work. Although the advice is plentiful, those providing it may base their guidance not on solid information but rather on their own perspectives. Clinical psychologists, for example, may develop advice after working with a variety of clients on their problems. Likewise, identifying patterns of behavior drawn by surveying college students has limitations.

Nonetheless, some of the "popular" authors can provide helpful, down-to earth, practical advice. One author whose approach works well from a wellness model is Barbara DeAngelis (1992), author of Are You the One for Me? Knowing Who's Right and Avoiding Who's Wrong. DeAngelis advises her readers to develop a compatibility checklist along 10 dimensions, identifying qualities that are important to them in each category. When two people are in an actual relationship, assessing compatibility takes time, as some things are learned early in a relationship and others over a period of months, if not longer.

sex in society 10.1

Compatibility List

According to author Barbara DeAngelis (1992), "Your Compatibility List can help you understand what is and what isn't working between you and your mate, and make it easier to decide whether it's time to separate. If you're looking for a new relationship, your Compatibility List acts like a shopping list, directing you toward partners who are right for you and helping you avoid partners you don't need and who will be a waste of time." Here is her list:

Directions: Use the following 10 categories to identify qualities you possess and those you want in a partner. Being as specific as possible will make the list more useful. When comparing results, you need to keep in mind how flexible you can be, how frequently you need traits to be exhibited, and which aspects of a relationship may work even if you two don't match.

1. *Physical style:* appearance, eating habits, personal fitness habits, personal hygiene
   Example: I exercise regularly. I would want a partner who likes to work out and exercise.

2. *Emotional style:* attitudes toward romance and affection, expression of emotions, approach to relationships
   Example: I'm very affectionate and need a lot of support. I would want a partner who would be affectionate and care about my interests.

3. *Social style:* personality traits, ways of interacting with others
   Example: I'm very outgoing and love to have family and friends around. I would not want a partner who only wanted to be with me and stay at home.

4. *Intellectual style:* educational background, attitude toward learning, world affairs
   Example: I'm a college graduate and read the newspaper daily. I also love books, both fiction and nonfiction. I would want a partner who is aware of what is going on in the world and also loves to read. My partner would have to at least have an associate's degree, although I would prefer someone who has finished a 4-year college program.

5. *Sexual style:* attitudes, skill, ability to enjoy sex
   Example: I love to try new things and be adventurous. I would want a partner who enjoys sex and is creative.

6. Communication style: patterns of communication, attitude toward talking, other forms of expression

Example: I know that I tend to scream when I'm angry.

7. My family is a bunch of screamers. While I may need to work on that behavior, I'd need someone who would understand that the screaming is more style than substance and wouldn't let the volume get to him [her].

8. Professional/financial style: relationship with money, attitudes toward success, work, and organizational habits
   Example: I work hard and budget my money carefully, never owing more than a couple hundred dollars on a credit card. I couldn't be with someone who gambles and is always in debt. Personal growth style: attitudes toward self-improvement, ability to be introspective and change, willingness to work on a relationship
   Example: I tend to think a lot about what I value and how I came to be who I am. If a relationship is important to me, I would do anything—even seek professional help if necessary—to make it work. I wouldn't want a partner who couldn't look at how we were getting along and work on the relationship.

9. Spiritual style: attitudes toward a higher power, spiritual practices, philosophy of life, moral views
   Example: I'm very involved with my church, working with youth groups and helping at local shelters. My partner wouldn't have to be exactly the same faith but would have to respect my beliefs and have a sense of his or her own.

10. Interests and hobbies
    Example: I love to travel, and I do my best to take at least one exciting vacation to some place new each year. I would want a partner who also likes to travel, or at least would be willing to travel.

After reviewing your list, think about how open you are to changing any of your answers. If you are without a partner, thinking about your interests becomes valuable in assessing how well you two match. As you get to know someone, finding dissimilar answers and styles in too many areas highlights a lack of compatibility. Most important, not all areas are equally important.

Jealousy

Healthy relationships are based on trust and respect. Unfortunately, many believe the destructive myth that jealousy shows how much someone loves the other person. Jealousy is neither a sign of love nor a healthy way of showing love but instead results from a number of factors: low self-esteem, fear of loss, bruised pride, insecurity, and, in some cases, a sense of "lost property" (Hatfield & Rapson, 1996). Individuals may react with feelings of jealousy in response to behaviors they find threatening. For example, a woman may get upset at seeing her boyfriend be kissed by a female friend. Another woman may not care about gestures of affection but not be able to handle a current boyfriend even having a cup of coffee with a woman he used to date. Jealousy, particularly if allowed to become out of control and increasingly intense, can spell the end of a relationship.

Men and women have been found to respond to feelings of jealousy in different ways. Jealous women are more likely to focus on the emotional involvement of their partner with another person, whereas men may focus on the sexual activity of their partner with another person. Researchers continue to find gender differences in how distressing infidelity becomes to the relationship, with women identifying emotional infidelity as the most distressing and men choosing sexual infidelity (Cann, Mangum, & Wells, 2001; Buss, Larse, Westen, & Semmelroth, 1992). Men are more likely to respond with rage and violence, and women are more likely to blame themselves and display more possessive behavior (Hatfield & Rapson, 1996).

When asked in a classroom setting, college students have voiced the opinion that some amount of jealousy is good for a relationship and shows love for the partner. In actuality, the foundation for jealous feelings is not based on love, and these feelings are not healthy for a relationship. Couples can learn healthy ways of dealing with jealousy to strengthen their relationship. Some communicate openly about the triggers for jealous feelings and together develop a strategy to minimize the triggers. For example, if Trent feels jealous when Sara talks to an old boyfriend at parties, she could start including him in the conversations. Couples can use the feeling of jealousy as a trigger to evaluate their relationship and make improvements where needed. Jealousy can be a reminder to pay more attention to a partner and the relationship. Each partner can also decrease jealous feelings by working to improve his/her confidence and self esteem. Honest, open communication and working on strategies to decrease jealousy will turn the destructive force of jealousy into a way to strengthen the relationship.

Love

Love is tied closely to our expectations for a relationship and has long been a topic for songwriters and researchers. Studies on love have attempted to classify, develop theory, examine love styles, make cross-cultural comparisons, and recognize the complexity of love.

Finding a comfortable definition of love is not easy. Some advise of the need to differentiate "love" and "lust." Others talk about being able to tell the difference between "love" and "infatuation."

personal exploration activity

Let's Have Some Fun Together

An important element of a healthy relationship is laughing and having playful, fun times together. Some experts believe that when a couple stops laughing together, this signals trouble in the relationship. Doing new and unusual things together activates the brain's reward system flooding it with the same chemicals released in early love (Parker-Pope, 2010). Laughing and playing together helps couples strengthen their bond. It takes creativity and work to make sure you do interesting activities that strengthen a relationship. The purpose of this activity is to develop a creative list of interesting things to do with a date or your partner so you can keep the joy and excitement in your relationship.

Your goal is to make a list of 30 activities that you would enjoy doing with a date or partner. They should not be expensive and should be easily accessible—you should not have to travel great distances to do these. First, list as many as you can think of that you would enjoy. Once you have exhausted your own ideas, start interviewing your friends and acquaintances to see what they can add to your list. Only add those that you would really like to do. When you have interviewed as many people as possible, share your list with your partner and put a check by those activities your partner would also enjoy doing. Decide which ones you want to do first and try to add one new activity each week. If you are not in a relationship at the present time, try these with your dates or with your friends. You should experience more laughter and enjoyment in your times together.

Theories of Love

In his classic book, The Art of Loving, Eric Fromm (1956) asserts that before we can love another, we must learn to love ourselves. It is important not to confuse self love with conceit, which is actually a result of a lack of self-love. A person who does not love him or herself spends much time trying to convince him or herself and others how amazing he or she is. When we truly learn to love and accept ourselves, we have no need to convince other of

Shared interests are important to a relationship.

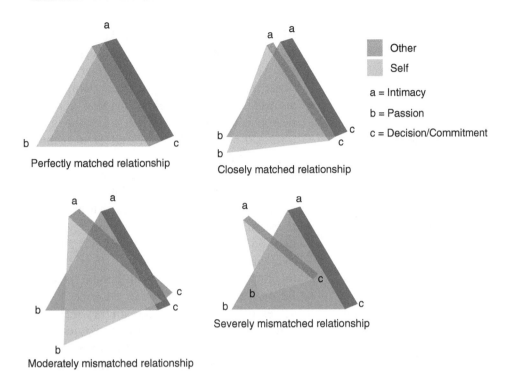

Other
Self
a = Intimacy
b = Passion
c = Decision/Commitment

Perfectly matched relationship

Closely matched relationship

Severely mismatched relationship

Moderately mismatched relationship

Figure 10.1 *Sternberg's Triangular Theory of Love*

Source: Sternberg, R. (1986) A triangular theory of love. Psychological Review, 93, 119–35. Sternberg R. (1988) Triangular love. In R. Sternberg and M. Barnes (eds.) The Psychology of Love. New Haven, CT: Yale Univ. Press.

our "greatness" and are capable of fully giving to another. Loving someone who has no self-love is similar to having a relationship with a vacuum. This person will take all they can from you (vacuum you) in an attempt to fill him or herself with love and will give you little or nothing in return. Fromm also believes love is a decision, not a feeling or emotion. We decide to whom and when we will give our love. Since love is a decision, we will not just fall out of love with someone but will decide to continue loving or to stop loving someone. There are many reasons we choose to stop loving someone including betrayal, loss of trust, lack of intimacy, and not having our needs met. It is very reassuring to know that love will not just disappear suddenly.

Sternberg's Triangular Theory of Love

Source: Callista Lee

Robert Sternberg's (1988) triangular theory of love is built on three components: intimacy, passion, and commitment. By **"intimacy,"** Sternberg is referring to the emotional closeness the couple shares. It includes wanting what is best for one's partner, experiencing empathy for their feelings, holding them in high regard, giving and receiving emotional support, being able to count on one another in times of need,

and being able to share private thoughts and feelings. It is the friendship component of love.

By **"passion,"** Sternberg is referring to both mental and physical arousal. It includes sexual arousal but also the desire to and excitement of sharing time together. Whether or not the couple is sexually active, they enjoy kissing and affectionate touching. Lastly, **"commitment"** is descriptive of the couple's active decision to be with and stay together as a romantic couple. Commitment is demonstrated by working through conflicts rather than walking away, and the efforts involved in maintaining a loving, mutually satisfying, and lasting relationship. For each of the three components, Sternberg has developed a self-rating scale of fifteen items to determine an individual's score. Couples who are "closely matched" will have similar scores on each of the three components (see Figure 10.1). Sternberg's research has found that couples who are happiest are closely matched.

In Sternberg's model, the ideal relationship is built when the couple achieves strength in all three components, which he refers to as **Consummate love**. Couples that manage to maintain all three components are the most long-lasting and happiest (Acevedo & Aron, 2009). In addition to the consummate type of love, Sternberg identifies seven others (shown in Figure 10.2):

Liking = Intimacy only. Think of friends who love each other but are not romantic. This may also apply to lovers who once had passion but allowed it to dissipate. A couple with "intimacy only" may have a weak level of commitment but not enough to sustain a long-term romantic connection.

Infatuation = Passion only. These couples are high on the neurochemistry of new romantic relationships but have not developed a strong component of intimacy or commitment. They may want to spend all of their time together and enjoy a fun, sexually charged romance but it is not one that is built to last. The lack of intimacy means that they don't really know each other very well and are probably basing their feelings of love based on sexual attraction and their own projections of who their partner is, rather than who their partner actually is. They may use words of commitment ("I want to be with you forever"), but when conflict arises they are more likely to break up than put in the efforts to get through it together in a way that is mutually respectful and satisfying.

Empty love = Commitment only. This may be a couple who is in an arranged marriage, hoping that intimacy and passion will develop later, or it may be a couple who once felt more intimacy and passion but now just have their promises to each other and the community

(through a legal marriage) keeping them together. They likely care about one another but would not consider their partner as their "best friend." Some empty love relationships are truly unhealthy, such as one in which one person is not interested but the other is an obsessed stalker. Only the stalker is feeling the commitment!

Nonlove = None of the three components. Sternberg brings this up to point out that there are a small number of couples that are weak in passion, commitment, *and* intimacy. This may be experienced prior to breaking up or by a continuing couple who just feels "stuck" together because of financial, family, or other factors, but wouldn't really describe themselves as being "in love" though they may still care about the well-being of their partner.

Romantic love = Passion + Intimacy. These couples are enjoying a wonderful romance that is destined to break up either because circumstances change (the vacation they met on ends, they return home from college or go off to college separately, one decides they want to get serious but the other doesn't, etc.) or they find that they are unable to conquer their differences. They may consciously choose to avoid committing to a long-term relationship or may actually marry (or make other declarations of commitment) but find that their commitment was not as strong as they thought it was when times get tough. It is also possible that their relationship will grow as commitment is added.

Fatuous love = Passion + commitment. This isn't a word that you hear very often, meaning foolish or pointless, which sounds pretty harsh. Sternberg is basing this on his own common American expectations that love *should* include a strong emotional connection and friendship (See the box, Love in Cultural Context). These couples may not like or admire each other all that much. They are not likely to share much private information with one another.

Companionate love = Intimacy + Commitment. What is missing from these relationships is the heat of passion. This could be totally acceptable for a couple who are largely asexual, but most of us would find it to be lacking. It is often *expected* that elderly people will have companionate love relationships, forgetting that most elderly people do continue to enjoy passion. Still, a companionate relationship can be wonderfully comfortable.

Consummate love = Passion + Intimacy + Passion. Here we are, back where we started, with Sternberg's completed love triangle. Research has found that not only is this type of love relatively rare, but also difficult to maintain over time. But for those who achieve it, it is a very happy experience.

Researchers have also found that, of the three components, passion is the one most likely to be high initially, with intimacy taking more time to develop as the couple gets to know each other, and finally developing commitment, which can keep the relationship going long after the initial flames of passion die down. Yes, it is natural for passion to cool off, but that doesn't mean that it is gone forever. Couples need to practice ways of keeping passion alive, such as engaging in shared, exciting activities that get their hearts and lungs working. Remember what you read about the physiological arousal in the section on attraction? These systems are at work throughout your life and the life of your romantic relationships.

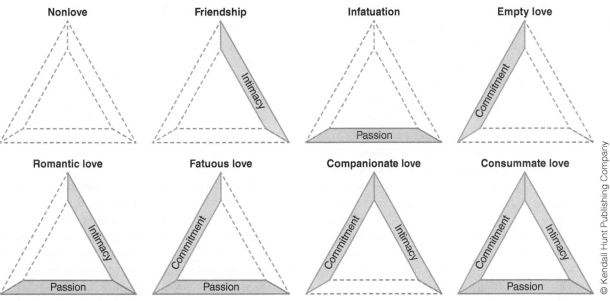

Figure 10.2

Styles of Love

Source: Callista Lee

Canadian sociologist John Allen Lee developed a theory of love in the 1970s which suggests that people follow at least one of six psychological scripts in relating to their partners in love.

Eros love—Much like Sternberg's Infatuation, Eros love is erotic and very passionate. Because high levels of passion cannot be maintained for a long time (usually cooling off after eighteen to twenty-four months), these relationships will be hot but brief unless another style of love is added. Eros lovers tend

to believe in love at first sight and emphasize physical attractiveness and romantic behaviors. Most relationships begin in an Eros style. Best partners for Eros lovers are other Eros lovers; worst matches are with Pragma lovers.

Ludus love—Ludus is the Greek word for play. Ludus lovers enjoy the game of seduction and the joy of new relationships more than the depth to be found in longer-term relationships. They tend to "play the field" and move from relationship to relationship relatively quickly, often leaving their partners feeling blindsided by their abrupt departure just as the relationship was settling into being very gratifying. Ludus lovers are not a "best match" for anyone, although they may get along well with other Ludus lovers.

Storge love—In Greek, storge (STOR-GAY) means natural affection; this style of love is characterized by a strong friendship (Sternberg's Intimacy). These relationships generally take a long time to develop, in contract to those of Ludus or Eros types. Passion may not be a central feature in these relationships, but partners are happy with their peace, stability, and security that this romantic friendship affords. Best partners for Storge lovers are other Storge lovers; worst matches are with Ludus or Mania lovers.

Mania love—Just like it sounds, this is a "madness" in which the mania lover is possessive, dependent, and often controlling. They tend to feel unlovable and constantly fear that their lover is about to leave them. These relationships are full of emotional turmoil, extreme (unrealistic) jealousy, and sometimes extreme obsession. Partners of mania lovers may at first feel excited to be so intensely loved and needed but eventually realize that they are being controlled by an insecure, clingy partner. This creates a self-fulfilling prophecy to the mania lover who may resort to extreme measures to hang onto their partner: threats of suicide, actual suicide attempts, or violence against the partner or others. Mania lovers are not a "best match" for anyone, but they may get on well with other Mania lovers.

Pragma love—Greek for business, pragma love is practical. Partners decide to love based upon their own list of requirements (compatibility, attractiveness, education level, social status, income, race, religion, etc.). While committing to a partner who makes good sense on paper may seem like a great idea, we find that these relationships are lacking in a very important way—lack of emotional intimacy, which is important for bonding. Pragma lovers are best with other Pragma lovers; worst with Eros and Ludus.

Agape love—Greek for brotherly or divine love, this is more of an altruistic goal rather than a realistically satisfying love style. It is a style of selflessness in which one enjoys giving without expecting anything in return. While loving in an agape way is sometimes satisfying, what we seek in our romantic relationships is a two-way sharing of emotional support and other resources. Agape asks for nothing. You need to ask for *something* in your relationships! Some people claim to be agape lovers but in truth *do* expect something in return for all that they do to support their partners, and feel resentful when they get nothing in return. Being honest with yourself and your partner about your needs is essential to developing and maintaining a psychologically healthy relationship. Agape lovers aren't a "best match" for anyone, but may find happiness with Eros, Storge, or Pragma lovers.

These Styles of Love (Lee, 1973, 1977, 1988) apply to both heterosexual and same-sex couples.

From Theory to Practice

Most of us want to find a partner with whom we can make a relationship work. Not all relationships function in exactly the same way, yet some characteristics predict a greater likelihood of "success." The style of love may change as people age. The style of love may improve with experience. The style of love may interfere with one's getting into and sustaining the kind of relationship desired. Recognizing your values, style, and how well you "match" to your partner, therefore, becomes valuable as you seek out love and a partner.

Pepper Schwartz (2001) has identified many myths about successful relationships that warrant being questioned. A few examples are "You can't be in love with two people at the same time," "Little annoying habits are unimportant in long-term relationships," and "You should always be

100 percent honest with your partner." Because human relationships are complex, she takes issues with commonly held guidelines governing behavior.

Loving more than one person can happen as we commit to a partner yet hold loving feelings for a past partner. Deciding to act on those feelings is different from having them. When couples date, they may not mind that one person is neat while the other messy; living in a home with two very different styles of where to place clothes, papers, and other items or different attitudes toward personal hygiene may prove more challenging than they had when dating. Finally, although most people feel that honesty in a relationship is fundamental to building trust and intimacy, Schwartz argues that there are times when information may need to be kept secret for the health of the relationship. Individuals are entitled to some areas of privacy, and partners may really only want to know information that they can deal with. Schwartz does caution that there are times, however, when keeping secrets can be destructive to the relationship. For example, if one person had unsafe sex outside the relationship, putting their partner's health in jeopardy, getting medical attention and discussing the situation are imperative. If real feedback is needed about behaviors such as drinking, the intimate partner is in an ideal situation to provide it. And for those for whom honesty is viewed as the key component of the relationship, keeping secrets from a partner is fundamentally incompatible with maintaining an intimate relationship.

Love in Cultural Context

Source: Callista Lee

Passionate love is a human emotion found throughout the world, but romantic love, which combines passion with friendship, is most likely found in cultures that value individualism over collectivism. However, persons who are extreme in their own personal individualism are less likely to experience "being in love" due to their inability to share intimacy. Such people are likely to endorse the *ludic* style of love.

Individualism values self-interest and the interests of one's immediate family, personal autonomy, and making one's own decisions. Most Western cultures are individualistic. Collectivism encourages individuals to subordinate their personal interests to the interests of the group (family, extended family, employer, neighborhood, clan, etc.), making decisions with input from the group (especially elders), and being loyal to the group which, in turn, looks out for them. Most Asian and Arab cultures are collectivistic.

"From an individualistic view, each person is a separate entity; from a collectivistic view, the individual is a part of more extended relationships. When one f as an individual with boundaries and separate from other people, loving for someone else is the chance to break through those boundaries and escape the loneliness caused by being a separate individual. Love becomes the bridge that connects a person to another one. This connection, however, implies a person's freedom. If a relationship does not give him/her what they expect, it is their choice whether to leave the relationship. This is why people in individualistic cultures place a great emphasis on romantic love.

From a collectivistic perspective, people emphasize the bonds that they already have. Since each person is a part of the relationships, people do not expect it as necessary to verbally confirm those bonds by asking if another loves them or by announcing their love to someone else. Their love is expressed more by what they do than by what they say (Dion & Dion, 2006)."

—Victor Karandashev (2015)

In a study comparing Americans with Russians and Lithuanians (deMunck, Korotayev, deMunck, & Khaltourina, 2011), Americans included friendship in their definitions of romantic love. But the Russians and Lithuanians (collectivistic cultures) viewed romantic love more as Sternberg views infatuation:

an unreal fairytale that is either going to end when its flame of passion burns out or develop gradually toward a more realistic love that includes friendship and commitment. Perhaps more interesting is that the Russians and Lithuanians reported falling in love more quickly than did the Americans. They found that 90 percent of Lithuanians reported that they fell in love within a month or less, whereas Americans fell in love within a couple of months to a year. This is likely linked both to the differences in how love is defined as well as cultural differences in how love is thought about and expressed.

Researchers have also found cross-cultural differences in the level of intimacy that couples experiences over the years of their romantic relationships. In the US, marriages tend to start out with a relatively high level of intimacy that is valued enough for partners to make efforts to keep it high, all the while maintaining their separate identities. But in Japan, marriages begin with a much lower level of intimacy, focused more on the obligations spouses have toward one another and their families. Their intimacy tends to develop later much later in life after those who depend upon them (such as parents and grandparents) die and they have more time to devote to one another (Ingersoll-Dayton, Campbell, Kurokawa, & Saito, 1996). Schmitt and colleagues (2009) compared over 15,000 individuals in forty-eight countries and found the lowest levels of emotional investment in Tanzania, Hong Kong, and Japan (all are in East Asia), and the highest levels of emotional investment in the US,

Slovenia, and Cypress (more individualistic cultures of the Western world).

Expressions of love differ around the world as well. Americans who tend to be individualistic stress the need to express verbally, saying "I love you" frequently. But Filipinos and Filipino-Americans come from a more collectivistic culture that stresses more indirect expressions of love. Saying, "I love you" is reserved for special occasions, but in everyday life they will express their love indirectly, through doing. They reveal their love by sharing a laugh, listening to one another attentively, being nonjudgmental, keeping their promises, and other kind acts (Nadal, 2012). Of course, Americans engage in these loving behaviors too, but they tend to focus on the direct verbal expressions and may miss some of the many nonverbal, more indirect ways their partner expresses their love and commitment. Filipinos do not find it necessary to focus on direct verbal affirmations of love, finding it to be excessive or "too American."

Because there are many cultural differences in how we experience and express love, it is very important for couples who are made up of people from different cultures to openly discuss their expectations. There are also likely be to a lot of differences in how they see parenting, the relationship with in-laws, gender roles, how to celebrate holidays, and religious traditions. It can a big challenge to accept, honor, and respect what is important to their partner from another culture.

■ Sexual Activity within Relationships

Premarital sex Usually refers to coitus, sexual intercourse, before marriage

Extramarital sex Usually refers to coitus, sexual intercourse, outside marriage

Monogamy Commonly used to refer to having one sexual partner, whether married to that person or not

In the context of relationships, individuals decide on preferences for particular behaviors, frequency of activity, and whether their behavior will occur exclusively with one partner. Research on the timing of sexual activity has often been framed with a heterosexual and marital bias. Hence, students can find reports on **premarital sex**, coitus occurring before marriage, and **extramarital sex**, coitus occurring outside of marriage. The demographics in the United States, however, indicate that there are currently more unmarried adults than at other times in history, with an estimated three-quarters of unmarried men and two-thirds of unmarried women engaging in some form of partnered sex over the course of a year (Waite & Joyner, 2001). Consequently, making marriage as the central core from which other situations vary can be problematic.

Because of such realities, terms that are more generic and focus on the primary relationship become preferred. The term **monogamy** by strict definition refers to the practice of having one spouse at a time, but more commonly it refers to having one sexual partner. Despite much of the research on sexual behavior outside the primary relationship using the term *extramarital,* the terms **dyadic**, referring to the couple, and **extradyadic**, referring to sexual activity with someone other than the primary partner, are preferred and considered to be less biased (Wiederman, 2001a).

Christopher and Sprecher (2000) reviewed years of research focused on sexuality within relationships. As couples were together longer, whether married or in long-term gay and lesbian relationships, there was a decline in the frequency with which they engaged in lovemaking. Researchers also found that sexual satisfaction is associated with relationship satisfaction, regardless of the sexual orientation of the couple. Cohabiting couples and those dating had slightly lower levels of sexual satisfaction when compared with married couples. Factors such as race, religion, and social status were not related to the frequency of sexual activity or sexual satisfaction.

Waite and Joyner (2001), in analyzing data from the National Health and Social Life Survey, propose that couples bring different expectations about sex to their relationships depending on whether they are married, cohabiting, or dating. For married individuals, there is a long-term contract with each being able to learn what pleases the other; satisfying a spouse enhances the emotional intimacy of the relationship. Cohabiters have a lower level of commitment to each other and may not feel as compelled to develop partner-specific skills. Single individuals may be dating more than one person, aware that a long-term relationship may or may not be possible, yet the connection may be sexual regardless. Overall, viewing a relationship to be long-term, being emotionally invested in it, and being sexually exclusive were hypothesized to increase emotional satisfaction and physical pleasure from sex. As with other research, commitment becomes an important variable for both men and women when examining their emotional satisfaction with the relationship. The researchers found that physical pleasure and emotional satisfaction were higher when the sex was used to express love for the partner.

Regardless of the relationship status, the body releases the bonding chemical oxytocin and arginine vasopressin (AVP) in response to sexual intimacy. We feel closer and experience warmer feelings for the partner after sexual intercourse (Trimarchi, 2013). This is an important consequence to consider when choosing whether to be sexually intimate with a partner. Do you really want this person to feel bonded to you? Do you want this person to feel warm, fond feelings for you? And, is this a person you like enough to want to feel bonded and close to? Never-married, young adults can and do decide to remain virgins. Primarily, researchers have identified that young adults may not feel that enough love is present in the relationship, they express a fear of sexually transmitted diseases and unwanted pregnancies, their belief system supports virginity, and/or personal feelings of insecurity and inadequacy interfere with experiencing coitus (Christopher & Sprecher, 2000). What is critical is that decisions to be sexually active involve mutual consent and comfort. For some, a solid, committed relationship is key.

Americans have strong views on extradyadic and extramarital sex. When surveyed on how they viewed "married people having an affair, the majority of Americans (88%) choose the answer "morally wrong" (Pew Research. 2014). Formal researchers have looked at married and cohabiting couples, and although those who cohabit have higher rates of extradyadic sex than married couples, and the rates for married couples in contemporary studies are relatively low, there are still significant numbers of people

Dyadic sex Referring to the sexual behavior of a couple, the two people in a relationship

Extradyadic sex Referring to sexual behavior outside the primary relationship. This term replaces *extramarital sex,* which is confined to heterosexual marriages.

who have had sex with someone other than their spouse at least once. The variables found to be associated with more permissive extramarital attitudes are high education, low religiosity, premarital sexual permissiveness, and being male (Christopher & Sprecher, 2000). According to one survey, twenty-one percent of males and nineteen percent of females admitted to have extramarital sex (Chalabi, 2015).

Abusive Relationships

Source: Callista Lee

Abusive relationships can occur in any age group, among partners of any sexual orientation, and are more complicated than most people think. About one in four women and one in nine men have experienced sexual violence, physical violence, and/or stalking by an intimate partner (CDC, 2016). Of those victimized by an intimate partner, more women than men suffer negative effects:

	Females (%)	Males (%)
• Feeling fearful	62	18
• Concern for their safety	57	17
• Symptoms of PTSD	52	17

Physical abuse may begin with something "mild" such as a slap, a shove, or a pinch intended to hurt. These "mild" behaviors should not be ignored or minimized because they may signal the beginning of more serious abuse. Likewise, it is common for abuse to start out with verbal slams intended to cause emotional pain, embarrassment, humiliation, or to control a partner. In addition to physical abuse, there are many other behaviors that are abusive:

Emotional abuse may include one or more of the following:

- *Minimization and blame*—not accepting responsibility for their actions; making hurtful jokes; blaming all problems on the partner; acting like abusive behavior is normal in relationships; insisting that partner's feelings are not a big deal; making untrue accusations
- *Intimidation*—yelling/screaming; using a threatening tone or words; destroying objects (intimidating because you could be the next object of violence); displaying weapons in a threatening manner; threatening self-harm

or harm to partner or their family, friends, or pets; actually harming pets or engaging in self-harm as a way to control the partner; threatening to publicly "out" a partner
- *Possessiveness*—groundless accusations of cheating; using jealousy as a sign of love; not letting partner spend time with family or friends; requiring partner to check in frequently; telling partner how to act or dress; not letting partner have private time
- *Humiliation*—putting the partner down; name calling; making partner feel like they are crazy (gaslighting); embarrassing partner in front of others
- *Domination*—treating partner like a child, property, or servant; making all decisions and rules for the relationship; controlling how the partner spends their time; having expectations that nobody could meet
- *Isolation*—making partner account for their whereabouts; depriving them of private time with family and friends; insisting that nobody will believe them if they report their abusive behavior
- *Using children*—make partner fear that they will lose custody if they leave the abusive partner; threatening to report you to children's services although you've done nothing wrong; turning children against you/encouraging children to mock you

Sexual abuse—bragging about your private sex life to others; comparing you to other partners in a disparaging way; using coercion to get partner to engage in sexual activities they do not enjoy; having sex with others to make partner jealous; using drugs or alcohol to take advantage of a partner sexually; ignoring a partner's "no"; forcing a partner into sexual acts to which they have not consented

Economic abuse—preventing partner from getting or keeping a job; controlling all of the couple's funds; borrowing money with no intention of paying it back; stealing money; using partner's credit without permission; running up debt without agreement from partner; putting assets in their own name so the partner is financially dependent on them; failing to pay bills that they had agreed to pay without discussing it … leaving the partner on the hook for those debts; lying about their income and expenses to take advantage of the partner; putting partner's name only on debts but not assets.

Why don't people leave abusive relationships sooner?

When learning about abusive relationships a common response is to wonder why anyone would stay in such a relationship. There are many reasons, including:

- Financial dependence
- Sociocultural obligation
- Having nowhere to go to
- Fear of harm to the children
- Fear that the abuse will become more violent if they leave
- Feelings of low self-worth or being unlovable
- Believing that the abuser is "not who my partner really is"
- Believing that the abuse is temporary and that the causes can be fixed
- Loving the partner and not wanting to hurt them

At this point you may be thinking "hold on, how could someone continue loving a person who was so bad to them? Why would they care if they hurt the feelings of their abuser?"

Keep in mind that this was someone they fell in love with; someone they enjoyed lots of fun with, had great sex, enjoyed the same activities together, shared ideals, shared secrets, and made plans for the future. This person made them feel special and loved. Abusers don't go around wearing actual red flags, nor do they often appear to have dark secrets when you first get to know them. They act like reasonable people and can be very charming, affectionate, good listeners … all those things you've been looking for. The relationship starts out like most relationships do, in a "honeymoon phase." Both partners are high on love, and if they notice any flaws in their partner they find them easy to forgive…nothing to worry about. But at some point every relationship will face a time of conflict. Healthy relationships get through these times of conflict by talking about it and coming up with solutions that make each person feel respected and cared for. In contrast, in abusive relationships rational problem solving doesn't work and the tension in the relationship continues to build. Psychologist Lenore Walker (1979) identified a **Cycle of Abuse**, (Figure 10.3) which describes the cycle that keeps victims of abuse trapped. She built this model based on the testimonies from battered women from both her clinical practice as well as research. Her model has become the standard for understanding abusive relationships in all sorts of romantic couples.

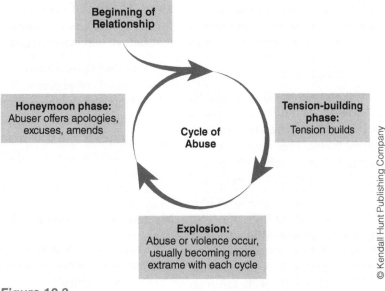

Figure 10.3

As stated already, the relationship begins in a **Honeymoon phase** in which love blooms and everyone is happy. But when conflict occurs, it remains unsolved and tension gradually increases. This is called the **Tension-Building phase**. This phase can last for weeks, months, or even years in some cases. During this time, both partners are feeling tense and/or irritated. There are often small fights or "mild" instances of physical or other sorts of abuse. The victim-to-be often finds himself/herself in a situation in which they are trying to help their beloved to get through their problems so that life can go back to the happy days of the Honeymoon phase. There is deep concern for the partner, and when they "lose it" they are generally excused because they are going through a difficult time. The bad behavior may be attributed to alcohol, drug use, or extreme stress. But at some point there is an escalation into the **Explosion phase**, during which there is one or more acts of obvious abuse. The abuser is seen as being "out of control" in a bout of physical, sexual, and/or emotional aggression. This stage is the shortest of the three phases. The victim is stunned and confused by feelings of disbelief and anxiety. They will generally isolate themselves while trying to figure out and cope with what has happened. If they ask for help, it will usually be after several days…unless they wind up in an emergency room sooner.

For the abuser, there is relief from the tension they had been feeling for the weeks or months of the tension-building phase. Most commonly, they will be quick to apologize, ask for forgiveness, and promise that such a thing will never happen again. This is while the victim is still trying to make sense of the abuse. The abuser may become extra sweet, bring home gifts, and/or arrange for special activities they know their partner enjoys.

The victim wants to believe it will never happen again. After all, they did not fall in love with an abusive person. This was an aberration. They fell in love with someone sweet, kind, generous, fun, loving…all those wonderful things. They want to believe that their beloved is "back" from that bad place. And they cautiously begin to enjoy **another Honeymoon phase**, which begins the cycle again. During the next tension-building phase, they may try new strategies to help their partner get through their struggles, they may suggest getting help, but the abuser will have excuses for not getting help and is likely to blame the victim for their problems. They will likely ramp up the emotional abuse to keep their victim "walking on eggshells." And finally, there will be another explosion phase. As victims move through these phases, they become less and less sure of themselves, often feeling embarrassed to tell family and friends. If they tell family or friends and hear advice like "don't put up with that—break up with them" they are most likely to isolate from those friends saying, "but you don't understand…I love them, I want to help them, *they* want to do better, I just need to give them more time…" Why, you ask? Because they remember the delight of the original honeymoon phase, and the subsequent honeymoon phases. They know how wonderful their partner can be; they want that person back. They may also feel partly to blame and want to redeem themselves by helping to heal their partner. As time goes by, it also becomes embarrassing to admit that they have stayed for so long without solving the problems in the relationship. It is not uncommon for victims of partner abuse to develop a form of posttraumatic stress disorder (PTSD) called "battered partner syndrome" which adds to their difficulty in managing their lives and making decisions clearly. They may feel that there is no way out and that nobody will understand or respect them.

Unfortunately, **none of the strategies that people use to help an abusive partner seem to work very well**, and so the cycle continues until the victim leaves the relationship. To make matters worse for the victim, leaving carries with it additional risk. Abuse of this sort is all about power and control over the victim. Often, the abuser cannot tolerate losing that control by allowing their partner to simply walk away. The risk of violence is extremely high at this time. Psychologists Dugan & Hock (2006) suggest that **before leaving a victim must prepare by**:

1. Assessing the abuser's danger level, based on past acts of violence;
2. Having an escape plan, not just to leave the home they share with the abuser but also the workplace and new residence;
3. Creating a network of support of trusted people;
4. Obtaining a legal restraining order;

Ms. Lee adds that after they leave, the next step is to:

5. Create an emotional, verbal, and physical strategy for coping with the abuser's pleas for them to return.

The temptation to go back to the abuser is strong for most victims. Victims will return seven times on average (TheHotline.org, 2014), before they finally leave forever. The problem with returning is that the violence escalates; things do not get better regardless of what the abusive partner has promised. If they accept responsibility for their actions and promise to go to therapy, encourage them go do that work. But do not return based on promises. Changing these abusive attitudes and behaviors will take a long time and a lot of sustained effort. Couples counseling is *not* recommended for partners in abusive relationships because abuse is not a "relationship problem" (TheHotline.org, 2014). In couples counseling, both partners should feel and actually *be* safe, physically and emotionally; they must be free to speak their truth. This is not a safe space for a victim in an abusive relationship. Their partner can easily use what they said in therapy against them once they are back at home. Even if they are living separately, couples counseling should not be attempted until the abuse is fully addressed. Instead, abusers should be in a Battering Intervention and Prevention Program (BIPP). Most counties have at least one. Victims should seek therapy through their local victims' services organization. You can call 211 in your county to get referrals for services near you.

Helping a Someone Who is in an Abusive Relationship

For friends and family who want to be supportive of a loved one trying to cope with an abusive relationship, patience is a must. To be most helpful, counselors recommend (Loveisrespect.org, 2017) that you **educate yourself** more about domestic abuse. Remember that the relationship began in love and that memories of the good times may be clouding the memories of the bad times. You will want to agree with your friend that there are good things about the relationship; it's not ALL bad. But **let them know that you are concerned** about the mean behaviors you have observed, and ask if they want to talk. If they don't, just let them know you will be there if they should change their mind. When they *are* ready to talk, **listen and support their decisions**, even if you believe they are not making the *best* decisions. Remember that their abuser has been emotionally manipulating them to not trust their own minds. You

don't want to be another person telling them what to do and how to feel. But do feel free to **model healthy behaviors** for them, and to let them know that you believe *they* are the best person to decide what to do about their situation. This demonstrates that you believe in them, and it may help with their battered sense of self-esteem.

Be prepared to **encourage even the smallest steps they make** toward becoming independent of their abusive partner. And **help them search for options** that are specific to their needs (housing, financial assistance, medical or mental health services, legal aid, child services, etc.). **Encourage them to practice self-care and to create a safety plan**. Remember that you cannot fix the problem for your friend/loved-one. But do **practice self-care for your own well-being**. You may experience vicarious trauma by seeing your friend hurting and imagining what they are going through.

Who are These Abusers?

They are more likely to be male than female, but some females do abuse males and some lesbians do abuse their partners as well. According to the American Psychological Association (2013), there are several warning signs that a person *may* become abusive:

- Aggression during their youth
- Anger and hostility toward others
- Desire for power and control in relationships
- Belief in strict gender roles (male dominance)
- Depression
- Few friends and isolated from others
- Young age
- Insecurity
- Unemployment

Preventing Abusive Relationships

The Centers for Disease Control (CDC) recommends that children should learn relationship skills and conflict resolution strategies (2011) early in life. Learning to view both male and female partners as equals, worthy of respect, is also recommended. In a society in which women are economic and social equals to men, abuse is less likely (Jewkes, 2002). In a healthy relationship, both partners are equally empowered to make their commitment to the relationship of their own free choice, each and every day.

healthy sex hints 10.2

Guidelines for Healthy Relationships

Both people in a relationship have the right to

Be treated as an equal
Ask for what they want.
Be accepted for who they are.
Be treated with respect.
Express their thoughts and feelings without criticism.
Not be forced to do anything.
Feel safe when alone with each other.
Give and receive expressions of affection.
Make some mistakes and be forgiven.
Say no and not feel guilty.
Have fun.

No one in the relationship has the right to

Tell the other person where and when he or she can go out.
Act like a boss and order the other person around.
Degrade and humiliate the other person, in either public or private.
Isolate the other from friends and family.
Pressure the other to give up interests and goals.
Read the partner's personal materials without permission, search private property, or follow the other around.
Physically intimidate and harm the other person.
Use sex as a bargaining tool

▮ Sexual Orientation and Relationships

Love and relationships among gay, lesbian, and bisexual adults have been subject to many myths. Perhaps one of the biggest problems lies in the secrecy involved. To be open about the relationship poses barriers that heterosexual couples seldom face. This translates into day-to-day losses such as relating stories of weekend fun with coworkers on Monday and the larger risk of losing one's job if coworkers find out about the gay or lesbian orientation. As José explains in Case Study 10.1, there can be a heavy emotional price to pay for having to keep a love relationship secret from friends and family.

Research comparing heterosexual couples and gay and lesbian couples has revealed that the differences in values one brings to a love relationship are tied more closely to gender than sexual orientation (Peplau, 1981; Metz,

Rosser, & Strapko, 1994). Similarly, gender was a more significant variable when examining differences in styles of conflict resolution. There are fewer verbal attacks, less belligerence and more of an effort to diffuse the argument when conflict occurs in same sex relationships than in heterosexual relationships (Gottman, Levenson, Swanson, Swanson, Tyson, & Yoshimoto, 2003).

Perhaps in response to the realization that gender role stereotyping is problematic when both partners are of the same sex, same-sex relationships tend to reject the traditional marriage model. Compared to heterosexual couples, gay and lesbian relationships are more egalitarian, sharing household responsibilities more evenly, sharing more common interests and spending more time together (Parker- Pope, 2010; Peplau, 1981).

Breaking Up and Ending Relationships

Romantic relationships end for a variety of reasons. For college students, the reasons may include being too busy with academics and sports or music commitments, transferring schools and being apart, finding someone new who excites you and with whom you want to get involved, getting pressure from family because a partner is of an "unacceptable background," and other reasons. Sometimes a crisis tests a relationship, and where one partner expected support, none was forthcoming. Whatever the reason, for at least one of the partners, the relationship wasn't working.

As discussed earlier, the end of a relationship is a perfect time to evaluate what you did and did not like in the previous relationship and your previous partner. You can use this failed relationship to refine your "must have" list for your next relationship. Take some time between relationships so you can spend time alone and with your friends. Use this period of time to reacquaint yourself with "you"-identifying what "you" think, believe and enjoy, not what "we" think, believe and enjoy. All that you learn about your wants and needs can be used to develop a better, healthier relationship when you find the person who is worthy of you.

For some college students dealing with the end of a relationship, it may be important to seek help from campus counseling centers. Whereas some students seem able to accept the end of the relationship, and move on, others find it extremely difficult to continue with their studies. College students may also need to seek counseling when their parents divorce and/or remarry. Some parents wait until their children are out of the house before initiating separation and divorce. Universities recognize the need to provide psychological health services to students.

Academic success can certainly be compromised by the energy diverted from studying to healing "a broken heart" or managing the array of emotions connected to seeing loved ones end their relationship.

case study 10.1

José and Marco, both 26

I'm the only son in my family and until recently was the middle child. My older sister was married, and my younger one is single. When my older sister died, my younger sister Selena and I felt increased pressure from our parents to provide grandchildren. My mother, in particular, is very religious and goes to church every day. She prays for her family, and her faith helped her deal with my sister's death. Now she prays to be blessed with a grandchild. Only one of us is going to be able answer those prayers—and Selena doesn't even have a boyfriend.

I get angry at my situation sometimes and realize that things might be easier if I would come out to my parents. On the other hand, my mother is very religious, and the church hasn't been all that welcoming. My father never gets into deep conversations, and I fear his disappointment. They've met Marco but just think he's one of my good friends. Since they live in Texas and I'm in San Francisco, it's easier to maintain the lie. Marco and I have caller ID on the phone, so we usually can tell who's calling before answering. The "right" person answers the phone.

My parents think I live alone and just have had little success dating women. I took a female friend to my senior prom, but other than her, I've never introduced my family to a girlfriend. They seem to be comfortable accepting my stories, although my mother tells me I should "settle down" and make a family.

When my sister died, it was hard to go home and not have Marco with me. And it continues to be hard to visit family without my partner. Straight people don't have to play these games. I'm getting sick of the secrets and know that I cut myself off from family because I think I am afraid they may totally reject me. I could not face the loss of my family. I may be wrong, but I'm just not ready to take the risk.

Critical Thinking

If you are heterosexual, compare your life to Jose's. What losses does he suffer that you do not have to experience? Imagine how your family would respond if you told them you were gay. Would they be loving and accepting? How would you feel about bringing your partner home with you and how would your family and friends react?

Communication

Communication The process by which information is exchanged between individuals through a common system of symbols, signs, and behaviors

Feedback A verbal or nonverbal response sent from a person receiving a message to the person sending that message

Dialogue An exchange of information in communication

Communication is defined as the process by which information is exchanged between individuals through a common system of symbols, signs, or behaviors. It involves all the modes of behavior that an individual uses to affect another person. It encompasses spoken and written words as well as nonverbal messages such as gestures, facial expressions, bodily messages or signals, and artistic symbols (Watzlawick, Beaven, & Jackson, 1967).

Communicating, as Pam and Doug show us in Case Study 10.2, involves a whole range of issues from emotional comfort and security, to cultural considerations, and finally to discrete behavioral skills. Communicating about sexuality-related issues is even more complex and often more difficult because of this. Communication is the foundation of healthy sexuality. It is essential to obtaining sexual information for oneself as well as communicating information to others. Sexual communication poses

Pam and Doug: Irreconcilable Differences or Poor Communication?

Pam was a non-traditional student in one of Dr. Blonna's online Human Sexuality classes. She and Doug agreed to be interviewed by Dr. Blonna for this book. After 25 years of marriage, Pam and Doug separated for six months because of "irreconcilable differences." Pam asked Doug to move out of their house so she could rethink their relationship. During that time they each began individual counseling, and after a couple of months started seeing a sex therapist together. It soon became apparent to the therapist that Doug and Pam had lost the desire to communicate effectively. After a few sessions with the therapist Doug and Pam began to realize how poor communication contributed to their marital problems. They are back together now and had this to say.

Dr. Blonna: "Could either of you please describe how communication was related to your problems?"

Doug: "I guess I'll start. I always thought Pam and I had sex problems. Our therapist showed me that the problems had as much to do with communication as sex."

Dr. Blonna: "In what ways?"

Pam: "Well, for one, he made us realize that we had just stopped talking about sex years ago."

Doug: "Not only about sex–we really stopped communicating about most things. We were both so angry most of the time that we just stopped talking and merely co-existed in the same house for over 10 years."

Dr. Blonna: "Ten years! Tell me about your sex life during this time."

Pam: "What sex life? I thought I had lost all of my sexual desire. At first I kept telling myself that it would return once the kids were older and in school. Then I told myself it would return when the kids moved out of the house and went away to college. When they left last year and I still did not feel any passion for Doug I wanted out. I needed to find out where my desire had gone."

Dr. Blonna: "So the two of you did have an enjoyable sex life in the beginning?"

Doug: "Yeah, it was good. It wasn't perfect. Pam and I were both raised in very strict households where sex wasn't discussed much and we had a lot of hang-ups about things like oral sex, but we enjoyed the physical and emotional aspects of intercourse."

Dr. Blonna: "So what happened?"

Pam: "Once the kids came and I had to stop working, our relationship changed and we never really talked about it or how we would work around it. I was angry because Doug had a low-level position in his firm and didn't earn what I expected he would. He was angry because

case study
10.2

Critical Thinking

Pam and Doug's story illustrates how important it is to communicate clearly when issues and problems in a relationship arise. How did failing to discuss other issues in their marriage influence their sexual relationship?

I never lost the 20 extra pounds from the second baby, and things just escalated from there."

Doug: "Yeah, neither one of us really knew how to talk about the things that were bothering us, so they just festered and grew. Eventually our problems seemed so great that I didn't know where to start to begin addressing them."

Dr. Blonna: "So you just gave up?"

Pam: "Yeah. I just assumed that this was what happened when couples had kids and were married for more than 10 years. I just immersed myself in my children and my home and Doug spent more and more time at work and on the golf course."

Dr. Blonna: "So how did it turn around?"

Doug: "After Pam asked me to leave and I was on my own for a couple of months I realized how much I loved and respected her. I really missed her."

Pam: "I felt the same way. I guess that beneath the years of anger and holding back our feelings we really did love each other. I had never been in therapy and my therapist helped me explore all of the things I had been holding inside for so long."

Doug: "It was hard for me to talk with a therapist. I didn't want to admit that I was equally at fault for the dissolution of my marriage. He worked with me on my communication skills; asking for the things that I want and need in our relationship and it feels good."

Pam: "Yeah, after 25 years together, I feel that I can argue with Doug in a healthy way and assert myself without hurting him. It has paid off in dividends in the bedroom. I can't believe that at 50 I am enjoying sex so much. Empty nest, what empty nest?"

unique challenges because of the difficulty of communicating in general, plus the personal nature of sexuality. Communicating effectively requires skill, patience, and commitment, as well as an understanding and mastery of sexual information. Honest and accurate sexual communication is essential in developing and maintaining good relationships and fostering healthy sexuality.

Effective communication is a circular process that involves sending and receiving coded messages, as illustrated in Figure 10.4. A sender, wishing to communicate, puts the idea and feeling of the message into a form that can be transmitted. This process of formulating a message, choosing appropriate words, symbols, tone, and expressions to represent it is called **encoding**. The receiver perceives and translates the message using his or her personal storehouse of knowledge and experience in a process called **decoding**.

Encoding Selecting the signs, symbols, emotions, and words to transmit a message

Decoding The use of knowledge, memory, language, context, and personal history and experience to interpret a message

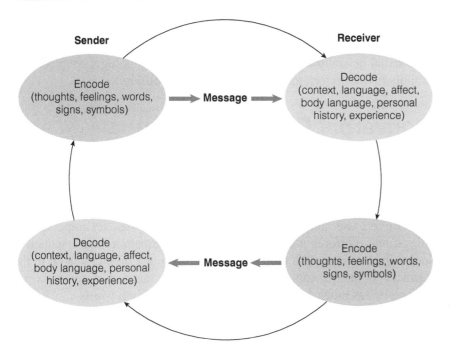

Figure 10.4 *A Circular Model of Communication* **A** circular model of communication assumes that senders and receivers provide feedback to each other.

Encoding and decoding take place within the context of the communicator's interpersonal and physical relationship. What is being said involves not only the actual message but also the physical environment of the communication as well as the relationship of the sender and receiver. A sender might alter the message depending on whether the environment is friendly or unfriendly, familiar or unfamiliar, safe or unsafe, formal or informal (Sawyer & Behnke, 2002).

In addition, a sender might send a different message in the same environment, depending on the nature of the relationship with the receiver. The message might be affected by whether the sender and receiver are friends or enemies, strangers or known to each other, peers or of unequal status (Sawyer & Behnke, 2002). Communication involves sending and receiving both verbal and nonverbal messages. Each type of message is capable of transmitting information, and is part of the encoding and decoding process.

Verbal Communication

Verbal communication is two-dimensional in that it involves transmitting both thoughts and feelings through words. The *cognitive* domain is concerned with communicating our thoughts about things. The *affective* domain involves putting our feelings into words. Many people find communicating cognitive information easier than expressing feelings.

Specificity is crucial in effective verbal communication. The more specific the message, the more likely it is to be transmitted clearly. Vocabulary plays a big part in the specificity of our verbal communication. Having a large working vocabulary allows us to specify exactly what we want to say.

One of the things that makes sexual communication difficult is the lack of a common sexual vocabulary. U.S. culture has no uniform set of agreed-on words, phrases, and sexual language level. Often we are unsure of the proper terminology for sexual topics such as anatomy and physiology and sexual behaviors. Insecurity about sexual terminology, coupled with emotional discomfort, makes talking about sex difficult.

Nonverbal Communication

Body language Sending intentional or unintentional messages through body postures and movements

How we say things is just as important as *what* we actually say. **Body language** describes the nonverbal messages we send through posture, gestures, movement, and physical appearance, including adornment. Our body language intentionally or unintentionally sends messages to receivers (Andersen 1999).

Lovers use nonverbal communication to express feelings, ask for things, and reinforce pleasurable activities. A moan, a hug, a seductive look—these can speak a thousand words. Placing a partner's hand in the correct spot or squeezing it when you are being touched as you want can accomplish as much as explaining these things through words.

■ Body Language

Positive, or open, body language is demonstrated by a relaxed posture, steady eye contact, nods of the head, and an occasional smile or happy expression. These are cues that you are an approachable sender or a receptive receiver (McGinty et al., 2003).

Negative, or closed, body language has visible signs of tension such as clenched fists or tight jaw muscles, a closed posture (arms folded, body shifted sideways, and the like), and facial expressions ranging from anger to disbelief. Negative body language can indicate either apathy or disturbance about something.

■ Silence

Silence is a form of nonverbal communication that can be either a source of stress or a sign of comfort. Silence also can be used to hurt and control

Paralanguage

Source: Callista Lee

Paralanguage is another term for nonverbal communication that includes intonation, pitch, and speed of speaking, hesitation noises, gestures, eye contact, and facial expression. These are all factors that can enhance or even change the meaning of words and/ or can convey information without the use of words. Partners may come to a relationship with a difference of agreement about what certain nonverbal messages mean; this is especially true when there is a cultural difference. For example, for traditional Latinos, men are expected to be the initiators of sexual activity but most Latino couples share decisions about which sexual activities they will engage in and contracep-

tive use, such as condoms (Wood & Price, 1997). If a female partner did not understand the expectation that the male is the one who initiates sex, her overtures toward sex could easily be misinterpreted as being overly aggressive sexually, and this could then lead to his changing his valuation of her.

Eye contact is another important feature of paralanguage. Couples with the highest levels of agreement (lack of conflict) tend to have the most eye contact with each other, while couples in conflict tend to avoid direct eye contact in most communications. However, we have probably all seen an angry stare used to threaten or demean someone.

sex in society 10.2

He Said/She Said

Do men and women communicate differently? Research about this subject over the past 20 years has yielded mixed results. Men and women are socialized differently, and many researchers believe this difference emerges in the way we communicate. Women are socialized to show their feelings, whereas men have been taught to keep their feelings hidden (Michaud & Warner, 1997). Men have been taught to keep their fears and doubts disguised, because showing these is considered a sign of weakness. Men are socialized to believe that admitting weakness is unmanly (Tannen, 1990).

These beliefs can affect the way we communicate with our partners. Wives send clearer and more emotional messages than their husbands do (Noller & Fitzpatrick, 1991). Wives tend to frame their message in an emotional context, whereas husbands deemphasize affect and focus instead on issues and facts. Husbands send more neutral, less expressive messages that are harder to interpret (Tannen, 1990).

Michaud and Warner (1997) found that men and women communicate differently when dealing with problems. When dealing with "troubles talk," these researchers found that women were much more likely to offer sympathy than men were. Men were much more likely to tell a joke. Women were much more

likely to be supportive, whereas men were more likely to avoid the trouble. Lastly, Tannen (1990) found that women were much more likely to listen as a way to offer support, whereas men were much more likely to try to "solve" the problem by offering advice.

McGinty, Knox, and Zusman (2003) found that female college students were more likely to engage in nonverbal feedback and were more proficient at using it than their male counterparts. Female college students in the study were also more proficient at decoding nonverbal feedback than the males who participated. McGinty et al., (2003) also found that males and females differ in how they communicate according to the nature of the relationship. There were significant differences in the communication patterns of students in "involved" versus "casual" relationships. The former group was significantly more concerned about nonverbal communication than the latter. The involved students also demonstrated greater skill in communicating nonverbally with their partners than the casual daters did (McGinty et al., 2003). Involved daters were also "less confused" about their communications than the casual daters were, and reported "working harder" on communicating (both verbally and nonverbally) clearly (McGinty et al., 2003).

people. Silence is a stressor when wordless pauses are perceived as signs of a breakdown in communication.

Conversely, silence communicates comfort and acceptance between friends and lovers who understand that a loving bond is present despite a lack of conversation. Silence is a necessary part of effective communication that is often overlooked. We need time to listen, digest, and understand messages. Silence allows us time to reflect as we formulate our thoughts and words.

Touch

A firm handshake, a reassuring touch on the arm, a gentle squeeze of the buttocks, the placing of a partner's hand on the genitals or breast—all convey messages without speaking a single word (McBurney, 2002). Appropriately used, touch adds another dimension of communication that sometimes reaches deeper than mere words.

Often we find it easier to communicate our sexual desires through touch than words. For example, a man might take his partner's hand and place it on his penis and squeeze it rather than ask, "Please squeeze my penis this hard."

True intimacy doesn't require constant talking. Holding hands and walking silently can communicate love, trust, and a variety of other emotions.

A woman might draw her partner's head upon her breast rather than ask, "Please suck on my nipples." A person might moan or groan rather than say, "I like it when you suck on my penis like that," or "It feels good when you rub my clitoris like that." When used inappropriately, however, the effects of touch can be devastating. A pat on the head can be a sign of endearment to a child but can embarrass or infuriate another adult. A squeeze on your friend's shoulder can show him you understand his problems and care about him. The same squeeze on your secretary's shoulder, however, can convey an entirely different meaning. A pat on a teammate's buttocks can show appreciation of a great play or an extreme effort. The same pat on a coworker's buttocks can be perceived as sexual harassment.

Despite the nature or length of the relationship, however, research shows that men and women often misread emotional cues and misinterpret nonverbal messages (Senecal, Murard, & Hess, 2003). This makes it particularly important to take responsibility for any perceived miscommunication and initiate a dialogue with one's partner to clear this up.

Verbal Skills

Open-Ended Questions

Open-ended questions
Sentences that require information from the other person

Open-ended questions are excellent for initiating a dialogue because they cannot be answered with a simple yes/no response. Imagine that you want to explore how your partner likes to be touched. You initiate, using an open-ended question such as, "Tell me more about how you like to be touched," or "What else can I do to make you feel good?" Open-ended questions require information from the other person. Your partner can't respond with a simple yes/no answer.

Maximize Your Use of the Following Types of Open-Ended Questions and Statements:

"Tell me what you like about this."
"Tell me more about what you didn't like about that."
"How do you feel about this?"
"What are your thoughts about that?"
"Describe that more fully."
"What are your thoughts about. . . .?"
"Explain that more completely."
"What made you decide to do that?"

Open-ended questions will get your partner talking and draw out additional detail and emotion.

I Language

"I" language Taking responsibility for feelings by saying "I feel" versus "You make me feel"

Using **"I" language** is a great way to start a dialogue, especially when discussing sexual concerns. When using "I" language, communicators take responsibility for their feelings. For example, let's say your boyfriend has made fun of your outfit in front of three other mutual friends. Rather than blame your boyfriend by saying, "You really made me feel bad," you

sex in society 10.3

Cultural Considerations in Communication

Communicating effectively requires awareness of, and sensitivity to, various cultural influences related to verbal and nonverbal communication. The following are a few examples of common cultural considerations to keep in mind.

Verbal Communication

Cultural groups and subcultures do not necessarily share a common language. Although English is the first language spoken by most Americans, and common discourse is the level most frequently used to communicate, this is not the case for many individuals and groups. For many Americans, English is a second language, and common discourse (including slang) is often misunderstood. For these Americans, certain subjects, words, and gestures may be misunderstood or taboo.

For Americans traveling abroad for pleasure or business, this consideration is even more important. Sharing personal information, using hand gestures, squeezing an arm, and giving a peck on the cheek are all examples of communication behaviors that are common to everyday discourse among Americans. These would be considered major gaffes when used by Americans traveling in such places as China and Japan (Dou & Clark, 1999).

Perception of time and the relationship of the past, the present, and the future also vary by culture. The predominant culture in the United States is time-urgent and future-oriented. Being aware of the present and doing something now to plan for the future (such as exercising now to prevent heart disease in the future) are commonly accepted.

In daily life, people are oriented to specific times of the day and strict schedules. Some other cultures are much less interested in time and are not as oriented to specific schedules. For example, many Native American homes do not even have clocks, as people of some tribes are more concerned about the present and live one day at a time (Ivey, D'Andrea, Ivey, & Simek-Morgan, 2002).

Nonverbal Communication

A variety of nonverbal factors also vary from culture to culture. Cultures differ in their norms for territoriality and personal space. In general, people of Arabic, Southern European, and African origins sit or stand relatively close to each other when talking. People of Asian, Northern European, and North American countries are more comfortable being farther apart when they are talking (Ivey et al., 2002).

Body language varies significantly according to culture. The dominant U.S. culture places a high value on direct eye contact when speaking. In contrast, Native Americans consider continuous direct eye contact to be insulting and disrespectful. Rules about eye contact also vary by gender in certain cultures. In Islamic cultures, women are taught to avert the eyes, whereas eye contact is OK for men. The meaning and acceptability of a myriad of other nonverbal behaviors, such as pointing fingers, shaking hands, and other forms of touch, vary by culture (Ivey, D'Andrea, Ivey et al., 2002).

could say, "I felt bad when you criticized my outfit in front of our friends." Rather than blame your friend for what you are feeling, express you own your feelings and state them in "I" language.

The situation and feelings about what happened should be stated in clear, simple terms. General statements like "I hate it when you treat me like a sex object" or "I hate it when you do things like that" should be avoided. Good communicators specify exactly what the other person did that they dislike. It's better to say things like "I don't like you to talk about my sexual behavior or level of desire in front of your friends," or "I really feel like a fool when you talk about my sexual needs in front of my friends." Specifying exactly *what* you dislike (talking about sexual needs) and the context (in front of your friends) clarifies the situation and leaves no room for misunderstanding.

From Opening Lines to "I Love You"

Source: Callista Lee

Forget the clever or overtly sexual opening lines; most people don't appreciate them. Both men and women prefer something straightforwardly honest like, "Since we are both here alone, do you care to join me?" or "Hi!" You can easily relate to the environment like, "Have you heard this band before?" or "Have you taken other psychology classes?" and of course, "Want to dance?" The *least* effective lines are sexually blunt like, "You are so HOT!" or really corny like, "Didn't we meet in a previous life?" (Kleinke, Meeker, & Staneski, 1986).

Most people (male, female, straight, gay, bi) report that their first moves toward sexual activity tend to be nonverbal. But as discussed in Chapter 9, **California college students are required to get a clear "yes" for any sexual activity**. So that means we have to move out of our comfort zones a little to use more verbal communication. But this doesn't have to make things legalistic or clinical. It can be *very* sexy to ask, "May I kiss you?" as you look lovingly into their eyes. As you get more practiced at asking for what you want, it will become easier and feel more natural. People like being desired ... by asking for a verbal "yes" you are making it clear that you desire them and that you respect them as a human being.

LGBT people have an added step in making initial moves in that they have to figure out if the person they are attracted to is open to an LGBT relationship. They have to use their "gaydar" (gay radar)—nonverbal cues that a person is LGBT or pansexual.

To become more intimate requires letting one's guard down; being vulnerable. **Relationships in which we share ourselves intimately are built on trust.** The most common way we built trust in relationships is through mutual self-disclosure. Because women have been socialized to share their feelings, they tend to find this easier than do a lot of men, who are socialized to hide their more tender emotions. During the process of self-disclosure, we not only help our partners to understand us better but we also tend to improve our own self-awareness by putting it into words. The ability to share private thoughts and feelings, *especially positive ones*, can enhance relationships (MacNeil & Byers, 2009). Initial feelings that you can trust a person make it easier to self-disclose, and then if those self-disclosures are handled in a respectful and caring manner, this increases trust, which then tends to make future disclosures easier. Trust is important for many reasons that may seem obvious, plus some that might not be. If you receive a communication that is unexpected or ambiguous (unclear), your level of trust will likely affect how you interpret it. For example, if your partner says, "I'm really tired and would rather just stay home alone tonight" you may wonder if they are moving toward breaking up with you if you have little trust in them. But if trust is high, you are more likely to take them at their word that they are just tired and in need of some space. Accepting that your partner can't always be there to meet your needs is a way to show that you care about their well-being as well as your own.

Besides determining whether there is mutual interest and getting consent, what do lovers need to talk about? Likes and dislikes, of course, since we cannot read each other's minds. And the type of relationship we want. But we also need to consider risks of pregnancy and STIs. It's a good idea to just be ready with a condom so that when you say that you want to use one there is no excuse of needing to go out to the store to get one. But you should talk about *why* you want to use a condom. As you will learn in Chapter 12, many STIs show no symptoms even while the infected person's illness is contagious to others. So, your discussion might be as short as, You: "I want us to use condoms because I've learned some really scary things about STIs." Your partner: "Okay."

Asking your partner *if* they have been tested or *when* they were tested is useful information, but one never knows if they picked up something from another partner between then and now. You would also have to ask *which* STIs they were tested for. You can't assume that if they got tested for HIV that they were also tested for Chlamydia, Gonorrhea, HPV, or Hepatitis. **Until you are both agreed that**

your sexual relationship will be monogamous and you've both been tested for all of the common STIs (and TRUST one another to tell the truth even if is not pretty), you are going to need to use condoms. That is true even for some virgins—yes, some people who have never "had sex" (by their definition) may have engaged in sexual behaviors that could transmit an STI. Some people believe that you need to drill a potential partner about how many partners they've had in the past or what they did with previous partners. A more important thing to know would be what their past "safe sex" practices have been. They may have been very careful with thirty partners or taken big risks with just three; the number really isn't the important thing to know when considering risks of STIs. Keep in mind that asking for this kind of self-disclosure may be too much for a new relationship to handle, with each person wondering if their truth will freak their potential partner out. It is that fear that leads people to avoid the truth. And once you have lied, how do you later tell the truth? Consider offering to share what you are comfortable sharing about yourself and let them decide what they are comfortable sharing. If you don't get enough information to help you feel emotionally and physically safe saying "yes," then don't! The sex can be delayed, even if it means a disappointment for now. How the two of you handle that disappointment can tell you a lot about whether or not this person is a good match for you right now.

Using "I" language when trying to meet others shows the other person that you are being responsible for your feelings and you really care: "Hi, I'm Rich. I find myself agreeing with a lot of your viewpoints about things. I really liked what you said in political science class today. Can we talk about it over a cup of coffee in the Student Center?"

Simple Declarative Statements

Sometimes simple **declarative statements** about a sexual topic can initiate a dialogue. These are not as direct as the previous two techniques because they do not specifically require a response. They can be useful, however, especially to test the waters to see how someone feels or what he or she thinks about some sexual topic. Imagine you just read some sexually provocative story in a magazine and are interested in discussing it with your partner. You could simply state this as a declarative sentence: "I just read a fascinating story in this magazine about what men desire most in sexual relationships." By tossing out this simple declarative statement, you could assess whether your partner wants to pursue the discussion and gauge his or her feelings about it. You might follow up with an open-ended statement or let it pass if your partner shows no interest.

Declarative statement A verbal initiating technique that does not require a response to a message

Yes/No Questions

The weakest way to initiate a dialogue—and the way most of us start conversations—is to ask direct **yes/no questions**. These are questions that can be answered by a simple yes or no. They don't require explanation or embellishment in the way that open-ended statements and paraphrasing do. Although they are useful for verifying facts ("Do you like it when I touch you like this?" "Does this feel good?"), when they are overused, they can shut down a dialogue.

Yes/no questions A verbal initiating technique involving a question that requires only a yes or no response

Listening Skills

Passive listening One-way listening; provides no feedback

There are two types of listening: passive and active. In **passive listening** the listener merely soaks in what the initiator of the message is sending. Passive listening is what we do when watching television, a movie, the radio, and so on. It is one-way communication. Although passive listening can be an effective way to receive sexual information, it is not the most effective form of listening to another person when trying to establish or maintain a dialogue.

Active listening Listening with understanding and providing feedback

Active listening is much better than passive listening for dealing with interpersonal communication because, by definition, it requires feedback. Active listeners show that they are listening by providing both nonverbal and verbal feedback. For this reason, active listening is demanding. It takes a lot of energy and concentration, and the listener can easily get distracted and lose interest.

Letting the sender know that the receiver is listening actively can be accomplished through a variety of nonverbal cues. First, the listener adopts a relaxed pose and maintains eye contact. Additional techniques include nodding the head and smiling. Simple verbal cues such as "uh huh," combined with eye contact and head nodding, are enough to let the speaker know the receiver is listening.

Responding Skills

The message receiver reacts to the initiator's message and encodes some type of feedback using verbal or nonverbal communication. If the message was understood and no further clarification is necessary, the receiver can make a simple declarative statement, acknowledging the message with agreement, disagreement, or new information. If the receiver disagrees, or has problems, he or she can use **"I" language** to express opinions. An example is "I hear what you're saying, and I understand your point, but I disagree with that position. I see it differently."

Often, responding skills go beyond merely providing feedback and are used to get additional information needed to understand an issue or to solve a problem. Keeping the conversation going or requesting more information relies on being able to draw more information out of the initiator. Open-ended statements, paraphrasing, and simple yes/no questions, discussed earlier in the chapter, can be used to respond as well as initiate. An additional responding technique that can be powerful is mirroring.

■ Open-Ended Statements

The open-ended statement is an excellent responding technique because it provides feedback and also keeps the dialogue going. A response such as, "I hear what you're saying—tell me more about how you feel about masturbation," lets the sender know you are with him or her and want additional information.

Paraphrasing

Paraphrasing lets senders know you are listening but goes one step further by giving them an idea of how you interpret their message. For instance, a response such as "What I heard you say is that you can accept masturbation as a form of sexual release in general but personally don't feel good about it" lets the sender know you are listening and also provides the opportunity for the sender to know what you think he or she said. The sender usually will let you know if your interpretation is accurate or if you missed the point.

Mirroring

A powerful technique for providing feedback and keeping a person talking is **mirroring**—restating the person's exact words while mimicking the body posturing. This is done intentionally for impact. Mirroring is useful when someone says something that has strong emotional connotations. The message was so powerful that you do not want to risk weakening or misinterpreting it. Let's say a friend tells you she was so angry at the lewd comments a stranger made to her as she walked by him that she felt she could kill him. You would mirror it by saying, "You were so angry you felt you could kill him!" This usually prompts the person to continue and go into the greater detail you desire.

Mirroring Restating the message exactly, including body language

Yes/No Questions

The weakest type of response in a dialogue—and the way most of us seek additional information about something—is to ask direct yes/no questions.

Barriers to Sexual Communication

Most of the barriers to effective sexual communication are related to the skills discussed previously in this chapter, and include failure to initiate, picking an inappropriate time or place, not being specific enough, lack of active listening and assertiveness, saying no when we mean yes, and failing to make requests. Although these barriers may seem insurmountable, in fact they can be overcome if you are aware of their presence, have the desire to overcome them, and are willing to work on improving your communication skills and changing them.

Failing to Initiate

One of the biggest barriers to effective sexual communication is failing to initiate. Initiating any conversation, let alone a sexual one, requires that you first realize that it is your responsibility to initiate the conversation. Whether you want to meet someone new who attracts you or discuss something with your long-term lover, you cannot wait and assume the other person will get the ball rolling for you. Failing to initiate is your problem, not the receiver's.

Taking the time to clear things up, before they are allowed to progress, can prevent problems from escalating.

Often, however, situational constraints prevent this. Other people may be around, you're in the middle of something else, or you don't have enough time right then. In these cases, you should tell the other person you need some time alone with him or her to discuss something important. The two of you should be in a neutral territory where you feel safe and emotionally strong, with enough time so neither of you feels rushed. In the case of meeting someone new, initiators should wait until they can speak to the person alone, away from friends.

Lack of Specificity

Being critical of a partner's behavior at times is normal in any long-term relationship. Being critical of someone's *behavior,* however, is different from being critical of the person. A sure-fire way to sabotage an attempt to discuss sexual concerns is to criticize the partner rather than the behavior. It is important to criticize the behavior, not the person. People have to understand that the other still loves them but does not like a certain behavior. The partner probably is unaware of how the behavior affects the other. The more precision in describing exactly what a person did or said, the better is the chance of clearing up the problem without hurting the person's feelings. "I really feel hurt when you reject my sexual advances" is a lot easier to deal with than "You're a jerk for rejecting me." Healthy sexuality revolves around effective communication, based on personal knowledge and the desire to communicate honestly.

Lack of Assertiveness

Assertiveness Pursuing one's own needs and wants without infringing on others

Aggressiveness Pursuing one's own wants and needs without regard for the rights of others

Assertiveness is a positive attribute, based on mutual respect and democracy in relationships. Assertiveness means understanding one's own wants and needs and pursuing them without infringing on others' ability to do the same. **Aggressiveness,** on the other hand, means pursuing one's needs and wants without regard to how this affects the rights of the others. Often, aggressive people get their needs met at the expense of others. Nonassertive people fail to pursue their needs and wants while allowing others to meet theirs. They fail to stick up for their rights and allow others to take advantage of them, often denying what is going on (Smith, 1993).

Assertiveness is important to effective communication. Many people are not assertive because they confuse assertiveness with aggressiveness. In an attempt to control what they perceive as aggressiveness, they act nonassertively and fail to meet their needs while allowing hostility and frustration to build up inside themselves, weakening their communication and relationships. Often, lack of assertiveness is based in religious, cultural, or gender role expectations, and transcends lack of skill or desire to assert oneself. Some cultures require subjugating one's personal desires to those of the dominant partner in the relationship.

In many cultures, the male partner is the dominant member of the couple. Women are expected to put their needs behind those of their partner and behave in ways expected of them. Respecting the wishes of the partner and the culture is taught to be more important than one's own needs. The conflict between these traditional ways of behaving, and U.S. cultural values focusing on the individual and self-actualization, is a source of stress and sexual dissatisfaction for many women.

healthy sex hints 10.3

Assert Yourself With the DESC Technique

The DESC model is a powerful tool for helping you make requests, deliver criticism more effectively, and become more precise in your assertiveness. The DESC model has four steps:

1. *D—describe:* Paint a verbal picture of the situation or the other person's behavior that is a source of stress. Be as precise as possible: "Honey, when you use language like 'I'm feeling horny—let's fuck,'. . . ."
2. *E—express:* Express your feelings about the incident using "I" language: "I feel seedy and cheap" or "I feel very uncomfortable."
3. *S—specify:* Be specific in identifying alternative ways that you would prefer the person to speak or behave: "I'd like you to soften your language and say, 'I'm feeling sexy—let's make love.'"
4. *C—consequences:* Identify the consequences that will follow if the person does (pro) or doesn't (con) comply with your wishes: "In the future, if you do soften your language, I'll be much more likely to get in the mood and want to make love with you (pro)." "If you don't, and you continue to use such crude language, I can't guarantee that I won't be turned off and not feel sexy." When using this model, precision is important in describing the other person's offending behavior or actions. As mentioned previously in this chapter, focus your criticism on the offensive behavior, not the person (Bower and Bower, 1976; Greenberg, 2003).

Saying Yes When We Mean No

When people are nonassertive, they say yes to others' demands when they really want to say no. They spend an inordinate amount of time pleasing others without being reciprocated. They forsake their sexual needs and wants while granting the partner's desires. Although sharing and sacrificing are important to relationships, they become a problem when this behavior is always one-way and not reciprocated.

When people are nonassertive, they are filled with resentment and hostility toward their partner as a result. It's a vicious cycle. Originally, in an attempt to avoid conflict, discomfort, or hurting the partner's feelings, they say yes when they really mean no. This response temporarily relieves them from feeling guilty.

Unfortunately, however, when they do this, they get trapped into doing things they really don't want to do. When this result happens, they begin to feel miserable because they've lost control of their lives and lost their self-respect. Not only do they feel stressed because of this situation, but it also affects their sexual response. Desire and arousal are difficult when a person feels stressed and angry. The only way to stop the cycle is to begin to say no. This brings us full circle to the same situation as the initial one: having to say no. If people are assertive to begin with, they can avoid the aggravation and stress.

healthy sex hints 10.4

Saying No

Saying no isn't always easy, but it is essential if you are to be assertive and reduce your stress. You have the right to say no. The following are clear guidelines:

1. *Face the other person from a normal distance.* If you are too far away, you may appear timid. If you crowd the person, you border on aggressiveness.
2. *Look the person directly in the eyes.* Averting eye contact is a sure giveaway that you'll cave in.
3. *Keep your head up and your body relaxed.* Don't be a shrinking violet.
4. *Speak clearly and firmly, at a volume that can be heard clearly.*
5. *Just say no.* You don't have to clarify why.
6. *Be prepared to repeat it.* Sometimes people are persistent. Be prepared to say it again.
7. *Stick to your guns.* Don't give in. It gets easier with practice.

If you feel a need to explain why you are declining, here are a few tips for setting the stage:

1. Thank the person for the offer: "Gee, thanks, but *no.* I really can't [don't want to] . . ."
2. Express appreciation: "I really appreciate the offer, but *no.* I'm not interested/too busy/ don't want any . . ."
3. Affirm your friendship: "I enjoy your company, and I'd like to do something together, but *no.*"
4. Reject the offer, not the person: "Please don't take this personally. I like you, but *no, I don't . . .*"

■ Failing to Make Requests

Assertiveness is directly related to requesting things you desire and saying no to things you don't want to do. People have many reasons for not making explicit sexual requests. As we've already discussed, language poses a unique barrier. Feeling comfortable with sexual language is important, and finding a comfortable language level helps. If sex has been a taboo topic of conversation while growing up, it may be difficult to talk about openly. People enter their first relationship without having had the benefit of knowing that talking about sex is OK. Shaking this taboo is sometimes difficult. You can become more comfortable by proceeding slowly, acknowledging your fears and discomfort, and allowing yourself to take chances and grow out of your old ways of thinking and feeling.

Another barrier is not taking responsibility for one's wants, needs, and feelings. First, the individual has to find out who he or she is as a sexual person. Then the person has to accept this. The third step is to share it with the partner. The partner can't know who the other is, what he or she needs, and how to please that person without the other person's taking responsibility to communicate this.

Our sexuality is continually growing and evolving. A married student expressed it this way in class:

> *My wife is always saying that she shouldn't have to explain what she wants sexually. We've been together for 10 years, and I should*

*know how to please her and what her needs are. I have a hard time
with this. My own needs change from day to day and from sexual
encounter to sexual encounter. One day I may want her to take
the lead and initiate sex and be dominant while I lie back and let
her take me. The next time we make love, I might want to initiate.
I know she's the same way, but I can't tell in advance without her
communicating her desires to me.*

We need to take responsibility for what we're feeling and make requests
accordingly, using "I" language.

❧ *Emotional Wellness* ❧

Emotional wellness affects the ability to communicate clearly. Communicating effectively is difficult even under the best of circumstances. Communicating about sexuality poses unique challenges because of the sensitive nature of the topic. Even though people may want to communicate more effectively, emotions sometimes get in the way. They might feel embarrassed talking about their most intimate desires, thoughts, and feelings. They also might feel guilty about some of these things. These emotions often make it difficult to think clearly and logically. A first step in sexual communication is to identify how we are feeling and to take responsibility for owning these feelings. Once we assume ownership for our feelings, we can use "I" language to communicate them to our intimate partner.

Digital Communication

Texting, emailing, and posting on social media sites have added another dimension to communication and communicating about sex. They are similar but very different from face-to-face communication.

They are different in three very real ways; feedback, permanence and the private vs public nature of the communication.

Permanence - When someone sends a text message, email, or social media post, there is a permanent record of the exchange. While something communicated face-to-face or over the telephone is usually private and temporary (in most cases the exchange is not intentionally recorded), texts, emails, and posts on social media are permanent. Things that are texted, emailed, or posted cannot be assumed to be private messages.

While this may not seem like a big deal in the heat-of-the-moment, the permanence of texts, emails, and posts allows them to re-surface without the benefit of context and other factors that would clarify the intent and meaning of the communication. One only has to look at the 2016 Presidential campaign to see how texts, email messages, and social media posts from both candidates were taken out of context and interpreted many different ways.

Feedback - Because texting, emailing, and blogging do not involve face-to-face communication, it makes it much easier to say something one might not say if they were looking into the eyes of the receiver. In addition to transmitting information, communicating face-to-face provides a rich source of feedback in regarding how the receiver is receiving the message. Posture, eye contact, and energy (or lack of it) are all transmitted by the sender along with the words. So, when someone says something, the person they are communicating the message to can also get a sense of *how* they are saying it from the way they face you, look at you, and address you. The same can be said of the receiver of a message. The sender can get a sense of how the message is being received by the receiver's posture, eye contact, and energy.

This is entirely missing from texting, emailing, and posting on social media. To make up for this, imogis, spacing, capital letters, bold face text, use of exclamation points, question marks, and other symbols are used to transmit the nuances of body language and tone. These non-face-to-face feedback replacers often do not have the same power of face-to-face feedback.

Public vs Private Space- Posting on social media sites such as Face-Book takes things (pictures, messages, other content) out of the private realm and puts it out there in the social realm for everyone else to see in addition to the receiver. Young people and college students often express romantic or sexual feelings for their partners, communicate intimate messages, and announce things to the public about their relationship.

In addition, posting on social media sites among people who are dating differs from face-to-face communication because it moves previously private dating communications into public spaces, gives dating partners and their social networks 24/7 access to one another. It also allows for the instant spread of information to their social networks. Sometimes partners' networks receive the information before the partner does (Reed & Safyer, 2015, Subrahmanyam & Smahel, 2011).

These differences require partners to set personal guidelines regarding how they want to use digital communication. Issues such as, "Is it okay to text each other all day?", or to post certain types of pictures etc.

On the positive side, digital communication enhances the ease of communication from anywhere around the globe. It facilitates keeping partners in touch and gives them the ability to communicate 24/7 at the push of a button.

All of these differences require care and attention beyond the realm of face-to-face communication.

Handling Conflicts Effectively

It is not so much about what couples argue about that makes or breaks the relationship, but how they argue. If you go to couples counseling, you will learn the **validating style** of conflict resolution, which allows for each person to feel safe in expressing their thoughts and feelings about a complaint, with a partner who is actively listening. Once the listener demonstrates that they have heard and understood the complaint, they may express how they think and feel about it, while their partner listens actively. This tends to lead to agreements about how to solve the problem in a way that respects both people. It has long been assumed that this is the "best" communication

style for couples striving to get through a conflict to a solution that is acceptable to both of them.

But Gottman (2008) learned that there are two other styles that work very well for some couples. The **volatile style** may look bad to outsiders, but these

Validating style Conflicts are resolved through calm discussion and compromise, using many of the verbal skills discussed in this chapter.

Volatile style These couples appear to be fighting, bickering, and squabbling a lot, and may get into loud shouting matches more often than other couples.

are people who don't hold back. They are passionate both in their conflicts as well as in their lovemaking. One key to this style working effectively is that both partners feel strong enough to hold their own in an argument and that neither needs peace and quiet to be happy.

The other factor that determines whether or not this style will work well for a couple is whether they can be respectful while arguing. Those who descend into contempt and disrespect will hurt one another, perhaps beyond repair.

The third type of couple uses a **conflict-avoiding style** in which they just don't let things bother them enough to argue very often. Of course, this is only going to work if both partners are on the same page. If you have one conflict avoider and the other is more validating or more volatile, there will be frustration all around. For the couples who make this work, we find that they are just able to "let things go."

While all three styles can work for some couples, some researchers have found that the validating style is more effective overall than the volatile style (Holman & Jarvis, 2003), and so it has been the style practiced in couples counseling.

Gottman and his research teams have also found four communication warning signs that often signal the impending doom of a romantic relationship, which they refer to as the "four horsemen of the relationship apocalypse" (Gottman, 1994; Gottman & Gottman, 2008; Gottman & Silver, 2000). They are:

Criticism—this goes beyond simple complaining to outright attacking the partner's speech, character, or actions. There are a lot of "you" statements (as opposed to "I" statements) and blaming.

Contempt—Disrespect, disgust, or hate expressed in place of love and admiration that was once shared. The focus becomes abusive, and again there are a lot of "you" attacks. Treating others with disrespect and mocking them with sarcasm are forms of contempt. So are hostile humor, name-calling, mimicking, and/or body language such as eye-rolling and sneering. Gottman believes this to be the most destructive of the four communication warning signs because of the damage it does to the partner who is the target of the contempt.

Defensiveness—Partners refuse to accept responsibility for their part in conflicts. It is impossible to solve a problem in which nobody is to blame because there is no behavior to change. People who communicate defensively will blame others for their own behavior rather than accepting even partial responsibility. They may also disagree with their partner's complaint, insisting that their partner's point of view is invalid. Many defensive communicators will fail to truly hear their partner and instead just keep repeating their position over and over so that there is no progress. And another common practice is "cross-complaining," in which they ignore their partner's complaint and bring up their own complaint. Again, no progress toward a solution.

Stonewalling—Men appear to use this method more often than women. Perhaps it relates to their "strong and silent" socialization. It is a form of passive-aggression in which they just appear to not respond to the complaining partner. It may send the message that "your problems do not concern me enough to respond" or "I'm not interested in working on the relationship so you can like it or leave it." Gottman views this as the culmination of the first three danger signs, which mostly occurs as a relationship is nearing its end.

Observations of thousands of couples have allowed Dr. Gottman to determine that these four patterns of communication are accurate for predicting divorce, 90 percent of the time (Prooyen, 2017). Of course, these signs do not have to mean that a relationship is doomed. If both parties are willing to get help to learn and practice more validating communication, they may be able to heal and rebuild their relationship over time.

Conflict-avoiding style These relationships find success in maintaining a shared sense of agreement, and placing low importance on areas of disagreement.

References

Acevedo, A. & Aron, A. (2009). Does a long term relationship kill romantic love? Review of General Psychology, 13, 1, pp. 59–65.

Andersen, P. A. (1999). *Nonverbal communication: Form and function.* Mountain View, CA: Mayfield.

Arnst, C. (2005). Better loving through chemistry. Business Week, 3956. Hillsdale, NJ: Erlbaum.

Berscheid, E., & Walster, W. (1974). Physical attractiveness. In L. Berkowitz (Ed.), *Advances in experimental social psychology* (Vol. 7). New York: Academic Press.

Boostin, J. (2010, February 12). The big business of on line dating. Available on line: www.CNBC.com

Botting, D., & Botting, K. (1996). *Sex appeal.* New York: St. Martin's.

Bower, S. A., & Bower, G. H. (1976). *Asserting yourself: A practical guide for positive change.* Reading, MA: Addison-Wesley.

Buss, D. M., Larse, R. J., Westen, D., & Semmelroth, J. (1992). Sex differences in jealousy: Evolution, physiology, and psychology. *Psychological Science, 3,* 251–255.

Byrne, D. (1971). The attraction paradigm. New York: Academic Press.

Cann, A., Mangum, J., & Wells, M. (2001, August). Distress in response to relationship infidelity: The roles of gender and attitudes about relationships. Journal of Sex Research, *38*(3), 185–190.

Carducci, B. (2000, Jan.). Shyness: the new solution. Psychology Today.

Centers for Disease Control (2011). Understanding intimate partner violence-fact sheet. Retrieved from www.cdc.gov

Chalabi, M. (2015, July 15). Sorting through the numbers on infidelity. Retrieved from http://www.npr.org

Christopher, F. S., & Sprecher, S. (2000, November). Sexuality in marriage, dating, and other relationships: A decade review. *Journal of Marriage and the Family, 62,* 999–1017.

Clifford, S. (2009, January 27) Teaching Teenagers about harassment. New York Times.

Corbett, S. (2001, October 14). When Debbie met Christina, who then became Chris. *New York Times Magazine,* Section 6, pp. 84–87.

DeAngelis, B. (1992). *Are you the one for me? Knowing who's right and avoiding who's wrong.* New York: Dell.

Dion, K. L., & Dion, K. K. (1987). Belief in a just world and physical attractiveness stereotyping. *Journal of Personality and Social Psychology, 52,* 775–780.

Dou, W. L., & Clark, W. (1999, Summer–Fall). Appreciating the diversity in multicultural communication styles. *Business Forum, 24*(3–4), 54–62.

Downey, G., & Feldman, S. I. (1996). Implications of rejection sensitivity for intimate relationships. *Journal of Personality and Social Psychology, 70*(6), 1327–1343.

Egan, J. (2003, November 23). Love in the time of no time. *New York Times Magazine,* p. 66.

Fisher, H. (1993). *Anatomy of love: The national history of monogamy, adultery, and divorce.* London: Simon & Schuster.

Francese, T. (2001, November). The battered woman's experience and theories of violence. Class presentation by the Passaic County Office of Women, William Paterson University.

Freedner, N., Freed, L., Yang, Y., & Austin, S. (2002, December). Dating violence among gay, lesbian, and bisexual adolescents: Results from a community survey. *Journal of Adolescent Health,* 469–474.

Fromm, E. (1956). The Art of Loving. New York: Harper Row.

Gottman, J. Levenson, R., Swanson, C., Swanson, K., Tyson, R. & Yoshimoto, D. (2003). Observing gay, lesbian, and heterosexual couples' relationships: mathematical modeling of conflict interactions. *Journal of Homosexuality,* 45, pp 65–91.

Greenberg, J. S. (2003). *Comprehensive stress management* (8th ed.). Boston: McGraw-Hill.

Hatfield, E., & Rapson, R. L. (1996). Love and sex: *Cross cultural perspectives.* Boston: Allyn & Bacon.

Hatfield, E., & Sprecher, S. (1986). *Mirror, mirror. . . . The importance of looks in everyday life.* Albany: State University of New York Press.

Henderson, L., Zimbardo, P., & Rodino, E. (2001). Painful shyness in children and adults [Online]. American Psychological Association. Retrieved from http://helping.apa.org.

Hendrick, S., Foote, F. J., & Slapion-Foote, J. (1984). Do men and women love differently? *Journal of Social and Personal Relationships,* 1, 177–180.

Ivey, A. E., D'Andrea, M. D., Ivey, M. B., & Simek-Morgan, L. (2002). *Theories of counseling and psychotherapy: A multicultural perspective* (5th ed.). Boston: Allyn & Bacon.

Kohl, J. V., & Francouer, R. T. (1995). *The scent of eros: Mysteries of odor in human sexuality.* New York: Continuum.

Lee, J. (1988). Love styles. In R. Sternberg & M. Barnes (Eds.), *The psychology of love.* New Haven, CT: Yale University Press.

Lewis, R. (2010). Emotional intimacy among men. *Journal of Social Issues, 34*(1)

McBurney, L. (2002, Spring). Touch me—not there! How to be sensual without necessarily being sexual. *Marriage Partnership, 19*(1), 26–29.

McClintock, E. (2011). Handsome wants as handsome does: Physical attractiveness and gender differences in revealed sexual preferences. *Biodemography and Social Biology*, 57, 221–257.

McGinty, K., Knox, D., & Zusman, M. E. (2003, March).

Marano, H. E.(2005, Jan/Feb.). What's a shy guy to do? *Psychology Today,* 38(1).

Metz, M. E., Rosser, B. R., & Strapko, N. (1994, November). Differences in conflict-resolution styles among heterosexual, gay, and lesbian couples. *Journal of Sex Research, 31*(4), 293.

Michael, R. T., Gagnon, J. H., Laumann, E. O., & Kolata, G. (1994). *Sex in America.* New York: Little, Brown.

Michaud, S. L., & Warner, R. M. (1997, October). Gender differences in self-reported troubles talk. *Sex Roles: A Journal of Research, 37* (7–8), 527–541.

Noller, P., & Fitzpatrick, M. A. (1991). Marital communication. In A. Booth (Ed.), *Contemporary families: Looking backward, looking forward.* Minneapolis: Council on Family Relations.

Nonverbal and verbal communication in "involved" and "casual" relationships among college students. College Student Journal, 37(1), 68–72.

Parker-Pope, T, (2010). For Better: how the surprising science of happy couples can help your marriage succeed. New York, NY, Plume.

Peplau, L. (1981, March). What homosexuals want in relationships. *Psychology Today, 28,* 37–38.

Reed, L.A., Tolman, R.M., Safyer, P. (2015). Too close for comfort: Attachment insecurity and electronic intrusion in college students' dating relationships. HYPERLINK "http://www.sciencedirect.com.ezproxy.wpunj.edu/science/journal/07475632" \o "Go to Computers in Human Behavior on ScienceDirect" Computers in Human Behavior, HYPERLINK "http://www.sciencedirect.com.ezproxy.wpunj.edu/science/journal/07475632/50/supp/C" \o "Go to table of contents for this volume/issue" Volume 50, September 2015, Pages 431–438.

Sawyer, C. R., & Behnke, R. R. (2002, Fall). Behavioral inhibition and the communication of public speaking state anxiety. *Western Journal of Communication, 66*(4), 12–23.

Schwartz, P. (2001). *Everything you know about love and sex is wrong: 25 relationship myths redefined to achieve happiness and fulfillment in your intimate life.* New York: Perigee.

Senecal, S., Murard, N., & Hess, U. (2003, January). Do you know what I feel? Partners' predictions and judgements of each other's emotional reactions to emotion-eliciting situations. *Sex Roles: A Journal of Research,* 21–38.

Smith, E., Becker, M., Byrne, D., & Przybyla, D. (1993). Sexual attitudes of males and females as predictors of interpersonal attraction and marital compatibility. *Journal of Applied Social Psychology, 23*(13), 1011–1034.

Smith, J. C. (1993). *Creative stress management.* Englewood Cliffs, NJ: Prentice Hall.

Sternberg, R. (1986). A triangular theory of love. *Psychological Review, 93,* 119–135.

K. Subrahmanyam, D. Smahel (2011). Digital youth: The role of media in development. Springer, New York, NY (2011)

Tannen, D. (1990). *You just don't know: Women and men in conversation.* New York: Morrow.

Tackett, S., Nelson, L., & Busby, D. (2013). Shyness and relationship satisfaction: Evaluating the associations between shyness, self-esteem, and relationship satisfaction in couples. *The American Journal of Family Therapy, 41,* 34–45

Trimarchi, M. (2013). 10 Steps to a more intimate relationship. Available on line: http://health.howstuffworks.com

University of Florida (2013). Types of intimacy. Retrieved from http://www.counseling.ufl.edu/

University of Michigan(2009, April 29). Seven-Year itch? Boredom can hurt a marriage. Retrieved from http://www.sciencedaily.com/

Waite, L. J., & Joyner, K. (2001). Emotional and physical satisfaction with sex in married, cohabiting, and dating sexual unions: Do men and women differ? In E. O. Laumann & R. Michael (Eds.), *Sex, love and health in America.* Chicago: University of Chicago Press.

Wheeless, L. R., Wheeless, V. E., & Baus, R. (1984). Sexual Communication, Communication Satisfaction, and Solidarity in the Developmental Stages of Intimate Relationships, *Western Journal of Speech Communication, 48*(3), pg. 224.

Wiederman, M. W. (2001). Mate selection: What determines peoples' choice of particular partners? In *Understanding sexuality research.* Belmont, CA: Wadsworth/Thomson Learning.

Wike, R. (2014, January 14). *French more accepting of infidelity than people in other countries.* Retrieved from http://pewresearch.org

Zimbardo, P. G. (1977). *Shyness.* Reading, MA: Addison-Wesley.

Chapter
eleven

Fertility Control

Student Learning Objectives

After reading this chapter, students will be able to:

- ☞ Differentiate the following terms: fertility control, contraception, birth control, and family planning.
- ☞ Compare the perfect use (theoretical effectiveness) and the effectiveness of typical (actual) use.
- ☞ Determine personal level of risk for unintended pregnancy.
- ☞ Develop a personal plan for controlling fertility.
- ☞ Evaluate a variety of fertility control methods.
- ☞ Determine which methods work best for different types of users.
- ☞ Describe how fertility control requires change over the life cycle.
- ☞ Identify which methods work best in reducing the risks for STD and HIV infection.
- ☞ Evaluate the health aspects of various fertility control methods.

**case study
11.1**

Critical Thinking

Sterilization is often something college students can't envision, yet it remains a very popular form of birth control worldwide. Could you imagine either you or your partner being sterilized after having had the children you wanted?

Joe's 34, Vasectomy

The best present I ever gave myself was my vasectomy. I belong to an HMO, and it cost me a dollar to have it done. I'll always feel it was the best dollar I ever spent. I guess I've used almost every method available with my wife and my girlfriends before I got married. All these methods had one problem or another, so I promised myself that after the kids were born, I'd take responsibility and get a vasectomy.

The week after my second son was born, I told my wife I wanted to have it done. She was glad that we could stop using condoms and fertility awareness and supported my decision. The procedure was uneventful. I was in and out in 1 hour. The only glitch was that the anesthesiologist had to give me three shots of painkiller before they could make the incision.

After about 16 weeks, my follow-up tests were negative, and we had sex for the first time without worry of my wife getting pregnant. The first time was in the shower. It was great. I can't remember the last time we made love in the shower. Getting the vasectomy was the biggest boost to our sex life in the past 10 years!

Family planning Postponing children until the optimal point in one's life

Many people use the terms *birth control, contraception,* and *family planning* interchangeably when referring to controlling fertility. Although the three terms are similar because they refer to strategies for preventing unintended pregnancy, they are vastly different in terms of their nature and scope. Although most people probably agree that avoiding unintended pregnancy is a good idea, how to accomplish this goal generates tremendous disagreement.

Family planning implies the desire to have children at some point in time. Planning a family involves postponing childbearing until it is desired, spacing subsequent births and avoiding pregnancy at other times. As discussed in Chapter 13, family planning may also include all the reproductive technologies available to facilitate a pregnancy as well as adoption. Family planning does not refer to specific methods or techniques to avoid unintended pregnancy.

Contraception Methods designed to prevent conception

Contraception refers to all methods designed to prevent conception or fertilization. Contraceptive methods work by preventing the sperm and egg from uniting to cause fertilization. These methods include noninsertive sexual activity, barrier methods, hormonal contraception, withdrawal, fertility awareness, and sterilization. How effective these methods are ranges from "not very" to "almost complete" at the other end of the spectrum.

Birth control The broadest term covering all methods designed to prevent the birth of a child

Birth control is a broad term encompassing all methods designed to prevent pregnancy and birth. It includes all contraceptive methods, what may be considered postconceptive methods, and abortion, which is designed to interrupt an established pregnancy. At its most literal, birth control also includes infanticide, although such a practice is generally viewed with repugnance and considered a crime.

Effectiveness: Perfect Use and Typical Use

One of the most important questions regarding any method of fertility control is "How effective is it?" Effectiveness is measured in two ways: theoretical use and actual use.

The **perfect use (also called theoretical)** of any fertility control method estimates how it should work if it is used consistently and correctly. It is the ideal effectiveness of the method, determined through laboratory research and experimental studies. Perfect use effectiveness research designs attempt to control for as many variables as possible that may interfere with correct and consistent use. Failure of the method accounts for most of the ineffectiveness. Perfect use reflects the percentage of women who will become pregnant in one year even though they use this method perfectly.

The **typical use effectiveness (also called actual)** of any fertility control method is how it actually works when real people use it under normal circumstances. Typical use reflects the percentage of women who become pregnant during their first year of use. Both women who use the method correctly and those who do not are represented in this percentage. When considering the contraceptive choice, this number is the most relevant number and will be listed first in each contraceptive section (Zieman, Hatcher, Allen, Lathrop & Haddad, 2016).

Perfect use effectiveness The percentage of women who will become pregnant in one year even though they use the method effectively

Typical use effectiveness The percentage of women who get pregnant while using a contraceptive method for 1 year

Choosing a Method

The best method is the one the person or couple uses consistently and correctly. It is the one that those involved are happy with, that offers the level of protection desired, and that fits the needs of those involved at this point in life. For college students today, choices about fertility control overlap with concerns about STD/HIV risk reduction. Some methods are highly effective in their ability to prevent pregnancy yet offer no protection against STDs thus requiring condom use with the method for some couples.

From a public health standpoint, overall costs become a factor in providing services to those least able to pay. Title X of the Public Health Service Act was designed to make comprehensive voluntary family planning services available. Today clinics that are funded through Title X provide services to 25% of women who obtain contraceptives services (Guttmacher Institute, 2016.) As women seek newer, more expensive methods and clinics and programs struggle with smaller budgets, the issue of "choice" and making methods available becomes ever more challenging.

It is important to realize that needs will change over time. Therefore, people would do well to review their fertility control needs periodically and make changes accordingly. Table 11.1 provides a summary of contraceptive methods.

Table 11.1 Comparison Typical Effectiveness of Contraceptive Methods

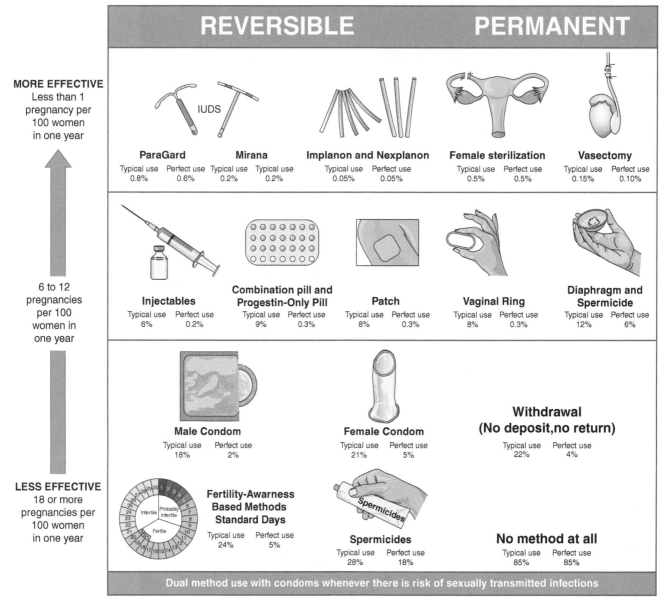

MORE EFFECTIVE	REVERSIBLE				PERMANENT	

MORE EFFECTIVE
Less than 1 pregnancy per 100 women in one year

IUDS		**Implanon and Nexplanon**	**Female sterilization**	**Vasectomy**
ParaGard	**Mirana**			
Typical use 0.8% — Perfect use 0.6%	Typical use 0.2% — Typical use 0.2%	Typical use 0.05% — Perfect use 0.05%	Typical use 0.5% — Perfect use 0.5%	Typical use 0.15% — Perfect use 0.10%

6 to 12 pregnancies per 100 women in one year

Injectables	**Combination pill and Progestin-Only Pill**	**Patch**	**Vaginal Ring**	**Diaphragm and Spermicide**
Typical use 6% — Perfect use 0.2%	Typical use 9% — Perfect use 0.3%	Typical use 8% — Perfect use 0.3%	Typical use 8% — Perfect use 0.3%	Typical use 12% — Perfect use 6%

LESS EFFECTIVE
18 or more pregnancies per 100 women in one year

Male Condom	**Female Condom**	**Withdrawal (No deposit, no return)**
Typical use 18% — Perfect use 2%	Typical use 21% — Perfect use 5%	Typical use 22% — Perfect use 4%

Fertility-Awarness Based Methods Standard Days	**Spermicides**	**No method at all**
Typical use 24% — Perfect use 5%	Typical use 28% — Perfect use 18%	Typical use 85% — Perfect use 85%

Dual method use with condoms whenever there is risk of sexually transmitted infections

Reprinted by permission of Managingcontraception.com

❧ *Physical and Intellectual Wellness* ❧

Making good decisions about controlling fertility is a multifaceted process. Choosing the most effective method, long acting reversible contraception, makes the most intellectual sense for those who do not want to get pregnant. It is essential that you learn how you and your partner's bodies function. So much information is now accessible on the Internet, making learning about anatomy, physiology, and the biochemistry of the human body and health less of a mystery. Teaching about and providing birth control at the time of Margaret Sanger's pioneering efforts in the early 1900s was viewed as obscene, landing her in jail. Today a variety of sources of information are available to help you decide what is best for you.

Fertility control, first, is affected by one's level of physical well being. Overall physical health influences the fertility methods available to you. For example, physical conditions such as hypertension and diabetes are contraindications for oral contraceptives. Health status also affects how you use certain methods.

Consistent and proper use of fertility control methods can enhance physical wellbeing. Practicing fertility control carries less risk to a woman than getting pregnant and having a child. The risk of dying associated with pregnancy and childbirth is significantly greater than that for using fertility control.

Certain methods impart specific health-enhancing benefits. Hormonal contraception offers protective effects against a variety of diseases including ovarian cancer and endometrial, along with possible improvement for acne and menstrual cramps. Barrier contraceptives reduce the risk of cervical cancer, as well as some STDs.

Intrauterine Devices

The intrauterine device (IUD)-also called intrauterine contraceptive- is the most commonly used reversible contraception in the world and is among the safest and most effective methods of contraception available today. The IUD works primarily by preventing the sperm from fertilizing the egg. IUDs are not abortifacients, meaning they do not function by ending a pregnancy. They combine a foreign body and the effect of either copper or the hormone levonorgestrel to prevent pregnancy.

The copper IUD (Paragard T 380A) works as a spermicide. The copper inhibits sperm motility so that sperm rarely reach the fallopian tube and therefore are unable to fertilize the ovum. Some advantages of the copper IUD include probable protection against endometrial cancer and possible protection against cervical cancer. The risk for ectopic pregnancy is reduced and once the IUD is removed, there is a quick return to fertility. The copper IUD contains no hormones so there are no hormonal side effects. Once inserted, it is effective for 10–12 years but can be removed at any time if pregnancy becomes desirable. The disadvantages of the copper IUD include increased menstrual flow and possible increased dysmenorrhea (painful menstruation). These side effects may decrease over time. Copper IUDs can be inserted up to 5 days after intercourse to act as emergency contraception (Zieman et al., 2016).

The hormonal IUD (Mirena, Liletta, and Skyla) works primarily by causing the cervical mucous to thicken thus preventing the sperm from reaching the ovum. In addition, the hormones cause a change in uterine and tubal fluids that impairs the movement of the sperm and the ovum. There are also changes to the endometrium that prevent implantation of a fertilized ovum. For some women, the hormones prevent ovulation. The advantages of the hormonal IUD include decreased menstrual flow and for some women, loss of menstruation. Hormonal IUDs decrease the risk of endometrial cancer and fibroids. There is also a decreased risk of ectopic pregnancy and pelvic inflammatory disease. There are some

sex in society 11.1

Intrauterine Devices Here and Abroad

When teaching undergraduates about intrauterine devices, faculty may get met with blank faces from those who have never heard of such an item nor could imagine having one inserted into the uterus. One of the original IUDs, the Dalkon Shield,was responsible for a variety of painful and deadly complications for early users. Although new designs have improved effectiveness and greatly minimized side effects, the method received a lot of "bad press," and lost favor among many women. The Dalkon Shield became infamous for its serious design flaw: a porous, multifilament string upon which bacteria could travel into the uterus of users, leading to sepsis, injury, miscarriage, and death. Modern Intrauterine devices (IUDs) use monofilament strings that eliminate this serious risk.

In the 1970s, the Dalkon Shield was a commonly prescribed IUD but after the serious side effects were discovered, a civil law suit was filed by users and their families. The company that made the Dalkon Shield lost the civil lawsuit, subsequently took the product off the market and went out of business.

Unfortunately, many safe IUDs were discontinued because of the costs involved in litigation, even though the companies that produced these products were found innocent of any liability claims. The IUD has now once more become more popular in the United States with three hormonal IUDs and one copper IUD available. IUDs account for 10 percent of contraception use in the United States(Buhling, Zite, Lotke, Black, 2014).

Worldwide, the IUD is the most widely used reversible contraceptive providing 14 percent of all contraception.

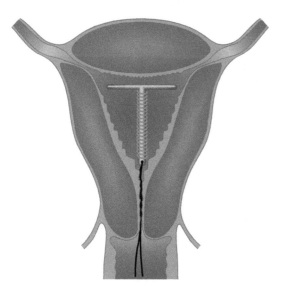

Figure 11.1 *An inserted IUD.*

disadvantages related to the hormones that include headaches, acne, depression and anxiety (Zieman et al., 2016). Figure 11.1 shows an inserted IUD.

Intrauterine devices have the advantage of providing long-term effectiveness. The longest lasting IUD is the copper IUD that can be worn for up to 10 years. The hormonal IUD Mirena can be worn for at least o 5 years, while Skyla and Liletta are effective for at least 3 years. The 5–10 years of contraception costing typically $475–$800 makes both types of IUDs cost effective. The IUDs are safe, very effective, long lasting but easily reversible contraception. In addition, the IUD is convenient and allows spontaneous sexual activity. The IUD is an excellent contraceptive for most women, including teens, who cannot or do not want to take hormones and for women who have and have not had children. IUDs can also be used by women who have had one or more STDs, who have had an ectopic pregnancy and those who are not in monogamous relationships. However, IUDs do not protect against STDs, so condoms will need to be used if the woman has multiple partners or is in a non-monogamous relationships (Zieman et al., 2016; Hatcher et al., 2011).

The IUD is so effective that it can be thought of as reversible sterilization. Typical use effectiveness and perfect-use effectiveness of IUDs are similar. Typical use effectiveness of the copper IUD is 99.2 and perfect use effectiveness is 99.4. For the Mirena, Liletta and Skyla the perfect and typical effectiveness rates are the same, 99.9 percent (Zieman et al., 2016).

Women who want an IUD should choose a health care provider experienced in inserting IUDs. The provider will measure the size and depth of the uterus and will then place the IUD into the uterus using an insertion device. Once the IUD is in place in the uterus, the provider will locate the string attached to the IUD that passes through the cervix into the vagina and trim it to a shorter length. The woman can feel the string to make sure the IUD is in place and should do so each month after her menstrual period ends. Although the woman can find the string with her finger, her sexual partner will not feel the string during intercourse. If the woman experiences bleeding or extreme cramping or cannot find the string, she must go back to the provider immediately.

Hormonal Contraceptives

The methods that prevent the release of an egg are hormonal. Focusing on managing a woman's ovulation has been extremely popular over the years. Hormones can be taken orally, implanted under the skin, by injection, by vaginal insertion, and via a patch.

Contraceptive Implants

Contraceptive implants are among the most effective contraceptive available with a typical and perfect use failure rate of only .05 % making them equal to the IUD and sterilization. Implanon and Nexplanon, the contraceptive implants available in the US, consist of a single rod approximately 4 centimeters long and 2 millimeters in diameter, which is designed to provide hormonally controlled protection for up to 3 years (Planned Parenthood, 2013). The implant releases progestin and within 24 hours of insertion is thought to be reliable. Similar to birth control pills, it works by inhibiting ovulation, thickening cervical mucus so that sperm are inhibited in their travel, and altering the endometrium so that it cannot support a fertilized egg (Zieman et al., 2016; Hatcher et al., 2011). User satisfaction is high for this method perhaps due to the ease of use, relief of dysmenorrhea and discreetness of method. Like other hormonal forms of birth control, it offers no protection against sexually transmitted infection. Irregular bleeding and headaches are the most reported disadvantages.

Oral Contraceptives

Oral contraceptives are formulated as combination pills of synthetic estrogen and progesterone, or progestin-only pills (POPs), commonly referred to as minipills. Combination pills are the most commonly used oral contraceptives. The combinations and levels of hormones contained in birth control pills have been changing constantly since their introduction in the early 1960s. Pills that are currently available contain the minimum levels of hormones necessary to carry out their intended functions and are much lower

Birth control pills come in containers that are easy to use and allow you to see if you've missed any.

than the original formulations. This has resulted in a safer pill with fewer side effects (Hatcher et al,. 2011). In fact, using the birth control pill is safer than carrying a pregnancy to term. The risk of death in healthy, young, nonsmokers is 240 times lower than death from pregnancy related complications (American College of Obstetricians and Gynecologists, 2013).

Combination birth control pills work in several ways. The progestins in the combination oral contraception provide most of the contraceptive effect by suppressing ovulation and causing the cervical mucus to thicken. The progestins stop the pituitary gland from secreting leutinizing hormone (LH), the hormone that induces ovulation. Estrogen also contributes to stopping ovulation by suppressing the release of follicle stimulating hormone (FSH), which is necessary for the release of a mature ovum (Hatcher et al., 2011).

Normally, levels of estrogen, FSH, and leutinizing hormone (LH) are low during the initial phases of the menstrual cycle. The hypothalamus senses this and triggers the pituitary gland to secrete estrogen, FSH, and LH just prior to midcycle. If there is no surge of these substances, there is no release of a mature ovum.

Oral contraceptives are highly effective in controlling fertility. The typical effectiveness is 91 percent; perfect use effectiveness is over 99 percent. The drop off is associated with human error in failing to take pills consistently and correctly. For women who correctly and consistently use the pill, even the first year failure rate is less than 1% (Hatcher et al, 2011). The key to success is highly motivated pill users who may even go so far as to set a daily alarm to make sure they take the pill on time.

Traditionally, birth control pills were packaged in 28-pill packages that included seven hormone free placebo pills designed to help keep the woman on schedule. Women now have many more choices with varying numbers of active pills and hormone free pills. Seasonal has 84 consecutive hormone pills with 7 placebo pills. This allows the woman to have only 4 periods of menstrual bleeding per year. Yaz and Loestrin-24 have 24 days of hormone pills and only 4 days of placebo. Lybrel, has no hormone free days allowing users to avoid having a menstrual period for a full year (Zieman et al., 2016).

Women are instructed to use a quick start method when prescribed the pill. Using quick start, the woman takes her first pill immediately in the health care provider's office and must then use back up contraception, such as a condom, for 7 days (Zieman et al., 2016). This appears to improve the likelihood that she will continue taking the pill (Plastino & Sulak, 2008). The woman will then take a pill each day until she has consumed them all. The length of time will depend on what type of hormone regimen she has chosen.

Consistent use is crucial for maximum effectiveness. The woman should try to take the pill at the same time each day. This will help develop the habit of taking one pill each day, keep the same amount of hormones in the blood level, and ensure consistent use. Some women prefer to take the pill each morning as part of their ritual for getting ready for school or work. Others take it at night as part of a night-time sleep ritual. Taking the pill at night can help reduce the nausea some women experience. The time is up to her. Taking the birth control pill should become part of her lifestyle, just like brushing her teeth. It needs to become so routine that she doesn't even have to think about it.

If a pill is missed, the woman should immediately take the missed pill and resume her regular schedule. Missing one pill will not compromise the effectiveness of the method. Missing two pills, however, does reduce the effectiveness of oral contraceptives, and a backup fertility control method such as condoms will be necessary. If she misses two pills, she should take two immediately and two the next day. After that, she should continue to take one each day until they are all gone.

Long-Acting Combination Pills   In 2003, the FDA approved an oral contraceptive called Seasonale. Women take tablets with combination hormones for 84 days, followed by 1 week of placebo tablets, making a 91-day regimen. Women using Seasonale will get their periods four times per year, rather than the monthly periods associated with traditional birth control pills. An advantage is that it may be more effective and easier to remember because hormones are take each day. Many women enjoy having fewer periods. Having fewer periods has no negative health effects (Zieman et al., 2016).

Progestin-Only Pills   Also it referred to as *minipills,* progestin-only pills are to be taken every day. The same precautions and instructions for missed combination pills apply to the minipill. Progestin, the same artificial progesterone used in combination pills, is taken by itself. It works primarily by thickening the cervical mucous which prevents the sperm from entering the uterus (Zieman et al., 2016).

Advantages   Birth control pills offer many advantages for women. There is no interruption during sexual activity allowing more spontaneity. They are frequently prescribed for women with irregular periods to regulate the menstrual cycle as well as to provide fertility control protection. Other menstrual advantages include lessening of cramps, decreasing the amount of bleeding, decreasing symptoms of PMS, and eliminating ovulation pain. While taking hormonal contraception females have what is referred to as withdrawal bleeding instead of a true menstrual period. Other benefits are the decrease in the risks of both ovarian and endometrial cancer thus protecting a woman from two causes of infertility. Hormonal contraceptives decrease a female's risk of dying from colon cancer and decreases benign breast conditions such as cysts. The pill is also beneficial in the treatment of acne and will decrease menstrual migraine headaches and iron deficiency anemia (Zieman et al., 2016; Hatcher et al., 2011).

Disadvantages   Some women experience negative side effects when taking oral contraceptives. The most common side effects mimic symptoms attributed to pregnancy: nausea, vomiting, breast tenderness, and headaches. A loss of sex drive and anorgasmia are also possible side effects. Although hormonal contraceptives can have some side effects, there are also myths about side

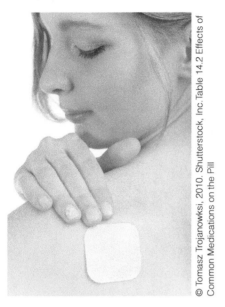

© Tomasz Trojanowksi, 2010. Shutterstock, Inc. Table 14.2 Effects of Common Medications on the Pill

The patch can be placed on the shoulder, arm, or abdomen, but never on the breast.

effects of the pill. One myth is that the pill decreases fertility when taken for a long time. The opposite is actually true; the pill protects women from some of the causes of infertility such as endometriosis, fibroids and cancer of the ovaries and endometrium, It is also a myth that the pill can harm a fetus if taken while pregnant. One major worry for many women is that the pill may cause weight gain. This is also not true as shown in studies comparing pill users and non pill users. There is also no increased risk of breast cancer among pill users, another scary myth. (Zieman et al., 2016; Hatcher et al., 2011).

Many of the side effects of the pill can be minimized or eliminated by changing the formula or brand of pill. Combination pills differ slightly by manufacturer in the amounts of estrogen and progesterone. If the combination of these hormones in the present pill is causing unacceptable side effects, the health care provider can change the prescription and the woman can try a different formulation. The birth control pill also can interact with other medications. Some drugs decrease the effectiveness of hormonal contraception thus increasing the risk of pregnancy. In some cases, hormonal contraceptives lessen the effectiveness of the other medications. It is important for a woman to tell her health care provider that she is taking hormonal contraceptives when any other drug is being prescribed to check for interactions.

Oral contraceptives are not recommended for women who have a history of high blood pressure or stroke; blood clots or a history of blood clots; have or had breast cancer; women who have severe migraines; and women who are over 35 and smoke 15 cigarettes or more a day. Women who smoke should quit smoking to allow them to safely use hormonal contraceptives. It is important to remember that the majority of young healthy women are good candidates for hormone based contraception (Zieman et al., 2016).

Although, as with any medication, the risks associated with oral contraceptives have to be considered, most of them can be reduced through proper screening of the woman by a health care professional. The benefits far outweigh the risks.

Birth Control Patch

The birth control patch administers hormones through the skin, and has effectiveness rates similar to birth control pills. The patch is thin, beige in color, and measures 1.75 inches on each side. A woman wears a patch for 1 week, replaces it on the same day for 3 consecutive weeks, and is "patch-free" during the fourth week (Planned Parenthood, 2017). One advantage of the patch is that it may be easier for women who forget to take a daily pill. The disadvantages are similar to the pill and include possible headaches, nausea and breast tenderness. In addition, some women experience skin irritation at the site of application. As with all the forms of hormonal contraception, the effectiveness for pregnancy prevention is high (91% typical use and 99 percent perfect use), but there is no protection against STDs (Zieman et al., 2016, Hatcher et al., 2011).

Women have two options for the first cycle of using the patch; start within 5 days of first day of period or start the patch on the day they are most likely to remember to change it each week. If she starts the patch later than five days after her period begins, she will also need to use 7 days of additional protection. Women can apply the patch to the buttocks, lower abdomen, upper torso, or upper arm. *The patch may not be applied to the breasts.* The manufacturer advises that the patch not be put where makeup, lotions, or creams are applied. The adhesive on the patch is designed to last the week, regardless of showering or bathing, swimming, exercise, or humidity.

Vaginal Contraceptive Ring (NuvaRing)

The NuvaRing works on the principle of a woman having a 28-day cycle: 3 weeks of hormonal control followed by 1 week of no hormones thus allowing withdrawal bleeding. The NuvaRing appears similar to the plastic ring at the end of the female condom, and it is inserted by the woman deep into the vagina, where it remains for 3 weeks. Insertion is relatively simple, involving folding the ring and pushing it up the vagina. At the end of the 3-week period, the ring is removed by hooking the index finger under the ring and pulling it out. Couples do not feel the ring, and it rarely falls out. As with other hormonal contraceptives, the typical use effectiveness is 91 percent and perfect use effectiveness 99 percent. When first using the ring, it can be inserted at any time but seven days of back up contraception must be used (Zieman et al., 2016).

A major advantage of the vaginal contraceptive ring is that the woman only has to remember to put it in and take it out once a month. This may be easier for some women to remember. Additional advantages are that most women do not experience weight gain and the ring is not visible, thus allowing contraceptive privacy. Possible disadvantages are similar to the pill: headaches and nausea. (Zieman, 2016: Hatcher et al., 2011).

Injectable Contraceptive

Depo-Provera, the most commonly used injectable contraceptive, is a progestin-only hormonal contraceptive. Its action is the same as the mini-pill. A major advantage of Depo-Provera over these other methods is the way in which it is administered: by injection every 3 months. The injections can be administered in either the arm or the buttocks. A single injection provides 3 months' worth of protection.

Depo-Provera has one of the highest typical use effectiveness rates of all fertility control methods, at 94% typical use and a perfect use of 99 percent. This rate can be attributed mostly to the nature of administering the product. There is no room for actual-use error. Once the shot is administered, the user doesn't have to remember to do anything. Depo-Provera works by inhibiting ovulation, thickening the cervical mucus to block sperm, thinning the uterine lining and slowing tubal motility (Zieman et al., 2016).

Advantages of Depro-Provera include decreased menstrual blood, loss of menstruation by half of all users, and after five years of use, 80 percent of women have no menstrual period. Women have a decrease in PMS, menstrual cramps and endometriosis. Because Depo-Provera does not contain estrogen, it does not produce many of the disadvantages associated with combination pills. Nevertheless, it does require a woman to visit a health care provider every three months which can be burdensome for some women. It can cause progressive weight gain, 5.4 pounds average during the first year; 16 pounds after three years. It also produces scanty

Table 11.2 Comparison of Newer Contraceptive Methods

Device	Monthly Injectable	Implant	Intrauterine System	Ring	Patch
Office visits	Once/month	Insertion/ removal	Insertion/ removal	Prescription	Prescription
Easily reversible	Yes	Yes	Yes	Yes	Yes
Dosing frequency*	Once/month	3–5 years	1–10 years	Every 4 weeks	Weekly
User controlled	No	No	No	Yes	Yes
Discreet	Yes	Sometimes	Yes	Yes	Sometimes

*The type of hormonal implant and intrauterine device/system will determine the dosing frequency.

Sources: Adapted from Baylor College of Medicine (2002) and Planned Parenthood Federation of America (2003).

Amenorrhea Absence of menstruation at some time after a female has reached menses

menstrual flow and **amenorrhea** in some women and irregular but long periods in others. Prolonged use of Depo-Provera may result in temporary and usually reversible loss of bone density. It is also long acting and return to fertility after last shot takes on average ten months, delaying pregnancy for those who are ready to become pregnant. Some women also experience an increase in depression when using Depo-Provera (Zieman et al., 2016; Hatcher et al., 2011)

Emergency Contraception—Back up for Contraception Failure

The most effective emergency contraception in the Copper T IUD and can be inserted up to 5 days after unprotected intercourse. It will then also provide long term protection against pregnancy. Ten time fewer pregnancies will occur when using the Copper T IUD as emergency contraception than when emergency contraceptive pills are used. If pills are used as emergency contraception, they will be progestin only hormones taken as a single pill. Emergency contraceptive pills are now available in the US on the shelf in the family planning aisle with no age restriction. Some of the choices include Plan B One Step, and Next Choice One Dose, My Way and Take Action. Ella is the most effective emergency contraceptive pill but a prescription is needed for ella. It is wise for all sexually active women to buy a supply in advance in case it is needed since it is designed to be administered as soon as possible after unprotected intercourse. It is most effective when used within 12 hours but can be used up to 5 days after unprotected sex. The sooner it is used, the more effective it will be. The early administration of the pills works to delay or prevent ovulation, inhibit fertilization or may at times prevent implantation of a fertilized egg. It never works to disrupt an implanted pregnancy and therefore is not an abortion. Nausea and vomiting are side effects experienced by 13–29% of women. Taking emergency contraception, even for multiple times, has no effect on future pregnancies or fertility nor does it cause birth defects if the woman is pregnant when she takes it. However, emergency contraception is not recommended for routine use since it is less effective than many contraceptives. If a woman does not get her menstrual period within 3 weeks, it is recommended that she take a pregnancy test (Hatcher et al., 2011). Overall, the rate of effectiveness is between 75 and 89 percent (Zieman et al., 2016).

Male Condom

The male condom is one of the oldest known fertility devices. Three types of condoms are currently available in the United States: latex, polyurethane, and natural lamb membrane. As more aggressive efforts were made to reduce the incidence of HIV/AIDS, condom promotion around the world has increased. Along with that has come more creative marketing, packaging, and choices, including shapes, colors, thickness and sizes. Each type is manufactured under stringent quality control and tested electronically before being sold (Hatcher et al., 2011). Almost all tested condoms meet the stringent standards with no differences found based on price, thickness or manufacturing country (Consumers Union, 2009). Condoms are easily transportable, an appealing feature, but should not be stored too long (one month maximum) in a wallet (Zieman, 2016).

The male condom works by covering the penis and trapping the ejaculate, thereby preventing it from being deposited in the vagina. A major advantage of condoms is that they reduce the risk of transmitting STD organisms that might be present in the ejaculate, vaginal fluids, vagina or on the penis. In addition, some men have more ejaculatory control with condoms, making intercourse more pleasurable (Zieman et al., 2016).

If a couple plans to use condoms as a primary birth control, they are advised to buy emergency contraceptive pills in advance to have in case the condom slips or breaks. The condom slipping or breaking happens in approximately 3–5 percent of all acts of intercourse using a condom (Zieman et al., 2016).

Latex Condoms   Latex condoms come in a variety of shapes, colors, and sizes. Latex condoms come individually wrapped in foil or other sealed packets. They are rolled up to the size of a half-dollar or are folded.

Latex condoms can be lubricated or non-lubricated. Spermicidal condoms are no longer recommended since they provide no additional protection against pregnancy and STD's (Zieman, 2016). Most non-lubricated latex condoms are dusted with powder or cornstarch to facilitate putting them on an erect penis. Latex condoms come in a variety of shapes. The traditional shape is a long, uniform sheath, with a rounded end and now, condoms that are tapered toward the closed end are also available. Each of these shapes comes with the choice of a reservoir tip, a small nipple that protrudes about 3/4 inch at the sealed end, to catch the ejaculate. Latex condoms also can be scented or unscented, flavored or unflavored, colored or transparent, and ribbed or smooth.

Form-fitting condoms generally mimic the shape of the penis. They are wider at the opening and taper to their narrowest dimension close to the

Pinch or twist the tip of the condom, leaving one-half inch at the tip to catch the semen.

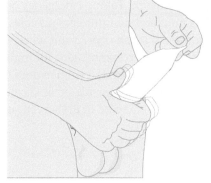

Holding the tip, unroll the condom.

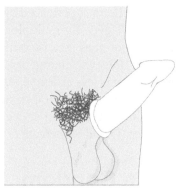

Unroll the condom until it reaches the pubic hairs.

Figure 11.2 *How to Use a Condom*

end, where they flare out again in the shape of the glans of the penis. They tend to fit more snuggly than traditionally shaped condoms.

Typical use effectiveness of the condom is 82 percent although perfect use effectiveness is 98 percent. Stringent manufacturing standards ensure uniformly high quality. The most common reason for condom failure is that couples do not use a condom during every act of intercourse. Two other contributors to failure are slippage and breakage of condom which happens in 3–5 percent of all acts of intercourse. Latex condoms are less likely to slip or break than are the polyurethane condoms. Vigorous sex can break the condoms and should be a consideration while using condoms (Zieman, et al., 2016). Proper condom technique will help prevent failure. (Hatcher, et al., 2011). Figure 11.2 describes the steps involved in using a male condom properly.

Some men and women are allergic to latex and itch, become dry, burn, and develop a rash when exposed to it. These people may not be able to use latex condoms (or diaphragms). They are good candidates for natural membrane condoms or the female condom. However, the natural membrane condoms may not provide the same level of STD protection as latex and polyurethane condoms (Zieman et al., 2016).

The marketing of condoms has become creative and diversified over the years. Durex's Performa and Trojan's Extended Pleasure are marketed to help males prolong excitement and delay ejaculation. By placing benzocaine, a mild anesthetic, inside the tip of the condom, the medication can numb the head of the penis yet not be transferred externally to one's partner. Condoms are also produced in flavors such as chocolate and mint, to encourage their usage during oral sex. Other condoms are marketed to the gay community along with messages about their value as part of safer sex practices.

Natural Lamb Membrane Condoms Unlike their latex cousins, natural lamb membrane condoms are not uniformly manufactured from scratch. They are made from the intestines of commercially slaughtered lambs. They are shipped to the condom manufacturer, where they are cleaned and inspected prior to being cut and sealed at one end. Even though each condom is slightly different from the next, they all must pass safety inspections and are held to the same standards as latex condoms.

Natural membrane condoms tend to fit more loosely than latex condoms. Some secure themselves to the penis with the help of a small elastic band sewn into the base. Others are snugger and grip the penis much like a latex condom. Natural lamb condoms are wet. They are sealed in a foil or other pouch with more liquid than latex condoms to keep them from deteriorating.

Natural lamb condoms offer an entirely different feel than their latex cousins. They simulate human tissue as closely as is possible. The combination of the material (lamb membrane), its wetness, and the loose fit makes natural lamb condoms feel almost like the lining of the vagina or mouth.

Condoms come in different colors and styles.

© dino o, 2010. Shutterstock, Inc.

As a cautionary note, studies have shown that the surface of natural skin condoms contains small pores that permit the passage of viruses, including the hepatitis B virus, herpes simplex virus, and HIV (Centers for Disease Control, 2011). Sperm, however, are not able to penetrate these pores because sperm are much larger than viruses.

Female Condom

The female condom is a loose-fitting polyurethane sheath that is inserted into the vagina, covering its walls and protruding over the vulva. The female condom works by containing a man's semen after he ejaculates into his partner's vagina. It also offers protection against STD bacteria or viruses that might be in the man's semen or on the penis.

Female condoms are made from a polyurethane material that is similar to latex but is less penetrable. The female condom is lubricated with a silicon based lubricant. Unlike the male condom, it does not come in different shapes, sizes, colors, or flavors. Female condoms are uniform in size and have a ring at both ends. The rings help with insertion and to ensure a proper fit. The ring at the closed end loops around the cervix, anchoring it in place in a way that is similar to a diaphragm, although the female condom does not require a prescription. The female condom is inserted like a diaphragm. You first fold the ring in half, then insert it similar to the way a tampon is inserted and finally you check to feel the inner ring notch against the cervix (see Figure 11.3).

A major advantage of the female condom is that it provides women a reliable source of nonprescription protection against both pregnancy and STDs. A woman does not have to rely on her partner for this protection; she can control the method. It can also be inserted up to 8 hours prior to intercourse adding convenience and sexual spontaneity as an advantage. A disadvantage of the female condom is that it costs more than a male condom. Like the male condom, it can be used only once. It is considered at least as effective as the male condom in preventing transmission of STDs, including HIV.

The typical use effectiveness of female condoms is 79 percent; perfect use effectiveness is 95 percent; (Zieman et al., 2016; Hatcher et al., 2011). Researchers found that the female condom rarely breaks, although slippage occurs in approximately 1 in 10 uses, and women may be exposed to semen

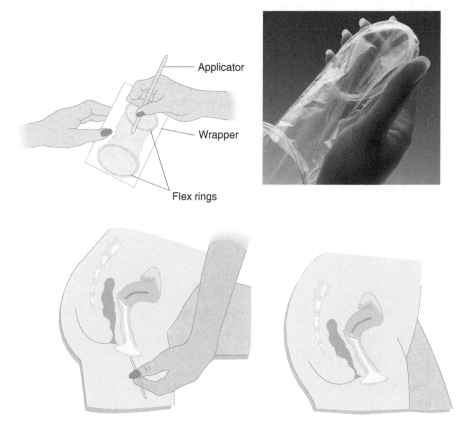

Figure 11.3 *Inserting a Female Condom*

in up to 1 in 5 uses. Furthermore, a woman is most likely to be exposed to semen if she and her partner experience mechanical problems with the condom, if there is a large disparity between the size of the penis and the size of the woman's vagina, and if intercourse is very active (Guttmacher Institute, 2003). Couples should not use a male condom at the same time they are using the female condom as it will increase the risk of breakage (Zieman et al., 2016). As with the male condoms, couples should have emergency contraception available in case the condom slips, or the female is exposed to semen.

Diaphragm and Cervical Cap

The diaphragm is a spring-loaded silicon dome shaped device that is inserted into the vagina and anchored between the wall of the vagina and the cervix (see Figure 11.4). It is non-lubricated, so before insertion, 2–3 teaspoons of spermicide must be placed around the rim and on the inside of the dome for it to work properly. It is not designed to form an impenetrable barrier against the cervix. It works by covering the cervix and thereby blocking access of most sperm to the egg. Any sperm that are able to get around the edge of the diaphragm are immobilized by the spermicide contained in the dome. The diaphragm should be left in place for at least six but no more than 24 hours after intercourse. A condom or extra spermicide should be used for every additional act of intercourse.

healthy sex hints 11.1

Eroticizing Condom Use

Condoms have been making a steady resurgence as a contraceptive method, yet many couples still find condom use unacceptable or not as desirable as making love without one. The following tips on eroticizing condom use might change your thinking about them.

1. It's all in your head (the one on your shoulders).
   - Start to examine your thoughts about condoms.
   - Don't buy into the myth that you can't have great sex if you use a condom.
2. Be prepared.
   - Keep a supply of condoms handy.
   - Distribute packets in the bedroom chest, living room end table, downstairs and upstairs bathrooms, and other places where you might have intercourse.
3. Practice condom use by yourself.
   - Men: Masturbate using a condom (this will help you get used to the feel); practice putting one on under a variety of conditions (in the dark, with lights, one-handed, and so forth)
   - Women: Practice putting a condom on a simulated penis (such as a banana); practice putting one on with your mouth. It can add a fun element to condom use when the female put it on the penis.
4. Try several styles/brands.
   - Find a favorite size, scent, brand and style that feels right for you. This makes condom use safer since a too large condom may slip off and a too small condom may be uncomfortable
5. Use extra lubrication.
   - Smear some water or silicon-based lubricant on the outside before penetration. This will help prevent the condom from breaking. Never put lubricant inside the condom
6. Make condom use (and penetration) just one part of lovemaking.
   - Read Chapter 6 about viewing lovemaking as a gourmet meal (you can enjoy a lot of erotic delights before even putting on the condom).
7. Immediately after ejaculation and before the loss of erection, hold the condom firmly against the base of your penis and pull out.
   - Check for breakage and dispose. If breakage is found, immediately use emergency contraception.
8. Take turns with birth control.
   - Trade off responsibility every month (male condoms this month, female condoms or oral sex the next month, and so on), and you might find using a condom less objectionable.

A diaphragm must be fitted by an experienced health care professional. This person can determine the proper size to fit into the vagina so the diaphragm will rest comfortably between the cervix and the top portion of the vagina. Diaphragms should be refitted if the woman gains or loses more than 10 pounds, has an abortion, or has a full-term pregnancy (Hatcher et al., 2011).

Typical use effectiveness is 88 percent—higher than the male condom; perfect use effectiveness of diaphragms is 94 percent. As with condoms, the drop off in effectiveness is primarily a result of human error associated

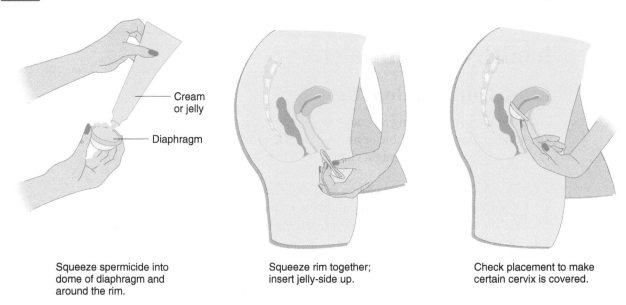

Cream or jelly

Diaphragm

Squeeze spermicide into dome of diaphragm and around the rim.

Squeeze rim together; insert jelly-side up.

Check placement to make certain cervix is covered.

Figure 11.4 *The Diaphragm and How to Insert It*

with incorrect and inconsistent use. It is recommended that women obtain emergency contraception as a backup in advance (Zieman et al., 2016; Hatcher et al., 2011).

Cervical Cap

The cervical cap is a small, thimble-shaped plastic or rubber cap that fits snugly against the cervix through suction. It is available in three sizes and must be fitted by a health care professional. It works in a fashion similar to the diaphragm, blocking the passage of sperm while utilizing spermicidal jelly as a backup to immobilize sperm that may enter around its rim.

The cervical cap differs from the diaphragm in these ways:

- The cervical cap anchors to the cervix through suction rather than by pressing against the walls of the vagina and the cervix the way the diaphragm does.
- The cap is much smaller and less conspicuous than the diaphragm.

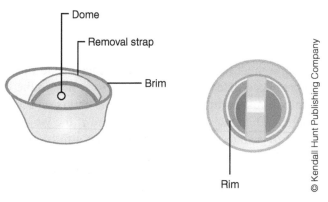

Dome

Removal strap

Brim

Rim

© Kendall Hunt Publishing Company

The cervical cap fits snugly against the cervix.

- The cap requires less spermicide (because of its smaller size).
- The cap does not require additional spermicide with additional episodes of intercourse.

Theoretical effectiveness of the cervical cap is comparable to that of other vaginal barrier methods, those being the female condom, diaphragm, and sponge. However, the cervical cap does not work as well for women who have given birth compared to those who have not. The perfect-use failure rate in the first year for parous women (those who have given birth) is 26 percent compared to 9 percent for nulliparous women (those who have not given birth). The typical-use failure rate, by comparison, for parous women is 40 percent in the first year of use, compared to 20 percent for nulliparous women (Nelson et al., 2000). It is advised, therefore, that emergency contraception be kept as a backup at times of possible failure.

The cervical cap may be inserted up to 6 hours prior to intercourse. It must remain in place at least 6–8 hours but no more than 48 hours after the male ejaculates.

Coitus Interruptus (Withdrawal; Pulling Out)

Coitus interruptus is one of the most commonly used and least understood of all the fertility control strategies. *Coitus interruptus* is a Latin term, literally meaning interrupting intercourse by withdrawing the penis prior to ejaculation.

For a typical, user the probability of pregnancy is about 22% during the first year of use (Hatcher et al., 2011). Two factors seem to contribute to the relatively low typical use effectiveness: human error (not withdrawing the penis in time) and use of the method during peak fertility (mid-cycle versus other times during a woman's menstrual cycle). There is some controversy over whether the pre-ejaculate contains sperm. In two studies no sperm were found in the pre-ejaculate and in two other studies small amounts of sperm were found. Though the number of sperm found were low, there were enough to possibly cause a pregnancy even if the male withdraws his penis before ejaculating (Hatcher et al., 2011).

The number of couples having ever used coitus interruptus as their method is increasing. In 2008, over half of women surveyed answered that they had ever used this method compared to only one in four in 1992 (Hatcher et al., 2011). For women who cannot risk getting pregnant, this is not a reliable choice since it is at the bottom of list of contraceptives in effectiveness. Some users argue that coitus interruptus is free, readily available, and a "natural," "effective" method of fertility control. In a sense, this belief is true. Coitus interruptus is free, it is always available, and it is relatively effective (78 percent versus 15 percent for "hope and a prayer"). Nonetheless, couples would be much wiser to choose a method with higher reliability and STD protection.

You'll remember from Chapter 3 that orgasm in men is a two-step process. The first step, ejaculatory inevitability, begins with the man feeling the contractions initiating the expulsion of semen that occurs during the next step, emission. Many couples, especially sexually inexperienced ones, overestimate the man's ability to withdraw his penis in time if he waits for ejaculatory inevitability. Timing the removal of the penis so closely sets the stage for method failure. This is difficult for sexually inexperienced men to do. Simultaneously, a woman worried about whether her partner will "pull out" in time cannot fully relax and enjoy the lovemaking. (It is possible for couples to practice the timing of withdrawal by having the female use a backup method of birth control.)

Another way to do coitus interruptus is to withdraw prior to any sense of ejaculatory inevitability and finish with a non-penetrative sexual method (such as masturbation) or oral-genital sex. This offers more variety in your sexual experience and reduces the risk of unintended pregnancy. You are able to enjoy vaginal intercourse while reducing the risk of pregnancy.

We suggest that all men who intend to use coitus interruptus urinate before they initiate any sexual activity. Also, we recommend that during sexual arousal and plateau, the couple remove any existing pre-ejaculatory fluid (with a tissue or orally) before intromission of the penis. This will remove some of the fluid. These precautions should also be repeated if more than one act of intercourse occurs.

The last thing to consider with coitus interruptus is your fertility status. One way to increase the effectiveness of coitus interruptus is to limit its use to less fertile times of the menstrual cycle. Avoiding intercourse during peak fertility times will increase its effectiveness.

With typical use effectiveness of 78 percent (Hatcher, 2011), 22 in 100 women using this method in their first year will get pregnant. This effectiveness compares poorly with other contraceptives that are available and offers no protection against transmission of STDs and HIV. This method usually is recommended for couples in disease-free, monogamous relationships for whom a pregnancy would perhaps not be ideal but would be acceptable. For all other couples, having emergency contraception available is essential in case of failure to withdraw before ejaculation begins.

Vaginal Contraceptive Sponge

The vaginal sponge is a soft, white, polyurethane sponge filled with spermicide. It works the same way as the diaphragm and cervical cap: It creates a double barrier (absorbent polyurethane sponge and spermicide) that blocks and absorbs sperm while chemically deactivating them. The sponge needs to be moistened with 1–2 tablespoons of water and inserted deep in the vagina like a diaphragm.

The sponge works for 24 hours even with multiple acts of intercourse so it can be inserted before sexual activity. Women who use the sponge need to wait for 6 hours after intercourse to remove the sponge and should avoid leaving it in for over 24 hours due to the risk of toxic shock syndrome (Hatcher et al., 2011). With the sponge, no additional applications of spermicide are needed if additional ejaculations occur within that time period. This feature allows greater flexibility in sexual activity without the need for using additional spermicides.

A major advantage of the sponge is that it is a nonprescription device. Sponges typically cost $5 unless obtained for free at a family planning clinic. Like the diaphragm and the cervical cap, the vaginal contraceptive sponge provides a protective barrier against the cervix. If used many times a day the nonoxynol-9 in the sponge may irritate the vaginal lining and make users more at risk for STD and HIV transmission (Planned Parenthood, 2013).

For women who have never had children, the vaginal contraceptive sponge is similar in effectiveness to the diaphragm and the cervical cap. Its typical effectiveness is 88 percent, and perfect use effectiveness is 91 percent. It is less effective in women who have previously had a child (Zieman et al., 2016; Hatcher, 2011). It is advised, therefore, that emergency contraception be kept as a backup at times of possible failure.

Spermicides

A wide variety of chemical spermicides are available as stand-alone fertility control methods or to be used in conjunction with mechanical barriers as previously discussed. They all work by immobilizing and killing sperm, though they vary in form and method of application. They are available as nonprescription fertility control devices at most drug stores. It was previously thought that nonoxynol-9 was also effective in killing the organisms that cause syphilis, gonorrhea, and genital herpes, HIV/AIDS, and other STDs. To the contrary, the frequent use (more than two times a day) of nonoxynol-9 may actually increase the prospects of infection transmission due to irritating the skin (Hatcher et al., 2011).

The best-known spermicides are foams, gels, and creams. These work by creating a chemical barrier suspended in a shaving-cream-like foam, clear gel, or smooth cream. All three are inserted into the vagina, near the cervix, using a cylindrical applicator (see Figure 11.5). They create an immediate, effective chemical barrier against sperm. These spermicides may be inserted no more than 1 hour prior to intercourse.

Spermicidal film is different, however, because it is not immediately effective. It takes about 15 minutes to transform from its original shape into an effervescent liquid once inserted into the vagina (VCF Contraceptive. com, 2016).

Spermicidal suppositories are waxlike cylinders about the size of earplugs. They are applied in the same way as rectal suppositories, except

Selected spermacide products

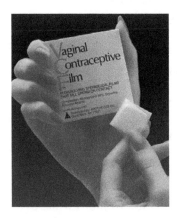
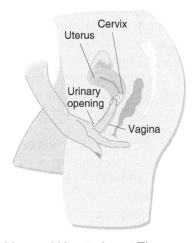

Figure 11.5 *Selected Spermicides and How to Insert Them*

into the vagina. Like film, the suppository requires about 15 minutes to liquefy after insertion into the vagina.

The effectiveness of vaginal spermicides is similar regardless of the specific type. Foam, gel, cream, film, and suppositories are much the same in outcome. The typical use effectiveness of spermicides is 72 percent; perfect use effectiveness is 82 percent.

Women who are at high risk for HIV should not use spermicides because these products may actually increase the risk of transmission. Spermicides should also be avoided by women who are not willing to accept the high risk of failure. To improve effectiveness, spermicides can be combined with condoms.

Fertility Awareness

Fertility awareness Natural family planning

Fertility awareness, also known as *natural family planning* and the *rhythm method,* is a strategy based on avoiding unprotected intercourse during peak fertility. Peak fertility can be estimated by combining knowledge about an individual woman's menstrual cycle with the latest scientific findings about egg and sperm viability. The four fertility awareness methods are calendar, basal body temperature, cervical mucus, and combined. Each of these methods requires understanding of the specific woman's menstrual cycle and her fertile periods, discussed in Chapter 13. Perfect-use effectiveness data for individual fertility awareness methods are shown in Table 11.1.

Calendar Method   The calendar method of fertility awareness uses the menstrual cycle history to estimate future ovulation. Once a woman can estimate the day she is likely to ovulate, she can build a **safe zone** around this day by factoring in how long an egg (24 hours) and sperm (5 days) can live. This safe zone represents days prior to and after ovulation when the presence of live sperm could result in fertilization.

Safe zone A fertility awareness concept that factors ovulation and length of time sperm and eggs can live as a time to avoid intercourse

Cervical Mucus Method   The cervical mucus method works by checking changes in cervical mucus during the menstrual cycle to predict ovulation. Mucus present in the cervix and vagina cause changes described as "wet" or "dry." In general, wet conditions represent fertile, unsafe days, and dry conditions designate infertile, safe days.

As a caution, production of mucus and vaginal/vulval wetness can be altered by antihistamines and other medications, douching, vaginal infection, contraceptive foam, jelly, and lubricants. For maximum effectiveness, this method should be combined with the calendar method to cross-validate the conclusion. For instance, if your calendar indicates that you are approaching midcycle and you don't feel the characteristic wetness, something may have altered your production of mucus. When in doubt, use a backup method.

Basal Body Temperature   To practice this method, you will need a basal body thermometer. This method relies on recognizing the slight, but measurable, change in basal **body temperature (BBT)** associated with ovulation (Hatcher et al., 1998).

Basal body temperature (BBT) The lowest body temperature of a healthy person during waking hours

Because this method does not predict ovulation (it notes when ovulation occurs), sexual activity prior to temperature changes may result in unintended pregnancy. Therefore, this method is best used in combination with either the calendar or the cervical mucus method, which help predict ovulation. The temperature charts should match the calendar charting of safe and unsafe days and the characteristics of wet and dry mucus.

Non-penetrative Sexual Release

Non-penetrative activities are sometimes referred to as **outercourse** and include massage, masturbation, manual stimulation of one's partner, and the like. These activities provide sexual release but do not involve vaginal penetration (McDonough, 1995). It is important to understand that there are lots of ways to be sexual without risking pregnancy.

Outercourse Nonpenetrative sexual activities such as massage and masturbation

The typical use effectiveness of sexual activities that do not involve vaginal penetration has not been established. f vaginal penetration doesn't occur, no mechanism is available for live sperm to reach a mature ovum. Perfect use effectiveness, therefore, should approach 100 percent.

Unprotected anal intercourse is not included in this group because, although it doesn't involve vaginal penetration, the close proximity of the anus could allow migration of fluids across the perineum and into the vagina. Ejaculating near the vagina is discouraged for this reason.

Celibacy/Abstinence

The first category of non-penetrative methods is celibacy and abstinence. These two terms are often used interchangeably, yet their meanings are distinct. Although the definition of celibacy means to avoid sexual relations, the term is often most associated with a religious decision not to marry. Abstinence refers to practicing self-restraint and, in the area of fertility control, not having sexual intercourse. Abstinence is an important method for reducing unintended pregnancy and STD's. Individuals choose abstinence for a variety of reasons throughout the life span. People often assume that celibacy and abstinence mean total avoidance of all forms of sexual release. This is not true. A person can be celibate or abstain from sexual intercourse but still masturbate or use other forms of non--penetrative behaviors to release sexual tension (Norris, 1996).

Many researchers have addressed the issue of failure rates of abstinence, partially in an attempt to counter the rhetoric that only abstinence is 100 percent effective. As with any method, perfect use effectiveness rates differ from typical use effectiveness rates. User failure rates are connected to how correctly and consistently the method is used. If an individual practices abstinence at a particular point in time, that person will never become pregnant or get a partner pregnant. When abstinence as a method fails, it is because of user failure (Pinkerton, 2001).

Outercourse Activities

Couples may choose to touch each other in a variety of ways that do not risk pregnancy. For example, the sucking, licking and rubbing, and tongue probing associated with kissing are pleasurable while imposing no risk for pregnancy. Kissing usually is associated with hugging and rubbing. Once commonly referred to as petting, these activities can take on new meaning when visualized as a viable form of fertility control. Hugging and rubbing, even with the clothes on, can be intensely pleasurable and can be carried to the point of orgasm with no risk of pregnancy. With a little imagination, these safe sex activities can be erotic and provide a satisfying outlet for sexual desire by themselves or when other fertility control methods are unavailable.

Somewhat riskier are activities in which partners are partially clothed or naked. The risk is that it puts the participants in a very tempting situation that may be difficult to control. Non-genital massage is a great sensual delight and can be a stand-alone sensual activity or part of activities culminating with orgasm. Partners can manually stimulate each other to orgasm without worrying about conception. Sex toys also offer a safe, low-pregnancy-risk sexual option

The various forms of oral-genital sexual contact (fellatio, cunnilingus, anilingus) offer a sexual option with low risk for pregnancy. Unlike abstinence and non-enetrative sexual behavior, however, oral-genital sexual contact can pose risks of disease transmission. We will discuss these risks in detail in Chapter 6.

The mechanical devices use latex and polyurethane barriers to cover the penis (male condom), line the vagina (female condom), or protect the cervix (diaphragm, sponge, cervical cap). The chemical devices either provide a stand alone spermicidal barrier that covers the cervix (foam, suppositories, film) or are used in combination with a mechanical device (gel/diaphragm or cap, spermicide impregnated in sponge, spermicidal lubricant for condoms.

Barrier methods Nonsurgical contraceptive measures that prevent the sperm and egg from uniting

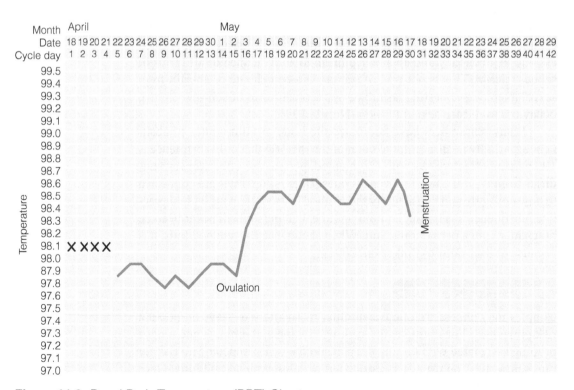

Figure 11.6 *Basal Body Temperature (BBT) Chart*

Future Methods for Males

It should be obvious that the hormonal discussion so far focuses solely on the female body. Over the years, the research question has been posited as to whether hormonal control of male sperm production would be possible. Giving synthetic androgens to men, whether orally, by injection, or by implant, could theoretically reduce sperm production. Finding the right reduction in testosterone without affecting a man's sex drive and causing other side effects is the challenge. Gossypol, made from cottonseed oil, has been shown in large studies to stop sperm production without changing testosterone levels. Another promising option for further research is anticancer drugs that reduce normal sperm production. This challenging research is continuing but it does not appear that any new options for male contraception will be available any time soon (Hatcher et al., 2011).

Permanent Birth Control

Sterilization is the most common form of contraception used today in the United States and in the rest of the world (Hatcher et al., 2011). The sterilization methods that prevent sperm from reaching the ova consist of vasectomy and tubal sterilization. Sterilization does not prevent sperm and ova from being released. It works by blocking the path of either the sperm or the egg as a result of surgical removal of a small section of the vas deferens (vasectomy) in the male or fallopian tubes (laproscopic, mini-laparotomy, and hysteroscopic) in the female The ends of the vas deferens and fallopian tubes are closed in a variety of ways including sealing with heat, using rings or clips or stitching shut.

> Sterilization Techniques (vasectomy and tubal ligation) that prevent sperm from reaching ova

All sterilization procedures should be viewed as permanent, because once these structures have been surgically altered, there is no guarantee that they can be rejoined. Ova or sperm that are produced after sterilization cannot continue their journey, so they die, break down, and are excreted from the body as waste products.

Both male and female sterilization have a typical and perfect use effectiveness rates of higher than 99 percent.

Of the two procedures, vasectomy is the simplest and significantly less costly than female sterilization. Vasectomies are performed as outpatient visits and last no longer than 30 minutes. Female sterilization is also relatively simple and usually takes under an hour to perform.

Both procedures require a conference with the person desiring sterilization to ensure that he or she understands the permanence of the procedure. The majority of women and men do not regret their decision to have the sterilization procedures. However, for both sexes regret was more common in those who chose to have the procedure before age 30. A change in life circumstances during the rest of the reproductive years may contribute to this regret and caution is advised (Hatcher et al., 2011).

Vasectomy

No major preoperative testing procedures are done for a vasectomy. The patient is given a local anesthetic in the scrotal skin, not the vas deferens and remains awake throughout the entire procedure (see Figure 11.7).

> Vasectomy A male sterilization procedure in which the vas deferens are cut and tied, clipped or heated to block the transport of sperm

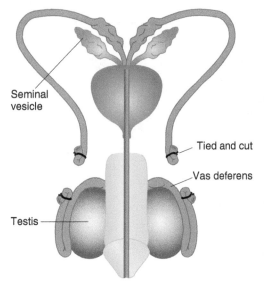

Seminal vesicle

Tied and cut

Vas deferens

Testis

Figure 11.7 *Vasectomy*

The physician locates the vas deferens and makes a small puncture in the scrotal sac, isolates the vas deferens and cuts out a small piece. The two surfaces are then clipped, treated with heat or tied off and the scrotal incisions closed. (Cutie & Dorgara, 2012). The same procedure is repeated on the other vas deferens. The patient is instructed to rest for a short time and is then free to leave. The entire outpatient stay is usually no more than an hour.

It is recommended that patients rest for 2 days, and wait a week before having intercourse or exercising strenuously. Sperm will remain in the body of many men for as long as 3 months requiring use of a condom or other back up method of birth control. Men are instructed to bring a semen specimen in for analysis after 3 months and a minimum of 20 ejaculations. This is the most reliable way to make sure there are no remaining sperm in the body and if the test is negative, intercourse is safe without a backup method (Cutie & Dorgara, 2012).

Side effects of a vasectomy are relatively mild; the most common are pain and tenderness. These can be minimized or controlled by wearing scrotal support (brief style underwear) and keeping an icepack on the scrotum for 4 hours to reduce the chances of swelling, bleeding or pain. Analgesics can also help reduce discomfort (Hatcher et al., 2011).

Female Sterilization

There are three commonly used methods of female sterilization, laparoscopy, mini laparotomy and hysteroscopic. The laparoscopy and mini laparotomy are surgical procedures and are often call a tubal ligation or having your tubes tied. The hysteroscopic procedure is not a surgical procedure but involves inserting a device in the fallopian tubes.

Laparoscopy (tubal ligation)is an outpatient procedure using either general or spinal anesthesia. A small incision is made near the navel, and a laparoscope is inserted to locate the fallopian tubes. The surgeon then uses rings or clips or heat to close the fallopian tube and then repeats this procedure on the other fallopian tube (see Figure 11.8). Women go home the day of the procedure. This method results in an almost invisible scar and allows women to return to normal activity quickly, within 1–2 days (Bratton & Dutton, 2017; Planned Parenthood, 2017).

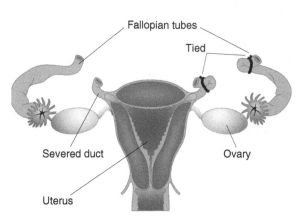

Fallopian tubes

Tied

Severed duct

Ovary

Uterus

Figure 11.8 *Tubal Ligation*

Mini-laparotomy A female sterilization procedure performed following the birth of a child in which the fallopian tubes are cut to block transport of the egg

The **mini-laparotomy (tubal ligation)**, surgical procedure occurs 1–2 days after childbirth and requires either general or local anesthesia. A small incision is made in the abdomen to remove a section of the each fallopian tube. The woman will not have to extend her hospital stay after birth so it is a convenient time for many women. The procedure only takes 20–30 minutes and women usually recover within 1–2 days (Bratton & Dutton, 2017; Planned Parenthood, 2017).

The hysteroscopic procedure was initiated in 2002, when Essure received FDA approval as a new method of sterilization for women. The advantage to the method is that it can be performed as an outpatient procedure without the use of general anesthesia or incision since the path for insertion is through the vagina, cervix, and uterus. A physician inserts a small metal spring into each fallopian tube. The coils lead to the development of scar tissue in the tube, which effectively blocks the passageway. Because it takes approximately 3 months for the fallopian tubes to become blocked, women are advised to use a backup method of birth control until their health care provider confirms that the tubes are blocked with scar tissue. (Bratton & Dutton, 2017; Planned Parenthood, 2017).

The advantages of sterilization include decreased risk of ovarian cancer and decreased worry about pregnancy. The disadvantages are that it is permanent so women need to be certain this is what they want (Zieman et al., 2016).

Laparoscopy Sterilization A female sterilization procedure done at a time other than childbirth in which a surgical instrument is used to cut and tie back the fallopian tubes to block passage of the ova and thereby prevent fertilization

Laparoscope A flexible surgical instrument with a cameralike attachment that can be inserted into the abdomen to view the fallopian tubes and other organs

Seminal vesicle Testis Tied and cut Vas deferens

Terminating an Established Pregnancy

Established pregnancies can be terminated through surgical and medical means. Abortion is defined as the termination, spontaneous or induced, of an established pregnancy and relates to viability. A viable fetus, if born, has a reasonable chance of living. In the United States the time definition for viability is 24 weeks (gestational age starting at conception).

About one-third of all abortions are *spontaneous abortions,* or miscarriages. They result from a variety of conditions ranging from physical trauma to a breakdown of the uterine lining. *Induced abortions* account for the remaining two-thirds. Nearly half of all pregnancies in the United States in 2011 were unintended and of these, about 40 percent ended in abortion (Guttmacher, 2017). At this rate, by age 45 more than one third of all American women will have had an abortion (Guttmacher, 2013). The good news is that the rate of abortion has been steadily dropping and in 2014, the rate was lowest observed since 1973 when abortion became legal (Guttmacher, 2017). In an abortion, the endometrium, placenta, and embryo or fetus are removed from the uterus. Abortion procedures are of several types, related to the length of the pregnancy and other extenuating circumstances.

Induced abortions have been legal in the United States since 1973, when two U.S. Supreme Court decisions, *Roe v. Wade* and *Doe v. Bolton,* determined that the decision to have a first-trimester abortion need concern only a woman and her physician. States could not use legislation to deny a woman's choice of first trimester abortions. The ruling did allow states the ability to set standards for second- and third-trimester abortions. The overwhelming majority of women (90 percent) who terminate their pregnancies do so in the first trimester and more than 60% take place at or before eight weeks (Hatcher, 2011). For women who have had prenatal screenings and receive information about serious health problems in the fetus, a second

Abortion Termination of an established pregnancy through surgical or nonsurgical techniques

Viability Fetus has a reasonable chance of living outside of the uterus usually at age of 24 weeks

case study 11.2

Critical Thinking

How do you feel about the decision that Mindy and Michael made about the pregnancy? What if they hadn't agreed to the same resolution to the unplanned pregnancy? How do you think you would have handled the same situation?

Mindy's Experience with Abortion

Mindy, 29, is a successful small business owner. She has been married to Bob about 5 years, and they have a 2-year-old daughter. This is the account of her decision to have an abortion.

I grew up in a small town and was raised to think that abortion was killing. I remember seeing those films about little babies being tossed out in the garbage after their mothers had abortions and all the posters and billboards with pictures of fully developed fetuses and the headings "Abortion is murder." I couldn't imagine anyone ever having an abortion. But then I got pregnant and began to look at things differently.

I was away at college. I was a 19-year-old sophomore and had been having sex with my boyfriend, Michael, for about 6 months. We were using my diaphragm for birth control, and, to tell you the truth, I don't ever remember having any problems with it. I used it faithfully, every time we had sex.

I couldn't believe I was pregnant. I was frantic. I must have had five pregnancy tests until I finally accepted the fact. I couldn't have this baby! I cried for 2 days, and Michael was very supportive. Sometimes we cried together as we tried to figure out what to do. I knew in my heart that I wasn't ready to be a mother. I still had 3 years of school left, plus graduate school. I had no job, no time, and psychologically just couldn't handle it.

I went to a local abortion clinic. The people were great. They gave me all the information I needed, I took tests, and they assured me that because I was only 6 weeks pregnant, the procedure they would use was safe and relatively simple. I scheduled an appointment and went home to think about it.

It wasn't an easy decision, but I felt I had no acceptable choice. I didn't think I could handle being pregnant, having a baby, and then give it up for adoption or foster care. I didn't want to tell my parents. I wasn't sure how they'd react and didn't want to jeopardize my being away at school.

They were paying for everything, and I wasn't sure if they'd force me to drop out.

I felt relief after my abortion. I wished I hadn't gotten pregnant and didn't have to make the decision, but sometimes life doesn't always work out the way you plan. I knew I was lucky to finish the school year, and graduate on time 2 years later. Now, 10 years later and the mother of a 2-year-old girl, I know I never could have been the mom I am now. Although it was a tough decision, it was the right one for me.

trimester abortion becomes an option, particularly since amniocentesis results are not returned until the 18th week of gestation or later.

Third-trimester abortions remain very rare yet are extremely controversial and have been the focus of much legal wrangling and debate. The term *late-term* abortion is applied to cases where the viability of the fetus is not possible, and an attempted birth will leave serious health problems for the mother, resulting in termination during the third trimester.

Surgical Abortions

Surgical methods include vacuum aspiration, dilation and curettage (D&C), dilation and evacuation (D&E)

Vacuum Aspiration

Vacuum aspiration is the most widely used procedure for early abortions. This type of abortion can be performed in a medical office or clinic for pregnancies less than 14 weeks gestation (Hatcher et al., 2011). This is an outpatient procedure using local anesthesia and cost on average $450 (Guttmacher, 2017). Aspiration is done with either a hand held suction device or a suction machine that gently removes the contents of the uterus. A curette, a narrow metal loop, is sometimes used after the suction to remove any remaining contents of the uterus. When the curette is used, some call the procedure a D & C, dilation and curettage (Planned Parenthood, 2013).

A vacuum aspiration abortion usually can be performed in approximately 5–10 minutes. It is safe and usually causes few side effects. Figure 11.9 (see page 320) shows this procedure.

Vacuum aspiration An induced abortion procedure in which uterine contents are removed by suction; used for early abortions

Cannula A tapered, strawlike tube used in the vacuum aspiration method of abortion

♋ *Emotional and Spiritual Wellness* ♋

Spirituality plays a big role in how people evaluate fertility control methods and which ones they ultimately choose. Religions have various beliefs regarding fertility control, with variations from division to division, and sometimes region to region. From a broad perspective, all decisions about pregnancy relate to the underlying theme of interconnectedness. The decision to create a new life or to prevent the unintended creation of life is fundamentally a spiritual issue.

The decision to end a pregnancy is not made lightly. Some women don't even tell the male involved, choosing only to seek support from close friends. Deciding to have an abortion may be kept secret from parents and siblings as well. Both males and females may need counseling to deal with the emotional aspects of the decisions they've made.

When couples confront second-trimester abortions, they may find privacy not an option. Family, friends, and coworkers may have been aware of a planned pregnancy. Explanations about deciding to have a second-trimester abortion can be very difficult to share. Again, counseling and support groups can be very helpful.

Dilation and Evacuation (D&E)

Dilation and evacuation (D&E), usually performed later than 14 weeks, combines vacuum aspiration and medical instruments to gently remove the contents of the uterus. In preparation for the procedure, practitioners may insert a laminaria several hours to days prior to the procedure. The laminaria is made of dried seaweed that expands and gently dilates the woman's cervix. (Zieman et al., 2016; Hatcher et al., 2011).

Like first-trimester abortions, women seek to terminate pregnancies in the second trimester for a variety of reasons. As discussed in Chapter 13,

Dilation and evacuation (D&E) A second-trimester abortion procedure in which the cervix is first dilated, and then the fetus removed by suction and medical instruments

Medical abortion

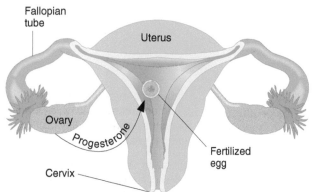

Progesterone, a hormone produced by the ovaries, is necessary for the implantation and development of a fertilized egg.

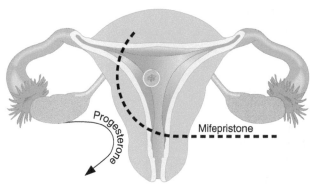

Taken early in pregnancy mifepristone blocks the action of progesterone and makes the body react as if it isn't pregnant.

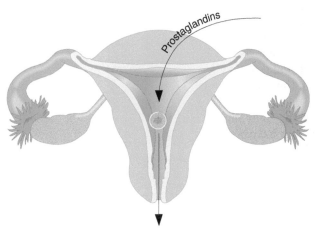

Prostaglandins, taken two days later, cause the uterus to contract and the cervix to soften and dilate. As a result, the fertilized egg is expelled in 97% of the cases.

Vacuum aspiration

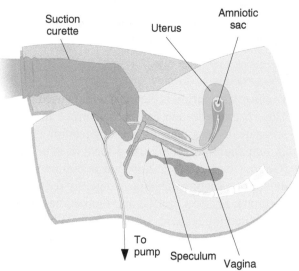

Figure 11.9 *Abortion Methods Used in Early Gestation*

couples do not get the results of prenatal screening tests such as amniocentesis or chorionic villus sampling until the second trimester.

Surgical abortions are very safe procedures. The risk of death from childbirth is 11 times higher than that of abortions performed before 20 weeks (Planned Parenthood, 2013). Since the legalization of abortion in 1973, the death rate for the procedure has dropped steadily.

Medication Abortions

Medication abortions account for 31 percent of all nonhospital abortions and have a high acceptability rate among women who have experienced them. Of those who had a medical abortion, eighty-four percent said they would choose a medical abortion over a surgical abortion if they faced the choice again (Guttmacher, 2017; Christen-Maitre, Bouchard, & Spitz, 2000; Guttmacher, 2011). Medication abortions can be performed until the tenth week of pregnancy (Guttmacher, 2017). These abortions do not involve surgical intervention but rather the use of medications to terminate a pregnancy. Figure 11.9 illustrates this method. Abortions can be induced by administering agents that work two ways: (a) by initiating the breakdown of the endometrium, making it impossible to sustain the pregnancy and (b) by causing the uterus to contract and expel its contents.

RU-486 is the drug mifepristone and was marketed in 2000 as Mifeprex. It is an antiprogester one drug that works by blocking the absorption of progesterone, the hormone necessary for continued viability of the endometrium. If progesterone is blocked, the uterine lining will no longer

RU-486 Known as the "abortion pill"; mifepristone, a drug used to induce menstruation by blocking the absorption of progesterone and thereby preventing the uterine lining from supporting an embryo

support fetal development. A second drug, misoprostol (a type of prostaglandin), is administered at home 24 to 48 hours later, causing uterine contractions. These contractions usually cause the uterine lining and products of conception to be sloughed off within 4–5 hours but it may take longer (Planned Parenthood, 2017).

■ After the Abortion

Deciding to terminate a pregnancy is a decision women, often along with their partners, make with great thought. The three most common reasons for choosing to have an abortion- each cited by three fourths of patients—were concern for or responsibility to other individuals; the inability to afford raising a child and the belief that a baby would interfere with school, work or caring for independents. Fifty percent said they did not want to be a single parent or were having relationship problems (Guttmacher, 2017). Although, the reasons are many, the one similarity for all is that *this* pregnancy is unwanted. Most women report the immediate feeling of relief, with the abortion representing the end to a crisis pregnancy. Ideally women would not have to make this very difficult decision. Free access to birth control could be a way to help women avoid unplanned pregnancies. A 2012 study found that free access to birth control would prevent as many as half of all abortions in the U.S. (Pierpert, Madden, Allsworth & Secure, 2012).

Over the years those who oppose abortion have suggested that women suffer long term mental health issues after an abortion calling it "postabortion syndrome". Scientific evidence has never supported this and a new, large rigorous study in Denmark has found no higher rates of mental health problems among women in the 12 months after the abortion than in the 9 months prior to the abortion (Guttmacher, 2011b). Furthermore, leading experts have determined that in women who have an unplanned

sex in society 11.3

Some Facts about Abortion

Despite abortion being legal in the United States since Roe v. Wade in 1973, many women hesitate to talk openly about a procedure that an estimated 926,200 million American women experienced in 2014. Consider the following facts:

- Forty-five percent of pregnancies among women in the United States are unintended, with 40% of them ending in abortion.
- More than half of U.S. women obtaining abortions are in their 20's, with teens representing 12 percent of those seeking abortions.
- Women who have never been married and are not living with a partner have 46% of all abortions

- Fifty-nine percent of abortions are among women who already have at least one child.
- Fifty-one percent of women having abortions used a contraceptive method during the month they became pregnant.
- Ninety percent of all U.S. counties lack an abortion provider; 39% of all women live in these counties.
- Two-third of abortions occur at eight weeks of pregnancy or earlier; eighty-nine percent occur in the first 12 weeks.

Source: Guttmacher Institute (2017).

pregnancy, those who have an abortion have no greater mental health issue than those who have the baby (Guttmacher, 2017). The American Psychiatric Association (2000) does not even recognize "post abortion syndrome and it is not included in the most recent *Diagnostic and Statistical Manual,* which characterizes recognized psychological illnesses. Critics claim that much of the available data on the purported syndrome has come from "expert witnesses" in congressional hearings and anecdotal reports from physicians, clinicians, and women who have incurred ill effects after having abortions. In repeated studies since the early 1980's, leading experts have concluded that abortion does not pose a threat to a woman's mental health (Guttamacher, 2011).

After the abortion, women are advised to start contraception immediately. For women who desire an IUD, the abortion is an ideal time to insert the IUD. Abortion follow-up may include referral for post-abortion counseling and group therapy for women who need these services to cope with their distress.

The decision to have an abortion is not an easy one to make. It is a complex moral and ethical decision that most women (and men) take seriously. The decision has both immediate- and long-term consequences that need to be taken into account. Overall, the decision to terminate an unwanted pregnancy becomes one of the many decisions couples make over the course of their reproductive years.

References

American College of Obstetricians and Gynecologist (2013, May). *Half of all women are unaware that pregnancy is more dangerous than contraception.* Retrieved from http://www.acog.org

American College of Obstetricians and Gynecologist (2014, July). *Progestin-only hormonal birth control: Pills and injections.* Retrieved from http://www.acog.org

American Psychiatric Association. (2013). *Diagnostic and statistical manual* (5th ed., text revision). Washington, DC.

Braaten, K. & Dutton, C. (2017). *Permanent sterilization procedures for women.* Retrieved from http://www.uptodate.com

Buhling, K., Zite, N., Lotke, P., & Black, K. (2014, March). Worldwide use of intrauterine contraception: A review. *Contraception,* 89 (3).

Centers for Disease Control (2011, January). *Sexually transmitted diseases.* Available: www.cdc.gov

Christin-Maitre, S., Bouchard, P., & Spitz, M. (2000). Medical termination of pregnancy. *The New England Journal of Medicine.* 342 (13), 946–954.

Consumers Union. (2009, December). Seven of 20 condoms tested earned a perfect score: extra protection. *Consumer Reports.*

Cutie, C. & Dorgara, T. (2013). *Vasectomy (beyond the basics). Patient information.* Retrieved from http://uptodate.com

Guttmacher Institute. (2003, January). Nowhere but up: Rising costs for Title X clinics. *Issues in Brief.* Retrieved from http://www.guttmacher.org

Guttmacher Institute (2003, September). *Method related problems account for most of the failures of the female condom.* Retrieved from http://www.guttmacher.org

Guttmacher Institute (2011, January, 31). *Comprehensive new study finds no causal link between abortion and mental health problems.* Retrieved from http://www.guttmacher.org

Guttmacher Institute (2013, January). *Induced abortion in the United States.* Retrieved from http://www.guttmacher.org

Guttmacher Institute (2016, September). *Publically funded family planning services in the United States* Retrieved from http://www.guttmacher.org

Guttmacher Institute (2017, January). *Induced abortion in the United States*. Retrieved from http://www.guttmacher.org

Hatcher, R. A., Trussel, J., Stewart, F. Nelson, A, Cates, W., Kowal, D. & Policar, M. (2011). *Contraceptive technology* (20th ed.). New York: Arden Media.

McDonough, P., (1995, September/October). The safest sex. *Psychology Today*, 47–49.

Norris, K, (1996, September). Celibate passion. *Utne Reader*, 51–53.

Piepert, J, Madden, T., Allsworth, J. & Secura, G. (2012). *Obsterics & Gynecology*. 120(6),1291–7.

Planned Parenthood Federation of America (2013). *Contraceptive implants*. Retrieved from http://www.plannedparenthood.org

Planned Parenthood Federation of America (2013). *Contraceptive sponge*. Retrieved from http://www.plannedparenthood.org

Planned Parenthood Federation of America (2017). *Birth control patch*. Retrieved from http://www.plannedparenthood.org

Planned Parenthood Federation of America (2017). *The abortion pill*. Retrieved from http://www.plannedparenthood.org

Planned Parenthood Federation of America (2017). *In clinic abortion procedures*. Retrieved from http://www.plannedparenthood.org

Planned Parenthood Federation of America (2017). *Sterilization for women*. Retrieved from http://www.plannedparenthood.org

Planned Parenthood Federation of America (2017). *Birth control patch*. Retrieved from http://www.plannedparenthood.org

Planned Parenthood Federation of America (2017). *The abortion pill*. Retrieved from http://www.plannedparenthood.org

Planned Parenthood Federation of America (2017). *In clinic abortion procedures*. Retrieved from http://www.plannedparenthood.org

Planned Parenthood Federation of America (2017). *Sterilization for women*. Retrieved from http://www.plannedparenthood.org

VCF Contraceptive (2017). *VCF contraceptive film*. Retrieved from http:// VCFContraceptive.org

Zieman, M. Hatcher, R., Allen, a., Lathrop, E., & Haddad, L. (2016). *Managing Contraception 2016*. Bridging the Gap Foundation.

Chapter
twelve

Sexually Transmitted Infections (STIs)

Student Learning Objectives

After reading this chapter, students will be able to

- ☞ Describe the major STI trends of the past decade.
- ☞ Diagram and describe the Pyramid of Risk for STI/HIV infection.
- ☞ Explain how demographic variables are related to STI/HIV risk.
- ☞ Evaluate the relationship between sexual/medical history and STI/HIV risk.
- ☞ Assess a variety of sexual lifestyles and the continuum of risk for STI that they represent.
- ☞ Evaluate the risks inherent in a variety of sexual behaviors.
- ☞ Develop a personal plan for reducing the risk for STI/HIV infection.
- ☞ Describe the major modes of STI/HIV transmission.
- ☞ Describe the major symptoms associated with STI/HIV infection.
- ☞ Describe the epidemiology of a variety of STIs.
- ☞ Show awareness of the cause of each STI: bacteria, virus, parasite

Introduction

Sexually Transmitted Infections (STIs) Infections that are spread from person to person through sexual contact.

Sexually Transmitted Infections (STIs), previously referred to as sexually transmitted diseases (STDs), or venereal diseases (VD), are usually spread from person to person via sexual contact. We say "usually" because there are a few that can *also* be spread via contaminated clothing or bedding (scabies and pubic lice) or by sharing damp towels (trichomoniasis) with infected persons. Besides being transmitted from an infected person to another person via sexual intercourse, most STIs can be transmitted via oral sex too. So while oral sex may be "safe" in terms of pregnancy, it is *not* safe regarding STIs. And infections that move from the genitals into the bloodstream (syphilis, HIV, Hepatitis B) can also be transmitted via shared injection needles or open cuts.

In this chapter we will also cover some genital infections that don't require contact with an infected person or material (Yeast, Jock Itch, and most cases of Bacterial Vaginitis) even though they are not technically "sexually transmitted" infections.

Epidemic Levels of infection in populations that exceed those normally expected for that population

We face an **epidemic** of STIs in the U.S. today, with about 20 Million new cases each year (**incidence**) adding up to a total of about 110 Million Americans currently living with STIs (**prevalence**), despite all public health efforts to keep STI rates low (CDC, 2013). The U.S. Centers for Disease Control (CDC) reports that Syphilis, Chlamydia and Gonorrhea have all risen sharply in recent years (CDC, 2019). Many young people don't take these three infections very seriously because they can all be cured by treatment with the appropriate antibiotic medication. But in order to be cured, a person must first go and be tested for them. In many cases the infected person doesn't even know that they *are* infected because the symptoms come and go, or are mild, or even absent altogether. Although the least common of these three, syphilis is the most upsetting because of the large spike in cases of **congenital syphilis** which can cause serious birth defects and illnesses to a baby. The infant can be cured of the active syphilis infection but the damage done while it was developing in the womb cannot be undone. The CDC attributes the recent rise in STIs to several factors which include decreased condom use and cuts to STI programs at the federal, state, and local levels.

Congenital syphilis is acquired by the fetus from the mother's infected blood passing through the placenta into the umbilical cord.

Probably the most alarming fact to learn about STIs is that so many can infect you, and even cause permanent damage to your reproductive system (or other bodily systems) without you even knowing that you are sick. As you read through the descriptions of each of the STIs covered in this chapter, be on the look-out for those that are often "invisible" – having no obvious symptoms. It is because of these "invisible" STIs that condoms should *always* be used by non-monogamous partners and that **sexually active** persons should be tested for *all* of the common STIs at least once a year, whether they have symptoms or not. Couples wishing to stop using condoms must agree to remain **monogamous** and to get tested before stopping condom use.

Sexually active means that a person has had sex with another person. It is not a judgement about how many partners or how many times the person has had sex. Just once is "active." And "sex" includes oral, anal, and vaginal.

Monogamous Only having sex with one partner during the course of the relationship.

When we look at who is most affected by STIs, the first thing to show up in the data is the high number of cases among young people (ages 15-24); young people account for half of all new cases each year. We also

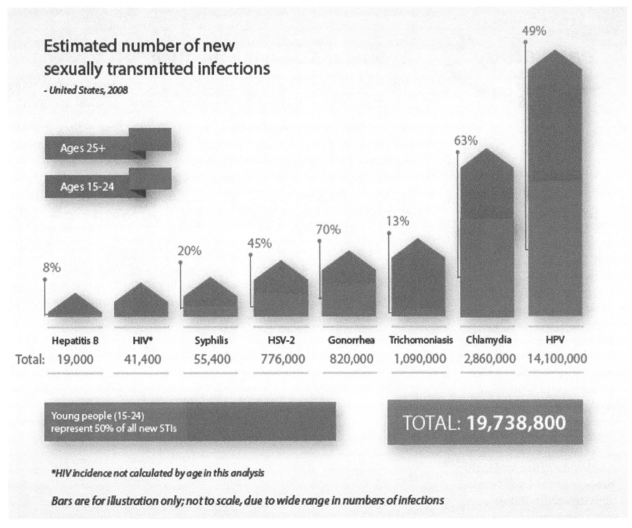

Estimated number of new sexually transmitted infections
- United States, 2008

Ages 25+

Ages 15-24

	Hepatitis B	HIV*	Syphilis	HSV-2	Gonorrhea	Trichomoniasis	Chlamydia	HPV
	8%	20%	45%	70%	13%	63%	49%	
Total:	19,000	41,400	55,400	776,000	820,000	1,090,000	2,860,000	14,100,000

Young people (15-24) represent 50% of all new STIs

TOTAL: 19,738,800

*HIV incidence not calculated by age in this analysis

Bars are for illustration only; not to scale, due to wide range in numbers of infections

CDC estimates that there are more than 19.7 million new STIs in the United States each year. While most of these STIs will not cause harm, some have the potential to cause serious health problems, especially if not diagnosed and treated early. Young people (ages 15-24) are particularly affected, accounting for half (50 percent) of all new STIs, although they represent just 25 percent of the sexually experienced population.

Source: https://www.cdc.gov/std/stats/sti-estimates-fact-sheet-feb-2013.pdf

see an overrepresentation of cases among most racial minorities. While Asian and White Americans tend to have the lowest rates of most STIs, rates are *much* higher among African Americans, Native Americans, and Pacific Islanders. These differences are largely attributable to lack of access to affordable health care and quality health education, especially among those living in poverty.

Fortunately for you, your College Health Center provides testing for all of the common STIs and can provide treatment for most of them too. You have already paid the Health Fee, so make an appointment today! Fortunately for you, your College Health Center provides testing for all of the common STIs and can provide treatment for most of them too. You have already paid the Health Fee, so make an appointment today!

case study 12.1

Yolanda: Assessing the Risk

Yolanda, a student in a human sexuality class, expressed the following concerns about finding out about her sex partners' medical histories:

It looks like I'm going to have to spend a lot more time getting to know my sex partners before I take a chance of having sex with them without condoms. Up until today I thought I was a responsible lady because I'm on the pill and take responsibility for my sexuality. I always thought the pill would protect me against STIs. Boy, was I wrong. I never realized that there was so much to find out about a guy before you could tell if he was a threat to you.

I used to try to sneak a look to see if he had any symptoms, but now you're saying there are lots of other things that are important about his sexual past that I need to know about. I'm not sure what I'm going to do, but I know I'll never let any guy in there bareback until I can answer all those questions about him.

Critical Thinking

As Yolanda points out, reducing risk for acquiring an STI involves both personal action and understanding the risks posed by your partner. Understanding your partner's sexual lifestyle and medical history in order to make an informed decision regarding their STI threat is not an easy task. What specific steps would you take to find out about your partner's sexual lifestyle and medical history? How long do you think this process would take? How would this process impact your sexual activities with that person?

Diagnosis and Epidemiology of Common STIs

Bacterial STIs—Curable with the Right Antibiotic Medications

Source: Callista Lee

The following STIs can be cured with antibiotic medicines prescribed by the doctor who diagnoses them.

There are a few patient behaviors that get in the way of effectively treating bacterial infections:

a. Infected individuals fail to get tested because they don't have obvious symptoms; we call these infections "invisible."

b. Infected individuals assume that once they feel better it is okay to stop taking the prescribed antibiotics. But feeling better only means that the antibiotics have *started* to work; they haven't fully eradicated the bacteria yet. By allowing some of the bacteria to live, despite partial antibiotic treatment, you may be helping to create a "super strain" that will be even more difficult to cure by antibiotics in the future. And you may infect a future sexual partner with this "super strain." This is true of all bacterial illnesses, not just STIs. Always take the full course of medication prescribed by your doctor. You should never have "left over" antibiotic medicines.

c. Patients may assume that since they are taking antibiotics for some other bacterial infection (example—strep throat or a bladder infection), they don't need a separate antibiotic medicine for their STI. But each bacterial infection responds only to certain antibiotic medicines, at certain doses. Follow doctor's instructions and ask questions if you have any.

d. Before prescribing an antibiotic medicine, your doctor will ask if you are taking any other medications. Too many contraceptive users say "No" because they don't think of their contraceptive method as medicine. But if you are on any of the hormonal contraceptives (pills, implant, patch, shots, cervical ring, hormonal IUD) be sure to say "Yes, I'm on the _____ for birth control." *Some* antibiotics may interfere with the effectiveness of your contraceptive method; your doctor needs to take that into consideration before prescribing the antibiotic for your bacterial infection.

e. Failing to return for a follow-up visit so the doctor can confirm that the bacterial infection is, indeed, cured. Always ask your doctor if you should return for a follow-up test after you finish your antibiotics.

◼ Syphilis

Syphilis is a blood-borne STI caused by infection with *Treponema pallidum,* a corkscrew-shaped bacterium. A **spirochete** type of bacteria, the *T. pallidum* is easily killed by penicillin and other broad-spectrum antibiotics. It is unique among STI organisms because its corkscrew shape and motility facilitate its entry into the bloodstream.

Syphilis An STI caused by the spirochete bacterium *Treponema pallidum*

Spirochete A mobile, flexible, corkscrew-shaped bacterium of the genus *Spirocheta,* one type of which causes syphilis

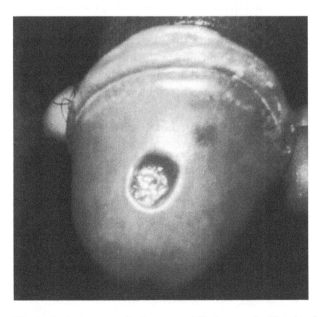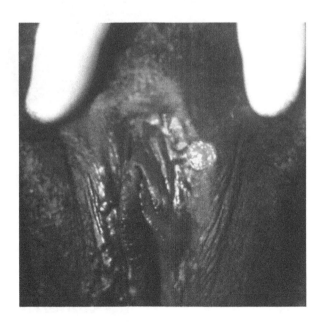

The typical chancre of primary syphilis is round with raised edges and painless; it is often internal and goes unobserved.

Source: Centers for Disease Control and Prevention, Division of STD Prevention

Chancre A painless, indurated primary lesion of early syphilis

Congenital syphilis The disease acquired by the fetus in the womb and present at birth

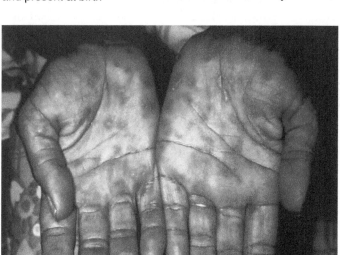

The typical rash associated with secondary syphilis is bilateral (on both hands or feet instead of just one), discolored, and raised.

Source: Centers for Disease Control and Prevention, Division of STD Prevention

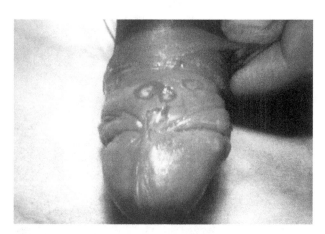

Unlike syphilis, the ulcers of chancroid are irregular in shape and painful.

Source: Centers for Disease Control and Prevention

After exposure to the bacterium, it enters the body through breaks in the skin or by penetrating intact skin, and from there passes into the bloodstream. Once in the bloodstream, it can move freely throughout the body. The usual incubation period for syphilis is 3 to 4 weeks, but it can be as short as 10 days or as long as 90 days (DSTD, 2013d).

After the incubation period, a **chancre** appears at the spot where the organism entered. The primary chancre is painless and disappears within 1 to 5 weeks without treatment. Often it is internal (inside the vagina, mouth, or rectum). Because of this, many people who become infected with syphilis don't realize it. An infected person's blood test will detect antibodies to the syphilis spirochete a short time after the primary chancre appears. Fluid from chancres can also be used to diagnose early syphilis. A specimen of the fluid can be examined under a dark field microscope. If infected, the specimen should be teeming with spirochetes, moving in their typical corkscrew motion (DSTD 2011e).

About 6 weeks later a generalized rash appears. The rash varies from being highly noticeable, covering the entire trunk, to a mild eruption on the hands or feet. As with the chancre, the rash disappears without treatment after 2 to 6 weeks.

In about 25 percent of the cases, a second rash appears and also goes away without treatment. At this point, those who are infected enter the latency period, during which time they are infected but have no symptoms. Although asymptomatic, they are capable of transmitting the infection only by donating blood. However, since all blood drawn on patients in the United States is tested for syphilis, no cases of the disease have been detected this way in decades. Syphilis can also be passed across the placenta by a pregnant woman passing the infection to her developing fetus, resulting in **congenital syphilis**. A requirement of routine prenatal care is a blood test for syphilis. Most adult women with health insurance get this test early in their pregnancies. If it is positive, they can be treated. Treatment of the mother almost always results in treating her developing fetus (DSTD, 2011e).

Gonorrhea

Gonorrhea A sexually transmitted infection caused by the bacteria *Neisseria gonorrheae*

Gonorrhea infection is very similar to Chlamydia clinically. Following sexual exposure, the organism incubates from 1 to 30 days. Most people who develop symptoms notice them within 1 to 3 days. The initial symptoms are

Sex in Society 12.1

The Tuskegee Study: It Couldn't Happen Here—or Could It?

In 1932, the U.S. Public Health Service (USPHS) embarked on one of the most tragic experiments ever conducted by a government on its own people. From 1932 to 1970, in Macon County, Alabama, the USPHS conducted a study under the guidance of the Tuskegee Institute (which, ironically, is one of the nation's most prestigious black academic institutions) on the history of syphilis in blacks.

Syphilis, it was hypothesized, progressed differently in blacks than whites. The study originally was intended to be a short-term investigation (6 to 9 months' duration) but evolved into a 40-year project that followed the subjects well beyond the initial stages of their disease through latency into complications and ultimately to their deaths.

Much of what we know about the disease, how it spreads, its complications, and how it attacks the body and kills comes from the Tuskegee Study.

The study followed 600 black subjects (399 infected men and 201 uninfected controls) for 40 years. Treatment was withheld intentionally from these men, even after they were diagnosed with serious, life-threatening complications of the disease. None of them benefited from penicillin as the effective treatment of choice in 1951. The USPHS devised elaborate plans to keep track of these men (and to continue to withhold treatment) even after they moved from Alabama to other states.

In 1966, Peter Buxtun, an investigator for the USPHS, brought the matter before the then-director of the Division of Venereal Diseases, Peter Brown. Given the moral climate and racial turmoil of the 1960s and the immorality of such an experiment, Buxtun pleaded that something be done. A special committee was impaneled within the USPHS to discuss the study. The committee ruled in favor of continuing the study to its natural end point.

Buxtun's pleas went unheeded, and the experiment continued. Not until Buxtun leaked his story to an Associated Press writer and it broke on the front pages of the *Washington Post* in 1972 was something done. In 1973, a special subcommittee of the U.S. Congress, chaired by Edward Kennedy (D-MA) began to investigate the matter.

The committee found the USPHS culpable, the study was terminated, and special regulations concerning conducting government experiments were drawn up. These regulations now serve as guidelines for handling human subjects in any government-financed study. Surviving participants of the Tuskegee Study and their heirs filed a $1.8 billion class action lawsuit. The government settled the suit out of court for $10 million (Jones, 1993).

the same as those associated with Chlamydia. Discharge and burning upon urination are the most common symptoms in men. Gonorrhea symptoms—heavy discharge, yellowish-green in color, and severe burning are usually are more severe than those associated with Chlamydia. The symptoms usually are enough to cause men with the infection to seek treatment. Up to 20 percent of men have no symptoms. About 50 percent of women infected with gonorrhea are asymptomatic, and a small percentage will notice a discharge or have irritation of the vulva.

In women, gonorrhea often results in complications, the most common of which is PID (pelvic inflammatory disease)—occurring in approximately 15 percent of all women with untreated gonorrhea. These women, as with those who develop PID from chlamydia, have an increased risk for chronic pain, ectopic pregnancy, sterility, and even death. Less than 1 percent of men with untreated gonorrhea develop disseminated gonococcal infection and/or epididymitis. Like chlamydia, gonorrhea is easy to treat (DSTD, 2013c).

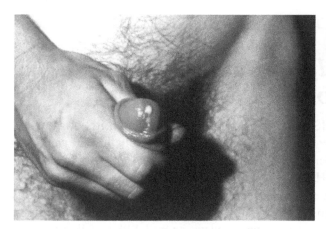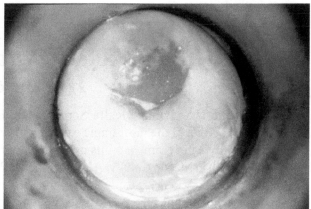

Gonorrhea infection typically produces a profuse, thick, yellow-green discharge, but it can also mimic the milder symptoms of chlamydia. Infection in the cervix, throat, or rectum is often asymptomatic.

Source: Centers for Disease Control and Prevention, Division of STD Prevention

Treatment

Increases in drug-resistant strains of gonorrhea, particularly those acquired in Asia or the Pacific, including Hawaii, require have treatment regimens be changed to inhibit the development of antibiotic resistant strains of *N. gonorrhoeae*. Patients infected with *N. gonorrhoeae* frequently are co-infected with *C. trachomatis;* this finding has led to the recommendation that patients treated for gonococcal infection also be treated routinely with a regimen that is effective against uncomplicated chlamydial infection. (DSTD, 2011).

✎ *Intellectual and Emotional Wellness* ✎

High-level intellectual wellness is the cornerstone of effective prevention of STIs. Knowing the risks and how to reduce them is critical to preventing STIs. This knowledge includes information about personal behavior and also about lifestyles and demographic risks. Intellectual wellness also fosters enhanced decision making. Reducing the risks for STI is all about personal choice. Because STIs are sexually transmitted, their prevention and control are more than just a medical matter. STIs involve our most intimate emotions. Knowing about prevention and seeking treatment are one thing. Working through the anxiety, fear, and guilt, and a host of other emotions that interfere with clear thinking about STIs is another thing. Emotional health can help us deal with the emotions that can cloud rational thinking.

Chlamydia

Chlamydia is a sexually transmitted disease caused by the *Chlamydia trachomatis* organism. It is transmitted through contact with infected semen or cervical mucus. It also can be passed through oral contact (usually fellatio) with infected mucus patches in the throat.

healthy sex hints 12.1

NAATs: Tests for Chlamydia

A recent advance in chlamydia and gonorrhea testing is the nucleic acid amplification tests (NAATs). These tests detect the presence of chlamydia through DNA testing.

They actually identify nucleic acid sequences that are specific to chlamydia. Unlike smear or culture tests, NAATs do not require viable organisms to diagnose the disease.

The specimens are easily obtained through urine samples.

Patients do not need to be symptomatic to obtain specimens, and samples can be collected anywhere urine collection can be performed. The beauty of NAATs is that it reduces dependence on invasive tests and allows public health programs to expand testing into locations such as schools where other means of testing were unacceptable. A classic study in a Philadelphia school-based clinic setting demonstrated a yield of more than 20 percent among students tested (Bertrami, 2002).

Another advantage of NAATs is their ability to test for gonorrhea infection at the same time using the same specimen. The same Philadelphia study found that almost half of students infected with chlamydia had coexistent gonorrhea infection. These gonorrhea infections would often go undetected with traditional tests that only checked for chlamydia. The ability to test for both infections simultaneously using an easy-to-obtain urine specimen represents a major breakthrough in STD testing and a major tool in the prevention of gonorrhea and chlamydia (MMWR, 2002).

During sexual contact, the organisms are passed by person-to-person contact with the infected ejaculate or mucus. Incubation is from 1 to 30 days. The initial symptoms of chlamydia in men are a scanty, clear to milky-white discharge from the penis, and burning upon urination. Some women notice a scanty, clear to milky-white discharge and irritation of the vulva. Seventy-five percent of women and 50 percent of men usually have no symptoms for chlamydia. This is why screening sexually active women and their sex partners for chlamydia in a variety of health care facilities that serve them is the basis for the government's prevention program for the disease.

In the 1960s and 1970s, chlamydia infection was believed to be a relatively minor problem. Men with the infection were often referred to as having "nonspecific urethritis" and were not counseled extensively regarding the necessity to have their sexual partners examined. Chlamydia, however, was discovered to be a major source of **PID** (pelvic inflammatory disease). Up to 20 percent of all women with *C. trachomatis* infection will develop PID.

PID The acronym for *pelvic inflammatory disease,* a generic term that can apply to any STI that produces the characteristic symptoms of infection

Pelvic Inflammatory Disease (PID)

PID isn't actually an STI itself, but it is usually a *consequence of an STI,* generally untreated chlamydia or gonorrhea that have traveled into the uterus and fallopian tubes. PID is a very serious bacterial infection that can lead to chronic pelvic pain, ectopic pregnancy, infertility, and/or tubo-ovarian abscess (which can lead to life-threatening sepsis if untreated). Symptoms may include:
sepsis if untreated). Symptoms may include:

- Pain in your lower abdomen and pelvis
- Heavy vaginal discharge with an unpleasant odor

- Abnormal uterine bleeding, especially during or after intercourse, or between menstrual cycles
- Pain or bleeding during intercourse
- Fever, sometimes with chills
- Painful or difficult urination

If symptoms include severe abdominal pain, a fever of 101 degrees or higher, nausea, and vomiting, go to an Urgent Care or Emergency Room right away. For less severe symptoms, see your doctor as soon as possible. Patients are treated with heavy doses of antibiotics, and about half must be hospitalized. Without treatment, the patient may die.

Epididymitis

In about 1 percent males with chlamydia, the bacteria may travel up the urethra to the vas deferens to settle in the epididymis (where sperm are stored after being made in the testicles) where it can cause the serious infection of the epididymitis (Morse et al., 1990). Other causes of **epididymitis** include the bacterium *E. coli*, the mumps virus, or, in rare cases, tuberculosis. Symptoms of epididymitis include:

- Pain in the scrotum, sometimes moving to the rest of the groin
- Swelling and redness in the testicle
- Blood in the semen
- Fever and chills
- Pain when urinating

Medical treatment depends upon the cause of the infection, but to manage symptoms the man should:

- Rest
- Elevate the scrotum
- Apply ice packs to the affected area
- Drink plenty of fluids
- Take anti-inflammatory medications for the pain

If epididymitis is not treated, an abscess may form on the scrotum, which can rupture. And in rare cases, infertility may result.

Bacterial Vaginosis (BV)

Source: Callista Lee

Bacterial Vaginosis is very common and may be caused by one of a few different bacteria. Some are from the vagina itself, but become problematic when there is an overgrowth of them; often *Gardnerella vaginalis*. Also, some bacteria that live without any problem in a person's anus can cause trouble in the vagina. These anal bacteria are why we teach girls to wipe from front to back after they have used the toilet; so anal bacteria don't migrate to the vagina. Another way they can migrate is on the fingers, mouth, penis, or sex toy of a sex partner who first touches the anus and, later, the vagina. Before you get too creeped out, remember that these bacteria are microscopic. We are NOT talking about moving fecal matter to the vagina! These bacteria are too small to see.

Symptoms usually include a thin, watery vaginal discharge that is gray or white with a fishy odor. There may be itching around the vagina and even burning during urination. Unfortunately, 50-75 percent of women will have mild or no symptoms.

Others will have symptoms, but will try using over-the-counter (OTC) non-prescription Yeast Infection creams, but because BV is not caused by yeast, this medication won't cure it. Because it is bacterial, antibiotics are needed to cure it.

While BV doesn't cause big problems for most women, it can cause very serious problems to pregnant women and their fetuses. And having BV puts a woman at greater risk for contracting other STIs because of the irritation of vaginal tissue.

Non-gonococcal Urethritis (NGU)

Non-gonococcal urethritis (NGU) is diagnosed when *Neisseria gonorrhea* is ruled out as the causative agent of discharge and burning in a male. In most cases, a negative lab test for gonorrhea and the presence of symptoms is enough to diagnose NGU. NGU is also a surrogate measure of chlamydia in men, as more than half of all cases of NGU are attributable to *C. trachomatis*. In some cases, a test for *C. trachomatis* is done.

NGU presents the same symptoms as chlamydia infection in men and is treated using the same treatment schedule recommended for chlamydia.

Non-gonococcal urethritis (NGU) An infection in the urethra of males, usually caused by chlamydia bacteria

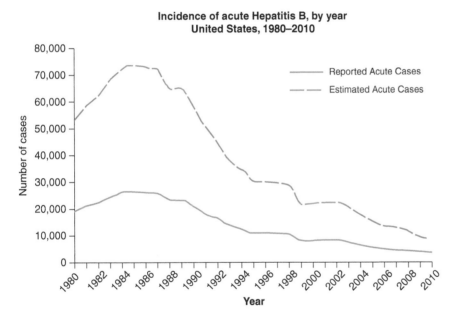

Figure 12.1 *Incidence of Acute Hepatitis B by Year United states, 1980–2010*

Source: (DSTD 2012 L). Centers for Disease Control and Prevention, Division of Viral Hepatitis

Parasitic—Curable with Medication Specific to Each

Source: Callista Lee

Generally, a person infected with any of these will have symptoms that will leave them eager to see a doctor, but some cases may be mild, leaving the person hoping it will go away on its own. Only Thrichomoniasis requires a prescription medication; others can be purchased at a pharmacy over-the-counter (OTC) without a prescription if you are certain about which one you have. All of these *may* be contracted without sexual contact, but sexual contact greatly increases the risk of infection.

■ Trichomoniasis (Trich)

Trichomonas vaginalis is a one-celled protozoan that generally causes more discomfort in women than in men. Females will likely experience several of these symptoms: frothy, unpleasant-smelling vaginal discharge; menstrual spotting; vaginal itching or burning; genital redness or swelling; a frequent urge to urinate; and/or pain during urination or sexual intercourse. Most men will not experience any symptoms, but those who do may experience a discharge from the urethra, pain during urination or after ejaculation, and a frequent urge to urinate. Because most men won't feel any symptoms, they are often hesitant to take the medication to cure it, and so they infect their female partners again. Although this infection is usually sexually transmitted, there have also been cases of it surviving on damp towels (warm climates) long enough to infect the next user. Treatment is a short-term dose of a medication that often leaves patients feeling light-headed and mildly nauseous, and it is important to avoid all alcoholic drinks for at least seven-two hours after treatment to avoid severe nausea and vomiting. Sex should be avoided for a full week after all partners have finished treatment. In rare cases, untreated trichomoniasis has led to PID.

■ Yeast Infection and Jock Itch

These infections are not believed to be sexually transmitted, but rather an overgrowth of a normally occurring fungus (yeast) found throughout many regions of the body, especially those that stay warm and moist. A specific kind of yeast called *Candida albicans* causes most yeast infections. These infections are easily treatable. Symptoms of **vaginal yeast infections** may include vaginal itching, swelling around the vagina, burning during urination or sex, pain during sex, soreness of the vagina and vulva, redness or a rash on the legs right near the vulva, and a clumpy white discharge that smells "yeasty." For women, risk of infection is greater if she takes antibiotics, is pregnant, diabetic, has a weakened immune system, has a poor diet (too much sugary food), is suffering from lack of sleep, is under ongoing stress, has hormonal imbalances, or wears tight-fitting nonbreathable underwear (and outerwear). Except for pregnancy and hormonal imbalances, the same risk factors apply to males for **Jock Itch**. A yeast rash can also occur in other warm moist areas such as underarms or under droopy breasts.

Today's OTC creams or vaginal suppositories are often designed for one to three-day treatment of vaginal yeast infections. Some more stubborn cases may require a full seven-day treatment. In even more stubborn or severe cases, an oral medication may be prescribed. Changes in lifestyle to reduce the risk factors are also important. Although **Jock Itch** may be caused by that same sort of yeast, it is more often caused by another fungus, *Trichophyton rubrum*, and is described as

"a fungal infection that affects the skin of your genitals, inner thighs and buttocks. Jock itch causes an itchy, red, often ring-shaped rash in these warm, moist areas of your body. Jock itch gets its name because it is common in people who sweat a lot, as do athletes. It also is more likely to occur in people who are overweight. Although often uncomfortable and bothersome, jock itch usually isn't serious. Keeping your groin area clean and dry and applying topical antifungal medications usually are sufficient to treat jock itch" (https://www.mayoclinic.org/diseases-conditions/jock-itch/symptoms-causes/syc-20353807).

Pubic Lice aka Crabs (Pediculosis)

Infection with **pubic lice**, commonly called *crabs,* is caused by infestation of *Phthirius pubis.* The lice are transmitted during sexual contact from the infested pubic hair of one person to the other. In rarer instances, the lice are transmitted from contaminated bedding, clothing, and towels that people share.

> **Pubic lice** *Phthirius pubis;* small insects (metazoan) that infest the host's pubic hair

Female lice lay eggs, called *nits,* which attach to the shaft of the pubic hair of the exposed individual. The incubation period for lice is between 24 and 48 hours, at which time the eggs hatch and another batch of lice spread throughout the pubic hair.

Symptoms of pubic lice are (a) visual confirmation of the lice, (b) intense itching of the pubic and perianal area, (c) skin irritation, and (d) secondary sores and erosions from scratching. Although infestation rarely leads to complications, persons with pubic lice sometimes develop secondary infections from their intense scratching (DSTD, 2011h).

Treatment of lice consists of special shampoos that kill the lice on the skin and hair. The shampoos are applied to the affected areas, allowed to sit for up to 10 minutes, and rinsed off thoroughly. Bedding, clothing, and other contaminated articles must be washed and dried thoroughly under hot settings or dry-cleaned. Fumigation of the person's house is not necessary (DSTD 2011h).

Scabies

Like crabs, **scabies** is caused by infestation with a mite. This mite, *Sarcoptes scabies,* is transmitted in the same way as pubic lice. Symptoms are similar with one notable exception: S. scabies actually burrows under the skin of an infected person and feeds on cellular matter (DSTD, 2011h).

Diagnosis usually consists of identifying the mite's burrows under the skin.

Because of the burrowing of the mites involved in scabies, treatment involves applying a lotion (similar to the shampoos used in pubic lice) that is left on the skin for 8 to 14 hours before being washed off. More than one application of the lotion may be required (DSTD, 2011H).

Viral—Treatable with Medication but Not Curable

Source: Callista Lee

Unfortunately, modern medicine has not yet been able to cure *any* viral diseases. Instead, rest and/or medicines can help your body's immune system to fight it off, or at least manage the symptoms. Also important, is following a healthy lifestyle (eating well, getting adequate rest, appropriate exercise, avoiding stress, and limiting alcohol and other recreational drugs). Some viral infections will eventually be vanquished by your immune system while others may stay with you for life. Learning how to live with the infection is important to your physical, emotional, and social health. There are currently vaccines available to help your immune system prevent infections of HPV and Hepatitis B. Although there is no vaccine in sight for HIV, retroviral treatments have been becoming much more effective.

case study 12.2

Critical Thinking

What makes the potential transmission of a past viral condition such as herpes different from a past bacterial infection such as gonorrhea?

Susan, an HSV Sufferer

Susan was a woman one of the authors met while conducting a self-help group for persons suffering with genital herpes. Susan had just found out that the ulcerative genital infection she had was caused by HSV. She came to the group to learn how to manage her disease.

I was shocked when my doctor told me I had herpes. I couldn't figure out how I got it, since I've been sexually involved with just my boyfriend for the past 6 months and he doesn't have any symptoms.

The doctor explained that my present boyfriend might not even have given it to me. [The doctor] explained that since I had several other sex partners since beginning to have intercourse at 19 years old, any of those guys could have given it to me. He said I might not have had any initial symptoms or might have missed them because they were so mild.

Now, because I've been stressed out—a new job, graduate school, getting engaged, moving into a house—the herpes is coming back. He suggested that I come here and learn about how to cope with it if I keep getting recurrences. I'm so stressed, but I know this is also the worst thing for me if I want to help my body keep it under control. Please help me!

■ HSV (Herpes I and II)

Genital herpes An infection caused by exposure to the herpes simplex virus type 1 or type 2 through sexual contact

Genital herpes infection is caused by exposure to the herpes simplex virus type 1 (HSV 1) or herpes simplex virus type 2 (HSV 2) through sexual contact. HSV 1 initially was associated with oral infection and HSV 2 with genital infection. Over the past 25 years, however, the increased popularity of oral sex has led to an almost equal probability of contracting either form from the genital area.

A 2- to 12-day incubation period follows transmission of the virus. The initial symptoms (also known as the primary outbreak) start as discrete grouped **vesicles**. After a short time (a few hours to a few days), the vesicles break open, merge with each other, and form painful ulcers, which drain and crust over. The entire first episode takes 15 to 20 days. Often, a systemic,

Vesicles Fluid-filled blisters

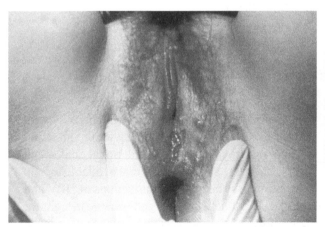
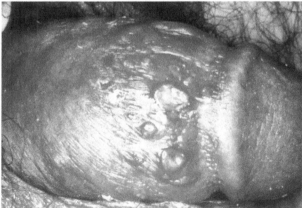

The primary symptoms of herpes are fluid-filled vesicles that break open to form painful, highly infectious ulcers. *Source:* Centers for Disease Control and Prevention; Division of STD Prevention

healthy sex hints 12.2

Self-Help for People with Genital Herpes

Most people with genital herpes are able to manage their infections and prevent spreading their infection to others.

The following tips will help you do just that.

If you are taking acyclovir or other herpes medication on a maintenance schedule and it helps reduce recurring episodes of infection, continue taking the medicine as prescribed.

1. At the first hint of prodromal symptoms, consider yourself infectious and capable of spreading your infection. During this time, abstain from intercourse, engage in non-genital sexual pleasuring, or use condoms.

2. Treat any outbreak as you would the flu (another viral infection), with bed rest and over-the-counter pain relievers.

3. Keep your genitals clean and dry. Take short baths, pat your genitals with a towel, and use a hair dryer to dry the area thoroughly.

4. Avoid pantyhose, tight underwear, and binding clothes until the blisters crust over and dry up. If you can, take a day or two off during the worst symptoms, stay in bed, and avoid wearing clothes.

5. Do not cover the blisters with petroleum jelly or other cream that blocks air from drying the area.

6. Minimize stress, as it delays healing.

flulike syndrome accompanies the primary outbreak. The symptoms of this syndrome, known as the **prodrome**, include aches, fever, and malaise.

Recurring outbreaks occur in most sufferers on an average of five to eight times per year and last approximately 10 days per episode. Recurrences often are preceded by the same prodromal syndrome that accompanies the primary episode. The frequency and severity of recurring episodes diminish with time.

Genital herpes in adults tends to be a self-limiting, albeit painful, STD. It is a much more serious condition among newborns (infected as they pass through the birth canal) and those whose immune systems are compromised because of HIV infection (DSTD, 2013b). Genital HSV infection has no cure but can be managed successfully with the use of antiviral drugs.

As with the other viral STIs, most treatment regimens focus on slowing the replication of the virus and boosting the immune system. Treatment also includes techniques to speed drying and healing of the vesicles and blisters associated with the infection.

Prodrome A systemic, flulike syndrome that accompanies genital herpes infection

HPV - Human Papilloma Virus (Genital Warts, Genital Cancer)

Genital warts, also known as venereal warts, are caused by infection with the **human papilloma virus (HPV)**. There are at least 46 known varieties of HPV. Of these, at least 12 types of the virus are associated with genital infection. The virus is spread through direct contact with an infected person's genital warts during sexual contact.

Genital warts An STI caused by the HPV or human papilloma virus

Human papilloma virus (HPV) A condition spread through direct contact with an infected person's genital warts during sexual contact

The genital warts associated with HPV infection can get large enough to block the openings of the urethra, vagina or anus. *Source:* Centers for Disease Control and Prevention, National Center for HIV/AIDS, Viral Hepatitis, STD, and TB Prevention, Division of STD Prevention

Autoinnoculate To self inflict the spread of disease from one body part to another

Cervical intraepithelial neoplasms (CIN) Tumors or growths within the cervical membrane tissues

The average incubation period for genital warts is 3 months from the time of exposure. The initial warts can be isolated or appear in clusters on the genitals and perianal area. The warts vary in size from 1/8 inch to considerably larger, and in some cases growths become so large that they cause deformity of genital structures. Growths can **autoinnoculate** adjoining tissue. These "kissing lesions" are often found on the labia or under the foreskin of uncircumcised men. Infection with warts is not painful, but continued growth can cause a painful obstruction of the vaginal, anal, or urethral opening.

Estimates of infection with no symptoms vary from 10 to 45 percent of infected individuals. Most HPV infections are temporary, and symptoms resolve by the body's immune response. Although studies have shown that most cases of HPV are undetectable after 2 years, reactivation of the virus can occur (DSTD, 2013a), (Ho, Bierman, Beardsley, Chang, & Burk, 1998).

The major concern associated with HPV is the increased risk for cancer. Cervical infection with HPV is associated with at least 80 percent of all cervical cancer cases (Schiffman, 1992; Woodman et al., 2001). Women with HPV infection of the cervix are 10 times more likely to develop cervical cancer than women without the infection (Schiffman, 1992). As many as 10 percent of women with cervical HPV infections will develop **cervical intraepithelial neoplasms (CINs)** within 1 year. HPV types 16, 18, and 31 have been found in all types of genital cancers. HPV 16 is responsible for more than half of all cases of cervical cancer. Four HPV types, 16, 18, 31, and 45, account for 80 percent of all cervical cancer associated with HPV (Ciaran et al., 2003; DSTD, 2000).

Human Papillomavirus (HPV) - The Most Common STI

Source: Callista Lee

The body's immune system clears most HPV naturally within two years (about 90 percent), though some infections persist. While there is no treatment for the virus itself, there are treatments for the serious diseases that HPV can cause, including genital warts, cervical, and other cancers.

Most sexually active men and women will get HPV at some point in their lives. This means that everyone is at risk for the potential outcomes of HPV and many may benefit from the prevention that the HPV vaccine provides. HPV vaccines are routinely recommended for 11 or 12 year old boys and girls, and protect against some of the most common types of HPV that can lead to disease and cancer, including most cervical cancers. CDC recommends that all teen girls and women through age 26 get vaccinated, as well as all teen boys and men through age 21 (and through age 26 for gay, bisexual, and other men who have sex with men). HPV vaccines are most effective if they are provided before an individual ever has sex.

Source: https://www.cdc.gov/std/stats/sti-estimates-fact-sheet-feb-2013.pdf

Hepatitis B Virus (HBV)

Hepatitis B virus (HBV) infection is another blood-borne disease transmitted through activities that involve percutaneous (i.e., puncture through the skin) or mucosal contact with infectious blood or body fluids (e.g., semen, saliva), including

Hepatitis B virus (HBV) A disease caused by contact with infected blood; often associated with unprotected sex with multiple partners

- Sex with an infected partner
- Injection drug use that involves sharing needles, syringes, or drug-preparation equipment
- Birth to an infected mother
- Contact with blood or open sores of an infected person
- Needle sticks or sharp instrument exposures
- Sharing items such as razors or toothbrushes with an infected person

HBV is not spread through food or water, sharing eating utensils, breastfeeding, hugging, kissing, hand holding, coughing, or sneezing (DSTD, 2012L).

 healthy sex hints 12.3

Should I Get the HBV Vaccine?

A vaccine for HBV has been available since 1981. At first, the vaccine was recommended for use by those whose work caused them to come in contact with potentially contaminated blood (such as health care workers and those living with persons infected with HBV). It is now recognized that many other persons are potentially at risk through drug-related behavior and sexual activity with infected persons and should consider becoming vaccinated. The vaccine is now recommended that the following populations:

- All infants, beginning at birth
- All children aged <19 years who have not been vaccinated previously
- Susceptible sex partners of Hepatitis B surface antigen (HBsAg)-positive persons
- Sexually active persons who are not in a long-term, mutually monogamous relationship (e.g., >1 sex partner during the previous 6 months)
- Persons seeking evaluation or treatment for a sexually transmitted infection
- Men who have sex with men
- Injection drug users
- Susceptible household contacts of HBsAg-positive persons
- Health care and public safety workers at risk for exposure to blood or blood-contaminated body fluids
- Persons with end-stage kidney disease
- Residents and staff of facilities for developmentally disabled persons
- Persons with chronic liver disease
- Persons with HIV infection
- Travelers to foreign countries where HBV is common
- Unvaccinated adults with diabetes mellitus who are aged 19 through 59 years (discretion of clinicians for unvaccinated adults with diabetes mellitus who are aged ≥60 years)
- All other persons seeking protection from HBV infection—acknowledgment of a specific risk factor is not a requirement for vaccination (DSTD 2012 L).

HBV is a serious viral disease that attacks the liver and can cause extreme illness and even death. HBV can cause acute infection or not be apparent. To most people, infection with hepatitis B is not clinically apparent. Between 10 and 68 percent of all cases are chronic **carriers**; the infected individuals have the disease and are capable of spreading it but have no noticeable symptoms. When they do notice their symptoms, they usually have jaundice, dark urine, fever, malaise, and moderate liver enlargement with tenderness.

Carriers Individuals who have a given disease and are capable of passing it on but have no apparent symptoms

Diagnosis is made through a combination of a clinical examination and a blood test indicating the presence of hepatitis B surface antigen (HBsAG). Chronic infection can lead to cirrhosis of the liver and liver cancer (DSTD 2012L).

The following populations are at increased risk of becoming infected with HBV:

- Infants born to infected mothers
- Sex partners of infected persons
- Sexually active persons who are not in a long-term, mutually monogamous relationship (e.g., >1 sex partner during the previous 6 months)
- Men who have sex with men
- Injection drug users
- Household contacts of persons with chronic HBV infection (DSTD, 2012L).

HBV infection has no cure because, like HIV, it is caused by a virus. For acute infection, no medication is available; treatment is designed to reduce the pain and suffering associated with the symptoms.

HIV/AIDS

Source: Callista Lee

Transmission & Diagnosis

HIV is a virus that interferes with the human immune system's ability to fight off infection and disease. When a person is infected with HIV, their medical diagnosis is "HIV+." If the HIV infection is not treated relatively quickly and aggressively with modern anti-retroviral medications (ART) it will eventually cause so much damage to the immune system that the patient will find it very difficult to fight off infections and will qualify for a diagnosis of **AIDS**. The AIDS diagnosis no longer means that the patient is without hope and about to die. Rather, it signals the patient's need for more aggressive medical treatment and lifestyle changes to better combat the HIV living in the bloodstream.

The immune system's ability to fight infection is measured by how many T-cells (also called CD-4 cells) are found in a cubic milliliter of blood. T-cells are a type of white blood cell that travels throughout your body along with the red blood cells and other substances found in blood. The normal T-cell count for a healthy young adult is usually between 1,000 to 1,600. During times of illness or stress it will be lower but will come up again once you are well. Once in the bloodstream, HIV attaches itself to the T-cells and takes them over; stopping them from doing their work in fighting infections and causing them to become nurseries for more HIV cells. The AIDS diagnosis is not given until the T-cell count is 200 or below, *and* the patient is suffering from at least one of a long list of **opportunistic infections**. You can search online for a list of them; most are infections you have probably never heard of. That is because these infections are easy for a healthy immune system to fight off...so easy that you wouldn't even know that germ found its way into your body. The list includes certain types of cancers, certain types of pneumonia, certain parasitic infections (they may affect your lungs, your digestive system or even your brain), as well as unusually invasive Candidiasis (yeast) infections of the esophagus (swallowing tube) or trachea or bronchia (breathing tubes) or deeper lung tissues. Herpes infections in which the blisters just won't heal may also be a sign of a compromised immune system. There is a condition called HIV Wasting Syndrome in which the patient is ill with diarrhea, fever, weakness, and serious weight loss that lasts for over 30 days.

Because HIV lives in the bloodstream, and specifically on/in T-cells, the body fluids of an HIV+ person that include T-cells will be infectious to others. The good news is that we don't come into contact with these fluids on a casual basis. **The infectious fluids include:**

- Blood
- Semen
- Vaginal fluids
- Breast Milk
- Anal fluids
- And other fluids that have blood in them due to infection or injury

So what fluids does that leave out? Sweat, tears, healthy urine, normal mucus, normal saliva, skin oils. None of these can transmit HIV.

How do these infectious fluids allow HIV into your bloodstream?

- Sexual activity is the most common way
  - Anal Intercourse (77% risk each time, unprotected)
  - Vaginal intercourse (68% risk each time, unprotected)
  - Oral-Genital sex (15% risk each time, unprotected)
- Sharing injection needles (55% risk each time the needle is used after an infected person uses that same needle)
- Pregnant Mother to Child (30% risk if no precautions are taken)
  - Less than 3% risk if mother is on ART, birth is Caesarian, and mother does not breastfeed
- Open cuts or sores, other breaks in the skin (data not available)

The risk data above was provided by Orange County's AIDS Services Foundation, recently renamed, "Radiant Health Centers."

The only way that you can know whether you have been infected with HIV is to have an HIV test. The initial testing can be done with blood or a mouth swab. Both of these tests are looking for your body's **antibodies** to HIV, not HIV itself.

Each time you get sick with influenza it is because the influenza virus has mutated so that your existing antibodies won't recognize it. Your immune system has to create new antibodies for the new version of the virus. You'll feel sick until your immune system is able to knock out that new strain of the influenza virus. HIV mutates quickly too; that is one of the reasons researchers have not been able to come up with a vaccine to prevent HIV (vaccines stimulate the immune system to create antibodies). **HIV antibody tests** are quick and easy. The OraSure mouth swab makes results available in just 20 minutes. (While HIV is not in your mouth, the antibodies *are*.) There is a Rapid HIV Blood test too, but most blood tests have to be sent off to a lab which may delay your results for a week or two. For people concerned that they had unsafe contact with a person known to have HIV, there is an Early Test (NAAT/RNA) available, which tests for HIV itself. Check with your local clinic to find out which test is best for you.

If your HIV antibody test is negative (meaning you do NOT have antibodies to HIV) then you will be encouraged to come back in a few of months to be retested, and to avoid taking additional risks. That is because it takes time for the immune system to create the antibodies. Some people may create them within a 3-4 weeks of infection while many others take up to 3 months. A very small number of people don't create them until 5 or 6 months after infection. If you have heard of a six-month waiting period, this is what that was about. ***Don't* wait 6 months to get tested.** If you want to be tested after waiting just 2 weeks, that is fine. Just know that if your test is negative you still need to come back for re-testing later.

If you test positive for HIV antibodies, a second type of test that looks for antibodies will be done using a small sample of blood from your arm. If this second test (the Western Blot test) comes back positive

Antibodies are cells created by the immune system in response to a viral infection. Each type of viral infection will lead the immune system to create a specific antibody to attack the virus causing that infection. Afterward, the antibodies stay in the system in case you encounter that virus again.

1 in 7 living with HIV

are **unaware** of their infection.

Source: https://www.hiv.gov/hiv-basics/overview/data-and-trends/statistics

you will be diagnosed as HIV+ and counseled about appropriate medical treatment for your condition.

Progression of HIV to AIDS

- Primary HIV Infection
  - You won't know you have HIV unless you get tested for the antibodies
  - Although there will be no symptoms of illness the person may be infectious to others in as soon as a few days after infection
- Acute HIV Infection
  - Within 2-4 weeks people infected with HIV may experience a flu-like illness which may last for a few weeks.
  - Whether the person feels sick or not, they are **highly infectious** during this early stage of infection because they have a lot of HIV in their bodies and it is actively making a home for itself in the T-cells.
  - If the person has tested HIV+, they begin medication at this time to help the immune system fight off the effects of HIV.
- Clinical Latency – less HIV activity
  - Even without medical treatment this period may last for up to 10 years or longer. HIV is active but reproducing itself at relatively low levels. The person's immune system is slowly being compromised and they are still very contagious to others who take in their infected fluids.

- Anti-Retroviral Therapy (ART) is designed to hold patients at this level, even managing to keep T-cell numbers in a relatively healthy range and keeping the viral load of HIV so low as to be undetectable.
- At the end of this phase, a person's viral load starts to go up and the T-cell count begins to go down. Various illnesses may begin to trouble the person and they will require treatment for those illnesses.
- Acquired immunodeficiency syndrome (AIDS)
  - The most severe phase of HIV infection, with at *least* one but usually more opportunistic infections due to low T-cell count (200 or less). They are often unable to work and may need to be hospitalized from time to time.
  - Common symptoms of this stage include fever, chills, sweats, swollen lymph glands, weakness, diarrhea and weight loss.
  - Without aggressive medical treatment survival is typically only about 3 years. HIV does not kill directly; the opportunistic infections kill.
  - Viral load is very high and the person is highly infectious. But remember, it is still just those infectious fluids mentioned earlier that contain HIV and are therefore dangerous to others. You can still spend time with them, share meals with them, hug them, play with them, etc.

Living With HIV

Because of all that medical researchers and doctors have learned about treating HIV, it is now considered a manageable disease, much like other chronic diseases like diabetes. It *does* take a toll on your health and your lifespan *is* likely to be shorter than it would have been without HIV, but one can live a productive and fulfilling life while living with HIV. And like living with diabetes, treatment involves not just medicines but also changes in lifestyle (healthy eating, exercise, reducing stress, getting good quality sleep, quitting smoking, reducing alcohol, etc.), as well as learning how to cope emotionally and socially. Some important tasks for the person living with HIV include:

- Seeking out a medical care team specializing in HIV

- Finding funding (HIV treatment is very expensive) programs
- Sticking to the medication regimen and coping with side effects
- Counseling to help develop healthier attitudes and behaviors
- Deciding who to tell
- Practicing safer sex, starting with telling partners their HIV status
- Dealing with HIV stigma and related anxiety or depression
- Realizing how precious life is; making life choices that improve daily life

HIV is certainly not the most common STI you can catch, but it is the most serious and certainly the most expensive. Prevention should be your priority.

Local, National, and International Epidemiology and History of HIV

Source: Callista Lee

In 2016, about 38,700 new cases of HIV were diagnosed to bring the total number of Americans living with HIV up to about 1.1 Million. Gay, bisexual and other men who have sex with men made up the largest group with about 26,000 new HIV cases that year. But the American experience with HIV/AIDS is not typical for the world and it is important to understand that. ***Worldwide, the most common way that people become infected with HIV is via heterosexual sex.*** It is only in North America that it has been perceived as a "gay disease" because only here did it appear to be limited to the gay male population when it first showed up. HIV is a mutation of SIV (Simian Immunodeficiency virus – a monkey virus). Scientists believe this mutation occurred around 1920 when SIV passed into humans during hunting, and butchering monkeys for meat. By 1959 HIV was definitely its own separate virus, able to infect humans (Avert, 2019). Researchers have only recently concluded that HIV went from Zaire (in Africa) to Haiti (in the Caribbean) back in 1967; then to New York in 1971 and to San Francisco in 1976 (McNeil, 2016). It took until the early 1980s before it caused enough immunodeficiency illness in the U.S. to draw the attention of the public. For a short time it was known as Gay-related Immunodeficiency Disease (GRID) because most suffering from it were men who had sex with other men. Shortly thereafter, researchers identified HIV as the cause of the mystery illness and understood that this virus was not specific to gay men, or to any specific type of sexual behavior. And about that time it was showing up around the world. A particular individual, "Gaétan Dugas, a globe-trotting, sexually insatiable French Canadian flight attendant" (McNeil, 2016, p.1) was blamed for being "patient zero" and accused of being responsible for the whole American HIV trauma. He didn't live long enough to suffer from that blame. It wasn't until 2016 that researchers were able to clear his name. He did die from HIV infection, but the strain he died from was already in New York before he began frequenting gay bars there in 1974. He could not have brought it from Africa; it was already here.

HIV began in Africa where it continues to ravage the populations of some countries today. Swaziland, Lesotho, Botswana, and South Africa have the highest rates of HIV/AIDS in the world. The U.S. falls 24th on the list of countries with the highest rates of HIV/AIDS (Chepkemoi, 2019). At least one likely reason that we place on that list is because our nation was slow to sound the alarm, slow to urge condom use and testing, and slow to make funding available to fight it. We don't like talking about sexually transmitted diseases. Canadians and Europeans were much

	Orange Co. 2009	OC 2018	Los Angeles Co. 2016
Number of new cases	300 (8.2/100K)	280 (4.4/100K)	1949 (19/100K)
Male	90.6%	88.6%	89%
Female	8.2%	9.6%	11%
Transgender		1.8%	unavailable
Black	5.1%	3.9%	25%
Hispanic	45.9%	54.6%	48%
White	42%	30%	18%
Asian	6%	10.7%	5%
Other			4%
0-18 years old	2.4%	1.8%	0-19 = 3%
19-25 years old	20.2%	27.5%	20-29 = 36%
26-35 years old	27.5%	31.4%	30-39 = 29%
36-45 years old	30.2%	18.6%	40-49 = 18%
46-55 years old	15.1%	12.1%	50-59 = 11%
56 years and older	4.5%	8.6%	60+ = 3%
Men having sex with men	78.9%	67.1%	84%
Heterosexual contact	10%	15.4%	9%
Injection Drug use	3.9%	6.8%	5%
MSM & IDU	5.4%	3.6%	3%
Other/Unknown transmission	1.8%	7.1%	<1%

The data above is from the Orange County and Los Angeles County Health Agencies, respectively.
http://www.ochealthinfo.com/civicax/filebank/blobdload.aspx?BlobID=92260
http://publichealth.lacounty.gov/dhsp/Reports/HIV/2017_AnnualHIVSurv_Report_FINAL_2018Nov15.pdf

more proactive in educating their populations about the prevention of HIV/AIDS in schools, through medical caregivers, and television.

People living with HIV are found throughout the country, including right here in Orange County. Those known to be living with HIV numbered 6,369 in 2018, up from 4,057 in 2009 (OC Health, 2019). This growth is not necessarily bad news, because the numbers of those living with HIV has go up when the numbers of patients dying due to AIDS goes down, and the numbers of new cases have stopped rising each year. Numbers of new infections in OC were at a high of 97 in 2009 but starting in 2014, numbers came down to 60 new diagnoses per year and they have stayed at that level or lower through 2018. As with many illnesses, researchers find racial and social disparities when it comes to who gets sick and what sort of care they receive. Health Education and Medi-

cal care is unevenly available throughout the nation, including California. Although many Americans still view HIV as a gay white man's disease, the fact is that it is a *human* disease that can affect anyone who has unprotected sex or shares needles. Rates of new cases (cases per 100,000 persons) were highest San Juan Capistrano (21.80) Santa Ana (19.5) and lowest in Huntington Beach (3.9) in 2016. Not all cities were included in the analysis due to low numbers of population. Let's compare those newly infected in OC with those in LA County.

Please note that there are many significant population differences between LA and OC. For example, there is a much larger African American population in LA County so it makes sense that their percent of new cases among the Black population would be higher than in OC. Compare our local numbers to the following national data.

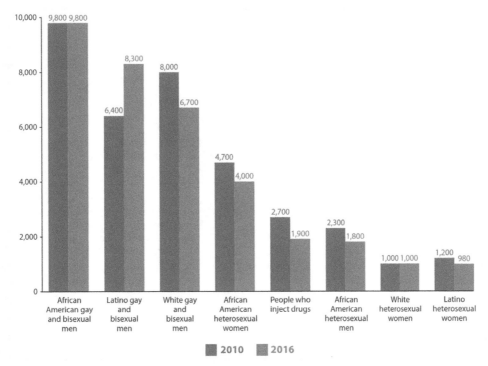

Source: https://www.hiv.gov/hiv-basics/overview/data-and-trends/statistics

As you can see, new HIV cases in white gay/bisexual men decreased, numbers in African-American gay/bisexual males remained stable, but increased in Hispanic/Latino gay/bisexual men. Heterosexuals accounted for 24% of the new cases, a decrease of 8-9%. New cases among injectable drug users also decreased. African American and Hispanics/Latinos are disproportionately affected, meaning that the rates of infection in this groups are high when compared to how many of them there are in the population. Not shown in the figure is an interesting observation that the Southern region of the country accounts for more than half of new HIV cases. There are "hotspots" of HIV infection in the U.S. with more than 50% of the cases occurring in just 48 counties with the U.S. plus Washington D.C., and Puerto Rico. The CDC estimates that 1 in 7 infected Americans is unaware of their HIV status (HIV.gov, 2019). This last statistic is a scary one because it means that these individuals are likely infecting others unknowingly. Each of us has a responsibility to protect our health.

STI Prevention and Risk Reduction

Personal health STI prevention programs focus largely on individual behavior as the basis for risk reduction. Many of these programs emphasize "safer sex" (using condoms consistently and correctly and verifying HIV status through testing) as the primary prevention approach (Crosby et al, 2003). Others stress abstinence from sexual intercourse as the preferred preventive approach (Howard & McCabe, 1990).

The problem with compartmentalizing STI risks is that it fails to acknowledge that personal and community risks have a synergistic effect. We propose a new way to conceptualize the relationship between community and personal risks as pyramidal in nature, consisting of various public and personal factors that build upon each other. Figure 12.2 illustrates this Pyramid of Risk.

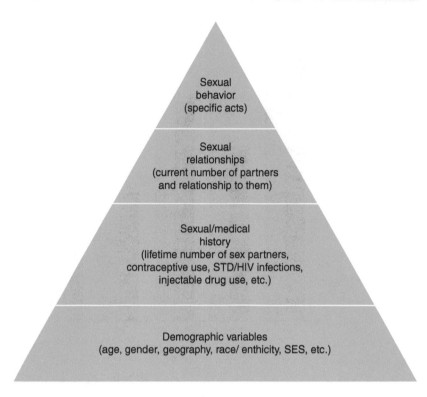

Figure 12.2 *A Pyramid of Risk for STIs* To assess one's true risk of acquiring STIs, demographic and sexual/medical history risks must be combined with behavioral and lifestyle factors.

Demographic Variables and the Distribution of STI

Sexual lifestyle The interaction between types and numbers of current sex partners

The foundation of the pyramid is made up of **demographic** variables that influence STI risk. These are generally beyond our individual control. The next level of risk revolves around the sexual and medical history of ourselves or our partners. Because these risks are part of a person's past, they also cannot be changed. They are the history that each of us brings to any sexual encounter. The third level of risk represents a person's current **sexual lifestyle**, the interaction between the types and numbers of current sex partners. The last level of risk is the one most educators focus on: personal sexual behavior. Most risk reduction pamphlets provide a laundry list of sexual behaviors that range from low risk to high risk. Although the four levels of factors influence STI risk independently, the interaction of levels can have a synergistic effect that can increase or reduce personal risk dramatically.

Seven major demographic variables that contribute to STI risk are age, gender, sexual orientation, injecting drug user (IDU; the clustering of injectable drug users in communities), geography, socioeconomic status (SES), and race/ethnicity.

Age

Estimates suggest that young people aged 15–24 years acquire nearly half of all new STIs.[1] Compared with older adults, sexually active adolescents aged 15–19 years and young adults aged 20–24 years are at higher risk of acquiring STIs for a combination of behavioral, biological, and cultural reasons (DSTD, 2012m).

Some age-related STI considerations are:

- People tend to have sex with partners in their general age groups. Since the 14-24 year old group has the highest rates of infection having sex with members of this group increases risk.
- The earlier the onset of intercourse (first time a person has sexual intercourse), the greater their potential exposure to different sex partners over their lifetime. Individuals who initiate sexual activity earlier are more likely to have more sex partners over a lifetime.
- Adolescents and young adults are more likely than older adults to engage in unprotected sexual intercourse.
- The transformation zone in women (the end of the cervix, where cervical tissue meets vaginal tissue) is most exposed during adolescence, and this tissue is most susceptible to STI infection in general and viral infection (cancer-causing) in particular (DSTD 2005c, Wallis, 2005, Bearman et al., 2004, Sipkin et al., 2003, DSTD, 2000; Quinn & Cates, 1993; Alan Guttmacher Institute, 1991).

Gender

The risk for STIs is different for men and women. Biological gender is a risk factor related to the genetic, anatomical, and physiological differences between men and women (Kennedy, Scarlett, Duer, & Chu, 1995). Women face a greater risk than men for both acquiring a sexually transmitted infection and developing complications for several reasons:

- Heterosexual women are receptive sexually—vaginally, orally, and anally. This greatly increases their risks for initial infection by exposing a greater surface area of mucosal tissue (Quinn & Cates, 1993). Once infected with most STIs, heterosexual women tend to be asymptomatic more often than heterosexual men. (Morse, Moreland, & Thompson, 1990).
- Because of the asymptomatic nature of STIs in women, more women than men do not seek treatment during the initial stages of infection. This delayed access to treatment results in progression of the disease and a greater likelihood of developing complications (Bonaviglia, 2000). For example, about 15 percent of women develop complications associated with gonorrhea or chlamydia versus less than 1 percent of men (Morse et al., 1990).
- Menstruation plays a role in facilitating the movement of pathogens from the lower reproductive tract (below the cervix) to the upper parts, facilitating the development of complications. Women face the added risk of passing on their infection to their developing fetus during pregnancy or newborn through childbirth (Smeltzer & Whipple, 1991).

Sexual Orientation

Risks for STIs are affected by a person's sexual orientation. The risks that heterosexual women face accrue as a result of their anatomy and physiology, which facilitate exposure to disease agents. Sexual exposure results in infection without symptoms, and menstruation facilitates infection.

Endemic A 20 percent level of ongoing infection within a specific population

Gay and bisexual men have some of the risks that heterosexual women do. They are receptive sexually and tend to have asymptomatic infections. This facilitates the development and spread of disease. In addition, certain diseases, such as HIV and hepatitis B, exist in **endemic** levels in the gay community (Bucharcz et al., 2005). These diseases are incurable and capable of causing death.

Heterosexual men are at less risk than heterosexual women and gay men for a variety of reasons. First, their symptoms tend to be more obvious because these men usually are the insertive sexual partners and develop external symptoms.

Of the four groups, lesbian women have the lowest rates of infection. Gay women tend to have fewer sexual partners over the course of their lifetime, and they do not engage in vaginal or anal intercourse (Kennedy et al., 1995).

IDU

IDU The acronym for *injectable drug user*

The risk for STI is becoming increasingly related to the prevalence of **IDUs** (injectable drug users) in a community (Powelson et al., 2000, Bachmann et al., 2000). Drug use is associated with increased STD/HIV risk in two ways.

- Psychoactive drugs impair users' ability to make good decisions regarding sexual behavior.
- Injectable drug use often involves needle sharing between users.

The drug most often involved is injectable heroin.

Urban/Rural and Geographic Differences

STIs including HIV are disproportionately higher in urban areas than in rural or suburban locations **(DSTD, 2005).** "Core urban populations" may be a major contributing factor for higher STI rates in urban communities and disproportionately high personal risk, despite individual behavior (Bearman et al, 2004, Wallis, 2005, Garnett & Anderson, 1996). The rate of acquisition of gonorrhea, for instance, in core urban populations is as much as 300 times higher than in the rest of the population (Rice, Roberts, & Handsfield, 1991).

With a high level of infection and prevalence of deadly diseases, any sexual activity (even so-called safer sex) between or with members of this population carries a higher degree of risk than the same behavior with non–core group people.

❧ *Intellectual and Emotional Wellness* ❧

STIs used to be called "social diseases" because of the nature of sexual transmission.

Social wellness is a major preventive strategy against STIs. Being in a mutually exclusive, monogamous, disease-free relationship is the best prevention against STIs. In the United States, the quality of one's social environment seems to be directly proportional to socioeconomic status (SES). As SES rises, most Americans seek out safer, healthier communities, and safe communities carry much lower risk for STIs. High-risk/low-wellness communities should be targeted for STD prevention and treatment services and programs.

Socioeconomic Status

(SES) To a large extent, STIs mimic other chronic diseases. SES can either facilitate or hinder access to preventive and interventive STD health care. People of lower SES tend to lack enabling factors related to prevention and treatment of STIs such as health care insurance and access to treatment services (Gallet, 2002, Santelli et al., 2000). Even though free public clinics are available, they may not be utilized promptly because poor people often lack access to transportation, don't have sick days if they are employed, or are unaware of the availability of free care (Donelan et al., 1996).

Race/Ethnicity

African Americans and Hispanics continue to have the highest rates of STD infection in the United States. Rates for almost all STIs are substantially higher for these groups than for whites. Risk for certain STIs like gonorrhea and syphilis are as much as 30 times higher for African Americans than for whites (DSTD, 2005).

Although disease rates in general are higher for blacks and Hispanics than whites, racial/ethnic differences are often markers for social class and poverty (Navarro, 1990). Poverty, especially that which affects the urban poor, is the true risk factor. The increased problem of STIs in minority populations in inner cities may stem in part from the unequal distribution of poverty, not race or ethnicity (Navarro, 1990). A greater proportion of blacks and Hispanics/Latinos live at or below poverty than whites. Socioeconomic differentials (often referred to as *class differentials*) are larger than race differentials in **morbidity**. When studies control for SES differentials, racial differences in disease distribution drop markedly. The problem of STIs in minority populations in inner cities is a result, in part, of the unequal distribution of SES (Fortenberry, 2002, Navarro, 1990).

Morbidity The relative incidence of a disease

Sexual/Medical History

The next level of risk on the pyramid is sexual medical history. This is something we cannot control because it has occurred in the past. Yet, a person's sexual and medical history can greatly influence the present level of risk for STIs (Manhart et al., 2004, Holloway, 2005). The following are sexual/medical factors most associated with the current risk for STIs:

Lifetime number of sexual partners. In general, the greater the number, the higher the risk.

Contraceptive use. Barrier contraceptive users have the lowest rates of infection. They are followed by other contraceptive users and nonusers, who have the highest risk (Manhart et al., 2004).

History of IDU. Persons with a history of IDU have an increased **incidence** of infection with blood-borne diseases, particularly HIV and hepatitis B (Alter & Margolis, 1990; Finelli et al., 1993).

Incidence The number of new cases of a disease during a specific time period

Prior STI history. Persons who have been infected with STIs in the past are more likely to become infected again than those who have never been infected **(Manhart et al, 2004).**

■ Sexual Relationships

Sexual relationship refers to the connections between people rather than the specific behaviors in which they engage. In general, the risk for STIs/HIV decreases as sexual relationships move away from multiple, anonymous, sexual encounters toward monogamous (with uninfected partner), trusting partnerships (Wallis, 2005, Bearman et al., 2004, Metzler et al., 2000, Lauman et al., 1994).

STI/HIV sexual relationship risks are specifically related to overall numbers of partners and the quality of the relationship (trust, understanding, and knowledge of one's partner). Figure 12.3 shows the continuum of risks for sexual relationships. There are two dimensions of lifestyle of partner risk: familiarity risk and exclusivity risk.

Familiarity risk. Familiarity risk is synonymous with *anonymity.* Studies show that the less familiar one is with the sex partner (the greater the anonymity), the greater is the risk. (Manhart et al, 2005, Bearman et al, 2004, Laumann et al, 1994).

Exclusivity risk. Laumann et al. (1994) call the second variable *exclusivity*—the quality of the sexual relationship. Exclusivity, they believe, has to be examined for *both* partners. For exclusivity to work, both partners have to be uninfected and monogamous. Subjects (and partners) who were not sexually exclusive were at increased risk for acquiring an STI (Manhart et al, 2005, Bearman et al, 2004, Lauman et al., 1994).

The highest risks were associated with the "interaction of risky partners" (lack of exclusivity and familiarity) and many partners. This sexual lifestyle, which combines multiple partners with anonymous sexual encounters, creates a deadly synergy that increases the risk exponentially (Manhart et al, 2005, Bearman et al, 2004, Lauman et. al, 1994).

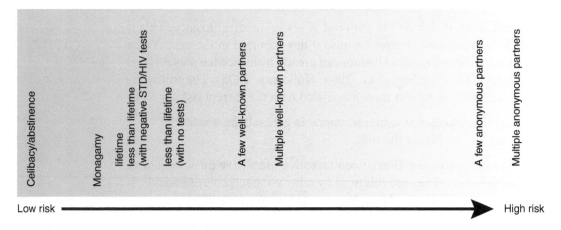

Figure 12.3 *Continuum of Risk for Sexual Relationships STI risks increase as relationships become less familiar and exclusive.*

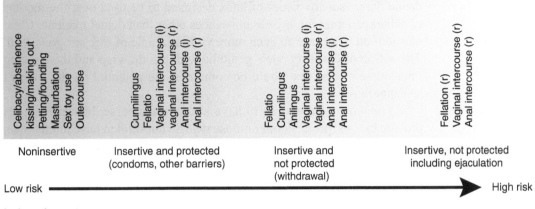

i = insertive partner
r = receptive partner

Figure 12.4 *A Continuum of Risk for Sexual Behaviors* STI risks increase as sexual activities become unprotected and receptive.

Sexual Behavior

At the top of the Pyramid of Risk is sexual behavior. In general, as illustrated in Figure 12.4, the risks increase as behaviors incorporate unprotected insertion and ejaculation. The lower-risk behaviors are non-penetrative and do not involve an exchange of bodily fluids. As we move along the continuum of risk, the behaviors reflect attempts to utilize barrier protection against infectious agents. The highest risk behavior is receptive anal penetration including ejaculation, which consists of unprotected ejaculation of semen into the delicate, non-lubricated tissue of the rectum. This allows direct access of infectious STI agents to the bloodstream.

Theoretically, as Figure 12.4 illustrates, the risk for STI is greater for the receptive partner of any sexual activity (MMWR, 2001, Manhart et al, 2005)

A Closer Look at Sexual Behaviors and STI Risk

Much remains to be known about the relative safety of various sexual behaviors. For instance, a wealth of literature documents the degree of protection condoms provide in preventing STIs. Little, however, has been written concerning the effects of non-penetrative sexual activity and withdrawal. Some of these activities now are included in "safer sex" methods, instead of "safe sex" behaviors because of the lack of adequate documentation on their effectiveness.

The effects of some of the more bizarre techniques haven't been documented at all. Consider the recommendation of some safe sex educators of the use of dental dams and clear plastic food wraps to prevent the transmission of STIs through cunnilingus, fellatio, and vaginal intercourse. We do not advocate these measures because they are untested and not intended for those purposes. No evidence is available to suggest that they work. In fact, the American Dental Association issued a disclaimer concerning using dental dams (square pieces of latex designed to be used over the mouths of dental patients) for any circumstances other than dental hygiene. Clear plastic food wraps are an even more vivid example of safe sex gone mad. The notion of covering one's genitalia with plastic wrap and then having intercourse or oral sex would be comical if the potential results weren't so dangerous.

For those who choose to have sexual intercourse, barrier methods provide the best protection. For those who do not want to have intercourse, a variety of non-penetrative sexual activities offer close to 100 percent effectiveness against STIs.

Condoms

If worn properly and used consistently, condoms (both male and female) help protect the wearer against some STI infection by preventing direct contact between the penis and cervical, vaginal, rectal, or pharyngeal secretions or lesions. They also protect against exposure to penile lesions, discharges, and infected semen. Proper use for preventing STIs requires putting them on prior to any sexual contact, and they must remain intact throughout sexual activity.

Condoms are more effective against sexually transmitted infections such as gonorrhea, chlamydia, trichomoniasis, and HIV, which are transmitted by fluids from mucosal surfaces and from semen (and therefore captured or blocked by the condom) than STIs transmitted by skin-to-skin contact such as HPV, herpes simplex virus (HSV), syphilis, and chancroid (MMWR 2001). The organisms of the latter diseases and others live in outcrops of blisters, warts, and lesions that could exist in areas that condoms do not protect (MMWR, 2001). In laboratory studies, male latex condoms have been shown to block the larger bacterial pathogens (gonorrhea and chlamydia) and, to a lesser extent, smaller viral organisms (such as HIV, HSV, and HPV) (Grimes & Cates, 1990; Conant, Hardy, Sernatinger, Spicer, & Levy, 1986; Minuk, Bohme, & Bowen, 1986). Similar findings have not been found for natural membrane condoms. Although they block the passage of sperm and are similar in their ability to prevent pregnancy, their pores are large enough to allow the passage of some STI organisms. Natural membrane condoms should not be the first choice for the prevention of STIs unless one is allergic to latex (MMWR, 2001).

Condoms lubricated with Nonxynol 9 (N-9) spermicides have not been found to be any more effective than other lubricated condoms in protecting against the transmission of HIV and other STIs (Richardson, 2002). Additional findings regarding condoms lubricated with N-9 are; spermicide-coated condoms cost more, have a shorter shelf-life than other lubricated condoms, and have been associated with urinary tract infection in young women (MMWR 2001).

Women-Centered Barriers

Although the male condom is the most reliable form of barrier protection against STIs, studies show that the women who stand to benefit the most do not use them consistently and correctly. The least consistent users of the male condom are adolescent women, women with a history of STI, and lower-SES women (who generally have less power and equality in their sexual relationships with men and have less negotiating skill) (Rosenberg & Gollub, 1992). This problem could be dramatically lessened, if not eliminated, if more women were to use female barriers consistently and correctly.

Clinical studies of the effectiveness of female condoms in preventing STIs are very limited **but** their theoretical effectiveness against STIs is high (Green & Gollub, 2003). Laboratory studies have demonstrated the effectiveness of the female condom in blocking viruses. Female condoms are recommended for use when male condoms cannot be used properly (Green & Gollub, 2003).

In both laboratory and STI clinic studies, the following rates of effectiveness were reported for the sponge, diaphragm, and spermicides:

- An overall reduced STI infection rate among barrier users compared to non-barrier users
- Lower STI infection rates (87 percent lower) for women using barriers and attending health maintenance organizations (HMOs) than nonusers
- Lower STI infection rates (61 percent lower than nonusers) for women attending STI clinics who used barriers
- Up to 70 percent effectiveness against gonorrhea when using barriers
- Up to 40 percent effectiveness against chlamydia when using barriers

Even though condoms have a higher rate of theoretical effectiveness against STIs, the women who need them the most use them less consistently and correctly. Woman-centered barriers, though theoretically less effective against STIs, provided greater actual effectiveness for women who used them instead of the male condom (Rosenberg & Golub, 1992).

personal Exploration Activity

My Most Persuasive Reasons to Wait to Have Sex

Although there are many great reasons to have sexual intercourse, there are also some really good reasons to wait. One of the best ways to avoid an STI is to limit your sexual partners. This activity will help you practice being assertive about why you want to wait to have sex.

This will be more fun if you can find a friend to role-play this with you. It will be even more fun if you find a friend of the opposite sex. Tell your friend that you would like for him or her to act out the following scenario with you. You are playing the parts of a couple who disagree when to become sexually active. One partner is ready to become sexually intimate, but the other partner wants to stay monogamous and to wait at least 4 months to be tested for HIV/AIDS and STIs before becoming intimate. Your friend will play the role of trying to persuade you to have sex, and your role is to give your friend all of the good reasons that you two should wait. Once you have finished, decide who was the most persuasive and discuss other good arguments you could have used. The more we practice assertively telling a partner what we need, the more likely we are to do it in our "real" relationships.

Non-penetrative Sexual Behaviors

The effectiveness of non-penetrative sexual activity in preventing STIs is relatively undocumented. Effectiveness in preventing STIs is generalized from the hypothesized ability of these methods to prevent unintended pregnancy by preventing the deposit of live sperm into the vagina. Because these methods exclude penetration and ejaculation, their ability to prevent pregnancy is very high (theoretically close to 100 percent).

Methods such as masturbation, use of sex toys, and even oral-genital sexual contact in preventing the transmission of STIs have not been scientifically studied and documented. Do they work? No one knows for sure. When theorizing about their ability to prevent STIs, one can say that, because they do not involve penetration and STIs, they must offer a high level of protection against STIs as well. We are not as totally convinced of this hypothesis as some other safer sex educators are.

These facts are why we present sexual behaviors on a continuum of risk from low to high. No behavior except celibacy is completely risk-free. Viewing sexual activity in this way will allow you to examine the risk of specific behaviors in the context of other sexual activities. You also must evaluate any behavior within the context of the relationship you have with your partner. The less you know about your partner, the more risky any behavior becomes.

◼ Using the Pyramid to Reduce Risks

The pyramid model presented earlier in the chapter shows that the risk for STIs combines personal lifestyle and behavior, past sexual history, and demographic factors. Focusing on just one set of factors and ignoring the others isn't enough. Though a person can never dismiss personal behavior as crucial to the success of prevention activities, other factors affect personal risk despite the most exemplary personal behavior. For example, in certain core areas, individuals have 300 times more risk for acquiring infection simply by virtue of community risk factors **(Potterat et al., 1985)**. Even if you are rather conservative in your behavior, if you live and interact sexually in such an area, engaging in any sexual activity carries a higher risk of becoming infected and engaging in risky sexual behavior may be life-threatening. This demographic influence might make risk reduction measures much different from someone who lives in a lower-risk area.

Fighting STIs: Prevention, Diagnosis, and Prompt Treatment

Source: Callista Lee

Because STIs are preventable, significant reductions in new infections are not only possible, they are urgently needed. Prevention can minimize the negative, long-term consequences of STIs and also reduce healthcare costs.

The high incidence and overall prevalence of STIs in the general population suggests that many Americans are at substantial risk of exposure to STIs, underscoring the need for STI prevention.

Abstaining from sex, reducing the number of sexual partners, and consistently and correctly using condoms are all effective STI prevention strategies. Safe, effective vaccines are also available to prevent HBV and some types of HPV that cause disease and cancer. And for all individuals who are sexually active—particularly young people—STI screening and prompt treatment (if infected) are critical to protect a person's health and prevent transmission to others.

CDC's STI screening recommendations: If you are sexually active, be sure to talk to your healthcare provider about STI testing and which tests may be right for you.

- All adults and adolescents should be tested at least once for HIV.
- Annual chlamydia screening for all sexually active women age twenty-five and under, as well as older women with risk factors such as new or multiple sex partners.
- Yearly gonorrhea screening for at-risk sexually active women (e.g., those with new or multiple sex partners, and women who live in communities with a high burden of disease).
- Syphilis, HIV, chlamydia, and hepatitis B screening for all pregnant women, and gonorrhea screening for at-risk pregnant women at the first prenatal visit, to protect the health of mothers and their infants.
- Trichomoniasis screening should be conducted at least annually for all HIV-infected women.
- Screening at least once a year for syphilis, chlamydia, gonorrhea, and HIV for all sexually active gay men, bisexual men, and other men who have sex with men (MSM). MSM who have multiple or anonymous partners should be screened more frequently for STIs (e.g., at three to six month intervals). In addition, MSM who have sex in conjunction with illicit drug use (particularly methamphetamine use) or whose sex partners participate in these activities should be screened more frequently.

Source: https://www.cdc.gov/std/stats/sti-estimates-fact-sheet-feb-2013.pdf

References

Alan Guttmacher Institute. (1991). *Sex and America's teenagers.* New York: Author.

Alter, M., & Margolis, H. (1990). The emergence of hepatitis B as a sexually transmitted disease. *Medical Clinics of North America, 6,* 1529–1541.

Avert. 2019. "Origin of HIV and AIDS." Accessed November 22, 2019. https://www.avert.org/professionals/history-hiv-aids/origin

Bachmann, L.H., Lewis, I., Allen R. (2000). Risk and prevalence of treatable sexually transmitted diseases at a Birmingham substance abuse treatment facility. *American Journal of Public Health* v. 90 no. 10 (October 2000) pp. 1615–18.

Bonavoglia, A (2000).Making love in the dark. *Ms.* v. 10 no. 5 (August/September 2000) pp. 54–9

Cameron, D. W., et al. (1991). Condom use prevents genital ulcers in women working as prostitutes: Influences of human immunodeficiency virus infection. *Sexually Transmitted Diseases, 18,* 188–194.

Centers for Disease Control and Prevention. 2013. "CDC Fact Sheet: Incidence, Prevalence, and Cost of Sexually Transmitted Infections in the United States.". Accessed November 22, 2019. https://www.cdc.gov/std/stats/STI-Estimates-Fact-Sheet-Feb-2013.pdf

Centers for Disease Control and Prevention. 2018. "Sexually Transmitted Disease Surveillance 2017." Accessed November 22, 2019. https://www.cdc.gov/std/stats17/minorities.htm

Centers for Disease Control and Prevention. October 8, 2019. "New CDC Report: STDs Continue to Rise in the U.S. Press Release." Accessed November 22, 2019. https://www.cdc.gov/nchhstp/newsroom/2019/2018-std-surveillance-report-press-release.html

Ciaran, B. J., Woodman, S. C., Rollason, T. P., Winter, H., Bailey, A., Yates, M., & Young, L. S. (2003, January 4). Human papillomavirus type 18 and rapidly progressing cervical intraepithelial neoplasia: Mechanisms of disease. *The Lancet, 361*(9351), 40.

Chepkemoi, J. January 21, 2019. "Countries With the Highest Rates of HIV/AIDs." *WorldAtlas.* Accessed November 22, 2019. worldatlas.com/articles/countries-with-the-highest-rates-of-hiv-aids.html

Conant, M., Hardy, D., Sernatinger, J., Spicer, D., & Levy, J. (1986). Condoms prevent transmission of AIDS-associated retrovirus. *Journal of the American Medical Association, 255,* 1706.

Crosby, R. A., DiClemente, R. J., Wingood G. M. (2003). Value of Consistent Condom Use:

A Study of Sexually Transmitted Disease Prevention Among African American Adolescent Females. *American Journal of Public Health* v. 93 no. 6 (June 2003) pp. 901–2.

DSTD (2000). *Tracking the hidden epidemics: Trends in STIs in the United States 2000.* Atlanta: Public Health Service. Atlanta GA: Centers for Disease Control and Prevention, National Center for HIV/AIDS, Viral Hepatitis, STD, and TB Prevention, Division of STD Prevention.

DSTD (2013a). *Genital HPV Infection-CDC Fact Sheet.* Atlanta GA: Centers for Disease Control and Prevention, National Center for HIV/AIDS, Viral Hepatitis, STD, and TB Prevention, Division of STD Prevention. available online at: http://www.cdc.gov/std/HPV/STDFact-HPV.htm

DSTD (2013b). *Genital Herpes- CDC Fact Sheet.* Atlanta GA: Centers for Disease Control and Prevention, National Center for HIV/AIDS, Viral Hepatitis, STD, and TB Prevention, Division of STD Prevention. available online at: http://www.cdc.gov/std/Herpes/STDFact-Herpes.htm

DSTD (2013c). *Gonorrhea- CDC Fact Sheet.* Atlanta GA: Centers for Disease Control and Prevention, National Center for HIV/AIDS, Viral Hepatitis, STD, and TB Prevention, Division of STD Prevention. available online at: http://www.cdc.gov/std/Gonorrhea/STDFact-gonorrhea.htm

DSTD (2013d). *Syphilis- CDC Fact Sheet.* Atlanta GA: Centers for Disease Control and Prevention, National Center for HIV/AIDS, Viral Hepatitis, STD, and TB Prevention, Division of STD Prevention. available online at: http://www.cdc.gov/std/syphilis/STDFact-Syphilis.htm

DSTD (2012*l*). *Hepatitis B Facts for Health Professionals.* Atlanta GA: Centers for Disease Control and Prevention, National Center for HIV/AIDS, Viral Hepatitis, STD, and TB Prevention, Division of STD Prevention. Available online at: http://www.cdc.gov/hepatitis/HBV/HBVfaq.htm#overview

DSTD (2012m). *STIs in Adolescents and Young Adults.* Atlanta GA: Centers for Disease Control and Prevention, National Center for HIV/AIDS, Viral Hepatitis, STD, and TB Prevention, Division of STD Prevention. Available online at http://www.cdc.gov/std/stats11/adol.htm

DSTD (2011e). *Sexually Transmitted Disease Treatment Guidelines: Gonococcal Infections.* Atlanta GA: Centers for Disease Control and Prevention, National Center for HIV/AIDS, Viral Hepatitis, STD, and TB Prevention, Division of STD Prevention. Available online at: http://www.cdc.gov/std/treatment/2010/gonococcal-infections.htm

DSTD (2011h). *Sexually Transmitted Disease Treatment Guidelines: Diseases Characterized by Urethritis and Cervicitis.* Atlanta GA: Centers for Disease Control and Prevention, National Center for HIV/AIDS, Viral Hepatitis, STD, and TB Prevention, Division of STD Prevention. Available online at: http://www.cdc.gov/std/treatment/2010/ectoparasitic.htm

DSTD (2005). Trends in Reportable Sexually Transmitted Diseases in the United States, 2004. National Surveillance Data for Chlamydia, Gonorrhea, and Syphilis. Available online at: http://www.cdc.gov/std/stats/trends2004.htm

Donelan, K., Blendon, R. J., Hill, C. A., et al. (1996). Whatever happened to the health insurance crisis in the United States? Voices from a national survey. *Journal of the American Medical Association, 276,* 1346–1350.

Fortenberry J. D. (2002). Clinic-based Service Programs for Increasing Responsible Sexual Behavior. *The Journal of Sex Research* v. 39 no. 1 (February 2002) pp. 63–6.

Gallet, C.A. (2002). A note on the determinants of sexually transmitted disease rates. *The Social Science Journal* v. 39 no. 4 (2002) p. 613–16.

Garnett, G. P., & Anderson, R. M. (1996). Core-group transmission of STIs. *Sexually Transmitted Diseases, 20*(4), 181–191.

Golden et al. (2003). HIV/STD Risks in Young Men Who Have Sex With Men Who Do Not Disclose Their Sexual Orientation—Six U.S. Cities, 1994–2000. JAMA v. 289 no. 8 (February 26 2003) pp. 975–7.

Green, Y., Gollub, E (2001). CDC promotes the female condom for HIV/STD prevention. *American Journal of Public Health* v. 91 no. 11 (November 2001) p. 1732–3.

Grimes, D. A., & Cates, W. (1990). Family planning and sexually transmitted diseases. In K. K. Holmes, P. A. Mardh, P. F. Sparling, P. Wiesner, W. Cates, S. M. Lemon, & W. E. Stamm (Eds.), *Sexually transmitted diseases* (2nd ed., pp.1087–1094). New York: McGraw-Hill.

HIV.gov. 2019. "U.S. Statistics." Accessed November 22, 2019. https://www.hiv.gov/ hiv-basics/overview/data-and-trends/statistics

Holloway, L.R. (2005). What You Should Know Before Having Sex. *Ebony* v. 60 no. 10 (August 2005) p. 118, 120, 122–3.

Howard, M., & McCabe, J. B. (1990). Helping teenagers postpone sexual involvement. *Family Planning Perspectives, 22,* 21–26.

Jones, J. (1993). *Bad Blood: The Tuskegee Study—A Tragedy of Race and Medicine.* New York City, NY; Free Press.

Kennedy, M. B., Scarlett, M. I., Duer, A. C., & Chu, S. Y. (1995). Assessing HIV risk among women who have sex with women: Scientific and communication issues. *Journal of the American Medical Women's Association, 50,* 103–107.

Kodner, CM., Nasraty, S. (2004). Management of Genital Warts. *American Family Physician* v. 70 no. 12 (December 15 2004) pp. 2335–42.

Kuyoh, M.A., Toroitich-Ruto, C., Grimes D.A., Schulz, K.F., Gallo, M.F. (2003). Sponge vs. diaphragm for contraception. *Contraception,* Jan2003, Vol. 67 Issue 1, pp. 15–19.

Laumann, E. O., Gagnon, J. H., Michael, R. Y., & Michaels, S. (1994). *The social organization of sexuality: Sexual practices in the United States.* Chicago: University of Chicago Press.

LosAngeles County.gov. 2018. "Annual HIV survey." Accessed November 22, 2019. http://publichealth.lacounty.gov/dhsp/ Reports/HIV/2017_AnnualHIVSurv_Report_ FINAL_2018Nov15.pdf

McNeil Jr., D.G. 2016. "HIV Appeared in the U.S. Long Before "Patient Zero." Accessed November 22, 2019. https://www.nytimes. com/2016/10/27/health/hiv-patient-zero-genetic-analysis.html

Metzler, C.W., Biglan, A., Noell, J. (2000). A randomized controlled trial of a behavioral intervention to reduce high-risk sexual behavior among adolescents in STD clinics. *Behavior Therapy* v. 31 no. 1 (Winter 2000).

Minuk, G., Bohme, G., & Bowen, T. (1986). Condoms and hepatitis B virus infection. *Annals of Internal Medicine, 104,* 584.

MMWR (2001). Revised guidelines for HIV Counseling, testing and referral.

MMWR. (2002, October 18). Screening tests to detect chlamydia and gonorrhea infections. Morbidity and Mortality Weekly Report, 51 (RR-15). Atlanta: U.S. Department of Health and Human Services, Centers for Disease Control and Prevention, Division of STD.

MMWR. (2002, May). 2002: Sexually transmitted disease: Treatment guidelines. *Mortality and Morbidity Weekly Report, 51* (RR-6).

National Center for Infectious Disease. (2003). Hepatitis surveillance 1980–2001 [Online]. Available: www.cdc.gov/ ncidod/diseases/ hepatitis/resource/dz_burden02.htm.

Navarro, N. (1990). Race or class: Mortality differentials in the United States. *Lancet, 336,* 1238–1240.

Orange County Health Care Agency. 2019. "2018 HIV Disease Fact Sheet." Accessed November 22, 2019. http://www. ochealthinfo.com/civicax/filebank/blobdload. aspx?BlobID=92260

Potterat, R., Rothenberg, R., Woodhouse, D. E., Muth, J. B., Pratts, C. I., & Fogle, J. S. (1985). Gonorrhea as a social disease. *Sexually Transmitted Diseases, 1,* 25–32.

Powelson, M., Fletcher, JF. (2000). Sexually transmitted diseases, drug use, & risky behavior among Miami-Dade County jail detainees. *Corrections Today* v. 62 no. 6 (October 2000) pp. 108–13, 122

Quinn, T., & Cates, W. (1993). Epidemiology of STIs in the 1990s. In T. Quinn (Ed.), *Sexually transmitted diseases.* New York: Raven.

Ramos, R., Shain, R. N., & Johnson, L. (1995). Men I mess with don't have anything to do with AIDS: Using ethnotheory to understand sexual risk perception. *Sociology Quarterly, 36,* 483–505.

Richardson B.A. (2002). Nonoxynol-9 as a vaginal mircrobicide for prevention of sexually transmitted infections. *JAMA* 2002;287:1171–2.

Rosenberg, M. J., & Gollub, E. L. (1992). Commentary: Methods women can use that may prevent sexually transmitted disease, including HIV. *American Journal of Public Health, 82*(11), 1473–1478.

Santelli, J.S., Lowry, R, Brener, ND (2000). The association of sexual behaviors with socioeconomic status, family structure, and race/ethnicity among US adolescents *American Journal of Public Health* v. 90 no. 10 (October 2000) pp. 1582–8.

Smeltzer, S., & Whipple, B. (1991). Women & HIV. *Journal of Nursing, 4,* 249–256.

Taylor, M., Prescott, L. Brown, J., Wong, W., Allen, M., Broussard, D., Lori, P. (2005). Activities to increase provider awareness of early syphilis in men who have sex with men in 8 cities, 2000-2004. *Sexually Transmitted Diseases,* Oct, 2005 Supplement, Vol. 32, pp. S24–S29.

Weinstock H., Berman S, Cates W. Sexually transmitted diseases among American youth: incidence and prevalence estimates, 2000. *Perspectives on Sexual and Reproductive Health* 2004; 36(1): 6–10.

Chapter
thirteen

Fertility, Pregnancy, and Parenting

Student Learning Objectives

After reading this chapter, students will be able to

- Discuss parenting readiness and how parenting style affects psychological development.
- Describe the process of conception.
- Describe normal developmental characteristics during the three trimesters of pregnancy.
- Assess the influence of a variety of negative personal behaviors (such as alcohol use) on prenatal development.
- Describe personal health behaviors that enhance pregnancy outcomes.
- Identify a variety of alternatives to traditional conception and parenting.
- Describe a variety of factors related to infertility.
- Describe the process of childbirth.
- Evaluate options for labor and delivery.
- Discuss pros and cons of parenting styles.

personal exploration activity

The World's Greatest Parent

Taking care of a baby before it is born is essential to the well-being of the child. However, the hard work has just begun. Parenting is complex and challenging, and often we are totally unprepared for the job. The following interview activity will help you begin the process of determining what you will need to do to be an effective, loving parent.

It is time to put your friends to work again to help you gather some ideas about healthy and unhealthy parenting. Interview five of your friends or acquaintances using the following questions, recording all of their answers in a journal.

What are the characteristics of a good parent?
1. What are the characteristics of a poor parent?
2. What are some things your parents or friend's parents did that you would like to do with your children?
3. What are some things your parents or friend's parents did that you will not do with your children?
4. How did your parents or friends' parents handle sexuality that you will also do with your children?
5. How did your parents or friends' parents handle sexuality that you will not do with your children?
6. In what activities will you encourage your children to participate?
7. What activities will you discourage your children from participating in?

When you have finished interviewing, review your list and add ideas you have about each question. Can you incorporate the ideas you gathered so you can be "the world's greatest parent"?

To Parent or Not to Parent

The decision about whether or not to have children may be the most life changing and important decisions one will ever make. While most people think very carefully about who and when to marry, many never closely examine whether they really want to take on the awesome responsibility of having and raising a child. However, unlike marriage where divorce is an option, a child is a lifelong responsibility. Some individuals and/or couples care for a friends' child for the weekend or get a dog to help assess how well they work individually and as a couple with the responsibilities of caring for a dependent. If after careful examination, they decide to become parents, they then face the decisions of how many children to have, when to have them, and how far apart to space them, all aspects of **family planning**. With reproductive technologies becoming more familiar and accessible, prenatal screenings more widespread, and better prenatal care more available, prospective parents have the opportunity to improve the health and welfare of

Family planning The conscious effort of deciding to have a family, including when to have children, how many, and how far apart to space them

sex in society 13.1

Who Makes Appropriate Parents?

Society makes judgments about who would make appropriate parents, with the ideal not matching up well to the diverse realities of American families. Income, age, marital status, and sexual orientation become a few of the focal points for commentary and public policy.

Many couples are waiting until later in life to have children but this approach has its drawbacks. Although it is no longer unusual to see "gray-haired parents "at PTA meetings of elementary- aged children, women in particular still struggle with their "biological clocks." Sylvia Ann Hewlett (2002), in the book *Creating a Life: Professional Women and the Quest for Children,* reported on a national survey of high achieving women. She found that 42 percent of these women working in corporate America still did not have children at age 40. Although admittedly some women in the group chose a professional career with no thoughts of having children, others found themselves childless by circumstance. The decision to become a parent after age 35 for women can mean greater reliance on infertility programs, with or without success, not to mention great financial expense. The concept of a "ticking biological clock" does not affect men in the same way. At the same time, being close to two generations older than a child can impact family dynamics.

When lesbian and gay couples choose to parent, they often find themselves being judged by a culture that traditionally has defined parenthood as a heterosexual right. Psychological studies have shown that good parenting is the key ingredient to raising healthy children, not the sexual orientation of the parents. The concern that having gay or lesbian parents will deprive a child of the opposite sex's influence is common yet without a scientific basis.

The American Academy of Pediatrics issued a statement in 2002 supporting co-parent and second-parent adoptions by same-sex couples: "There is a considerable body of professional literature that suggest children with parents who are homosexual have the same advantages and the same expectations for health, adjustment, and development as children whose parents are heterosexual." In addition to adoption, lesbian couples may choose to use artificial insemination with donor sperm to create their families. As described in Case Study 13.1, lesbian couples today have more options for bearing children and sharing in the joys of parenthood.

their babies. In addition, if biological parenthood is not possible, adoption opportunities exist both within and outside the United States.

Not everyone wants to be a parent. The number of those choosing not to have children appears to be increasing. Today nearly one- in- five American women reaches the end of her childbearing years never bearing children, compared to one in ten in 1970 (US Census, 2015). The explanations for this increase include a decrease in social pressure for women to have children, better economic opportunities for women and better contraception choices. Among women in their forties, an equal number are childless either by choice or because they cannot have children. In 2002, among those 40–44, six percent were childless by choice, six percent wanted children but were infertile and 2% were hoping to have them in the future (Livingston & Cohen, 2010). These numbers do not even include all of the males who do not choose to have children. The overall birth rate in the U.S. declined eight percent between 2007 and 2010. The birth rate for those 15–44 was the lowest since 1920, perhaps currently due to the great recession (Livingston & Cohen, 2012).

U.S. Birth Rates Continue to Drop

Source: Callista Lee

Usually birth rates would climb back up after the economy recovers, but many factors have been different this time. The Great Recession began in December 2007. With the aid of the federal government, major industries recovered financially, and unemployment rates have gradually dropped, but most workers have not seen significant gains in income and some have seen decreases. Many young couples today face crushing student debt and impossibly high housing costs. For most Americans, times are still tough. Millennials have been accused of ruining businesses because they don't spend enough. But in a 2018 paper by the Federal Reserve Bank, authors report that "Younger people are spending less because they have less money to spend" and "Millennials are less well off than members of earlier generations when they were young, with lower earnings, fewer assets, and less wealth," write authors Christopher Kurz, Geng Li and Daniel J. Vine (in Blumberg, 2018). So much for the bragging of politicians about how great the economy is! The US birth rate has not only failed to "bounce back" after the end of the recession but has continued to go down, to the lowest number of births in thirty years. The only group in which births have increased is women aged 40-44 (NVSS, 2018). At the same time, the preterm births (birth at less than thirty-seven weeks) has increased over all age groups, as has the number of low birthweight babies; both are indicators of a need for better access to prenatal care.

At the same time that would-be parents are feeling economic pressures and better access to healthcare, the social stigma of remaining childless has been decreasing. We now differentiate between being "childless" (wishing you had kids) and being "childfree" (having made a choice to not have children). Still, nearly half of American pregnancies are unintended, meaning we still have a lot of work to do regarding sexuality education and access to family planning services. Unintended pregnancy rates are highest among low-income women, women aged 18-24, cohabiting women, and women of color. In 2011, 42 percent of unintended pregnancies (excluding miscarriages) ended in abortion, and 58 percent ended in birth (Guttmacher, 2019). The Personal Assessment for this chapter (at the website) uses the Wellness Model to help you determine your readiness to be a parent.

case study 13.1

The Joy of Matthew

Elizabeth, 30

I remember when I came out as a lesbian to my family and friends—it took a little while to live openly and share my life with those closest to me. I also thought that as a lesbian I had to give up my dreams of owning a home, getting married, and having kids. Then I met Maria, and everything changed. Maria and I have been together for 6 years now and have built a really fulfilling life together. We have a home, we got married, and we have our wonderful son, Matthew.

Maria and I were together 3 years before we decided to begin building our family. We know gay and lesbian couples who have adopted children, others who have children from previous marriages, and those who had a child biologically together. After a lot of discussions, we decided to have our own biological child. There we were with all those eggs, but no sperm. We needed a donor.

After even more discussion—and I mean lots of talking and soul searching—we decided that Maria would be the biological mother. I know

Critical Thinking

What do you see as unique child-rearing issues for gay and lesbian parents? Do you think there are unique "growing-up" issues for children of lesbian and gay parents? If so, what are they?

that many couples "plan" their children, but for two prospective parents of the same gender, the planning is more complicated and takes on a lot of the same issues faced by infertile heterosexual couples. We had to know when Maria was fertile and then inseminate her at the right time. And as with all couples trying to create a pregnancy, success does not necessarily happen right away. It took nearly 9 months before Maria became pregnant. Believe me, this baby was planned and so very wanted!

Luckily, we had found our way to a gay-friendly health clinic that referred us to a helpful physician. With donor sperm, insemination took place at home. We're not quite sure yet what we're going to tell Matthew about how he was conceived, but since he's a baby, we have time to figure out how best to explain things. Even though friends may be curious about the donor, they've been really understanding and respect our privacy.

For now we're just basking in the joys (and challenges!) of parenthood. Maria is breastfeeding Matthew, but we share all other parenting roles. Our son has a hyphenated last name representing both of us, and I have legally adopted him to ensure I have the same parental rights as Maria. Maria is "Mama" to Matthew, and I'm "E-Mom" for "Elizabeth Mom." But the other night, he pointed at Maria and said, "Mama," then pointed at me and said, "Mama." He gets it. Smart kid.

Almost as wonderful as Matthew himself has been the growing awareness that people see and accept us as the loving family we are. While there is certainly much more that needs to happen when it comes to lesbian and gay rights, we feel very lucky to live at a time where there is so much more acceptance and understanding. We have a great support network of family and friends. We always had great support from our doctor, and the birthing experience at the hospital was totally positive. We haven't experienced any homophobia as we meet other families, and we have families with all different structures in our life. All we hear over and over again is what a great kid Matthew is. People could care less that he's got two moms instead of a mom and a dad. That's pretty neat.

Matthew is safe, secure, and totally loved by his two moms and the wonderful people we're lucky enough to have in our lives.

Becoming Pregnant

Source: Callista Lee

In way of review from Chapter 2, a woman's ovary releases an egg (ovum) approximately once per cycle, and this process is referred to as **ovulation**. It occurs about two weeks before the beginning of her next period. Because it can be risky business to rely on trial and error to guess when that might be, many women who are hoping to get pregnant will study fertility awareness methods to help them get a better idea of when ovulation is about to happen. The textbook's website will link you to more information about the fertility awareness methods that are most effective. There are a number of apps available, but most of them rely on the calendar method (counting the days of your cycles), which is not very accurate.

Ovulation The release of an egg from the ovary.

The best predictor of ovulation is a combination of the Calendar, Mucus, and Temperature Methods (Planned Parenthood, 2019).

While most women only ovulate about once a month, men are making new sperm daily. So, the couple must determine days of best fertility based on the woman's ovulations. Getting the sperm and the egg together is just part of the process, however. **Conception** (successful **fertilization** of the ovum by a sperm) is not the same as pregnancy. A fertilized egg will not survive for more than a week or so on its own. Some will break down and fail at the stage of early cell division just days after fertiliza-tion. Others will begin development but will fail to implant in the wall of the uterus. And some will implant but fail to continue growing there; no placenta will develop. Researchers estimate that only about half of all fertilized eggs achieve full development in nature (UCSF Health, 2019). For the process to become a pregnancy, it must successfully implant into the wall of the uterus, stimulating the uterus to develop the placenta, which connects the embryo to the mother's blood supply, as a source of nutrients and oxygen needed for survival.

Fertilization/conception Union of the sperm and ovum.

Conception

Fallopian tubes Conduits connected to the uterus through which the egg passes into the uterus during ovulation. Fertilization usually takes place at the outer third of the tube

Conception results from the successful journey of a group of sperm to the outer third of the **fallopian tube**. After being deposited in the vagina, ideally close to the cervix, sperm must make their way into the uterus, over to and up the fallopian tube where the ovum is waiting. Pregnancy is most likely to happen when intercourse occurs within six days before ovulation.

A normal ejaculation usually contains between 250 and 500 million sperm. Although only one sperm penetrates the membrane of the ovum at conception, millions are needed for conception. For a male to be considered fertile, the sperm count must be 15 million/milliliter of semen, there must be a high number of sperm with normal shaped oval heads and long tails and at least 40% of sperm are moving- wriggling and swimming (Mayo Clinic, 2015). Sperm survive best in an alkaline environment, and many die when confronting the acidity of the male urethra and female vagina. Continued losses result from sperm not heading toward the correct tube (the two tubes alternate in egg production each month). Finally, the much smaller group reaches the ovum. Consequently, though the sperm count starts at millions, only a few thousand make it to the fallopian tube, and a couple hundred get close to the ovum.

Descriptions of conception have often left mental images of the valiant, strong, surviving sperm successfully attacking and breaking through the membrane of the ovum. Research has demonstrated that the process is more complicated. A mature ovum will release the chemical **allurin**, which attracts the sperm. The sperm that ultimately penetrates the outer membrane of the ovum is able to do so because of **fertilin**, a protein on its plasma membrane (Sherwood, 2004). The ovum extends microvilli up from its surface, which hold down the sperm and push other sperm away. Finally, the egg pulls the sperm inside toward its nucleus. This process and its aftermath are depicted in Figure 13.1.

Sterility The permanent inability to reproduce

Fraternal twins will result if two eggs are released and both are fertilized by different sperm, and identical twins will be produced if one egg splits and develops into two embryos. Fraternal twins are no more alike than siblings but identical twins have same eye color, hair color and blood type. Identical twins may even share a placenta during development. Having twins does run in families but it is a myth that twins

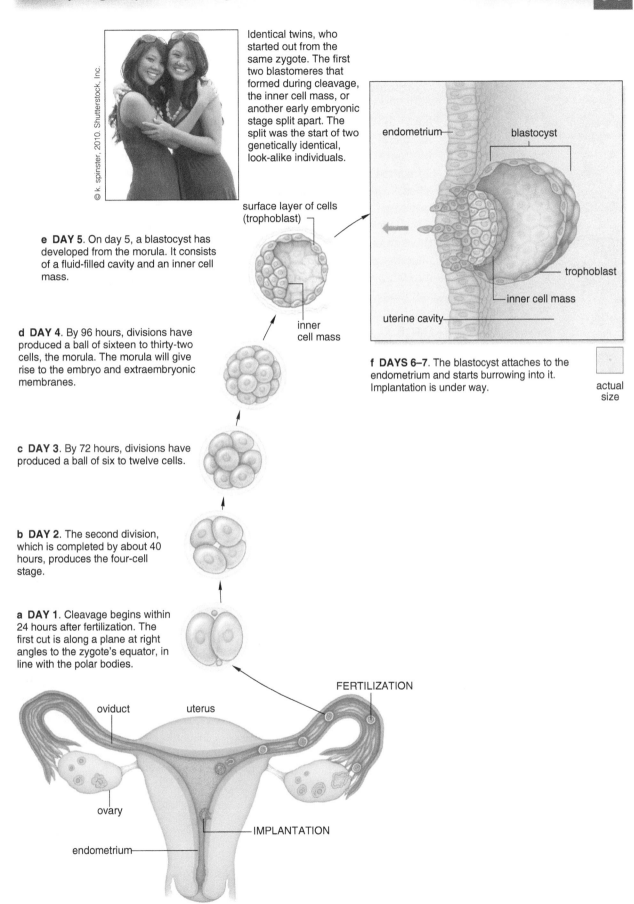

Identical twins, who started out from the same zygote. The first two blastomeres that formed during cleavage, the inner cell mass, or another early embryonic stage split apart. The split was the start of two genetically identical, look-alike individuals.

© k. spinster, 2010. Shutterstock, Inc.

endometrium

blastocyst

trophoblast

inner cell mass

uterine cavity

surface layer of cells (trophoblast)

e DAY 5. On day 5, a blastocyst has developed from the morula. It consists of a fluid-filled cavity and an inner cell mass.

inner cell mass

d DAY 4. By 96 hours, divisions have produced a ball of sixteen to thirty-two cells, the morula. The morula will give rise to the embryo and extraembryonic membranes.

f DAYS 6–7. The blastocyst attaches to the endometrium and starts burrowing into it. Implantation is under way.

actual size

c DAY 3. By 72 hours, divisions have produced a ball of six to twelve cells.

b DAY 2. The second division, which is completed by about 40 hours, produces the four-cell stage.

a DAY 1. Cleavage begins within 24 hours after fertilization. The first cut is along a plane at right angles to the zygote's equator, in line with the polar bodies.

FERTILIZATION

oviduct   uterus

ovary

IMPLANTATION

endometrium

Figure 13.1 *Fertilization in the Fallopian Tube*

skip a generation. Age is a contributing factor to having twins. Women older than 30 are more likely to release more than one ova increasing the chance for fraternal twins (American College of Obstetricians and Gynecologist, 2012).

The fertilized egg, beginning a process of rapid cell division, travels down the fallopian tube over 3 to 4 days and sometimes longer, reaching the uterus, where it will attach to the uterine wall in a process called **implantation**. During this time, cell division is occurring constantly. Once implanted, the fertilized egg, now referred to as an **embryo**, will be nourished through the remaining term of the pregnancy. After 8 weeks, the structure is referred to as a **fetus**.

The environment within the uterus is highly protected. The fetus floats in, and is protected by, **amniotic fluid**. The **placenta**, an organ of interchange that attaches to the uterine wall, passes oxygen and nutrients through the umbilical cord to the fetus and passes waste products and carbon dioxide back to the mother. Unfortunately, as will be discussed later, numerous toxins may also cross the placenta and damage the fetus in a variety of ways.

Infertility

Vasectomy The surgical sterilization of the male that involves cutting and tying off the vas deferens

Although pregnancy and childbirth are "natural" occurrences, they don't occur easily for all couples. Infertility affects as many as 10–18 percent of all couples in the United States (Alvero, 2017). Based on surveys conducted by the National Center for Health Statistics (NCHS) in 2017, 7.5 million women (12 percent) between ages 15 and 44 had an impaired ability to have children; eleven percent of women had used an infertility service (Centers for Disease Control, 2017).

Infertility is the inability to conceive or impregnate after 1 year of regularly engaging in sexual intercourse without the use of birth control. Infertility rates have increased in recent years probably due to couples choosing to have children at a later age. The peak age for fertility is 20 to 24 when 86% of couples will conceive in 12 months of unprotected sex. As age increases the percentage declines as follows: age 25–29—78% will conceive in 1 year, age 30–34—63% will conceive in 1 year and it falls to 52% for age 35–39. After age 40, fertility declines progressively and more rapidly (MD Consult, 2007, Medical Clinics of North America, 2008). Both male and female fertility decline with age. For females, subtle infertility begins at 30, after age 37 the rate increases dramatically and by the mid 40's, pregnancy is extremely unlikely. Male infertility also increases greatly at age 37. Approximately forty percent of infertility are related to female factors, forty percent related to male factors, and twenty percent are either a combination of male and female factors or unknown (Alvero, 2017). On occasion, individuals may know or suspect that they may have difficulty or be unable to reproduce. For others the knowledge comes as a painful reality. Over half of women described infertility as the most upsetting experience of their lives. Many will experience emotions similar to those experienced when grieving for any important loss. Typical reactions include depression, anger, frustration, and perceived loss of control over one's life (Miller, 2012). In recent years, reproductive technologies have greatly expanded to enable couples to biologically become parents. The pregnancies that result, though, come at great physical, emotional, and financial cost and do not always result in a successful birth.

Prevention of infertility has become an important focus in educating future parents. Behavioral changes prior to attempting to become parents can have very positive impacts on decreasing the risk of infertility. Reducing the risk of STD's by minimizing the number of sexual partners, using barrier contraception and screening regularly for STD's can greatly decrease the female's risk for scarring the fallopian tubes. Maintaining a healthy weight (body mass index 18-25) all throughout life increases the probability of normal ovulation. Being overweight (body mass index over 25) or

sex in society 13.2

Ethical Issues and Reproductive Technologies

Among attempts to have a child, surrogate motherhood remains an option—albeit a controversial one. The case of Mary Beth Whitehead in 1986 brought the complicated issues of surrogacy to national attention. Whitehead had signed a contract with a New Jersey couple and was artificially inseminated with the husband's sperm. After giving birth to a baby girl, Whitehead decided that she didn't want to give up the child for adoption. The courts became involved, and the story spread across the popular media. For a while the baby girl even had two names. The outcome of the court case was that the child was given to the adoptive parents, with Whitehead being granted visitation rights.

As a result of this case, a number of legal and ethical issues were brought to national attention. To some people, the use of surrogate mothers extends the array of reproductive options for infertile couples. It represents a choice that is both private and not much different from traditional adoption. To others, it represents exploitation of women's bodies. Those who are able to pay hire women whose need of income may be paramount. The contractual elements, fees involved, and possible legal challenges all contribute to the debate over surrogate mothering.

Another public case had to do with John and Luanne Buzzanca. After 6 years of infertility treatments, the couple turned to a laboratory that supplied donor sperm and ova, paid a surrogate, and finally became parents in San Francisco in April 1995. Shortly after the birth, John filed for divorce and refused to make child support payments on the grounds that he wasn't the baby's father in any true legal sense, despite having earlier signed a contract agreeing to the child's

birth. The Superior Court agreed, claiming that baby Jaycee had been conceived in a petri dish, from anonymous donors, and carried and delivered by a surrogate mother with no genetic ties to her. Consequently, according to California law, not only was John not the father, but Luanne was not the legal mother. By California law, the child had no parents.

A petition filed with the California Court of Appeals for the Fourth Circuit (March 1998), however, resulted in the determination that both John and Luanne Buzzanca were the legal parents of Jaycee (Vorzimer, O'Hara, & Shafton, 1998). As a result of that ruling, individuals who use assisted reproductive technologies and intend to be considered the parents can finalize their parental rights before the child is born, regardless of whether they use a traditional or a gestational surrogate. Specific to this case, because John Buzzanca initially had consented to using donor sperm and a surrogate to produce a child, he was viewed as the father and, therefore, has financial responsibilities to Jaycee.

In January, 2009, Nadya Suleman, a single mother of 6 gave birth to an additional 8 children conceived through invitro fertilization. These births ignited a controversy over the ethics of implanting multiple ova when the guidelines recommend implanting only 2 embryos in young women. This prompted the California Medical Board to investigate the fertility doctor to determine if the standards of medical practice had been violated. These births also created much debate over the issue of a single mom with no source of income choosing have so many children through invitro fertilization.

underweight (body mass index of 17 or less) is associated with infertility due to lack of ovulation.

Smoking is the most common lifestyle choice that decreases the chances of getting pregnant (Alvero, 2017). Moderate exercise and responsible alcohol use are also important health habits. Moderate exercise increases and enzyme that protects sperm. Those who exercise heavily more than 7 hours a week and consume high intakes of alcohol delay conception (Hornstein & Gibbons, 2008). Individuals are urged to take control and practice healthy behaviors to maintain their reproductive ability thus giving themselves the choice of whether to have children or not.

In vitro fertilization (IVF)
A procedure in which ova are removed from the woman's body and fertilized with sperm in a laboratory; the embryo is surgically implanted into her uterus.

When a woman's fallopian tubes remain blocked, **in vitro fertilization (IVF)**, the most effective form of assisted reproductive technology, becomes an option. Her ovaries are first stimulated using hormones, so that more than one ovum matures each month. After surgically removing the eggs, they are joined with sperm in a laboratory. Often more than one embryo will be placed directly into the woman's uterus if the woman is over 35. for those under 35, the recommendation is that no more than 2 be place in the uterus. Generally, the more embryos that are transplanted, the higher the rate of success. However, placing more than one embryo also carries the risk of multiple births (Van Voorhis, 2007). Transferring a single embryo rather than multiple ones is an option that will reduce this risk of multiple births and the chance of premature delivery (CDC, 2017).

Some couples confront the reality that a pregnancy will result only from the use of donor sperm or donor ova. Fertility clinics can provide information to couples that allow them to choose donors who match them in physical appearance, background, and interests. Because college students are considered young and healthy, they may be approached as possible donors. You may find advertisements in your college newspaper seeking sperm and ova donors. For women in particular, the money offered is enticing and intended to compensate for the health risks involved. High doses of hormones are prescribed, which stimulate multiple ovulations. The ova are harvested and then retrieved surgically. Both hormone ingestion and surgery carry some risk to the woman's health.

Assisted reproductive technology (ART) Infertility interventions in which a laboratory is involved with the union of the sperm and egg

The **assisted reproductive technology (ART)** refers to fertility treatments in which both eggs and sperm are handled by a laboratory. The federal government requires all medical centers in the United States that use ART to report data to the CDC on an annual basis. Assisted reproduction can stem from a couple's fresh eggs and sperm, donor eggs and sperm, "thawed" embryos, and so forth. The latest data from the CDC shows a deceasing success rate as women age. For those under 35, the live birth rate is 40 percent, the highest rate. The success rate for other ages is: 32 percent for those 35-37, 21 percent for ages 38-40, and only 2 percent for those 44 and older (CDC, 2017). Overall, about half of all couples who go through the rigors of these procedures are able to take a baby home. The success decreases as the woman ages. This is not the information most people hear when the discussion of assisted reproductive technology takes place. Infertile couples come to learn that attempts do not mean automatic success and that multiple births with their concomitant issues are a risk (Van Voorhis, 2007).

Couples spend varying amounts of time, money, and certainly emotional energy being tested and evaluated for the causes of the infertility. Those who consider IVF can expect to pay $12,000–$17,000 for each

Anthony's Story of Infertility

Anthony, 40

Looking back on it now, it all seems so distant. My wife and I married in September of 2005. We planned a perfect life together, filled with love and joy. We thought that most of this joy would come from the children we planned on having.

I don't know whether it was the combination of my going back to college full-time and the pressures of conceiving or whether it just wasn't "God's time" (a phrase we held to that kept our faith), but getting pregnant just wasn't happening. At first we kidded about it. Then we decided to pay more attention to having sex around my wife's ovulation date. Purchasing and using the special thermometer that allowed us to take her basal body temperature was the beginning of a host of infertility treatments. We came to hate that word infertility as much as the constant advice to "relax."

One year passed, and no pregnancy. I thought about how my brother's infertility was remedied by an operation to remove a varicocele. Six months after his surgery, his wife became pregnant. The operation had helped his sperm count, which had been both low and with slow-motility sperm.

Now it was my turn. I delivered more sperm samples to a variety of medical centers than I care to remember! I had such anxiety as I tried to ejaculate into cups, being in public medical facilities with what seemed to be everyone knowing what I was doing. It was determined that I was a candidate for varicocele surgery. Finally our problems would be solved! I had the surgery and hoped to become a father soon. No such luck.

My wife was given two fertility drugs to improve our chances of children but neither worked. She was then scheduled for a laparoscopy to allow the doctors to see what was going on. It turned out that she had endometriosis, cysts on her ovaries, and one of her fallopian tubes was smaller than the other. All these problems were described as "fixable" and, paired with my problem, could have explained why we weren't getting pregnant. After the necessary surgery, we regained our hope.

Months and months of trying came and went. Negative pregnancy tests . . . trying again . . . waiting and hoping that she wouldn't get her period. Anger and sadness when her period came. And trying again. Lovemaking became a job. We were so upset that we were often no-shows at family christenings and children's birthday parties.

After a period of time, the doctor suggested artificial insemination with my sperm. My wife would be put on fertility drugs to increase her chances of ovulation. I would provide a sample—legal masturbation, as I called it—and the sperm would be injected into my wife using a long syringe. We agreed to the procedures. Each time we prayed and prayed yet continued to get negative results.

Not being ready to consider adoption—people were kindly suggesting that to us—we enrolled at the reproductive clinic at a local hospital, known for its successes with infertile couples. I was now 33 years old, finished with college, and fortunately employed at a place with good health benefits. The doctors there suggested in vitro fertilization. We agreed. I had to inject

Critical Thinking

Anthony's case highlights the lengths couples may go to in their attempts to reproduce.

With health care so costly, should limits be placed on what options individuals and couples can exercise? How far would you be willing to go to have a baby when the time is right for you?

Anthony's triplet girls.

fertility drugs into my wife's buttocks for 21 straight days prior to "the day." Prayer got me through that. Retrieval of the eggs was successful, and we were told that there were seven excellent embryos. The doctors would put three back into my wife's uterus.

My wife had to be monitored daily at the hospital, giving blood and having ultrasounds. The egg retrieval was done on March 17, Saint Patrick's Day. The embryos were put back on March 20, the first day of spring. We would have to wait 14 days for the results. Those were the longest 14 days of our lives.

On Easter Sunday we received the exciting news that she was pregnant! Tests conducted 2 weeks later confirmed that she was carrying triplets. We were grateful . . . scared . . . overwhelmed. There was never a question that, despite the high risks associated with multiple births, we would keep all three babies.

After 20 weeks of bed rest and daily monitoring, my wife gave birth, with me at her side, to three beautiful girls. The road was long and bumpy. It took almost 6 years of trying. Although we had been angry, sad, and frustrated, we never lost our faith. We supported each other from start to finish. And now I live with the four most beautiful women in the world, all coming in "God's time."

attempt. Multiple cycles are typically needed with twenty-two percent of cycles resulting in a live birth (Medline Plus, 2016; Mayo Clinic, 2015). Class differences become readily apparent, as those with financial resources and better health insurance plans clearly have an advantage.

Preconception Health for Parents

Source: Callista Lee

Ideally, both parents will work at achieving optimal health *before* pregnancy occurs. Smokers need to quit and partyers need to learn how to have fun without getting drunk or stoned. All that good advice that doctors and health educators always advise should be heeded as a couple gets ready for pregnancy. Making life changes to improve diet, exercise, weight, sleep, coping with stress, and other health habits are more important than ever. Waiting until pregnancy or even until after birth just makes these changes all the more stressful. Some people think that they need a baby in front of them to inspire them to make

difficult lifestyle changes, but the baby needs parents who have already proven themselves to be up for the task. A woman hoping to get pregnant should see her doctor to make sure her body is in good health for a pregnancy. She will probably be prescribed folic acid supplements to reduce the risk of neural tube defects that can occur in early pregnancy (American College of Obstetricians and Gynecologists, 2015). Waiting to make improvements in health until after she is pregnant can carry great risk, as the heart and nervous system are in critical periods of development often before a woman even realizes that she is pregnant.

Pregnancy

Confirming a pregnancy in years past meant that a woman had to see her physician, have a urine test, and wait for days for the results. Today, determining whether a woman is pregnant is as simple as purchasing a home pregnancy kit at the local pharmacy. Home pregnancy kits are designed to detect the presence of **human chorionic gonadotropin (hCG)**, a hormone present in the urine of pregnant women. Because this hormone is secreted as the fertilized egg implants in the uterus, early testing can confirm a pregnancy. Many kits can be used reliably within a day or two of a missed period, although reliability improves if used a week after a period is missed (Consumers Union, 2003b). Overall, a woman must be aware that her period was due to have early feedback that she is pregnant.

Human chorionic gonadotropin (hCG) A hormone secreted during pregnancy that shows up in the urine of pregnant women; the basis for determining pregnancy using home kits

Although home pregnancy tests are 85 to 95 percent accurate, medical laboratory tests are the most accurate. Urine and blood tests for pregnancy detection are available from a caregiver. One of the test, the quantitative test, can detect pregnancy as quickly as 6–8 days after ovulation (MD Consult, 2012). Women should follow up a positive pregnancy test with a visit to a physician. A pelvic exam will indicate an enlarged uterus associated with pregnancy and also will allow the physician to estimate the duration of the pregnancy and project a birth date.

Many women never realize they are pregnant since fifty percent of pregnancies are unplanned and of these fertilized eggs, almost half die and are aborted spontaneously (miscarry) before the woman even suspects she is pregnant. Of the women who know they are pregnant, the miscarriage rate is 10–20% with most occurring before the seventh week. The majority of miscarriages are caused by chromosome issues that prevent the fetus from developing. Other factors that can cause a miscarriage include heavy smoking and alcohol use, illegal drug use, being overweight or underweight, and environmental toxins (Storch, 2012).

Gestation

A pregnancy is measured from the first day of a woman's last menstrual period, with the expected period of **gestation** averaging 40 weeks. A normal birth will take place between the 38th and 42nd week. Deliveries before 38 weeks are considered premature, and after 42 weeks, the extended time may threaten the health of the baby, so labor may be induced. A mathematical calculation called the *Naegele's rule* is used by obstetricians, nurse midwives, and other health care providers to help estimate the expected date of birth. To calculate the estimated due date, take the first day of the last menstrual period, subtract 3 months, and then add 1 year and 7 days. (Women need to keep track of their menstrual cycles as a general health practice, but especially around pregnancy.) For example: Jessica's last period began on February 2. Subtracting 3 months brings her to November 2, and adding 7 days makes her estimated due date November 9.

Gestation The period of time representing pregnancy and development of fetus from conception to birth

Tubal ligation The surgical sterilization of the female that involves cutting and tying off the fallopian tubes

Pregnancies are divided into trimesters, each having unique characteristics. Figure 13.2 is a time line showing features of each.

Fetal development

Weeks		
First trimester	0	Conception
	2	Implantation; cell differentiation
	4	Heart is forming and begins to function Central nervous system is forming
	6	Sex organs are forming; male and female differentiated by 8th week
	8	Ears, eyes, arms, and legs are forming
	10	Embryo responds to stimulation; form is recognizably human
	12	Vital organs are basically formed and working
Second trimester	14	Circulatory system is operating
	16	Mother can feel movements Fetus' sex organs are distinct
	18	
	20	Hair is forming on body and head
	22	
	24	Fetus demonstrates sucking movements, vigorous body movements; eyelashes and eyebrows appear; skin is thin, wrinkled, translucent
Third trimester	26	Eyes open
	28	Suvival outside womb is possible
	30	Layer of fat starts forming beneath skin
	32	
	34	Survival outside womb is probable
	36	
	38	Birth

Figure 13.2 *Fetal Development*

First Trimester

During the first trimester of the pregnancy, all structures and systems develop in rudimentary form. At the end of 3 months, the fetus has arms, legs, feet, toes, fingers, and the vital organs and body systems are functioning. The mother's taking drugs during the first trimester can have a particularly damaging effect on the fetus. One overpowering argument for planning a pregnancy lies in the fact that without planning, the mother unintentionally may be taking medications with **teratogenic effects**, causing fetal malformations. As suggested earlier, women who are trying to get pregnant should take care of themselves as if they are already pregnant. This will help protect the developing embryo during that time between conception and when pregnancy is determined. For example, as discussed earlier, women need to take folic acid supplements prior to getting pregnant and during the pregnancy to prevent neural tube defects. Neural tube development is complete within 28 days after conception and this is often before the woman knows she is pregnant. Taking preconception folic acid supplements would reduce neural tube defects by 50%. (MD Consult, 2007). At the end of the first trimester, the fetus is approximately 4 inches in length and weighs approximately 1 ounce. At this point, the hands are more developed than the feet and the arms are longer than the legs. The bones and muscles are beginning to grow, the genitalia are clearly formed into female and male, and the skin is almost transparent (ACOG, 2015).

Second Trimester

The second trimester is marked by growth and maturation of all the fetal systems. As the fetus grows in size and the uterus stretches, the mother's pregnancy becomes evident. During the fifth month of pregnancy, fetal movement is usually active enough for the mother to feel and the fetus sleeps and wakes regularly. In females, the eggs have formed in the ovaries and in males the testicles begin to descend from the abdomen into the scrotal sac. By the end of the second trimester, the fetus is close to 12 inches long and weighs between 1 and 1.5 pounds. The sex organs are apparent, as is body hair, including eyebrows and eyelashes. The eyes begin to open and the lungs are fully formed but not functioning. Neonatal intensive care units, equipped with the proper medications and technology, can help some babies born prematurely at the end of the sixth month of pregnancy to survive (ACOG, 2011).

Third Trimester

During the third trimester, the fetal systems continue to grow and mature. Early in this trimester, the fetus kicks and stretches and responds to sound.

Teratogenic effects Side effects of drugs and other substances that cause birth defects

STAGES
EMBRYO DEVELOPMENT

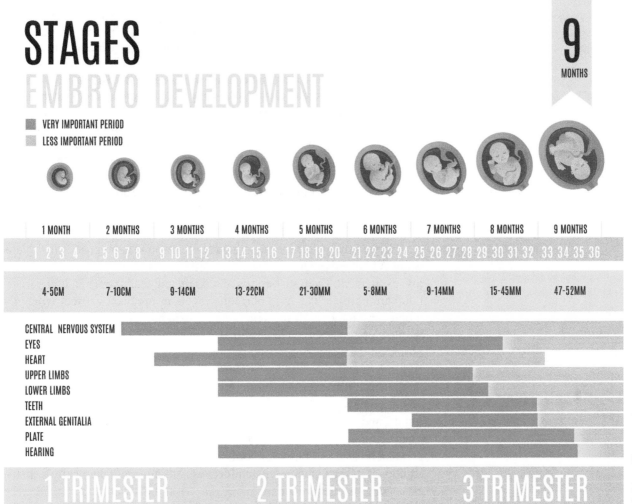

9 MONTHS

■ VERY IMPORTANT PERIOD
■ LESS IMPORTANT PERIOD

1 MONTH	2 MONTHS	3 MONTHS	4 MONTHS	5 MONTHS	6 MONTHS	7 MONTHS	8 MONTHS	9 MONTHS
1 2 3 4	5 6 7 8	9 10 11 12	13 14 15 16	17 18 19 20	21 22 23 24	25 26 27 28	29 30 31 32	33 34 35 36
4-5CM	7-10CM	9-14CM	13-22CM	21-30MM	5-8MM	9-14MM	15-45MM	47-52MM

CENTRAL NERVOUS SYSTEM
EYES
HEART
UPPER LIMBS
LOWER LIMBS
TEETH
EXTERNAL GENITALIA
PLATE
HEARING

1 TRIMESTER   2 TRIMESTER   3 TRIMESTER

Sabelskaya/Shutterstock.com

The embryo/fetus is most susceptible to teratogenic effects during the time periods shown in brown.

The eyes open and close and react to light. The taste buds develop and the fetus can distinguish sweet and sour taste. The mother may even feel the baby hiccup. With all the major development finished, the fetus rapidly gains weight and in the ninth month gains ½ pound per week. The fetus will usually turn and settle into a head down position for birth. The lungs are fully developed and ready to function on their own (ACOG, 2011). At birth, the average baby weighs 8 pounds and is approximately 20 inches in length.

Physical, Psychological, and Social Effects of Pregnancy

Clearly, pregnancy has a powerful impact on health. The woman experiences a number of physical changes as her body responds to the physical demands of the pregnancy. Carrying an ever larger baby in the front of one's body puts demands on all the systems. Pregnancy and childbirth may well be the greatest physical challenges in a woman's life.

Pregnancy and childbirth clearly have an impact on a woman's health, and parenting affects the health of all caregivers. The mere fact that pregnant women are advised to gain between 25 and 35 pounds to have a healthy baby can put a strain on many body systems. Blood pressure may increase. Respiration becomes more labored. Muscles and ligaments must stretch. Throughout pregnancy, women report varying degrees of fatigue, shortness of breath, heartburn, indigestion, nausea, gas, constipation, headaches, leg cramps, backaches, water retention, varicose veins, and difficulty sleeping. Nerves may be impinged upon by the developing fetus; sciatica is a common complaint. Maintaining a healthy pregnancy requires good prenatal care, focusing on nutrition, exercise, and monitored use of medication. Any problems that develop can then hopefully be managed without harm to the developing fetus.

Emotionally, fathers and mothers both respond to pregnancy in various ways. A planned pregnancy should connect to positive feelings—happiness, joy, excitement. Even so, periods of anxiety and fear about pending parenthood are normal. The high hormone levels in pregnancy affect women's moods and may result in being weepy, irritable, and upset but for many women, pregnancy is a wonderful and amazing period in their lives. As the projected date of birth gets closer and closer, pending parenthood, or the addition of another child to the family, becomes all the more real. Couples might have difficulty concentrating on anything but the soon-to-arrive baby.

Pregnancy may affect social relationships as well. Because the birth of a child, and having children, changes our lives in so many ways, some people report feeling awkward around those who have not had the experience of pregnancy. Once children are born, relationships may go through periods of additional strain. Couples with children are talking about their baby's smallest accomplishment or where to buy diapers at the lowest expense, whereas childfree couples may be discussing their latest vacation. Continuing to be able to relate to each other's lifestyle can test the bounds of friendship.

Relationships with family members also may change. Excited grandparents can be a tremendous source of support. Relations between adult children and their parents may improve as the new parents come to better understand the roles of mother and father. In some situations, however, grandparents offer unsolicited advice and become controlling. Something as basic as naming a child and honoring relatives can be a source of tension.

Couples can manage the stresses associated with pregnancy, and later child rearing itself, by communicating openly. Private time to share what can be an intensely spiritual event becomes important. Couples also need time away from the baby to help maintain their bond and the strength of their relationship.

Sexual Activity during Pregnancy

Sexual activity, harmless in a normal pregnancy, can continue throughout the pregnancy. Changing hormones may cause an increase in some women's level of desire and a decrease for others. Beginning in the 4th month of pregnancy women are advised to not lie on their backs, therefore positions for intercourse may need to change. For many couples, intercourse continues

Prenatal Care

Source: Callista Lee

As soon as pregnancy is confirmed, the woman should ask for a referral to an OB-GYN doctor (a doctor specializing in Obstetrics and Gynecology). In addition to helping a pregnant woman manage her own general health, her OB-GYN will perform medical tests to check on the well-being of the developing fetus and provide education for both parents (assuming the father wants to be involved) about pregnancy health issues and preparing for birth. A **nurse-midwife**, birth coach, or **doula** may also provide education, services, and support. Prenatal visits to a healthcare provider usually include a physical exam, weight checks, and providing a urine sample. Depending on the stage of the pregnancy, healthcare providers may also carry out blood tests and imaging tests, such as ultrasound exams. These visits also include discussions about the mother's health, the fetus's health, and any questions about the pregnancy. Having a healthy pregnancy is one of the best ways to promote a healthy birth. Getting early and regular prenatal care improves the chances of a healthy pregnancy (NIH, 2017).

Nurse-midwife Certified nurse-midwives/certified midwives are skilled health professionals who practice in a wide variety of clinical settings, diagnosing and treating patients as well as referring them to a specialist, if required. They are a vital part of the healthcare team and collaborate closely with physicians.

Doula A person who provides emotional and physical support to you during your pregnancy and childbirth. Doulas are not medical professionals. They don't deliver babies or provide medical care. A certified doula has taken a training program and passed an exam in how to help pregnant women and their families during this exciting but challenging experience.

until the birth of the child but not for all. However, sharing intimacy is always important and pregnancy is no exception. Couples can achieve non sexual intimacy by romancing one another with long walks and candle light dinners. Physical intimacy can be achieved in ways other than intercourse such as erotic kisses, hugging, massage and oral sex.

If a pregnancy has been determined to be high-risk, a physician may advise modifications in lovemaking patterns. Sexual activity causes increased uterine activity, perhaps due to orgasm, nipple stimulation, or prostaglandins in semen. Women who are at risk for preterm labor or who have previously lost a pregnancy are often advised to either use condoms or avoid intercourse (Gabbe, 2012).

Substances to Avoid during Pregnancy

Because so many substances can cross the placenta, pregnant women are advised not to take any drug, even over the counter drugs, without first consulting a physician. Public health messages have been created to make women aware of the dangers of consuming alcohol and smoking during pregnancy. Increasing awareness is the first strategy. Actually getting women to stop drinking and smoking is more difficult.

It is estimated that getting women to stop smoking during pregnancy would reduce infant deaths by five percent and reduce the number of low birth weight infants by 10 percent. (Rayburn & Phelan, 2008). Smoking cigarettes and inhaling secondhand smoke both affect the health of the fetus negatively. Cigarette smoke reduces the amount of oxygen in the bloodstream, adversely affecting fetal growth and nicotine decreases uterine blood flow. These effects contribute to the increase in risk of low birth weight,

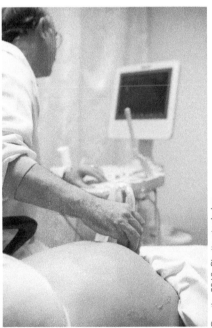

© ustin, 2010. Shutterstock, Inc.

Ultrasound testing can determine position of the baby, abnormalities, and often the sex.

premature birth, still birth, sudden infant death syndrome and respiratory illness for the infant (Gabbe, 2012).

According to the Centers for Disease Control and Prevention, Fetal Alcohol Syndrome cost the United States more than $4 billion dollars per year (CDC, 2015). Because no level of drinking is known to be safe, pregnant women are encouraged to abstain totally. Women who are trying to become pregnant or who use poor birth control also should not drink since they may be pregnant for a few weeks before they know it (Gabbe, 2012). The blood alcohol concentration (BAC) of the mother is the same as that of the fetus, so the impact to the fetus is greater. The higher the alcohol intake the greater the impact and the greater the lifelong problems associated with this intake. An occasional glass of wine or a beer has not been shown to have this impact. Yet, there is a risk and it may not be worth taking.

Fetal alcohol syndrome (FAS) is a cluster of effects found in babies as a result of their mother's drinking. Heavy drinking is a major risk to the fetus and a reduction, even in mid pregnancy can have a beneficial effect (Gabbe, 2012). Children born with FAS have a small head, abnormal facial features, sleep disorders, short stature, a wide space between the eyes and between the nose and upper lip, and behavioral and intellectual impairment.

Women who abuse cocaine, heroin, and other opiates risk having babies addicted to the abused substance. What is less well known is that many other drugs can have damaging effects.

Fetal alcohol syndrome Effects on embryo and fetus of pregnant woman's alcohol consumption; symptoms include facial abnormalities, behavioral and intellectual impairment

 Environmental/Occupational Wellness

When women become pregnant, they need to determine whether their work surroundings are free of toxins and other pollutants that may affect the fetus. For example, exposure to radiation can damage the fetus. Some women who were smokers stop during their pregnancies but unfortunately return to smoking once the baby is born. Not only are they then harming themselves, but the quality of the air is unhealthy for the baby.

Ideally, new parents should be given support by their employers. Some companies are considered "family-friendly" and provide leave to new parents, birth parents, and adoptive parents. On-site day care is available at some private and public institutions. Flexible work schedules are recognized as valuable to the ever increasing number of working parents. Overall, however, the United States is not in the forefront of providing quality day care and family support compared to other industrialized nations.

Childbirth

Childbirth encompasses labor and delivery. Although the baby is born from the mother's body, the experience is increasingly viewed as one to be shared by the couple. Stories of experiences with childbirth vary from couple to couple, woman to woman, and birth to birth, even for the same woman.

For much of history, women helped women birth their babies. With the advent of "modern medicine," obstetricians began to deliver babies. Mothers left their other children at home, went to a hospital, and gave birth, while the fathers waited in the expectant fathers' waiting room. By the end of the 20th century, birthing became an extended family event with much greater support and participation from partners, family, and friends.

Depending to some extent on geography and the availability of health care providers, couples do have choices as to where and how their baby is born. Most babies in the United States are born in hospitals. Establishing a relationship with a private gynecologist/obstetrician, hospital clinic, or birthing center will determine where the baby is born. Although facilities share some fundamental aspects of delivery, they can have philosophical differences in practice and procedures. Being informed about the staff, facilities, and philosophy will enhance the birth experience. The type of health insurance, if any, that the couple has may be the driving force in making a choice.

The Childbirth Process

Childbirth is a three-phase process, shown in Figure 13.3, occurring over a 12- to 14-hour period on average. Some women have a rapid labor, delivering even before they can make it to the hospital. Others report long labors of

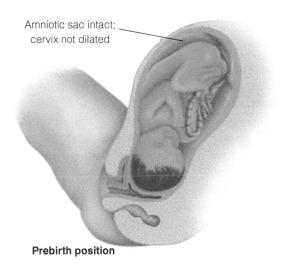

Amniotic sac intact; cervix not dilated

Stage 1
Dilation

Amniotic sac bursts; cervix dilates

Prebirth position

Stage 3
Delivery of placenta

Stage 2
Delivery of baby

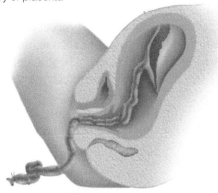

Placenta separates from uterus and is delivered

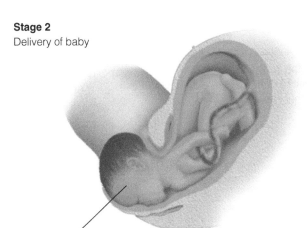

Fetus's head turns, crowns, and is delivered

Figure 13.3 *Stages of Childbirth*

30 or more hours. The length of labor is affected by many factors including fetal size, fetal position, epidural use and the mother's body mass index (Gabbe, 2012). The first stage of labor is the longest; it also tends to be longer for a first delivery than subsequent births. A number of signs indicate that labor is beginning:

- The uterus begins to contract. As labor progresses, these contractions become more regular, closer together in time, and more intense.
- The thick mucous plug that has been covering the cervix, protecting the pregnancy, is dislodged. Because this mucus can be stained with blood, it sometimes is referred to as a "bloody show."
- Rupture of the amniotic membranes releases much of the amniotic fluid in the uterus that has protected the baby, and it trickles or gushes from the vagina. Not all women experience loss of amniotic fluid early in labor; it may happen later in the process. Other women may think their membranes have ruptured but actually may be experiencing urinary incontinence from all the pressure. Because the risk of infection increases after the rupture of membranes, women who think their "water has broken" should get in touch with their health care provider.

First Stage

The first stage of labor is the longest of the three stages and is divided into early and active labor. In early labor the cervix begins to dilate and mild to moderate contractions begin. This part of the labor can last hours or even days. This is followed by active labor where the cervix dilates to 10 centimeters (4 inches), the diameter needed for safe passage of the baby's head. During active labor, which often lasts eight hours, the contractions get stronger and closer together. **Effacement**, the thinning of the cervix, also takes place during this phase. The end of the first stage of labor, called transition, is marked by the most intense contractions, and the woman now often feels the urge to push (Mayo Clinic, 2016).

Effacement Thinning of the cervix during first stage of labor

Second Stage

The second stage of labor involves the actual birth. This is a short stage for some women—one to three pushes and the baby is out and for others it may last several hours. An **episiotomy**, once performed routinely, is now performed only when absolutely necessary because the procedure increases the mothers risk for perineal and vaginal trauma and anal sphincter disruption. Based on the evidence showing a lack of maternal benefits of having an episiotomy, currently only 10-17% of births involves an episiotomy compared to 87% in 1976. (Gabbe, 2012). Once the head is out of the vagina, the baby's airway will be cleared and the umbilical cord will be checked to make sure it is free. The rest of the baby will then emerge into the world.

Episiotomy The surgical cutting of the perineum to facilitate childbirth now considered medically unnecessary

Third Stage

The third stage of labor consists of delivery of the placenta, which had been attached to the uterine wall, and the umbilical cord, which has been cut at the baby's abdomen but remains attached to the placenta at the other end. Delivery of the placenta, sometime called **afterbirth**, takes about 5–30 minutes. During the third stage, women may experience the rush of emotions associated with the birth itself and holding their newborn. The mother can breast-feed her infant during the delivery of the placenta. The first moments and hours after the birth of the child are very important in the maternal-infant attachment process. There should be as many opportunities as possible for the new parents to be with their newborn immediately after birth and as often as possible in the next few days. This bonding process is characterized by fondling, kissing, cuddling and gazing at the infant. Modern hospitals can encourage this bonding by having flexible hours for fathers, infant rooming with the mother and supporting breast-feeding (Gabbe, 2002).

> **Afterbirth** The placenta, umbilical cord, which has been cut at the baby's abdomen but attached to the placenta, and membranes expelled after the birth of a child

Delivery Options

Couples now have a variety of delivery options that include not only the traditional method but also birthing centers, home births, and cesarean deliveries.

Traditional Delivery

What has come to be viewed as traditional today is different from the traditional delivery of years ago. Both mother and father are typically present at the delivery, which takes place in a hospital. Some fathers film and photograph their child's first minutes. Prior to that, couples attend prepared childbirth classes that teach about pregnancy and childbirth. Taking childbirth education classes such as Lamaze helps a woman reduce the fear and pain often associated with labor. Childbirth education gives the woman and her partner/coach the tools to help her relax, improve her labor and delivery and perhaps even decrease the need for pain medication.

Some women come to their deliveries with a "coach," who may not necessarily be the father of the child. For lesbian couples, the partner helps with the birth. Some women want their own mothers or sisters to be present. Whatever the circumstance, most hospitals have modified their obstetrical practices to allow for one or more family members or designated friends to participate in the birth.

Many hospitals offer family centered care where the woman goes through labor, delivery and recovery all in the same room. Often it is a very home like setting where the partner stays with the woman and after the birth, the baby sleeps in the room. There is also often the option of the "in hospital birthing center" that is either in or next to the hospital. These also offer a home like atmosphere with the advantage of being close to medical help if needed (Conaway, 2012).

Hospital births afford both mother and baby the availability of technology and monitoring. Some facilities also are known for their neonatal intensive care units, which become particularly important if the baby is at high risk—premature, physical deformities, infant in other than head-first position, blood incompatibility between mother and fetus, **toxemia**, multiple births, and so on.

> **Toxemia** A highly dangerous condition during pregnancy when high blood pressure occurs

Hospitals are set up to give women a lot of attention, with specialized nurses to care for the mother and the baby. Hospital births give women more options for managing pain. Although individuals may have decided beforehand what their philosophy of birth is, the true test comes during labor. Some women manage their pain well and find that the breathing techniques they learned in their childbirth classes prepared them well. Relaxation techniques and hypnosis also can be helpful in managing the discomfort associated with labor.

Epidural anesthetic An injection of a drug into the spinal cord during labor to dull pain

The most popular pain relief is the **epidural anesthetic** used by 60% of women (Silva & Halpern, 2010). The epidural which relieves pain in 10–20 minutes can be administered once a woman has dilated to 5 centimeters. This numbs her abdominal area, removing pain and discomfort while allowing labor to progress. Women who have an epidural must remain in bed. Its advantage is that the dosage of the drug is monitored in such a way so that the woman regains the capacity to push the baby out at the time of delivery. However, an epidural may decrease her ability to push effectively.

Birthing Centers

Birthing centers gained in popularity with the growth of the women's movement in the 1970s. Women were taking an increased role in the birth of their own babies and asking for changes to traditional delivery. Birthing centers were operated by nurse midwives who worked under the supervision of obstetricians, in close physical proximity to hospitals.

The unique feature of birthing centers is the belief that the woman, with the support of her partner, should have as much control over the birthing process as possible. They were the first places where the space for deliveries was "homey," incorporating birthing beds, wallpapered rooms, and rocking chairs. They also cut back on the use of fetal heart monitors so the woman could move around more easily during the first stage of labor. Women could take showers, eat lightly, and have family, including their other children, with them. They often have Jacuzzis or tubs where the mother can relax.

Birthing centers do not provide anesthesia so women will not have the option of an epidural or pain medication (Conaway, 2012). Women who deliver at birthing centers usually are screened to rule out high risk cases. Multiple births, health conditions that warrant close medical monitoring—for example, diabetes and heart conditions—and being over 40 years of age are situations in which a hospital birth is encouraged or required.

As hospitals have increasingly embraced some of the offerings of birthing centers—leaving women to labor and deliver in one room, making those rooms more attractive and less stereotypically hospital-like, having nurse midwives on staff—free-standing birthing centers away from hospitals may be a less attractive option now.

Home Births

Delivering babies at home may be a personal choice or may result from rapid labor. Lay midwives have delivered many babies at home. Today, the attitude toward home birth is that it puts the life and welfare of both the baby and mother at risk. Because of the risk of charges of medical malpractice, obstetricians do not conduct home births, and only a select number of licensed nurse midwives will do so. In contrast, the majority of the world's babies are born at home, particularly in non-industrialized countries.

Cesarean Deliveries

Cesarean delivery, or **c-section**, is a surgical procedure done for a variety of reasons related to the health and survival of either the mother or the baby, or both. In 2014, nearly 1 in 3 live births in the US was a cesarean birth, a 60 percent increase since 1996 (ACOG, 2014). C-sections are generally done when the baby is in a **breech position**—feet or buttocks presenting first. Other indications for cesarean delivery are incompatibility between the baby's head size and size of the mother's pelvis, a large baby, signs of fetal distress, weak contractions of the uterus and prolonged labor, or problems with the placenta and identified bleeding. If the surgery is performed under emergency conditions, such as a detached placenta, general anesthesia is administered. In other situations, where time allows, anesthesia can be given with an epidural, which allows the mother to remain awake and, in many hospitals, her partner to be present. In an effort to decrease the number of unnecessary cesarean births, the American College of Obstetricians and Gynecologists is now recommending that women with low-risk pregnancies be allowed to spend more time in the first stage of labor. Evidence shows that labor progresses more slowly than once thought so women should not be rushed into a cesarean. Once a woman has a c-section her later births are usually also cesarean (ACOG, 2014).

Cesarean delivery (c-section) The surgical form of childbirth in which an incision is made through the abdomen and uterus to deliver the baby, placenta and umbilical cord

Breech position A birth position in which the buttocks or foot rather than the baby's head presents at the cervix

Postpartum

The *postpartum* period represents the time after the birth, with all its various dimensions of change.

Women, whether breastfeeding or bottle feeding, will experience marked changes in their hormone levels, which in turn affect emotions. Levels of estrogen and progesterone drop rapidly within 24 hours and then continue dropping until the body reaches its pre-pregnancy levels. It is normal to experience unexplained sadness, often termed "baby blues," after birth. For some, the blues last a few hours; for others, they can last for 1 to 2 weeks. Postpartum depression (PPD) can start after the birth and affects up to 15 percent of mothers. Women may have feelings of anxiety and deep sadness. Some may not have any interest in their babies, whereas others become overly worried. There appears to be an association between depression prior to pregnancy or during pregnancy and experiencing post partum depression (Informed Health Online, 2012).

One of the major adjustments postpartum is the effect of lack of sleep on the body. Some newborns wake to eat every 2 to 3 hours, and for those women who breastfeed, the burden of being available and awake cannot be equally divided. Anthony, in Case Study 13.1, later shared that for the 1st year with his triplets, there was never 1 hour when all three were asleep at the same time! Prolonged sleep deprivation affects mood, energy, interest in socializing, and ability to concentrate.

One very positive change for most women is the loss of some of the weight they gained during pregnancy. Immediately after birth, a woman will lose 10-13 pounds from the combination of the weight of the baby, placenta, amniotic fluid, and blood loss. By the six week milestone, 28% of women will be at their pre-pregnant weight (Gabbe, 2002).

Adjustment in this period also includes a reassessing of roles—parent, partner, individual. Who comes first? Fatigue for the parents, with the simultaneous constancy of attending to a baby, may interfere with any

Lochia The uterine discharge that is released over a period of weeks after childbirth

desire to resume lovemaking. After birth, the uterus produces a bloody discharge called **lochia**, which can be on again/off again for weeks. If a woman has an episiotomy or cesarean section, the incision will also need to heal. As a result, physicians will often advise women to wait until their first postpartum medical appointment usually 4–6 weeks, before resuming sexual intercourse. Overall, any sexual activity can be reintroduced into a couple's lifestyle once the woman and her partner feel comfortable. Once sexual intercourse is resumed, the couple will need reliable birth control, even if breastfeeding. Good choices include any progestin only hormonal contraception or an IUD. For the health of the mother and next baby, it is probably best to wait 18–24 months before becoming pregnant again (Mayo Clinic, 2015).

■ Breastfeeding

Women today are strongly being encouraged to breastfeed their babies, even for a short period of time. The American Academy of Pediatrics recommend babies be exclusively breast-fed for 6 months, continuing for at least one year while the World Health Organization recommends breast-feeding continue for two years (CDC, 2015). Even women who have a career can continue to breast feed once they return to work. Techniques such as decreasing the amount of times they nurse and pumping breast milk to leave for caretakers can give women the option to continue breast-feeding (Gabbe, 2002).

Breast milk is tailored to meet the nutritional needs of the infant and brings numerous health benefits. Perhaps one of the greatest benefits of breast feeding is that it reduces the risk for sudden infant death syndrome and death from other causes. Breast feeding improves an infant's immune response, reduces the risk for a variety of chronic diseases, contributes to better cognitive skills, stimulates bonding between mother and child and promotes better health in premature infants. Additional benefits include allergy prevention, lower asthma risk, and better mouth and tooth development in the baby. Breast-feeding is thought to give the baby better control of its intake, thereby reducing later obesity. Breast-feeding also benefits the mother in a variety of ways. Post partum depression risks are lower and bone density increases. The breast-feeding mother will also burn 450–500 extra calories a day, helping her return more quickly to her pre-pregnancy weight. In addition, her uterus will also shrink faster. Women who breast-feed lower their risks for ovarian cancer and breast cancer (American Academy of Pediatrics, 2012). Breast-feeding may also have a calming effect on mothers, allowing an easier transition into motherhood. Oxytocin spikes during breast-feeding and this may have an anti-anxiety effect and help promote bonding with the baby. Breast-feeding may even be a mood elevator (Rabin, 2006). In addition to all of the health benefits, breast-feeding is convenient and is less expensive than formula. In our "Go Green" world, breast-feeding is the environmentally friendly choice (Leung & Sauve, 2005).

Not all women want to breast-feed, and they need to know that improved formulas do provide the essential nutrients needed by the new-born. Mothers have many choices in types of formulas that are available for infants who are less than twelve months old. These formulas vary in nutritional and calorie content, taste and cost.

Once children become a fact of life, notions of family expand and change. Relationships with parents, employers, and friends take on new dimensions and demands.

Caring for children is a 24-hour job, not easily filled by one person. Will parenting responsibilities be shared? Will we work well as a team to care for and raise our child ? What networks of support are in place? Will the mother work? Is child care available? Play groups? Recognizing what is required helps promote social health.

Parenthood can convey a sense of purpose and add meaning to life. Parents often discover new meaning in life/death issues as they become responsible for another human being. Parenthood brings with it an ongoing assessment of the relationship to one's child. Is the child like me? Does that matter? Can I love this child? Can I help him/her grow and be free to live his/her own life? What happens when parents die? If children die?

Although answering some of these questions may be uncomfortable and difficult, doing so is essential to plan for responsible parenthood. Parents need to have a will and designate guardians. Some children know of adults who became their godparents, yet those individuals may or may not assume an active role throughout their lives.

Adoption

Source: Callista Lee

Making one's child available for adoption may be a good option for some birth parents who are not able to parent their children themselves. The vast majority of mothers who face unplanned births will choose to parent their children themselves, because it is so emotionally difficult to let go of one's child, even if that was the plan before the birth. But it may ultimately be the most *loving* thing they can do if they are truly not able to be a good parent at that time in their life. Adoption specialists avoid using the phrase "giving up a child" when working with mothers considering adoption and prefer "choosing adoption" or "allowing others to parent my child." It empowers the mother making this difficult decision. Socially, a lot of pressure is put on mothers to raise their children themselves, even those who are still children themselves. Accusations like "you must not love your child" can cut like a knife.

Long ago in the past, a mother choosing adoption might not even get to see her baby after the birth. People thought that it would be too painful. But the opposite turned out to be true. We have learned that before a mother can say "goodbye" to her child (and to process it in her own mind), she must first say "hello." She has the opportunity to hold, feed, bathe, and name her baby. The adoptive parents may change the name, but she will always have the birth certificate with the name she chose. Of course, if she doesn't want to, she doesn't have to. But many decades of just snatching babies away from their mothers and then adopting them out to strangers they would never meet proved to be associated with ongoing emotional trauma for birth mothers (and some birth fathers as well). And as their children came of age, they had no way of finding their birth parents if they chose to do so. The situation is much different today with "open adoption." Open simply means that the process includes lots of choices. The birth mother may have a say in choosing among preapproved adoptive families, meeting them, and discussing whether or not there will be any ongoing communication between them after the adoption. Parents wanting to adopt a baby are more likely to be chosen by birth parents if they agree to this "open" process. And many are happy to do so. They get to know the person who has blessed them with a child. When such adoptions are handled by adoption agencies, it is standard that the birth-mother will have a social worker looking out for her best interests and the adopting couple (or individual) will have their own social worker helping them to prepare for their experience, so that there is no conflict of interest in matching birth parents with adopting parents.

Sometimes people choose to skip the adoption agency and go right to an attorney. This makes a lot of sense when the birth mother has already identified an adoptive family, such as a relative or friend. When going through an attorney, there are fewer steps to go through, including a lack of required counseling. In California agency adoptions, once the final parental relinquishment papers are signed there is no changing one's mind. The adoption is final. And so plenty of time and care is taken to make sure the birth parent is ready to make that decision. Social workers have reported that they always have their birth parent clients make a parenting plan in addition to an adoption plan, because in most cases their teen and other young birth mothers usually can't bring themselves to go through with the adoption plan. At least they've been prepared for what parenting will be like.

In attorney adoptions, the "final" relinquishment papers aren't quite as final. The birth mother has several months in which she may change her mind and contest the adoption. This sounds cruel to the adopting family, but it is set up this way to guard against birth parents feeling coerced or rushed by the attorney or the adopting couple. In any case, the adopting parents must undergo a home inspection and other steps to determine that they will be providing a safe and stable home for the child. And either way, the adopting family pays the fees. Typical adoption agency fees range from US$20,000-US$40,000 (Adoption.com, 2019). This covers the costs of medical care and other services for birth mothers, social workers, legal fees, educational outreach, and running the agency. If you are concerned about making some corporation rich off your adoption, seek out your local County Agency or another nonprofit adoption agency. Birth parents pay nothing for choosing adoption. International adoptions may cost more or less than domestic adoptions, depending upon how eager the foreign country is to find adoptive parents for their orphaned children.

Another way of adopting, which results in a better chance of getting a child and in a shorter length of time, is to adopt a child who is in foster care and determined by the court to be available for adoption. Single and LGBT parents are more likely to go this route because birth parents are less likely to choose singles or LGBTs to parent their baby. And adoption from foster care costs little or nothing.

Parenting

Source: Callista Lee

Most parents will go by a default path and raise their children the way their parents raised them. It takes time, lots of effort, and guidance to learn how to do things differently. Parenting classes are available at colleges, but also through county government agencies and private nonprofit agencies. Of course, no book or instructor can help you with every situation; they can only teach you methods and strategies that have proven effective. Your personality and assumptions play an important role. Psychologists have identified four types of parenting styles, and each associates with a different outcome. These are, briefly, as follows:

- **Authoritarian parenting leads to a passive child with low self-esteem**
  - Authoritarian parents combine a low level of warmth with strict discipline. Rules and decisions are rarely explained, and in some cases may change without notice. The parents control the child's autonomy. They don't include children in problem solving, so children don't learn how to behave in novel situations. Sometimes their children become hostile or aggressive. Some become good liars to avoid punishment. Children behave out of fear rather than an appreciation for safety concerns or the well-being of others.

- **Permissive parenting leads to a rebellious child; often unhappy**
  - Permissive parents provide a lot of warmth but very little control. They hate to see their children upset, and so they give in to tantrums, which lead to more tantrums. Their children are more likely to have health problems because they don't

enforce healthy behaviors. Because children need limits, they often act out, even violently, to get their parents to act like parents instead of tall friends. These children often have problems in school because they have not been taught to work hard to solve problems, or to appreciate reasonable authority and rules.

- **Uninvolved parenting leads to an unhappy child with low self-esteem**
  - Uninvolved parents seem to expect children to raise themselves. Their style is both low warmth and low level of control. There are few rules and little guidance. The children grow up craving attention and may act out to receive it. The parents may neglect the child's needs, not intentionally but because they are overwhelmed with their own lives. These children are often behind in school because of a lack of parental support and involvement in their learning attempts.

- **Authoritative parenting leads to a cooperative child with healthy self-esteem**
  - The Authoritative style include both warmth and control. They explain to their children

why there are certain rules. They may involve a child in discussions of what a fair punishment would be for breaking them. They teach their children how to make good decisions, especially as they grow older and need to learn how to make their own choices. Logical consequences are used instead of punishments. Praise and encouragement foster good behavior. Children learn how to evaluate safety risks based on parental modeling.

As you can see, the authoritative style is the most effective at raising a child who will be a happy and responsible adult. Books on parenting (and even episodes of Super Nanny!) teach the methods for approaching parenting from an authoritative style, where the parent is the authority by virtue of their life experience, but they are not the dictator of the family. They understand that children need to learn that there are consequences for their actions and how to solve problems in novel situations. Rules are created for reasons of safety and general well-being in the family, rather than to feed the parent's ego. They are preparing their children to be builders of their own lives.

References

American Academy of Pediatrics. (2002). *Policy on same sex adoption.* Retrieved from http://www.aap.org/policy/02008t.htm.

American College of Obstetricians and Gynecologists (2012, June). *Evaluating Infertility. Frequently Asked Questions (FAQ 136).* Retrieved from http://www.acog.org

American College of Obstetricians and Gynecologists (2012, June). *Having Twins. Frequently Asked Questions (FAQ 092).* Retrieved from http://www.acog.org

American College of Obstetricians and Gynecologists (2014, February). *Nation's Ob-Gyns take aim at preventing cesareans.* Retrieved from http://www.acog.org

American College of Obstetricians and Gynecologists (2015, June). *Exercise during pregnancy. Frequently Asked Questions (FAQ 131).* Retrieved from http://www.acog.org

American College of Obstetricians and Gynecologists (2015, June). *Prenatal development: How your baby grows. Frequently Asked Questions (FAQ 156).* Retrieved from http://www.acog.org

American College of Obstetricians and Gynecologists (2015, September). *Diagnostic tests for birth defects. Frequently Asked Questions (FAQ 164).* Retrieved from http://www.acog.org

Brassard, M. Ainmek, Y., & Baillargeon, J. (2008). Basic infertility including polycystic ovary syndrome, *Medical Clinics of North America,* 92 (50), 1163–1192.

Carson, M. & Ehrenthal, D. (2008). Medical issues from preconception through delivery: A roadmap for the internist. *Medical Clinics of North America,* 92(5).

Centers for Disease Control and Prevention. (2015). *Fetal alcohol spectrum disorders.* Retrieved from http:// www.cdc.gov.

Centers for Disease Control and Prevention (2015). *Breastfeeding.* Retrieved from http://www.cdc.gov

Centers for Disease Control and Prevention (2016). *Infertility*. Retrieved from http://www.cdc.gov

Centers for Disease Control and Prevention (2017). *Assisted reproductive technology*. Retrieved from http:// www.cdc.gov.

Conaway, B. (2012, December 2). How do you want to deliver your baby? *WebMD*. Retrieved from http://webmd.com

First Consult. (2013). *Pregnancy: medical topics:first consult*. Retrieved from http://www.mdconsult.com

Gabbe (2007). *Gabbe: Obstretrics-normal and problem pregnancies*. 5th edition. Churchill Livingston, Inc.

Gabbe (2012). *Gabbe:Obstretrics-normal and problem pregnancies*. 6th edition. Churchill Livingston, Inc.

Hewlett, S. A. (2002). *Creating a life: Professional women and the quest for children*. New York: Hyperion.

Hornstein, M. & Gibbons, W. (2008). *Initial Infertility consultation in couples planning pregnancy: Lifestyle factors*. Retrieved from www.utdol.com

Informed Health Online (2012). *Postpartum depression*. Retrieved from http://www.ncbi.nlm.nih.gov

Johns Hopkins Medicine (2017). *Calculating a due date*. Retrieved from http://www.hopkinsmedicine.org

Leung, A. & Sauve, R. (2005). Breast is best for babies. *Journal of the National Medical Association*. 1010–1019.

Livingston, G. & Cohn, D. (2010). *More women without children*. Pew Research Center Publications Retrieved from http://pewresearch.org

Livingston, G. & Cohn, D. (2012). Immigrant women lead recent drop in U.S. births and birth rates. *Pew Research Social & Demographic Trends*. Retrieved from http://www.pewsocialtrends.org

Livingston, G. (2014). In terms of childlessness, US ranks near the top worldwide. *Pew Research Center*. Retrieved from http://www.pewresearch.org

Livingston, G. (2015). Childlessness falls, family size grows among highly educated women. *Pew Research Center*. Retrieved from http://www.pewsocialtrends.org

Livingston, G. (2015). Childlessness. *Pew Research Center*. Retrieved from http://www.pewsocialtrends.org

Mayo Clinic (2015). *Healthy sperm: Improving your fertility*. Retrieved from http://mayoclinic.com

Mayo Clinic (2015). *Labor & delivery, postpartum care*. Retrieved from http://www.mayoclinic.com

Mayo Clinic (2016). *Stages of labor. Baby its time*. Retrieved from http://mayoclinic.com

Mayo Clinic (2016). *Miscarriage*. Retrieved from http://www.mayoclinic.com

MD Consult (2005). *Clinical Topic Tours- Infertility*. Retrieved from http://www.Mdconsult.com

MD Consult (2007). *Evaluation of the infertile couple*. Retrieved from http://www.MDConsult.com

MD Consult (2007). *Pregancy*. Retrieved from http://www.MDConsult.com

MD Consult (2012). *Pregancy tests-how do pregnancy test work?*. Retrieved from http://www.MDConsult.com

Medical Clinics of North America (2008, September) *Infertility*. 92 (5).

Medline Plus (2016). *Invitro fertilization*. Retrieved from http://www.medlineplus.gov

Miller, C. (2012). *The emotional strain of infertility*. Retrieved from http://www.intelhealth.com

Murkoff, H., Eisenberg, A., & Hathaway, S. (2002). *What to expect when you're expecting*. New York: Workman.

National Center for Health Statistics (2014). *Birth-methods of delivery*. Retrieved from http://www.cdc.gov

Rabin, R. (2006, June 13) Breast-Feed or Else. The New York Times.

Rayburn, W. & Phelan, S. (2008). Promoting Healthy Habits in Pregnancy. *Obstetrics and Gynecology Clinics*. (35) 3.

Silva, M. & Halpern, S.(2010). Epidural analgesia for labor: Current techniques. *Local, Regional Anesthesia, 3*, 143–153.

Storch, S. (2012). Miscarriage. *MedlinePlus*. Retrieved from http://http://www.nlm.nih.gov/medlineplus

Van Voorhis, B. (2007). In vitro fertilization. *New England Journal of Medicine*. 356 (4). 379–385.

US Census Bureau (2014, June). *Current population survey: historical time table*. Retrieved from http://www.census.org

US Census Bureau (2015, April). *Fertility*. Retrieved from http://www.census.org

Chapter *fourteen*

From Kinky to Paraphilic

Student Learning Objectives

After reading this chapter, students will be able to

- ☞ Distinguish between the following sexual variations; normative sexual behavior, atypical sexual behavior, and paraphiliac sexual behavior.
- ☞ Assess their own attitudes, values, and beliefs about what is normal.
- ☞ Describe the key characteristics of a variety of paraphilias.
- ☞ Evaluate the health risks associated with body piercing.
- ☞ Differentiate transvestic fetishism and transsexualism (gender dysphoria).
- ☞ Describe the origins of atypical sexual behavior and paraphilias.
- ☞ Evaluate various ways of treating atypical sexual behaviors and paraphilias.
- ☞ Discuss differences between Sado-Masochim Disorders and BDSM play

case study 14.1

Greg: Exhibitionism or Mooning?

Greg was the first client assigned to Dr. Blonna during the supervised clinical training component of the master's degree in counseling. Greg was on probation as a first-time sex offender convicted of exhibitionism. As a condition of parole, Greg had to seek counseling for a prescribed period of time. In Dr. Blonna's words:

I'll never forget Greg. I was a 25-year-old man, not too much older than Greg. I was still working through issues related to my own sexuality and found Greg quite a challenge. He was referred to counseling because he had been arrested for exposing himself to a young woman.

It was hard for me to understand the significance of exhibitionism. I had been raised as a typical man of the 1950s and 1960s and viewed exhibitionism with amusement more than a clinician's understanding of it as a paraphilia. Indeed, I was only a few years removed from engaging in mooning and streaking as fraternity pranks. In time, my work with Greg crystallized the significance of his behavior and the furtive nature of exhibitionism.

Greg was a reluctant client at first. He did not want to be in counseling, and the first couple of sessions were almost totally devoid of any conversation. Gradually we began to establish a relationship, and Greg started to talk about his exhibitionism. It became quite evident after that point that Greg's behavior was vastly different from mooning and other juvenile sexual behavior that, although offensive, has an entirely different motivation. Mooning, streaking, and other prank public displays of nudity are not intended to serve as sexual come-ons. Greg's behavior had an entirely different purpose.

Greg was immature—both socially and sexually retarded. He was painfully shy, could not communicate with women effectively, and had limited dating experience. His sexual experience was limited to auto-erotic activities and a handful of sexual liaisons with prostitutes. He lacked self-esteem and self-confidence, and had a hard time maintaining eye contact. He also admitted, while in counseling, that he was a voyeur and had masturbated several times while watching a few women in his neighborhood get undressed. He had a couple of peeping vantage points that allowed him to peer into the windows of apartment buildings in his neighborhood.

After seeing Greg for several sessions, it was obvious that exposing himself was his way of coming on to women sexually. He really believed that women, upon seeing his nakedness (and throbbing erection) would literally throw themselves at his feet and perform oral sex on him or ask him back to their place to have intercourse. He believed that his "manhood" would speak for itself and make traditional forms of establishing a sexual relationship unnecessary. In reality, Greg lacked the conversational and other social skills necessary to meet women and establish a sexual relationship.

Critical Thinking

Many people experiment with a host of sexual behaviors and participate in sexual pranks such as "mooning." When you read Greg's case study, however, it becomes obvious how Greg's behavior varies from these more typical sexual activities. What makes Greg's behavior exhibitionistic instead of a prank? How does Greg's exhibitionism impact the rest of his life?

As we can see with the illustration of Greg, sometimes there is a fine line between what is considered "normal" sexual behavior and what isn't. Normative behavior can be classified as sociological, biological, psychological, and statistical. Sexual behavior that is *sociologically* normal falls within the laws, mores, and customs of a society. Most of this behavior is culturally defined and passed from one generation to the next as a result of socialization. *Biologically* normal behavior is characterized as healthy and natural, and helps perpetuate the species in positive ways. *Psychologically* normal sexual behavior is sexual activity that does not result in emotional distress or in neurotic or psychotic functioning. Finally, behavior that is considered normal *statistically* is sexual behavior in which the majority of people engage.

Given these four categories of "normality," defining abnormal sexual behavior might seem easy. Anything falling outside the parameters established by these four categories would be considered "abnormal." The words *normal* and *abnormal* are commonly used labels because they characterize sexual behavior in easy-to-understand, stereotypical patterns. Furthermore, dichotomizing normal and abnormal makes it easier to stigmatize and discriminate against people who are not in the norm. A more commonly accepted term to describe behaviors that the majority of the population does not practice is atypical sexual behavior. Atypical sexual behavior is described as behavior that is not statistically typical. It could also be referred to as a sexual variation. The terms atypical sexual behavior or sexual variations do not carry the same pejorative tone as abnormal (Levinson, 2003).

Paraphilia An unusual or atypical sexual behavior that becomes the focal point for an obsessive preoccupation or need. Having a Paraphilia is considered "Criterion A" for a Paraphilic Disorder, which is more serious.

Kinky or Disordered

Kinky or Disordered?

Source: Callista Lee

For this chapter, think of sexual behaviors on a continuum, starting with typical sexual behavior, then moving onto less common or "kind of kinky" behavior, and then to atypical behavior (very kinky) that is considered "paraphilic" by the psychological community, and then finally to the mental health diagnosis of a **Paraphilic Disorder**. What differentiates extremely kinky (or paraphilia) behavior from a disorder is that the paraphilic disorder causes distress or impairment in functioning or that the sexual practice inherently involves nonconsenting individuals (APA, 2013). The DSM-V (the most recent diagnostic manual of the American Psychiatric Association) specifically lists just eight Paraphilic Disorders: exhibitionistic disorder, fetishistic disorder, frotteuristic disorder, pedophilic disorder, sexual masochism disorder, sexual sadism disorder, transvestic disorder, and voyeuristic disorder (APA, 2013).

There are many other paraphilias that they are *not* specifically discussed in the DSM-V, because they are relatively rare and don't often rise to the level of a disorder. Some examples include: telephone scatologia (obscene telephone calls), necrophilia (sex with a dead person), zoophilia (sex with animals), coprophilia (sexual contact with feces), klismophilia (sexualized enemas), Asphyxiophilia (sexual attraction to asphyxia; also called breath control play), Xenophilia (sex with foreigners, or aliens), Pyrophilia (sexual arousal from setting and/or watch-

Paraphilic disorder In addition to meeting the criteria of a Paraphilia (Criterion A), a Paraphilic Disorder also includes another diagnostic requirement: that the paraphilia causes distress or impairment in functioning or that the sexual practice inherently involves nonconsenting individuals (Criterion B).

ing fires), Macrophilia (sexual attraction to larger people or extremely large body parts). You can do an online search for an even longer list (https://www.psychologistanywhereanytime.com/) after you finish reading this chapter.

A lot of people will respond to sexual behaviors that they find not-at-all-sexy or even repulsive as "sick." But sexologists remind us that the range human sexual behaviors is vast. The notion of "normal" is very much embedded in culture, and within each culture there is a wide range of individual sexual behaviors. We tend to think of kissing, for example as totally normal, even expected for lovers. But there are cultures in which the mouth is viewed as a dirty or a dangerous chewing device. Bringing your mouth close to someone's face could be considered weird, gross, or even a threat that you mean to bite them (Bever, 2015). Cultural considerations must always be part of a mental health diagnosis. The Paraphilic Disorders discussed in this chapter would be considered atypical and problematic worldwide because of "Criteria B"—the psychological and/or physical harm to the self or others.

> Typical Sexual Behavior → Less Typical, Kinky → Atypical,
> Very Kinky → Atypical, Paraphilic Disorder

© Kendall Hunt Publishing Company

Exhibitionistic Disorder

Exhibitionistic Disorder deriving sexual arousal by exposing one's genitals to unsuspecting strangers

The paraphiliac focus of **Exhibitionistic Disorder** involves deriving sexual arousal by exposing one's genitals to unsuspecting strangers. The overwhelming majority of people with this paraphilia are men between 18 and 40 years of age. Sometimes the person masturbates while exposing himself or fantasizing exposing himself (APA, 2013). Often the sexual gratification is derived from the sheer shock value of the act and the reaction from the victim. The greater the reaction, the more the person has proven his masculinity.

Men who reveal exhibitionism tend to be shy, passive, and sexually inhibited. Exhibitionism is generally perceived to be unrelated to rape or sexual assault. In some instances, the man with this paraphilia believes that his victim will be sexually aroused by his nakedness and that it will provoke a sexual encounter with her. Most are heterosexual and enjoy sex with their partners. They tend to be highly sexed individuals and 15% have coexistant paraphilias that involve some form of physical contact (Morrison , 2014).

Exhibitionism is often confused with "mooning" (baring one's buttocks to unsuspecting passersby). Generally, those who moon do not derive sexual gratification from the act, and it usually is a prank typically associated with adolescents.

In a sense, exhibitionism is culturally disparate. Male and female exotic dancers get paid to expose themselves. Nude or partially nude dancing and other forms of exotic entertaining are designed to be sexually arousing and are legal, yet streaking, which is not sexual, is illegal.

Voyeuristic Disorder

Voyeuristic Disorder Deriving sexual pleasure from observing unsuspecting individuals undressing or engaging in sexual activities

The paraphiliac focus of **Voyeuristic Disorder** is exactly the opposite of exhibitionism. The voyeur derives sexual excitement and pleasure from observing unsuspecting people (usually strangers) who are naked, disrobing, getting dressed, or in the act of having sex. The pleasure is derived from the act of "peeping" and is not intended to lead to an encounter with the unsuspecting stranger. Sexual release usually occurs through masturbation either while peeping or later with the voyeuristic memory of the encounter. The person may fantasize having sex with the stranger (APA, 2013).

Voyeuristic behavior can be depicted along a continuum. At the extreme is the person who can achieve sexual release only by observing others having sex. At the other end of the continuum is the person who watches others to augment sexual pleasure with a partner. This person might get turned on by watching exotic entertainers to fuel a sexual episode with a partner.

Fetishistic Disorder

The paraphiliac focus of **Fetishistic Disorder** is deriving sexual arousal and gratification from nonliving objects and body parts not normally associated with sexual behavior (feet etc.) (Morrison, 2014, APA, 2013). The overwhelming majority of people with fetishes consists of men who derive sexual pleasure from items of women's clothing such as underwear, bras, stockings, shoes, and boots. Typically, the man with paraphiliac fetishism masturbates while holding, stroking, smelling, or licking the object. To a lesser extent, the person may ask his partner (or pay a prostitute) to wear the item of clothing while they engage in sex or while he masturbates (APA, 2013).

Fetishistic Disorder Deriving sexual pleasure from inanimate objects

A person with a true paraphiliac fetish usually strongly prefers and needs the object to experience sexual desire. Often, a person with a fetish is unable to obtain or sustain an erection without the object being present. Fetishes often are linked to significant childhood experiences and are in place by adolescence (APA, 2013).

Frotteuristic Disorder

The paraphiliac focus of **Frotteuristic Disorder** is deriving sexual arousal and pleasure from rubbing one's genitals against an unsuspecting, non-consenting person. The male rubs his genitals against his victim's buttocks and thighs while simultaneously fondling her breasts or genitalia, or both. This typically occurs in crowded public places such as busy sidewalks, subways, buses, and other public places where the perpetrator can make a quick escape and avoid arrest (APA, 2013).

Frotteuristic Disorder Deriving sexual pleasure from rubbing up against unsuspecting and unwilling victims

✨ Environmental/Occupational Wellness ✨

The overwhelming majority of paraphiliacs are harmless, and as long as their behavior is private and with consenting adults, it does not represent a threat to society. In other instances it does. Legislation was passed in New Jersey and a host of other states to protect children from sex offenders in their communities. The New Jersey legislation, "Megan's Law," was enacted in response to the brutal murder of a young girl, Megan Kanka, by a neighbor who was a known sex offender. Essentially, the new law requires that neighbors be notified that a convicted sex offender has moved into their neighborhood. The hope is that such notification will enable parents and other neighbors to protect their children by keeping them away from the sex offender. In 1994, 12 new laws were enacted in California specifically targeting sex offenders. Provisions of these laws include, among others, a state-maintained toll-free phone number that alerts people to registered sex offenders living in their area, stiffer penalties for first-time offenders convicted of child molestation or rape, and the barring of unsupervised visits of sex offenders to their children.

▉ Pedophilic Disorder

Pedophilic Disorder Engaging in sexual activity with or fantasizing about prepubescent children

The legal aspects of **Pedophilic Disorder** are discussed in detail in Chapter 9. The paraphiliac focus of pedophilia is fantasizing about engaging in sexual activity with a prepubescent child. Those sexually attracted to girls, in general, prefer 8- to 10-year-olds. Those attracted to boys favor slightly older children. The two subtypes of pedophilia are (a) exclusive (individuals who are sexually attracted to children only) and (b) nonexclusive (individuals who are sexually attracted to both adults and children) (APA, 2013). A pedophilia arousal pattern refers to the act of fantasizing about and becoming aroused by thoughts of sexual contact with children. A pedophilia behavior pattern refers to acting on the arousal (Oliver, 2005).

Individuals with pedophilia show a wide range of sexual activity with their victims. Not all pedophiles are child molesters. According to the law, a pedophile is an individual who fantasizes about sexual contact with children, whereas a child molester actually commits that act in some form (Davis, McShane, & Williams, 1995). This does not always have to include actual physical contact with a child and may include possessing pornographic material of prepubescent children (Williams, 2014).

Most pedophiles masturbate while watching their victims undress, fondle themselves, or engage in sexual activities with another child or an adult. These activities can be live (paying children to perform in person or observing live sex shows broadcast over the Internet) or available through print (magazines, newspapers, and the like) and other electronic media (including movies, videotapes, and CD-ROMs).

Child molesters engage in a variety of sexual activities with their victims. This may consist of rubbing or fondling the child or performing oral sex on the child (Williams, 2014). Other child molesters penetrate the child's mouth, vagina, or rectum with their fingers, penis, or a foreign object. Some people with pedophilia obtain these sexual favors by gaining their victims' trust, affection, or loyalty. Others use physical force and psychological pressure and terror to obtain sex and control their victims (APA, 2013).

Numerous state and federal laws have made the possession of any sexual image of kids under age 18 illegal. Nonetheless, the underground market for all forms of child pornography and prostitution is thriving (Kaplan, 1997). Pedophiles have victimized their own children, stepchildren, foster children, or relatives' children. Less often victims are children adopted through foreign services, bought through underground slave trade, or exchanged with other pedophiles.

People with pedophilia have been known to use extraordinary means to obtain child pornography or actual live victims. In recent years, several pedophiles have made headlines by arranging encounters with children while posing as adolescents in Internet chat rooms.

Pedophilia usually is chronic and is more difficult to treat than other paraphilias. The recidivism rate for men attracted to boys is more than twice that of men attracted to girls (Davis et al., 1995). Public outrage and increased law enforcement efforts directed toward child sex offenders has resulted in a wealth of information regarding the association of pedophilia to sexual offenses against children. Despite advances in this type of knowledge, much remains to be learned about pedophilia, including its prevalence in the general population, cross-cultural manifestations, and etiology (Seto, 2004).

Sexual Masochism Disorder

The paraphiliac focus of **Sexual Masochism Disorder** is deriving arousal and pleasure through being beaten, bound, humiliated (physically or mentally), or made to suffer in some other fashion (APA, 2013). Although fantasizing about being the victim of masochistic acts is common, true paraphilia involves engaging in the behaviors.

Many different masochistic acts typically are sought with a partner. These include being bound (physical restraint involving being tied, strapped, taped, chained, or handcuffed), spanked, bitten, paddled, whipped, beaten, shocked with an electrical current, cut, or pierced/pinned (infibulation). Another common masochistic desire is to be humiliated by being urinated or defecated on, to be forced to crawl and bark like a dog, and to be verbally abused **Infantilism** involves being treated like an infant and forced to wear a diaper.

The last category of masochistic paraphilia involves **hypoxyphilia** (also known as *autoerotic asphyxia*), or oxygen deprivation, by noose or wire (ligature), chest compression, plastic bag, mask, or chemical (such as amyl nitrate, a powerful vasodilator that reduces the flow of oxygen to the brain). This behavior is particularly dangerous because mishaps in applying these procedures for sexual arousal could result in death. Little is known about this behavior, since information about individual cases is usually derived from postmortem physical and psychological evaluations of the victim. Investigation is made even more difficult by the victim's family attempting to cover up the sexual nature of the death (Downing & Nobs, 2004).

It does not seem that hypoxyphilia is attempted suicide (Hickman, 2002). Rather, in most cases it is accidental, a result of ritualized autoeroticism where oxygen deprivation is part of the sexual attraction and risk-taking. Most people who engage in autoerotic asphyxia are males with a history of sexual abuse, physical abuse, choking behavior (sometimes associated with asthma), exposure to traumatic family experiences, and other risk-taking (Downing & Nobs, 2004).

Sometimes, individuals with sexual masochism engage in masochistic acts by themselves. They self-inflict pain and humiliation through pinning, binding, shocking, or engaging in hypoxyphilia. Men with sexual masochism often concurrently have fetishism, transvestic fetishism, or sexual masochism (APA, 2013).

Sexual Masochism Disorder
Deriving sexual pleasure from being humiliated or forced to suffer pain

Infantilism Deriving sexual pleasure from being treated like an infant

Hypoxyphilia Deriving sexual pleasure from activities that involve oxygen deprivation

❧ *Physical Wellness* ❧

The continuum of atypical sexual behavior, as we've discussed, ranges from the relatively benign (occasional use of a fetish object) to the very dangerous (sadomasochistic beatings and torture). As we've mentioned throughout this text, healthy sexuality promotes physical well-being and behaviors that enhance health. Engaging in many of the atypical sexual behaviors can put your physical health in jeopardy. It is crucial to follow all of the warnings associated with these behaviors. There are ways to reduce the physical health risks associated with atypical sexual behavior.

Sexual Sadism Disorder

Sexual sadism Deriving sexual pleasure from inflicting pain or humiliation

The paraphiliac focus of **sexual sadism** involves deriving sexual arousal and pleasure by inflicting physical or psychological pain and suffering on another person. The person may engage in sadistic activities with either a willing victim (usually someone with sexual masochism) or a nonconsenting victim (APA, 2013). Sexual sadism incorporates a range of acts, including all of those discussed previously under the topic of sexual masochism. In extreme cases, people with sexual sadism seek sexual arousal through extreme brutality, torture, mutilation, and murder.

Typically, they engage in such behavior with nonconsenting victims and have had the condition for several years. The fantasies of sexual sadism usually are present in childhood, and the behavior begins in early adulthood and becomes chronic.

healthy sex hints 14.1

Reducing the Health Risks Associated with Body-Piercing

Body-piercing, like other forms of adornment such as tattooing, branding, and ear-piercing, carries some risk. The risks vary and are related to the body part being pierced, the piercing equipment, sterilization procedures used (or lack thereof), and the skill of the provider. The following hints can help reduce the risks associated with body-piercing:

1. Think long and hard about your motivation for getting your body pierced. Make sure you understand the risks associated with the procedure.
2. Talk with people who have had piercing done. Ask what kind of experiences they had.
3. Before getting pierced, ask your physician about vaccination for hepatitis B, a blood-borne infection passed through contaminated needles.
4. Do not pierce yourself or let an inexperienced person (such as your best friend, who pierced her own ears) pierce you.
5. Go to a reputable piercing parlor that has been in business for some time. Ask for references from former customers.
6. Make sure the piercing parlor you choose uses an autoclave (a tabletop sterilizing device that uses heat and pressure to kill germs) to sterilize equipment. Ask to see the certificate verifying that the autoclave has been recently inspected. If only boiling water is used to clean equipment, head for the door.
7. If a tattoo artist uses individually sealed, sterile needles, ask him or her to open these in front of you. Request the same for the containers of ink being used for your tattoo.
8. Talk to your physician to learn about special considerations concerning the body part being pierced. Particularly risky parts (because of increased likelihood of infection or permanent damage) are the eyelids, the tongue, the nipples, the clitoris, and the frenulum of the penis.
9. Don't have piercing done if you are pregnant or nursing.
10. Follow after-care instructions to the letter. If you suspect infection, consult a doctor immediately.
11. Wear only jewelry that is 14K gold, niobium, or surgical-grade stainless steel. These contain fewer alloys and are less likely to cause allergic reactions.

Source: Association of Professional Piercers (2002), *Procedure manual* (Chamblee, GA: Author).

Transvestic Disorder

Transvestic Disorder differs from other forms of fetishism in that the fetishist derives sexual arousal by cross-dressing (dressing up as a female or wearing an article of female clothing). The transvestic fetishist typically masturbates to orgasm while dressed in that clothing.

Transvestic Disorder Deriving sexual pleasure from wearing women's clothing

❧ *Emotional Wellness* ❧

The difference between someone who engages in atypical sexual behavior and the true paraphiliac is in the emotional distress and social dysfunction the latter experiences. An individual or couple can engage in almost all of the atypical behaviors of paraphiliacs without this representing a paraphiliac sexual condition. A person can be emotionally healthy and still enjoy an occasional walk on the wild side. Actually, some people engage in atypical sexual activities to add a spark to their sex lives. When the behavior becomes an obsession, however, and carries with it emotional distress and social dysfunction, it becomes a paraphiliac sexual disorder.

The disorder is known only in males. It runs the full spectrum of behavior from routinely wearing a single item of female clothing (such as silk panties) under the male clothing, to spending thousands of dollars on customized gowns and makeup and participating in the transvestic subculture (APA, 2013).

sex in society 14.1

The Underground World

In the 1970s Lou Reed, an avant garde artist and the lead singer for the Velvet Underground, sang about taking a walk on the wild side. The wild side in this case was the underground world of transsexuals—a world replete with its own bars, clubs, magazines, and clothing outlets.

Today you still can experience this underground world on certain streets in every major city in the United States, from New Orleans to New York City to San Francisco, and find a world filled with all of the transpeople—transsexuals, transvestites, and the transgendered. You'll find boutiques catering to transsexuals that carry everything in "women's" clothing from panties to feather boas in sizes designed to fit the average truck driver. You'll also find shoe stores that cater to spiked heels in sizes 10, 11, and 12 in every width. At night these districts come alive as clubgoers of all sexual persuasions flock to see their favorite female impersonators, although some of the actors and actresses already have gone through sex reassignment surgery and can hardly be called impersonators.

The World Wide Web has opened the globe to the transcommunity. You now can view entire catalogs of merchandise on your computer and shop from the privacy of your own home. There are social organizations, self-help groups, political action committees, legal aid societies, chat rooms, list serves, travel clubs (they find the best places for transpeople to vacation), auto clubs, discount purchasing cooperatives—and the list goes on and on. The amazing thing is that most of these people, places, and services operate outside the realization of mainstream society.

Men with transvestic fetishism do not have gender dysphoria (think they are really females), and most are heterosexual in sexual orientation. When not cross-dressed, men with transvestic fetishism look like the average man. Men who do not have transvestic fetishism but occasionally like to put on articles of female clothing often do so with the willing participation of their female partners.

The Origin and Treatment of Atypical Sexual Behavior

There are many different theories regarding the causes and treatment of atypical sexual behavior and paraphilias. Implied in "atypical" is the need to fix something that is wrong. Therefore, we reemphasize the difference among individuals who occasionally engage in behaviors that are atypical and cause no harm to another person and individuals who have paraphilias that cause themselves and others pain and suffering. The difference lies in the psychological distress and impairment in social, occupational, and other functioning between the two types of behavior.

Etiology

Many explanations have been set forth for the causes of atypical sexual behavior and paraphilias. Three of the more commonly accepted views revolve around (1) a psychoanalytic appraisal, (2) a behaviorist explanation, and (3) an eclectic etiology.

Psychoanalytic Appraisal

A classic psychoanalytic explanation for atypical or paraphiliac sexual behavior is the fixation of libidinal energy at a specific point in development. An individual becomes "stuck" and, with advancing age, constantly

Ethical Considerations

Source: Callista Lee

When it comes to those with paraphilic disorders, there is no argument that people suffering from psychological and behavior problems should receive treatment if it is desired. But what if they don't want to be cured? Those who commit crimes related to their paraphilic disorders generally face jail time. What is controversial is whether they should be allowed to return to the community after serving their time in jail. Convicted sex offenders are required to be listed their state's Sex Offender Registry so that community members can look up their neighborhood to see how many reside in their neighborhoods. You can check your neighborhood at https://www.meganslaw.ca.gov/. Is it fair though that ALL sex offenders should be on this list for life even if their risk of reoffending is low? In an article in the Journal of the American Academy of Psychiatry and the Law Online (First, 2014), the author asks readers to consider the risk to persons diagnosed with a Paraphilic Disorder of finding themselves locked up in a forensic psychiatric facility, possibly for life, after having already completed their prison sentence because a *diagnosis* suggests that they are high risk for reoffending. At what point would they be able to prove themselves well enough to be allowed back into society? And what sorts of psychiatric treatments can we ethically subject them to without their consent?

regresses to that point in psychosexual development. The immature level of sexual development is a result of not having been allowed the full expression and passage of libidinal energy at the age-appropriate stage.

Sexual masochists' need to be humiliated by having their partner urinate or defecate on them, for instance, is attributed to unresolved issues at the anal stage of development. Perhaps this person was rushed through toilet training or belittled for soiling his underpants. Whatever the specific issue, the unresolved transition through this period results in the fixation of sexuality at this stage of development.

Behaviorism

The behaviorist focuses on some facet of learning, and argues that atypical sexual behavior and paraphilia stem from some associative learning experience. Perhaps it was extremely harsh parental punishment for some minor sexual act such as observing Mom in the shower or being caught masturbating. Or it may be pairing an act (observing a woman undressing, for instance) with a pleasurable sexual experience (such as masturbation) that is positively reinforcing. This type of behavior is likely to be repeated.

Eclectic Perspective

John Money (Money & Lamacz, 1989) offers an eclectic explanation to atypical sexual behavior and paraphilia. He has developed a biosocial theory of sexual and gender development (see Chapter 4) based on what he called "lovemaps" ("templates" in the brain for patterns of eroticism and love). These templates, according to Money, are developed between 5 and 8 years of age as a result of biological and psychosocial forces.

During this period of development, Money believes children begin to link sex, love, and lust. The child usually develops a normal, healthy connection between romantic love and lust (sexual desire). Each of us has a unique lovemap based on a combination of biology (genetic inheritance, gonadal and hormonal influences) and psychosocial learning (parental and other models of love and affection). Healthy lovemaps are imprinted in our brain and create our idealized lover, love affair, and erotic imagery.

Atypical sexual behavior and paraphilia, according to Money, are a result of a distorted or "vandalized" lovemap that does not make a healthy connection between romantic love and lust. Love and lust are imprinted as disparate entities.

Because the two are not linked, sexual desire (lust) is not attached to normal romantic involvements but, rather, becomes attached to the inanimate objects, humiliating behavior, and the like, that evolve into paraphilias. Sexual desire is something apart from intimacy and affection. Lovemaps can become distorted for a variety of reasons including incest, physical abuse, extremely harsh parental punishments for normal sexual activity in childhood, repressive parental attitudes, and lack of displays of affection between parents.

Treatment

Most paraphiliacs enter treatment as a result of being arrested for their behavior. They do not seek treatment on their own or enter willingly. Paraphilias

personal exploration activity

Is It Really So Bad?

It is really easy to react negatively when we hear of some "different" sexual behavior and to immediately label it as harmful. However, even though we may never want to engage in any paraphiliac sexual behavior, many of the behaviors cause no real harm to the person or others. The goal of this activity is to try to identify those behaviors that are truly harmful from those that, however odd they seem, are really rather harmless.

Take a sheet of paper and label three columns—one "harmless," one "harmful," and one "both harmful and harmless." As you continue to read about the different behaviors, try to keep an open mind and forget the judgments you have already formed about these behaviors. After reading about each behavior, list it in the column where it seems to fit the best. Notice what factors cause you to give each the label you assign. Based on what label you give each behavior, do you think there should be criminal penalties for the behavior?

Keep in mind that many of these behaviors carry severe criminal penalties or at least very negative social attitudes. Is it possible that our society is overreacting because the behaviors do not fit what most consider normal? Should our laws and attitudes be changed for those you listed in the harmless category?

are extremely difficult to treat, and "cure rates" are low. Regardless of which view one holds regarding the etiology of paraphilias, most experts agree that atypical and paraphiliac behavior originates early in life, manifests itself in fantasy and desire, and evolves into full-blown behavior and lifestyle by young adulthood. As such, the person has a long history of behavior that has been reinforced over time through pleasure (masturbation or other sources of orgasm). The prognosis for eliminating such behavior is not good. In a study of 435 juvenile sex offenders, Zolondek and colleagues (2001) found that 10 percent to 30 percent were involved in exhibitionism, fetishism, frottage, voyeurism, obscene phone calls, and phone sex. Williams (2014) found that 15–25% of all men with Pedophilic Disorder revert to their per-incarceration behavior within a few years of being released from jail.

Biomedical and Surgical Treatment

One way to treat people with paraphilia is to attempt to lower their level of sexual desire through chemical (drugs) and surgical (castration) procedures. Drug therapy consists of administering drugs that either inhibit the production of testosterone or block its effects on the brain. As we discussed in Chapters 2 and 3, testosterone is the main androgen linked to sexual desire in men and women. Drugs such as cyproterone acetate (CPA) and medrohxyprogesterone (MPA-Depo-Provera) interfere with the effects of progesterone. They have been shown to have limited effectiveness in treating pedophiles, rapists, and other male sex offenders (Wincze, Bansal, & Malamud, 1986; Cooper, 1986). Until the 1980s, castration was used to reduce the sexual desire of sex offenders. The surgical removal of the testicles eliminates the production of most testosterone but does not prevent sexual excitement and erection (Nobre, Wiegel, Bach et al., 2004).

Although decreasing testosterone levels lowers sexual desire, it does not eliminate desire entirely. Also, no evidence is available to show that reducing testosterone levels, and thus sexual desire, has any permanent effect on the focus of sexual behavior. Testosterone is linked with sexual desire, not sexual orientation or the focus of sexual activity. Drug therapy seems to work by lessening the compulsion to engage in paraphiliac behavior (Walen & Roth, 1987). It doesn't eliminate the desire but, in conjunction with other approaches invoking the patient's support system, helps control the desire enough to allow intervention.

Behavior Modification

Behavior modification is used to desensitize paraphiliacs to their paraphilias and sensitize them to new, aversive stimuli. **Aversion therapy** is a behavior modification technique that pairs an aversive stimulus (such as electric shock) with the behavior that is targeted for change (Hermans, Dirikx, and Vansteenwegenin, 2005). Covert sensitization is a type of aversion therapy sometimes used with paraphiliacs. In **covert sensitization,** an aversive fantasy (not behavior) is paired with the paraphiliac fantasy in an attempt to extinguish it. For example, a voyeur is asked to visualize a past fantasy that accompanied one of the voyeuristic episodes. As the person visualizes the pleasing fantasy (say, peeping on an unsuspecting woman), the therapist introduces an aversive fantasy image (such as vomiting uncontrollably). By pairing the new aversive image (the vomiting) with the previously arousing image (peeping at the victim), the therapist links the negative image to the paraphilia.

Aversion therapy A behavior modification technique that pairs an aversive stimulus with the behavior targeted for change

Covert sensitization A type of behavior modification in which an aversive fantasy is paired with the paraphiliac fantasy in an attempt to extinguish it

❧ *Intellectual Wellness* ❧

High-level intellectual functioning can help a person know when an atypical behavior pattern represents a true paraphilia. Knowledge can help people understand that they have a problem and how to seek help in dealing with it. Paraphilias, however, tend to have such a strong hold over people that knowledge alone usually isn't enough to motivate them to seek help. Even so, knowledge can play a part in helping them learn how to live with their obsession and channel it into more acceptable forms of expression.

Skills Training

The focus of skills training is to enhance interpersonal skills. Paraphiliacs often rely on the paraphilia because of their inability to engage in satisfying interpersonal sexual relationships. Often they lack the self-esteem, confidence, and behavioral skills to meet potential sex partners and cultivate sexually satisfying relationships.

In skills training, they learn a variety of behaviors ranging from communicating (how to initiate conversations, meet new people, and the like) to coping with stress. As individuals become more proficient with these skills, they can learn to rely less and less on their paraphilia for sexual arousal (Zilbergeld, 1992).

People who engage in atypical sexual activity (particularly partnered activities) can be socially healthy. They may engage in atypical activities to add spice to their sex lives. Most people with full-blown paraphilias, however, are not doing well socially. Their paraphilia often originated from disordered social functioning and learning. The paraphilia takes the place of functional adult social and sexual relationships. Many paraphiliacs experience sexual release through solitary masturbation in the presence of their paraphiliac object of desire.

Safe, Sane and Consensual BDSM

Source: Callista Lee

What are the differences between kinky sex play and a paraphilic disorder?

When considering whether you or someone you know (or see in a movie) is just atypical in their sexual behavior or whether they would meet the criteria for a paraphilic disorder, remember the criteria for diagnosis:

Criteria A: The sexual behavior is atypical, ongoing (at least six months), has an obsessive-compulsive nature, and is the primary focus of their sexuality.

and

Criteria B: The paraphilia causes distress or impairment in functioning **or** that the sexual practice inherently involves nonconsenting individuals

Atypical sexual behavior is not necessarily problematic, even if the person is really into it and has a whole room devoted to their BDSM (Bondage, Domination/submission, Sado-Masochism) or fetishistic hobbies or lifestyle. There are clear markers for where it crosses the line. Healthy players always follow these rules:

Safety—The people involved learn what is safe (both physically and emotionally) and what is not. There are methods of binding or even suspending a partner that can be safe, but if you do it wrong you can cause harm. The same goes for spanking, flogging, and other behaviors. BDSM clubs sometimes offer

"Safe Play" classes, and there are a variety of books on the subject. There is some controversy in the community about what constitutes harm. Some people are totally fine with bruises or welts or even cuts that take a few days to heal, while others feel that lasting marks goes too far. One important area of concern is "breath play." There are those who insist that temporarily restricting or cutting off air supply can be safe as long as you don't let your partner pass out. But loss of consciousness is not the only risk. At the website, you'll find a lengthy article about the risk of heart attack during breath play. It can come on without warning, even in a healthy young person. It is caused by the brain and heart panicking when oxygen to the brain gets low. The chemical chaos can lead to cardiac arrest.

Sanity—Players know and respect the difference between fantasy and reality. They understand and respect physical, intellectual, and emotional limits. They know the importance of communication, and they talk with their partners ahead of time about what turns them and what is off-limits. BDSM players are known for being excellent communicators, often spending a good deal of time discussing their turn-ons, turn-offs, and fantasies with one another before they get around to getting into a "scene."

Consent—Even a couple playing master and slave respect a person's "no." The slave is not an actual slave; it's a role play. To stay "in scene," they often choose safe-words or safe-signals to communicate important information like "this is too much, we need to go back to something less intense" or "I really have to pee" or "STOP." The usual words like "no, don't, please don't" may be part of the role play so terms like "red" for stop or "yellow" for less intense please may be used. We know a gentleman who likes to use the word "jail" as his safe word. That says "stop!" to him no matter how sexually and emotionally into a scene he may be. He proudly brags that no submissive of his has ever had to use that safe word because he pays close attention to their responses and backs off when it appears that they are too close to their limits. But consent is not just about keeping people out of jail. The purpose of BDSM play is for both partners to have a good time. No kind of sex is fun for a person who is not consenting.

50 Shades of Grey was *not* Safe, Sane, or Consensual—It is despised in the BDSM community because it misrepresents them. Christian Grey has mental problems linked to his traumatic childhood. He makes it clear that he is unable to have a healthy relationship with a woman. He does not respect

Anastasia's boundaries. He breaks into her home, and he attempts to control her even though she has not given consent to be controlled. In real life, she should have run far, far away from him and never looked back. But like so many romantic fantasies, he is cured simply by finding the right woman to love and be loved by. Believing in such a fantasy is not safe *or* sane.

Warning to beginning BDSM players—Beware of charming strangers. Sometimes people who don't play by the rules will infiltrate a BDSM club, meet an unsuspecting submissive, get them alone, and abuse them. To make matters worse, they may gaslight them by insisting that the victim actually enjoyed going beyond their limits. Victims are often afraid to report the abuser because they feel foolish for having gotten themselves into the situation. While not everyone is comfortable playing in a public club, it is much safer than going home with someone you don't know well. **Listen to your gut** and excuse yourself quickly from any situation that feels wrong, even if you can't explain it intellectually. Learn about safety precautions and engage in lots of conversation before agreeing to "play" with someone.

References

American Psychiatric Association (APA). (2013). *The diagnostic and statistical manual of mental disorders* (5th ed.) Washington, DC: Author.

Cooper, A. J. (1986). Progesterone in the treatment of male sex offenders: A review. *Canadian Journal of Psychiatry, 31,* 73–79.

Cusack, J. (1996). The murky world of Internet porn: The "Orchid Club" shakes up the law. *World Press Review, 43*(11), 8–10.

Davis, L., McShane, M. D., & Williams, F. P. (1995). Controlling computer access to pornography: Special conditions for sex offenders. *Federal Probation, 59*(2), 43–48.

Downing, L., Nobus, D. (2004). The Iconography of Asphyxiophilia: From Fantasmatic Fetish to Forensic Fact. *Paragraph*, Oct 2004, Vol. 15 Issue 3, pages 265–280

Friedman, R. C. (1998, January 19). Gender identity. *Psychiatric News: Viewpoints* [Online]. Available: www.payxh.org/pnews/98-01019/gender.html.

Hickman, W. (2002, August 8). A real swinger—Part IV (autoerotic asphyxiation cases). *Mondau Business Briefings.*

Hermans, D., Dirikx, T., Vansteenwegenin, D. (2005). Reinstatement of fear responses in human aversive conditioning. *Behaviour Research and Therapy* v. 43 no. 4 (April 2005) p. 533–51

Kaplan, D. E. (1997). New cybercop tricks to fight child porn: Police struggle against an online onslaught. *U S.News & World Report, 122*(20), 29.

Levinson, J. (2003). Sexual Perversity. *The Monist* 86 no1 30–54 Ja 2003

Money, J., & Wiedcking, C. (1980). Gender identity/role: Normal differentiation and its transpositions. In Nobre, P. J., Wiegel, M., Bach, M., Weisberg, R. B., Brown, T. A., Wincze, J. P., Barlow, D. H. (2004). Determinants of sexual arousal and accuracy of its self-estimation in sexually functional males. *J Sex Res*. Nov 2004: 41(4): 363–71.

Oliver, B. E. (2005). Thoughts on Combating Pedophilia in Non-Offending Adolescents. *Archives of Sexual Behavior* v. 34 no. 1 (February 2005) p. 3–5.

Seto, M. C. (2004) Sexual Offenses Against Children. *Annual Review of Sex Research* v. 15 (2004) p. 321–61

Wolman & J. Money (Eds.), (1998). *Handbook of human sexuality.*Englewood Cliffs, NJ: Prentice Hall.

Walen, S., & Roth, D. (1987). A cognitive approach. In J. H. Geer & W. T. O'Donohue (Eds.), *Theories of human sexuality.* New York: Plenum.

Wincze, J., Bansal, S., & Malamud, M. (1986). Effects of medroxprogesterone acetate on subjective arousal, arousal to erotic stimulation, and nocturnal penile tumescence in male sex offenders. *Archives of Sexual Behavior, 15,* 293–306.

Zilbergeld, B. (1992). *Male sexuality: A guide to sexual fulfillment.*Boston: Little, Brown.

Zolondek, S. C., Abel, G. G., Northey, W. F. (2001). *Journal of Interpersonal Violence* v. 16 no. 1 (January 2001) pp. 73–85.

Chapter *fifteen*

Sex Work

Student Learning Objectives

After reading this chapter, students will be able to:

- Explain how pornography has affected advances in technology.
- Differentiate pornography, erotica, and obscenity.
- Discuss how technological advances have combined with other historical trends to create a new commercialization of sex.
- Describe some of the problems inherent in policing the Internet for sexual victimization and exploitation.
- Evaluate the effectiveness of blocking tools that parents can use to limit children's access to Internet- or television-based sexual material.
- Evaluate the effects of sexually explicit materials on sexual behavior.
- Discuss the well-being of sex workers.
- Describe the pros and cons of decriminalizing sex work.

Sexualized Media

Source: Callista Lee

People have been sharing sexual imagery for thousands of years, from cave drawings to stone carvings to pottery to hand-written books and finally to books churned out by printing presses. But **pornography** didn't really take off as big business until after the invention of the photograph in 1826. Since that time, pornographers have been at or near the forefront of new technologies, moving them forward by adopting them while they were still new and expensive (there have always been people willing to pay for porn), keeping the new media alive as it eventually became more affordable for other content and use by the masses. We've seen this play out several times since the invention of the photographic negative in 1839, a new technology that allowed for multiple copies to be printed from a glass negative. Prior to that, every photo was one of a kind. The first known nude photos *for sale* were made in Paris in 1840 (just one year later!) and sold widely throughout the city, often by women who hid them under their skirts. Just twenty years later, there were 400 shops in Paris selling pornographic photos (The School of Life, 2019). The first *entertainer* to appear in such a photo was American stage actress and poet, Adah Isaacs Menken (1835-1868). Although her life was not long, she lives on in her poetry, the annals of 1800's American and European theater, and the famous photo in which she appears to be naked, strapped to a running horse (Britannica, 2019). After still photos came moving pictures, and pornographers were quick to expand into that quickly growing business. One of the earliest films was French, "Le Coucher de la Mariée," made in 1896, showing a woman doing a striptease. In the early days of porn movies, viewers had to either go to a theater that played them (often in seedy parts of town) or own a private projector, which was very expensive and uncommon. But again, new technology came along to bring porn to the masses. "In 1958 a young British glam photographer, Harrison Marks, began making 8 mm short films of women undressing and posing topless...The Super 8 camera was cheap and extremely easy to use and, because of this convenience, became standard in the porn industry" (Glass, 2014). At the same time, families began making home movies and bought projectors with which they could view them.

In the 1970s, the video cassette debuted; two types actually, Betamax and VHS. They were expensive. but porn users were happy to pay for the convenience and privacy of just popping a cassette into their player and watching it on the television at home. With that, porn movie theaters were on the way out. As a consumer you had to make a choice between them when you bought a videotape player. Betamax made higher quality recordings but were limited to just sixty minutes each. VHS quality was not as good, but offered three hours of footage. Pornographers chose VHS to get more porn per tape, and so viewers bought VHS players; it was porn that killed the Betamax. Through the late 1970s, most videotape sales were pornographic. Hollywood wanted to keep its viewers in the theaters. But eventually movies were put on VHS because that was what their viewers were demanding. They already had porn at home and wanted other content too. When it came to close captioning for videos, again porn helped lead the way. It seems that viewers actually wanted to know what the actors were saying above the "sound of smashing flesh and guttural moans" (Glass, 2014). One has to wonder if the only users of close captioning had been those viewers with hearing difficulties, whether close captioning would have become as normalized as quickly as it did.

As the Internet showed up in average people's homes, the **chat room** became the new way for people to share their erotic fantasies and photos. "A 1990s study of Usenet discussion groups suggested that five in six images shared were pornographic" (Hartford, 2019). Sharing photos takes more bandwidth than text, so again the pornographers became leaders in calling for more because their customers were willing to pay for it. As more homes got onto the Internet, more services became available, including newer ways to enjoy and share pornography. Online porn providers were pioneers in video file compression and even user-friendly payment systems. By implementing online credit-card verification systems, they

Pornography A depiction of lewd material or erotic behavior designed to cause sexual arousal

Chat rooms Live e-mail discussion lines in which a person can communicate with others by typing messages

Bandwidth a measure of the amount of information a fiber-optic cable can transmit

paved the way for businesses like iTunes, eBay, and Amazon (Glass, 2014). And porn providers were the first to offer online subscription-based services, online and on cable TV. The growth of online porn has been huge, with 70,000 adult websites in 2001 to more than 4.2 million today in the just the US alone (Glass, 2014). As we've seen in many businesses, consolidation of many providers into one or just a few huge providers (like Pornhub, owned by Mindgeek) has been an effective way to make money for people at the top. Because of the relative lack of competition between providers and the fact that many people are making and giving away their own home-based porn, there has been radical change in working conditions for porn actors. There is now greater pressure for them to do more work (and work they don't enjoy) for less pay…something we've seen happening in many industries over the past couple of decades. And while sites like Pornhub collect money every time someone streams their content, the actors are generally paid a one-time fee at the time of production. The new union for porn actors, the International Entertainment Adult Union (IEAU), is hoping to file a class action lawsuit on behalf of its members to change that.

Another technology that the porn industry has taken advantage of is the instant camera. Sexting didn't begin with SnapChat; it began with photos that would develop without the photographer having to take them to a photo shop or drugstore to be developed. And before Tinder, there were those annoying ads for "sexy single ladies" targeted to your geolocation. Today, pornographers are eagerly awaiting updates in Artificial Intelligence (AI) and Virtual Reality (VR) technology that will allow them to transmit not just sounds and pictures but also smell, taste, and touch.

Who is buying porn?

A report published in Huffpost (2013) states that

- 12 percent of websites are pornographic
- 35 percent of internet downloads include pornographic content
- 25 percent of online search engine requests relate to sexuality
- 40 million Americans describe themselves as regular porn viewers
- The average age of first exposure to pornography is eleven years old.

One positive aspect of this proliferation of high-speed internet access was its ability to provide accurate, nonbiased information on sexuality (Edwards, 1996). As Fisher and Barak (2002) point out, Internet-based sexuality education programs can offer significant resources and expert instruction, and they can reach massive audiences in a very cost-effective manner. The Internet also opens up many exciting venues for conducting sex research. Mustanski (2002) explains that the anonymity and accessibility of the Internet, along with access to very large sample sizes, make sexual survey research very attractive.

On the down side, the Internet is so large and powerful that it is almost impossible to police. It brings graphic, sadomasochistic, live video clips into the living room. It connects 45-year-old pedophiles with potential victims through chat rooms. Couple this technology with a much more permissive culture, and you have an entirely different sexual landscape today than at any time in U.S. history. It is a no-holds-barred culture in which almost anything goes—and much of it goes into our living rooms, bedrooms, and offices via these new technologies. Although all of these things existed before 1990, now the low cost has allowed Americans to be exposed to almost any sexual idea, theme, or image in the privacy of the home. Nearly anything goes—especially if it sells.

Unfortunately, the Internet also provides access to hard-to-find materials that aren't readily available and are often illegal. This cornucopia of sexually explicit materials includes pedophilia, bondage, sadomasochism, and sex with animals (Elmer-Dewitti, 1995).

Internet-based sexually oriented materials are difficult to supervise. With more than 40 million sites (the number grows by thousands daily) and nearly universal access, the Internet provides global access to sexually oriented material. A consumer who has a connection to the Web can access sexually oriented chat rooms, still pictures (X-rated stills of anything desired, including kiddie porn), video clips (short sections of sex films), and live sex shows (the viewer becomes part of the audience from his or her living room) that can originate from anywhere around the globe.

A person can connect with a live sex show from Denmark, a sadist or masochist from Asia, or a housewife selling still pictures of herself engaging in fellatio with her husband in Australia. Although this may sound too good to be true to an adult who enjoys pornography, it can cause much concern for the average parent of a teenage son or daughter. Technology is available to block minors' access to adult Internet sites. These barriers, however, work only if parents and other adults using home PCs install them and check up on them regularly. Problems remain, however, even with these technological aids in place.

∾ *Emotional Wellness* ∾

Not only is sexual information available in unprecedented amounts, but sexual counseling, therapy, and self-help also are within the average person's reach. As sex comes into the open, so does sexual healing. Online chat rooms, self-help groups, and other computerized services offer increasing opportunities for dealing with sexual concerns and problems.

Web sites are available catering to all people and interests. Gay people who need help to come out of the closet can find help and link up with others around the country or around the corner. Transgendered people no longer have to feel alone. They have their own Web sites and referral networks a mere mouse-click away. Although electronic resources will never take the place of a live helping relationship, the technological innovations and resources available to average individuals can greatly improve their emotional wellness by providing easy access to information and services that were not available a decade ago.

∾ *Social Wellness* ∾

Many argue that the current sexual climate in the United States impacts negatively on our social wellness as individuals and as a culture. Everything from child-rearing to productivity in the workplace, they say, becomes harder as parents, employers, and government have to compete against the lure and distraction of sexual availability. It is more difficult, they argue, to uphold standards of decency and social relationships in the face of a no-holds-barred societal attitude toward sex. Others disagree. They argue that greater sexual freedom and availability of sexual information and services empowers people and fosters understanding of their sexuality. Social wellness, they say, is thereby enhanced because sexuality, a natural part of life, is allowed its full expression. This allows people to understand their sexuality better and develop higher levels of social wellness.

How is Pornography Defined?

Although *pornography, erotica,* and *obscenity* have been used interchangeably, these terms mean entirely different things.

Pornography

Derived from the Latin roots *porne* (prostitute) and *graphos* (depicting), the literal translation of pornography is a depiction in writing or pictures of prostitutes or prostitution.

It refers more commonly to any depiction of lewd material or erotic behavior designed to cause sexual arousal. In U.S. culture, the connotation of pornography and pornographic materials is usually negative, even though most people admit they get sexually excited while viewing it.

Erotica

Derived from the Greek word *erotikos* (love poem), **erotic** means devoted to or tending to arouse sexual love or desire. Erotic materials depict beauty, love, sensuousness, voluptuousness, and the like. In U.S. culture (and most others around the world), the depiction of erotica and erotic materials tends to be positive. This judgment is subjective, however. Some people do not distinguish pornography from erotica, and lump them together.

Erotic Devoted to arousing sexual love or desire

In real life, separating some pornographic materials from erotica is difficult. Often, the context of the material helps to define it. For instance, one could view two films, an X-rated porn film and a sex ed video. Each film portrays a heterosexual couple having sex. Both films have graphic displays of nudity, masturbation, oral sex, and intercourse in various positions. What is the difference? Are the films pornographic or erotic?

The porno film makes little mention of love or expressions of caring. The relationship between the partners may be unknown or casual. The sexual acts may be forced or seemingly initiated by one partner for his or her own gratification. The genitalia are overemphasized, with close-ups of the coupled genitalia. Most porn films end with a mandatory, degrading ejaculation in the face of the female.

The sex education video emphasizes communication. The couple talks to each other. They ask what each one desires, whether something feels good, and the like. They take their time. Their intent is mutual pleasuring. They equally participate and initiate. The narration describes what is happening. The partners proceed through the various acts and show their appreciation, caring, and kindness. These videos do not include genital close-ups and orgasm. They do not show "in-your-face" ejaculation.

One could almost use a continuum to evaluate sexually explicit materials. Pornographic materials would represent one extreme and instructional sex education materials would be at the other end, with erotica in the middle. To complicate matters, one must also consider whether the material is obscene.

Obscenity

Obscenity is derived from the Latin word *obscenus,* which means dirty, filthy, and disgusting. Obscene materials repel the senses and are abhorrent

Obscenity Material that is abhorrent to moral virtue and accepted norms of social behavior

to morality, virtue, and accepted norms of societal behavior. In 1966, the U.S. Supreme Court defined obscene materials as meeting three criteria:

- The dominant theme had to appeal to a purely erotic interest in sex.
- The material had to be offensive to contemporary community standards.
- The material had to be without serious literary, artistic, political, or scientific value.

This definition posed serious difficulties in interpretation, and numerous challenges have been brought to bear. In 1973, the Supreme Court reversed its ruling using the three original criteria. In *Miller v. California,* the Court decided that only one criterion was necessary to define obscenity: local community standards. Each community had to decide for itself whether specific materials were offensive by its standards. The producers, actors, distributors, and sellers of materials that a community defines as obscene are all subject to prosecution even if the materials were produced in another community. This criterion is still in effect today. It is troubling because it gives a vocal minority in a community the ability to declare anything from skimpy bathing suits to Michelangelo's *Venus de Milo* obscene.

In general, materials described as erotic are not perceived as obscene and usually are not the target of prosecution. Obscene materials, in contrast, are considered to be subcategories of pornography. The overwhelming majority of Americans believe that adults should have access to sexually explicit material, both erotic and pornographic, depicting sexual activity between consenting adults (Diamond & Dannemiller, 1989).

Support for obscene materials is much less. These materials usually depict themes other than sexual activity between consenting adults. Materials that involve children, rape, sadomasochism, and similar themes are more often those that fail to meet community standards.

Prostitution

Prostitution The exchange of sexual services for money

Prostitution has been around since the dawn of civilization. The earliest written accounts are in the Bible. Jesus himself took time to protect a prostitute from a stone-throwing crowd who would persecute her. Prostitution is illegal in the United States except in Nevada, where it is regulated and limited to certain counties.

It is very difficult to estimate the number of persons who currently work, or have ever worked as prostitutes in the United States. There are many reasons for this. The definition of prostitution varies from state-to-state making reporting difficult. There is no accurate way to sample the general population and organizations such as The Bureau for Labor Statistics do not have data on prostitution as a work category. Most estimates of the incidence of prostitution come from law enforcement and reports of prostitutes who get arrested. National arrest figures in the United States average about 100,000 annually. The National Task Force on Prostitution suggests that over one million people in the US have worked as prostitutes in the United States, or about 1% of American women (ProCon.Org, 2013).

In Nevada and other places where prostitution is legal, prostitutes are called *sex workers,* and they are employed in the sex worker industry.

Prostitution is legal in many European, Asian, African, and South American countries, where it is considered a victimless crime.

Small numbers of prostitutes in the United States have organized in an attempt to try to legalize it in all 50 states. Legalization, they believe, will help protect prostitutes, ensure better working conditions, extend benefits such as disability and Social Security, and help them reduce their risk for contracting a variety of sexually transmitted diseases, including HIV (ProCon.org, 2013, Prostitutes' Education Network, 2003). It also will free police to spend more time on other forms of crime, relieve the courts of a tremendous burden, and allow women to use their bodies the way they want to.

Although people tend to assume that all prostitutes are women, men and women alike engage in exchanging sex for money, food, shelter, drugs, or other resources. They can be subcategorized. Prostitutes who literally solicit clients off the streets are called *hookers* (females) and *hustlers* (males), although the labels could apply to either gender. These prostitutes also are known as *streetwalkers*. They generally are at the lower end of the social order of prostitutes.

In a major study of eight major metropolitan areas, (San Diego, Seattle, Dallas, Denver, Washington, DC, Kansas City, Atlanta, and Miami), the Urban Institute reported (Dank et al, 2014) that the underground commercial sex economy (UCSE) has changed significantly over time. It used to mainly consist of street prostitution, whereas over the last decade, a majority of the business is now run through the Internet. This has driven most street prostitutes off of the street and onto online sex sites and chat rooms where they advertise their services. Law enforcement officials believed that the Internet has shifted many of the adults and minors previously found on the street indoors. This has resulted in somewhat hiding the prevalence of the issue, as the number of adults and children visible on the streets has decreased in some areas (Dank et al, 2014).

In their report entitled, Estimating the Size of the Underground and Commercial Sex Industry in the United States. The Institute noted that in addition to this major trend there has been a shift away from an industry run mostly by individuals to one that is very connected to gangs and professional syndicates (Dank et al, 2014). With the exception of street prostitutes, most sex workers are connected to organized groups that control the industry. The report found that in addition to street prostitution, the UCSE includes brothels, massage parlors, escort services.

Street Prostitution

There are two different levels of street prostitutes. The first group is made up of those addicted to crack cocaine, methamphetamine, heroin and cocaine. These men and women are usually involved in prostitution to support their drug habits and their physical condition and unattractiveness generally puts them at the lowest price point for commercial sex. These individuals mostly perform oral sex for $5 to $10 in cars, hallways, and other locations (Dank et al, 2014).

The next level of street prostitution is managed by pimps. Pimps serve as the conduit for connecting customers with prostitutes. Most of these

case study
15.1

Critical Thinking

How would you handle a situation where you had strong sexual desires for particular behaviors that your sexual partner didn't share?

Edgar: Paying for Sex

Edgar, 43, married, identifies as Hispanic.

Married for 20 years, Edgar has two children, ages 13 and 16. He is a middle manager in an insurance company. He describes his relationship with his wife as intimate and committed but feels the passion in their relationship died several years ago. Although they have sex about once a week or every other week, it isn't very exciting and he wants more. He frequents massage parlors about twice a month, paying for a massage that includes masturbation and usually fellatio.

I guess you could say that sex for me has never been all that exciting. Except for the prostitutes I used to pay for when I was in Vietnam, I was sexually inexperienced. I didn't have sex until I enlisted in the army at 18 and went to Vietnam. When I returned, I got a job in an insurance company and went to college at night.

I met my wife at the insurance company during the first month I worked there, and we got married about a year after that. The first year or so, things were OK. My wife wasn't very interested in sex, and we probably had intercourse about once a week that first year. She's pretty conservative and isn't into oral sex or anything kinky. I really didn't know what to expect of married life. My dad never really talked about sex with me, and I was too embarrassed to talk to my friends about it in much detail. My first son was born after a year, and things slowed down a little more with my wife.

I was in New York for a training program for my current job. I guess it was about 10 years ago. I remember walking around Times Square and going into the bookstores and bars. I passed a massage parlor, and the guy out front was passing out coupons for a special deal. I said, "What the heck," and went in. I had been curious about these massage parlors and was feeling horny. No one there knew me, so I took a chance. I picked out my masseuse and went into our little room.

After undressing, she started to rub my back, and before long her touches became a lot more intimate. She asked if I wanted her to jerk me off, and I said yes. I had to pay her a little more but it was worth it. The next night I went into a different place and found out I could get a blow job for about $20. The masseuse there was unattractive, but, boy, could she give head. It reminded me of my experiences in Vietnam.

When I returned home to Virginia from my training program, I began to seek out massage parlors in Richmond and other places within a reasonable drive from my home. I've been doing this at least once a month more than 10 years. My wife doesn't know, and the cost isn't too much. I'm basically happily married and love my kids. I wish I had more sex with my wife and she was into oral sex, but I don't think she'll change. She won't even talk about seeing a sex therapist, so I keep doing what I'm doing. I don't have a problem with it, and it probably keeps my marriage going.

customers viewed the prostitutes online through websites and chatrooms. They place a call asking to arrange a meeting and the pimp sets the connection up. The actual sex can take place in a variety of settings controlled by the pimp. Prostitutes who work with pimps are generally not addicted to drugs and are healthier and more attractive than their drug-addicted peers. Because of this, and the fact that the pimp takes a cut of the transaction, costs are higher than for drug-addicted street prostitutes. These prostitutes typically charge around $60 to $120 per hour for sexual intercourse (Dank et al, 2014).

Most street and Internet pimps are independent agents who usually do not work closely with organized crime . They have their own social networks that share information about cities' markets and warn one another about law enforcement activity. They also trade or buy prostitutes between each other.

The study found that pimps, brothels, and escort services often employed drivers, secretaries, nannies, and other non-sex workers to keep operations running smoothly. In addition they paid off hotel managers and law enforcement agents with money or sexual services to help facilitate sexual encounters and evade prosecution (Dank et al, 2014).

Streetwalking has many unwritten rules, which concern respecting other prostitutes' work areas (also known as "turf"), outwitting undercover police officers, avoiding sadists and murderers, and trying to avoid STDs/HIV. Because of these "rules," streetwalkers often work for pimps (a type of business agent) who help control some of these problems in exchange for a share of the profits.

Street pimps vary in their approach to working with hookers and hustlers. Some provide valuable protection and care for their workers to some extent. Others are thinly disguised sadists and criminals who dominate their hookers and hustlers through drugs, violence, and fear. In the netherworld of streetwalking, violence and death are never far away.

Brothel A house of prostitution

Brothels

Prior to 1920, large **brothels** could be found in every major American city. Many were elegant facilities where customers (overwhelmingly male) could have a drink, eat dinner, play cards, socialize with peers and the prostitutes, and have sex.

Typically, brothels were set up like hotels, with socializing downstairs and sex negotiated in upstairs rooms. Repeat business was the norm, and clients were generally recruited by word of mouth (Petersen, 1999). As a result of legislation and the sweeping moral reform of the early 1920s, most brothels were closed, driving prostitution into the streets or the massage parlors. Brothels still exist in Nevada and, on a much smaller scale, most major metropolitan areas.

Brothels have undergone a resurgence in the 2000s because of their connection to organized family groups. Rather than operating out of grand hotels or other more opulent settings, most brothels today operate out of private residences in almost every community. Dank et al, 2014 reports that brothels are now primarily operated by individuals from Mexico, Guatemala, Honduras, or El Salvador and managed by individual families, rather than large criminal networks.

Prostitution is one of the world's oldest professions.

Brothels are typically run by Latinos and comprised primarily of Latinas. Brothels predominantly target Latino men and workers associated with the brothel hand out business cards that say "construction" or "restaurant" with a phone number. When men call the phone number, they are sent to a location, which is typically a house located in a poor neighborhood. Prices are about $20 to $25 for 15 minutes. Half the proceeds go to the "house" or person(s) running the brothel and the sex worker keeps the other half.

Law enforcement agents reported that most women working in the brothels were working voluntarily, but had been smuggled to the United States when they were minors and then forced into the underground commercial sex trade to pay off their smuggling debts. Many stayed in the brothels because of the lack of other viable employment opportunities and fear of being deported (Dank et al, 2014).

Massage Parlors

Prostitutes who work in massage parlors are referred to as *hookers* and *hustlers* but also may be known as *masseuses*. Most massage parlors are fronts for houses of prostitution, where, in addition to a massage, clients are able to receive masturbation, oral sex, and sometimes sexual intercourse.

Most clients of massage parlors walk in off the street and pay cash for a massage and either masturbation or oral sex. Their visit usually lasts 30 minutes and the minimum massage fee costs anywhere from $20 to $50. Additional sex acts are negotiated between the customer and the masseuse and typically mimic the price range charged by pimp-run street prostitutes (around $60 to $120 per hour for oral sex or sexual intercourse). Massage parlors usually have procedures that help screen for potential undercover police activities. For example, they require that customers sign a form indicating that they are not police officers. Clients pay for the massage in advance, with no mention of sexual "extras" until the later stages of the massage. The overwhelming majority of prostitutes working in massage parlors are female.

The Urban Institute Report (Dank et al, 2014) reported that in 2014, the massage parlor business was being run almost exclusively by highly organized Chinese nationals advertising Chinese women and with direct links back to China. This is a major shift away from massage parlor activity in previous years where massage parlors were more diverse. Massage parlors operate similar to escort services in that the owner charges a "house fee" to rent the room and a charge per sexual activity. Any amount tipped would go to the woman performing the act. It is not unusual for a family or owner to operate multiple massage parlors in a given city. Owners often rotate women through the different parlors and advertise their services primarily on the internet (Dank et al, 2014).

Escort Services

In theory, escort services involve the legal practice of "escorting" a client to dinner, a show, a political affair, and the like, for a fee. In reality, most escort services derive their primary business through "out-call" male and female prostitution.

The prostitutes that work for escort services are considered a "higher class" than those who work on the street or in brothels and massage parlors. They charge anywhere from $150 to $500 just to show, and then charge an additional several hundred to several thousand to perform a variety of sex acts. Escorts can make up to $10,000 in one week for five to six dates and upwards of six figures in a year (Dank et al, 2014).

Unlike most other venues within the UCSE, with the exception of massage parlors, escort services accept credit cards and provide a receipt for services rendered. Escort services owners are very careful and thoughtful in their business structure, investments, and business practices in order to evade law enforcement. People who operate escort services are both domestic and foreign national men and women and range from individuals to larger organized criminal enterprises, including gangs.

As with other venues of the UCSE, the internet has also greatly expanded the reach of escort services that previously advertised in print media. Because running an internet business requires a website, various kinds of software and accounts , and constant maintenance, most prostitutes connect with escort agencies who provide all of these services for a cut of the profits. There is usually a 60–40, or in some cases an 80–20, split between the prostitute and the agency (Dank et al, 2014).

Exotic Dancers, Strippers, and Live Sex Performers

In the 1980s–1990s the strip club industry changed from a hodge-podge of seedy bars to a very upscale industry operating "Gentlemen's Clubs" that catered to upscale business professionals aged 25–65. The atmosphere of such clubs is comparable to a country club replete with limousine service, five-star dining, smoking rooms, champagne and conference centers.

According to the Association of Club Executives, a national trade association comprised of club owners and professionals, a single gentlemen's club in a major metropolitan area can gross between $10–20 million per year. A small club in a rural area (Less than 5000 square feet) can generate over a million dollars while cities in secondary markets such as Cleveland or Pittsburgh boast clubs that gross approximately $2 million per year. The majority of adult dance clubs are not owned by large consortiums nor are they connected with organized crime as is the common public perception. Most owners are average business men and women who own a single club (Spencer, 2016).

About 4,000 gentlemen's clubs currently operate in the United States. The industry employs about 400,000 strippers who work as independent contractors. The average earnings for a stripper ranges from $70,000–$100,000 annually (Statistic Brain.com, 2016).

One study actually found that one quarter of the 300 strippers interviewed had university degrees and about 14% were paying for undergraduate or graduate courses with their earnings. Most enjoy their work. Rather than being pressured into becoming a stripper, most voluntarily chose the profession because it fit in with their lifestyle, afforded a lot of job flexibility, and paid well (Holden, 2010).

The Well-Being of Sex Workers

Source: Callista Lee

Because it is illegal, nobody knows how many people (mostly women and girls) are victims of sex trafficking, but it is estimated to be in the millions and to account for about a third if international criminal activity (Walker-Rodrguez & Hill, 2011). It usually involves "deception, fraud, coercion, force or exploitation by the sex trafficker" (Schauer & Wheaton, 2006, p. 148). It is not something that only happens to females in poor countries, although they are at greater risk; it happens to American girls as well, right here in Orange County, California. According to the Los Angeles Times "The 2017 and 2018 victim demographic report from the Orange County Human Trafficking Task Force reveals 365 sex trafficking cases within our county. These women are minors and minorities, many ridden with poverty that keeps them entrapped with limited opportunities to leave and receive support" (Nestor, 2019). Fortunately, the county justice system takes these crimes very seriously and has devoted special resources to police, prosecutors, and victims' advocacy services. However, even when social services or law enforcement are able to rescue a sex trafficking victim there is not always a happy ending. They must deal with the trauma they experienced, and may find that their families are too ashamed to welcome them back home. Some were already on the outs with their families before they were picked up by traffickers…runaways, juvenile delinquents, drug abusers. Repeated exposure to sexual violence may result in severe psychological consequences, requiring years of treatment and support. Of the types of sex work described in this chapter, trafficked workers can be found in any type of setting but are *least* likely found in high-end Escort Services, legal brothels, exotic dancing, and most pornography. It is just too hard to hide them away from someone who would be able to help them in those settings. Because of increased concerns for victims of sex trafficking and because arresting prostitutes has led to an ineffective revolving-door justice system, law enforcement focus in many regions has turned to the traffickers and pimps. Customers are sometimes arrested, but penalties tend to be light unless they were found with a minor. Any sex with a minor is legally a sexual assault.

Leaving sex work isn't easy for those who entered it voluntarily, either. Even if you have a great cover story for family and friends, how do you come up with work history for a legitimate employer? Do you just claim to have been supported by a partner or family member for those years? Admitting to a background in sex work generally doesn't go over well with employers. *If* they hire you, they may use it against you to exploit you. Some workers are clever enough to plan ahead by saving their money so that they can afford to go to college or vocational training after leaving the sex trade. But if they worked in the porn industry they also have to worry about being recognized, and harassed because of it. This is something that people sharing videos of themselves for free online should also consider. Once its on the Internet, it is available forever.

Research into the backgrounds of those who go into sex work has found disturbing similarities. Many were sexually molested as children and/or neglected by parents. Some learned that they could get their physical, social, and/or psychological needs met by going along with what the molester wanted; a perfect training ground for selling sex as a teen or adult. This was found to be true for both males and females (Denenberg, 1997; Sanders, O'Neill & Pitcher, 2009). Drug abuse is often blamed for people choosing this type of work for good reason, as research has found that drug abuse began *before* the first experiences with prostitution in the vast majority of cases of drug abusing prostitutes (Potterat et al. 2004; Weber et al. 2004). And because of unhealthy childhood and/or adolescent experiences, many sex workers find it difficult to develop or maintain healthy friendships or romantic relationships, despite their ability to compartmentalize their work from their personal lives.

But not everyone involved in sex work has that unfortunate background. Recent studies have found that having a high sensation-seeking personality may lead to some people engaging in this type of work (Ley, 2017), especially as social norms have become more accepting of sexuality. Unfortunately, there is a shortage of psychological research on the mental health of sex workers by the type of work they do. They tend to all be lumped together. There is certainly a different experience and level of risk for a drug addict working the streets compared to an exotic dancer, porn star, or high-end out-call worker. There was, however, a Swiss study in 2005 of 4,000 legally registered sex workers. Findings included that "45 percent of sex workers reported no desire to quit, and that the single most common reason for doing sex work was "liking the job," endorsed by 37 percent, while the least common was "being forced," endorsed by 1.6 percent" (Vrangalova, 2014). Besides liking the job, other common reasons for choosing sex work included the following: Can't find another job, 29 percent; Supporting the family, 26 percent; Paying off debt, 24 percent; and Drugs, 22 percent. Of course, the situation in Switzerland is different, with sex work being legal there. While those findings don't sound *so* bad, 50 percent of the sex workers reported mental health problems, whereas we expect about 20-25 percent in the general population. Most common were anxiety (34 percent), mood disorders (30 percent), and PTSD (13 percent). The researchers found that the mental health disorders were clustered by the type of sex work done and their national origin. "On one end of the spectrum were the women in Cluster 4 ($n = 30$). These were virtually all non-European, working out of studios or brothels, and experiencing low levels of social support, and high levels of pressure, violence, and rape as part of their work (though very little of it outside of the work context). Their mental health was in poor shape: 90 percent had at least one psychiatric issue. On the other end on the spectrum were the women in Cluster 3 ($n = 42$). They were of mixed European origin, worked mostly in studios

or as escorts, experienced high levels of social support, and relatively little violence, pressure or rape outside of work, and little to none within sex work. Their mental health was quite admirable. They were very similar to the general U.S. female population in prevalence of depression or any psychiatric diagnosis" (Vrangalova, 2014). It appears clear from this research that experiencing a high level of violence in their work as well as being an immigrant were associated with mental health problems, and *not* the performance of sex work itself. Hopefully we will see research in the US like this in the not too distant future.

Those who argue for the legalization of sex work argue that it will decrease the level of violence; increase access to social, medical, and psychiatric services; allow workers the benefits of legal employment such as Social Security, Unemployment Insurance, and worker safety regulations; the opportunity to unionize; decrease drug abuse; decrease STIs; and remove the incentive for trafficking.

Those who argue against legalization claim that those in favor of legalization are living a fairy tale; that the criminal element will always be involved, violence is hopelessly linked to sex work; that it demeans the workers, and morally harms society. They also argue that testing sex workers for STIs and requiring the use of condoms will lead to a false sense of safety for both workers and clients because condoms are not 100 percent effective and some workers will fail to use them every time.

Both sex workers and some human rights organizations, such as Amnesty International, support decriminalization. But others, such as the founder of Girls Educational and Mentoring Services, a nonprofit for sexually exploited women in New York, Rachel Lloyd, say there is nothing that will equalize the power imbalances in the sex industry and that it is inherently exploitative. "The folks who end up in the commercial sex industry are the folks who are the most vulnerable and the most desperate" (Garsd, 2019).

People on both sides of the debate tend to agree that sex workers should not be treated like criminals and that the people who exploit them are the real problem.

case study 15.2

Kim: Working Her Way through College as an Exotic Dancer

Last year my lover Danielle convinced me to apply for a job as an exotic dancer at a local men's club.

She had been doing it for a few months, and the money was great. She said that with my exotic Asian looks I'd make a fortune in tips if I was willing to act a little. I didn't want to do it, but Danielle said she'd be there a lot to make sure nobody hassled me when I danced. Besides, she said, if I got the job, they occasionally had two girls dance at the same time, and we could try this if I wanted to.

I got the job, and the money really was good, and the bouncers kind of adopted me because they knew I was Danielle's lover. I was a nervous wreck the first night I had to dance. The first set was a near-disaster. I didn't want to make eye contact with the customers because I thought they'd know I wasn't straight, and I was worried that they'd really be obnoxious. I didn't dance too well, either. I think I earned about $7 in tips, mostly out of sympathy.

The next night was better. I had a couple of drinks before going on, and Danielle was there, so I danced for her. She told me to relax and fantasize that she was the only person in the bar. It started to be a real a turn-on, and I relaxed and really got into the music. The guys in the bar went crazy and were all holding dollar bills to stick into my G-string. That was a real turn-off, but the manager and the bouncers made sure that things didn't get out of hand. They told me to smile, and if I let the guys touch my breasts and butt, I'd get more tips. I took their advice and brought home close to $300 that first night. I average about $150 in tips on a typical night.

I don't really like it when the customers proposition me, but it comes with the territory. I'd say about 30 percent of the guys hit on me, but I've learned how to cope with it by smiling, telling them I like guys but love women, and move on. Most of them can deal with that, and it probably feeds their fantasies when they go home and jerk off or have sex with their wives.

Danielle and I have talked about opening a bar of our own when we graduate this year. We want to do something upscale that caters to women's fantasies and dance in the club together as well as manage the place. There is a ton of money to be made in this line of work.

Critical Thinking

Dancers and club operators would describe what they do as providing erotic entertainment and not engaging in sexual activities with customers. How would you characterize Kim's behavior at work?

❧ *Environmental/Occupational Wellness* ❧

In the majority of non-sex-based business, participating in sexually oriented activities (Internet use, telephone sex, and the like), even on lunch or break time, is grounds for dismissal. Many corporations and other workplaces routinely screen workers' computer and telephone records to monitor such activities.

Tech Sex

Telephone Sex

In 2015 there were between five and 10 major companies in the field employing around 100 in-house staff and over 1,000 freelancers (part-time telephone sex workers). These companies average over 500,000 clients paying between $2.00–3.00 per minute. Annual revenue in America is in the hundreds of millions of dollars each year (Morris, 2016).

Today, with free pornography readily available online, and anyone willing to pay for virtual sex can watch performers live over a webcam it is a wonder that phone sex still exists. Even sex work researchers express surprise at the industry's continued existence. Mayyasi (2016) reports that many of the sex magazines that advertised phone sex numbers have disappeared.

Phone sex offers something different from porn and webcams. While there are no market industry reports on the size of the business, phone sex seems to have adapted to the Internet rather than fallen victim to it. Instead of using porn magazines to locate call numbers, customers can now go to phone sex websites where operators post their pictures and describe their "specialty" (anything from fetishes to masturbation) (Leonard, R. (2016).

Two things related to the unique nature of phone sex seem responsible for keeping it alive (1) anonymity, and (2) it is a live, real-time experience (Leonard, R. (2016).

Phone sex involves speaking with a live person in real time. Most phone sex customers are men in their 40s who like the sound of

personal exploration activity

Is Sex Selling to You?

Most states have laws that forbid selling sex. But there are definitely no laws forbidding using sex to sell. You are constantly bombarded by ads using sex to grab your attention. This activity will help you increase your awareness of just how often sex is used to sell a product to you and help you decide whether you want to support the products using this tactic.

For the next month, every time you thumb through a magazine, look at the newspaper, or view any other print material that has advertisements, look for the ads that use sex to sell. The sex part may be in the form of a couple embracing, a sexy guy wearing no shirt, and so forth. Evaluate what they are trying to sell and whether the product is really related to the picture. Put a Post-it or some type of marker on the page with your evaluation and stack all evaluated material in one place. At the end of the month, look at all of the pages you have marked. Were the majority of ads just using sex to sell the product? Do you agree with this technique? If not, are these products you will avoid buying because of their blatant use of sex in a commercial way? Are these ads influencing the way you view sexuality?

a woman's voice but are too intimidated by the face-to-face contact required when interacting with prostitutes or webcam hosts. Being able to interact live from the safe place of the other end of a telephone line is something that has not gone out of favor in a certain segment of the market (Morris, 2016).

Mayyasi (2016) noted that for many persons with disabilities, the phone sex industry is very appealing. The anonymity of the calls allows for telephone sex operators to come in all sizes, shapes, ages, and physical conditions. While many phone sex operators choose their profession out of personal preference, the industry seems to have particular appeal to individuals (mainly women) who can't access the traditional job market (Mayyasi, 2016).

Cable Television and DVDs

The advent of cable television and home DVD/VCRs has almost single-handedly caused the near-extinction of the "porno movie theater." Cable

case study 15.3

Critical Thinking

Is Ed helping or hurting his son's healthy sexual development in his approach to viewing X-rated materials?

Ed

Ed, a continuing education student, recalls his response to finding an X-rated video in the VCR in the family room after a sleepover his 14-year-old son had the night before.

I was cleaning the basement family room. The VCR light was on, so I ejected the film and, much to my surprise, found an X-rated video in it. I figured my son and his friends had watched it the night before, so I talked with him about it when he came home from school. I asked him if it was his, and he said it was one of his friend's father's tapes. His buddy had brought it over for the guys to watch.

I told him that I was more upset over him leaving it in the basement where his 10-year-old brother could have viewed it than the fact that he had seen it. I asked him what he thought of the movie, and he told me that it was a real turn-on.

I reemphasized to him that his mother and I still didn't want him to begin having intercourse until he was older and found a girlfriend he cared about and it would be exclusive. I also reassured him that I understood his natural curiosity about sex and sexual behavior and that masturbation was an acceptable outlet. I also wanted to be sure that he understood that X-rated films are fantasy sex and that he shouldn't confuse what he saw on some of these tapes with reality. I explained that these tapes are designed to cater to our fantasies but that real sex between two people involves talking, negotiating, and caring.

He said he understood and didn't really expect that sex would be like the film. He said that some of the stuff on the film was too kinky for him anyway. I sometimes worry that my approach is too casual, but Ed is a very responsible boy and seems to treat girls with respect. I feel that if I make too big a deal out of this, it will become a forbidden-fruit deal and he'll want to watch them even more.

television has literally brought the world of soft-core and hard-core pornography into Middle America's living room. Twenty years ago, viewing pornography entailed either a trip to the local X-rated movie house or threading a super-8 film into the old family projector, setting up the screen, and hoping kids (or parents) wouldn't discover you watching the movie.

Today, virtually every cable television service provider has at least one soft-core channel that serves up late-evening viewing of "non-penetrative" (penetration and ejaculation scenes have been edited out) versions of X-rated films. Many of the larger metropolitan-area cable television companies also offer X-rated (penetration and ejaculation are shown) channels for home viewing. These channels typically are offered for an extra charge (premium) that rarely exceeds $15 per month, thereby ensuring access to nearly all markets. In 1996, the Federal Telecommunications Law was passed, limiting the hours for airing these channels to between 10 P.M. and 6 A.M. All companies also are required to provide devices that deny transmission without a code that can be entered to activate the service.

✦ *Physical Wellness* ✦

Critics of media portrayals of what is sensual, beautiful, and sexual claim these set unrealistic standards of perfection and a physical ideal that is unattainable for most people. Proponents of sexy media themes and personalities view these positively.

The widespread interest in lifting weights, exercising, and eating healthfully comes in part from images of physical beauty personified by models and popular media personalities (such as Madonna), who promote these behaviors as contributing to their sexiness. You can scarcely pass a women's or men's magazine that doesn't portray the virtues of working out to sculpt a "sexy" body. In a sense, then, the fitness craze, which generally enhances physical wellness, is fueled by the same sexual climate that has also produced many negative sexual images.

healthy sex hints 15.1

Computer Blocking Software
Source: Callista Lee

Parental Control software changes frequently to keep up with the technology. To find out what is rated as "best," do an internet search for "Best Parental Control Software."

For 2019, PC Magazine rated ten products based on price, whether there was a limit to the number of devices or children it could be applied to, and whether it offered the following features: content filter, filtering for https sites, access scheduling, social network monitoring, and remote management. For each product, in-depth professional reviews were included. Prices ranged from US$14.99 to US$100 with most under US$40. Whatever software you choose, be sure to check settings from time to time to make sure that it is doing all that you want it to do.

Source: https://www.pcmag.com/roundup/240282/the-best-parental-control-software

Effects of Pornography and Sexually Explicit Material

As long as pornography has been available, there have been attempts to regulate it, citing that it leads to a variety of social maladies including rape, sexual harassment, degradation and exploitation of women, and weakening of the moral fiber of America. Two presidential commissions on pornography and obscenity have been impaneled over the past 25 years to examine the effects of viewing such material.

The first commission was designated in 1970 by President Richard Nixon. The commission was charged with examining whether exposure to pornography could cause personal harm or lead to sexual violence. It found that exposure to pornography and obscene materials did not cause personal harm or contribute to sexual violence.

The second commission, impaneled by President Ronald Reagan in the early 1980s, had a similar charge. The Meese Commission found that exposure to nonviolent pornography was not harmful and did not lead to sexual aggression and violence (Attorney General's Commission on Pornography, 1986; Petersen, 1999).

A secondary finding of the commission, however, touched off a great deal of controversy among human sexuality professionals. This finding was the claim that the most prevalent forms of pornography were violent in nature and that exposure to this material had a causal relationship to sexual violence.

Since that time several studies have found no conclusive evidence to support this claim (Wright et al., 2016).

Within the past decade there is mounting evidence of an association between neural changes associated with traditional addictions and those associated with internet addiction. These neural changes associated with internet addiction have been found in some people who are heavy viewers of internet pornography.

Internet addiction, like substance addiction seems to affect the reward circuitry in human brains that could lead to a loss of control in some individuals. Internet addiction is viewed as a form of behavioral addiction. Future research needs to address whether or not there are specific differences between substance and behavioral addiction including internet pornography addiction (Love et al, 2015).

In a study of adolescent pornography use, after controlling for other variables, viewing sexually-explicit material online accounted for between less than 4 % of the total variance in sexual behavior among adolescents. The authors conclude that viewing sexually-explicit material online was just one factor among many that may influence youth sexual behaviors (Nursing Standard, 2015).

A study of internet pornography use among college men found that men who reported high levels of sexual behavior were also highly likely to be regular consumers of pornography. Unlike the common stereotypical perception that men who use pornography are socially isolated and use it as a substitute for actual sexual behavior with partners, the study's results suggested that high pornography use was associated with high levels of partnered sexual activity. In addition, college men who were internet pornography users reported that this was consistent with their overall sexual ethics and personality (Carroll et al, 2014).

Carroll et al, 2014 did not report similar findings with college women. The results for college women were unlike the results for men where pornography use, acceptance, and partnered sexual activities were connected. Women with multiple sexual partners tended to be infrequent and casual users of pornography. Internet pornography use was more common among within a couple context.

Since the last Presidential Commission research finding have consistently shown that the overwhelming majority of pornography viewers report no problems or difficulties due to their use. When porn users do report problems, they relate primarily to their relationships, their culture, their morals and their personal functioning, not to porn itself. In other words, using pornography may be a symptom of personal and relationship problems, but there is no conclusive evidence that it is the cause of the problems (Ley, 2014).

In studies that have been replicated around the world, greater access to pornography is actually associated with a decrease in sex crimes. Even the most bizarre, scary types of sexual fantasy, have no proven connection to people's actual behavior. While it would seem to be common sense that viewing deviant, scary, or illegal sexual activities online would lead to engaging in them the research does not support this.

Studies show that fantasy is more likely to reduce the likelihood that people will act out scary, dangerous desires. Ley (2014) explains that something like thinking about choking your boss doesn't increase the chances you will actually do it. In fact, fantasizing about doing it probably dissipates the tension making it easier for you to go back to work and face your boss. Sexual fantasies work the same way, whether they are in your head or on the computer screen (Ley, 2014).

✃ *Spiritual Wellness* ✃

Our nation's *moral fabric* is a term used by all presidents (including George W. Bush as well as Nixon and Reagan) to describe our standards as a society. It refers to our values, attitudes, and beliefs about moral issues that reflect our spiritual health as a nation. Religious leaders and others concerned with the moral fabric of America claim that the widespread availability of pornography, both online and through other sources, reflects our moral bankruptcy as a society. Our spirituality, they say, suffers when sex becomes a commodity instead of an intimate bond that connects people through love and commitment. Those who represent the opposing view cite the absence of evidence connecting greater sexual availability and permissiveness with moral decay.

These claims were instantly refuted by sex researchers and professional organizations (Board of Directors, 1987). Researchers argued that studies of the sexual content of samples of pornographic material revealed that between 4 and 16 percent contained violent themes or scenes depicting violence (Slade, 1986). Professional organizations

422

decried the supposed causal link between viewing violent pornography and sexual violence, citing the lack of substantiating evidence within the commission's report or in the professional literature.

℘ *Intellectual Wellness* ℘

One positive outcome of greater accessibility to sexual resources coupled with the technological innovations of the past decade is the incredible explosion in information technology. Our ability to conduct research, gather information, process what we've found, and share resources has never been better. Average people working from home on a personal computer can tap into the greatest minds of our time without leaving home. This has the potential to greatly enhance our intellectual well-being. We have unprecedented access to information about any facet of sexuality, in the privacy of our own home.

References

Adult video, cable market surges. (1995). *Broadcasting & Cable, 125*(13) 47.

Ashe, D. (2009). Dani.cash Frequently Asked questions. http://www.dannicash.com/info/faq_unlogged.cfm

Attorney General's Commission on Pornography. (1986). *Report on pornography and obscenity.* Washington, DC: U.S. Department of Justice.

Board of Directors of the Society for the Scientific Study of Sex. (1987). SSSS responds to the U.S. Attorney General's Commission on Pornography. *Journal of Sex Research*, 23(2), 284–285.

Bond, J.M., Wehner, M. (2015). The wonderful, weird, and kinky world of VR porn. The Daily Dot. Feb 5, 2015 available online at: www.dailydot.com/authors/john-michael-bond/

Bradlee, N. C. (1997). The Bradlee files. *Newsweek, 126*(13), 82–88.

Dank, M., Khan, B., Downey, P. Kotonias, C., Mayer. D., Owens, C., Pacifici, L, Yu, L. (2014). Estimating the Size of the Underground and Commercial Sex Industry in the United States: The Urban Institute Research Report, March 2014. Copyright © March 2014. Washington DC: The Urban Institute.

Guarding young Web-surfers: Don't count on special software to protect kids' privacy. (1997 September). *Consumer Reports, 62*(9), 17.

Heavy breathing: Phone sex. (1994). *Economist, 332*(7874), 71.

Horrigan, J.B., Duggan, M (2015). Home Broadband 2015. Numbers, Facts and Trends Shaping the World. Research Center, December 21, 2015, Available at: http://www.pewinternet.org/2015/12/21/2015/Home-Broadband-2015/

Holden, M (2010). Study Finds Quarter of UK Lap Dancers Have Degrees. Reuters.Com, August 27, 2010. available online : http://www.reuters.com/article/us-britain-lapdancing-idUSTRE67Q2YW20100827

Holmes, D (2015). Pornhub launches 'Netflix for porn' subscription service. The Guardian. Thursday 6 August 2015

Huffington Post (2013). Porn Sites Get More Visitors Than Netflix, Amazon And Twitter Combined. Technology, 05.04.2013. available online: http://www.huffingtonpost.com/2013/05/03/internet-porn-stats_n_3187682.html

Is your kid caught up in the Web? How to find the best parts and avoid the others. (1997, May). *Consumer Reports, 65*(5), 27–32.

Kaplan, J. (1995). The Triumph of Calvinism. (September 18), New York, 46–57.

Leonard, R. (2016). The History of Phone Sex. Chatline Guide. April 5, 2016. available

online:http://www.chatlineguide.com/
history-of-phone-sex/

Ley D. J. (2014). Common Sense about the
Effects of Pornography. Psychology
Today. https://www.psychologytoday.
com/blog/women-who-stray/201402/
common-sense-about-the-effects-pornography

Love, T, Laier, C, Brand, M, Hatch, L, Hajela, R.
(2015). Neuroscience of Internet Pornography
Addiction: A Review and Update. Behavioral
Sciences , Vol 5, Iss 3, pp. 388–433 (2015)
Behavioral Sciences , Vol 5, Iss 3, Pp 388-433
(2015).

Masters, W. H., & Johnson, V. E. (1966). Human
sexual response. Boston: Little, Brown.

McWilliams, P. (1998). Ain't nobody's business if
you do: The absurdity of consensual crimes in
a free country. Santa Monica, CA: Prelude.

Mayyasi, A (2016). The Life of a Phone Sex
Operator. Prececonomics. Aug 10, 2016
available online: https://priceonomics.com/
the-life-of-a-phone-sex-operator/

Morris, C. (2014). Porn Industry Feeling Upbeat
About 2014. NBC News.com JAN 14
2014. available online: http://www
.nbcnews.com/business/business-news/
porn-industry-feeling-upbeat-about-2014-n9076

Morris, C. (2015). Things are looking up in
America's porn industry. NBC News.com
JAN 20 2015. available online: http://www
.nbcnews.com/business/business-news/things-
are-looking-americas-porn-industry-n289431

Masters, W. H., & Johnson, V. E. (1966). *Human
sexual response.* Boston: Little, Brown.

McWilliams, P. (1998). *Ain't nobody's business if
you do: The absurdity of consensual crimes in
a free country.* Santa Monica, CA: Prelude.

Nursing Standard Ed., (2013). Watching
pornography has small effect on young
people's sexual behavior. Nursing Standard
(2015). May 15, 2013, Vol. 27 Issue 37,
p17, 1 p.

ProCon.Org (2013). Estimated number of
prostitutes. ProCon.Org, Legal Prostitution.
8/28/2013, available online: http://
prostitution.procon.org/view.answers.
php?questionID=000095

Prostitutes' Education Network. (2003). Home
page [Online]. Available: www.bayswan.org/
index.html.

Shrage, L. (1996, Spring). Prostitution and the
case for decriminalization. *Dissent.*

Slade, J. (1986). Violence in the hard-core
pornographic film: A historical survey.
Journal of Communication, 34(3), 148–163.

Spenser, A (2013). The Erotic Economy.
Las Vegas: RCI Hospitality Holdings Inc.

StatisticBrain.Com .(2016). Strip Club Statistics.
StatisticBrain.com, September, 6, 2016.
available online: http://www.statisticbrain.
com/strip-club-statistics/

Willoughby, B.J., Carroll, J.S, Nelson, L.J.,
Padilla-Walker, L.M. (2014). Associations
between relational sexual behavior,
pornography use, and pornography
acceptance among US college students.
Culture, Health & Sexuality, Volume 16,
Issue 9, pp. 23–36.

Wright, P, Tokunaga, R.S., Kraus, A. (2016). A
Meta-Analysis of Pornography Consumption
and Actual Acts of Sexual Aggression in
General Population Studies. Journal of
Communication. Feb2016, Vol. 66 Issue 1,
p183–205. 23p. 2 Charts

Chapter

sixteen

Sexual Dysfunction, Sex Therapy, *and* Sexual Enhancement

Student Learning Objectives

After reading this chapter, students will be able to:

- ☞ Describe the relationship between sexual dysfunctions and the phases of the sexual response cycle.
- ☞ Describe the key components of sexual desire disorders.
- ☞ Describe the key components of sexual arousal disorders.
- ☞ Describe the main elements of orgasmic disorders.
- ☞ Describe the main elements of sexual pain disorders.
- ☞ Evaluate recent criticisms of the current conceptualizations of sexual disorders based on the classic sexual response cycle.
- ☞ Describe the medical, pharmacological, behavioral, socio-cultural and psychological causes and treatments of sexual dysfunction.

From *Healthy Sexuality*, 4th edition, by Richard Blonna and Lillian Cook Carter. © 2017 by Richard Blonna and Lillian Cook Carter. Reprinted by permission of Kendall Hunt Publishing Company.

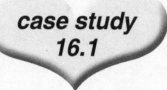

case study 16.1

Orgasmic Disorders: Christine

Christine is a college senior. She has been having sex with her boyfriend, Nick, for about 3 months and has not been able to have an orgasm yet. She met with Dr. Blonna.

I'm not sure whether I have a problem, but I've been having sex with my boyfriend, Nick, since the end of the spring semester—about 3 months—and haven't had an orgasm yet.

He's a real nice guy, and I think I love him. I've been dating lots of guys since my boyfriend Tom and I broke up 3 years ago, and Nick is very special. I met him at the college gym, and we were instantly attracted to each other. He is in great shape, is very outgoing, a former athlete, and has a great sense of humor. In a way, he's a great big kid, always joking.

We started having sex from the first date and all spring made love about three to five times a week, but I never had an orgasm with him. Even though I don't come, sex with him is a lot of laughs. The only problem is that he kind of rushes through it and doesn't last very long. I haven't said anything because I kind of hoped he would get better with time.

During the summer, things cooled off because he had a summer house with a bunch of fraternity brothers and was at the shore every weekend (Friday to Sunday night) from Memorial Day to mid- September. I went down a few times but was really turned off because everyone did nothing but get drunk, act out, and sleep the days away.

Since September, we've picked up where we left off last spring, but I still can't come with him. When I masturbate by myself, I have satisfying orgasms, but not with Nick. I'm afraid that if I tell him, he'll get upset and maybe our relationship will suffer. The problem is that I like him a lot and would like the relationship to grow, but the sex is a real problem. I'm not sure what to do about the relationship.

Critical Thinking

The fact that Christine can achieve orgasm through masturbation is solid evidence that her orgasmic problems have more to do with Nick, and her relationship with him than with herself. What would you recommend Christine do in light of this?

Sexual Dysfunctions

Source: Callista Lee

Sexual dysfunctions, as Christine's case illustrates, are complex phenomena that include physical sexual responses as well as relationship factors, past history, physical health, thoughts, and emotions. According to the American Psychiatric Association's diagnostic manual (DSM-V), **sexual dysfunctions** are a group of disorders that are typically characterized by a clinically significant disturbance in a person's ability to respond sexually or to experience sexual pleasure. Christine is experiencing disappointment about her sexual response, but does her lack of orgasm qualify for a diagnosis of sexual dysfunction? Let's explore the depth and range of problems in sexual responding a bit more deeply to find out.

Sexual dysfunctions A group of disorders that are typically characterized by a clinically significant disturbance in a person's ability to respond sexually or to experience sexual pleasure.

Sensory arousal combines with emotional arousal (limbic system) and conscious thought (cerebral cortex) as our sensing, feeling, thinking brain triggers and directs the organs, glands, and tissues that regulate our sexual response. Although something as common as developing and maintaining an erection seems like a fairly primitive response, in reality it is a complex result of many reactions within a complicated interdependent system. As such, sexual response isn't always an all-or-nothing phenomenon. Levels of performance and satisfaction vary.

Everyone experiences some level of dysfunction throughout the course of life. It is produced by illness, stress, fatigue, or a variety of other causes. Dysfunction is not just a heterosexual issue, either. Gay, lesbian, and bisexual people also experience sexual dysfunction (Lemonick, 2004).

Our perception, gender role, and beliefs about aging all factor into determining whether a sexual problem is or is not a dysfunction. As we'll describe, one of the mediating factors in determining dysfunction is whether the "problem" causes emotional distress or relationship difficulties. One's perception of the issue plays a big part in determining whether it even *is* a problem. If a person or partner does not perceive a sexual "problem" (premature ejaculation, for example) as troubling, is it a dysfunction or even a problem?

Gender role also factors into the mix. For years, women were taught that they were not supposed to initiate sex. Does a woman who wants sex but won't ask for it from her partner because she thinks this isn't the "proper" thing to do have a sexual dysfunction? What about our expectations of sex as we age? If we expect a decline in sexual performance and response because we view this as a normal part of aging, do these changes constitute a dysfunction? We'll address these and many other questions in this chapter.

Basson et al., (2000) carry the issue of gender-based differences a step further. They argue that emotional factors and intimacy issues are the central issues in understanding sexual response and subsequent dysfunction in women. Women, according to these researchers, are much more likely than men to have intimacy issues as the basis of low sexual desire and sexual arousal disorders. In fact, as we will examine in more detail later in this chapter, Basson et al., found that many women who have low sexual desire have no problem becoming aroused physiologically (evidence of lubrication and so forth) and achieving orgasm.

If you recall from Chapter 5, sexual functioning combines physical, intellectual, emotional, social, spiritual, and environmental well-being. We need a minimum level of physical health to ensure that all of the component body parts and systems are able to perform the myriad tasks necessary for sexual response to occur. The health of our social relationships impacts on our ability to trust our partner, relax, and let the sexual response happen. Our emotional health contributes to our self-esteem, feeling good about ourselves, and feeling comfortable with our partner. Our intellectual health contributes to being able to understand and improve our sexual technique and to make informed choices about fertility control and protecting ourselves against STDs. Our spirituality helps us connect with our inner sexuality and others in a deeper way. And a healthy environment allows us to feel safe and comfortable in our sexual space. Stevenson (2002), in an eloquent editorial, describes the interplay of the mind-body continuum in sexual response and dysfunction. He explains how the body does not exist independent of the mind and how sexual dysfunctions can never be diagnosed independently without an examination of the whole person.

Physical/Medical Causes of Sexual Dysfunction

Research findings over the past decade concerning the causes of sexual dysfunctions have created a dramatic change in our understanding of these conditions and approach to their treatment. In the past, sexual dysfunctions (particularly **erectile dysfunction**, formerly known as *impotence*) had been thought to be caused primarily by psychological factors. Most experts in the field now believe the exact opposite, especially regarding erectile disorder. Sexual dysfunction can be caused by a host of physical causes, ranging from disease and injury to the side effects of legal and illegal drugs (Goldstein, I., Auerbach, S., Palma-Nathan, H., Rajfer, J., Fitch, W., Schmitt, L. (2000). Goldstein, 2000; Johnson, Phelps, Cottler, 2004; Kloner & Padma, 2005; McCabe, 2004; Richardson, 1991).

Recent studies show that understanding sexual dysfunction may not be such a simple either-or phenomenon. It may well be that dysfunction in men is primarily related to blood flow and physical causes (therefore very amenable to pharmacological fixes such as Viagra), whereas problems in women are more related to psychosocial issues such as intimacy (Basson, 2002, Johnson, 2004, Enserink, 2005, *Drug Week*, 2001). The differences may be so great that prominent researchers in the field are calling for a reexamination of the nature of sexual response in women to shed light on how to treat sexual dysfunctions. This may ultimately change the very way dysfunctions are diagnosed and treated in men and women (Basson, 2002, Lieblum, 2000).

Erectile dysfunction A disturbance or disorder related to obtaining an erection

■ Cardiovascular Disease

In a study of approximately 1,300 men in the Massachusetts Male Aging Study, nearly half of the subjects (all were between 40 and 70 years of age) had experienced erectile difficulties in the previous 6 months (Heapes, 1994). Furthermore, men being treated for heart disease and high blood pressure were up to four times more likely to be completely impotent than men without these conditions. These findings implicate vascular problems (blood flow) as the major culprit in erectile problems. All forms of cardiovascular disease rob the blood and body of adequate oxygen through circulation, contributing to increased risk for sexual dysfunction (Kloner & Padma, 2005).

Behaviors that increase the risk for cardiovascular disease also can increase the likelihood of incurring erectile disorders. Smokers have been found to be four times more likely than nonsmokers to have severe erectile dysfunction (Heapes, 1994).

■ Other Diseases

Other physical causes of sexual dysfunction range from structural defects or changes (congenital abnormality of the penis or vagina, scar tissue, fibroids, tumors), to sexually transmitted disease, endocrine disorders, neurological problems, and spinal cord injury, to deficiency diseases (insufficient hormonal production, malnutrition, vitamin deficiency), to allergic reactions (say, to

© visi.stock, 2010. Shutterstock, Inc.

Aerobic exercise can reduce the risk for developing certain sexual dysfunctions.

spermicide). These and other medical causes can affect any or all of the phases of the sexual response cycle, resulting in a wide variety of sexual dysfunctions. Table 16.1 describes a variety of chronic diseases and disabilities and their effects on sexual functioning.

❧ *Physical Wellness* ❧

High-level physical wellness can enhance sexual performance and satisfaction and lessen the risk for dysfunction. Physical wellness plays a crucial role in the desire and excitement phases of sexual response. Physical wellness is also linked to vasocongestion, as blood flow leading to engorgement of genital tissue and lubrication are affected adversely by obesity, arteriosclerosis, and other physical health problems. Being fit (especially attaining high levels of cardiovascular fitness) and maintaining recommended body composition promote efficient vasocongestion.

Table 16.1 Effects of Select Medical Physical Conditions on Sexual Response

Condition	Effects of Sexual Response
Cardiovascular disease	*Men and women: sexual arousal disorder; loss of sexual desire*
Spinal cord injuries	*Vary according to severity and location* *Men: often lose ability to have typical erections (may have "reflex" erections); often lose ability to ejaculate* *Women: decreased vaginal lubrication; lose genital and orgasmic sensations*
Complications from surgery (hysterectomy, cesarean section, tubal ligation, episiotomy)	*Women: damage to nerves and blood vessels involved in vasocongestion; sexual arousal disorder, orgasmic disorder.*
Multiple sclerosis and other neurogenic diseases	*Men: loss of erections and ejaculation* *Women: orgasmic disorder*
Diabetes	*Men: male erectile disorder; small percentage suffers from retrograde ejaculation and less intense ejaculation* *Women: varies—some experience less lubrication and sexual arousal disorder; female orgasmic disorder*

Cancer
  Breast
  Cervix
  Uterus
 	
  Prostate
  Testicles
 	
  Anorexia
  Bulimia
	
	Vary based on treatment and psychological reactions
	Minimal if treated early (bleeding; discharge)
	Vary according to amount of scarring; hysterectomy is sometimes related to sexual desire disorder in women who feel a diminished sense of femininity
	Can cause sexual arousal disorder and orgasmic disorder
	Infertility; no physiological changes but psychological stress is related to sexual desire disorder in some men who feel a diminished masculinity
	Sexual desire disorders; sexual arousal disorders
	Sexual desire disorder

Source: McCabe 2004, Heiman, 2002a; Lewis Rosen, Goldstein, 2005; Kloner & Padma, 2005; O'Donohue and Geer (1993); Lowinson, Ruis, Millman, and Langrod (1992); Kita (2001).

healthy sex hints 16.1

Enhancing Male Potency by Increasing Wellness

Greg Gutfield (1994) summarized findings from studies documenting the effects of a healthy lifestyle on sexual potency. These findings show that many of the roadblocks to good sex can be removed through simple lifestyle changes aimed at improving overall health status.

Three of the major culprits in sexual potency—heart disease, diabetes, and high blood pressure—often can be prevented by regular exercise and a healthy diet. Both of these also aid tremendously in weight management and controlling obesity, a major risk factor for all three conditions. The common denominator is *vascular health.* Impaired blood flow leads to poor sexual response. Increasing exercise and eating a healthy diet (low-fat, high-carbohydrate, moderate protein) enhances blood flow and vascular health.

Stress is another factor that can undermine sexual potency. Chronic stress can lower testosterone, the key hormone related to sexual desire. Less testosterone means less sexual desire. Stress also can make us angry. Men who respond to stressors by losing control and getting angry were much more likely to suffer from erectile disorder then men who were not angry. Of the men who scored highest on measures of anger, 35 percent reported moderate erectile disorder and 20 percent complete erectile disorder.

Stress management and relaxation will help moderate testosterone levels, reduce anger, and help restore potency.

Smoking increases the likelihood of erectile dysfunction and is a major risk factor in cardiovascular disease (Heapes, 1994). Smokers are four times as likely as nonsmokers to develop complete erectile disorder. The negative effects of smoking can be reversed by quitting.

Use it or lose it. "The more erections you have, the more you're likely to have" (Gutfield, 1994). Having at least three erections per week can reduce the risk for erectile disorder. Erections improve blood flow to the penis. Frequent erections help promote circulation and bring oxygen-rich blood to the area.

To improve your erectile function, make these three simple lifestyle changes:

1. Exercise regularly.
2. Eat a balanced diet.
3. Stop smoking.

Injuries and Surgery

Certain injuries also can cause erectile disorder and other forms of sexual dysfunction. An estimated 600,000 or more cases of erectile dysfunction are attributed to accidents and injuries to the underside of the penis (Parker-Pope, 2002; Kita, 2001). Athletic injuries resulting from being kicked or struck in the groin can damage the area. Extensive bicycle riding (100-mile rides) can damage the blood vessels on the underside of the penis. Falls that crush the penis against an object (such as a railing or fence) can damage the blood vessels that supply blood to the penis.

Female-centered sex therapists suggest that such injuries to women can also damage nerves and blood vessels in the pelvic region associated with sexual response in women. "Straddle" injury trauma associated with accidents such as falls from gymnastic balance beams and narrow bicycle seats can affect blood flow and nerve transmissions in women also (Parker-Pope, 2002; Kita, 2001).

Sexual dysfunction can also be traced to nerve and blood vessel damage associated with surgery. Common surgical procedures such as episiotomy, cesarean section, hysterectomy, and tubal ligations are often related to subsequent sexual dysfunctions. Cosmetic surgery involving the pelvic area (genital, cosmetic surgery, vaginal tightening, and labial reconstruction) is also associated with some forms of female sexual dysfunction (Kita, 2001).

Prescription Drug Interactions

The effects of prescribed and over-the-counter drugs are many and varied. They range from decreased vaginal lubrication associated with antihistamines (over-the-counter use by allergy sufferers) to erectile dysfunction associated with certain forms of anti-hypertensive medication. The commonly prescribed antidepressant drug Prozac (fluoxetine) has been shown to cause erectile disorder and **anorgasmia** in small numbers of male and female users, respectively (Rosen, 1991). Table 16.2 outlines common medical drugs and their associated sexual dysfunctions.

Anorgasmia An inability to achieve orgasm

Table 16.2 The Effects of Select Medical Drugs on Sexual Response

Drug	Medical Use	Effect on Sexual Response
Hormones Estrogen and Progesterone	Replacement therapy in menopause; birth control; prostate cancer prescription	May decrease sexual desire in women; sexual arousal disorder in men
Steroids Diannabol and others	Treatment for hypogonad disorder (deficiency in gonadal function); promote growth; treatment for aplastic anemia	*Men:* atrophy of testicles; cessation of sperm production; growth of breasts; sexual desire disorder *Women:* masculination of clitoris; excessive facial and body hair
Hypertensive medications Diamox Catapres Inderal Tanormin	Control high blood pressure	Loss of sexual desire; sexual arousal disorders; orgasmic disorders
Gastrointestinal drugs Tagament Librax	Treat gastrointestinal distress and similar problems	Decreased sexual desire; sexual arousal disorders
Antihistamines	Control allergic reactions, stop runny nose, itchy eyes	Inhibit lubrication; painful intercourse
Psychiatric medications (major tranquilizers)	Control psychotic episodes	Decreased sexual desire; sexual arousal disorders; orgasmic disorders

Source: Heiman 2002a, Enserink 2005, Witters, Venturell, and Hanson (1992); Jones and Jones (1977); Masters, Johnson & Kolodny (1996); O'Donohue and Geer (1993); Lowinson et al., (1992).

Synergistic effect An enhanced, unpredictable drug effect caused by combining two or more substances

Anyone who takes these drugs should have a thorough understanding of their potential sexual side effects. A potential complication associated with taking medications is the effect of combining two or more medications. The effects can range from a simple additive effect (the effect of one medication added to the effect of the other) to a **synergistic effect** (the effects of two or more drugs creating a third, enhanced, and often unpredictable effect), which can be associated with sexual dysfunction. This possibility can be especially troubling for people with chronic diseases who must take more than one medication regularly. They must guard against mixing over-the-counter medications with alcohol or illegal substances, as well as medically prescribed drugs.

◼ Psychotropic Drugs

Psychotropic drugs Substances that are mind-altering

Mind-altering drugs, both legal and illegal, have the potential to affect sexual response. The complexity of our vascular, neurological, and endocrine interactions during sexual response makes us particularly susceptible to the effects of psychoactive substances. The sexually-related side effects of psychoactive drugs are variable. As with all psychoactive drugs, the user's psychological well-being and environment can affect the outcome of the drug experience. A placebo effect can occur if a user has certain expectations for the drug (Johnson et al., 2004).

Depressants

Tranquilizers, barbiturates, and alcohol are all central nervous system (CNS) depressants. They reduce, depress, or slow down brain and nervous system functioning. Although they are all classified as depressants, their intended use and effects are different. Barbiturates and alcohol have a more diffuse, less targeted effect on the nervous system. Benzodiazepines (the most frequently prescribed tranquilizers selectively target neural receptors. In addition, tranquilizers and barbiturates are prescribed as medical drugs for treating psychological disorders. Their social use is illegal. Alcohol is a legal, nonmedical drug whose primary use is social.)

Tranquilizers originally were divided into two categories: minor (primarily used to treat anxiety and insomnia) and major (antipsychotic drugs used to treat severe mental illness such as schizophrenia). Benzodiazepines (Valium-like drugs) are the most frequently prescribed CNS depressants. The pharmacologic effects of benzodiazepines are so different from those of the antipsychotic drugs that the terms *minor* and *major tranquilizers* are rarely used today. The primary medical use of Valium-like drugs is to reduce anxiety and treat neuroses. They work by depressing limbic functioning and thereby altering mood. Because these drugs can reduce anxiety and improve mood, they sometimes are used by people in an attempt to enhance sexual desire.

Barbiturates have a less specific, more diffuse sedative/hypnotic effect on depressing nervous system functioning. Barbiturates are used primarily as sedatives to treat insomnia. Barbiturates are rarely used to treat anxiety these days, having been replaced by safer drugs (such as the benzodiazepines). In low doses, barbiturates can induce a lazy, sleepy state. Because of this, barbiturates sometimes are used incorrectly and illegally to enhance sexual response by inducing a relaxed, less inhibited state of mind. In high, toxic doses, barbiturates can induce coma.

healthy sex hints 16.2

Dealing with Side Effects of Drugs

Drugs have many different effects. The *intended effect* is the desired outcome of taking the product. The intended effect of hypertension medication, for example, is to lower blood pressure. *Side effects* are secondary outcomes that result from taking the medication. Some side effects are beneficial, such as regulation of the menstrual cycle when taking oral contraceptives.

The drug is intended to prevent the release of an ovum, and, as a side effect, it regulates the menstrual cycle. Many side effects, however, are not beneficial for sexual response. A side effect of some hypertension medication, for instance, is a reduction in sexual desire. All drug manufacturers are required by law to provide information about side effects concerning their products. Pharmacists also are required to discuss side effects with consumers.

Ultimately, you have the responsibility for making sense of it all. Here are some tips for understanding possible adverse side effects of prescriptions:

1. Make sure you know what disease or condition you have been diagnosed as having *before* you leave your health care provider.
2. Be sure you know the name of your medication and its intended effects.
3. Understand exactly how to take it (dosage schedule, contraindications, and so forth).
4. Ask your health care provider, "What possible effects will taking this medication have on my sexual response?"
5. If the medication carries any potentially negative sexual side effects, ask, "What other medication can I take that will treat my disease [or condition] without affecting my sexual response?"
6. When you pick up your prescription, read the package insert. Ask the pharmacist to clear up any questions you have about the medication.

If you experience any negative side effects that detract from the quality of your life, go back to your health care provider.

The alcohol people drink is more precisely termed ethyl alcohol, also known as ethanol. **Ethyl alcohol** is available either in its pure form, grain alcohol, or more commonly as the active ingredient in a wide variety of alcoholic beverages. Alcohol is a strong central nervous system depressant.

Ethyl alcohol A grain alcohol that is a central nervous system depressant

Unlike the other categories of depressants (tranquilizers and barbiturates), alcohol is not a prescription medical drug with specific intended effects. Alcohol creates a sedative/hypnotic effect similar to that of barbiturates. Alcohol decreases the inhibitory centers of the brain and is used primarily for its ability to reduce inhibitions (USDHHS, 2000). Therefore, people often use alcohol to enhance sexual desire (Georgea, W.H., et al. (2011) . In larger doses, alcohol has effects similar to those of other depressant drugs.

When a person consumes an alcoholic beverage, about 20 percent of the alcohol enters the bloodstream immediately through the stomach lining. The remainder enters the body when the stomach's contents enter the intestines. Because the brain has a large blood supply, it absorbs a lot of alcohol (USDHHS, 2000). The measurement of alcohol content of blood in circulation is termed **blood alcohol concentration (BAC)**.

Blood alcohol concentration (BAC) A measurement of percentage of alcohol in blood; also termed *blood alcohol level* (BAL)

Why Women Get Drunk Faster than Men

Source: Callista Lee

Have you ever wondered if there is a scientific reason for why women seem to get drunk faster than men do? Are they just "lightweights," or is it just a body mass difference?

Well, yes, size does matter. But there is another reason; something that women can't do anything about: women produce smaller quantities of an enzyme called **alcohol dehydrogenase (ADH)**. It is produced by the liver, and it breaks down alcohol in the bloodstream. With less of it in their blood, more alcohol is free to get into the brain and other organs.

In addition, most women carry more body fat but less water than most men do. Fat retains alcohol, while water disperses it; another reason that women are affected more dramatically by alcohol more than men

Sip for sip, women are getting more alcohol to the brain than men are, which puts them at greater risk for a variety of alcohol-related health problems, including alcohol addiction, liver disease, and damage to the heart and nerves.

Gender-based differences in the effects of alcohol on health were unknown until 1990 because researchers had focused almost entirely on men. It was assumed that alcoholism was a mostly male problem, and so nobody wondered whether effects of alcohol might be different in women.

Recently, researchers have begun to research how alcohol affects the brains of men and women differently, and whether reasons for drinking tend to be different between men and women. If you plan a career in counseling or just know people with alcohol problems, you will want to read up on this new research.

Source: https://www.bbc.com/future/article/20180618-why-alcohol-affects-women-more-than-men

Alcohol dehydrogenase (ADH) An enzyme that breaks down alcohol; women have less of this than men do.

Small elevations in BAC are characterized by a "mellow" state, in which the body is relaxed and the person is less inhibited than usual. At this stage, sexual desire—and sexual performance—may be enhanced. Sobczak (2011) found contradictory evidence when studying the effects of alcohol on women's sexual functioning. Findings from laboratory studies show that while women's physiological sexual arousal is suppressed at relatively low BAC levels, women are more likely to report increased sexual arousal.

In other words, even in the absence of physiological evidence of arousal (lubrication etc.) women still reported that low levels of alcohol made them feel more aroused. With increased alcohol intake, however, the person's judgment rapidly becomes impaired, which impacts sexual decisions. Because alcohol is classified as a depressant, the initial high may be followed by a low. Some drinkers become suicidal. Sobczak (2011) found that heavy use however is more likely to impair overall sexual satisfaction. Women who habitually drink may believe that alcohol facilitates sexual activity, and may even drink for this reason. However, they are not necessarily having more sex or even enjoying it more (Sobczak, 2011).

Physiological responses (including sexual performance) are compromised with increasing BACs. The person may have trouble walking a straight line and maintaining balance, and the speech may become slurred. Sometimes the person vomits. At higher levels, the drinker may pass out. Chronic drinkers often have a problem with erectile dysfunction. Alcohol intoxication can even result in death. Because of the many variables—gender, weight, food consumption, simultaneous use with other medications, and so forth—the actual effects vary from person to person and cannot be predicted.

The legal drinking age is 21 in all states. Also, because of the high accident rates involving drinking and driving, laws are becoming more restrictive. A person is considered legally intoxicated at BAC levels between 0.08 and 0.10 percent, depending on the state. Sexual assault, rape, domestic violence, and crime in general are also associated with overuse of alcohol. *Moderation* is the operative word (Higher Ed. Center, 2003; Weschler, Eun, Kuo et al., 2002, Fisher, Cullen, & Turner, 2000). In Chapter 16 we talk more about alcohol-related violence.

Stimulant Drugs

Stimulants work by increasing or speeding up nervous system functioning. Three major physiological effects of stimulants are higher energy and alertness, heightened cognitive functioning, and less appetite. The major legal stimulant drugs are **amphetamines**, which come in a wide variety of brands. The major illegal stimulants are designer amphetamines (chemically synthesized variants of legal products) and cocaine (in powder and crack forms). Amphetamines are available by prescription for three intended medical purposes: treatment of narcolepsy (inadvertent falling asleep), attention deficit hyperactivity disorder (ADHD), and weight reduction.

Amphetamines A central nervous system stimulant that is administered by ingestion, injection, snorting, or inhalation

People often use stimulants illegally in an effort to enhance sexual response. Cocaine and intravenous injection of amphetamines have been reported to create an intense burst of energy that users have described as "orgasmic." Users also report that amphetamines can help prolong sexual activity. The use of stimulants seems to interfere with the brain's ability to trigger orgasm. Although these drugs might enhance the excitement and plateau stages, some users are unable to achieve orgasm under any circumstances (Goldberg, 2006).

Hallucinogens

Hallucinogens are a class of drugs that distort the perception of reality by altering the perception of all sensory inputs—sights, sounds, tastes, touches, and smells. Hallucinogens work by interfering with the normal function of sensory processing systems within the brain. Routine interpretation of sensory input is altered, causing hallucinations.

Hallucinogens A class of drugs that distort the perception of reality by altering the perception of all sensory inputs

Some people use hallucinogens to improve their sexual response by enhancing the perception of touch and other sensations. Users also report a sense of time distortion; sexual activities seem to last longer. Three of the best-known hallucinogens are lysergic acid diethylamide (LSD), methylene-dioxymethamphetamine (MDMA), and phencyclidine (PCP). Hallucinogens are illegal except as part of certain American Indian tribal ceremonies.

© Yuri Arcurs, 2010. Shutterstock, Inc.

Marijuana

For many years, marijuana, or cannabis, was classified as a mild hallucinogen. Most drug authorities now place marijuana and its variants (hashish and hash oil) in its own category because of the varied effects. The effects of marijuana result in

Although alcohol in limited amounts can reduce inhibitions, excess consumption can make sexual arousal difficult.

part from the varying amounts of the active ingredient, tetra-hydrocannabinol (THC). High levels of THC can produce a mild hallucinogenic effect, which leads to changes in perception of sensory stimuli. Users report a heightened sensitivity to visual and auditory stimuli and an increased craving for certain kinds of foods.

The effects of marijuana on sexual response are variable. Many users report increased sexual pleasure because of enhanced sensations, as well as a distortion of space and time. This creates a "time warp" in which the sexual act seems to hang suspended.

Other users, in contrast, report that the same mildly hallucinogenic state creates a kind of paranoia that cancels out these same effects. The loss of control brought on by the distortion of perception of time and space is frightening and can diminish sexual pleasure and disorders in sexual response. Long-term marijuana use has been shown to lower testosterone (the sex hormone most related to sexual desire) and sperm levels. In one review of the literature, researchers found that the frequency of marijuana use in women was unrelated to sexual problems. Men who reported daily use of marijuana reported a higher incidence of the following problems: (1) inability to reach orgasm, (2) reaching orgasm too quickly, and (3) reaching orgasm too slowly (Vijay et al., Shamloul, 2013). In another, ln another review of the literature on marijuana use and sexual functioning, Shamlou (2011) found that cannabis use may negatively impact male sexual performance because of its effects on receptor cells in the penis. Cannabis use may have an antagonizing effect on these receptors in the penis, making it more difficult for a man to achieve and maintain an erection (Shamlou, 2011). More research is needed in this area. Previous studies examining the effects of cannabis use on male sexual function have been limited and many of these studies have produced contradictory results. While some studies have indicated cannabis could have beneficial effects in enhancing erectile function, other studies have found the opposite (Shamlou, 2011).

Narcotics

Narcotic drugs are pain killers. They work by diminishing the transmission of pain throughout the nerve pathway. The common opium-derivative narcotics are opium, heroin, and codeine. A common myth concerning heroin addicts is that they are sexually aggressive. To the contrary, one of the side effects of heroin addiction is a diminished interest in sex.

Cautions

Any illegal drug carries the potential for toxicity, overdose, and serious physical danger because illegal substances are not regulated or controlled. Therefore, a person has no idea where or how the substance was produced, and there is no way to quantify the amount of the active ingredient in the drug or the presence of any additives. Marijuana, for instance, has varying amounts of THC and can be cured or mixed with a variety of other substances. Heroin and cocaine can be "cut" (diluting the original volume and pure form by adding ingredients to increase the volume) with anything ranging from talcum powder to rat poison.

Vaping Illness and the Black Market

Source: Callista Lee

Nicotine is an addictive drug that can cause sexual dysfuntion by its effect of narrowing blood vessels throughout the body. When the sex organs are deprived of adequate blood flow vasocongestion suffers. The sudden flurry of mysterious vaping-related lung infections during 2019 led to a panic about teens vaping candy-flavored tobacco oils. Some states rushed to ban the sales of any flavor vape other than "original"/ tobacco flavor. Health providers had been sounding the alarm about this new way the tobacco industry was luring young people into using their products for a couple of years, and this sudden onset of illnesses (some ending in death) were exactly the motivation that the lawmakers needed to act. But in all the talk about teens being lured into becoming tobacco addicts, the fact that most of the illnesses were among vapers who used marijuana, not tobacco, was lost in the public discourse. After several months of study, researchers learned that the vast majority of those who came down with the life-threatening mystery illness had used black-market marijuana products, purchased on the street rather than in a legal marijuana store. The most often cited black-market brand was Dank Vapes, but fourteen other brands were listed as well. The producers had used vitamin e acetate to thicken their product vape oils; vitamin e can be good for your skin but has no business being in the lungs.

It should be noted that about 10 percent of those who became ill had no THC in their systems and reported using only tobacco vapes, so tobacco vaping is still not considered safe. It is unknown whether those illnesses can be linked to black-market sources. And vaping tobacco is still linked to tobacco addiction, just like smoking cigarettes.

How can you tell if you are buying a black-market/counterfeit vape? First: Look at where you are buying it. Second: It will generally be much cheaper than regulated brands.

Source: https://www.washingtonpost.com/health/2019 /09/07/what-we-know-about-mysterious-vaping-linked- illnesses-deaths/

Psychological Causes of Sexual Dysfunction

Besides being correlated with health problems ranging from cardiovascular disease to substance abuse, sexual problems and dysfunction also appears to be associated with personal psychological well-being and relationship stability (Heiman, 2002b). The two basic psychological causes of sexual dysfunction are (a) prior learning and (b) immediate causes. **Prior learning** refers to factors related to childhood development. *Immediate causes* are factors that have their origins later than childhood learning.

Prior learning Factors relating to childhood development

Prior Learning

Most theorists agree that childhood learning shapes many of our fundamental attitudes, values, and beliefs about sexuality. Humans are capable of experiencing sexual and sensual pleasure from birth to death. Infants of both sexes seem to derive great pleasure from touching and rubbing their genitals against bedding and clothing. They also seem to thrive when physical bonding, breastfeeding, and other forms of intimate physical touch are established early in infancy (Montague, 1977). When this seemingly innate sexual potential is thwarted through overt or covert child-rearing practices, the seeds of subsequent sexual problems in adulthood are planted.

The messages we receive during childhood—particularly those from our parents and other primary caregivers—contribute heavily to healthy or

Table 16.3 The Effects of Select Psychoactive Substances on Sexual Response

Drug	Chronic Use or Effects of Small Dosage	High Dosage
Depressants		
Benzodiazepines *Valium* *Librium* *Tranxene*	Diminished anxiety and improved social and sexual functioning	Loss of interest in sex
Barbiturates *Amytal* *Nembutal* *Luminal* *Seconal* *Tuinal*	Cerebral disinhibition; increased relaxation	Loss of desire; sexual arousal disorders; loss of motor control
Alcohol	Cerebral disinhibition; increased relaxation	After time, loss of desire; sexual arousal disorders; loss of motor control
Stimulants		
Amphetamines Cocaine	Increased energy and interest in sex; ability to prolong sexual activities; "rush" similar to orgasm	After time, loss of desire and interest; loss of control; orgasmic disorders
Hallucinogens		
Marijuana LSD MDMA	Heightened awareness and sensations; time distortion (sex seems to last longer)	Decrease in testosterone; loss of desire
Narcotics		
Opium Heroin Morphine Methadone Codeine	Feelings of warmth; reduction in aggression; sleepy/mellow state	Loss of desire; sexual arousal disorders; orgasmic disorders

unhealthy psychosexual development. Sex therapists widely report the relationship between severe anti-sex parenting and the development of sexual dysfunction in later life. Children who are reared in environments where nudity, masturbation, and childhood inquiry and discussion of sexuality are severely punished are more likely to develop sexual problems than their peers who are reared in more tolerant environments.

In one study, adults with the former type of childhood histories were less interested in sex, derived less pleasure from sexual relations, had more inhibitions about sexual expression, and had higher levels of shame, guilt, anxiety, and disgust than those with less rigid backgrounds (Purcell, 1985). The "sex-as-sin" message and subsequent sexual problems came from a strict or orthodox religious orientation; the more rigidly orthodox, the greater the extent of dysfunction.

Even covert practices can sabotage the development of healthy sexuality. Parents who are uneasy about sexuality may choose to deal with this subject by ignoring it. Saying nothing still sends a strong message to children about sexuality. Omitting such an integral part of life from all discussion leaves a void that children clearly perceive. They learn early that something must be wrong, shameful, or dirty about sex if it doesn't ever come up as a topic of conversation. Students often report anecdotally in class their feelings that their parents must have made love only once (for their conception) or as many times as they have siblings, because they never discussed sexuality, their desire for each other, or other sexual themes when the children were around.

Other messages about sexuality relate to gender role expectations. Males and females in U.S. culture often are reared with different sets of sexual standards and expectations. Rather than viewing sexual needs and expression as a human universal, they are reared with the belief that men and women have differing needs and wants that are gender-specific. Society also has different rules and codes of conduct concerning how to satisfy these needs. Men are expected to be more assertive in pursuing their sexual needs. Women are expected to be more demure, to rely on men to pursue them and satisfy them.

These gender role expectations can create anxiety, shame, guilt, and fear—all attributes that detract from sexual pleasure. As early as 1970, Masters and Johnson (1970) noted that rigid sex roles and a double standard concerning sexual expression were often at the root of much of their clients' sexual dysfunction.

Fifteen years later, another study found that nontraditional, less rigid gender roles were related positively to increased enjoyment with sex, greater levels of experimentation with sexual positions, oral sex, initiation of sexual encounters, and assertion of one's sexual needs and wants (Kobilinsky & Palmeter, 1984).

Male sexual dysfunction is often related to performance anxiety stemming from rigid male gender role socialization. (Zilbergeld, 1992). Many men grow up with an idealized picture of male sexuality that positions men as all-knowing, ever-ready, and being responsible for initiating sexual encounters and pleasing their partners. This view puts tremendous pressure on men to live up to those expectations.

Immediate Causes

Immediate causes of sexual dysfunction are identified as (a) failure to engage in effective sexual behavior because of either ignorance or unconscious avoidance; (b) anxiety related to performance, fear of failure, or perceived inability to please a partner; (c) perceptual and intellectual defenses against erotic feelings; (d) failure to communicate effectively with one's partner; and (e) stress and fatigue.

Ignorance/Avoidance

Failure to engage in effective sexual behavior often arises from simple ignorance. Sexual dysfunctions related to the arousal and orgasm phase often are related to lack of knowledge concerning effective techniques for achieving optimal levels of stimulation. Ignorance is often compounded by shame and guilt related to sexual experimentation, assertiveness, and admission of what is arousing. Some people unconsciously avoid exploration of the sensual and erotic and fail to take advantage of opportunities to explore sexual satisfaction.

Achieving sexual pleasure is a skill that can improve with better technique. If one perceives sexual activity as something that is learned rather than innate, and allows oneself to pursue self-improvement, many sexual problems and dysfunctions can be remedied. All five phases of sexual response can be enhanced by improving technique. People can learn how to increase desire, enhance arousal, maximize plateau, increase the likelihood of orgasm (and multiple orgasms), and enjoy resolution and the refractory period.

Good communication can enhance technique, especially when practicing with a partner and discovering what works with him or her. But, as one man said, "The way I got to become such a good lover was that I practiced a lot by myself when I was at home." Through introspection, guided readings, practice activities, and a variety of other techniques, technique and performance can be enhanced.

⤳ *Social Wellness* ⤳

Sex with another person is a unique social experience that cannot be separated from the emotions the two people bring to the encounter. High-level social wellness revolves around healthy relationships. And healthy relationships are based on trust, respect, commitment, love, and affection. Good sex flows out of this safe and protected context. When trust, respect, and affection are displaced by mistrust, disrespect, and fear, relationship problems ensue. Communication, which is central to good sex, often breaks down when couples are having relationship problems. When sexual needs and desires are not communicated clearly, sexual response suffers.

Performance Anxiety

Sexual anxiety resulting from fear of failure, the demand for performance, or an excessive need to please one's partner can literally shortcircuit sexual response. Any type of anxiety interferes with the ability to relax and allow vasocongestion and other sexual processes to occur. Anxiety can interfere with the level of sexual desire and ability to get aroused and to create sufficient stimulation to trigger orgasm. Anxiety interferes with the ability to become fully involved in the moment, not allowing one to be immersed in the sexual episode.

Anxiety related to a current sexual encounter is often rooted in past sexual episodes. Failure to become sufficiently aroused and maintain an erection in the past often leads to anxiety related to the present ability to perform satisfactorily. Being asked to perform sexually on demand can create resentment and anxiety related to current functioning. In a sense, anxiety fosters the anticipation of failure.

Anxiety is perhaps the greatest psychological factor associated with erectile disorder. Although **performance anxiety** is often characterized as a "male problem" because men usually are viewed as responsible for their partner's orgasm, women also suffer from this malady. The person worries

Performance anxiety Fear, worry, or panic associated with one's perceived sexual behavior over every facet of the sexual encounter: "Am I attractive enough . . . sexy enough?" "Is my penis big enough?" "Are my breasts large enough?" "Is my underwear sexy?" "Will I be able to get [sustain] an erection?" "Will my technique work?" "What if he [she] asks me to do something I'm not comfortable with or know how to do?" "Will we come together?" These and countless other thoughts and concerns set up an expectation-anxiety performance feedback loop that initiates and perpetuates sexual problems. The expectation of failure or poor performance produces anxiety ranging from mild worry to panic.

Defenses

Anxiety also contributes to the perceptual and intellectual defense against erotic feelings called **spectatoring**. Spectatoring occurs when the person becomes an outside observer of his or her own sexual encounter. In a sense, the sexual encounter is reduced to an intellectual activity in which the participant steps away and critically analyzes his or her own behavior.

Spectatoring Becoming an outside observer of one's own sexual encounter while it is occurring

Whether driven by narcissistic preoccupation with self, voyeurism, or performance anxiety, spectatoring turns the participant into an observer of his or her own sexual encounter. In a sense, the spectator examines the performance of self or partner rather than becoming fully involved in the sensations and experiences. The result is a lack of enjoyment in the experience, as well as dysfunction with any phase in the response cycle.

Communication Problems

We sometimes have trouble communicating our sexual desires, needs, and wants because of feelings of shame, guilt, or fear. Maybe we have learned that sex and sexual needs are a taboo subject.

Furthermore, we may be uncomfortable with the language of sexuality. Our culture does not have a common sexual language. This makes it difficult to understand, articulate, and communicate about sexuality with our partners. Consequently, we suppress our needs and problems, anger and resentment build, and eventually this repression short-circuits the delicate balance among the neurological, vascular, and endocrine factors necessary in the sexual response.

Stress and Fatigue

Finally, stress and fatigue can precipitate sexual dysfunction. When associated with other aspects of life such as work, child-rearing demands, money problems, and poor health, stress and fatigue can rob a person of vital energy and a zest for living. Stress and fatigue can affect all phases of the sexual response cycle. When men are stressed, their testosterone levels drop. Testosterone, you may recall, is the hormone most related to the level of sexual desire.

When these men participated in stress management activities, their testosterone levels and levels of sexual desire returned to normal (Singer-Kaplan, 1974). Common sense tells us that when we are tired and stressed, the last thing we seem to be interested in is sex. For the sexual response to begin and orgasm to occur, people need to relax and let the body take over. This reaction often is not possible if a person is feeling overwhelmed or just needs a good night's sleep.

Open communication is essential for dealing with sexual problems.

❧ *Occupational Wellness* ❧

Work-related stress is often associated with low sexual desire. Other job-related issues ranging from rotating shifts to excessive travel and long-standing separation (such as in military assignments) are also implicated in sexual dysfunction. As we have seen, injury and illness are also associated with sexual dysfunction. Some jobs and work sites are more risky than others and can indeed be hazardous to one's health.

Types of Sexual Dysfunctions

The APA (2013) classifies sexual dysfunctions as the lifelong type, acquired type, generalized type, and situational type. *Lifelong disorders* have been present since the onset of sexual functioning. *Acquired disorders* have developed after a period of normal functioning. *Generalized dysfunctions* are not limited to specific types of stimulation, situations, or partners. *Situational dysfunctions* are limited to certain types of stimulation, situations, or partners. The APA classification of sexual dysfunctions is based on traditional models of sexual response and a four-phase conceptualization of human sexual response: desire, excitement, orgasm, and resolution.

The *desire phase* originates with fantasizing and thinking about engaging in sexual activities. Sexual dysfunctions that relate to this phase are called *sexual desire disorders*.

The *excitement phase* is characterized by the buildup of sexual excitement and tension, manifested through vasocongestion. Penile tumescence and erection are physical evidence of desire in men. In women, vaginal lubrication and expansion and swelling of the vulva indicate arousal. Sexual dysfunctions related to this stage are called *sexual arousal disorders*.

In the *orgasm phase,* built-up sexual tension is released, followed immediately by psychological feelings of satisfaction and satiation. Sexual dysfunctions related to this phase are referred to as *orgasmic disorders.*

The *resolution phase* is characterized by a physiological return to the predesire stage. *Sexual pain disorders* may be present during intercourse or in the resolution phase.

Dysfunction versus Disinterest

When discussing sexual dysfunctions, we must recognize the normal continuum of sexual interest and desire in all people. Some people are much more interested in sexual activity than others. The level of interest, desire, and fantasy are variable and are not the only criteria for a diagnosis of sexual dysfunction. To qualify for a diagnosis of either hypoactive sexual desire disorder or sexual aversion disorder, the condition must (a) be persistent and recurrent, (b) cause marked distress or interpersonal difficulty, and (c) not be the result of another medical or physical condition.

Little interest in sexual activity, low desire, and no fantasizing aren't necessarily dysfunctional unless they are accompanied by the three diagnostic criteria. Individuals with low levels of sexual desire still can be happy and productive, and can sustain satisfying long-term relationships as long as their partners have similar sexual traits.

Hypoactive sexual desire disorder should not be confused with voluntary celibacy or abstinence. Some people perceive celibacy as a sexual dysfunction because they believe it is "abnormal" and abstinence is "unnatural." Celibacy is not a sexual dysfunction. Not all celibate people lack sexual interest and desire. Most of us choose to be celibate and abstain from sexual activity at times in our lives, for a variety of reasons.

Dziegielewski (2014) explains that multiple factors need to be considered in diagnosing sexual desire and arousal problems, including the relationship with the sexual partner, prior sexual abuse and past negative sexual experiences, poor sexual body image (small breast size for women and small penis size for men), internalized negative emotions about sexuality, life stress, fatigue, mental health issues such as anxiety and depression, and medication or medical conditions.

Sexual Desire Disorders

Sexual desire disorders include hypoactive sexual desire disorder and sexual aversion disorder.

Male Hypoactive Sexual Desire Disorder

Male Hypoactive sexual desire disorder is a dysfunction characterized by very low levels (or complete absence) of sexual desire. Individuals with this condition do not initiate sexual activity and may engage in sexual relations only begrudgingly at the insistence of their partner. They have little or no motivation to seek sexual stimulation and are increasingly undisturbed by this lack of opportunity.

Three APA (2013) criteria are necessary to diagnose hypoactive sexual desire disorder: (a) persistent or recurrent deficiency or absence of sexual fantasy or desire for sexual activity; (b) marked psychological

Male Hypoactive sexual desire disorder A dysfunction characterized by very low or complete absence of sexual desire

Sexual Aversion Disorder

Source: Callista Lee

Sexual aversion disorder can occur in either men or women. It goes beyond a lack of desire, to an active feeling of wanting to distance oneself from sex. As in the Case Study of Josh, below, it can be an aversion to just a particular sexual behavior that is so distressing that it affects other sexual functioning. Sexual Aversion is an anxiety-based disorder that may be expressed simply as an avoidance of partnered sexual behaviors or may involve symptoms characteristic of a panic attack such as a racing heart, difficulty breathing, a feeling of doom or loss of control, nausea, weakness, feeling sweaty, or having the chills. Aversion is a conditioned response, and most cases involve someone who has experienced sexual trauma in the past or grew up in a home where they were taught to be fearful of sex.

or interpersonal distress attributable to the disorder; and (c) no other psychological disorder (such as major depression or posttraumatic stress disorder), medical condition, or direct physiological effects of a drug or medication. Both low/absent desire for sex and deficient/absent sexual thoughts or fantasies are required for a diagnosis of the disorder (Dziegielewski (2014).

The onset of hypoactive sexual desire disorder can be as early as puberty but usually begins in adulthood, after a period of adequate sexual interest. This dysfunction often is associated with chronic stress, interpersonal difficulties, and problems related to intimacy and commitment.

Although loss of sexual desire can be chronic or episodic, depending on the underlying relationship and psychological problems, hypoactive sexual desire disorder is a chronic condition. Temporary loss of sexual desire is a common byproduct of recovery from depressive disorders (Warnock, 2005; Sceifo, 2002).

Sexual Arousal Disorders

Sexual arousal disorders differ from sexual desire disorders in that the latter are related to lack of desire and the former to the inability to achieve sufficient levels of arousal. The arousal phase of sexual response depends on vasocongestion, which affects erection in men and vaginal lubrication and expansion and swelling of the external genitalia in women. Vasocongestion involves a complex interplay between psychological variables (desire, trust, affection) and physiological variables (unrestricted blood vessels, a healthy endocrine system). Similarly, the causes of sexual dysfunction related to vasocongestion can be psychological, physiological, or both (Fisher, 2004; Munarriz, Kim, Goldstein et al., 2002).

Female Sexual Interest/Arousal Arousal Disorder

Female sexual interest/arousal disorder (FSIAD) represents the fusion of two older diagnoses: hypoactive sexual desire disorder and female sexual arousal disorder. This disorder was renamed because there is a high overlap between desire and arousal and some experts think of desire as just the cognitive component of arousal (Morrison, 2014). The major characteristic of this female dysfunction is the persistent or recurrent inability to attain or

Sexual Aversion Disorder: The Case of Josh

Josh, a senior, is an excellent student; he works for a large investment firm. He is finishing his degree in finance. He grew up in a strict, conservative family and remembers being severely punished for masturbating when he was a child. He came to the office of one of the authors to seek guidance concerning a sexual problem he had. Josh began by saying, "I feel really strange talking to you about this, but you seem very understanding and I need to talk to someone." After receiving some reassurances and permission, he began his story.

I met this wonderful woman, Suzanne, at work this semester. She is 30 years old, divorced with no kids, and is one of the stock traders for the company. She is gorgeous, funny, and bright. We hit it off immediately. I'm not a virgin, and I've been engaged in the past, but I'm hardly what you'd call sexually experienced. I like sex and all that, but I'm kind of conservative and not into any kinky stuff. Intercourse is okay, but oral sex repulses me. I start to get nauseous just thinking about it.

Anyway, Suzanne and I began dating, and from the start she was very passionate. She wanted to have sex on our first date, but I held off, told her I was tired and needed to get up early the next day. I wasn't ready for her and needed time to get to know her. I was surprised she wanted to see me again, but she did, and we talked about my need to get to know her better before we began to have sex. She said she really liked me and it was OK—we wouldn't rush into a sexual relationship.

After about a month, we finally had sex. We went back to her place after dinner and a movie, and she had a glass of wine. We started to kiss and undress, and everything was great until she started to kiss me on the chest and stomach. I felt her head begin to go lower, and as she reached my penis, I began to stiffen up and push her away. I guess she thought I was teasing, because she persisted and even laughed. When I began to lose my erection, she knew something was wrong and stopped. I was so embarrassed I didn't know what to say.

She told me it was OK, that we'd try to work it out, but I just couldn't perform that night. I told her we'd have intercourse the next time, but I just couldn't enjoy oral sex. I really like her and want to make this relationship work. My fiancée broke our engagement because of this same issue three years ago, and I don't want to lose Suzanne.

Critical Thinking

It is not uncommon for couples to differ in terms of what they need or want to be sexually satisfied. What advice would you give Josh and Suzanne for dealing with the issue of oral sex?

maintain sufficient vaginal lubrication and swelling to complete the sexual activity. Vasocongestion is impaired, and the vagina and external genitalia do not become fully engorged with blood. As a result, penetration is restricted, which may result in painful intercourse, avoidance of sexual relations, and a disturbance of the relationship. Female sexual arousal disorder is often accompanied by a sexual desire disorder and female orgasmic disorder.

The three APA diagnostic criteria for this disorder include lower desire for sexual activity than her partner with absence or reduced frequency or intensity of at least three of six indicators for a minimum duration of approximately 6 months (APA 2013, Dziegielewski (2014).

Women who have sexual arousal disorder simply do not become sufficiently aroused to have or enjoy sexual relations. Sexual arousal disorder often is accompanied by sexual desire disorders and female orgasmic disorder (Fass, 2004, Basson, 2002).

Male Erectile Disorder

Often called *impotence,* male erectile disorder is the persistent or recurring inability to attain or maintain an adequate erection for the completion of sexual activity. Erectile disorder is related to a complex interplay of physiological and interpersonal issues and has different patterns. Some men with the disorder are unable to attain an erection at all. Others are able to get an erection but lose it upon penetration. A third group of males are able to attain an erection and complete penetration but lose their erection during thrusting. Some men with this condition report having morning erections or being able to attain erection during masturbation. Others are unable to attain an erection through masturbation (Swindle, Cameron, Lockhart, 2004). About 40 percent of men over the age of 40 and up to 70 percent of men 70 years old or older suffer from erectile disorder (Goldstein, 2000).

The three APA diagnostic criteria for male erectile disorder are (a) marked distress or interpersonal difficulty, (b) no other coexisting psychological condition, and (c) no direct physiological effects of a substance or preexisting medical condition. Men who have male erectile disorder often are anxious, fear failure, and doubt their sexual performance. These psychological concerns often result in lack of sexual excitement and pleasure, avoidance of sexual intercourse, and disturbance in sexual and marital relationships (APA, 2013).

Isolated episodes of inability to obtain an erection are almost universal among men. The reasons include, among others, stress, fatigue, depression, and anxiety (Goldstein, 2000).

■ Orgasmic Disorders

Orgasmic disorders Dysfunctions related to the orgasm phase of sexual response

Orgasmic disorders are dysfunctions related to the orgasm phase of sexual response. These disorders center on the inability of men and women to release pent-up sexual tension through orgasm. These people are interested in sexual relations and are able to become sexually aroused. Their problems relate to their inability to move to the next stage of sexual response, orgasm.

Female Orgasmic Disorder

Formerly known as *inhibited female orgasm,* female orgasmic disorder is a persistent or recurring delay in or absence of orgasm following a typical excitement phase. Three specific APA criteria must be met to diagnose this condition: (a) the absence of orgasm following a "normal" excitement phase, (b) accompanying marked distress or interpersonal difficulty, and

(c) not the result of another medical or psychological condition or direct physiological effects of a substance (APA, 2013).

The "normal" excitement phase is highly variable. The clinician has to assess what is a normal excitement phase for any given patient. This assessment takes into account the woman's sexual experience, history, and the level and adequacy of stimulation she receives. A normal excitement phase for one woman may be markedly different from that of another woman (Basson, 2002).

Because the female capacity for orgasm increases with age, female orgasmic disorder is more prevalent in younger women. As women experience more variety of sexual stimulation, become more knowledgeable about their bodies, and better communicate their needs to their partner, they tend to gain orgasmic facility. Most female orgasmic disorder is lifelong rather than acquired, as women who learn to be orgasmic rarely lose this capacity.

When orgasmic disorders are situational, they often are related to issues such as stress, fatigue, overindulgence of food or drink, or relationship problems such as poor communication and poor technique. Many, if not most, women do not receive enough direct clitoral stimulation through back-and-forth vaginal thrusting. Vaginal intercourse alone does not always provide enough clitoral stimulation for orgasm (Johnson, 2004; Hite, 1977).

Emphasis on intercourse (especially the man-on-top position) as the only acceptable sexual outlet for women can be the root of the problem. Often, women who are unable to achieve an orgasm through vaginal intercourse find that they can achieve it during cunnilingus or masturbation or with additional manual clitoral stimulation during coitus. Some educators and therapists call women who never have had an orgasm "preorgasmic," implying that all women are inherently capable of achieving orgasm. These professionals prefer to view the inability to orgasm as a developmental learning issue versus a dysfunction (Barbach, 1982; Dodson, 1974).

❧ *Emotional Wellness* ❧

Emotions are related intimately to sexual response. All phases of the sexual response cycle are subject to the effects of emotions. Sexual interest and desire are fueled by positive emotions such as happiness, love, joy, respect, and trust. Negative emotions (especially directed at a partner), such as anxiety, anger, hate, fear, disgust, and mistrust, make interest and desire difficult at best and impossible for most. For the body to respond properly, the mind must let go and relax. Arousal and orgasm also are affected by our emotions. The ability to prolong and enjoy sex is affected in part by emotions. Relaxing and becoming immersed in the sensuality of the plateau stage are difficult if we are feeling anxious, rushed, fearful, or angry. We just want to hurry up and get it over with. When we can relax, let down our guard, and allow our senses free rein, we can enjoy the plateau.

Orgasm is contingent on the buildup of tension through adequate stimulation. It is triggered when we give up mental control and allow our body to be swept along in the ecstasy of physical pleasuring. This is difficult if we are on guard, tense, angry, or resentful.

Resolution might be considered a thankful end to a resentful experience in which partners uncouple, roll over, and fall asleep. Or the resolution phase can be a special time. Lovers who are emotionally healthy can bask in the afterglow of loving time spent pleasuring each other.

Delayed Ejaculation

Delayed Ejaculation A persistent or recurrent delay in or absence of orgasm following a normal excitement phase

Formerly known as Male Orgasmic Disorder this disorder is a persistent or recurrent delay in or absence of ejaculation following a normal excitement phase. As for female orgasmic disorder, the three APA diagnostic criteria that must be met in making this diagnosis are (a) absence of ejaculation following a "normal" excitement phase, (b) marked distress or interpersonal difficulty, and (c) not the result of a preexisting medical or psychological condition or physiological effects of a medication or other drug.

Men who have this condition have a marked delay or the inability to achieve ejaculation, when engaging in partnered sexual activity, despite the presence of adequate sexual stimulation and the desire to ejaculate. They usually are able to reach ejaculation if intercourse is accompanied by manual or oral stimulation of the penis. In less common manifestations, the men are able to experience ejaculation only after a substantial amount of noncoital stimulation. A smaller group of men with Delayed Ejaculation are able to ejaculate only through masturbation or upon waking from an erotic dream (APA, 2013).

Men who have Delayed Ejaculation are able to experience pleasure during the excitement phase of sexual activity and enjoy the beginnings of a sexual encounter but rapidly lose interest. For these men, thrusting and prolonging sexual activity are a chore rather than a pleasure. Many men with Delayed Ejaculation have a pattern of paraphiliac sexual arousal and are unable to experience orgasm without the object of their desire.

Premature Ejaculation

Premature ejaculation The persistent or recurring early onset of orgasm and ejaculation

Another male orgasmic disorder is **premature ejaculation**, the persistent or recurring onset of orgasm and ejaculation shortly after penetration or before the man wishes it. The condition is diagnosed after the following three APA (2013) criteria have been met: (a) the clinician must take into account factors that affect the duration of the excitement phase such as age, novelty of the partner or scenario, and the frequency of activity; (b) accompanying marked distress and interpersonal difficulty; and (c) not a result of the effects of a substance.

Sometimes premature ejaculation is related to the level of desire and excitement. An extremely high level of sexual arousal can trigger orgasm prematurely and does not represent the true disorder. Occasional episodes are common and are not a problem if they do not cause marked distress and interpersonal difficulty. Also, specific exercises can be practiced to delay orgasm.

With sexual experience and aging, most men learn to delay orgasm. As with women, this technique is related to learning from experience and better sexual communication. Some men continue to have premature ejaculation under all circumstances. Others incur this disorder only when they are with a new partner. Premature ejaculation can create tension and discord in sexual relationships and deter single men from dating and initiating new relationships because of fear and performance anxiety.

Sexual Pain Disorders

Genito-Pelvic Pain/Penetration Disorder

Genito-Pelvic Pain/Penetration Disorder is a new disorder that combines two former ones; Dyspareunia and Vaginismus and is associated with genital pain during sexual intercourse. It may be present before, during, or after sexual intercourse and can affect both men and women. Symptoms range from mild discomfort to sharp pain (Phillips, 2000). The pain is the recurrent or persistent involuntary contraction of the perineal muscles surrounding the outer third of the vagina during attempted penetration with a penis, finger, tampon, or speculum. In some cases, even the anticipation of vaginal penetration can cause muscle spasms. Symptoms range from mild discomfort and tightness to severe contractions and cramping (APA, 2013).

Genital pain associated with sexual intercourse (such as STDs or scar tissue) or substance use. It is accompanied by painful, involuntary contractions of the outer third of the vagina during attempted penetration.

Three APA (2013) diagnostic criteria include the following components (1) difficulty having intercourse, (2) genito-pelvic pain, (3) fear of pain or vaginal penetration, and (4) tension of the pelvic floor muscles.

Sexual pain disorders are not the result of insufficient excitement (which can account for insufficient lubrication and erection and tense muscles) or poor technique. Nor are they a result of medical conditions that affect sexual functioning (APA, 2013). Sexual pain disorder is diagnosed when these other conditions are ruled out and the pain has no clear-cut physiological or medical basis (Phillips, 2000).

Sexual pain usually is discovered upon first gynecological examination or the onset of sexual intercourse. It is more common in young women than older women but can become chronic if it is not treated. It is a primary contributing factor to unconsummated marriages and can limit the development of relationships. Vaginismus is more common in women who have negative attitudes about sex, as well as females who have a history of sexual abuse or trauma (Phillips, 2000, Basson, 2002).

A Survey of Sexual Dysfunction

At a meeting of the Office of Research on Women's Health, National Institutes of Health, the director of the Partnership for Women's Health at Columbia, Marianne Legato (1999), reported that 43 percent of women and 30 percent of men have some sexual dysfunction. Figure 16.1 presents the various problems by gender. Many of these problems respond well to various treatments.

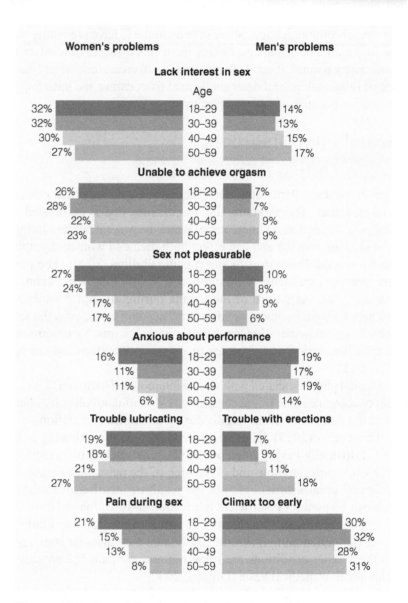

Figure 16.1 *Sexual Dysfunction by Gender and Age*

Source: National Health and Life Survey, 1992.

Treating Sexual Dysfunctions

Because the origin and nature of sexual dysfunction are multifaceted, diagnosis and treatment are also usually multifaceted. Treating impaired sexual functioning is complex, with many interdependent components. Sexual dysfunction can be caused by physical problems (for example, arteriosclerosis, which impairs vasocongestion), emotional disorders (excessive stress or negative emotions), spiritual distress (no longer being in love with a partner, lack of self-love), or simple ignorance (poor technique, inadequate stimulation).

Often, sex therapy and enhancement involve all four components. In 1959, Masters and Johnson developed a systematic approach to sex therapy that incorporated an extensive physical examination (to root out organic causes) and individual and couple counseling in the treatment of sexual dysfunction.

Most sex therapists take an extensive medical history, and many incorporate a physical examination as part of the diagnostic work-up of their patients. The individual and couple approaches to counseling and treatment have many variations.

Treating Sexual Dysfunction Related to Medical Conditions

The first step in treating medically related sexual dysfunction is to properly diagnose the condition. A thorough medical examination, combined with a detailed sexual/medical history, guides the therapist in diagnosis. The overwhelming majority of cases of erectile disorder are caused by medical conditions and respond to medical treatment (Lewis et al., 2005; De Tejada, 2002).

Viagra, Levitra, and Cialis

Since 1998, three drugs have been introduced in the United States for the treatment of erectile disorder. These drugs have revolutionized the treatment of erectile disorder. Their appeal lies primarily in their ease of use. Prior to the advent of these drugs, erectile disorder was treated primarily through drug injection therapy, vacuum pumps, and surgical implants. As we'll see later in this chapter, all three of these treatments were invasive, and interrupted lovemaking in one way or another. The discovery of drug therapy for erectile disorder, one of the most common forms of sexual dysfunction, will go down as one of the medical breakthroughs of the twentieth century.

Viagra, the trade name for Sildenafil, was the first of the three drugs to go in the United States in April 1998. The recommended dose of Sidenafil/pill varies but following ingestion Viagra goes to work in about 30 minutes. The effects last for 3–5 hours with a 4-hour average duration (Wooten, 2004).

Viagra The drug sildenafil, prescribed for the treatment of erectile disorder

Viagra immediately became one of the best-selling drugs ever to hit the marketplace. The response to the drug by men who have erectile disorder was staggering. After 3 weeks on the market, Viagra was being prescribed at a rate of at least 10,000 prescriptions a day (Handy, 1998). By the year 2000 over 20 million prescriptions for the drug were being filled worldwide (Rosen & McKenna, 2002).

Unlike injectable drugs, pumps, and implants that produce an erection regardless of a man's level of desire, Viagra enables the production of an erection if desire is present. In other words, Viagra does not produce desire. It is a sexual arousal drug. Viagra works in consort with sexual desire to produce erections. Once a man feels the desire for intercourse, Viagra allows arousal and erections to proceed (Wooten, 2004). If a man is not interested in sex or has little sexual desire, Viagra will not work effectively. Viagra is effective only if a man is sexually aroused and NOS has been released (Wooten, 2004).

As we discussed in Chapter 7, the muscular and vascular changes of erection are controlled by a complex chemical reaction involving nitric

Guanosine triphosphate A chemical that controls the muscular and vascular changes of erection

oxide synthase (NOS) and the conversion of **guanosine triphosphate** (GTP) into guanosine monophasphate (GMP). This starts a chain reaction resulting in the relaxation of smooth muscle tissue in the penile tissue, allowing it to engorge with blood (Rosen & McKenna, 2002; Wooten, 2004).

During sexual arousal, if the man feels sexual desire, GMP is released from cells in the penis that are stimulated by the brain and nervous system. The GMP triggers receptor cells in the spongy erectile tissue, allowing muscles there to relax and penile arteries to dilate. As the erectile tissue expands, it squeezes shut the veins responsible for removing the blood to the area. After orgasm, GMP is broken down by a normally occurring enzyme called *phosphodiesterase 5* (PDE5) (Rosen & McKenna, 2002; Wooten, 2004).

Most men with erectile disorder don't produce enough GMP to override the ever-present PDE5. Their erectile tissue doesn't expand enough to squeeze the veins shut, and consequently the penis does not attain complete erection. Viagra works by suppressing the effects of PDE5, allowing even a limited amount of GMP to cause erections (Rosen & McKenna, 2002).

Another important thing to know about Viagra is that "more" is not better. Viagra is generally prescribed in either 50 or 100-milligram tablets but can be effective in as small as 25 mg. doses (Wooten, 2004). The correct dose is the smallest needed to create the desired effect. The penis has a limited number of receptors for GMP, and the body can process only so much of it. Taking a bigger dose of Viagra will not allow more GMP to be processed than the body can handle. Men who are not having problems with GMP production will not obtain any enhanced erectile effects from taking the drug, because the body is already processing as much GMP as it can handle. Any enhanced erectile response reported probably is placebo effect rather than an effect of Viagra (Handy, 1998).

Levitra (Vardenafil) and Cialis (Tadalafil)

Levitra (Vardenafil) and Cialis (Tadalafil) work basically the same way as Viagra but differ primarily in their specificity, absorption, and potency. The specificity of these three drugs relates primarily to their ability to target the PDE 5 enzyme while not affecting other PDE enzymes. A side effect of Viagra is to influence other PDE enzymes while targeting PDE 5. For example, the PDE 6 enzyme is involved in retinal function and color recognition. A common side effect of Viagra is mild abnormal vision due to it influencing PDE 6 as well as PDE 5. Both Levitra and Cialis are more specific in their ability to target PDE 5. Neither is associated with the mild vision disturbances associated with Viagra. Of the three drugs, Cialis is the only one whose absorption is unaffected by food. Food definitely influences the absorption of Viagra and because of this it should be taken on an empty stomach. While Levitra can be taken with or without food, studies have shown that high-fat meals can delay its absorption (Rosen & McKenna, 2002; Wooten, 2004). The last variable, potency, refers to the duration of effectiveness of the medication. As we mentioned, Viagra takes about 30 minutes to work and the effects last about 4 hours. Levitra becomes effective about 25 minutes after ingestion and lasts up to about 24 hours. In one clinical study of Levitra, some subjects were able to obtain erections that were suitable for intercourse as early as 16 minutes after dosing

sex in society 16.1

Why No Viagra for Women?

If Viagra and other drugs have been so effective in reversing the effects of PDE-5 in men, thereby enhancing sexual arousal, why don't they work similar magic in women? There are two main reasons for Viagra's limited effectiveness in treating women's sexual dysfunction; (1) Viagra is a drug to enhance sexual arousal, not sexual desire, (2) most women with a diagnosed sexual dysfunction do not have problems with vasocongestion.

In Chapter 5 we clearly established the link between nitric oxide synthase (NOS) and sexual response in men and women. In men, NOS is released in the spongy erectile tissue of the penis. In women, it is produced in the erectile tissue of the vestibular bulbs, the body and crura of the clitoris and in the tissue of the walls of the vagina (O'Connell, Sanjeevan, Hutson (2005). In both men and women NOS converts guanosine triphosphate (GTP) to guanosine monophosphate (GMP) and starts a chain reaction initiating vasocongestion and sexual arousal (Rosen & McKenna, 2002). In this chapter we discussed how PDE-5, a normally-occurring enzyme, is responsible for degrading GMP and reversing vasocongestion once we either reach orgasm or cease stimulation. As we've seen in this chapter, most problems related to male sexual arousal are not related to lack of desire; they are linked to the breakdown of GMP by PDE-5. Viagra works wonders in correcting this.

The main reason that Viagra seems to be less of a breakthrough for women than for men is that for most women with a sexual dysfunction, vasocongestion is already occurring. For the majority of women seeking sex therapy, vasocongestion is not the issue (Basson et al., 2000).

(Padma-Nathan, Kaufman, & Taylor, 2003). Cialis is the most long-lasting of the three drugs. Cialis begins to work after 30 minutes and is effective between 24–36 hours (Wooten, 2004). During this time a user can achieve additional erections without having to take another does of the medication.

The most common side effects of these drugs are headache and facial flushing. As mentioned, Viagra use has been associated with altered vision. The dosages for all three drugs vary. Consult your physician for the appropriate dose, schedule, and use of these and any drugs (Wooten, 2004).

Drug Injections

Prior to Viagra, most medically caused erectile disorders were treated with self-injections of a drug (alprostadil, a synthetic prostaglandin, is a common one) directly into the penis. The drug works by relaxing the muscles of the spongy erectile tissue, allowing the arteries to dilate and engorgement to occur. Men (and often their partners) were taught how to administer the injections using tiny needles similar to the ones diabetics use to inject insulin. The injections produce a pinprick sensation that patients usually tolerate well.

Unlike Viagra, injection treatment produces an erection without requiring the brain to initiate it through sexual desire. The injections lead to erections in approximately 15 minutes. The medication is premeasured in doses that will produce erections that last for approximately an hour (Goldstein et al., 2000).

Another method of delivering alprostadil involves inserting tiny pellets of the drug directly into the urethra. A small plastic tube containing a plunger product is inserted about 1 inch into the urethra. When the plunger is pushed, it releases the drug, which resembles tiny rabbit food pellets, into the urethra. Within 10 minutes the drug begins to take effect (Goldstein et al., 2000).

Vacuum Pumps

Prior to Viagra and injectable drug therapy, vacuum pumps and surgical implants were used to treat erectile disorder. The vacuum pump is a flexible plastic sleeve that is placed over the penis and secured at the base of the lubricated penis with an elastic band. Suction is applied to the sleeve, by mouth or a small hand pump, through a tube that connects at the other end. The pump draws blood into the penis, filling the erectile tissue and thereby causing an erection. Once the man achieves a sufficient erection, the sleeve is removed and the band is kept in place to trap the blood for about half an hour (Raina, Agawarl, Ausmundson, et al., 2005).

Implants and Other Surgery

Implant treatment involves the surgical implantation of an inflatable penile prosthesis. The device consists of two hollow cylinders connected to a fluid-filled reservoir and a pump. The cylinders are implanted in the shaft of the penis, the reservoir in the abdomen, and the pump in the scrotum. When the man desires an erection, he activates the pump, which fills the cylinders and causes erection. After intercourse, he turns a valve, which empties the cylinders back into the reservoir. Figure 16.2 depicts a penis pump. Implant surgery is considered radical treatment and should be considered only if other forms of treatment fail (Montague, 2000). It can lead to permanent damage that could make a natural erection impossible.

Finally, some structural problems in sexual anatomy may have to be corrected with surgery. Examples are removing scar tissue and freeing adhesions that cause pain during intercourse.

Hormone Treatments

Certain medical conditions, particularly those of the endocrine system, respond to medication or hormone replacement therapy. Correcting a hormonal imbalance that might affect disorders of sexual arousal might best be treated through the oral administration of hormone replacement therapy. Sometimes endocrine glands need help in being stimulated to begin producing adequate amounts of sex hormones.

Medications are available that activate endocrine glands to release their hormones. Although testosterone is often considered a male hormone, both men and women have testosterone, and it is believed to play an important role in libido. As levels of this hormone

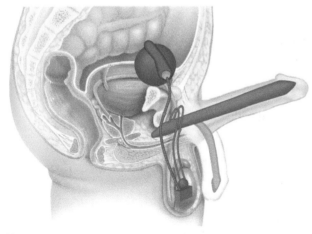

Figure 16.2 *Penis Pump* The penis pump uses a closed system consisting of a hydraulic pump (hidden in the testes), a fluid reservoir (concealed in the abdominal cavity), and expandable chambers (hidden in the penis). To produce an erection, fluid is pumped from the reservoir to the chambers.

decline with age, sexual interest may wane. Many women are helped by taking testosterone, in low enough doses to prevent any male secondary characteristics to develop. Also, estrogen improves vaginal lubrication in postmenopausal women.

Other Medical Treatments

Still other sexual dysfunctions are related to a disease that can be treated or cured with medication. Sexual pain disorders associated with sexually transmitted infection, for instance, respond quite well to treatment or cure of the underlying disease condition. Sexual arousal disorders related to cardiovascular problems such as arteriosclerosis often can be improved through medication designed to change blood biochemistry and improve the flow of blood and blood pressure.

Treating Psychosocially Based Sexual Dysfunction

Several different sex therapy approaches can be applied when the origin of the dysfunction is psychosocial in nature. The therapeutic approach has four main variables:

- The therapist's theoretical framework
- Duration and schedule of treatment
- Individual versus couple or group approach
- Use of surrogates

Sex therapists come from a variety of backgrounds. Some are physicians with advanced training in psychiatry, sex therapy, psychoanalysis, or counseling. Others are psychologists, psychoanalysts, counselors, and social workers. No uniform credentials are required for sex therapists across the United States; credentialing requirements vary from state to state. Each of these professionals has a philosophical and theoretical framework regarding sex therapy that guides his or her work.

Psychoanalysts, for example, take a psychodynamic approach to treatment that is grounded in the work of Freud. A basic element in their approach is helping the client gain insight into the origin of his or her problem (Kring, 2000). Counselors using a behaviorist approach, in contrast, do not believe it is necessary to delve deeply into their clients' past to help them gain insight into the origin of their problem. Rather, the behaviorist focuses on the here and now and examines the nature of the problem, how the client perceives it, and how it directly affects the person's quality of life.

The therapist's theoretical framework is intimately related to the duration and schedule of therapy. A psychoanalyst might spend several sessions just getting to know the client and establishing trust while beginning to look back into his or her past. A Masters and Johnson–trained therapist team would be finished with therapy by that time because the approach is to get right down to the business of treating the presenting problem in an intensive 2-week program.

Some sex therapists work only with individuals. Most however, believe that sexual dysfunction can be understood and treated only within the context of the relationship. Couples are seen together and individually,

PLISSIT Model of Sex Therapy

Source: Callista Lee

A simplified way of understanding sex therapy is to view it through the PLISSIT Model. PLISSIT stands for:

- Permission
- Limited information
- Specific suggestions
- Intensive therapy

The first guideline of the PLISSIT model is that the therapist only takes the client into as much depth as they want and need. Sometimes all a couple or individual needs is to learn how to give themselves permission to own their own sexuality; to define what is normal and pleasurable for them rather than trying to achieve some outside standard. Permission may be all that they need to solve their issues—no need to go further.

A therapist may also find that they need information about how the sexual response works, effects of medications they are on, whatever topics relate to their sexual problems. Specific Suggestions are the kinds of skills and homework that most people think of when they think of sex therapy. Again, the therapist only guides clients through techniques that will be helpful to their particular problems. Common techniques are directed masturbation (to not only learn more about one's own sexual response but also to relieve sexual tension while working on other relationship issues), sensate focus (for self-awareness), the stop–start or the squeeze technique (for premature ejaculation), and the bridge maneuver (to increase likelihood of female orgasm during intercourse). Intensive Therapy may help a client deal with individual issues that are affecting their sex life, or it may be couple's therapy. Don't let the word "intensive" intimidate you. It just means that this level of therapeutic intervention tends to be more emotionally intense that the preceding levels. It also means that the therapist must be appropriately skilled in psychotherapy.

Sex surrogate A person who acts as a substitute sex partner during therapy

and treatment involves treating the couple as well as the individual. Others incorporate group therapy to help couples view their problems in a broader context (Corliss & Steptoe, 2004).

Finally, some sex therapists provide explicit help by using trained **sex surrogate** partners. Although these surrogates are sexually responsive trained professionals who serve as partners for clients, the American Association of Sex Educators, Counselors, and Therapists (AASECT, 1998), one of the leading professional groups charged with certifying sex therapists, does not recommend their use in the treatment of sexual dysfunctions.

Most sex therapy is eclectic, combining elements from various forms of psychotherapy, education, and medicine (Bach, Barlow, Wincze, 2004, Rosen, Seidman, Menza et al., 2004). Six common threads that seem to underlie the practice of sex therapy, regardless of the therapist's theoretical framework, are (a) permission-giving, (b) limited information, (c) specific suggestions, (d) selfawareness, (e) communication training, and (f) use of masturbation.

■ Permission-Giving

Permission-giving is the unconditional support the therapist offers for becoming a fully self-actualized sexual being. Clients are given permission to explore any thoughts, feelings, desires, fantasies, and behaviors that might enhance their sexual pleasure. They also are given permission not to engage in behaviors and relationships that undermine their sexual and other well-being.

Information-Giving

Information-giving or education is a key element in all forms of sex therapy. Because most people receive little or no formal sex education, they often are misinformed about simple issues that can undermine their sexual enjoyment, such as penis size, level of sexual activity, and effects of aging. Often, providing information, along with permission giving, is liberating enough to help people work their way out of some sexual dysfunctions.

Information-giving can include didactic sessions with the therapist related to the individual's specific concerns, guided reading (reading a prescribed set of materials), and viewing instructional videotapes. Providing limited information helps change negative attitudes, open lines of communication, and develop sexual skills necessary for enhancing performance and pleasure.

Specific Suggestions

Each person or couple has unique problems and needs that can be addressed through specific suggestions. The main technique in this regard is "homework assignments" with one's partner. The range of specific suggestions varies depending on the nature of the problem and the specific individual or couple involved. Usually these homework assignments require the couple to practice activities and techniques that the therapist has discussed with them. These often are coupled with communication activities designed to help couples open up and share their feelings with each other.

∽ *Intellectual Wellness* ∽

Many sexual problems are based on ignorance, illogical thinking, irrational expectations, and poor technique. Intellectual wellness is fostered through knowledge, logical thinking, rational expectations, and improved sexual technique. Much of sex therapy revolves around relearning what good sex is and what being a good lover means. These things can be taught. You can learn about sexual response and what to expect during lovemaking. You can learn to understand the factors that influence interest, desire, plateau, orgasm, and resolution and begin to set more realistic and logical expectations about lovemaking. You can learn techniques and practice your skills (by yourself or with your partner) and become a better lover.

Self-Awareness

Increased self-awareness is a natural outgrowth of permission- and information-giving. Many of the specific suggestions prescribed as homework help individuals and couples focus on their sensual/sexual response. This is the first time many clients have spent focusing on their sexual response and specific techniques related to sensual and sexual arousal.

One commonly used activity is called **sensate focus**. In the early stages of sex therapy, the couple is instructed to refrain from sexual activity involving genital contact. This approach is designed to relieve performance anxiety and other forms of anxiety and to allow the couple to focus on nongenital pleasuring.

Sensate focus Nongenital pleasuring used to heighten sensuality without sexual activity

personal exploration activity
A Great Sex Life

Unfortunately, many of us have just a few sexual issues and hang-ups that may cause our sex life to be less than great. However, there are many things we can do to increase our enjoyment and physical response so that we can have a better sex life. Your task is to find one or more methods to incorporate that would improve your sexual response.

While reading this chapter, compare your sexual response to various sexual disorders. Your goal is to find one that is similar to an issue that you may have experienced. Then choose a sexual therapy that you can try to see whether it improves the way you respond. You may choose one to do alone or with a partner. If you cannot find anything you need to improve, try one of the therapies just for fun. You may find something like sensate focus increases the enjoyment you already experience and may decide to incorporate it in your routine sexual activities. Look for some therapy that would increase pleasure or skill, and give it a try. Hopefully, you will find the results worth the work.

During the first phase of sensate focus (Figure 16.3), each partner is given a turn to explore the other's body. The breasts and genitals are off-limits. The intent is not to give sexual pleasure but instead to establish awareness of touch by paying attention to the textures, contours, and temperature of the partner and to attend to what it feels like to touch and be touched.

The partner doing the touching is in control and is not driven by the needs of the person being touched. The initial stage is supposed to be conducted as silently as possible. The person being touched is allowed to convey (either verbally or nonverbally) when the partner's touch makes him or her uncomfortable.

During the second phase of sensate focus, touch is extended to include the breasts and genitals. The couple receive instructions similar to those in the first phase and are advised to gradually expand the touch to include the genitals. The purpose is still to experience the sensation of touch and to discover what types of touch are most pleasurable.

A simple technique called *handriding* is used during this phase. This involves having one partner place his or her hand over the partner's and to guide it on an exploration of the other's body. The guiding hand nonverbally communicates by increasing or decreasing the pressure, changing the speed or type of motion, and holding the hand to linger. The idea is to help the partner who is doing the touching understand the preferences of the partner being touched without controlling the action. The partner doing the touching is still in control but is guided along.

In the third phase of sensate focus, the couple is asked to explore each other at the same time. Rather than take turns, the couple doubles the amount of sensory input by mutual exploration. This simulates real-life touching and allows the couple the opportunity to get lost in the sensations of touch without the pressure to have intercourse.

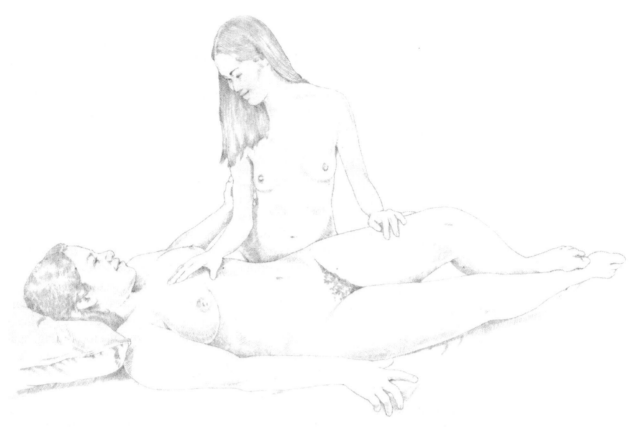

Figure 16.3 *Couple Practicing* Sensate Focus During the first stage of sensate focus, couples practice nongenital pleasuring.

In the last stage of sensate focus, the couple shifts to the female-on-top position without attempting full penetration of the penis. In this position, the woman can rub her clitoris directly against her partner and stimulate his penis with her vulva and vaginal opening. This position may or may not result in arousal and full erection in her partner. The purpose is not to cause full arousal and intercourse, but if an erection occurs, she can put the tip of the penis into her vaginal opening. The couple are instructed to continue to explore each other, using full body contact to explore the sensations of touch and arousal. After the couple has worked through the stages of sensate focus successfully and is comfortable with it, the two of them usually are ready to experience full intercourse without difficulty.

Communication Training

Couples can learn how to communicate nonverbally through sensate focus and other awareness-building activities. Often, nonverbal communication—such as placing a hand or other body part in a certain position or holding a partner to linger at what he or she is doing—can transmit information that will help treat sexual problems. Improving verbal communication—in particular, expressing needs and desires and communicating using "I" language instead of blaming one's partner—is integral to all forms of sex therapy. Communication building can occur during sessions with the therapist and as homework assignments.

Use of Masturbation

Sex therapy commonly includes masturbation, both individual and mutual. It can be used in sexual arousal disorders to help both partners explore the types, intensity, and duration of stimulation necessary for full arousal. It also can help the couple learn how to delay orgasm in cases of premature ejaculation.

A variation of masturbation used to treat premature ejaculation is the squeeze technique, illustrated in Figure 16.4. During manual stimulation of her partner, the woman is instructed to stop periodically and apply firm pressure for a few seconds to the frenulum and coronal ridge with her thumb and first and second fingers, respectively. This squeezing reduces her partner's urgency to ejaculate. She can continue to masturbate her partner, stopping periodically to squeeze. Through this technique her partner can learn to delay ejaculation.

Masturbation also can be used to treat female and male orgasmic disorder. Often these conditions are related to inadequate sexual stimulation. Through permission giving, sensate focus, and masturbation, men and women can learn the type, intensity, and duration of stimulation necessary for orgasm.

Treatment progresses from individual masturbation, to masturbation in the presence of the partner, to being masturbated by the partner, to using masturbation as a prelude to intercourse.

Masturbation, coupled with the use of increasingly larger dilators can be used to treat some cases of vaginismus. Women are taught to use permission giving, self-awareness, and masturbation to initiate sexual arousal and to use the varying sizes of dilators for 10 to 15 minutes at a time to introduce objects into her vagina. The goal is to work up to a penis-size dilator and then make the transition to a real penis.

Figure 16.4 *Squeeze Technique* During the squeeze technique, the partner's erect penis is periodically squeezed to inhibit ejaculation.

Vaginal and rectal dilators come in varying sizes and colors.

Image courtesy of CooperSurgical Milex Pessaries.

What Sex Therapy Is NOT

Source: Callista Lee

- **Sex therapy is NEVER about having sex with or in front of your therapist,** nor will it be recorded for your therapist to see. Any therapist who approaches a client for sex should be reported to the licensing board for their profession. Links to these organizations in California can be found on our textbook's website.

- Sex therapy is not about making you change in ways you do not want to change.

- Sex therapy will never involve treatments that have been condemned by the psychological or medical community as ineffective or harmful, such as gay conversion therapy. Such "therapies" are not effective in changing one's sexual orientation, but they *are* known to cause an increase in psychological distress.

The Best RX: A Healthy Lifestyle

Throughout this chapter and the textbook there has been a heavy emphasis on the importance of lifestyle in promoting healthy sexuality. This is especially true when preventing sexual dysfunctions. Many of the risks associated with key lifestyle factors related to sexual dysfunction can be reduced, especially if begun in early adulthood.

Chronic diseases such as obesity, diabetes, and hypertension, and the medications used to treat them have all been implicated in specific sexual dysfunctions. The risks associated with developing these chronic diseases and others can be reduced significantly by developing high level physical wellness through three key lifestyle behaviors:

1. Exercise regularly.
2. Eat a balanced diet.
3. Stop smoking.

Increasing exercise (especially aerobic) eating a healthy diet (low-fat, high-carbohydrate, moderate protein) and stopping smoking both reduces the risks associated with the three major chronic diseases but also enhances blood flow and vascular health, two keys to good sexual response.

As previously discussed, smoking increases the likelihood of erectile dysfunction in addition to being a major risk factor in cardiovascular disease. Smokers are four times as likely as nonsmokers to develop complete erectile disorder.

Chronic stress can lower testosterone, the key hormone related to sexual desire. Less testosterone means less sexual desire. Building high-level emotional wellbeing through meditation and other relaxation techniques can lower stress levels and enhance sexual desire and arousal. Stress management and relaxation will help moderate testosterone levels, reduce anger and other negative emotions, and help restore potency.

Curbing excessive drug use, both legal and illegal can reduce risk for experiencing sexual dysfunction. Although used for the purpose of achieving the *intended effect* (the desired outcome of taking the drug), *unintended side effects*. That effect sexual response can occur. This is especially true when taking multiple legal medications and/or mixing them with illegal drugs.

High-level social wellness helps build healthy relationships. Healthy relationships are based on trust, respect, commitment, love, and affection.

Good sex flows out of this safe and protected context. When trust, respect, and affection are displaced by mistrust, disrespect, and fear, relationship problems ensue. Communication, which is central to good sex, often breaks down when couples are having relationship problems. When sexual needs and desires are not communicated clearly, sexual response suffers.

High-level emotional wellbeing also helps reduce the risk of sexual dysfunction. As described in earlier chapters, the sexual response system relies on a fragile interconnectedness between things going on in both the mind and the body. Emotions are related intimately to sexual response. All phases of the sexual response cycle are subject to the effects of emotions. Sexual interest and desire are fueled by positive emotions such as happiness, love, joy, respect, and trust. Negative emotions (especially directed at a partner), such as anxiety, anger, hate, fear, disgust, and mistrust, make interest and desire difficult at best and impossible for most.

For the body to respond properly, the mind must let go and relax. Arousal is much more difficult when emotions like anxiety, anger, hate, fear, disgust, and mistrust, exist. The ability to prolong and enjoy sex and orgasm is contingent on the buildup of tension through adequate stimulation. It is triggered when we give up mental control and allow our body to be swept along in the ecstasy of physical pleasuring. This is difficult if we are on guard, tense, angry, or resentful.

High level intellectual well-being can help prevent sexual dysfunction. Many sexual problems are based on ignorance, illogical thinking, irrational expectations, and poor technique. Intellectual wellness is fostered through knowledge, logical thinking, rational expectations, and improved sexual technique.

A safe and supportive environment is also associated with reducing risks for sexual dysfunction. Being able to relax and allow sexual response to occur is much more difficult in an environment that is unstable or unsafe.

Lastly, high-level spiritual wellbeing can also reduce risks for sexual dysfunction. Spiritual wellbeing is all about interconnectedness. There is no greater example of interconnectedness that the uniting of sex partners in a mutually satisfying relationship based on respect, affection, trust. Being in the most connected (two human beings formed as one) of all relationships can trigger a deep sense of spirituality. The effects of participating in secular and religious activities that build high-level spiritual wellbeing can help strengthen the connection two lovers have, especially if they engage in these activities together.

References

American Association of Sex Educators, Counselors, and Therapists. (1998). *Ethical guidelines for sex therapists*. Washington, DC.

American Psychiatric Association (APA). (2013). *Diagnostic and statistical manual of mental illness* (5th ed). Washington, DC.

Bach, A. K., Barlow, D. H., Wincze, J. P. (2004). The Enhancing Effects of Manualized Treatment for Erectile Dysfunction Among Men Using Sildenafil: A Preliminary Investigation. *Behavior Therapy*, Winter 2004, 35 (1) pg. 55–73.

Barbach, L. (1982). *For each other: Sharing sexual intimacy*. Garden City, NY: Doubleday.

Basson, R., Berman, J., Burnett, A., Derogatis, L., Ferguson, D., Fourcoy, J., Goldstein, L.,

Graziotto, A., Heiman, J., Laan, E., Lieblum, S., Padma-Nathan, H., Rosen, R., Seagraves, K., Shabsigh, R., Sipsk, M., Wagner, G., & Whipple, B. (2000). Report of the International Consensus Development Conference on Female Sexual Dysfunction: Definitions and classifications. *Journal of Urology, 163,* 888–893.

Basson, R. (2004). Recent advances in women's sexual function and dysfunction. *Menopause.* 2004 Nov–Dec11(6):714–25.

Basson, R. (2002). Are our definitions of women's desire, arousal and sexual pain disorders too broad and our definition of orgasmic disorder too narrow? *J Sex Marital Ther.* 2002 July–Sept.28(4):289–300.

Berman, J. R., Berman, L. A., Lin, H., Flaherty, E., Leahy, N., Goldstein, I., Cantey-Kiser, J. (2001). Effect of sidenafil on subjective and physiologic parameters of the female sexual response in women and sexual arousal disorder. *Journal of Sex and Marital Therapy*, 27 pages 411–420.

Boschert, S. (2000, July). Women don't get a rise out of taking Viagra. *Ob Gyn News, 35*(13), 23–24.

Corliss, R., Steptoe, S. (2004). The Marriage Savers. *Time*, vol. 163, no. 3, Jan 19th 2004, pp. 88–92.

DeTejada, I. S. (2002). Molecular mechanisms for the regulation of penile smooth muscle contractility. *International Journal of Impotence Research* 2002 (14) Supplement 1, pp. 6–10.

Dodson, B. (1974). *Liberating masturbation.* New York: Dodson. *Drug Week.* (2001, August 24). Viagra-type drugs unlikely to solve many women's sexual response problems [Online]. Article A78895438. Available: NewsRX.net.

Dziegielewski, S. F.(2014). DSM-5 in Action. New York: John Wiley & Sons.

Enserink, M. (2005). Let's Talk About Sex—and Drugs. *Science* 308, June 10, 2005. pgs. 1578–1580.

Fisher, B. S., Cullen, F. T., & Turner, M. G. (2000). *The sexual victimization of college women.* Washington DC: U.S. Department of Justice.

Fisher, H. (2004). *Why we love; the nature and chemistry of romantic love.* New York: Henry Holt and Company.

Georgea, W.H., Davisa, K.C., Heimanb, J.R., Norrisa, J., Stonerc, S.A., Schachta, R.L., Hendershotd, C.S., Kajumolo K.F. (2011) Women's sexual arousal: Effects of high alcohol dosages and self-control instructions. *Hormones and Behavior*, Volume 59, Issue 5, May 2011, Pages 730–738

Goldstein, I., Auerbach, S., Palma-Nathan, H., Rajfer, J., Fitch, W., Schmitt, L. (2000). Axial penile rigidity as primary efficacy outcome during multi-institutional in-office dose titration clinical trials with alprostadil alfadex in patients with erectile dysfunction. *Int J Impot Res.* 2000 Aug 12; (4):205–11.

Goldstein, I. (2000). Male sexual circuitry. *Scientific American* August 2000, Vol. 283, Issue 2, pp. 70–75.

Goldberg, R. (2006). *Drugs across the spectrum.* Englewood, CO: Morton.

Gutfield, G. (1994). The prescription for male potency. *Prevention, 46*(11), 78–82.

Handy, B. (1998). The Viagra craze. *Time, 151*(17), 50–53.

Heapes, T. (1994). Smoking your sex life away. *Muscle & Fitness, 55*(4), 42. Heiman, J. R. (2002a). Sexual Dysfunction: Overview of Prevalence, Etiological Factors, and Treatments. *The Journal of Sex Research* v. 39 no. 1 (February 2002) p. 73–78.

Heiman, J. R. (2002b). Psychologic Treatments for Female Sexual Dysfunction: Are They Effective and Do We Need Them? *Archives of Sexual Behavior* Vol. 31 number 5, Oct. 2002, pp. 445–450.

Higher Education Center. (2003). *Sexual assault: Alcohol and other drugs.* http://www.Edc.org/hec/pubs/factsheets/fact_sheet1.html.

Hite, S. (1977). *The Hite report.* New York: Dell.

Johnson, J. (2004). Exposed at last; the truth about your clitoris. In Worcester N. Jones, H. B., & Jones, H. (1977). *Sensual drugs: Deprivation and rehabilitation of the mind.* London: Cambridge University Press, pp. 387–389.

Kita, J. (2001). The sex crusaders. *Men's Health, 16*(9), 98–106.

Kloner, R., Padma, N. H. (2005). Erectile Dysfunction in patients with coronary artery disease. *International Journal of Impotence Research*, Jun 2005, Vol. 17 Issue 3, p. 209–215.

Kobilinsky, S., & Palmeter, J. (1984). Sex role orientation, mother's expression of affection toward spouse and college women's attitudes towards sexual behaviors. *Journal of Sex Research, 20,* 32–43.

Kring, B. (2000). Psychotherapy of sexual dysfunction. *American Journal of Psychotherapy*, Vol 54 no. 1, Winter 2000, pp. 97–101.

Laan, E., Van Lunsen, R. H., Everaerd, W., Riley, A., Scott, E., Bodell, M. (2002). The enhancement of vaginal vasocongestion by sidenafil in healthy premenopausal women. *Journal of Women's Health and Gender-Based Medicine*, pp. 357–365.

Legato, M. (1999). *Summary: U.S. Department of Health and Human Services, Public Health Service, National Institutes of Health: A report of the task force on the NIH Women's Health Research Agenda for the 21st century. Vol. 1: Executive summary* [Online]. Available: www:4.od.nih.gov/orwh/report. pdf.

Lemonick, M. (2004). The Chemistry of Desire. *Time*, Jan 19th, 2004, pp. 62–68.

Lewis, J. H., Rosen, R., Goldstein, I. (2005). Erectile dysfunction. *Nursing*, February, 2005, 35(2) p. 64.

Lowinson, J. H., Ruiz, P., Millman, R. B., & Langrod, J. G. (1992). *Substance abuse: A comprehensive textbook* (2nd ed.). Baltimore: Williams & Wilkinson.

Masters, W. H, & Johnson, V. E. (1970). *Human sexual inadequacy.* Boston: Little, Brown.

Masters, W. H., Johnson, V. E., & Kolodny, R. (1996). *Human sexuality* (5th ed.). New York: HarperCollins.

McCabe, M. P. (2004). Exacerbation of Symptoms Among People With Multiple Sclerosis: Impact on Sexuality and Relationships Over Time. *Archives of Sexual Behavior*, December, 2004, 33 (6) pp. 593–601.

Montague, D. K. (2000). How to implant a threepiece inflatable penile prosthesis. *Urology Times*, Jul 2000, Vol. 28 Issue 7, pp. 32–34.

Montague, A. (1977). *Touching: The human significance of the skin.* New York: Harper & Row.

Munarriz, R., Kim, N. N., Goldstein, I., Traish, A. M. (2002). Biology of female sexual

function. *Urol Clin North Am.* 2002 Aug; 29(3):685–693.

National Council on Patient Information and Education (2001). Alcohol and Medications: Ask Before You Mix, publication #B-20, Washington, DC: National Council on Patient Information and Education.

O'Donohue, W., & Geer, J. H. (1993). *Handbook of sexual dysfunctions: Assessment and treatment.* Needham Heights, MA: Allyn & Bacon.

O'Connell, H. E., Sanjeevan, K, V., Hutson, J. M. (2005). Anatomy of the clitoris. *J Urol.* 2005 Oct; 174(4 Pt 1):1189–95.

Padma-Nathan, H., Kaufman, J., & Taylor, T. (2003, June 28–July 1). *Earliest time of onset of erections with vardenafil determined in an at-home setting.* Paper presented at the Second International Consultation on Erectile and Sexual Dysfunctions, Paris.

Parker-Pope, T. (2002). Studies link bicycling to impotence. *Wall Street Journal*, Oct 15th, 2002, p. D1.

Phillips, N. A. (2000). Female sexual dysfunction: evaluation and treatment. *American Family Physician*, Vol 62, number 1, July 2000, pp. 127–142.

Purcell, S. (1985, August 25). *The relationship between religious orthodoxy and marital sexual functioning.* Paper presented at annual meeting of American Psychological Association.

Raina, R., Agawarl, A., Ausmundson, S., Lakin, M., Nandipati, K. C., Montague, D. K., Mansour D., Zippe, C. D. (2005). Early use of vacuum constriction device following radical prostatectomy facilitates early sexual activity and potentially earlier return of erectile function. *International Journal of Impotence Res.* 2005 Aug 18, pp. 57–87.

Richardson, J. D.(1991). Medical causes of sexual dysfunction. *Medical Journal of Australia, 155,* 29–33.

Rosen, R. C., McKenna, K. E. (2002). PDE-5 Inhibition and sexual response; pharmacological mechanisms and clinical outcomes. *Annual Review of Sex Research.* Volume 13 pages, 36–88.

Rosen, R. C., Seidman, S. N., Menza, M.A., Shabsigh, R., Roose, S. P., Tseng, L. J., Orazem, J., Siegel, R. I. (2004). Quality of life, mood, and sexual function; a path analytic model of treatment effects in men with erectile dysfunction.. *International Journal of Impotence Research*, Aug 2004, Vol 16 Issue 4, pp. 334–340.

Scelfo, J. (2002). Bored with sleeping? Sleep and Sex. *Newsweek,* v. 140 no.3 (July 15, 2002) p. 45.

Shamlou, R. (2011). Queen's University researcher connects cannabis use and sexual dysfunction. *Life Science Weekly.* (Mar. 8, 2011): p. 199.

Singer-Kaplan, H. (1974). *The new sex therapy.* New York: Brunner/Mazel.Sobczak, J. A. (2011). Alcohol Use and Sexual Function in Women: A Literature Review Journal of Addictions Nursing , 20:71–85, 2009

Stevenson, R. W. D. (2002, January). Sexual dysfunction: Attending to the mind–body continuum. *Medical Aspects of Human Sexuality, 2,* 7–9.

Swindle, R. W., Cameron, A. E., Lockhart, D. C. (2004). The Psychological and Interpersonal Relationship Scales: Assessing Psychological and Relationship Outcomes Associated With Erectile Dysfunction and Its Treatment. *Archives of Sexual Behavior* Vol. 33, Issue 1, Feb. 2004, pp. 19–30.

United States Department of Health and Human Services USDHHS (2000). Alcohol and health: Tenth special report to the US Congress. *NIH Publication* 00-1583. Washington DC: US Government Printing Office.

Vijay, M. Kiran KumerPK, Narendra J. Shetty, S. (2013). Substance Use and Sexual Dysfunction. *Journal of Evolution of Medical and Dental Sciences.* 2013; Vol 2, November 04, Issue 44 pp. 8620–8628.

Warnock, J. (2005). Acquired, Generalized, Female Hypoactive Sexual Desire Disorder: I Had It, I Lost It, I Want It Back. *Psychiatric Times*, August, 2005, Vol. 22, Issue 9, pp. 45–52.

Weschler, H., Eun, L. J., Kuo, M., Sebring, M., Nelson, T. F., & Lee, H. (2002). Trends in college binge drinking during a period of increased prevention efforts: Findings from four Harvard School of Public Health college alcohol study surveys: 1993–2001. *Journal of American College Health,* 50(5), pp. 203–217.

Witters, W., Venturelli, P., & Hanson, P. (1992). *Drugs and society.* 3rd ed. Boston: Jones & Bartlett.

Wooten, J. M. (2004). Erectile Dysfunction. *RN,* October, 2004, No. 67 (10), pp. 40–45.

Zilbergeld, B. (1992). *The new male sexuality.* New York: Bantam.